CONNELL ON THE AGRICULTURAL HOLDINGS (SCOTLAND) ACTS

CONNELL ON THE AGRICULTURAL HOLDINGS (SCOTLAND) ACTS

Seventh Edition

Donald G. Rennie, obe, ma, llb, ws

Sir Crispin Agnew of Lochnaw Bt, qc

T & T CLARK
EDINBURGH
1996

T & T CLARK
59 GEORGE STREET
EDINBURGH EH2 2LQ
SCOTLAND

First published 1923
Second edition 1928
Third edition 1938
Fourth edition 1951
Fifth edition 1961
Sixth edition 1970
Seventh edition 1996

ISBN 0 567 00514 3

British Library Cataloguing-in-Publication Data
A catalogue record for this book is available from the British Library

Typeset by Fakenham Photosetting Ltd, Fakenham, Norfolk
Printed and bound in Great Britain by Hartnolls Limited, Bodmin, Cornwall

AUTHORS' PREFACE

This seventh edition of *Connell* was started by the late Mr Kenneth M. Campbell before his sad and untimely death. He set aside the work when he learned that it was proposed to consolidate the Agricultural Holdings Acts. Our task has been made easier by the extensive work carried out by Mr Campbell.

Following the pattern of the previous editions, the book begins with a general account of the provisions of the principal statute, the Agricultural Holdings (Scotland) Act 1991, and of the provisions of other statutes bearing on agricultural tenancies. Reference is made to earlier statutes which the 1991 Act consolidated and repealed. There is also a summary of the law and practice of agricultural arbitration and valuation in Scotland and notes on contractual resumption clauses and compulsory purchase of the tenant's interest in an agricultural lease.

The main change since the sixth edition was published in 1970 has been the impact of European Union directives and in particular the impact of the introduction of agricultural quotas. The text therefore now contains new sections dealing with the landlord and tenant aspects of milk quota and an annotated text of those parts of the Agriculture Act 1986 which relate to quota.

At the heart of the book is the annotated text of the Agricultural Holdings (Scotland) Act 1991, which has been prepared by Sir Crispin Agnew of Lochnaw.

The first fourteen chapters are the responsibility of Mr Rennie; the fifteenth, dealing with quotas and set aside, is the reponsibility of Sir Crispin Agnew.

The law is stated as at 31st December 1995.

Donald G. Rennie
Crispin Agnew of Lochnaw
June 1996

CONTENTS

Authors' Preface . . . . *v*
Table of Legislation . . . . *xiii*
Table of Cases . . . . *xxiii*

Chapter 1 The Object of the Acts 1
  Commencement and Dates of Operation of the Agricultural
    Holdings (Scotland) Acts 1
  Landlord and Tenant 2
  Holdings Affected 3
  Size of Holding 3
  Buildings 4
  Used for Agriculture 4
  Trade or Business 4
  Minimum Term of Lease 4
  Exceptions from Section 2 5
  Jurisdiction of Court and Arbiter 7
  Tacit Relocation 7
  Provision for Written Leases 8
  Provision and Maintenance of Fixed Equipment 8

Chapter 2 Review of Rent 11
  Demand for Arbitration 11
  Revision Period 11
  Appointment of Arbiter 12
  Basis of Rental Valuation 12
  The 'Normal' Basis – Open Market Rents of Comparable
    Holdings 13
  Valuing Out Premium Rents 13
  Factors to be Disregarded 14
  Information to be Provided to Arbiter 15
  Inspection 15
  Reasons for Award 15
  Form of Award 16
  Stated Case to Land Court 16
  Appeal to Land Court 16
  Absolute Right to Increase Rent 17

Chapter 3 Succession to Leases 18
  Leases not Transferable on Death: Special Destinations . . . 18
  Leases Terminating on Death of Tenant 18
  Special Destinations 18
  Bequest of Lease 19
  Intestate Succession 20

Executor's Title 20
Time-limits 21
Transfer to Executor 21
Termination if Tenancy not Transferred 22

Chapter 4   Notice to Quit and Notice of Intention to Quit . . 23
Restriction on Operation of Notices to Quit 25
Exclusion of Security of Tenure 25
The Seven Cases under Section 22(2) 26
Consent of Land Court to Notice to Quit 32
Termination of Interest of Successor 36
Schedule 2 – Grounds for Consent 37
The 'Fair and Reasonable Landlord' Provision 38

Chapter 5   Compensation for Improvements 41
Extent of the Right to Compensation for Improvements . . . 41
Improvements for which the 1991 Act allows Compensation . . 42
Improvements Requiring Consent (Part I) 43
Improvements Requiring Notice (Part II) 43
Temporary Improvements (Part III) 44
Artificial Manures and Feeding-stuffs 45
Eradication of Bracken, etc 46
Temporary Pasture. 47

Chapter 6   Further Provisions for Compensation 49
Compensation for Disturbance 49
Reorganisation of Tenant's Affairs 50
Early Resumption 51
High Farming 52
Ascertaining the Value of Improvements 52
'Substituted' Compensation for Improvements 54
Damage by Game – Deer, Pheasants, Partridges, Grouse and
    Black Game 54
Notices of Intention to Claim Compensation and Lodging of
    Particulars 55

Chapter 7   Miscellaneous Provisions 57
Variation of Terms of Tenancy 57
Freedom of Cropping 57
Tenant's Rights to Remove Fixtures 58
Penal Rent and/or Liquidated Damages 59
Irritancy 59
Record of Holding 59
Removing for Non-payment of Rent 60
Application for Certificate of Bad Husbandry 61
Effect on Notice to Quit of Agreement to Sell 61
Charging the Estate with Compensation 61

Chapter 8   Contracting Out 63
Avoiding Indefinite Security of Tenure 63

Chapter 9 **Market Gardens** 66

Chapter 10 **Contractual Resumption** 68

Chapter 11 **Compulsory Purchase** 74

Chapter 12 **Arbitration under the 1991 Act** 77
Claims by the Tenant 78
Claims by the Landlord 83
Particulars of Claims 83
Competency and Relevancy of Claims 84
Appointment of Arbiter 85
Disqualification and Removal of Arbiter 86
Minute of Submission 87
Procedure in Arbitration 87
Appointment of Clerk 88
Receiving Claims and Objections 88
Hearing and Inspection 89
Evidence 90
Stated Case 92
Note of Proposed Findings 94
Expenses 94
The Award 96
Reduction of Award 98

Chapter 13 **Valuation of Bound Sheep Stocks** 100
Lease Commencing before or on 6th November 1946 . . . 102
Lease Commencing after 6th November 1946 and before 1st
    December 1986 (Sch 9) 102
Lease Commencing on or after 1st December 1986 (Sch 10) . . 103
Procedural Matters 104

Chapter 14 **Arbitrations and Valuations (Outside the Act)**
    Generally Between Awaygoing and Incoming
    Tenants 106
The Subjects of Common Law Arbitration or Valuation . . . 107
Appointment of Arbiters and Oversman 109
Procedure and Principles of Valuation 110
The Duties of Arbiters and Oversman 110
Procedure in Making Valuations 111
Awaygoing Crop Valuations 111

Chapter 15 **Quotas and Set Aside** 112
Introduction 112
Milk Quotas 112
Sheep and Suckler Cow Annual Premium Quotas 121
Arable Areas Payment Scheme 122

Annotated Text of the Agricultural Holdings (Scotland) Act 1991 124
Arrangement of Sections 124
Part I: Agricultural Holdings 128

CONTENTS

Part II: Terms of Leases and Variations Thereof 131
Part III: Notice to Quit and Notice of Intention to Quit . . . 151
Part IV: Compensation for Improvements 170
Part V: Other Provisions Regarding Compensation 179
Part VI: Additional Payments 196
Part VII: Arbitration and Other Proceedings 202
Part VIII: Miscellaneous 211
Part IX: Supplementary 214
Schedule 1: Provisions Required in Leases 223
Schedule 2: Grounds for Consent to Operation of Notices to
            Quit a Tenancy where Section 25(3) Applies . . . 224
Schedule 3: 1923 Act Improvements for which Compensation
            May Be Payable 227
Schedule 4: 1931 Act Improvements for which Compensation
            May Be Payable 228
Schedule 5: New Improvements for which Compensation May
            Be Payable 229
Schedule 6: Market Garden Improvements 232
Schedule 7: Arbitrations 232
Schedule 8: Supplementary Provisions with Respect to Payments
            Under Section 56 237
Schedule 9: Valuation of Sheep Stock in Scotland in Respect of
            Old Leases 238
Schedule 10: Valuation of Sheep Stock on Scotland in Respect of
            Leases Entered into after December 1, 1986 . . . 241
Schedule 11: Consequential Amendments of Enactments . . . 244
Schedule 12: Transitionals and Savings 251
Schedule 13: Repeals and Revocations 252
Table of Derivations 254
Table of Destinations 257

Appendix 1: Forms for Use in Connection with the 1991 Act . . 262
Lists of Forms 262
A. Notices to Quit and Miscellaneous 265
B. Applications to the Secretary of State for Scotland 289
C. Arbitration Procedure 290
D. Additional Forms 306

Appendix 2: Extracts from the Agriculture Act 1986 310
Section 14: Compensation to outgoing tenants for milk quota:
            Scotland 310
Section 16: Rent arbitrations: milk quotas, Scotland 310
Schedule 2: Tenants' Compensation for Milk Quota: Scotland . 312

Appendix 3: Extract from the Succession (Scotland) Act 1964 . 327
Section 16: Provisions relating to leases 327

Appendix 4: Extracts from the Agriculture (Scotland) Act 1948 331
Fifth Schedule: Rules of Good Estate Management 331
Sixth Schedule: Rules of Good Husbandry 331

CONTENTS

Appendix 5: The Agricultural Holdings (Specification of Forms) (Scotland) Order 1991 333

Index. 341

TABLE OF LEGISLATION

Statutes

Note: A reference in **bold** indicates that the text of the section appears in full.

Acquisition of Land (Authorisation
    Procedure) (Scotland) Act 1947 (c 42)
    Schedule 2
        para 3 238
Act of Regulations 1695. 98
Administration of Justice (Scotland) Act
    1972 (c 59) 106, 302
    s 1 83
    s 3 . . . . 106, 204
        (1), (4). 106
Agricultural Holdings Act 1948 (c 63) . 157,
    166, 205, 235
    s 2 130
    Schedule 6
        para 1 234
Agricultural Holdings Act 1986 (c 5) . 3, 31,
    159, 166, 254
    ss 2, 3 5
    s 17(3) 255
    s 96(1) 4
    Schedule 2
        para 4 145
    Schedule 14
        para 25(8). 253
        para 26(11) 253
        para 33(8). 253
Agricultural Holdings (Amendment)
    (Scotland) Act 1983 (c 46) . . . 1, 2,
    15, 32, 144, 145, 161, 164, 203, 226,
    251, 253, 254
    s 2 . . . . 144, 254
        (d) 11
    s 3 255
    s 4(1), (2) 255
    s 5(1) 255
        (2) 256
    Schedule 1 256
Agricultural Holdings (Notices to Quit) Act
    1977 (c 12) 159
Agricultural Holdings (Scotland) Act 1883
    (c 62) 19, 41, 58, 220
    s 42. 221
Agricultural Holdings (Scotland) Act 1908
    (c 64) 3, 106, 148, 180
Agricultural Holdings (Scotland) Act 1923
    (c 10) . . . 1, 4, 136, 170, 171, 173,
    176–178, 185, 188, 217, 222, 227, 251
    s 3 177
    s 11. 55
    s 27. 153

s 35(1) 193
    Schedule 1
        para 29. 172
Agricultural Holdings (Scotland) Act 1949
    (c 75) . . 1, 2, 55, 71, 140, 155, 156,
    160, 165, 171–173, 178–180, 188, 199,
    217, 251, 252, 254, 292, 297, 313
    ss 1, 2 254
    s 3 254
        (1), (2) 71
    ss 4, 5 254
    s 6(1) 255
        (2) 190, 255
        (3), (4). 254
    ss 7, 8 254
    s 9 . . . . 135, 254
    s 10. 254
    s 11. 255
    s 12. 254
        (1) 193
    ss 13, 14 254
    ss 15, 16 255
    ss 17, 18 254
    s 19. 255
    s 20. 254
        (4) 140
    s 21. . . . . 142, 254
    ss 22, 23 254
    s 24. . . . . 152, 255
        (1) 152, 254
    ss 25, 26 255
    s 26A 255
    ss 27, 28, 30, 31 255
    s 32. . . . . 255, 269
    ss 33–41 255
    s 42. . . . . 181, 255
    s 43. 255
    s 44(1), (4) 255
    ss 45–50 255
    s 51. 255
        (2) 178
    ss 52–56 255
    s 57. 255
        (3) 255
    ss 58–61 255
    ss 63–65 255
    s 66. . . . . 181, 255
    ss 67, 68 255
    ss 69, 70 . . . . 256, 325
    s 73. 256

Agricultural Holdings (Scotland) Act
1949 (cont)
s 74. . . . . 202, 255
ss 75–78 255
s 79. 256
s 80. . . . . 212, 213, 256
ss 82–84 256
s 85. 256
  (1) 4
s 86. 256
s 87
  (1) 256
  (2) 255
ss 88–91 256
s 93. . . . . 221, 256
s 95. 256
s 96. 181
s 97. 256
s 99(2) 256
s 100 . . . . 149, 189, 190
s 101 256
Schedule 1 256
Schedule 2 . . . . 256, 267
Schedules 3–6 256
Schedule 7 244
Agricultural Holdings (Scotland) Act 1991
  (c 55) . 2, 42, 55, **124–252**, 310, 314,
  315, 323, 328
s 1 . . . 3, 4, **128**, 140, 185, 192, 211,
  217–219, 254, 313
  (1) 3, 113, 211, 315
s 2 . . . 2, 5–7, 24, 128, **129**, 130, 152,
  153, 155, 218, 254
  (1) 7, 74, 147, 156, 200
  (2) 5
    (b) 7
    (c) 164
  (3) 7, 82
s 3 . . 8, 63, 71, **130**, 132, 152, 173, 218,
  254
s 4 . . . 8, 10, 82, **131**, 146, 147, 190, 223,
  254, 262, 272–274
  (4) 190
s 5 . . 8–10, 59, 82, 131, **132–133**, 134,
  137, 146, 147, 231, 254, 262, 272, 308
  (1) 137, 138
  (2) 57, 63, 147
    (a) 9–10
  (3) 9, 63, 147, 264, 309
  (5) 82
s 6 . . . . 133, **134**, 254
s 7 . . . . . 63, **134**, 220, 254, 288
  (3) 77, 147
    (b) 176
  (4) 77
  (5)(a) 123
s 8 . . 52, 132, **137**, 174, 188, 189, 191,
  254, 263, 278, 286
  (3) 133, 278
  (4)(6)–(9) 133
s 9 . 54, 57, 135, **138**, 147, 193, 195, 254
  (2) 193

  (3) 194
s 10. . . . . . . **138–139**, 216, 254
s 11. . 19, 20, 36, 37, 63, **139**, 163, 183,
  216, 220, 254, 263, 279, 316, 327–330
  (3) 263, 279
  (6) 329
  (8) 20
s 12. . 1, 20, 36, 94, **141–142**, 254, 263,
  279, 280, 328
  (2) 20, 263, 280, 281
s 13. . . 11, 12, 17, 65, 74, 81, 83, 117,
  122, **142–144**, 146, 147, 183, 235, 237,
  254, 262, 274, 299, 310, 320
  (1) . 16, 146, 147, 203, 233, 234, 237,
  275
  (2) 88, 147, 187
  (3) 12, 13
  (4) 12, 13, 14, 97
  (8) 11
  (9) 81
s 14. 10, 11, 132, 134, 144, **146**, 147, 254
s 15. . . 17, 81, 83, **146**, 147, 237, 254,
  262, 274, 275
  (1) 12, 16, 144
s 16. . . . . 131, **147**, 254
s 17. . . . . . 78, 136, **147–148**, 254
  (1)(a), (b) 278
s 18. . 58, 63, 72, 80, 137, **148–149**, 155,
  176, 180, 181, 254, 262, 263, 276, 277
  (3) 277
s 19. . . . . . 63, 82, 109, **150**, 254
s 20. . . . . . 60, 139, **150**, 151, 255
s 21. . . 8, 11, 24, 36, 37, 131, **151–152**,
  158, 163, 164, 167, 255, 262, 265, 330
  (1) 23, 71
  (3) 23, 144, 159
    (c), (d) 154
  (4) 23
  (5) 23, 216, 265
  (6) 24, 32, 59, 220
  (7) 72, 149
s 22. . 25, **155–156**, 159, 160, 165, 166,
  188, 198, 255, 262, 265
  (1) . . 25, 30–32, 37, 49, 51, 65, 82,
  159, 160, 167, 169, 184, 196, 197, 262,
  267–269
  (2) 23, 159, 169, 268
    (a) 6, 26, 49, 184
    (b) 26, 35, 49, 75, 161, 162, 186, 266
    (c) 27, 49, 165, 184
    (d) . 25, 27–31, 49, 133, 151, 169,
  170, 184, 207, 208, 262, 288
    (e) . . . 25, 31, 49, 133, 184, 269
    (f) 32, 49, 184, 220, 330
    (g) 32, 36, 49, 51, 164, 262, 266, 267
s 23. . 31, 156, **159–160**, 255, 262, 268
  (1) 32
  (2) 25, 30, 158, 169, 207, 208, 266, 328
  (3) 26, 155, 269, 328
  (4) 156
  (6) 64
s 24. 38, 156, **160–161**, 164, 198, 226, 255

Agricultural Holdings (Scotland) Act
1991, s 24 (*cont*)
  (1) 32, 164, 266, 267
    (a) 32–33, 40, 50, 196
    (b) . .33, 39, 40, 51, 196–198, 267
    (c) . .33, 40, 51, 75, 196, 198, 199
    (d) 34–35, 40
    (e) . . 35–36, 39, 40, 51, 75, 157,
  197, 198, 267
  (2) 32, 40, 170
  (3) 40, 165, 166
s 25. . . 20, 36, 37, 155, 159, **163–164**,
  198, 224–226, 255, 329
  (1) 36, 156
  (2) 36, 160, 198, 262, 266
    (a) 156, 197
    (b) 156, 197, 266
    (c) 141, 267
    (d) 36, 197
    (f) 328
  (3) . . . 37, 40, 160, 197, 224, 226
    (b) 38, 226
  (4) 40, 161, 163
s 26. . 33, 61, 157, 159, **164–165**, 255
s 27. . . . . . 82, 163, 164, **165**, 255
s 28. . . . . 61, **166**, 255
  (2) 262, 271
s 29. . . .25, 81, 152, **167**, 168, 169, 185,
  192, 219, 255, 262, 270
  (1) 167
  (2) 270
s 30. . . 49, 76, 80, 160, 167, **168**, 169,
  184, 185, 219, 255, 262, 270
s 31. . . . 12, 72, 81, 144, 167, **168**, 192,
  219, 255
s 32. 30, 31, 157, 158, **169–170**, 208, 255
  (2) 30
  (3) 30, 31
  (4) 30
  (5) 30, 40
  (6) 31, 208
s 33. . **170–171**, 188, 217, 227–229, 255
  (1) 212
s 34. . 63, **171–172**, 176, 185, 191, 255,
  315
  (2) 79
  (4) 195
  (5 . . . . 48, 188
  (6) 48, 175
  (7) 53, 63, 178, 195
  (8) 79
s 35. . . . 53, 138, **173–174**, 255, 286
  (2) 94, 107
  (3) 262, 276
  (4) 181
s 36. . . . 145, 171, **175**, 188, 231, 255
  (4) 171, 173
s 37. . . 53, 79, **176**, 178, 255, 263, 281
  (2) 195
s 38. . . .53, 79, **177–178**, 231, 255, 263,
  282, 283
  (2) 44

  (3) 178
  (5) 195
s 39. . . . 171, **178–179**, 231, 255, 282
  (1) 263, 283
  (2) 78
  (3) 146, 147, 263, 283
s 40. . 171, 173, **179–180**, 182, 183, 231,
  232, 255
  (3) 212
  (4)(a) 148
s 41. . . 82, 171, 173, 180, **181–183**, 255
  (3)–(6) 184
s 42. . . 53, 171, 173, **183–184**, 195, 255
  (2) 83
s 43. . 32, 49, 63, 72, 80, **184–185**, 196,
  197, 255, 286, 330
  (4)(b) 80
  (6) 197, 198
  (7) 168, 169
s 44. . . 43, 60, 72, 80, 133, 137, 145,
  155, **187–188**, 255, 263, 284, 286, 330
  (2) 205
s 45. . . .60, 83, 133, 137, **189**, 190, 191,
  255, 263, 284, 287, 288, 330
  (1)(b) 190
  (3) 195
    (b) 190
s 46. . . . 137, **190**, 255, 262, 273, 274
  (2) 189
  (3) 262, 274
  (4) 189
s 47. . . . . . 189, **190–191**, 255
  (1) 83, 205
  (3) 285
s 48. . . . . 63, **191**, 255
s 49. . . . 72, 167, 169, **192**, 219, 255
  (1)(b) 72
  (3), (4) 129
s 50. . 173, **192–193**, 197, 198, 219, 255,
  324
s 51. . . . . 54, **193**, 255
  (1) 57, 195, 196
    (a) 138
s 52. .55, 63, 81, **194**, 255, 263, 277, 278
  (2)(b) 278
s 53. . . . . . . 44, 53, **195**, 255
  (2), (3) 45
s 54. . 35, 36, 49–51, 63, 80, 152, 167,
  168, 185, 186, 196–198, 199, 201, 255,
  262, 265–267, 286, 330
  (2) 237
s 55. .49, 76, 80, 152, **196–198**, 201, 255
  (1) 50, 51, 198
    (a) 75, 200, 267
    (b), (c) 267
  (2) 51, 198, 200
  (3) 76
  (4) 76, 201
  (5) 187, 193, 201
  (6) 76
s 56. 74, 198, **199**, 200, 201, 237, 238, 255
  (1) 200, 201, 237, 238

Agricultural Holdings (Scotland) Act
1991 (cont)
s 57. . . 74, 76, **199–200**, 201, 237, 255
  (4) 199
s 58. .51, 74, 80, 155, 199, **200–201**, 255
s 59. . . . . 74, 255
Pt VII (ss 60–72) 85
s 60. .63, 77–78, 84, 101, 106, 149, 150,
  176, 183, **202**, 203, 205, 206, 255, 323
  (1) 324, 325
  (2) 7, 77, 323, 324
s 61. . 92, 101, 106, 148, **202–203**, 211,
  232, 255, 263, 287
  (1) 197
  (2) . . 16, 17, 92, 144, 146, 147, 233,
  235–237
  (7) 84, 86, 101, 106, 107, 148, 202, 205
s 62. . . . 185, 188, 203, **204–205**, 255
  (2) 80, 83, 263, 285
  (4) 263, 288, 289
s 63. . . . . .85, **205–206**, 255
s 64. . . 78, 85, **206**, 215, 255, 323–325
s 65. . . . . .98, **206**, 256, 325
s 66. . . 27, 28, 31, 134, 157, 158, 160,
  170, **206–208**, 256
  (1) 28, 30, 169
  (a) 28, 29, 31
  (c) 28
  (2) 29
  (3) 29, 31, 170
  (4) 29, 30
s 67. . . . . 93, **208**, 256
s 68. . 98, 101, 128, 147, **208–209**, 211,
  217, 256, 330
  (1) 211
  (2) 80
s 69. . 101, 106, 128, 147, 208, 209, **210**,
  211, 217, 256
  (3) 235
s 70. . . 101, 128, 147, 208, 209, **210**,
  211, 217, 238, 241, 256
s 71. . . 101, 104, 128, 208, 209, **211**,
  217, 256
s 72. . .3, 101, 128, 208, 209, **211**, 217,
  256
s 73. . . . . **211–212**, 256
s 74. . 80, 197, 198, 202, **212**, 214, 256,
  325
s 75. . . . . . . 61, **212–213**, 216, 256
  (1)–(4), (6) 325
s 76. . . . . **213–214**, 256
s 77. . . . .**214**, 256
s 78. . 43, 172, 174, 176, 196, **214**, 235,
  256, 316
s 79. . . . . . . **214**, 223, 256, 311
s 80. . . . . 206, **215**, 256, 323–325
ss 81, 82 . . . .**215**, 256
s 83. . . . .**216**, 256
s 84. . . . . . . .11, **216**, 256, 326
  (4) 219, 263, 286
s 85. . 3, 18, 59, 64, 256, 307, 320, 321
s 85(1) . . 3–5, 21, 128–130, 135, 137,

140–142, 149, 151–153, 156, 168, 172,
173, 180, 188, 192, 193, 205, 209, 212,
214, **217–218**, 312–314, 329
  (4) 172
  (5) 152, 157
s 86. . . . .**222**, 256
s 87. . . . . **222**, 250, 256
s 88. . . . . **222**, 244, 256
s 89. . . . .**222**, 256
Schedule 1 .8, 68, 82, 131, 132, **223**, 256
  para 5 216
Schedule 2 37–40, 51, 141, 163, 164, 197,
  198, **224–226**, 256, 267
Pt I. 37–38
Pt II 37, 38
Pt III 36, 37
  para 1 164
Schedule 3 41–43, 78, 79, 170, 181, 189,
  227–228, 256
Pt I. 42, 79, 176
Pt II 42, 43–44, 79, 149, 177
  para 19. 178
Pt III .42, 44–45, 53, 172, 173, 180, 184,
  193
  para 29. 172
Schedule 4 41–43, 78, 79, 170, 181, 189,
  256
Pt I. 42, 79, 176
Pt II 42, 43–44, 79, 149, 177
Pt III .42, 44–45, 53, 172, 173, 180, 184,
  193
  para 28. 171
  para 29. 172
Schedule 5 . .41–43, 78, 171, 181, 189,
  211, **229–231**, 256, 302
Pt I. . . . 42, 79, 176, 263, 281, 285
Pt II . 42, 43–44, 78, 79, 149, 177, 178,
  263, 282, 283, 285
Pt III . . 42, 44–45, 107, 174, 180, 193,
  276, 285, 301, 308
  para 32. 171
Schedule 6 42, 45, 66–67, 179–181, 183,
  184, 189, 211, 231, **232**, 256
Schedule 7 . 85–87, 106, 116, 117, 169,
  203, 205, **232–234**, 256, 263, 290
  para 2 86
  para 3 290
  para 5 . 78, 83, 88, 205, 211, 263, 287
  (a) 288
  (b) 88
  para 6 91
  para 8 . . . . .96, 98, 291
  para 10. . . . . . . 15, 146, 147
  para 11. 16
  para 12(a). 97
  para 14. . . . . . . 97, 324, 325
  para 18. 293
  para 19. . . . . 88, 297
  para 20. . . 92, 147, 263, 287, 299
  para 21. . . . . . 93, 146, 147
  para 22. . . 17, 92, 144, 146, 147
  para 24. 98

Agricultural Holdings (Scotland) Act
1991 (cont)
Schedule 8   74, 199, 200, 201, **237–238**, 256
  para 1 74
Schedule 9 . . 101, 102–103, 104, 210,
238–241, 256, 304
Pts I–III 209
Schedule 10 . . 101, 103–104, 209, 210,
241–243, 256, 304
Pts I–III 209
Schedule 11 . . . . . 222, **244–250**
Schedule 12 . . . . .222, **250**
Schedule 13 222
Agricultural Holdings (Scotland)
Amendment Act 1910 (c 30) . . 204
Agricultural Land Sales (Restriction of
Notice to Quit) Act 1919 (c 63) . .61
Agriculture Act 1920 (c 76) 188
  s 10(3) 181
Agriculture Act 1958 (c 71) . . . 1, 2, 36,
154, 156, 161, 254
  s 2 144
  s 3 252
    (1) 255
    (2) 2, 255
    (3) 255
  s 6 2
    (1), (2) 140
  s 9(1) 254
  Schedule 1 252
  Pt II 165, 179
    paras 32, 33 254
    paras 34–36 255
    para 37 . . . . . . 160, 255
    para 38 . . . . . . 165, 255
    paras 40–43 255
Agriculture Act 1967 (c 22)
  s 26(1) 247
  s 27(5B) 247
  s 28(1)(a) 247
  s 29(3)(a) 247
    (4) 51, 156, 197, 198, 247
  s 48(2)(a) 248
  Schedule 3
    para 5 215
    para 7(5) 202, 203, 206,
248
Agriculture Act 1986 (c 49) 1, 2
  s 2(1)(a), (b) 119
  s 14 . . . .**310**, 326
    (a) 249
  s 15(3), (7) 148
  s 16 . . . 114, 117, 144, 249, **310–311**
    (2) 117
    (3) 118
      (b) 117
    (4), (6) 118
    (7) 214
  s 17(3) 254
  s 18(b) 249
  s 19(4) 249
  s 23 249

Schedule 2 . . . 118, 120, 174, 206,
310, **312–313**
  para 1 . . . . . . 250, 253, 311
  para 2 . . . . . . 117, 119, 311
    (1) 113
    (a) 119
    (2) 113, 114, 311
  para 3 . . . . 117, 119, 311, 312
    (1)(b) 250
  para 4 311
  para 7 250
  para 9 120
  para 10 215
    (1) 203, 250
  para 11 . . . . . . 118, 215, 250
    (4) 203, 236
    (5) 193
  para 12 . . . . 213, 250
Agriculture (Miscellaneous Provisions) Act
1963 (c 11) 2, 102, 254
  s 21 . . . . 253, 257
Agriculture (Miscellaneous Provisions) Act
1968 (c 34) 1, 2, 226, 254
  Pt II (ss 9–17) 253
  ss 9, 11 . . . . 163, 255
  s 12 255
    (2) 199
  ss 14–16 255
  s 17 . . . . 200, 255
    (3) 256
  Schedule 4 . . . . . . 253, 256
  Schedule 5 253
    paras 1, 5 255
    paras 6, 7 256
Agriculture (Miscellaneous Provisions) Act
1976 (c 55) 2, 170, 254
  s 13 . . . . 208, 253, 256
  s 14 . . . . 253, 255
    (6) 256
Agriculture (Safety, Health and Welfare
Provisions) Act 1956 (c 49)
  s 25(4) 133, 139, 245
    (5) 146, 245
    (10) 245
Agriculture (Scotland) Act 1948 (c 45). 173,
217, 254
  Pt I (ss 1–25) 2, 49, 222
  s 43(1) 55, 194
  s 52 . . . . 55, 252
  s 54 252
  s 64 . . . . . . 33, 161, 167, 200
  s 86(1) 3, 128
    (2) 219
  Schedule 5 . . 139, 162, 165, 218, **331**
  Schedule 6 . . .49, 137, 157, 158, 165,
218, **331–332**
Allotments (Scotland) Act 1922 (c 52). 252
Arbitration (Scotland) Act 1894 (c 13). 203
  ss 2–4 . . . .**109**, 204
Bankruptcy Act 1842 (c 122) 220
Bankruptcy (Scotland) Act 1913 (c 20) 59,
152

Bankruptcy (Scotland) Act 1985 (c 66) . 2,
  59, 152, 158, 217, 218
s 7 . . . . 32, 156, 182, 183
s 75(9) 158
Civil Evidence (Scotland) Act 1988 (c 32) 91
Coal Mining (Subsidence) Act 1957 (c 59)
s 10(1)(a). 245
Companies Act 1985 (c 6). 213
s 725(1) 256
Control of Pollution Act 1974 (c 40)
s 31B 61, 165
  (2)(a) 249
Conveyancing and Feudal Reform (Scotland)
  Act 1970 (c 35)
Schedule 1
  para 5(a) 248
Criminal Law Act 1977 (c 45)
s 31. 256
Criminal Procedure (Scotland) Act 1975
  (c 21)
s 289 256
Crofters Holdings (Scotland) Act 1886
  (c 29) 167, 313, 328
s 6 310
s 16. . . . . 316, 327, 328
s 33. 129
s 34. 321
Crofters (Scotland) Act 1955 (c 21). . 328
s 3(1) 313, 327, 328
  (2) 310, 313
s 5(3) 310
s 10. . . . . 316, 327
s 11. 316
  (5) 313
s 14(10) 244
s 37. 320
  (1) 244, 312
Schedule 2
  para 10. 244
Crofters (Scotland) Act 1961 (c 58)
s 13(1) 247
Crofters (Scotland) Act 1993 (c 44). . 310,
  313, 315
s 10. 328
Crofting Reform (Scotland) Act 1976 (c 21) .
  3, 314
Schedule 2
  para 25. . . . . 253, 256
Crown Proceedings Act 1947 (c 44)
s 21. 85
s 43(a). 84
Deer (Amendment) (Scotland) Act 1982
  (c 19) 55, 194
Finance Act 1975 (c 7) 329
Finance Act 1994 (c 9)
s 240 308
Hill Farming Act 1946 (c 73) .103, 147, 209,
  244, 254
s 9 244
ss 28–30 . . . . 252, 257
s 31. 252
Schedule 2 . . . . 252, 256

Horticulture Act 1960 (c 22)
s 1(1)(b) 247
Housing Act 1964 (c 56)
s 38(2) 231
Housing and Planning Act 1986 (c 63)
Schedule 8 36
  para 5 147
Schedule 11
  para 12. 147
Housing (Scotland) Act 1966 (c 49)
s 80(2) 231
Housing (Scotland) Act 1974 (c 45) . 231
Housing (Scotland) Act 1987 (c 26)
s 246 176
s 256 . . . . 146–147, 176, 179, 231
  (1), (3). 251
s 338(1) 251
Schedule 8
  para 13(1). 251
  (2) 230, 251
Housing (Scotland) Act 1988 (c 43)
Schedule 4
  para 6(a) 251
Hypothec Abolition (Scotland) Act 1880
  (c 12) 151
Income and Corporation Taxes Act 1988 (c 1)
Pt II (ss 21–43). 185
Interpretation Act 1978 (c 30)
s 7 . . . . 216, 326
s 16. 252
Schedule 1 208
Land Compensation (Scotland) Act 1963
  (c 51) 199
Pt I (ss 1–7). 238
Pt II (ss 8–11) 238
s 40. 238
Land Compensation (Scotland) Act 1973
  (c 56) 74, 75
s 31(3)(c). 248
s 44. . . . . .75, 76, 248
s 52. 248
s 55. . . . . .75–76, 248
  (2) 168, 200
  (8) 201
80(1) 248
Land Tenure Reform (Scotland) Act 1974
  (c 38) 160
s 8(5)(a) 249
s 17. 317
Lands Clauses Consolidation Act 1845
  (c 18)
s 114 74–76
Lands Clauses Consolidation (Scotland) Act
  1845 (c 19)
ss 56–60, 62–65, 67–70, 72, 74–79,
  83–87, 114, 115, 117 238
Law Reform (Miscellaneous Provisions)
  (Scotland) Act 1985 (c 73) . . 24, 59
s 4 154
s 7(1)(b) 154
  (2) 249
s 32. . . . . 253, 256

Limited Partnerships Act 1907 (c 24) . . 64
Livestock Rearing Act 1951 (c 18)
   s 1(2)(b) 252
Local Government (Scotland) Act 1973
   (c 65) 254
   s 228(4) 204
   (5) 253, 255
Market Gardeners' Compensation (Scotland)
   Act 1897 (c 22) 180
Matrimonial Homes (Family Protection)
   (Scotland) Act 1981 (c 59)
   s 13(8) 249
New Towns (Scotland) Act 1968 (c 16)
   s 7 200
   Schedule 6
     para 4 238
Opencast Coal Act 1958 (c 69)
   s 2 157
   s 14. 144
   s 14A 36, 245
   (6) 157, 161, 162
   s 24. . . . . . 174, 205, 231
   (10). 245
   s 25. . . . . 189, 190
   (3) 246
   s 26. . . . . 212, 231
   (6) 246
   s 27. 149
   (4) 246
   s 28. 212
   (6) 246
   s 52(2), (5) 246
   Schedule 6
     para 31. 246
   Schedule 7
     para 25(a) 246
Partnership Act 1890 (c 39)
   s 4(2) 38, 226, 315
Rating Act 1971 (c 39) 220
Recorded Delivery Service Act 1962 (c 27) .
   153, 216
Registration of Leases (Scotland) Act 1857
   (c 26) 212
Removal Terms (Scotland) Act 1886 (c 50) .
   153
   s 6 152
Rent (Scotland) Act 1984 (c 58)
   s 25(1)(iii) 249
Requirements of Writing (Scotland) Act
   1995 (c 7). 131, 214
Reserve and Auxiliary Forces (Protection of
   Civil Interests) Act 1951 (c 65). . 156
   s 21. . . . . 244, 252
   s 22(4)(a). 244
   s 24. . . . . 250, 252
   s 38(6)(a)(i) 244
Sheep Stocks Valuation (Scotland) Act 1937
   (c 34) . . . 101, 103, 209, 210, 252,
   254
   ss 1–4 257
Sheriff Courts (Scotland) Act 1907 (c 51)
   . . . . 23, 151–154, 265

Sheriff Courts (Scotland) Act 1971 (c 58)
   s 4 . . . . 255, 256
   s 49. 208
Small Landholders and Agricultural
   Holdings (Scotland) Act 1931 (c 44) . 2,
   167, 170, 171, 173, 176, 177, 217, 222,
   228, 328
   s 13. 196
   s 28(2) 177
   s 40. 173
   Schedule 1
     para 30. 172
Small Landholders (Scotland) Act 1911
   (c 49) . 187, 201, 217, 312, 313, 315,
   320, 321, 328
   s 2 . . . . 310, 313
   (1)(iii) 196
   (2) 313
   s 32. 313
   (1) 201, 310
   (7) 237, 310
   (8) 237
   (15). 200, 201
Succession (Scotland) Act 1964 (c 41). 1, 2,
   18–22, 139, 254
   Pt I (ss 1–7) 139
   s 14. . . 18, 20, 139, 141, 327, 328
   s 16. . . 18, 20, 21, 37, 140–142, 163,
   164, 186, 316, 326, **327–328**, 329
   (2) 20
   (c) 247
   (3) 22, 313
   (b) 21, 247
   (4) 22
   (a) 22
   (8) 141, 247
   (9) 247
   s 23(5) 36, 225
   s 29(2) 140, 247
   s 32(2) 329
   s 34(1) 254
   s 36(2) 18
   Schedule 1 . . . . . . 142, 329
   Schedule 2
     paras 19–21 . . . . . 253, 254
     para 22. . . . . 142, 253, 254
     para 23. 253
Term and Quarter Days (Scotland) Act 1990
   (c 22) . . 23, 24, 142, 151, 154, 211,
   221
   s 1 23
   (3) 24
   (5) 221
   (7) 23
Town and Country Planning (Scotland) Act
   1972 (c 52)
   s 24. 157
   ss 102, 110 200
   Schedule 21
     Pt II. 255
Tribunals and Inquiries Act 1971 (c 62) 15,
   86, 94, 275, 290, 296

Water Act 1989 (c 15)
  Schedule 25
    para 12. 255
Water (Scotland) Act 1980 (c 45)
  Pt V (ss 63–67). 213

s 65. 213
  (2), (4), (6)–(10) 213
Schedule 10 256
  Pt II. 251

Statutory Instruments

Agricultural Holdings (Scotland) Act 1949
  (Variation of First Schedule) Order 1978
  (SI 1978/798) 253, 254, 256
Agricultural Holdings (Scotland) Regulations
  1950 (SI 1950/1553) . . . 253, 254,
  255
Agricultural Holdings (Servicemen)
  (Scotland) Regulations 1952 (SI 1952/
  1338) 156
Agricultural Holdings (Specification of
  Forms) (Scotland) Order 1991
  (SI 1991/2154) 96, 204, 333
Agrcultural Records (Scotland) Regulations
  1948 (SI 1948/2817) 133
Agriculture (Adaptation of Enactments)
  (Scotland) Regulations 1979 (SI 1977/
  2007) 255
Arable Area Payment Regulations 1994
  (SI 1994/947) 123
Dairy Produce Quotas (Amendment)
  Regulations 1994 (SI 1994/2448) . 112,
  314
Dairy Produce Quotas (Amendment)
  Regulations 1994 (SI 1994/2919) . 112,
  314
Dairy Produce Quotas (Amendment)
  Regulations 1995 (SI 1995/254) . 112,
  314
Dairy Produce Quotas Regulations 1984
  (SI 1984/1047) 112
Dairy Produce Quotas Regulations 1986
  (SI 1986/470) 312, 313
Dairy Produce Quotas Regulations 1991
  (SI 1991/2232) 313
reg 2(1) 114
Schedule 9 . . . . 113, 114
Dairy Produce Quotas Regulations 1994
  (SI 1994/672) 112, 314
reg 2(1) 112, 113, 114
reg 7 . . . . 114, 323
  (1) 114
    (a) 114
  (2)(a), (b) 114
  (6)(iii) 314
regs 8(4), (5) 114
reg 10 . . . . 114, 117
  (a) 316
  (b)(ii) 115, 316
reg 11 114
  (2) 114
reg 12 115
reg 13(2) 120
regs 15(1), (3), (4). 120

Schedule 1
  para 6(5)(b) 320
Schedule 3 . . . . 115, 316
  para 1(3) 115
  para 2 319
    (1) 115, 117
  paras 3–19 116
  para 3(1)–(3) 115
  para 12. 115
  para 20. 116
  paras 21, 22, 25 117
  para 28. 115
Schedule 5
  para 5 115
Hill Farming Act 1946 (Variation of Second
  Schedule) (Scotland) Order 1986
  (SI 1986/1823) 209, 210, 253, 254, 256
Milk Quota (Calculation of Standard Quota)
  (Scotland) Amendment (No 2) Order
  1987 (SI 1987/870) 319
Milk Quota (Calculation of Standard Quota)
  (Scotland) Amendment Order 1988
  (SI 1988/714) 319
Milk Quota (Calculation of Standard Quota)
  (Scotland) Amendment Order 1990
  (SI 1990/943) 319
Milk Quota (Calculation of Standard Quota)
  (Scotland) Amendment Order 1991
  (SI 1991/2309) 319
Milk Quota (Calculation of Standard Quota)
  (Scotland) Amendment Order 1992
  (SI 1992/1152) 319
Milk Quota (Calculation of Standard Quota)
  (Scotland) Order 1986 (SI 1986/1475)
  318, 319
Set-Aside Access (Scotland) Regulations
  1994 (SI 1994/3085) 123
Set-Aside (Amendment) Regulations 1990
  (SI 1990/1716) 122
Set-Aside Regulations 1988 (SI 1988/1352)
  122
Sheep Annual Premium and Suckler Cow
  Premium Quotas (Amendment)
  Regulations 1993 (SI 1993/3036) . 121
reg 5(2) 122
Sheep Annual Premium and Suckler Cow
  Premium Quotas (Amendment)
  Regulations 1994 (SI 1994/2894) . 121
Sheep Annual Premium and Suckler Cow
  Premium Quotas Regulations 1993
  (SI 1993/1626) 121
regs 6(1), 7 122
regs 8, 9 121

TABLE OF LEGISLATION

European Regulations

Commission Regulation (EEC) 2293/92 123
Commission Regulation (EEC) 334/93 123
Commission Regulation (EEC) 536/93 112
Commission Regulation (EEC) 1756/93 112
Commission Regulation (EC) 470/94 . 112
Council Regulation (EEC) 804/68 . . 112
Council Regulation (EEC) 856/84 . . 112
Council Regulation (EEC) 857/84 art 3a 113
Council Regulation (EEC) 590/85 . . 323
Council Regulation (EEC) 2998/87. . 120
Council Regulation (EEC) 763/89 . . 113

Council Regulation (EEC) 764/89 . . 113
Council Regulation (EEC) 306/91 . . 114
Council Regulation (EEC) 1765/92. . 123
Council Regulation (EEC) 3950/92. . 112
  art 6 120
  art 9(c) 314
  (d) 112, 314
Council Regulation (EEC) 748/93 . . 112
Council Regulation (EEC) 1560/93. . 112
Council Regulation (EEC) 2055/93. . 113

TABLE OF CASES

Aberdeen Endowments Trust v Will 1985 SLT (Land Ct) 23. . . . 14, 16, 145, 204, 235
Adam v Smythe 1948 SC 445 235
Admiralty, The v Burns 1910 SC 531; 1910 1 SLT 277 . . . . .69, 71, 155
Allan v Thomson (1829) 7 S 784 136
Allan's Trs v Allan & Son (1891) 19 R 215 157
Allan-Fraser's Trs v Macpherson 1981 SLT (Land Ct) 17 130
Alston's Trs v Muir 1919 2 SLT 8. . . . . 136, 153
Altyre Estate Trs v McLay 1975 SLT (Land Ct) 12 . . . . 39, 162, 226
Anderson v Gibb 1991, unreported 83
—— v McCall (1866) 4 M 765 136
—— v Moray District Council 1978 SLT (Lands Tr) 37 75
—— v Tod 1809 Hume 842 136
Andrew v Smith (1983) Strathclyde RN 242 140
Arbroath Town Council v Carrie 1972 SLCR App 114 162
Armstrong & Co v McGregor & Co (1875) 2 R 339 136
Ashdale Land & Property Co Ltd v Manners [1992] 2 EGLR 5 130
Auckland, Lady v Dowie 1964 SLT (Land Ct) 20; 1965 SLT 76 194
Austin v Gibson 1979 SLT (Land Ct) 12 . . . . 133, 153, 165, 221
Avon County Council v Clothier (1977) 242 EG 1048 130
Bahamas International Trust Co Ltd v Threadgold [1974] 1 WLR 1514; [1974] 3 All ER 428;
    [1974] 3 All ER 881. 130
Baird's Exr v IRC 1991 SLT (Lands Tr) 9 329
Ballantyne v Brechin (1893) 1 SLT 306 151
Barbour v M'Douall 1914 SC 844. . . . . 148, 178, 186, 187, 316
Barns-Graham v Lamont 1971 SC 170; 1971 SLT 341. . . . . . . 34, 159, 198
Barr v Strang & Gardner 1935 SLT (Sh Ct) 10 . . . . 4, 219
Barrow Green Estate Co v Walker's Exrs [1954] 1 All ER 204 190
Bebington v Wildman [1921] 1 Ch 559 193
Beevers v Manson (1978) 37 P & CR 452 157
Bell v Forestry Commission 1980 SLCR App 116 141
—— v Graham 1908 SC 1060 . . . . 173, 236
—— v McCubbin [1989] EG 100 157
—— v Simpson 1965 SLT (Sh Ct) 9 209
Benington-Wood's Trs v Mackay 1969 SLT (Land Ct) 9 . . . . 161, 162
Bennett v Stone [1920] 1 Ch 266 221
Bennie v Mack (1832) 10 S 255 187
Bennion and National Provincial Banks' Arbitration (1965) 115 LJ 302 235
Bernays v Prosser [1963] 2 QB 592 . . . . 129, 218
Berwick v Baird [1930] 2 Ch 359 219
Bevan v Chambers (1896) 12 TLR 417 221
Beveridge and Ors v McAdam (1925) Sh Ct Rep 288 185
Bickerdike v Lucy [1920] 1 KB 707 . . . . 180, 220
Birmingham Corporation v West Midland Baptist (Trust) Association [1970] AC 874 . 201
Black v Clay (1894) 21 R (HL) 72. . . . . 153, 221
Black (Alexander) & Sons v Paterson 1968 SLT (Sh Ct) 64 . . . . . . 144, 219
Blair v Meikle (1934) Sh Ct Rep 224 173
Blay v Dadswell [1922] 1 KB 632 166
Boyd v McDonald 1958 SLCR 10. . . . . 144, 202
—— v Wilton [1957] 2 QB 277 190
Bradshaw v Bird [1920] 3 KB 144. 221
Brand's Trs v Brand's Trs (1876) 3 R (HL) 16 149
Breadalbane, Marquis of v Robertson 1914 SC 215 186
—— v Stewart (1904) 6 F (HL) 23 . . . . 154, 221
British Alcan Aluminium Co v Shaw 1987 SLCR 1 . . . . 144, 145

British Rail Pension Trustee Co Ltd v Wilson 1989 SLT 340 . . . . 151, 154
Broadland Properties Estates Ltd v Mann 1994 SLT (Land Ct) 7 . . . 117, 144, 311, 312
—— v —— Highland RN 449, 5th May 1995 312
Brodie v Ker; McCallum v McNair 1952 SC 216 . . . . 77, 151, 153, 202
Brown v Stoneman [1973] 1 WLR 459 158
Brown v Tiernan [1993] 1 EGLR 11 130
Broxburn Oil Co Ltd v Earl of Buchan (1926) 42 Sh Ct Rep 300 236
Brunskill v Atkinson 1884 Sol J 29 231
Buccleuch v Kennedy 1986 SLCR App 1 145
Buchanan v Buchanan 1983 SLT (Land Ct) 31 . . . . 161, 165
Budge v Gunn 1925 SLCR 74 . . . . 129, 219
—— v Hicks [1951] 2 KB 335 159
—— v Mackenzie (1934) Sh Ct Rep 168 202
Burnett v Gordon 1950 SLCR 9 163
Callander v Smith (1890) 2 F 1140 180
—— v —— (1900) 8 SLT 109 186
—— v Watherston 1970 SLT (Land Ct) 13 . . . . 153, 154
Cambusmore Estate Trust v Little 1991 SLT (Land Ct) 33 . . . . . . 121, 122, 165
Cameron v Duke of Argyll's Trs 1981 SLT (Land Ct) 2 . . . . 3, 129
—— v Ferrier (1912) Sh Ct Rep 220 208
Carnegie v Davidson 1966 SLT (Land Ct) 3 . . . . 39, 162
Carron Co v Donaldson (1858) 20 D 681 136–137
Carson v Cornwall County Council [1993] 1 EGLR 21 . . . . 120, 323
Cave v Page (1923) 67 SJ 659 172
Cayzer v Hamilton (No 2) 1995 SLCR 13 . . . . 156, 157
Chalmers' Tr v Dick's Tr 1909 SC 761 154
Chalmers Property Investment Co Ltd v MacColl 1951 SC 24 . . . . . 205, 235
Christison's Trs v Callender Brodie (1905) 8 F 928 220
Clark v Hume (1902) 5 F 252 187
Clarke v Smith 1981 SLCR App 84 . . . . 35, 161, 162
Coates v Diment [1951] 1 All ER 890 . . . . 155, 195
Coats v Logan 1985 SLT 221 . . . . 20, 140, 142, 329
Collett v Deeley (1949) 100 LJ 108 . . . . 235, 288
Combey v Gumbrill [1990] 2 EGLR 7 . . . . 131, 152
Commissioners of Crown Lands v Grant 1955 SLCR 25 . . . . 206, 215
Cooke (ED & AD) Bourne (Farms) Ltd v Mellows [1983] QB 104 . . . . . 205, 235
Cooper v Muirden 1950 SLCR 45 163
—— v Pearce [1896] 1 QB 562 220
Copeland v McQuaker 1973 SLT 186 . . . . 35, 159, 186, 187, 196, 198
Cormack v McIldowie's Exrs, 1974 SLT 178; 1975 SC 161; 1975 SLT 212 18, 130, 203, 329
Coutts v Barclay-Harvey 1956 SLT (Sh Ct) 54 . . . . 205, 221
Cowan v Wrayford [1953] 2 All ER 1138 159
Cowane's Hospital, Patrons of v Rennie 1966 SLCR App 147 162
Cowdray v Ferries 1919 SC (HL) 27 203
Cowe v Millar 1923; unreported 145
Craig and Anr, Applicants 1981 SLT (Land Ct) 12 . . . . 130, 202
Crawford v Dun 1981 SLT (Sh Ct) 66 . . . . 4, 129, 155
—— v McKinlay 1954 SLCR 39 162
Crichton-Stuart v Ogilvie 1914 SC 888 155
Crown Estate Commissioners v Gunn 1961 SLCR App 173 14
Cunningham v Fife County Council 1948 SC 439 219
Cushnie v Thomson 1954 SLCR 33 152
Dale v Hatfield Chase Corporation [1922] 2 KB 282 . . . . 187, 221
Datnow v Jones [1985] 2 EGLR 1 216
Davidson v Chiskan Estate Co Ltd 1952 SLCR 41 202
—— v Hunter (1888) Sh Ct Rep 33 46
Davies v Barber 1965 SLCR App 133 162
Dean v Secretary of State for War [1950] 1 All ER 344 186
Department of Agriculture for Scotland v Goodfellow 1931 SLT 388 153
Derby (Lord) and Fergusson's Contract, Re [1912] 1 Ch 479 . . . . . 219, 221
Dickson v Allison 1976 SLCR 108 34
—— v Boucher (1984) 269 EG 1159 157

Digby and Penny, In re [1932] 2 KB 491 159
Disraeli Agreement, Re [1939] Ch 382 . . . . 72, 155
Donaldson's Hospital v Esslemont 1925 SLT 92; 1925 SC 199 130
——— v ——— 1926 SC (HL) 68 203
Dow Agrochemicals Ltd v EA Lane (North Lynn) Ltd (1965) 192 EG 737 . . . 157, 162
Drummond v Thomson (1921) 37 Sh Ct Rep 180 220
Duff v Keith (1857) 19 D 713 220
Duguid v Muirhead 1926 SC 1078 . . . . 130, 152
Dunbar's Trs v Anderson 1985 SLCR 1 . . . . 144, 145
——— v Bruce (1900) 3 F 137 . . . . 129, 219
Duncan v Anderson 1985 SLCR 1 144
Dundas v Morison (1875) 20 D 225 220
Dundee Corporation v Guthrie 1969 SLT 93 . . . . 144, 235
Dunlop v Mundell 1943 SLT 286 . . . . 210, 236
Dunlop & Co v Meiklem (1876) 4 R 11 220
Dunn v Fidoe [1950] 2 All ER 685 128
Dunsinnan Estate Trs v Alexander 1978 SLCR App 146 141
Dyke, ex parte, in re Morrish (1882) 22 Ch 410 220
Eagle Star Insurance Co Ltd v Simpson 1984 SLT (Land Ct) 37 161
Eastern Angus Properties Ltd v Chivers & Sons Ltd 1960 SLCR 3 162
Edell v Dulieu [1924] AC 38 . . . . 136, 153, 159
Edinburgh Corporation v Gray 1948 SC 538; 1948 SLT 425 . . . . . 68, 71, 72, 155
Edinburgh, Lord Provost, etc v The Lord Advocate 1923 SLT 14 187
Edmonston v Smith 1986 SLCR 97 162
Edmonstone v Lamont 1975 SLT (Sh Ct) 57 155
Edmunds v Woollacott (1958) 109 LJ 204 158
Egerton v Rutter [1951] 1 KB 472 220
Elibank, Lord v Hay (1780) M 13869 151
Ellis v Lewin (1963) 107 SJ 851 236
Elphinstone, Lord v Monkland Iron Co (1886) 13 R (HL) 98 220
Evans v Glamorgan County Council (1912) 28 TLR 517 186
——— v Jones [1955] 2 QB 58 . . . . 189, 190
——— v Roper [1960] 1 WLR 814 162
——— v Tompkins [1994] 2 EGLR 6 130
Evans (FR) (Leeds) Ltd v English Electric Co Ltd (1977) 36 P & CR 185 . . . 144
——— v Webster (1962) LJ 703 235
Fairlie Yacht Slip Ltd v Lumsden 1977 SLT (Notes) 41 116
Fane v Murray 1995 SLT 567 . . . . 31, 158, 160, 208
Farrans (Construction) Ltd v Dunfermline District Council 1988 SLT 466 119
Farrer v Nelson (1860) 15 QBD 258 195
Farrow v Orttewell [1933] Ch 480 186
Faulks v Faulks [1992] 1 EGLR 9 119
Featherstone v Staples [1986] 2 All ER 461 156
Fenton v Howie 1951 SLCR 7 161
Ferguson v Norman (1837) 4 Bing NC 52 236
Findlay v Munro 1917 SC 419 . . . . 48, 53, 145
Fleming v Middle Ward of Lanark (1895) 23 R 98 169
Fletcher v Fletcher 1932 SLT (Sh Ct) 10 151
Forbes v Darling 1965 SLCR App 139 162
——— v Pratt 1923 SLT (Sh Ct) 91 185
——— v Ure (1856) 18 D 577 220
Forbes-Sempill's Trs v Brown 1954 SLCR 36 157
Forsyth-Grant v Salmon 1961 SC 54 . . . . 236, 299
Fothringham v Fotheringham 1987 SLT (Land Ct) 10 . . . . . 70–71, 155, 168, 179
Frankland v Capstick [1959] 1 All ER 209 205
Fraser v Murray's Trs 1954 SLCR 10 141
Fraser's (Alan) Trs v Macpherson 1981 SLT (Land Ct) 17 . . . . . . 160, 161
Fraser's Trs v Maule & Son (1904) 6 F 819 222
French v Elliott [1960] 1 WLR 40 . . . . 159, 265, 269, 270
Gairneybridge Farm and King, Applicants 1974 SLT (Land Ct) 8 130
Galbraith and Ors v Ardnacross Farming Co 1953 SLT (Notes) 30 202
Galbraith's Trs v Eglinton Iron Co (1868) 7 M 167 169

Gale v Bates (1864) 33 LJ Ex 235 136
Galloway, Earl of v Elliot 1926 SLT (Sh Ct) 123 185
—— v McClelland 1915 SC 1062 . . . . 173, 176, 231
Gardiner v Lord Abercromby (1893) 9 Sh Ct Rep 33 221
Garrow and Anr 1958 SLCR 13 209
Garvie's Trs v Garvie's Tutors 1975 SLT 94 . . . . 21, 140, 142, 329
—— v Still 1972 SLT 29 . . . . 140, 141
Gates v Blair 1923 SC 430 . . . . 167, 219
Geddes v Mackay 1971 SLCR App 94 162
Gemmell v Hodge 1974 SLT (Land Ct) 2 160
Gibson v Farie 1918 1 SLT 404 181
—— v Mackenzie 1961 SLCR 11 162
—— v Sherret 1928 SC 493 172
Gifford v Buchanan 1983 SLT 613 . . . . 21, 330
Gilmour v Cook 1975 SLT (Land Ct) 10 159
—— v Osborne's Trs 1951 SLCR 30 165
Gisbourne v Burton [1988] 3 WLR 921 . . . . 65, 160
Gladstone v Bower [1960] 2 QB 384 . . . . 5, 129
—— v Halliday, OH, 1981, unreported 140
Glencruitten Trs v Love 1966 SLT (Land Ct) 5 . . . . 70, 155
Gold v Jacques Amand Ltd [1992] 2 EGLR 1 129
Goldsack v Shore [1950] 1 KB 708 . . . . 7, 130, 202
Gordon Lennox Estate Co v Christie 1969 SLCR App 84 162
Gordon v Rankin 1972 SLT (Land Ct) 7 . . . . 153, 166, 219
Gore-Browne-Henderson's Trs v Grenfell 1968 SLT 237 135
Graham v Gardner 1966 SLT (Land Ct) 12 144
—— v Lamont 1970 SLT (Land Ct) 10 . . . . 162, 163
—— v Stirling 1922 SC 90 . . . . 131, 152, 153
—— v Wilson-Clarke 1962 SLCR 35 160
Grant v Broadlands Properties Estates Ltd 1955 SLCR 39 145
—— v Murray 1950 SLCR 3 162
Gray v Edinburgh University 1962 SC 157 131
—— v Low (1859) 21 D 293 220
Grewer v Moncur's Curator Bonis 1916 SC 764 . . . . 180, 220
Grieve & Sons v Barr 1954 SC 414 131
Grounds v AG of the Duchy of Lancaster [1989] 1 EGLR 6 319
Gulliver v Catt [1952] 2 QB 308 . . . . 189, 202
Haddo House Estate Trs v Davidson 1982 SLT (Land Ct) 17 226
Haggart and Brown, Joint Applicants 1983 SCLR 13 10
Halliday v Semple 1960 SLT (Sh Ct) 22 235
—— v William Fergusson & Sons and Ors 1961 SC 24 . . . . . . 157, 165
Hallinan, Lady v Jones & Jones [1985] CLY 38 . . . . 216, 325
Hamilton v Duke of Hamilton's Trs 1918 SC 282 219
—— v Lorimer 1959 SLCR 7 . . . . 152, 167
Hamilton's Trs, Duke of v Fleming (1870) 9 M 329 . . . . 177, 187
Hamilton Ogilvy v Elliot (1905) 7 F 1115 178
Hammon v Fairbrother [1956] 2 All ER 108 159
Hammond v Allen [1994] 1 All ER 307 133
Hammond, ex parte [1844] De G 93 220
Hannaford v Smallacombe [1994] 1 EGLR 9 . . . . 157, 158, 235
Harrison-Broadley v Smith [1964] 1 WLR 465; [1964] All ER 867 . . . . 64, 130
Hart v Cameron (1935) Sh Ct Rep 166 158
Harvey and Mann's Arbitration (1920) 89 LJ KB 687 186
Hemington v Walter (1949) 100 LJ 51 . . . . 156, 220
Hendry v Fordyce (1953) 69 Sh Ct Rep 191 116
—— v Walker 1927 SLT 333 . . . . 172, 185, 203
Hewson v Matthews (1950) 100 LJ 654 156
Hickson and Welch v Cann (1977) 40 P & CR 218 129
Hill v Wildfowl Trust (Holdings) Ltd 1995 SCLR 778 . . . . . . 133, 136, 202
Hoile v Sheriffs 1948 SLCR 24 169
Hollings v Swindell (1950) 155 EG 269 129
Holman v Peruvian Nitrate Co (1878) 5 R 657 136

Hopetoun, Earl of v Wright (1864) 2 M (HL) 35 153
Hoth v Cowan 1926 SC 58 154
Houison-Craufurd's Trs v Davies 1951 SC 1 . . . . 77, 130, 153, 202
Howie v David Lowe & Sons Ltd 1952 SLCR 14. 141
Howkins v Jardine [1951] 1 KB 614; [1951] 1 All ER 320. . . . . 128, 129
Hunter v Barron's Trs (1886) 13 R 883 222
Hunter v Miller (1862) 24 D 1011 137
Hutcheson v Wolfe-Murray 1980 SLCR 12 179
Hutchison v Buchanan 1980 SLT (Land Ct) 17 162
Imrie's Tr v Calder (1897) 25 R 15 220
Ingham v Fenton (1893) 10 TLR 113 222
Inglis v Inglis 1983 SC 8 . . . . 22, 329
—— v Moir's Tutors (1871) 10 M 204 195
Inland Revenue v Assessor for Lanarkshire 1930 SLT 164. 219
IRC v Clay [1914] 3 KB 466 13
—— v Graham's Trs 1971 SC (HL) 1 218
Irving v Church of Scotland General Trs 1960 SLCR 16 140
Jackson v Hall [1980] AC 854 226
Jamieson v Clark (1951) 67 Sh Ct Rep 17 . . . . 235, 288
Jardine-Paterson v Fraser 1974 SLT 93 329
Jenners Princes Street Edinburgh v Howe 1990 SLT (Land Ct) 26 . . . . . . 219, 226
Johnson v Gill 1978 SC 74 . . . . 116, 236
—— v Moreton [1980] AC 37; [1978] 3 All ER 37 . . . . . 18, 31, 63, 65, 149, 152
Johnston v Glasgow Corporation 1912 SC 300 116
—— v Malcolm 1923 SLT (Sh Ct) 81 186
Jones v Gates [1954] 1 WLR 222; [1954] 1 All ER 158. . . . . 157, 159
Kedwell v Flint & Co [1911] 1 KB 797 181
Kennedy v Johnstone 1956 SC 39. . . . . 18, 19, 139–140, 220
Kent v Conniff [1953] 1 QB 361 189–190
Kestell v Langmaid [1950] 1 KB 233. 186
Keswick v Wright 1924 SC 766 . . . . 150, 186
Kidd v Byrne (1875) 3 R 255 195
Kildrummy (Jersey) Ltd v Calder 1994 SLT 888 152
—— v —— (No 2) 1996 GWD 8–458 160
Kilmarnock Estates Ltd v Barr 1969 SLT (Land Ct) 10 . . . . 144, 145
Kininmonth v British Aluminium Co 1915 SC 271 155
Kinnaird Trust v Boyne 1985 SLCR 19 145
Kirkland v Gibson (1831) 9 S 596. 220
Kok Hoong v Leong Cheong Kweng Mines Ltd [1964] AC 993. . . . . . . 130, 152
Lancaster & Macnamara, In re [1918] 2 KB 472 219
Land v Sykes [1992] 1 EGLR 1 156
Lean v Inland Revenue 1926 SC 15 219
Leask v Grains 1981 SLT (Land Ct) 11 162
Lennox v Reid (1893) 21 R 77 151
Leschallas v Woolf [1908] 1 Ch 641 149
Lindsay-MacDougall v Peterson 1987 SLCR 59 162
Linton's (Andrew) Trs v Wemyss Landed Estates Co Ltd 1953 SLCR 14 140
Loganair v Reid 1960 SLCR 34 162
Lory v London Borough of Brent [1971] 1 All ER 1042 130
Lothian's (Marquis of) Trs v Johnston 1952 SLCR App 233 . . . . 140, 141
Love v Montgomerie and Logan 1982 SLT (Sh Ct) 60 . . . . 7, 130
Lovie v Davidson 1988 SLCR 13 162
Lower v Sorrell [1963] 1 QB 959 . . . . 129, 159
Lowther v Clifford [1927] 1 KB 130 180
Luss Estates Co v Campbell 1973 SLCR App 96 141
—— v Colquhoun 1982 SLCR 1 . . . . 156, 161
—— v Firkin Farm Co 1985 SLT (Land Ct) 17 . . . . 139, 165
Luttenberger v North Thoresby Farms Ltd [1993] 1 EGLR 3 . . . . . 152, 156, 157
Lyons v Anderson (1886) 13 R 1020 145
McBay v Birse 1965 SLT (Land Ct) 10 162
McCallum v McNair: see Brodie v Ker
McDiarmid v Secretary of State for Scotland 1970 SLT (Land Ct) 17 136

Macdonald *v* Macrae 1987 SLCR 72 226
McDouall's Trs *v* MacLeod 1949 SC 593 . . . . 151, 154
McGavin *v* Sturrock's Tr (1891) 18 R 576 220
McGhie *v* Lang and Anr 1953 SLCR 22 . . . . 3, 129
McGill *v* Bichan 1970 SLCR App 122 . . . . 153, 162
—— *v* —— 1982 SLCR 33 165
Macgregor *v* Board of Agriculture 1925 SC 613 186
MacGregor *v* Dunnett 1949 SC 510 129
McGregor (John) (Contractors) Ltd *v* Grampian Regional Council 1991 SLT 136 . . 119
McIntyre *v* Board of Agriculture 1916 SC 983 169
Maciver *v* Broadland Properties Estates Ltd 1994 SLCR 18 . . . . . . 144, 203, 204
M'Iver *v* M'Iver 1909 SC 639 220
McKenzie *v* Buchan (1889) 5 Sh Ct Rep 40 219
Mackenzie *v* Cameron (1894) 21 R 427 141
—— *v* Laird 1959 SC 266 . . . . 6, 130, 156
—— *v* Lyon 1984 SLT (Land Ct) 30 . . . . 39, 163, 226
—— *v* McGillivray 1921 SC 722; (1921) 58 SLR 488 . . . . 173, 175, 176, 222, 231
—— *v* Mackenzie 1969 SLCR App 86 162
—— *v* Tait 1951 SLCR 3 . . . . 161, 162
Mackessack & Son *v* Molleson (1886) 13 R 445 220
Mackie *v* Gardner 1973 SLT (Land Ct) 11 . . . . 147, 154
McKinley *v* Hutchison's Trs 1935 SLT 62 154
Mackinnon *v* Arran Estate Trust 1988 SLT 32 179
—— *v* Martin 1958 SLCR 19 140
Mackintosh *v* Lord Lovat (1886) 14 R 282 219
McLaren *v* Lawrie 1964 SLT (Land Ct) 10 162
Maclean *v* Galloway 1979 SLT (Sh Ct) 32 130
M'Lean's Tr *v* M'Lean (1850) 13 D 90 220
McLellan *v* McGregor 1952 SLCR 3 161
Macleod *v* Urquhart 1808 Hume 840 222
MacMaster *v* Esson 1921 SLCR 18 175
Macnab *v* Willison 1960 SLT (Notes) 25; 1960 SC 83 . . . . . . 133, 154
Macnabb *v* Anderson 1955 SC 38; 1957 SC 213 . . . . . . 158, 159
McNeill *v* Duke of Hamilton's Trs 1918 SC 221 . . . . 3, 129
Macpherson *v* Secretary of State for Scotland 1967 SLT (Land Ct) 9 209
McQuaker *v* Phoenix Assurance Co (1859) 21 D 794 236
McQuater *v* Fergusson 1911 SC 640 . . . . 175, 176, 236
McRobie *v* Halley 1984 SLCR 10 162
Magdalen College Oxford *v* Heritage [1974] 1 WLR 441 157
Main Calthorpe Settlement, Trs of the *v* Calder 1988 SLT (Land Ct) 30 163
Malcolm *v* McDougall 1916 SC 283 . . . . 3, 129, 219
Mann *v* Gardner (1991) 61 P & CR 1 145
Masters *v* Duveen [1923] 2 KB 729 180
Mears *v* Callender [1901] 2 Ch 388 . . . . 149, 176
Meggeson *v* Groves [1917] 1 Ch 158 . . . . 136, 137
Methven *v* Burn 1923 SLT (Sh Ct) 25 204
Metropolitan Properties Co Ltd *v* Woolridge (1968) 20 P & CR 64 145
Meux *v* Cobley [1892] 2 Ch 253 149
Millar *v* McRobbie 1949 SLT 2; 1949 SC 1 153
Miller *v* Muirhead (1894) 21 R 658 149
Miller's Trs *v* Berwickshire Assessor 1911 SC 908 187
Mills *v* Rose (1923) 68 SJ 420 172
Milne *v* Earl of Seafield 1981 SLT (Sh Ct) 37 153
Minister of Agriculture *v* Jenkins [1963] 2 QB 317 157
Ministry of Agiculture *v* Dean [1924] 1 KB 851 220
Mitchell-Gill *v* Buchan 1921 SC 390 . . . . 99, 236
Moffat *v* Young 1975 SLCR App 98 . . . . 160, 162
Moll *v* McGregor 1991 SLCR 1 145
—— *v* —— (*sub nom* Wallace *v* Moll) 1990 SLT (Land Ct) 59; 1989 SLCR 21 . . 144, 145
Moncrieffe *v* Ferguson (1890) 24 R 47 220
Montgomerie *v* Wilson 1924 SLT (Sh Ct) 48 . . . . 152, 153
Morris *v* Muirhead 1969 SLT 70 158

Morrison v Rendall 1986 SC 69 130
Morrison's Exrs v Rendall 1986 SC 69; 1989 SLT (Land Ct) 89 . . . . . 71, 152–154
Morrison-Low v Howison 1961 SLT (Sh Ct) 53 . . . . 157, 158, 270
—— v Paterson 1985 SLT 255; 1985 SC (HL) 49 . . . . . . 21, 140, 218, 328–330
Morse v Dixon (1917) 87 LJ KB 1 181
Morton, Earl of v Hamilton 1977 SLCR App 136 163
Morton's Trs, Earl of v Macdougall 1944 SC 410 195
Mountford v Hodkinson [1956] 1 WLR 422 156
Murray v Fane, Perth Sh Ct, 22nd April 1996 . . . . 133, 235, 309
—— v Nisbet 1967 SLT (Land Ct) 14 158
NCB v Drysdale 1989 SLT 825 130
Newman v Keedwell (1977) 33 P & CR 333 153
Nicholl's Trs v Maclarty 1971 SLCR 85. 158
Nuttall (Edmund) Ltd v Amec Projects Ltd 1993 SLT 255 236
O'Donnell v Heath 1995 SLT (Land Ct) 15 . . . . 160, 161
Officer v Nicolson 1807 Hume 827 136
Official Solicitor v Thomas [1986] 2 EGLR 1; (1986) 279 EG 407 . . . . . . 157, 158
Osler v Lansdowne (1885) 1 Sh Ct Rep 48 221
Paddock Investments v Lory (1975) 236 EG 803 . . . . 25, 157, 167
Pahl v Trevor [1992] 1 EGLR 22 130
Paynter v Rutherford and Ors 1940 SLT (Sh Ct) 18. 210
Peace (J & A) v Peace 1984 SLT (Land Ct) 6 162
Pearson and I'Anson, Re [1899] 2 QB 618 . . . . 176, 180
Pendreigh's Tr v Dewar (1871) 9 M 1037 221
Pennington-Ramsden v McWilliam [1982] CLY 28 235
Pentland v Hart 1967 SLT (Land Ct) 2 . . . . 133, 158
Pickford v Bishop (1975) 119 SJ 407 157
Pigott v Robson 1958 SLT 49 . . . . 71, 155
Poett v Henderson [1979] Central RN 11 226
Posthumus v Oosterward [1992] CMLR 336 116
Pott's Judicial Factor v Johnston 1952 SLCR 22 209
—— v Rutherford 1940 SLT (Sh Ct) 18. 209
Poyser and Mills Arbitration, Re [1964] 2 QB 467 . . . . 154, 216
Premier Dairies v Garlick [1920] 2 Ch 17 149
Preston v Norfolk County Council [1947] 1 KB 233 185
Price v Romilly [1960] 3 All ER 429 [1960] 1 WLR 1360 . . . . . . 50, 157, 158
Prior v J & A Henderson Ltd 1984 SLT (Land Ct) 51 161
Pucknowle Farms Ltd v Kane [1985] 3 All ER 790; (1985) 275 EG 1283 . . . 116, 319
Purser v Bailey [1967] 2 QB 500 . . . . 162, 166
—— v Worthing Local Board (1887) 18 QB 818 220
R v Agricultural Land Tribunal for Wales, ex parte Davies [1953] 1 All ER 1182 . . . 162
—— v Agricultural Land Tribunal (South Eastern Province), ex parte Palmer [1954] JPL
181 128–129
—— v Ministry of Agriculture, Fisheries and Food, ex parte Cox [1993] 1 EGLR 17 . . 315
Rae v Pringle 1990 Borders RN 27 165
Rae & Cooper v Davidson 1954 SC 361. 154
Ramsay v McLaren and Ors 1936 SLT 35 235
Reid v Dawson [1954] 3 All ER 498 130
—— v Duffus Estate Ltd 1955 SLCR 13 . . . . 141, 226
Reid's Exrs v Reid (1890) 17 R 519 46
Reid's Trs v Macpherson 1975 SLT 101 . . . . 19, 140, 220, 329
Renwick v Rodger 1988 SLT (Land Ct) 23. 179
Roberts v Magor (1953) 103 LJ 703 . . . . 149, 185
—— v Simpson (1954) 70 Sh Ct Rep 159 156
Robertson v Lindsay 1957 SLCR 3 163
—— v Ross & Co (1892) 19 R 967 169
Robertson's Trs v Cunningham 1951 SLT (Sh Ct) 89 . . . . . . 205, 235
Robinson v Rowbottom 1942 SLT (Sh Ct) 43. 219
Rochester and Chatham Joint Sewerage Board v Clinch [1925] Ch 753 . . . . 153, 166
Roger v Hutcheson 1922 SC (HL) 140 148
Roper v Prudential Assurance Co Ltd [1992] 1 EGLR 5 133
Ross v Donaldson 1983 SLT (Land Ct) 26. 165

Ross v Macdonald (1934) Sh Ct Rep 201 202
——— v Monteith (1786) M 15290 220
——— v Watson 1943 SC 406. 195
Rotherwick's Trs v Hope 1975 SLT 187. . . . . 21, 328
Rous v Mitchell [1991] 1 WLR 469 . . . . 152, 156
Rugby Joint Water Board v Shaw Fox [1973] AC 202 157
Russell v Freen (1835) 13 S 752 222
Russell & Harding's Arbitration, In re (1992) 67 SJ 123 219
Rutherford v Maurer [1962] 1 QB 16. . . . . 4, 129, 130
Salmon v Eastern Regional Hospital Board, Forfar Sheriff Court, 1960, unreported . . 219
Sangster v Noy (1867) 16 LT 157 154
Sanson v Chalmers 1965 SLCR 135 130
Sarris v Clark 1995 SLT 44 329
Saunders, Trs of v Ralph (1993) 66 P & CR 335 220
Saunders-Jacobs v Yates [1933] 2 KB 240 180
Scene Estate v Amos [1957] 2 All ER 325 . . . . 6, 130
Schofield v Hincks 58 LJ QB 147 220
Sclater v Horton [1954] 2 QB 1 144
Scott v Livingstone 1919 SC 1 154
——— v Scott 1927 SLT (Sh Ct) 6 154
Scott's Exrs v Hepburn (1876) 3 R 816 220
Scottish Discount Co Ltd v Blin 1985 SC 216. 149
Seafield, Earl of v Currie 1980 SLT (Land Ct) 10 . . . . 40, 163, 226
——— v Stewart 1985 SLT (Land Ct) 35 . . . . . . 145, 204, 235
Secretary of State for Scotland v Anderson 1967 SLCR App 117 . . . 103, 209
——— v Brown 1993 SLCR 41 206
——— v Campbell 1959 SLCR 49 69
——— v Davidson 1960 SLT (Land Ct) 7. 144
——— v Fraser 1954 SLCR 24 156
——— v John Jaffray and Ors 1957 SLCR 27 206
——— v Maclean 1950 SLCR 33. 138
——— v Prentice 1963 SLT (Sh Ct) 48 . . . . . 153, 167, 193, 219
——— v Sinclair 1960 SLCR 10 . . . . 133, 309
——— v ——— 1962 SLCR 6 144
——— v White 1967 SLCR App 133 209
——— v Young 1960 SLCR 31 13
Seggie v Haggart 1926 SLT (Sh Ct) 104 154
Sellick v Hellens [1928] LJ KB 214 159
Service v Forestry Commission of Argyll 1951 SLT (Sh Ct) 2 141
Shand v Christie's Trs 1987 SLCR 29 145
Sharpley v Manby [1942] 1 KB 217 . . . . 216, 326
Shaw-Mackenzie v Forbes 1957 SLCR 34 163
Shepherd and Anr v Lomas [1963] 1 WLR 962 158
Short v Greeves [1988] 08 EG 109 128
Simpson v Henderson 1944 SC 365 235
Sinclair v Clyne's Tr (1887) 15 R 185 . . . . 176, 220
——— v Mackintosh 1983 SLT (Land Ct) 29; 1982 SLCR 43 165
Skinner v Cooper 1971 SLCR App 83 162
Sloss v Agnew 1923 SLT (Sh Ct) 33 141
Smith v Grayton Estates Ltd 1960 SC 349 . . . . . . 64, 131, 153
Smith v Richmond [1899] AC 448 149
Somerville v Watson 1980 SLT (Land Ct) 14 162
Spencer-Nairn v IRC 1985 SLT (Lands Tr) 46 133
Stark v Edmonstone (1826) 5 S 45 136
Stevens v Sedgeman [1951] 2 KB 434 129
Stewart v Brims 1969 SLT (Sh Ct) 2 . . . . . . 158, 235, 270
——— v Maclaine (1899) 37 SLR 623 172
——— v Moir 1965 SLT (Land Ct) 11 . . . . . 153, 167, 193, 219
——— v Williamson 1910 SC (HL) 47 106
Stirrat and Anr v Whyte 1968 SLT 157 . . . . . . 64, 156, 219
Stone v Whitecombe (1980) 40 P & CR 296 130
Stonehaven v Adam 1970 SLT (Sh Ct) 43 219

Stoneman v Brown [1973] 1 WLR 459; [1973] 2 All ER 225 157
Stormonth-Darling v Young 1915 SC 44 219
Strachan v Hunter 1916 SC 901 . . . . 153, 154
—— v Robertson-Coupar 1989 SLT 488 . . . . 218, 219
Strachan's Tr v Harding 1990 SLT (Land Ct) 6 . . . . 175, 176
Strang v Abercairney Estates 1992 SLT (Land Ct) 32 235
—— v Stuart (1887) 14 R 637 221
Strathclyde Regional Council v Arneil 1987 SLCR 44 . . . . 144, 145
Stubbs v Hunt & Wrigley [1992] 1 EGLR 17 314
Suggett v Shaw 1987 SLT (Land Ct) 5 . . . . 88, 205, 211, 235
Sumnall v Statt (1985) 49 P & CR 367 158
Surrey County Council v Carson [1992] 1 EGLR 26 319
Swinborne v Andrews [1923] 2 KB 483 221
Sykes v Edgar 1974 SLT (Land Ct) 4; 1974 SLCR App 95 . . . . 39, 163
Tayleur v Wildin [1868] LR 3 Ex 303 159
Taylor v Brick 1982 SLT 25 . . . . 154, 156
—— v Burnett's Trs 1966 SLCR App 139 . . . . 133, 179
—— v Earl of Moray (1892) 19 R 399 219
—— v Fordyce 1918 SC 824 219
—— v Steel Maitland 1913 SC 562 . . . . 135, 180
Taylor's Tr v Paul (1880) 15 R 313 220
Teignmouth UDC v Elliott (1958) 108 LJ 204 157
Thomas v Jennings (1896) 66 LJ QB 5 149
Thomson v Earl of Galloway 1919 SC 611 194
—— v Lyall 1966 SLCR 136 140
—— v Murray 1990 SLT (Land Ct) 45 219
Tinball v Marshall [1922] EGD 396 185
Todd v Bowie (1902) 4 F 435 221
Tombs v Turvey (1923) 68 SJ 385; (1923) 93 LJ KB 785 . . . . 172, 221
Toms v Parnell 1948 SLCR 8 209
Towns v Anderson 1989 SLT (Land Ct) 17 145
Trotter v Torrance (1891) 18 R 848 155
Tuffnell and Nether Whitehaugh Co Ltd 1977 SLT (Land Ct) 14 . . . 57, 103, 147, 209
Turnbull v Millar 1942 SC 521 . . . . 43, 176, 282
Turner v Hutchinson (1860) 2 F & F 185 176
—— v Wilson 1954 SC 296 . . . . 155, 161
Turton v Turnbull [1934] 2 KB 197 159
Tustian v Johnston [1993] 2 All ER 673 133
Tweeddale, Marquis of v Brown (1821) 2 Mur 563 137
Twygen v Assessor for Tayside 1991 GWD 4-226 . . . . 180, 220
University College Oxford v Durdy [1982] Ch 413 235
University of Edinburgh v Craik 1954 SC 190 . . . . 162, 163
Urwick v Taylor [1969] EGD 1106 157
Van Grutten v Trevenen [1902] 2 KB 82 154
Verall v Farnes [1966] 1 WLR 1254 129
Wachauf v Bundesamt für Ernährung und Forstwirtschaft [1991] 1 CMLR 328 . . . 112
Waddell v Howat 1925 SC 484; 1925 SLT 403 . . . . 172, 219, 221
Waldie v Mungall (1896) 23 R 792 153
Walker v Crocker [1992] 1 EGLR 29 . . . . 205, 325
—— v Hendry 1925 SC 855 . . . . 153, 219
Walker &c v M'Knight (1886) 13 R 599 220
Walker's Trs v Manson (1886) 13 R 1198 . . . . 145, 177
Wallace v Moll 1989 SLCR 21 . . . . 65, 144
—— v Perth & Kinross Assessor 1975 SLT 118 220
Wallis, ex parte Sully, In re (1885) 14 QBD 950 220
Ward v Scott [1950] 66 TLR 340 156
Wardell v Usher (1841) 3 Scott (NR) 508 181
Ware v Davies (1932) 146 LT 130 231
Watters v Hunter 1927 SC 310; 1927 SLT 232 . . . . 154, 180, 220, 222
Watts v Yeend [1987] 1 WLR 323 130
Weatherall v Smith [1980] 1 WLR 1290; [1980] 2 All ER 530 129
Webster & Co v Cramond Iron Co (1872) 2 R 752 185

Westlake v Page [1926] 1 KB 298 185
Weston v Duke of Devonshire [1923] 12 LJCCR 74 193
Whittaker v Barker (1832) 1 C & M 113 221
Wight v Earl of Hopetoun (1864) 2 M (HL) 35 152
—— v Marquis of Lothian's Trs 1952 SLCR 22 140
Wilbraham v Colclough and Ors [1952] 1 All ER 979 216
Wildfowl and Wetlands Trust (Holdings) Ltd v Quinn 1994, unreported 78
Williams v Lewis [1915] 3 KB 493 136
Williamson v Stewart 1912 SC 235 . . . . 100, 101
Wilson v Love [1896] 1 QB 626 192
—— v Stewart (1853) 16 D 106 220
Wilson-Clarke v Graham 1963 SLT (Sh Ct) 2 158
Witham v Stockdale 1981 SLT (Land Ct) 27 . . . . 13, 144
Woodhouse, ex parte The Times, 18th June 1960 94
Yool v Shepherd 1914 SC 689 219
Young v Steven 1951 SLCR 10 161
Yuill v Semple 1954 SLCR 3 161

CHAPTER 1

THE OBJECT OF THE ACTS

The object of the Acts is to encourage the tenant to farm well and to make necessary improvements to his holding. This has been done by giving him substantial security of tenure and rights to compensation for (1) improvements, (2) disturbance, (3) damage by game, and (4) his fraction of milk quota. The Acts make important provisions with regard to the terms of leases and the rights and obligations of landlords and tenants in regard to the maintenance and repair of buildings and equipment on farms. There are also subordinate provisions relating to removing for non-payment of rent, the fixing of rent by arbitration, notice of termination of tenancy, bequest of lease, compensation for fixtures, freedom of cropping, sale of produce and market gardens, and the apportionment of milk quota.

The Acts up to and including the Agricultural Holdings (Scotland) Act 1949 progressively extended the tenant's rights in relation to security of tenure and compensation. Since then sometimes the landlord has been favoured and sometimes the tenant with the result that instead of a simple and coherent body of law applicable to all agricultural tenancies we find a number of situations where the rights of the parties depend either on the date that the lease commenced or the date on which the present tenant succeeded to the lease. The Agriculture Act 1958 was, to some extent, an attempt to redress the balance in favour of the landlord. It entitled the landlord to obtain an economic rent for his land. It enabled him, subject to certain limited rights open to heirs and legatees of the tenant, to terminate the lease at the tenant's death or at the expiry of the lease where the tenant died during its stipulated endurance, but these provisions were largely restricted by the Agriculture (Miscellaneous Provisions) Act 1968 mentioned below. It amended the provisions restricting the operation of notices to quit. It transferred to the Land Court certain powers which belonged under the previous Acts to the Secretary of State.

The Succession (Scotland) Act 1964, having abolished primogeniture, provided a new method of transferring a deceased tenant's lease to one of his heirs and introduced what is now section 12 of the Agricultural Holdings (Scotland) Act 1991 (the 1991 Act) to establish a procedure for intimation by the acquirer of a lease and for objection by the landlord.

The Agricultural Holdings (Amendment) (Scotland) Act 1983 set out a scheme for the review of rent and the conduct of rent arbitrations. The Agriculture Act 1986, passed following the introduction of milk quotas in 1984, made provision for the apportionment of the value of these quotas between landlord and tenant.

COMMENCEMENT AND DATES OF OPERATION OF THE AGRICULTURAL
HOLDINGS (SCOTLAND) ACTS

The Agricultural Holdings (Scotland) Act 1923 came into operation on 7th July 1923 but some of its provisions affected contracts entered into prior to

1

its commencement. The Small Landholders and Agricultural Holdings (Scotland) Act 1931 came into operation on 31st July 1931, but did not affect improvements made or begun before that date. The Agriculture (Scotland) Act 1948 came into operation on 1st November 1948. (We are here concerned with Part I only of the 1948 Act.) The Agricultural Holdings (Scotland) Act 1949 came into operation on 24th November 1949. In certain cases it is necessary to refer to, and found on, the repealed Acts; in some cases the Acts apply to contracts entered into after specified dates, and in others to contracts entered into after the commencement. The Agriculture Act 1958 received the Royal Assent on 1st August 1958 but all of its provisions did not immediately come into effect. The effect of section 6 (which related to succession to holdings) was postponed to 1st September 1958. Section 3(2) (which related to notices to quit) came into force on 1st November 1958. The Agriculture (Miscellaneous Provisions) Act 1963 received the Royal Assent and came into effect on 15th May 1963. The Succession (Scotland) Act 1964 received the Royal Assent on 10th June 1964 and came into effect on 10th September 1964. The Agriculture (Miscellaneous Provisions) Act 1968 received the Royal Assent and came into effect on 3rd July 1968. The Agriculture (Miscellaneous Provisions) Act 1976 received the Royal Assent on 15th November 1976 and sections 13 and 14 came into effect on 7th April 1978. The Agricultural Holdings (Amendment) (Scotland) Act 1983 received the Royal Assent on 13th May 1983 and came into effect on 13th July 1983. The Agriculture Act 1986 came into force on 25th July 1986. The 1991 Act, which is a consolidating Act and therefore not intended to effect any changes in the law, came into effect on 25th September 1991. It did not affect the Agriculture Act 1986, whose provisions remain in force. It also did not consolidate the Rules of Good Husbandry and the Rules of Good Estate Management, which still have to be found in the Agriculture (Scotland) Act 1948.

LANDLORD AND TENANT

'Landlord' means 'any person for the time being entitled to receive the rents and profits or to take possession of any agricultural holding'. 'Tenant' means 'the holder of land under a lease' and lease means generally 'a letting for a term of years, or for lives, or for lives and years, or from year to year'. In the case of sub-tenants as of others the period of let must not be less than one year. Even a let for a shorter period than from year to year (unless it be approved by the Secretary of State before being entered into) may give rise to a claim under the Act as if it were a lease of the land from year to year (section 2). If the principal tenant and sub-tenant are in the relation of landlord and tenant as defined in the Act, the sub-tenant appears to have right to such claims as are competent to a tenant.

'Landlord' and 'tenant' are defined as including the executor, assignees, legatee, disponee, guardian, *curator bonis*, tutor or permanent or interim trustee (within the meaning of the Bankruptcy (Scotland) Act 1985) of the landlord or tenant. This definition does not overrule the express terms of the lease providing for the exclusion of legatees, executors and assignees.

HOLDINGS AFFECTED

In section 1 of the 1991 Act an 'agricultural holding' is defined as meaning 'the aggregate of the agricultural land comprised in a lease, not being a lease under which the land is let to the tenant during his continuance in any office, appointment or employment held under the landlord'. This definition does not apply to sheep stock valuations for which section 72 provides a different definition. 'Agricultural land' is defined as 'land used for agriculture which is so used for the purposes of a trade or business and includes any other land which by virtue of a designation of the Secretary of State under section 86(1) of the Agriculture (Scotland) Act 1948, is agricultural land within the meaning of that Act'. 'Trade or business' is not limited to agricultural trade or business. The definition of 'agriculture' in section 85(1) of the 1991 Act seems designed to cover every arable, pastoral and livestock-raising activity. The effect of the definition is to include all areas of agricultural land comprised in a lease.

The phrase 'aggregate of agricultural land' used in the definition in section 1(1) might be thought to mean the sum of the areas of land included in the let and used for agriculture which together make up the holding without any non-agricultural areas in the same let.

It has been held in England, however, that the word 'aggregate' refers to the definition of agriculture in section 96 of the Agricultural Holdings Act 1986 (corresponding to section 85 of the 1991 Act) where various activities to be included are set out, and that it is these which are to be aggregated to determine if the tenancy is in substance a tenancy of an agricultural holding. If it is, then the whole subjects let are an agricultural holding, including any parts which are not used for agriculture. It is not now possible to have in the same tenancy subjects which are partly an agricultural holding and partly not. In *McGhie v Lang and Anr*[1] the Land Court took the view that it was possible to determine the extent of the agricultural holding by excision of the non-agricultural subjects included in the let, but in *Cameron v Duke of Argyll's Trs*[2] (a case under the Crofting Reform (Scotland) Act 1976), the court indicated that *McGhie* might require to be reconsidered and pointed out that the case of *McNeill v Duke of Hamilton's Trs*[3] followed in *McGhie*, was decided on the very different definition of agricultural holding contained in the Agricultural Holdings (Scotland) Act 1908 where subjects had to be wholly agricultural or pastoral. It is likely, therefore, that the Scottish courts will follow the English courts and apply the test of predominant user.

SIZE OF HOLDING

There is no minimum size for an agricultural holding. In *Malcolm v McDougall*,[4] the holding extended to a quarter of an acre and a share of grazing rights. In England, an allotment of half an acre was held to be an agricultural holding when the produce from it was sold and not consumed by the tenant.

1 1953 SLCR 22.
2 1981 SLT (Land Ct) 2.
3 1918 SC 221.
4 1916 SC 283.

BUILDINGS

In England, a building without land, other than that on which it stands, may be an agricultural holding. In Scotland, it was held in *Barr v Strang & Gardner*,[5] a sheriff court case under the Agricultural Holdings (Scotland) Act 1923, that a farmhouse with outbuildings and garden ground could not constitute an agricultural holding. The definition of holding in the 1923 Act was different: it referred to 'a piece of land', which was taken by the sheriff in *Barr* to mean land without buildings. The garden ground was not used for agriculture and so there was no piece of land with which the buildings could be used. 'Agricultural land' in section 1 of the 1991 Act would probably now be held to cover a building on its own which is used for agriculture, but there has been no decision on this.

USED FOR AGRICULTURE

Section 85(1) states various activities which are included in the term 'agriculture' but does not provide an exhaustive definition. Arable farming is not mentioned and it must be assumed that the matters specified are in addition to anything within the ordinary meaning of agriculture.

The use of the land for agriculture must not be contrary to the lease. 'Used for agriculture' is to be taken as lawfully so used.

TRADE OR BUSINESS

The use of the land must be commercial and not merely private, such as keeping horses for hunting or growing vegetables for consumption by the tenant or his family, as in the case of an allotment garden. An allotment other than an allotment garden, if used for a trade or business, may be an agricultural holding.

The trade or business does not have to be agricultural. In *Rutherford v Maurer*[6] land let for grazing horses belonging to a riding school was held to be an agricultural holding. The definition of agriculture in section 96(1) of the 1986 Act (as in section 85(1) of the Agricultural Holdings (Scotland) Act 1949) includes 'the use of land as grazing land' without stipulating that the grazing must be by livestock, and the Court of Appeal decided that it was not so restricted. The decision has been criticised but it has been followed in Scotland in the sheriff court case of *Crawford v Dun*,[7] when the grazing was also by horses belonging to a riding school.

MINIMUM TERM OF LEASE

A lease of an agricultural holding may not be created for a period shorter than from year to year without the prior approval of the Secretary of State, except in grazing and mowing lets for a specified period of less than a year or where the lease is in respect of land which the granter holds on a lease for a lesser period than from year to year.

5 1935 SLT (Sh Ct) 10.
6 [1962] 1 QB 16.
7 1981 SLT (Sh Ct) 66.

Prior to 1st November 1948 it was possible to avoid the application of the agricultural holdings legislation by granting a lease for less than a year. This was so even where a series of lets each for 364 days was granted. To prevent the use of this device section 2 provides that where under a lease entered into on or after 1st November 1948 agricultural land is let for a shorter period than from year to year and the circumstances are such that if the tenant were a tenant from year to year he would be a tenant of an agricultural holding, the lease is to take effect with the necessary modifications as if it were a lease from year to year.

It has been held in England that a lease for one year is for a shorter period than from year to year and that a let for more than one but less than two years is a greater interest than a tenancy from year to year and so outwith the corresponding section 2 of the 1986 Act. Since under section 3 of that Act, unlike the 1991 Act, tacit relocation applies only to lets of two years or more, a let of eighteen months did not give security of tenure. Whether subjects in Scotland let for more than one year and less than two years would be an agricultural holding depends on whether such a let would be for a 'term of years' and so within the definition of a lease in section 85(1). It is considered that it would so that a '*Gladstone v Bower*'[8] lease would not avoid security of tenure in Scotland.

EXCEPTIONS FROM SECTION 2

There are express exceptions under section 2 where:
(1) the let is made with the prior approval of the Secretary of State; or
(2) the let is made in contemplation of the use of the land only for grazing or mowing during some specified period of the year; or
(3) the let is granted by a person whose own interest is less than a tenancy from year to year and which has not become such by virtue of section 2.

(1) Secretary of State's approval

The Act does not indicate on what grounds the Secretary of State's approval should be given and this appears to be a matter for his discretion. It is commonly given to local authorities or others who have acquired land for a proposed development which is not due to commence for a year or two. It may also be given to private landlords who intend to farm the land themselves but are unable to do so immediately and would otherwise be unwilling to let except for seasonal grazings. It was suggested in an English case that approval might be sought by a landlord wishing to grant a tenancy for a total period. The approval must be given before the lease is entered into. The Secretary of State will not entertain an application for approval of an existing lease and even if he did it would not be within the section. Approval may be given to a number of successive lets but each must be approved separately.

(2) Seasonal grazing or mowing lets

Section 2(2) excludes from the effect of the section a lease of land entered into (whether or not the lease expressly so provides) in contemplation of the

8 [1960] 2 QB 384.

use of the land only for grazing or mowing during some specified period of the year.

The subsection makes an important exception from the security of tenure provisions of the Act. It has been much invoked and the subject of much litigation, mainly on the question of whether a let was a seasonal grazing let or a protected agricultural lease.

A specified period of a year includes any period of less than a year and may be for 364 days. A series of three-month lets without any break was also within the proviso although the series totalled more than five years as each let was a separate agreement and the parties did not contemplate renewal of the let although they may have expected it.

A let for six-month periods, however, implied at least a let for one year and so was outwith the proviso. The 'period of the year' may be sufficiently specified without stating dates for its beginning and end. A let for the 'grazing season' is for a specified period of the year although its actual duration depends on when the grass is adequate for grazing. Agricultural tenancies have been unintentionally created by landlords who mistakenly thought that a grazing let for a year or a cropping let for less than a year were outwith the protection of the Acts. The latter belief has been encouraged by the common practice of letting land to potato merchants or growers who do not normally in practice claim protected tenancies although they would be entitled to do so. There have also been numerous cases where lets which began as seasonal grazing lets have been converted into yearly protected tenancies by allowing the tenant to crop the land without making an agreement, such as is referred to in section 22(2)(a), or by allowing the tenant to remain in occupation after expiry of the seasonal let. Occupation outwith the specified period of the year may be regarded as no more than a privilege or concession as in *Mackenzie v Laird*[9] but it is clearly advisable for the landlord to require the tenant to remove his stock at the end of the period of let. If a let is within the subsection tacit relocation does not operate but if a tenant remains in occupation without any new agreement and rent is paid a new verbal lease from year to year may be inferred.

Agreements for seasonal grazing lets sometimes provide for the lets to be granted during several years in succession. This was the case in *Mackenzie* and it appears to have been accepted that it does not affect the application of the subsection, but the question was not a matter of argument and it will be safer to have a separate agreement for each season.

The inclusion of buildings in a let would tend to indicate that the parties contemplated more than grazing or mowing but it has been held in England that a gratuitous licence to use stabling was ancillary to a seasonal grazing let and did not exclude the subsection.

The phrase in the subsection, 'in contemplation of', was considered in *Scene Estate v Amos*[10] where it was held to mean more than mere expectation. Both parties must actually have understood the lease to be restricted as to use and period. In the case of written agreements what was contemplated by the parties must be gathered from the terms of the document and not from extrinsic evidence. The possible exception to this rule in England where the lease is silent does not apply in Scotland.

9 1959 SC 266.
10 [1957] 2 All ER 325.

(3) Sub-tenancies from tenants without protection of section 2(1)

Section 2(2)(b) excludes from the operation of the section a sub-let by a tenant under a lease for a shorter period than from year to year which has not taken effect as a lease from year to year by virtue of section 2(1).

This is a situation unlikely to be encountered. It has been held that a contract for the grazing of sheep for the winter season was an agricultural let and sub-letting was accordingly prohibited. It has, however, been held by the Land Court that a let of seasonal grazing does not amount to sub-letting.

JURISDICTION OF COURT AND ARBITER

Under section 2(3) any question as to the operation of section 2 in relation to any lease is to be determined by arbitration. A question of jurisdiction arises where there is a dispute as to whether a let is a seasonal grazing let or a protected tenancy. It has been held in England that the applicability of the section as opposed to its operation is a matter for the courts and it has been suggested that the kind of question which would be referred to arbitration under section 2 would be, for example, the modifications to be made to a lease converted by section 2(1) into a lease from year to year.

The Scottish authorities support the proposition that where the question is whether the subjects let are an agricultural holding or whether the parties are in the relationship of landlord and tenant, it is one for the court. In *Love v Montgomerie and Logan*[11] the Sheriff Principal, after referring to the Scottish authorities and *Goldsack v Shore*,[12] indicated that where a party averred that the let was a seasonal grazing let only, this was a matter for the court and not for the arbiter. The parties' averments in *Love* disclosed that the true issue between them was whether there was a grazing let or an agricultural lease. This was a question for the court alone and accordingly interdict was granted to prevent an arbiter from acting.

Any question referred to arbitration under the 1991 Act may be referred instead to the Land Court on a joint application under section 60(2). In such cases the court has only such jurisdiction as an arbiter would have. The Land Court has acted in a joint application on a question under section 2 to determine whether there was an agricultural tenancy. It may be questioned if the court would now make such a determination in view of the decision in *Love* and the Land Court's own decisions that it has no jurisdiction to determine status in relation to agricultural holdings and that parties cannot confer on it a jurisdiction which it does not have by statute.

TACIT RELOCATION

On the expiry of the contractual term of the lease at common law a lease for a year or more is held to be continued for a further year by tacit consent if neither party gives intimation to the contrary and the actings of the parties are not inconsistent with the continuation.

The effect of this tacit reletting or relocation is that 'all the stipulations and

11 1982 SLT (Sh Ct) 60.
12 [1950] 1 KB 708.

conditions of the original contract remain in force in so far as these are not inconsistent with any implied term of the renewed contract'.

Tacit relocation prolongs the existing lease and does not create a new lease.

The only effect of section 3 on the common law position is that the notice required to prevent continuation of the lease must comply with the requirements of section 21.

PROVISION FOR WRITTEN LEASES

Where there is no written lease embodying the terms of a tenancy, the landlord or the tenant is entitled by section 4 to request the other to enter into an agreement. If no such agreement is made, the matter can be referred to arbitration. A similar request and reference to arbitration can be made where a subsisting written lease entered into on or after 1st November 1948 or entered into before that date and held on tacit relocation contains no provision for one or more of the matters specified in Schedule 1 to the Act, or contains a provision inconsistent with that Schedule or with section 5 which deals with the liability for maintenance of fixed equipment. The agreement which is requested by the one party from the other, or is referred to arbitration, will be one containing provision for all the matters in Schedule 1 or provisions not inconsistent with that Schedule or with section 5. If there is no provision inconsistent with section 5 (as where the lease is silent on the subject of provision and maintenance of fixed equipment) section 4 does not give the arbiter power to provide for inclusion of the terms of section 5.

On any such reference under section 4 the arbiter must specify the terms of the existing tenancy and make provision for the matters specified in Schedule 1 insofar as the terms of the tenancy, as agreed between the landlord and the tenant, make no provision for them. These matters include names of parties, particulars of the holding referable to a map or plan, the term or terms for which the holding is let, the rent with the dates on which it is payable, and certain undertakings by landlord and tenant in the event of fire.

PROVISION AND MAINTENANCE OF FIXED EQUIPMENT

Common law

The landlord's main obligations at common law are 'to put the buildings on the farm in a proper state of repair' and 'to give the tenant such buildings as will enable him to cultivate the land'. The landlord does not appear to have a common law obligation to put drains in proper repair. The general principle is that buildings should be such as to last with ordinary care for the duration of the lease.

So far as repairs and renewals are concerned the tenant's common law obligation is to leave the buildings and other fixed equipment 'in such condition as he received them less ordinary wear and tear'. Renewal or replacement of fixed equipment rendered necessary by natural decay or fair wear and tear is the obligation of the landlord and 'there is no obligation upon the tenants to reconstruct or renew what has become worn out or was so through wear and tear or failure in the obligation of maintenance not attributable to their actings or omissions'.

The landlord's obligation at the commencement of the tenancy is thus more onerous than that of the tenant to leave the fixed equipment in tenantable condition at his waygoing.

It has been argued for landlords that some partial renewal of materials may be necessarily included in the tenant's repair obligation. The question has been considered by the Land Court in regard to fences which the tenant had to maintain 'ordinary wear and tear excepted', but it was held that if a stob is so decayed or wire so corroded as to be unserviceable it is for the landlord to replace it.

Where fixed equipment is damaged or decayed because of the tenant's actings or principally because of his failure to carry out maintenance obligations then he becomes responsible for the reconstruction or renewal required. If his failure to repair is a contributory factor then the landlord may recover damages.

In written leases entered into before 1st November 1948 the common law obligations are commonly varied and the question has frequently arisen as to whether the tenant has undertaken a renewal obligation. If the lease merely provides that the tenant accepts the fixed equipment as in good and tenantable condition the common law exception of natural decay and fair wear and tear will still apply at waygoing. It is a matter of interpretation in each case but it requires express stipulation for such liability to be transferred to the tenant.

Statutory obligations (s 5(2)(a))

In every lease entered into on or after 1st November 1948 there is deemed to be incorporated

> 'an undertaking by the landlord that, at the commencement of the tenancy or as soon as reasonably practicable thereafter, he will put the fixed equipment on the holding into a thorough state of repair, and will provide such buildings and other fixed equipment as will enable an occupier reasonably skilled in husbandry to maintain efficient production as respects both—
> (i) the kind of produce specified in the lease, or (failing such specification) in use to be produced on the holding, and
> (ii) the quality and quantity thereof,
> and that he will during the tenancy effect such replacement or renewal of the buildings or other fixed equipment as may be rendered necessary by natural decay or by fair wear and tear'.

The provisions place a heavy obligation on the landlord and as they are deemed to be incorporated in the lease they override any inconsistent provisions in it. It is, however, open to either party after the lease has been entered into to undertake to execute on behalf of the other party any work which the lease obliges that party to do. Agreements to this effect are permitted by section 5(3) and it is usual in any new let for such a contracting-out agreement to be entered into whereby the tenant undertakes the whole of the landlord's obligations in relation to fixed equipment. The prospective tenant is often taken bound by contract to enter into a lease and post-lease agreement. As the tenant's obligations to enter the contracting-out agreement are contemporaneous with his taking the lease it is doubtful if such an agreement complies with section 5(3).

Provisions in leases entered into after 1st November 1948 requiring a tenant to pay the whole or any part of the fire insurance premium are null and void.

Any question as to the liability of a landlord or tenant under section 5 is referred to arbitration. An arbiter cannot make an order *ad factum praestandum* but once he has made an award an action may be brought to compel the party responsible to carry out the work required. For a case on a landlord's liability under this section which was referred to the Land Court, see *Haggart and Brown, Joint Applicants.*[13]

In this respect the liability of a landlord under a lease entered into on or after 1st November 1948 is substantially greater than that of a landlord under a lease entered into before that date to which the provisions of section 5 do not apply. Under such old leases the common law provisions referred to above will, in the absence of stipulation to the contrary, apply but in the event of the landlord's failure to carry out his obligation for renewal or replacement of fixed equipment the tenant cannot compel him to do so and his remedy is to seek damages or abatement of rent.

By section 14 the arbiter may vary the rent where he considers such variation equitable on a reference under sections 4 or 5 of the Act.

13 1983 SCLR 13.

CHAPTER 2

REVIEW OF RENT

Since the security of tenure conferred by the 1991 Act allows an agricultural lease to continue after the end of its stipulated endurance provision is made for the revision of rent. Control of the level of rent is also required as security of tenure would be meaningless if the landlord could increase the rent at will. The parties cannot contract out of the statutory provisions for variation of rent when the lease is running on tacit relocation, although they are at liberty to do so during the initial contractual period of the lease.

Demand for Arbitration

Under section 13 of the 1991 Act either the landlord or the tenant may serve a written demand on the other for a reference to arbitration as to rent. The arbitration is to decide the question

> 'what rent should be payable in respect of the holding as from the next day after the date of the notice on which the tenancy could have been terminated by notice to quit (or notice of intention to quit) given [at the date of demanding the reference]....'.

In terms of section 21 of the 1991 Act the period of notice to quit or notice of intention to quit required is not less than one year nor more than two years, and the same period is required for a demand for rent arbitration which must also be served against a break or the contractual ish if the lease is current or the anniversary of the ish if the lease is on tacit relocation. The method of serving a demand for a reference is found in section 84. There is no specified form of demand but a suggested style is given in Appendix 1.

Revision Period

A reference to arbitration cannot lawfully be demanded if the consequent increase or reduction of the rent would take effect as from a date earlier than three years from the latest of:
(1) the commencement of the tenancy; or
(2) the date as from which there took effect a previous increase or reduction of rent (whether under section 13 or otherwise); or
(3) the date as from which there took effect a direction under section 13 that the rent should continue unchanged.

The minimum revision period was formerly five years but was reduced to three years by section 2(d) of the Agricultural Holdings (Amendment) (Scotland) Act 1983.

The following variations are to be disregarded for the purposes of section 13(8):
(1) any variation under section 14, ie where an arbiter is required to establish the terms of the tenancy and to make provision for the compulsory terms;

(2) an increase of rent under section 15(1) where the landlord has carried out certain improvements;

(3) a reduction of rent under section 31 where there has been a reduction in the size of the holding either because of a valid notice to quit part of the holding or a contractual resumption of part of the holding.

These accordingly do not interrupt the running of the three-year period. The position is different if there is a variation in the size of the holding by agreement or compulsory purchase or if the reduction of rent following a resumption is agreed by the parties and not fixed by arbitration under section 31. These cases are not provided for in the subsection and will have the effect of starting a new revision period running from the date of the variation.

Appointment of Arbiter

The arbiter must be appointed and accept office before the date when the alteration of rent is to take effect. It has been held in England that the arbiter's appointment is complete once it is made in writing and he has accepted office. It is unnecessary for an arbiter in Scotland to intimate formally his acceptance of office. In the case of appointment by the Secretary of State for Scotland the arbiter will have agreed to act before his letter of appointment is issued and the date of appointment is the date on that letter.

Basis of Rental Valuation

Section 13(3) lays down as the criterion for the arbiter that the rent properly payable is to be

> 'the rent at which, having regard to the terms of the tenancy ... the holding might reasonably be expected to be let in the open market by a willing landlord to a willing tenant, there being disregarded ... any effect on rent of the fact that the tenant who is a party to the arbitration is in occupation of the holding'.

Section 13 provides that 'normally' the criterion for determining rent shall be the open market basis but also that where the evidence available to the arbiter is in his opinion insufficient to enable him to determine the rent properly payable, or he is of the view that the open market for rents for comparable subjects in the surrounding area is distorted by scarcity of lets or by other factors, the rent properly payable for the purposes of section 13 shall be the rent which he would expect to be paid, in a market which was not affected by such distortion, having particular regard to certain specified factors.

The proper operation of the 'open market' basis of rent revisions depends upon the availability of evidence of lets in the open market in the area. The 1991 Act assumes that normally such evidence will be available and it is only where there is a lack of evidence or the arbiter considers the rents obtained to be distorted by scarcity or other factors that the provisions of section 13(4) fall to be applied. The other factors may include the so-called 'marriage' factor, that is the distortion of rents due to neighbouring farmers seeking to enlarge their enterprises and willing to pay a higher rent than they would without other land.

THE 'NORMAL' BASIS – OPEN MARKET RENTS OF COMPARABLE HOLDINGS

Where there is evidence of open market lets and the arbiter does not apply the provisions of section 13(4) the rent will be fixed in accordance with the provisions of section 13(3).

The interpretation of what is now section 13(4) was discussed by the Land Court in *Secretary of State for Scotland v Young*[1] where it was stated that a member of the court was now 'less in the position of relying upon his own expert knowledge and more in the position of assessing evidence of external circumstances'.

The rent to be fixed is the rent which a prospective tenant would pay for the farm and is not to be based on the existing state of occupation or standard of husbandry but on an assessment of the agricultural potentiality of the holding. The personal circumstances of the sitting tenant are irrelevant. The arbiter, who still has some limited discretion, must consider the terms of the lease of the holding under review and compare them with those of the allegedly comparable holdings. He must also compare the physical characteristics of the holdings, such as location, size, altitude, aspect, soil, rainfall, buildings and other fixed equipment, and access.

The importance of evidence of open market lets is emphasised in a number of Land Court cases and the best evidence is 'evidence of values at which transactions have recently been concluded by offer and acceptance in the open market after advertisement of the subjects'. Rents adjusted with sitting tenants are not the best evidence of open market rents and should not be used by the arbiter unless there is no evidence of open market lets.

A landlord may, on a long-term view, be wiser not to accept the highest rent offered but to prefer a tenant at a lower rent if he is more likely to maintain the fertility and productivity of the holding. The reference to what might reasonably be expected enables an arbiter to disregard freak offers. In *Witham v Stockdale*[2] the court indicated that where evidence was limited it was appropriate to have regard to the 'middle band' of offers rather than the highest offer even when that had been accepted. It is, however, a question of what is a reasonable expectation and not what is a reasonable rent and, as in *IRC v Clay*,[3] the phrase 'might reasonably be expected' is to be taken to refer to 'the expectations of properly qualified persons who have taken pains to inform themselves of all the particulars ascertainable about the property, its capabilities, the demand for it and the likely potential tenants'.

Where a holding is used partly for non-agricultural purposes such as letting of caravans the rent should reflect the actual use, but if the holding is used for agriculture only the rent should not be increased to take account of a potential non-agricultural use.

VALUING OUT PREMIUM RENTS

The scarcity of farms to let has frequently made it difficult or impossible for parties in rent arbitrations to produce evidence of open market lets of

1 1960 SLCR 31.
2 1981 SLT (Land Ct) 27.
3 [1914] 3 KB 466.

comparable holdings in the same area. It has also resulted in very high rents being offered simply in order to secure tenancies. The provisions of section 13(4) are designed to enable arbiters to have regard to other factors when there is insufficient evidence of open market lets and to exclude the premium or 'key money' element in rents distorted by scarcity of lets or other factors. When there is distortion of the market or insufficiency of evidence the rent properly payable is the rent which the arbiter would expect to be paid in a market which was not affected by the distortion of rents caused by scarcity or other factors.

In fixing the hypothetical rent the arbiter must still start by ascertaining the open market rental but then adjust this having particular but not exclusive regard to four factors:

(1) information about open market rents of comparable subjects outside the surrounding area. It is for the arbiter to determine what constitutes 'the surrounding area';
(2) the entire range of offers made for comparable subjects;
(3) sitting tenants' rents fixed by agreement for comparable subjects in the surrounding area; and
(4) the current economic conditions in the relevant sector of agriculture.

In *Crown Estate Commissioners v Gunn*[4] the Land Court expressed the view that 'an offerer in the open market will base his offer on an estimate of what the holding can be made to yield if properly farmed', but the statutory provisions recognise that rents offered may be greater than the productive capacity of the holding would justify and include a premium for possession. The provisions of section 13(4) are designed to exclude such premium but since they do not introduce a new criterion and merely allow for abatement of the open market rent the adjustment to be made is largely in the arbiter's discretion. If the scarcity of farms to let continues it is likely that arbiters will have to apply the section 13(4) factors in most cases rather than the 'normal' criterion of open market rents in the surrounding area. The arbiter will have to consider the evidence of open market comparisons and any evidence of the section 13(4) factors and decide whether the open market evidence is sufficient and undistorted. It is only when he is not so satisfied that he should take into account evidence of the section 13(4) factors. Guidance on the application of the factors in section 13(4) may be found in the decisions of the Land Court, especially *Aberdeen Endowments Trust v Will*[5] in which the Land Court specifically set out their judgment in a form designed to assist arbiters.

FACTORS TO BE DISREGARDED

The arbiter in fixing the new amount of the rent is not entitled to take account of the following.

(1) Any increase in the rental value of the holding which is due to improvements so far as they have been executed wholly or partly at the expense of the tenant without any equivalent allowance or benefit from the landlord in consideration of rent. If, however, the improvement was executed under an obligation imposed on the tenant by the lease then the

4 1961 SLCR App 173.
5 1985 SLT (Land Ct) 23.

effect of the improvement on the rental value can be taken into account. An 'improvement' is for this purpose an improvement executed at the tenant's expense. Tenants' improvements are to be disregarded whether or not the expense has been or will be reimbursed by government grant.

(2) An increase in the rental value of the holding due to improvements executed by the landlord insofar as the landlord has received or will receive government grant in respect of them.

(3) Any dilapidation or deterioration of or damage to fixed equipment or land caused or permitted by the tenant.

In practice, arbiters disregard tenants' improvements or dilapidation by valuing the holding as if the improvement did not exist or the dilapidation had not occurred. Dilapidations for which the landlord is responsible do not fall to be disregarded although the tenant may be able to require that they be made good. The adjustment for landlords' improvements which have been grant-aided is more complicated as only part of the improvements may fall to be disregarded. A rental value for the improvement should then be assessed and an appropriate proportion of this deducted from the rental of the whole.

INFORMATION TO BE PROVIDED TO ARBITER

The Land Court has indicated what information should be provided to an arbiter or the court in a rent arbitration or application.

'The information required would be copies of any written lease and any subsequent repair agreements to show who was responsible for repairs and renewals, a detailed list of the landlord's provisions of fixed equipment and of the improvements carried out by him with details of the grant which he received for these, a note of all the improvements carried out by the tenant so that we could ignore them when inspecting all the improvements and details of the basis on which the rent had been determined, eg by negotiation between landlord and tenant or by a statutory arbitration.'

INSPECTION

The arbiter should always make a full inspection of the holding and should be accompanied by both parties or their representatives. There is no statutory requirement for the arbiter to inspect allegedly comparable holdings. He should, however, satisfy himself either by inspection or on the strength of expert evidence as to whether the other holdings are truly comparable. If he is satisfied that they are not comparable or if he is already familiar with them, he may decline to inspect them.

REASONS FOR AWARD

Prior to the Agricultural Holdings (Amendment) (Scotland) Act 1983, there was no statutory obligation on an arbiter to state reasons for his award. If he was appointed by the Secretary of State he could, in terms of section 12 of the Tribunals and Inquiries Act 1971, be required to state reasons if so requested before the issue of the award. Paragraph 10 of Schedule 7 to the

1991 Act provides that an arbiter appointed by the Secretary of State or the Land Court to revise rent under section 13(1) shall, in making his award, state in writing his findings of fact and the reasons for his decision and shall make that statement available to the Secretary of State and the parties.

FORM OF AWARD

In terms of paragraph 11 of Schedule 7 to the 1991 Act, the form of award in an arbitration under the Act and any statement of reasons where this has to be given in a rent arbitration must be in such form as may be specified by the Secretary of State by statutory instrument. See Appendix 1 for the form of award and matters to be covered in the statement of reasons for a rent award. A decision of the Land Court does not require to be in the form required for an arbiter's award, but in *Aberdeen Endowments Trust* the court's note followed the same headings as those laid down in the statutory instrument and did so explicitly with a view to assisting arbiters.

There is now no need for either party to request reasons for the award in a rent arbitration if the arbiter was appointed by the Secretary of State. An arbiter appointed by joint submission cannot be required to give reasons for his award unless the submission so stipulates.

STATED CASE TO LAND COURT

Where the arbiter has been appointed in a rental arbitration by the Secretary of State or by the Land Court the arbiter may at any stage in the proceedings state a case to the Land Court on a question of law (but not valuation). The decision of the Land Court is final.

APPEAL TO LAND COURT

Section 61(2) provides for a right of appeal to the Scottish Land Court on any question of law or fact (including the amount of the award) by any party to a rent arbitration where the arbiter was appointed by the Secretary of State or the Land Court.

In such an appeal the Land Court will not disturb the arbiter's award unless the appellant can demonstrate that it was incorrect either in law or in the basis of calculation. Failure to provide all the information required in the prescribed form of award may be a ground of appeal but the appeal may be on amount only.

The provision for appeal to the Land Court does not apply where the arbiter in a rent arbitration is appointed by joint submission, nor does it apply to arbitrations other than rent arbitrations, but in that case the provision for application to the sheriff by stated case on a question of law during the course of the submission would apply.

The appeal must be brought within two months of the date of issue of the award.

ABSOLUTE RIGHT TO INCREASE RENT

Where the landlord has carried out any improvement of the nature specified in section 15(1) of the 1991 Act, the landlord is absolutely entitled to have the rent increased. These improvements are improvements carried out by the landlord at his own expense either at the request of the tenant or with the tenant's consent or in pursuance of an undertaking to carry out an improvement proposed by the tenant and approved by the Land Court or in compliance with a direction given by the Secretary of State under statutory powers.

In respect of any such improvement the landlord can serve a written notice on the tenant within six months from the completion of the improvement. If he does so, the rent of the holding is increased by an amount equal to the increase in the rental value of the holding attributable to the carrying out of the improvement. The date as from which the increase operates is the date of the completion of the improvement.

If the landlord obtained a state grant towards the cost of the improvement, that fact will not affect his right to an increase of rent under section 15. The arbiter will still have to determine the amount of the increase in the rental value of the holding, which is attributable to the carrying out of the improvement, but when that amount has been ascertained, it has to be 'reduced proportionately' by the amount of the state grant. The simplest interpretation of these words is that the amount by which the rent would be otherwise increased is to be reduced by a sum representing the portion of the increase which is due to the grant.

The rental value will have to be assessed on the same basis as under section 13. The provisions for appeal to the Land Court in section 61(2) do not apply to an arbitration under section 15, nor do the provisions for giving reasons or for a stated case to the Land Court under paragraphs 10 and 22 of Schedule 7 respectively.

CHAPTER 3

SUCCESSION TO LEASES

LEASES NOT TRANSFERABLE ON DEATH: SPECIAL DESTINATIONS

Under section 36(2) of the Succession (Scotland) Act 1964 the estate of a deceased person includes his interest as tenant 'under a tenancy or lease which was not expressed to expire on his death'.

Under the proviso (a) to the subsection a lease subject to a special destination is not treated as a part of the deceased's estate unless the destination was evacuated by will or otherwise. Accordingly if a lease is expressed to expire on the tenant's death or if it contains a special destination which has not been evacuated it does not form part of the deceased's estate. It does not vest in the executor under section 14 or become transferable by him under section 16, but will be transmitted to the substitute tenant called under the destination.

LEASES TERMINATING ON DEATH OF TENANT

At common law the succession of heirs can be excluded by making the lease a liferent one and although the view has been expressed that that is not possible in a lease of agricultural subjects it appears from the observations in *Cormack v McIldowie's Exrs*[1] that the court did not exclude the possibility of a liferent lease of agricultural subjects. It is thought that such a lease would not be a lease within the definition of that term in section 85 of the 1991 Act but this was not a matter before the court in *Cormack*. It may, however, be possible to have a lease expressed to expire on the tenant's death without granting a liferent lease if there is an express exclusion not only of assignees but of all heirs and successors. Before the changes made by the 1964 Act it was not possible to exclude the succession of the heir-at-law in a lease other than a liferent lease but it is cogently argued in Gill, *The Law of Agricultural Holdings in Scotland* (2nd edn), that it is now competent to contract out of the implied destination to heirs. *Kennedy v Johnstone*[2] held it competent to contract out of the statutory power to bequeath a lease and this decision was considered without adverse comment in *Johnson v Moreton*.[3] It may therefore be competent to exclude heirs on intestacy. It is now common for leases to provide for the exclusion of all successors but the validity of such exclusion has not yet been the subject of decision by the courts.

SPECIAL DESTINATIONS

Since leases subject to special destinations are excluded from the estate transferable under section 16, the question of definition of special destina-

1 1975 SC 161.
2 1956 SC 39.
3 [1980] AC 37.

tion is of importance. It was held in *Reid's Trs v Macpherson*[4] that a destination to 'A and his heirs excluding assignees and subtenants' was not a special destination. In *Cormack* the Second Division considered a destination to joint tenants and the survivor and the heirs of the survivor excluding heirs portioners, sub-tenants. It held that this also was not a special destination which was defined as 'one in which the particular property in the deed is disponed to the particular person (or persons) specifically nominated by the granter without regard to the normal operation of the law of succession on intestacy'. The restrictive nature of this definition has been the cause of some concern.

BEQUEST OF LEASE

At common law a tenant had no right to bequeath his lease but since the Agricultural Holdings (Scotland) Act 1883 there has been a statutory power of bequest. This is now contained in section 11 of the 1991 Act, in terms of which the tenant has the power of bequest to his son-in-law or daughter-in-law or any person 'who would be or would in any circumstances have been entitled to succeed to the estate on intestacy' by virtue of the Succession (Scotland) Act 1964.

The Court of Session held in *Kennedy* that contracting out of the power of bequest is permissible; and an express exclusion of legatees or of assignees (which term is held to include legatees) would preclude a tenant from bequeathing his lease. In practice therefore the right is of little value where there is a formal lease as assignees are normally excluded.

The right is subject to certain conditions.

(1) The legatee must intimate the bequest to the landlord within twenty-one days after the tenant's death, unless he is prevented, by some unavoidable cause, from doing so within that time, in which event notice must be given as soon as possible thereafter. Such notice imports acceptance by the legatee of the bequest.

(2) Within a month after receipt of the notice, the landlord may give a counter-notice refusing to receive the legatee as tenant. Failing the giving of such counter-notice the lease is binding on landlord and legatee as from the date of the death of the tenant. If the landlord gives a counter-notice, the legatee may apply to the Land Court to declare that he is tenant under the lease as from the date of death of the deceased tenant. If the landlord establishes a reasonable ground of objection, the Land Court must declare the bequest to be null and void but otherwise must make an order in terms of the application. Pending the court proceedings, the legatee shall, with the consent of the executor, have possession of the holding unless, on cause shown, the Land Court otherwise directs. The statute does not suggest any particular ground of objection to a legatee, and it is left to the Land Court to decide whether any ground stated by the landlord is reasonable. Objections have usually been on the grounds of the legatee's lack of training or experience in agriculture, his lack of financial resources to farm the holding, or his character or habits.

Where a bequest is not accepted or is declared null and void the right to the lease is treated as intestate estate of the deceased tenant and may be

4 1975 SLT 101.

transferred by the executor under section 16(2) of the 1964 Act within one year from the date of determination or withdrawal of the application. Where, however, the legatee accepted the bequest after the expiry of the twenty-one-day period and he was not prevented by unavoidable cause from giving notice within that period the predecessor of section 11(8) was held not to apply so that the right to the lease was not intestate estate which could be transferred by the executor: *Coats v Logan*.[5]

INTESTATE SUCCESSION

Where a lease is or is treated as intestate estate the deceased tenant's interest may be transferred by his executor under section 16 of the 1964 Act to any one of the persons entitled to succeed to the deceased's intestate estate or to claim legal rights on the prior of a surviving spouse. Such a person is referred to in section 12 of the 1991 Act as an 'acquirer' and must give notice to the landlord within twenty-one days after the date of acquisition unless prevented by unavoidable cause. It should be carefully noted that the notice must be given by or on behalf of the acquirer and not by or on behalf of the executors. If the landlord does not give counter-notice within one month the lease becomes binding on the landlord and acquirer as landlord and tenant as from the date of acquisition. If the landlord serves counter-notice the procedure differs from that in section 11 as it is not for the acquirer to make application to the Land Court for an order declaring him to be tenant but for the landlord to apply for an order terminating the lease. The application under section 12(2) may not be made before the expiration of one month from the giving of the counter-notice. There is no time-limit stated within which the landlord must make application.

If the Land Court is satisfied that the landlord has established any reasonable ground of objection it must make an order terminating the lease from such term of Whitsunday or Martinmas as it may specify. The grounds of objection are as for those against a bequest of the lease. If a landlord wishes to avoid the uncertainty of such an application, it may be better for him to accept the successor and then, if he is not a near relative of the deceased tenant, to give an incontestable notice to quit under section 25 of the 1991 Act (see above).

Pending the proceedings, the acquirer is to have possession of the holding with consent of the executor unless the Land Court on cause shown otherwise directs. A termination of the acquirer's interest in this way is to be treated, for the purposes of the statutory provisions as to compensation, as the termination of his tenancy; but he is not entitled to compensation for disturbance.

EXECUTOR'S TITLE

The executor's title to the lease is by virtue of 'confirmation thereto' – section 14 of the 1964 Act. The lease must be included in the inventory of the deceased tenant's estate and adequately described. If the lease is not included in the inventory the executor has no title to effect a transfer under

5 1985 SLT 221.

section 16 of the 1964 Act: *Rotherwick's Trs v Hope*.[6] It has been held that executors may validly assign the lease first and obtain confirmation later (*Garvie's Trs v Garvie's Tutors*)[7] but it is obviously advisable to confirm first. The transfer may be by assignation or docquet on confirmation.

The lease vests in the executor for administrative purposes only but he is 'tenant' in terms of section 85(1) of the 1991 Act and responsible for paying rent and for the other obligations in the lease until he effects the transfer to the acquirer.

TIME-LIMITS

The executor must transfer the lease within one year of the deceased's tenant's death or the date of determination or withdrawal of a legatee's application to the Land Court; otherwise the landlord may terminate the lease by notice under section 16(3)(b) of the 1964 Act. That subsection provides that a longer period than a year may be fixed by agreement between the landlord and executor or failing agreement by the sheriff on summary application. In *Gifford v Buchanan*[8] application was not made until after the year had expired and it was held that notice of transfer had been served too late. The Lord Justice-Clerk reserved his opinion on whether application must be made within one year. Lord Robertson thought that it must with Lord Grieve concurring.

If an executor fails to obtain confirmation within a year of the late tenant's death the landlord may obtain declarator that the lease is at an end.

The actings of the parties after the death of a tenant may be sufficient to constitute a new tenancy, as in *Morrison-Low v Paterson*[9] where the executors remained in possession, although they did not obtain confirmation. Rent was accepted for several years by the landlords. In the House of Lords Lord Keith of Kinkel said:

> 'In the ordinary case, there can be no doubt that where a proprietor admits someone into the possession of an agricultural holding, or maintains him in such possession without any pre-existing right thereto, and regularly accepts rent from him, there is an inescapable inference that a tenancy has been brought into existence, and it is of no moment that no particular occasion can be pointed to upon which the parties agreed to the one granting and the other taking a tenancy.'

TRANSFER TO EXECUTOR

The executor is very often among the category of persons eligible to acquire the interest in the lease. If he transfers it to himself, however, the transfer may be challenged by the other beneficiaries on the ground that he is *auctor in rem suam*, ie that he is acting in a situation where his duty as executor is in conflict with his interests as an individual. Unless he has the consent of all other interested parties the prospective acquirer should not accept or seek

6 1975 SLT 187.
7 1975 SLT 94.
8 1983 SLT 613.
9 1985 SLT 255.

appointment as executor. If he has already done so he should resign before the transfer is made: *Inglis v Inglis*.[10]

Termination if Tenancy not Transferred

If none of the heirs on intestacy wishes to take over the lease, as may be the case where there is an unprofitable lease or no 'near relative' successor, the executor may terminate the tenancy by notice under section 16(3). If the interest is not disposed of within one year of the tenant's death or such longer period as may be agreed or fixed by the sheriff, either the landlord or the executor may terminate the tenancy by such notice.

The notice to be given is notice in accordance with section 16(4) and not notice to quit or notice of removal. Section 16(4)(a) provides that notice in the case of an agricultural lease may be of such period as is agreed and failing agreement a period not less than one year nor more than two ending with a term of Whitsunday or Martinmas. The term chosen does not require to coincide with the contractual ish or an anniversary of it. Apart from the period the terms of the notice are not specified.

The termination of the tenancy by notice under section 16(3) does not prejudice the claims of either the landlord or tenant for compensation or damages in respect of termination of the lease or any rights under it, but any award of compensation or damages in respect of termination by the executor is enforceable only against the deceased's estate and not against the executor personally.

10 1983 SC 8.

CHAPTER 4

NOTICE TO QUIT AND NOTICE OF INTENTION TO QUIT

In terms of section 21(1) of the 1991 Act written notice of intention to terminate a tenancy must be given not less than one year nor more than two years before the termination of the lease. If the notice is given by the landlord it is known as a 'notice to quit', while if it is given by the tenant it is known as a 'notice of intention to quit'. The provisions of the subsection have effect notwithstanding any agreement or any provision in the lease to the contrary. Contracting out of the provisions with regard to notices to quit is incompetent and any agreement which amounts to contracting out of security of tenure is void. Although the parties cannot bind themselves in advance to a different period of notice they may agree on termination of the tenancy and, for example, accept notice of less than one year or more than two, provided that the agreement is acted upon. It is also competent for the tenant to renounce his tenancy unilaterally.

In terms of section 21(4) the provisions of the Sheriff Courts (Scotland) Act 1907 relating to removings are, in the case of an agricultural holding, to have effect subject to the provisions of the section. Where the 1907 Act provisions are inconsistent with those of section 21 of the 1991 Act it has been held that they are superseded by the latter.

The manner of service and form of notice to quit are specified in section 21(5) but there is no corresponding provision for notice of removal given by a tenant. In terms of section 21(3) a notice complies with the section if it is in writing and is a notice of intention to bring the lease to an end. Where the notice is to take effect at the termination of the stipulated endurance of the lease it must be given not less than one nor more than two years before that date. If the lease is running on tacit relocation it must similarly be given not less than one year nor more than two years before it is due to take effect. A simple letter by the tenant is sufficient so long as it clearly intimates that he does not consent to tacit relocation. Where such a letter intimated intention to remove at dates other than those specified in the lease but was accepted by the landlords this was treated as an agreement to vary the terms of ish.

The Term and Quarter Days (Scotland) Act 1990 regulates the dates of Whitsunday, Martinmas, Candlemas and Lammas and is intended to avoid the confusion and scope for error which formerly arose. The majority of the Act came into force on 13th July 1991. Section 1 of the Act provides that Whitsunday and Martinmas mean 28th May and 28th November and Candlemas and Lammas mean 28th February and 28th August for any enactment or rule of law whether entered into before or after the commencement of the 1990 Act. The words have the same meaning for the purposes of any lease, agreement or undertaking which is entered into or given or any document which is executed after 13th July 1991. Section 1(7) provides that if a lease, agreement, undertaking or document refers to a term day and also gives a specific date other than that defined in the Act, the date is to have effect and the specified term day is to be disregarded. If, for example, a lease

23

refers to the ish as Whitsunday (15th May), the lease will be taken to end at 15th May, not 28th May, and notice in terms of section 21 of the 1991 Act will have to be given against the earlier date. If, on the other hand, the word 'Whitsunday' is used without any further specification, notice must be given against 28th May.

Where the lease was entered into before 13th July 1991 and contains a reference to Whitsunday, Martinmas, Candlemas or Lammas, this is to mean 28th May, 28th November, 28th February and 28th August. These dates are to apply only if there is no other specification of which dates are intended by the parties to the contract.

Section 1(3) of the 1990 Act provides that a lease, agreement or undertaking may be either written or oral.

In summary, the position following the enactment of the 1990 Act is:
(1) if a date of ish is specified in the lease, that is the date against which notice to quit or notice of intention to quit must be given;
(2) if the term day only is given in the lease, notice must be given against 28th May or 28th November as the case may be.

The effect of the Act is therefore to sweep away the old law that it was open to the parties to give their own definition to Whitsunday and Martinmas. Although they may be so by specifying the dates of these terms in their lease, the effect of the Act is that if they rely simply on the words 'Whitsunday' and 'Martinmas' the statute defines these words for them.

Provision is made in the 1990 Act for the situation that the parties in fact intended some date other than that specified in the Act. A summary application could be made to the sheriff within one year after the passing of the Act (ie before 13th July 1991) for a declaration that the date intended in the lease was a specific date other than the date specified in the 1990 Act. If this date has passed without application to the sheriff having been made, the statutory dates apply whatever the original intention of the parties may have been.

In terms of section 21(6) of the 1991 Act a landlord's right to enforce an irritancy is not affected by the provisions of the section. Unless stipulated for in the lease no period of notice is required but simply notice that the irritancy has been incurred and that the tenant is required to remove. If the tenant does not do so the landlord may proceed with an action of declarator of irritancy and removing. An irritancy, particularly a general irritancy for any breach of the lease, is accordingly a dangerous provision from the tenant's point of view. If, as is usual, it makes no provision for the tenant's being given the opportunity to remedy the breach the landlord will be in a position to terminate the lease forthwith if the tenant is guilty of any breach. The principle of mutuality of contract may, however, prevent the landlord from enforcing an irritancy if he is himself in breach of his obligations under the lease. The provisions in the Law Reform (Miscellaneous Provisions) (Scotland) Act 1985, in terms of which an irritancy clause cannot be founded on in respect of a breach of contract capable of remedy until the party in default shall have been given a reasonable opportunity of remedying his breach, do not apply to leases of agricultural holdings.

The statutory provisions for notice to quit do not apply to a notice given under a power reserved in the lease for the landlord to resume land for building, planting, feuing, or other purposes not being agricultural purposes nor to lets for less than a year unless the lease takes effect as a lease from year to year under section 2 of the 1991 Act.

In a year to year tenancy by section 29 a notice to quit part of a holding is not invalid on the ground that it relates only to part if it is given for the purpose of adjusting the boundaries or amalgamating agricultural units or parts thereof or for the erection of farm labourers' cottages or other houses, allotments, tree planting, mineral working, making of reservoirs and certain purposes. In *Paddock Investments v Lory*[1] it was held that the words 'other houses' were qualified by the words 'farm labourers' so that this section does not help a landlord who wishes to get back part of the farm to sell to a developer.

Where the landlord gives notice to quit part of a holding under section 29 the tenant may choose to give counter-notice under section 22 so that the notice does not take effect without the consent of the Land Court.

If the tenant does not resist the notice to quit or if the Land Court consents to its operation the tenant may give counter-notice that he accepts the notice as notice to quit the entire holding. The counter-notice must be given within twenty-eight days of the giving of the notice to quit or of the Land Court's decision that it has effect.

Restriction on Operation of Notices to Quit

A tenant who receives notice to quit which does not state any of the reasons in section 22(2) may take steps to have the notice referred for the consent of the Land Court. This is done by the tenant, within one month of the giving of the notice to quit, serving on the landlord a counter-notice in writing, requiring that subsection (1) of section 22 shall apply to the notice to quit. If this is done the notice to quit is not effective unless it is consented to by the Land Court. A mere statement of objection to the notice or a refusal to go out will not be sufficient. The provision is peremptory and must be strictly followed.

Exclusion of Security of Tenure

The tenant's right to serve counter-notice under section 22(1) and so render the notice to quit ineffective without the Land Court's consent is excluded in the seven cases listed in section 22(2).

Where a landlord serves notice to quit under one of these cases he must make it clear on which of them he is relying and not only identify the paragraph relied on but quote its terms. The notice may refer to more than one of the paragraphs or both parts of paragraph (d) but paragraphs (d) and (e) are mutually exclusive. Ambiguity in the notice to quit will render it invalid.

A tenant who wishes to contest a notice to quit under section 22(2) should not serve counter-notice under section 22(1) but notice requiring arbitration under section 23(2) within one month after the notice to quit is served on him. If the arbiter's award is in the tenant's favour he should serve counter-notice under section 22(1) within one month of the date of the award. This is to prevent the landlord's notice to quit under section 22(2) taking effect as a

1 (1975) 236 EG 803.

plain notice to quit. It is arguable whether it would do so but it is safer for the tenant to serve counter-notice in any case.

If two notices to quit are given for different reasons it is possible for one of them to take effect although the other is suspended under section 23(3) pending arbitration. The tenant should therefore respond appropriately to both notices either by serving counter-notice or by requiring arbitration.

It has been held that a preliminary notice founded on in a notice to quit under the corresponding English provisions must be strictly construed against the landlord because of the possible forfeiture of the tenant's interest. This involved considerations of equity but the Scottish courts also require strict compliance with the statutory requirements both in respect of the notice to quit and any preliminary notice founded on.

THE SEVEN CASES UNDER SECTION 22(2)

(1) Cropping lets for definite and limited period (s 22(2)(a))

This case applies where permanent pasture which the landlord has been in the habit of letting for seasonal grazing or keeping in his own occupation is let for cropping for a definite and limited period and on condition that the tenant shall sow permanent grass seeds along with the last or waygoing crop. The object is to enable the owner to let for the purpose of renewing the permanent pasture without creating security of tenure. The provision has been little used and has the disadvantage for the landlord that he must serve notice to quit against the end of the definite and limited period and if he fails to do so this lease will continue by tacit relocation and the tenant will acquire security of tenure.

(2) Planning consent: non-agricultural use (s 22(2)(b))

This case applies where notice to quit is given expressly on the grounds that the land is required for non-agricultural use for which permission has been granted on an application under the town and country planning legislation or for which (otherwise than by virtue of any provision of that legislation) such permission is not required. The paragraph does not expressly state that the land must be required at the date of serving the notice but the wording 'notice to quit is given on the ground that the land *is* required' suggests that this is so. The landlord must show that there is a definite intention and prospect of non-agricultural use by himself or someone else. The use must be one for which planning permission has been granted or for which (for a reason other than a provision of the planning legislation) such permission is not required. Apart from use by the Crown, which is not subject to the Town and Country Planning Acts, there are unlikely to be many cases where planning permission is not required, except by virtue of provision in the Planning Acts.

The paragraph will not enable a landlord to terminate the lease of the whole holding if only a relatively small part is required for non-agricultural use and it is thought that the whole or substantially the whole holding must be the subject of any planning consent and be required for non-agricultural use. This is likely to prove a difficulty where only part of a farm is proposed to be developed for housing if there is no power of resumption.

(3) Certificate of bad husbandry (s 22(2)(c))

Where the Land Court has granted a certificate of bad husbandry the landlord can serve incontestable notice to quit under this paragraph. The notice to quit must be served within nine months of the application to the Land Court but cannot be served before the certificate is granted. If a certificate were granted after the expiry of the nine-month period it would not found a notice to quit under this paragraph.

(4) Non-compliance with demand to pay rent or remedy breach of lease (s 22(2)(d))

Paragraph (d) specifies two separate grounds for serving notice to quit, namely failure to comply with a demand for payment of rent within two months and failure to comply with a demand to remedy a breach of the lease which is capable of remedy.

Demand for rent. There is no statutory form of demand for payment of rent but it should quote the words of the paragraph and clearly require payment within two months. The rent must be due and unpaid at the date of serving the notice. It has been held in England that a demand was valid when posted immediately before this date when rent became due but was delivered and so served after the rent was due. In practice such demands will be sent by recorded delivery and unless the contrary is proved will be deemed to be served when they would be delivered in the ordinary course of post. In a case where the landlord had been in the habit of accepting payment by cheque sent by post it was held that a demand to pay within two months had been complied with when the cheque was posted within the two-month period but received after its expiry. If the tenant wishes to challenge the reason stated in the notice to quit, he must demand arbitration within one month.

Demand to remedy breach of lease. Section 22(2)(d) also provides for a landlord's serving notice to quit which does not need Land Court consent when the tenant has failed to comply with a demand in writing requiring him within a reasonable time to remedy any breach which was capable of being remedied of any term or condition of his tenancy which was not inconsistent with fulfilment of his responsibilities to farm in accordance with the rules of good husbandry.

This has been the most commonly invoked of all the provisions in section 22(2) and very often the landlord's demand has been served with a view to recovering possession of the farm, rather than obtaining compliance with the terms of the lease. The value of this procedure to a landlord has, however, been limited by the provision of section 66 in the case of demands requiring work of 'provision, repair, maintenance or replacement of fixed equipment'.

There is no prescribed form of demand but it should quote the words of the paragraph and clearly indicate to the tenant what is required of him. If it fails to do so the demand and the notice to quit founding on the demand will be invalid. Demands commonly include a list of alleged breaches and failure to remedy any of these will found a notice to quit.

The statutory remedy under section 22(2)(d) is not affected by the principle of mutuality of contract which precludes a landlord from enforcing an irritancy clause when he is himself in breach of his obligations under the lease. The landlord's demand may, however, be invalid if his own breach prevents the tenant from complying.

The time considered reasonable does not have to be stated in the demand but if no period is stated in a demand requiring work in respect of fixed equipment the tenant may ask an arbiter to state the period in terms of section 66 of the Act. There is not, as there is in England, a minimum period which will be considered reasonable. The question is one of fact to be determined by the arbiter in the circumstances of each case. It has been held by an arbiter that three days was a reasonable time within which to carry out work of carting materials which the tenant was obliged to do so under his lease. Where there were a number of alleged breaches it was held that the time allowed had to be reasonable for all of them to be remedied including items which were not enforceable.

The landlord's previous acquiescence in a breach, even for a period of eleven years, does not prevent him from requiring that it be remedied unless there is prejudice to the tenant which would found a plea of personal bar.

Arbiters have additional powers in relation to section 22(2)(d) demands which require work of 'provision, repair, maintenance or replacement of fixed equipment' but not in relation to other section 22(2)(d) demands.

The powers conferred on the arbiter in section 66(1) are:

(1) that the arbiter may in relation to all or any of the items specified in the demand, substitute for any period specified as the period within which the breach may be remedied such period as appears in all the circumstances to the arbiter to be a reasonable period;

(2) the arbiter may delete from the demand any item or part of an item as to which, having due regard to the interests of good husbandry and sound estate management, the arbiter is satisfied that it is unnecessary or unjustified;

(3) where no period is specified in the demand, the arbiter may specify in relation to all or any of the items so specified such period as appears to him reasonable; and

(4) he can substitute in the case of any item or part of an item specified in the demand, a different method, or material from that required in the demand.

It may be noted that although there is power to delete an item of a demand there is no general power to amend it, but only the limited power under section 66(1)(c) to specify a different method or material.

The arbiter's powers under section 66(1) may be invoked when the demand is received by means of an arbitration to fix the period and adjust the terms of the demand. There is not, however, a provision as there is in the corresponding English regulations, that arbitration on such a demand must be required within one month of the service of the demand. If a period for compliance is stated the tenant may prefer not to seek an extension under section 66(1)(a) but simply to argue that the time allowed was insufficient and that any notice to quit following on it was invalid.

It is obviously more satisfactory for a tenant to know the date by which he is required to carry out the work and it will be advisable for a landlord to state a period in a demand to which section 66 applies as there may otherwise be a reference to an arbiter to fix the period. It is competent simply to follow the statutory wording and to require the work to be done within a reasonable period.

The circumstances where the power of deletion is likely to be invoked are where there is an unreasonably large number of minor items or a requirement to carry out obsolete or uneconomic operations.

As the arbiter's power may be exercised in respect of any one of a series of items there may be different periods for different items and the extensions of the period for one item may not enable the tenant to escape the consequences of failure to deal with one of the other items.

Section 66(2) provides that when an arbiter specifies a period under section 66(1)(a) or the time for remedying a breach is extended under section 66(2) then the Land Court may on the application of the arbiter or the landlord specify a date for the termination of the tenancy by notice to quit in the event of the tenant's failure to remedy the breach within the period specified by the arbiter or the extended time being a date not earlier than

(1) the date on which the tenancy could have been terminated by notice to quit served on the expiry of the time originally specified in the demand, or if no time was specified, served at the date of giving demand; or

(2) six months after the expiry of the period specified by the arbiter or the extended time.

Section 66(3) provides that a notice to quit on a date specified by the Land Court under section 66(2) shall be served on the tenant within one month after the expiration of the period specified by the arbiter of the extended time and shall be valid notwithstanding that it is served less than twelve months before the date on which the tenancy is to be terminated or that that date is not the end of a year of the tenancy.

Thus, if a landlord required a tenant to remedy a breach by doing work on a building by 3rd May 1992 and the tenant satisfied the arbiter that this was not a long enough period and the arbiter allowed him to 3rd August 1992, then the landlord's original plan to serve notice to quit against Whitsunday 1993 would be thwarted, but under section 66(2) he could apply to the Land Court to authorise the serving of notice to quit against Whitsunday 1993 because he could have served notice against that term on the expiration of the original period and there is still over six months from the expiration of the period fixed by the arbiter. If, however, the arbiter had allowed to 3rd December 1992 for the work to be done, then the earliest date against which notice to quit could be authorised would be 3rd June 1993, being six months after the period allowed.

Section 66(4) provides that when notice to quit is given under section 22(2)(d) because of a tenant's alleged failure to remedy a breach within the time specified in the demand or extended by the arbiter and the arbiter considers that although the time originally specified or extended was reasonable, it would, because of any happening during that time, have been unreasonable to require the tenant to remedy the breach within that time, then the arbiter may treat the time as having been extended or further extended and make his award as if the time had not expired; and if the breach has not been remedied at the time of the award, the arbiter may extend the time by such period as he considers reasonable having regard to the length of the time that has elapsed since the service of the demand. So, if the tenant has done the work, but done it later than required, the arbiter can let him escape the notice to quit. If he has not done the work, the arbiter can allow him a longer time to do it, but this subsection applies only where the time allowed was reasonable but became unreasonable because of some happening.

The nature of this happening is not specified and the arbiter has a discretion as to the reasons which he may accept.

The section does not provide (as the English regulations do) that the running of the period is extended until the termination of the arbitration and may be extended by the arbiter thereafter. It is suggested in Gill, *The Law of Agricultural Holdings in Scotland* (2nd edn), that the purpose of the provisions would be frustrated if the demand were not suspended pending arbitration and it is understood that arbiters have in practice agreed to extend the period even when they considered it to be originally reasonable and the demand justified. It would clearly be open to the arbiter where the period stated was unreasonable to allow a longer period to take account of the time spent on the arbitration. If the time stated was originally reasonable and the arbiter did not extend it under section 66(1) the reference to arbitration would itself be a happening which would enable the arbiter to exercise his powers under section 66(4).

Where the tenant requires arbitration on only some of the items in a demand time continues to run on the unchallenged items.

Where a notice to quit is served by reason of alleged failure to remedy a breach which requires the doing of work of provision, repair, maintenance or replacement of fixed equipment section 32 provides a mechanism whereby the tenant who is in breach may give counter-notice requiring the landlord to apply to the Land Court for consent to the operation of the notice to quit. By section 32(5) the court must give its consent unless in all the circumstances it appears to it that a fair and reasonable landlord would not insist on possession. The section deals both with the situation where a tenant accepts that he is in breach and with the situation where he denies it. The section provides that the notice is not to have effect without the Land Court's consent if the tenant serves notices under subsections (2) or (3). The reason for the two subsections is that there are alternative courses open to the tenant. He can either go to the Land Court straight away without going to arbitration first or he can go to arbitration; if the arbiter finds against him he can go on to the Land Court. It is unlikely that many tenants will in effect concede that the landlord is going to succeed on the merits by going straight to the Land Court, but it would save the expense of going to arbitration with a hopeless case and in that event counter-notice can be given under subsection (2). Subsection (3) preserves the right to require arbitration under section 23(2) of the Act within one month of the giving of notice to quit. If that is done, the counter-notice under section 32(2) is of no effect. In most cases, a tenant who receives a notice to quit under section 22(2)(d) will require arbitration on the reasons stated in the notice. If he is unsuccessful in the arbitration and the notice to quit is held to be valid and effective, then he can still serve counter-notice under section 32(4). The counter-notice simply requires that the provisions of section 32(4) shall apply to the notice to quit and the effect of the counter-notice is that the notice to quit does not have effect without the consent of the Land Court. The procedure is similar to the counter-notice procedure under section 22(1) of the Act dealt with below.

Section 32(2) provides that after counter-notice a notice to quit is not to have effect '(whether as a notice to which section 22(1) of this Act does or does not apply)'. This is designed to deal with the possibility of a notice to quit being served which may operate either as a notice under section 22(2)(d) or as a plain notice to quit, so the effect of the words in parentheses is that the counter-notice serves as a counter-notice under section 22(1) as well.

Section 32(6) applies where notice to quit is given under section 66(3), that is served against the date specified by the Land Court after the arbiter has specified the time he thinks reasonable or extended the time under section 66(1)(a). A notice to quit under section 66(3) need not include a statement in accordance with section 22(2)(d) and accordingly a counter-notice under section 32(3) would not be competent but for the express provision of section 32(6) that counter-notice can be given.

The provisions in sections 32 and 66 have not been much invoked but they have had some effect in discouraging landlords from embarking on the section 22(2)(d) procedure.

In *Fane v Murray*[2] the First Division held that if the tenant wished to challenge the notice to remedy, he did not require to do so by arbitration initiated immediately after the notice to remedy is served on him. He may wait for the consequent notice to quit and then proceed to challenge the notice to remedy by arbitration under section 23.

(5) Irremediable breach (s 22(2)(e))

This case relates to the situation where the landlord's interest has been materially prejudiced by a breach of contract by the tenant which was not capable of being remedied in reasonable time and at economic cost. The term or condition which has been broken must not be inconsistent with the fulfilment by the tenant of his responsibilities to farm in accordance with the rules of good husbandry.

It is considered that the landlord's interest would be materially prejudiced if the value of his interest in the holding were considerably reduced by the tenant's breach. The corresponding English section does not contain reference to reasonable time or economic cost but cases under the Agricultural Holdings Act 1986 are relevant as they relate to breaches considered irremediable and the sections are otherwise similar. Examples of irremediable breaches are:

(1) breach of prohibition of assigning or sub-letting;
(2) the cutting of timber or mature hedges;
(3) the serious exhaustion of land by a succession of white straw crops.

A notice to quit must make clear that it is founding on paragraph (e) and not paragraph (d).

The operation of the corresponding English section is considered in *Johnson v Moreton*,[3] where it was argued that the serving of counter-notice to notice to quit was an irremediable breach of a condition in the lease whereby the tenant undertook not to serve counter-notice. The condition was, however, held to be invalid as simply a device to avoid security of tenure.

2 1995 SLT 567.
3 [1980] AC 37.

(6) Apparent insolvency (s 22(2)(f))

In this case the landlord can serve incontestable notice to quit on a tenant who has become apparently insolvent within the meaning of section 7 of the Bankruptcy (Scotland) Act 1985.

Most formal agricultural leases provide for irritancy on the tenant's bankruptcy and commonly this is worded to apply on notour bankruptcy in older leases and apparent insolvency in post-1985 leases. Section 21(6) of the 1991 Act provides that nothing in that section is to affect the right of a landlord of an agricultural holding to remove a tenant whose estate is sequestrated under the 1985 Act, or who by failure to pay rent or otherwise has incurred an irritancy. A landlord has, however, no common law right to irritate a lease on the tenant's bankruptcy and section 22(2)(f) does not create a statutory irritancy in that event. Accordingly, in the absence of a conventional irritancy the landlord will require to proceed by way of notice under section 22(2)(f).

(7) Non-near relative successor (s 22(2)(g))

This paragraph was introduced by the Agricultural Holdings (Amendment) (Scotland) Act 1983 and is dealt with under 'Termination of Interest of Successor'.

CONSENT OF LAND COURT TO NOTICE TO QUIT

The Land Court must consent to the operation of a notice to quit if it is satisfied on one of the five grounds stated in section 24(1), but by section 24(2) the court 'shall withhold consent to the operation of the notice to quit if in all the circumstances it appears to them that a fair and reasonable landlord would not insist on possession'.

The ground on which consent is sought under section 24(1) does not have to be stated in the notice to quit but such statement may be required in terms of section 43 to exclude payment of compensation for disturbance under that section.

In terms of section 23(1) the landlord's application for the Land Court's consent must be made within one month after the service of the tenant's counter-notice requiring that section 22(1) apply to the notice to quit. The application must specify the ground on which consent is sought. In section 24(1) applications the onus of proof is on the landlord.

The grounds for consent under section 24(1) are:

(1) Good husbandry (s 24(1)(a))

'the carrying out of the purpose for which the landlord proposes to terminate the tenancy is desirable in the interests of good husbandry as respects the land to which the notice relates, treated as a separate unit'.

This paragraph involves a comparison between the way in which the holding is being farmed by the tenant and the way in which it would be farmed if the tenancy were terminated. The court must not have regard to any land other than the holding to which the notice relates. The desirability of amalgamating the holding with other land would not be a relevant consideration. Evidence of the standard of other land farmed either by the landlord or proposed new occupier would, however, be relevant. Since the court is to assess the relative merits of the two systems it is not necessary to show that the tenant's farming is inefficient but only that the landlord's proposals are better for the holding. If the tenant is an efficient farmer, however, a landlord might fail on the fair and reasonable landlord provision. In practice such applications tend to involve averments of bad husbandry and may be combined with an application under section 26 for a certificate of bad husbandry.

(2) Sound estate management (s 24(1)(b))

'the carrying out thereof [of the purpose for which the landlord proposes to terminate the tenancy] is desirable in the interests of sound management of the estate of which that land consists or forms part'.

In this case also the court has to compare the present system with the landlord's proposals but it is not restricted to consideration of the land which is the subject of the notice to quit and must consider also the rest of the landlord's estate. The paragraph has commonly been invoked where the landlord proposes amalgamation with other land on his estate. The paragraph uses the term 'sound' estate management and not 'good' estate management and it is thought that sound estate management may involve matters not concerned, as are the rules of good estate management, with enabling an occupier to maintain efficient production but could involve sale of the holding or part of it in order to finance improvements on the rest of the estate.

Hardship to the tenant is not a relevant consideration in deciding if the purpose is desirable under this case but it is relevant under the 'fair and reasonable landlord' provision.

The landlord must have definite proposals for the use of the land he seeks to recover and his purpose must relate to the management of land and not merely the landlord's personal financial benefit. The paragraph does not enable a landlord to terminate the lease for the purpose of reletting on terms more favourable to himself. 'Estate' in this paragraph means only the landlord's estate and not other lands which have passed into other ownership although formerly part of a larger estate and still owned by members of the landlord's family. The holding may itself constitute the entire estate and an area of twenty-six acres is capable of being an estate. Where the holding is the estate, consideration of good husbandry may be relevant under this paragraph as well as under paragraph (a). An application may found on both paragraphs.

(3) Agricultural research, smallholdings or allotments (s 24(1)(c))

'the carrying out thereof is desirable for the purposes of agricultural research, education, experiment or demonstration, or for the purposes of the enactments relating to allotments, smallholdings or such holdings as are referred to in section 64 of the Agriculture (Scotland) Act 1948'.

The court has discretion to decide if one of the purposes in this paragraph is desirable presumably on grounds of public policy. The landlord seeking to use land for such purposes is likely to be a government department or educational institution but the paragraph will also apply to a private landlord.

(4) Greater hardship (s 24(1)(d))

'[T]hat greater hardship would be caused by withholding than by giving consent to the operation of the notice'.

This is the paragraph of section 24(1) most often founded on. It is also the most difficult on which to advise as to the prospects of success as the court must not merely decide whether hardship would be caused but also the relative degree of hardship which would result to each party if the notice did or did not take effect.

This involves balancing the personal circumstances of each party. Each party must show the whole extent of the hardship falling on that party. 'The Court must then consider the relative degrees of hardship and determine which is the greater'. If the degrees of hardship are the same the landlord must fail because the court has to be satisfied that greater hardship would be caused by withholding than by granting consent. The onus of proof is then on the landlord but it is for each party to show the hardship which would result to him.

In its note to *Dickson v Allison*[4] the Land Court indicated that

'no cases involve more anxious consideration than those such as the present. We have repeatedly held that regard must be had to the whole relevant circumstances including personal and family ones. Each such case must be decided on its particular own facts and circumstances'.

Hardship for this purpose is widely interpreted and is not restricted to financial hardship although that is usually an element of the hardship alleged. Hardship is something more than inconvenience but it may consist solely in the effect on agricultural operations. The normal operation of security of tenure does not of itself constitute hardship. Business hardship and hardship to a company are relevant.

It is not only hardship to the applicant and respondent which may be considered but the effect on their families, employees or even the beneficiaries of a trust.

In a number of cases consent has been granted to enable the landlord to sell the holding with vacant possession. Such applications are more likely to succeed where the landlord is elderly, has most of his capital invested in the holding and wishes to sell in order to increase an inadequate income. Much will, however, depend on the tenant's circumstances. Where he occupies other land and has substantial resources the loss of the holding will obviously involve less hardship than in the case of a tenant who stands to lose his house and livelihood.

Where, as is usual, financial hardship is alleged it is essential that the parties make full disclosure of their finances. Accounts when available should be produced and in any event the evidence should be corroborated. Where a tenant has several farms or buildings he should assist the court as to the profit attributable to the holding in question. In a number of cases the hardship alleged has been primarily or even wholly non-financial. In *Barns-Graham v Lamont*[5] a statement of the anticipated frustration of a long-standing plan for the landlord's son's career for which he had undergone prolonged training

4 1976 SLCR 108.
5 1971 SC 170.

was held to be a statement that the landlord would suffer hardship if his notice to quit did not take effect. In that case Lord Migdale said:

'hardship is a word of many meanings. It is not restricted to financial hardship or penury on the part of the landlord. . . . Upsetting the landlord's plans is a hardship to him and that is implicit in terms of the letter'.

The last sentence must be taken to mean that upsetting the landlord's plans amounted to hardship in the particular circumstances of the case. Merely to state that the landlord's plans will be frustrated if the notice does not have effect will not amount to a statement of hardship. See *Copeland v McQuaker*[6] at p 190 where the Sheriff Principal's interlocutor (affirmed on appeal) pointed out that the failure to take effect of a notice to quit must always to some extent frustrate a landlord's plans and held that a statement that this would be so did not amount to a statement of hardship.

Normally each party will seek to show the hardship which would be caused to him or his family or his employees but hardship is considered at large and the landlord's liability to pay an additional sum of four times the annual rent in terms of section 54 may involve financial hardship to him and be a reason for refusing his application.

In one case it was held to be economic hardship in the sense of the section for the landlord to have made a bad investment by paying too much for the holding. The court has not been disposed to grant consent where the hardship has been self-inflicted as where the landlord accepted a gift of the holding and was aware of the existence of the tenancy. In that case it was held that his hardship must be assessed from the point of view of the landlord without regard to the intentions of the former landlord.

It is doubtful if a tenant's failure to honour an agreement of contract out of security of tenure involves hardship on the landlord. Since such agreements are unenforceable and contrary to public policy it is thought that the court should not treat the breach of the agreement as a relevant factor in a greater hardship case and it has expressly not done so. In *Clarke v Smith*[7] where the holding had been acquired through the offices of the tenant who then obtained a tenancy which the landlords did not know gave security of tenure it was observed that since the tenancy was admitted these factors were no more than a make-weight but would have been more relevant had the court been required to consider the 'fair and reasonable landlord' provision. The same may apply to the breach of an unenforceable agreement contracting out of security of tenure.

The court will not terminate the tenancy if it appears that the hardship to the landlord will only emerge sometime in the future. In that case the application will be refused as premature.

(5) Non-agricultural use (s 24(1)(e))

'that the landlord proposes to terminate the tenancy for the purpose of the land being used for a use, other than for agriculture, not falling within section 22 (2)(b) of this Act'.

This case applies where the use to which the landlord proposes to put the land is a non-agricultural use but one which is a permitted use by virtue of

6 1973 SLT 186.
7 1981 SLCR App 84.

some provision in the Town and Country Planning Acts. The most obvious example is the planting of trees.

By section 14A of the Opencast Coal Act 1958, which was added by Schedule 8 to the Housing and Planning Act 1986, section 24(1)(e) does not apply where planning permission has been granted for opencast coal working but with a condition that the ground should be restored after extraction and that it be returned to agricultural use.

TERMINATION OF INTEREST OF SUCCESSOR

In addition to his rights of objection under sections 11 and 12 of the 1991 Act the landlord may under section 25 terminate the tenancy after the tenant's death by notice to quit but the extent of his rights will depend upon whether the successor is a near relative of the deceased tenant. 'Near relative' is defined in Part III of Schedule 2 to mean a surviving spouse or child of the deceased tenant, including a child adopted by him in pursuance of an adoption order (as defined in section 23(5) of the Succession (Scotland) Act 1964). A grandchild is therefore not a 'near relative' for the purposes of the section.

The landlord's right to terminate the lease of a non-near relative successor also depends on whether the successor acquired right to the lease after 1st August 1958 (the date of commencement of the Agriculture Act 1958).

If the successor acquired right before that date, section 25 of the 1991 Act has no application. This is because section 25(1) provides that the section is to apply where notice to quit is 'duly given' to a successor. Subsection (2)(d) provides that notice to quit is 'duly given' to a successor who was not a near relative if he acquired right to the lease after 1st August 1958. This means that the successor enjoys the same measure of security of tenure as the person from whom he acquired no later than 1st August 1958.

If, on the other hand, the successor who is not a near relative acquired right to the tenancy after 1st August 1984, section 25 does apply with the effect that it is open to the landlord to terminate the lease by an incontestable notice to quit.

Section 25(2) provides that notice to quit is duly given if it complies with section 21 of the Act, ie the normal provisions regarding notices to quit. In addition it must specify as its effective date:
(1) where, when the tenant acquired right to the lease it had two years or more to run, the term of outgo;
(2) where, when the tenant so acquired right, his lease had two years or less to run, the term of outgo or the corresponding term in any subsequent year being a date not less than one nor more than three years after the tenant's acquisition.

Section 22(2)(g) provides that a notice complying with these requirements excludes the counter-notice provisions requiring the Land Court to consent to the notice to quit.

It is not necessary to state the section in pursuance of which the notice is given.

If the notice to quit does not state that the tenancy is being terminated for the purpose of using the land for agriculture only, an additional payment will be due to the tenant under section 54 of the Act.

Section 25(3) applies where notice to quit is given to a tenant who is a near relative of the deceased tenant and has acquired right to the holding under section 16 of the 1964 Act or as legatee under section 11 of the 1991 Act.

This provides that a notice is duly given if it complies with section 21 of the Act which sets out the general provisions regarding notices to quit as its effective date, the contractual term of outgo. Where, when the tenant acquired right the lease had two years or less to run the notice must specify the term of outgo or the corresponding date in any subsequent year but this date must be not less than one nor more than three years after the tenant's acquisition.

The notice must also specify the case set out in Schedule 2 under which it is given.

The application of section 22(1) means that a near relative successor can serve counter-notice to the notice to quit which does not then take effect without the consent of the Land Court. The grounds on which the Land Court may consent to the operation of a notice under section 25 are set out in Schedule 2. Part I of this applies where the lease was entered into before 1st January 1984 and Part II where it was entered into on or after that date. The Land Court has a discretion to withhold its consent in Cases 1, 2, 3, 6 and 7, if it appears to it that a fair and reasonable landlord would not insist on possession.

SCHEDULE 2 – GROUNDS FOR CONSENT

Part I (pre-1984 leases)

Case 1. The tenant has neither sufficient training in agriculture nor sufficient experience in the farming of land to enable him to farm the holding with reasonable efficiency. The burden of proof lies upon the landlord.

Case 2. The holding or any agricultural unit of which it forms part is not a two-man unit; the landlord intends to use the holding for the purpose of effecting an amalgamation within two years after the termination of tenancy. The notice must specify the land with which the holding is to be amalgamated. Again the burden of proof lies on the landlord. Part III of Schedule 2 defines 'amalgamation' to mean 'a transaction for securing that agricultural land which is comprised in a holding to which a notice to quit relates and which together with other agricultural land could form an agricultural unit, shall be owned and occupied in conjunction with that other land'. 'Two-man unit' means 'an agricultural unit which in the opinion of the Land Court is capable of providing full-time employment for an individual occupying it and at least one other man'.

In deciding whether land is a two-man unit it is to be assumed that it is farmed under reasonably skilled management, that a system of husbandry suitable for the district is followed and that the greater part of the feeding stuffs required by any livestock kept on the unit is grown there. The effect of the statute is to impose an objective standard rather than the standard of farming actually being demonstrated.

In consenting to the operation of a notice to quit for the purpose of an amalgamation the court must impose such conditions as it thinks necessary for securing that the holding will within two years after the termination be amalgamated with the other land.

Case 3. The tenant is the occupier (either as owner or tenant) of agricultural land which is a two-man unit; is distinct from the holding and from any agricultural unit of which the holding forms part; and has been occupied by him since before the death of the tenant whom he succeeded. The notice must specify the other agricultural land. The occupation of the other unit must be by the tenant personally. Occupation by a partnership in which the tenant is a partner is insufficient. The burden of proof again lies on the landlord.

Part II (leases no earlier than 1984)

Case 4. The tenant does not have sufficient financial resources to enable him to farm the holding with reasonable efficiency. By section 25(3)(b) the burden of proof lies on the tenant which is reasonable as he is the person who knows the extent of the financial resources available to him.

Case 5. As in Case 1, the tenant has neither sufficient training in agriculture nor sufficient experience in the farming of land to enable him to farm the holding with reasonable efficiency but with the proviso that this case is not to apply where the tenant has been engaged throughout the period from the date of death of the previous tenant in a course of relevant training in agriculture which he is expected to complete satisfactorily within four years from the date of death and he has made arrangements for the holding to be farmed with reasonable efficiency until he completes the course. The burden of proof again lies on the tenant.

Case 6. The circumstances are as in Case 2 of Part I, so that the burden of proof lies on the landlord.

Case 7. The circumstances are as in Case 3 of Part I. Section 25(3)(b) makes specific provision for the burden of proof. The tenant is not required to prove that he is not the owner of any land, in accordance with the general principle that a party is not required to prove a negative.

For the purposes of Case 7 the occupation of agricultural land by a company controlled by the tenant is to be treated as occupation by the tenant and occupation by a Scottish partnership is to be treated as occupation by each of the partners. The Act specifically excludes the rule contained in section 4(2) of the Partnership Act 1890 that a Scottish partnership is an entity distinct from the partners constituting it.

THE 'FAIR AND REASONABLE LANDLORD' PROVISION

Notwithstanding that it is satisfied on one of the grounds in section 24 or that one of Cases 1, 2, 3, 6 or 7 of Schedule 2 applies, the Land Court must withhold consent to the operation of a notice to quit if it appears to it that a fair and reasonable landlord would not insist on possession.

Although this provision does not simply give the court a discretion to withhold consent there can obviously be widely differing views on what a fair and reasonable landlord would do. The Court has indicated that it is impossible to lay down any precise guidelines as to when the provision should be applied beyond saying that there must be strong reasons for doing so that go beyond the requirements of the principal sections. Questions of hardship to the tenant may be relevant in considering whether to apply the provision although they were not relevant to the principal section.

The decision whether to apply the provision does not turn on whether the tenant has discharged any onus of proof but the tenant must give the landlord due notice in the pleadings that he intends to rely on the provision. The Land Court's discretion to apply the provision has been exercised on very few occasions. There follow reported cases of instances in which the court applied the provisions and others in which it indicated that it would have been prepared to do so if it had not refused the consent sought on other grounds.

In *Carnegie v Davidson*[8] the landlord sought consent to a notice to quit under what is now section 24(1)(e) for the purposes of forestry whose success as a commercial venture was problematical. The landlord had other ground which he could have used and it was held that a fair and reasonable landlord would have done so rather than dispossess a tenant who was making full use of the land's agricultural potential.

In *Altyre Estate Trs v McLay*[9] consent was sought under what is now section 24(1)(b) on grounds of estate management. The holding was not viable on its own and the landlords proposed to amalgamate it with other land owned by them. The tenant owned a nearby farm which had been farmed with the holding for thirty years. The court was satisfied that the amalgamation was desirable in the interests of sound management of the landlord's estate. It took account, however, of the fact that the tenant was farming efficiently, that the loss of the holding would cause him considerable loss and inconvenience and that he had indicated his willingness to take on the tenancy of the amalgamated unit. In these circumstances the court withheld consent to the notice.

In *Mackenzie v Lyon*[10] consent was sought under what are now Cases 2 and 3 of Schedule 2. The ground in Case 3 (occupation of another two-man holding) was conceded and the tenant defended that part of the case on the fair and reasonable provision only. The court had some doubt if the landlord's case under Case 2 (amalgamation) was made out but it would have been entitled to succeed on the other ground if the provision were not applied. The court considered the future use of a unit comprising the landlord's adjoining land and the holding to be problematical. It was thought that expenditure on a steading and farmhouse would hardly be justified and that the proposed combined unit was more likely to be used as grazing land in conjunction with another farm or farms in the neighbourhood. It also took account of the fact that the landlords were not farmers and had acquired the land in connection with a sand and gravel business. The tenant and his family had been farming the holding successfully for some sixty years. The court referred to *Carnegie* and withheld consent.

In *Sykes v Edgar*[11] the application was for consent under what is now section 24(1)(b) (sound estate management) to notice to quit parts of two

8 1966 SLT (Land Ct) 3.
9 1975 SLT (Land Ct) 12.
10 1984 SLT (Land Ct) 30.
11 1974 SLT (Land Ct) 4.

hill farms on which the landlord wished to establish an elaborate scheme of shelter belts. Consent was refused and the court indicated that it would in any case have applied the provision because of the difficulties which the scheme would have caused for the tenant.

In *Earl of Seafield v Currie*[12] where an application under what is now Case 2 of Schedule 2 (proposed amalgamation) was refused the court indicated that it would otherwise have applied the provision 'in favour of a keen young tenant who is already doing his best to improve his farm'.

A provision in almost the same terms as that in section 24(2) is included in section 32(5) which has already been dealt with.

Section 24(3) provides that in consenting to the operation of a notice to quit the Land Court may, subject to section 25(4), impose conditions to ensure that the land is used for the purpose for which the landlord proposes to terminate the tenancy. Gill, *The Law of Agricultural Holdings in Scotland* (2nd edn), suggests that the imposition of conditions is competent only in cases under paragraphs (a), (b), (c) and (e) of the present section 24(1) since they refer to purposes for which the landlord seeks to terminate the tenancy and not under paragraph (d) which deals with greater hardship. Paragraphs (a) and (b), however, do not state explicitly the purpose for which the landlord seeks to terminate the lease but only that the carrying out of the purpose is desirable in the interests of good husbandry or the sound management of the landlord's estate. The purpose may be to farm himself or to let to another tenant or to sell. It does not have to be stated in the notice to quit and may only be disclosed in the application. The same applies in cases under paragraph (d) and if section 25(3) enables the court to require that the land be used for a purpose so stated in cases under paragraph (a) or (b) it would seem that it may also do so under paragraph (d). Section 24(3) does not, like section 25(4), limit the imposition of conditions to cases where consent is given on specified grounds. In practice the court has applied conditions in section 24(1)(d) cases.

12 1980 SLT (Land Ct) 10.

CHAPTER 5

COMPENSATION FOR IMPROVEMENTS

EXTENT OF THE RIGHT TO COMPENSATION FOR IMPROVEMENTS

Where the tenant has made one or more of the improvements comprised in Schedules 3, 4 or 5 to the 1991 Act he may be entitled, at the determination of the tenancy on his quitting the holding, to obtain from the landlord as compensation such sum as fairly represents the value of these improvements to *an* incoming tenant (not, *the* incoming tenant). Compensation is due though there may be no incoming tenant. The Act divides improvements into 'old improvements' and 'new improvements'. An 'old improvement' is one which:

(1) is within Schedule 3 to the Act being 'a 1923 Act improvement'; or
(2) is within Schedule 4 to the Act being 'a 1931 Act improvement'.

'A 1923 Act improvement' is one begun before 31st July 1931, and a '1931 Act improvement' is one begun before 1st November 1948, and on or after 31st July 1931. 'New improvements' are those within Schedule 5 to the Act and begun on or after 1st November 1948.

Where, however, the tenant undertook to execute the improvements in question, he is to receive compensation only where the lease was entered into on or after 1st January 1921.

The right to compensation for improvements may depend on the time at which they were made or begun, and in certain cases it may be necessary to fall back upon the repealed Acts, beginning with the original Agricultural Holdings (Scotland) Act 1883. There are cases in which improvements embraced in the Schedules have been made too early to enable compensation to be claimed.

The fact that an improvement was made during a previous tenancy does not, *ipso facto*, bar the right to claim, so long as the improvement is unexhausted, and so long as the tenant under the two tenancies is identical. Thus if a son succeeds his father in a lease which is running on relocation the son will be entitled at his waygoing to claim compensation for improvements carried out by his father. If, on the other hand, a new lease is granted to the son following the death of his father, compensation for the father's improvements will be forfeited, and instead the son may be rented on his father's improvements.

Compensation may be claimed even for improvements made by a previous tenant where, with the landlord's consent in writing and in pursuance of an agreement made before 1st November 1948, the tenant has paid compensation therefor. Questions have been raised as to whether a tenant who sub-lets part of his farm to a potato merchant or another farmer is entitled to claim compensation for manurial improvements effected by the sub-tenant. It is sometimes argued that the improvements must, to comply strictly with the terms of the repealed Acts, be made by 'the tenant' himself and by no one else. It is thought, however, that compensation should be awarded if an improvement has, in fact, been made. The principal tenant may have bound his sub-tenant to execute the improvements.

41

It has been suggested that, before compensation can be claimed, the tenant must have effected an improvement on the general condition of the holding. Though much can be said for this view on equitable grounds, it does not appear to be consistent with the scheme of the 1991 Act. Certain things are specified as 'improvements'. If these are effected, compensation is due up to the value to an incoming tenant, notwithstanding that, from some other operation or some neglect of the tenant the holding has otherwise suffered deterioration. This may be concluded from the fact that the statute directs that in assessing the amount of compensation certain things shall be taken into account in calculating the value of old improvements, namely 'benefit' allowed by the landlord, and the manurial value of crops sold off the farm within the last two years of the tenancy. If it had been the intention that the general condition of the holding was to be taken into account, the Act could have so provided. Instead, it directs that only two things shall be taken into account, and it seems clear that nothing else requires to be considered. This does not mean that the landlord has no remedy, because he may make claims for deterioration or dilapidations. Moreover, in certain cases, notably where state grants have been received there may be a reduction in the amount of, or exclusion of the right to compensation for improvements.

Conditions are attached to the tenant's rights to freedom of cropping and sale of produce. The question whether a tenant is exercising, or has exercised his rights:

(1) to dispose of the produce of the holding other than manure produced thereon; or,

(2) to practise any system of cropping of the arable land on the holding in such a manner as to injure or deteriorate his holding or to be likely to injure or deteriorate his holding

is determined by arbitration. The certificate of the arbiter as to his determination is to be conclusive proof of the facts therein stated. Where the tenant abides by his contract or by custom (in the absence of contract, for custom cannot override express contract) regarding the method of cropping and disposal of produce, the rules of common law will apply. Where, however, and insofar as the tenant exercises his statutory rights to freedom of cropping or sale of produce, and makes any of the improvements referred to, the arbiter may have to disallow compensation for these improvements insofar as they afford no more than suitable and adequate provision for protecting the holding from injury or deterioration.

IMPROVEMENTS FOR WHICH THE 1991 ACT ALLOWS COMPENSATION

The improvements are comprised in Schedules 3, 4 and 5 and as regards market gardens in Schedule 6.

The improvements in each Schedule are classified under Parts I, II and III. Part I improvements are those for which compensation is payable if the landlord's prior consent was obtained to their execution. Part II improvements are those for which compensation is payable if due notice was given to the landlord before their execution. Part III improvements are those for which compensation is payable without the consent of, or notice to the landlord.

Section 44 provides for compensation for the continuous adoption of a special standard of farming.

Compensation for Improvements

Improvements Requiring Consent (Part I)

Compensation for this class of improvement can be obtained only where the landlord has given consent in writing (which can be informal – section 78) to the execution of the improvement before it was begun. Such consent, however, does not imply that in all cases compensation would be payable on the basis of value to an incoming tenant, because the consent may be given 'unconditionally, or upon such terms as to compensation or otherwise as may be agreed upon between the landlord and the tenant'.

Sometimes, under a lease, the tenant is expressly permitted to execute some of the improvements embraced in this part of the Schedules. If the permissive clause is sufficiently specific it would probably be held equal to the 'consent in writing' which is required by this section. In such a case, the tenant, with permission, is free to do as he wishes, and, if he executes the improvements, he does so voluntarily, and under the permission and not under contract. Agreements giving a conditional right to compensation and giving no right were both held valid in *Turnbull v Millar*.[1]

In ascertaining the amount of compensation payable in respect of new improvement, the arbiter must take into consideration 'benefit' given or allowed by the landlord. This may not apply to substituted compensation (in the sense of compensation on an agreed scale) which, however, is confined to compensation for market garden improvements or compensation payable under agreements entered into before 1st January 1921.

The landlord's consent is required for 'alteration' of buildings in Schedules 3 and 4, but not for 'repair'. No such consent is required in Schedule 5.

The Schedules are applicable equally to market gardens and farms, but in the case of farms the 'erection, alteration or enlargement of buildings', requires consent under Schedules 3 and 4.

Improvements Requiring Notice (Part II)

In Schedule 3 the second class of improvements is covered by the single word 'drainage'. Schedule 4 transfers to this part among others the following improvements: formation of silos, making or improvement or roads and bridges, water courses, permanent fences, reclamation of waste land, and provision of sheep-dipping accommodation. It also includes the provision of electrical equipment other than moveable fittings and appliances and the repairing and renewal of embankments and sluices against floods. Schedule 5 introduces improvements relating, *inter alia*, to the erection of hay or sheaf sheds etc, the provision of fixed threshing mills, barn machinery and fixed dairying plant, the improvement of permanent pasture, sewage disposal and necessary repairs to fixed equipment other than repairs which the tenant is under an obligation to carry out.

Compensation can be claimed for the improvements in this part of the Schedule only where the statutory conditions are complied with. The tenant must have given written notice of his intention to execute the improvement, and of the manner in which he intended to do so, not more than three nor less than two months before beginning operations, in the case of 1923 Act

1 1942 SC 521.

improvements, and not more than six nor less than three months in the case of 1931 Act improvements. In the case of new improvements the tenant must give to the landlord not less than three months' notice in writing. Upon such notice being given, the landlord and the tenant may agree 'on the terms as to compensation or otherwise' on which the improvement is to be executed. The landlord may, however, after service of the notice, undertake to execute the improvement himself in the case of old improvements.

In the case of new improvements specified in Part II of Schedule 5 if, within one month of receiving notice from the tenant of his intention to carry out the improvement the landlord gives notice to the tenant that he objects to the making of the improvement or to the manner in which it is proposed to carry it out, the tenant may notify the landlord and make application to the Land Court for approval of the improvement. The Land Court may

(1) approve conditionally or unconditionally the improvement (and make terms as to compensation) or

(2) withhold approval.

Thereafter, within one month of receiving notice of a decision of the Land Court approving the improvement the landlord may undertake to carry out the improvement himself. If the landlord does not give notice of his intention to do so, or having given such notice the Land Court finds that he has failed to execute it, the tenant may carry out the work himself and be entitled to compensation therefor.

With reference to improvements under this part, section 38(2) allows parties, by lease or otherwise, to agree to dispense with notice. Mere acquiescence by the landlord after verbal intimation by the tenant does not infer such an agreement. It is open to doubt whether such an agreement can be proved otherwise than by writing.

As regards drainage, the most usual arrangement in practice has been for the landlord to supply the drain tiles, and for the tenant to do the work, including carting. Whether such an arrangement would bar the tenant's right to claim compensation is a question of some difficulty, especially where the tenancy is terminated within a few years after the improvement is executed. It is thought that it would not in view of the terms of section 53.

TEMPORARY IMPROVEMENTS (PART III)

The third class of improvements, and undoubtedly the class of which the greatest advantage has been taken, is that embraced in the third part of the Schedules. No consent of, or intimation to, the landlord is required before making improvements of this class.

It is sometimes found that leases require the tenant to give the landlord or his factor particulars of the manures and feeding-stuffs he proposes to use, along with analysis of the manures, as a condition of receiving compensation. It may also be laid down that compensation shall be limited to the average quantities used during the three years preceding the termination of the tenancy. In general, such conditions may be ignored: they cannot be enforced unless they fall within subsections (2) and (3) of section 53, which together protect the landlord and tenant from limitations, even by agreement, of the right to claim. The right to compensation for improvements is statutory. An unsuccessful attempt was made to refuse to pay compensation in respect that a tenant had failed to implement an obligation in the lease for a month's notice of intention to claim.

Nor can agreed compensation (according to a scale in a lease or otherwise) other than for market garden improvements in Schedule 6 be 'substituted' under leases entered into after 1st January 1921.

The most important of the improvements in this class are:

(1) Liming including chalking of land.
(2) Application to land of purchased manure and fertiliser whether organic or inorganic.
(3) Consumption on the holding of corn (whether produced on the holding or not) or of cake, or other feeding-stuff not produced on the holding by horses, cattle, sheep, pigs or poultry.
(4) Laying down temporary pasture with clover, grass, lucerne, sainfoin, or other seeds, sown more than two years prior to the termination of the tenancy insofar as the value of the temporary pasture on the holding at the time of quitting exceeds the value of the temporary pasture on the holding at the commencement of the tenancy for which the tenant did not pay compensation.
(5) In the case of old improvements only, repairs to buildings, being buildings necessary for the proper cultivation of the holding other than repairs which the tenant is bound under an obligation to execute.
(6) In the case of new improvements and the case of old improvements begun on or after 31st July 1931, the eradication of bracken, whins or gorse growing on a farm at the commencement of a tenancy and in the case of arable land, the removal of tree roots, boulders, stones or other like obstacles to cultivation.

ARTIFICIAL MANURES AND FEEDING-STUFFS

Most outgoing tenants have a claim for the application of fertilisers or other purchased manures and lime, and the consumption of feeding-stuffs not produced on the holding and corn produced and consumed on the holding.

In order to recover compensation for such improvements it is, of course, necessary for the tenant to prove that he has made them, and that a residual value is left unexhausted. The tenant should, therefore, carefully preserve his invoices and receipts for purchased fertilisers, manures and feeding-stuffs, especially those used in the later years of his tenancy. In the case of lime, it may be desirable to produce vouchers for all lime applied during the last seven years to ten years; in the case of manures and feeding-stuffs, vouchers for the last two or three years are generally sufficient. (This takes no account of cases where claims are put forward for continuous high farming, which is dealt with later). A claim having been duly made, it is usual for the tenant to submit his vouchers to the landlord (or his agent or factor) who may make an offer for settlement, and, if this is not accepted, the claim must be referred to arbitration. Particularly where the tenant has more than one farm the arbiter should be satisfied that the vouchers relate to manures and fertilisers applied to the holding or feeding-stuffs consumed thereon.

Each claim should be judged on its merits. A similar expenditure on each of two farms would not necessarily result in an improvement of the same value on both. Climatic conditions, the method of cropping, exhaustive or otherwise, and the question whether the produce is consumed on or removed from the land, each have an important bearing on the amount of residual value of such 'improvements'. Tables prepared by a standing committee appointed by the Secretary of State for Scotland, and brought up to date annually, are available as a guide.

It may be noticed that, in the case of manures and fertiliser, compensation is only allowed where these are 'purchased', while in the case of feeding-stuffs (except corn produced on the holding) all that is required is that they be such as were not produced on the holding (they might be produced on another holding of the claimant). In the case of corn produced and consumed on the holding there is often a difficulty regarding proof. The most satisfactory evidence is the production of a regularly kept barn book or record, but, where that is not available, arbiters are sometimes satisfied otherwise.

Compensation for purchased manures and feeding-stuffs is generally a proportion of the manurial value, so much per ton based on the unit values of the different constituents at the time when the claim arises in accordance with the standing committee's tables.

In dealing with claims for 'manurial improvements', it is frequently of importance to ascertain to what crops the manures were applied, and, as already mentioned, whether the crops have been consumed on or removed from the land. For example, if a certain quantity of manure were applied to an acre of turnips, and the same quantity to an acre of potatoes sold off, most arbiters would agree that the remaining improvement would be greater in the case of turnips.

It is also necessary, as a general rule, to ascertain what proportion of the feeding-stuffs was in the dung taken over by the incoming tenant at valuation because no compensation is due for such feeding-stuffs where they are included in dung not applied to the land. If a different course were followed, the awaygoing tenant would, in effect, be paid twice over.

A question has been raised whether compensation may be claimed for feeding-stuffs in dung which the tenant was bound to leave steelbow. Compensation has been awarded in such a case but the decision was not tested in court. In *Davidson v Hunter*,[2] the decision was based largely on the ground that manure taken over at a valuation was moveable, had not been, and might never be, applied to the land. In a question of succession, dunghills or manure prepared for being spread upon the land may be heritable from manifest purpose or intention. In *Reid's Exrs v Reid*[3] it was held that the dung on the farm was heritable, in a question between the heir and the executor of the tenant. 'Steelbow' dung left at a waygoing may be merely the equivalent of what was handed over steelbow at entry, and (assuming compensation to be payable) the question of 'benefit' may therefore arise. It may, however, be argued that a steelbow obligation is confined to the dung made from the produce of the farm.

ERADICATION OF BRACKEN, ETC

Questions may arise as to when bracken is 'eradicated'. If the bracken is reduced to such a condition that cultivation of arable or the grazing of

2 (1888) Sh Ct Rep 33.
3 (1890) 17 R 519.

pastoral land is restored, it is at least arguable that compensation should be allowed. The amount awarded would vary with the extent of the improvement effected. It is provided that compensation shall only be payable when the bracken or whins were growing at the commencement of the tenancy, this seeming to imply that it is simply an aspect of 'good husbandry' for a tenant to deal himself with any new development.

TEMPORARY PASTURE

The improvement consists in laying down temporary pasture with clover, grass, lucerne, sainfoin, or other seeds, sown more than two years prior to the termination of the tenancy, insofar as the value of the temporary pasture on the holding at the time of quitting exceeds the value of the temporary pasture on the holding at the commencement of the tenancy, for which the tenant claiming did not pay compensation. Suppose that, at a claimant's entry, there had been on the farm fifty acres of temporary pasture, and that he entered to that without payment, and that at quitting there were 100 acres of temporary pasture of the same kind, and sown not less than two years before quitting, the arbiter according to the scheme of the Act would allow compensation, not on the basis of the excess of fifty additional acres, but on the basis of the difference in the value of 100 acres over the value of the fifty acres. (If the tenant had paid for the fifty acres, then he would get compensation for the whole 100). The value of 100 acres might be less or more than the value of the fifty acres. The quality of the temporary pasture at · quitting has to be compared with the quality of that which was taken over at entry free of compensation. Probably the best definition of 'permanent pasture' is pasture which the tenant cannot break up under the terms of his tenancy, and all other grass may be described as temporary. The tenant's right to freedom of cropping does not include the breaking up of permanent pasture. The mixtures used for sowing down the two species of pasture vary greatly and experts often differ as to what constitutes a 'permanent' grass mixture and what a 'temporary', but, whatever its constituent grasses, the test above referred to is most useful in practice. Grass still remains 'temporary' even though it remains down for many years, provided only it can be broken up by the tenant. In England it has been held that the question of what is temporary pasture has been left unsettled by the Acts, and that it is a practical question for an arbiter.

Although the improvement is apparently the excess in value, the question of 'benefit' requires to be taken into account, excluding, however, from 'benefit' the value of the temporary pasture at entry, which has already been debited in the comparison of values.

Compensation is not due for the mere leaving of temporary pasture unless the tenant claiming laid it down, otherwise a tenant might claim for temporary pasture laid down not by him, but by his predecessor. On certain soils, well-laid down temporary pasture may improve in value over a course of years. There remains, however, the question of when the improvement was made or begun. It has been held that leaving down pasture which might have been broken up was not 'laying down pasture', to entitle the tenant to compensation. In comparing the condition of a holding at entry and outgo, the entry is to be taken as at the beginning of the last lease. If this view is sound compensation would not be payable for temporary pasture laid down under a previous lease. See, however, section 34(5) which provides that compensation may be allowed at the end of a lease for improvements effected during a previous lease in the name of the same tenant.

Section 34(6) provides that compensation should be payable notwithstanding that the pasture was laid down in contravention of the provisions of the lease or any agreement regarding cropping. In ascertaining the amount of compensation, however, the arbiter is directed to take into consideration any injury to or deterioration of the holding due to the contravention. An arbiter has the duty not merely to fix a figure more or less arbitrarily at which the pasture itself may be valued but also, if there is a breach of contract, to compare the condition in which the farm was left with the condition in which it would have been if the contract had been fulfilled.

Compensation in the case of 1931 Act improvements and new improvements is based on the increase in the value of the temporary pasture on the holding when compared with such pasture, 'at the commencement of the tenancy for which the tenant did not pay compensation'. The amendment made a material change on the pre-1931 position. It is difficult to say whether, in making the comparison, there should be taken into consideration temporary pasture less than two years old at the commencement of the tenancy. There is a good deal to be said for confining the clause throughout to temporary pasture as described there. In this view, the clause might be paraphrased thus:

> Laying down temporary pasture with seeds sown more than two years prior to the termination of the tenancy, insofar as the value of the temporary pasture (so laid down) on the holding, at the time of quitting exceeds the value of the temporary pasture on the holding at the commencement of the tenancy, which had been sown more than two years prior to such commencement, and for which the tenant did not pay compensation.

Here like is being compared with like. Upon the alternative view the value of the whole temporary pasture at entry, so far as not paid for, would fall to be set against the temporary pasture sown more than two years before quitting with a result probably unfortunate for the tenant. He is not entitled to claim, under the Act, for pasture laid down within the last two years of his tenancy, whereas the value of the pasture laid down within the two years immediately preceding his entry, if he paid no compensation or value therefor, would form a deduction. This seems to be contrary to equity. As to the expression 'the commencement of the tenancy' see *Findlay v Munro*.[4]

---

4 1917 SC 419.

CHAPTER 6

FURTHER PROVISIONS FOR COMPENSATION

COMPENSATION FOR DISTURBANCE

In general, by virtue of section 43 of the 1991 Act compensation is payable by a landlord to his tenant where

(1) the tenant quits possession after the landlord gives due notice to quit or notice of resumption; or

(2) the tenant gives counter-notice under section 30 of the Act that he accepts a notice duly given to quit part of the holding as notice to quit the entire holding.

This is called compensation for disturbance and amounts to a minimum of one year's net rent (ie gross rent less public burdens, but not minister's stipend) or a maximum of two years' net rent. Where the tenant has lawfully sub-let the whole or part of the holding, and has had to pay compensation for disturbance to the sub-tenant in consequence of a notice to quit given by the landlord, the tenant may, although not himself in occupation, have a claim against the landlord. The landlord is not bound to pay such compensation where notice to quit is given for the reasons specified in paragraphs (a) or (c) to (f) of section 22(2), which have already been dealt with. It is useful to refer to one case in particular since it is necessary also to examine part of the Agriculture (Scotland) Act 1948 which has not been consolidated in the 1991 Act. In this example, the provisions of section 22(1) of the 1991 Act are excluded by the operation of section 22(2)(c), namely where the Land Court, on an application made to it not more than nine months before the giving of the notice to quit, was satisfied in relation to the holding that the tenant was not fulfilling his responsibilities to farm in accordance with the rules of good husbandry, and certified that the court was so satisfied and that fact is stated in the notice. The rules of good husbandry are to be found in Schedule 6 to the Agriculture (Scotland) Act 1948.

Compensation will be payable unless the notice to quit states one or more of the reasons detailed under section 22(2)(a) or (c) to (f) of the 1991 Act for terminating the tenancy and, of course, the reasons stated must be true in fact. In an English case it was held sufficient that the notice referred to reasons as in paragraphs of the Act.

Where the notice to quit is under section 22(2)(b), ie a use for which planning permission has been granted, compensation for disturbance and an additional payment under section 54 are payable. Where the notice is under section 22(2)(g) compensation for disturbance will be payable but a section 54 payment may be excluded if the notice contains an appropriate statement in terms of section 55.

It will be observed that the words 'at the date of the notice' are frequently used in the Act. This generally refers to the conditions existing at or immediately prior to the notice. Anything done after serving the notice could not be assigned as a reason for serving it. If a tenant is to comply with a preliminary demand he must do so before the notice to quit has been served: see *Price v Romilly*.[1]

Further conditions must be fulfilled in order to recover compensation for disturbance in excess of one year's rent:

(1) if the tenant claims loss in respect of the sale of any goods, implements, fixtures, produce or stock he must have given the landlord one month's notice of the sale and also a reasonable opportunity of making a valuation thereof before the sale;

(2) loss or expense directly attributable to the quitting of the holding up to the amount of the claim must be proved.

A maximum of two years' net rent can be claimed where the loss and expense directly attributable to the quitting of the holding which the tenant unavoidably incurs upon or in connection with the sale or removal of his household goods, implements of husbandry, fixtures, farm produce or farm stock exceed one year's net rent. Any tenant contemplating a claim based on such loss would be well advised to have his stock valued independently prior to sale.

Where more than one year's rent is claimed, and it is proved that the loss and expense exceed one year's rent, there does not appear to be room for making any deduction: the arbiter will merely have to fix the compensation at the actual loss and expense.

The reorganisation payment provided for in section 54 is payable only where the tenant is entitled to compensation for disturbance, and the exclusion of disturbance payment will exclude the additional payment also. The additional payments are, however, for the reorganisation of the tenant's affairs and are not, like disturbance payments, in respect of loss or expenses incurred.

REORGANISATION OF TENANT'S AFFAIRS

Section 54 of the 1991 Act provides that where compensation for disturbance becomes payable by the landlord to the tenant of an agricultural holding there shall also be payable by the landlord to the tenant 'a sum to assist in the reorganisation of the tenant's affairs'. The amount of this sum is to be four times the annual rent of the holding or in the case of part of a holding the appropriate proportion, at the rate at which rent was payable immediately before the termination of the tenancy of the holding or part of the holding.

The question of what is the appropriate proportion is, failing agreement, to be determined by the Land Court on application by the tenant.

It will be noted that the additional payment is not due unless compensation for disturbance is payable. Where disturbance compensation is payable the additional sum is due unless the notice to quit contains a statement that it is given on one of the grounds stated in section 55(1) and either the tenant does not serve counter-notice or the Land Court consents to the operation of the notice to quit on one of these grounds.

The grounds stated in section 55(1) of the Act, which if stated in the notice to quit may exclude payment of the additional sum, are:

(1) that the purpose for which the landlord proposes to terminate the tenancy is desirable on any of the grounds mentioned in section 24(1)(a)

1 [1960] 3 All ER 429.

to (c). These are that it is in the interest of good husbandry, or sound estate management or for the purpose of agricultural research, education or the like or for smallholdings;

(2) that the landlord will suffer hardship;

(3) where the notice to quit is served on a 'near relative' successor, one of the grounds specified in Schedule 2.

Section 55(2) provides that the exemptions afforded by section 55(1) are not to apply in two circumstances even though the Land Court has consented to the operation of the notice to quit. These are:

(1) where the court's reasons include that it is satisfied under section 24(1)(e) of the Act (use of land for certain non-agricultural purposes); or

(2) where the court's reasons are or include that it is satisfied under section 24(1)(b) of the Act (sound management of estate) or Cases 1, 3, 5 and 7 of Schedule 2 (tenant's lack of training or experience or possession of other agricultural land) but would have been satisfied also under section 24(1)(e) of the Act (use of land for non-agricultural purposes) if that matter had been specified in the application for consent.

Where the court would have been satisfied as mentioned in paragraph (b) it must include a statement to that effect in its decision.

Payment of the additional sum is excluded where section 22(1) does not apply by virtue of section 29(4) of the Agriculture Act 1967 which relates to notices to quit served by the Secretary of State as landlord for boundary adjustments or an amalgamation. Section 29(4) of the 1967 Act applies only where the tenant has signed a lease acknowledging that the tenancy is subject to the provisions of the section.

The additional sum is not payable to a deceased tenant's successor who is not a near relative. If notice to quit is served under section 22(2)(g) of the 1991 Act and contains a statement that the tenancy is being terminated for one of the cases specified in Schedule 2 and the tenant disputes the statement, this must be referred to the Land Court on an application for consent to the notice to quit and not to arbitration.

The provisions of section 54 of the 1991 Act can obviously have important consequences for both landlords and tenants. A landlord will have to consider carefully the effect of any notice to quit which he may serve, as omission of the reason for its service may result in liability to pay a large sum to the tenant. A tenant who receives a notice to quit will require to consider its financial effects, depending on whether or not reasons are stated, and weigh up the advisability of contesting the notice or of accepting it and obtaining payment of the additional compensation.

EARLY RESUMPTION

Section 58 of the 1991 Act provides for additional compensation to be paid to a tenant where the landlord resumes part of the holding in terms of the lease. The additional payment is to be equal to the value of the additional benefit which the tenant would have received if the land had been resumed twelve months after the end of the year of tenancy current two months before the date of resumption. The current year of a tenancy for this purpose is the year from the term, corresponding to the term of ish, which occurs during the twelve months ending two months before the date of resumption. Thus a tenant with a Martinmas waygoing who had ground resumed at 5th December 1991 would be entitled to claim for the benefit he would have received if he had been allowed to remain until Martinmas 1992. The date two months back is 5th October 1991 and the current year is thus Martinmas 1990 to Martinmas 1991. If the resumption were at 30th January 1992 the current year would be Martinmas 1991 to Martinmas 1992 and the tenant could claim for the benefit he would have received if he had been allowed to remain until Martinmas 1993.

The amount of compensation will accordingly vary considerably depending on the date of resumption. The object is to give the tenant the benefit which he would have had if notice to quit and not notice of resumption had been served. The counting back two months to ascertain the year of tenancy derives from the assumption that at least two months' notice of resumption is required.

If the tenant unsuccessfully contests the resumption the date of his actual removal will almost inevitably be later than the resumption date. It is thought that in that event the amount of compensation should be reduced by the amount of the actual benefit which accrued to the tenant from his continued occupation.

HIGH FARMING

This heading is not used in the Act, but is short for 'the continuous adoption of a special standard or system of farming' for which compensation may be claimed subject to certain conditions. Compensation is awarded to the tenant who proves that the value of the holding to an incoming tenant has been increased during the tenancy by the continuous adoption of a standard of farming, or a system of farming, which has been more beneficial to the holding, than the standard or system required by the lease. This goes further than a mere allowance for cumulative fertility.

The conditions precedent to the recovery of such compensation are that
(1) there must have been a record of the condition of the holding as provided for under section 8 – compensation not being payable for anything done prior to the date of the record;
(2) the tenant must, not later than one month before the termination of the tenancy, give the landlord notice of intention to claim.

In assessing the compensation due allowance is to be made for any compensation agreed or awarded in respect of any improvement which has caused or contributed to the benefit. The tenant, therefore, would not be paid twice over for the same thing.

ASCERTAINING THE VALUE OF IMPROVEMENTS

In ascertaining the amount of compensation payable for any scheduled improvement, whether old or new, arbiters are directed to use the same basis of valuation, namely the value of the improvement to an incoming tenant, but there are the following differences and adjustments to be made on the basic values of old and new improvements.

(1) In the case of old improvements there must be deducted the value of any benefit which the landlord has given or allowed to the tenant in consideration of his carrying out the improvement. It should be observed that, although it is not essential that the benefit was expressly stated to be given in consideration of the tenant's carrying out the improvements, it is nevertheless necessary to prove that it was so given. The main effect of the words 'under the lease or otherwise' is to allow oral evidence, and they contemplate the possibility of 'benefit' being given during the currency, and not merely at the inception of the lease. Oral evidence may be led to prove that a benefit was given and the arbiter is entitled to decide on the facts adduced. In the case of new improvements, however, the benefit to be taken into account must be 'one which the landlord has agreed in writing'. 'Benefit' need not be in money. In *Findlay v Munro*[2] opinions were expressed that the right to take two successive white crops off land which had lain three years in grass was not a 'benefit'.

(2) Manuring is omitted as a matter to be taken into account in ascertaining compensation for new improvements. In respect of old improvements, however, a deduction must be made in respect of manuring as defined in the Act. The amount of deduction is the value of the manure required, by the lease or by custom, to be returned to the holding, in respect of any crops grown on and sold off or removed from the holding during the last two years of the tenancy, or other less time for which the tenancy has endured. In the general case, and apart from contract, nothing falls to be taken into account in respect of the awaygoing white crop, or where it is taken over by the incoming tenant at a valuation. It has not been the custom for the awaygoing tenant to return to the holding manure in respect of that crop, although, in many cases, the straw of the crop has, by contract, to be left steelbow. It should be noted, however, that this provision is not confined to the crops of the last two years; it extends to any crops sold off or removed from the holding in the last two years, whether grown in these years or not.

The term 'substituted compensation' may be used in two senses. The first is where compensation on an agreed scale or basis is allowed to take the place of statutory compensation. The second is where the tenant has a right to statutory compensation but agrees to accept compensation on a different basis.

The former kind of substituted compensation is now restricted by section 34(7) to improvements of the kind specified in Part III of Schedule 3 or Part III of Schedule 4 (whether on farms or market gardens) for which there is an agreement entered into before 1st January 1921 which allows fair and reasonable compensation. Substituted compensation is permitted only where the Act expressly so provides (section 53). Express provision for substituted compensation in the first sense is made in sections 34(7) and 42. Express provision for substituted compensation in the second sense is made in sections 35, 37 and 38. Agreements under these sections may provide for the sharing of the cost of permanent improvements and usually provide for the tenant's contribution to be written off over a stated period of years. In such cases the substituted compensation may, it is thought, be any sum of money which is not merely nominal or illusory.

The arbiter has also to take into account, for new improvements, any state

2 1917 SC 419.

grant which has been or will be made to the tenant in respect of the improvement.

No compensation is payable to a tenant for anything done under a direction under section 9 which enables an arbiter to vary the terms of a lease prohibiting the breaking of permanent pasture (section 51). Where permanent pasture has been ploughed up in pursuance of a direction the value of the tenant's pasture (ie what was laid down by him or paid for by him at his entry) shall be taken not to exceed the average value per hectare of the whole tenant's pasture at the termination of the tenancy.

'SUBSTITUTED' COMPENSATION FOR IMPROVEMENTS

In all cases, it is thought that the substituted compensation must be money – something that can be 'awarded' at the termination of the tenancy. Throughout the Act 'compensation' is to be 'payable'.

A difficult question is the ascertainment of what is fair and reasonable compensation, having regard to the circumstances at the time of making the agreement. That is a matter for the arbiter to decide subject to appeal to the court on a question of law.

The court held that a stipulation in a lease that compensation payable at quitting was subject to a deduction of the amount paid by the landlord to the previous tenant was not void.

DAMAGE BY GAME – DEER, PHEASANTS, PARTRIDGES, GROUSE AND BLACK GAME

At common law an agricultural tenant was not entitled to compensation for game damage unless he proved that the damage resulted from an increase in the stock of game. On taking the farm, it was assumed that he agreed to suffer, without compensation, such damage as would naturally result from the stock of game as it was when he entered. Lord Fullerton said: 'The true ground of damage seems to be not that the game is abundant, but that its abundance has been materially increased since the date of the lease.' This is not now the law, for compensation can be claimed where the damage exceeds 12p per hectare of the area over which the damage extends.

If the damage does not exceed that figure, no compensation is due. If it does exceed that figure, the full amount of the damage may be claimed without any deduction. It is no defence that the game came from the property of a neighbouring proprietor, even during close time. Practically the only case in which the landlord is not liable is where the agricultural tenant has permission in writing to kill the game. Where the right to kill and take the game is vested in some person other than the landlord, the landlord is entitled to be indemnified by the other person against claims for compensation on this ground. Even if the tenant enters into an agreement with his landlord not to claim compensation, he can repudiate the agreement, contracting out not being permitted under the statute. The tenant is entitled, however, to agree, after the damage has been caused, as to the amount of the compensation. Failing such agreement, the amount is to be fixed by arbitration.

No compensation can be claimed under the statute unless notice in writing is given to the landlord as soon as may be after the damage was first observed by the tenant, and a reasonable opportunity is given to the landlord to inspect the damage –

(1) in the case of damage to growing crop, before the crop is begun to be reaped, raised, or consumed; and

(2) in the case of damage to a crop reaped or raised, before it is begun to be removed from the land.

Notice in writing of the claim, together with the particulars thereof, must also be given to the landlord within one month after the expiration of the calendar year, or such other period of twelve months as by agreement between the landlord and tenant may be substituted therefor, in respect of which the claim is made.

Where the tenant of a holding consisting entirely of arable land and permanent pasture who did not have permission in writing to kill deer claimed compensation from a landlord for damage to crops by deer it was held that he was entitled to compensation notwithstanding that he had a statutory right to kill deer under section 43(1) of the Agriculture (Scotland) Act 1948 (now repealed by the Deer (Amendment) (Scotland) Act 1982). It was pointed out that section 52 of the 1948 Act preserved the tenant's right to compensation for damage by deer conferred by section 11 of the Agricultural Holdings (Scotland) Act 1923 of which section 52 of the 1991 Act is practically a re-enactment. As the 1949 Act (like the 1991 Act) is a consolidating Act it was held that it did not alter the tenant's previous rights.

NOTICES OF INTENTION TO CLAIM COMPENSATION AND LODGING OF PARTICULARS

Generally such notices must be in writing, but there are some exceptions. Again, generally, the notices must be in the hands of the person to whom they are addressed within the prescribed period, no matter when despatched, and the intervention of a Sunday makes no difference.

In order to recover compensation for improvements, no notice of intention to claim is required before the termination of the tenancy except in the case of compensation for improvement effected by following a special standard or system of farming. In such case notice of intention to claim must be given in writing to the landlord not less than one month before the determination of the tenancy.

Notice of intention to claim compensation for improvements must be given before the expiration of two months from the termination of the tenancy.

Landlord's claim for compensation for deterioration of holding

Notice in writing of intention to claim under the Act must be given not later than three months before the termination of the tenancy, but this is not necessary where the claim is made under the lease.

Compensation for damage by game

Notice must be given as soon as may be after the damage and the landlord given an opportunity of valuation. Further, notice in writing of the claim, together with particulars, must be given not later than one month after the expiration of the calendar year (ie 31st December) or such other period of twelve months as by agreement may be substituted therefor, in respect of which the claim is made. Notice given before the end of the appropriate period of twelve months is competent.

CHAPTER 7

MISCELLANEOUS PROVISIONS

VARIATION OF TERMS OF TENANCY

Permanent pasture

Either the landlord or the tenant can by section 9 of the 1991 Act demand a reference to arbitration on the question whether the amount of land required to be maintained as permanent pasture in terms of the lease should be reduced in the interests of full and efficient farming.

The arbiter may order a reduction in the area which the lease requires to be in permanent pasture but may stipulate that at the termination of the tenancy the tenant will leave in pasture an area not exceeding what the lease originally required. Section 51(1) excludes compensation for restoration of pasture in accordance with such a stipulation and requires averaging of the value of pasture (to prevent inferior pasture being treated as that for which compensation is excluded).

Continuance of lease not affected by variation of term

The addition of new terms or the variation of existing terms under the provisions of the Act noticed above does not have the effect of creating a new lease.

At common law an agreement to vary a lease running on tacit relocation is likely to have the effect of creating a new lease. The results can be important. The provisions of section 5(2) of the Act will apply and the basis of valuation of bound sheep stock may be affected: see *Tuffnell and Nether Whitehaugh Co Ltd*.[1]

FREEDOM OF CROPPING

No conditions can be imposed on a tenant, by lease or otherwise, to prevent him from practising any system of cropping of the arable land (which does not include land in grass which by the lease is to be retained in the same condition throughout the tenancy), or from disposing of the produce of the holding. These are statutory rights, and the tenant cannot be subjected to any penalty, forfeiture, or liability for exercising them.

There are, however, important conditions attending the exercise of these rights. The tenant must previously have made, or as soon as may be, make suitable and adequate provision to protect the holding from injury or deterioration, such provision in the case of disposal of produce, consisting in the return to the holding of the full equivalent manurial value of all crops sold off or removed from the holding in contravention of custom, lease or agreement.

These rights of freedom of cropping and disposal of produce do not apply –
(1) in the case of a tenancy from year to year, as respects the year before the

1 1977 SLT (Land Ct) 14.

57

tenant quits the holding, or any period after he has given or received notice to quit which results in his quitting the holding; or

(2) in any other case, as respects the year before the expiration of the lease.

It will be observed that the tenant is not bound to follow the rotation of cropping prescribed in his lease, nor, for that part, the rotation customary in the district, nor is he bound to consume on the farm the produce grown on it. A general obligation to follow the rules of good husbandry still holds good, but a tenant cannot be found guilty of a breach of these rules simply because he acts contrary to long-practised methods or to the express terms of his contract.

What is the meaning of 'full equivalent manurial value to the holding' of all crops sold or removed in contravention of custom, contract, or agreement? It has no necessary relation to cost. What is intended is restoration of fertility leaving the land in the condition in which it would have been had the crops not been removed. Assuming that the tenant is taken bound to have his turnips consumed by sheep, he can nevertheless sell and remove the turnips, but he must bring back the equivalent of their manurial value to the land.

If the tenant exercises these rights in such a manner as to injure or deteriorate the holding, the landlord may recover damages at waygoing or obtain interdict during the currency of the lease restraining the exercise of the rights in that manner. The question whether a tenant is exercising, or has exercised, his rights in such a manner as to injure or deteriorate the holding, or is likely to do so, falls to be determined by arbitration. A certificate by the arbiter as to his determination of the question will, in any proceedings including arbitrations, be conclusive proof of the facts stated in the certificate.

Tenant's Rights to Remove Fixtures

At common law there are two rules regarding fixtures:
(1) 'that whatever is fixed to the freehold land becomes part of the freehold or the inheritance'; and
(2) that 'whatever becomes part of the inheritance cannot be severed by a limited owner'.

An exception was made in the case of trade fixtures but this did not extend to agricultural fixtures (although the courts tended to favour tenants in deciding whether items were fixtures or not).

A statutory right to remove fixtures was introduced by the first Agricultural Holdings (Scotland) Act in 1883 and the present provisions are contained in section 18 of the 1991 Act. In terms of this section a tenant who, without being taken bound to do so, has erected any engine, machinery, fencing or other fixture or any building (other than a building in respect of which he is entitled to compensation under the Act or otherwise) which was not erected or affixed in place of some fixture or building belonging to the landlord, is entitled to remove the same before, or within six months or such other time as may be agreed, after the termination of the tenancy. Before the removal, however, he must pay all rent owing, and perform or satisfy all other obligations to the landlord; he must not do avoidable damage to any other building or other part of the holding and must make good any unavoidable damage. He must also give the landlord notice one month before both the exercise of the right and the termination of the tenancy of his intention to remove the fixtures and others, and any time within that month the landlord may, by notice in writing to the tenant, elect to purchase them at a value to be fixed, failing agreement, by a single arbiter. The basis of value is 'the value to an incoming tenant'.

It appears to be evident that the 'engine, machinery and fencing' here referred to must be of the nature of fixtures. The words 'or other fixture' indicate this. Ordinary moveable machinery would not, it is thought, be affected. Again 'any building' would probably not apply to a mere temporary wooden erection.

Ordinary wood and wire fencing and wooden structures not built into the ground would not seem to be 'fixtures' within the meaning of the Act. 'Fixtures' have frequently been defined in the courts.

> 'Whatever moves, or is capable of being moved, from place to place without injury, or change of nature in itself or in the subject with which it is connected, is moveable' (Bell's *Principles*, 1472).

PENAL RENT AND/OR LIQUIDATED DAMAGES

Since 1900 penal rents and liquidated damages have been placed in the same position as ordinary damages, ie they can be enforced only up to the amount of the actual loss sustained. This applies to penal rents or liquidated damages for breach or non-fulfilment of any of the terms or conditions in the lease. This does not prevent the landlord from enforcing such penalties as are not stated in money. In certain events he might stipulate for power to withdraw certain rights or privileges, or to irritate the lease.

IRRITANCY

In dealing with notice to quit, section 21(6) provides that nothing in that section is to affect the right of the landlord of an agricultural holding to remove a tenant whose estate has been sequestrated under the Bankruptcy (Scotland) Act 1985 or the Bankruptcy (Scotland) Act 1913 or who by failure to pay rent or otherwise has incurred irritancy of his lease or other liability to be removed.

The subsection does not confer any rights on the landlord other than those which he would otherwise enjoy at common law. It simply provides that these rights shall not be restricted by the provision that a tenancy shall not come to an end except by operation of a notice to quit. At common law, the bankruptcy of the tenant did not terminate the lease, so that unless there is a contractual stipulation entitling the landlord to terminate the lease on this ground, this section does not assist the landlord.

The provisions of the Law Reform (Miscellaneous Provisions) (Scotland) Act 1985 which provide broadly that a breach capable of remedy shall not entitle the landlord to terminate the lease unless the tenant has had an opportunity to remedy do not apply to tenancies of agricultural holdings.

RECORD OF HOLDING

Section 5 of the 1991 Act makes it obligatory to have a record of fixed equipment (defined in section 85) made in the case of all new leases. In addition the landlord or tenant is entitled, at any time, to require a record to be made of the condition of the fixed equipment on, and of the cultivation of, the holding. The tenant may also require that the record shall include any existing improvements executed by him or in respect of the carrying out of which he has, with the written consent of the landlord, paid compensation to an outgoing tenant. He may also require to be included any fixtures or buildings which under the Act he is entitled to remove. The record falls to be made by a person to be appointed by the Secretary of State, and is to be in such form as may be prescribed. The form of application to the Secretary of State makes no provision for the parties to agree on the appointment of a person of their choice, so that if the parties have agreed who the individual shall be they must make separate intimation of this to the Secretary of State. Farm records, exhaustive and well compiled, offer considerable advantages.

Such a record must be made
(1) before a tenant can claim compensation for the adoption of a special standard or system of cultivation (section 44) and the improvement must be made after the date of the record; and
(2) before a landlord can make a claim for dilapidations under section 45.

To be of permanent value a record must be exhaustive and, more than that, compiled and written so that it may convey to a reader years later a true picture of the state of the holding when it was written. Vagueness of description and general expressions capable of wide interpretation are to be deprecated. To say that a fence is 'not in very good repair' or that a certain building is 'inadequate' conveys very little useful information. A plan is useful; all fields, fences or hedges, and buildings should be numbered for identification and the references should be to an up-to-date Ordnance Survey plan; a schedule of cropping should be provided with particulars of temporary pasture; and details of construction, with repairs necessary, should be exactly given. Photographs may usefully be included in the record. Each field may be dealt with separately, with observations on its water supply, drains, state of cultivation and soil. Any further information, such as particulars of stock, its condition and quality and the quality of crops would be useful when eventually a comparison comes to be made with the state of the farm at a later date. Any consideration or allowances made by the landlord to the tenant, or vice versa, should be shown in the record.

It may sometimes occur that the landlord and tenant are not agreed on points arising in connection with the preparation of such a record, particularly with reference to 'improvements' for which the tenant is entitled to claim compensation, and 'fixtures or buildings' which the tenant is entitled to remove. Either party may apply to the Land Court to determine any question or difference arising. The cost of making the record is to be borne equally by the landlord and the tenant, unless they agree otherwise.

REMOVING FOR NON-PAYMENT OF RENT

When a tenant is six months in arrear with his rent, in terms of section 20, the landlord may raise an action in the sheriff court for his removal at the next ensuing term of Whitsunday or Martinmas. The only answer open to the tenant is to pay up or find security to the satisfaction of the sheriff for the arrears and for one year's additional rent. The tenant who is removed under this section has all the rights of an awaygoing tenant as if his lease had naturally expired at the quitting term. Accordingly, he will be entitled to all the rights and privileges specified in the lease. He is entitled to compensation for improvements. He is not entitled to compensation for disturbance as the liability to pay this only arises where the tenancy terminates by reason of either a notice to quit given by the landlord or a notice of intention to quit given by the tenant, and in consequence of such notice the tenant quits the holding.

APPLICATION FOR CERTIFICATE OF BAD HUSBANDRY

Section 26 provides that application for such a certificate must be made direct to the Land Court.

The court is directed to disregard any practice adopted by the tenant in compliance with any obligation imposed on him or accepted by him under section 31B of the Control of Pollution Act 1974. This relates to the restrictions which may be imposed on agricultural operations in nitrate-sensitive areas.

EFFECT ON NOTICE TO QUIT OF AGREEMENT TO SELL

Section 28, whose provisions originated in the Agricultural Land Sales (Restriction of Notice to Quit) Act 1919, deals with the situation where a notice to quit an agricultural holding or part of it has been given and during its currency a contract is made for the sale of the landlord's interest in the holding or any part of it. The general rule is that such a contract renders the notice to quit invalid. The parties may agree in writing whether on the conclusion of missives of sale the notice to quit is to continue in force or not. If they have not so agreed within three months ending with the date on which the contract is made the landlord is required to give the tenant written notice of the making of the contract of sale. He must do so within fourteen days of the making of the contract or before the expiry of the notice to quit if that is earlier.

The tenant may then within one month of receipt of the notice and before the expiration of the notice to quit give written notice to the landlord electing that the notice to quit continue in force. Otherwise the notice to quit is of no effect unless the landlord fails to give notice of the sale. The purpose of the section is obscure. It has been suggested that it was designed before the introduction of security of tenure to prevent a landlord giving notice to quit for the purpose of selling. The corresponding English section has, however, been the subject of adverse judicial criticism, and since the section does not apply where the contract of sale is made before the notice to quit is served the protection to a tenant before security of tenure was slight. The section is a trap for the unwary landlord and appears to serve no useful purpose.

CHARGING THE ESTATE WITH COMPENSATION

Section 75 of the 1991 Act authorises a proprietor to charge his estate with sums paid for compensation for old or new improvements, and also for disturbance. Application for such charge must be made to the Secretary of

State. The charge ranks after all prior charges and burdens heritably secured on the holding or estate. It is thought that compensation paid by agreement, where there is no arbitration, cannot be charged on the estate, because the necessary certificate must be granted by an arbiter.

Similarly, the section provides that when any sum has become payable to the tenant in respect of compensation where the landlord has failed to discharge his liability, the Secretary of State may make a charging order creating a charge on the holding. The Secretary of State may burden the holding with an annuity to repay the sum due.

CHAPTER 8

CONTRACTING OUT

In the absence of the express prohibition parties are generally free to contract out of the provisions of the Acts insofar as the public interest is not affected. They may not, however, do so, even if there is no express prohibition, if the contracting out is contrary to public policy. This was the decision by the House of Lords in *Johnson v Moreton*,[1] which concerned an attempt to exclude security of tenure by a scheme which involved the tenants agreeing not to serve counter-notice to notice to quit.

Possibly the most important matter on which contracting out is expressly permitted is the deemed incorporation in all leases of the provisions of section 5(2) of the 1991 Act. Under section 5(3) these provisions can be varied by subsequent agreement and this has become a very common practice and is usual with any new leases. It has been held competent to contract out of the provisions of section 18 regarding fixtures and buildings and the power of bequest in section 11.

It is not competent to contract out of:

(1) the provisions of section 3 for continuation of tenancies by tacit relocation;
(2) freedom of cropping (section 7);
(3) compensation for damage by game (section 52);
(4) the prohibition of penal rents (section 48);
(5) the provisions as to payment for implements and other items sold in quitting the holding (section 19);
(6) compensation for disturbance (section 43);
(7) the additional payments (section 54);
(8) the provisions as to arbitration (section 60);
(9) the provisions of the Act on compensation except where there is express provision in the Act excluding compensation or permitting contracting out. There is such provision for exclusion of compensation in section 34(7) and for substituted compensation as noted above.

It would be equivalent to contracting out if conditions were imposed on the tenant's rights to compensation, such as requiring him to give notice within a period not prescribed by the Act; not, however, conditions under which the tenant got certain benefits in consideration of which he undertook to effect the improvement.

If the tenant is bound by his lease to execute all repairs to buildings, he cannot claim compensation for doing so, notwithstanding that section 34 allows compensation for contracted-out improvements under leases entered into after 1st January 1921.

AVOIDING INDEFINITE SECURITY OF TENURE

Although it is incompetent to contract out of the security of tenure provisions of the Act, it is nevertheless possible to grant a let in such a way that it does

1 [1980] AC 37.

not continue indefinitely. Various methods have been devised for this purpose and are summarised as follows.

1 Agreement not a 'lease'

If the agreement does not satisfy the definition of 'lease' in section 85 the subjects let will not be an agricultural holding. See, for example, *Stirrat and Anr v Whyte*[2] where the let was indefinite and to terminate on sale.

2 Company

The let may be granted to a limited company in which the landlord holds a share or shares carrying voting rights which enable him to terminate the company's tenancy by giving notice of intention to quit or by allowing him to liquidate the company.

3 Partnership

A let to a firm normally terminates when the firm is dissolved. As the firm is in Scots law a separate person from the partners the let could be to a firm in which the landlord is a partner. For the position in England see the case of *Harrison-Broadley v Smith*.[3] From the landlord's point of view, apart from the obvious danger of incurring liability, there is the possibility that the partnership agreement would be treated as a sham if the parties did not in fact carry on business in common with a view of profit. Unless the landlord wishes to be able to terminate the lease at any time it is preferable to form a limited partnership under the Limited Partnerships Act 1907 in which the tenant is the general partner and the landlord the limited or sleeping partner. The agreement will be of a stipulated endurance to end when it is desired to terminate the lease. This method, like method 2 above, does not exclude security of tenure but limits the existence of the tenant. The lease may be on a year-to-year basis but the tenant will have security of tenure so long as it continues in existence. The method has been widely used and it is now usual for new leases to be on this basis.

4 Joint tenancy

In *Smith v Grayton Estates Ltd*[4] it was held that tacit relocation depends on implied consent and that one of two joint tenants could not insist on continuing when the other wished to give up. It may therefore be possible to avoid creating security of tenure by the landlord's granting a short tenancy jointly to the real tenant and nominee of the landlord who will be in a position to terminate the tenancy.

5 Sub-tenancy

A notice to quit which terminates a tenancy will also terminate any subtenancy. If the holding is let to a nominee of the landlord and he sub-lets to the real tenant the latter is not in a position to prevent termination of the tenancy (and with it his own sub-tenancy). In terms of section 23(6), where a tenant receives notice to quit and gives notice to quit to his sub-tenant, the

2 1968 SLT 157.
3 [1964] All ER 867.
4 1960 SC 349.

64

provisions of section 22(1) do not apply to the notice to the sub-tenant who cannot therefore serve an effectual counter-notice. It has been held in England in the case of *Gisbourne v Burton*[5] that such a device is not effective.

6 Letter of removal

Attempts have been made to exclude security of tenure by granting a missive of let in exchange for a letter of removal by the tenant. It has, however, been held in England that notice of removal cannot validly be given before the commencement of the tenancy and it was observed that such a notice would have the effect of defeating the purpose of the 1991 Act. In view of the decision of the House of Lords in *Johnson* this device would not be effective.

With any of the above methods there is the danger that the arrangement may be treated by the courts as a sham agreement and not be given effect. In *Wallace v Moll*[6] (a case relating to a provision for review of rent which did not comply with section 13) the Land Court recognised the principle in *Johnson* as applicable in Scotland and there is no reason why the cases which follow it and develop the concept of the sham transaction should not be followed in Scotland.

5 [1988] 3 WLR 921.
6 1989 SLCR 21.

CHAPTER 9

MARKET GARDENS

The improvements for which compensation may be claimed by tenants of market gardens are practically the same as those which may be claimed by ordinary agricultural tenants, with the difference that in their case certain additional improvements, which require neither the consent of nor notice to the landlord, are provided for by Schedule 6 to the 1991 Act, namely:

(1) planting of trees or bushes permanently set out;

(2) planting of strawberry plants;

(3) planting of asparagus, rhubarb, and other vegetable crops which continue productive for two or more years;

(4) erection, alteration or enlargement of buildings for the purpose of the trade or business of a market gardener.

The tenant of a market garden is entitled to remove all fruit trees and fruit bushes not permanently set out, subject to this condition, that if he fails to remove them before the termination of his tenancy, they remain the property of the landlord without compensation. In short, practically the whole provisions of the statute with reference to compensation for improvements, for disturbance, for game damage, fixtures and buildings, erected or acquired by the tenant, and notices to terminate tenancy, apply with the same force to market gardens as they apply to ordinary agricultural holdings with the additions referred to above. The tenant of a market garden is in a more favourable position than the ordinary agricultural tenant, as he may erect or enlarge buildings without the landlord's consent and claim compensation therefor at quitting, on the basis of the value to an incoming tenant.

The provisions of the Acts relating to substituted compensation (in the sense of compensation according to a previously agreed scale), continue to apply to market garden improvements but not to other improvements, except under agreements entered into prior to 1st January 1921.

A tenant of agricultural land who wishes to make any of the improvements which may be executed by tenants of market gardens, where the landlord refuses, or within a reasonable time fails to agree in writing, that the land shall be treated as a market garden, may apply to the Land Court who may direct that the land shall, in effect, be treated as market garden land, with right in the tenant to execute all market garden improvements thereon, or some only of these improvements. Such a direction may be given, subject to such conditions for the protection of the landlord as the Land Court thinks fit to impose. In all cases where a direction is given, the following provision, based on what is known as the Evesham custom, must apply: where notice to quit is given by the tenant he is not to be entitled to the compensation specified in the direction, unless he produces a substantial and otherwise suitable successor who is willing to accept the tenancy of the holding on the same terms and conditions, and pay to him, the outgoing tenant, all compensation payable under the statute, or under the contract of tenancy, and the landlord fails to accept that tenant within three months after the offer is made to him.

In the event of the landlord accepting the offer, the incoming tenant must pay to him all sums payable by the outgoing tenant, on the termination of the tenancy, for rent, or breach of contract, or otherwise in respect of the holding, and any amount so paid may be deducted by the incoming tenant from any compensation payable by him to the outgoing tenant.

If the direction relates only to part of a holding the direction may, on the application of the landlord, be made subject to the condition that the tenant shall consent to the division of the holding into two parts (one such part being the part to which the direction relates) to be held at rents agreed between the landlord and tenant, or failing agreement, determined by arbitration, but otherwise on the same terms and conditions as the original holding, so far as applicable. The new tenancy created by the acceptance by the landlord of a tenant on the terms and conditions of the existing tenancy, is not to be treated as a new tenancy for the purposes of the provisions of the Act relating to demands for arbitration as to rent.

CHAPTER 10

CONTRACTUAL RESUMPTION

The general principle is that a landlord, having made a grant, cannot subsequently derogate from that grant. If, therefore, the landlord who has given off a lease is to be entitled to get back part of what he has given he must be able to point either at a particular contractual stipulation or at an overriding statutory enactment permitting him to do so. Unless the parties have chosen to express their agreement in writing the landlord is extremely unlikely to be able to establish that he has a contractual right of resumption. Equally, if the lease is one which simply consists of the minimal statutory terms set out in Schedule 1 to the 1991 Act, the landlord will not be entitled to resume.

The first question is whether the lease in question contains a resumption clause. If it does, one must consider the precise terms of it.

The resumption clause must be scrutinised as part of a normal exercise in the construction of deeds to decide what the permitted purposes and circumstances of resumption may be.

It must then be determined whether what is proposed falls within the terms of the resumption clause. If it does not, the landlord is not entitled to carry through his proposed resumption. If it does, then in principle the landlord is entitled to resume, whether or not it seems fair that he should be entitled to do so. In *Edinburgh Corporation v Gray*[1] Lord President Cooper said:

'It is well to recall that a lease is a contract, and that the parties are free to make any lawful bargain they like, fair or unfair, consistently with the statutes. The landlord's reserved power to resume possession for some particular purpose (other than that of merely reletting to another tenant) has long been recognised in our decisions, textbooks and styles.'

In that case the landlords were a local authority. The lease conferred on the landlords power at all times to resume land from any part of the farm for any purpose whatever on certain conditions as to payment of compensation. Lord Cooper pointed out:

'The tenant has chosen to remain year after year on tacit relocation in the occupation of an arable farm in the suburbs of a large city, and he must long have known perfectly well that the risk of resumption for housing purposes was real and increasingly imminent, for the successive resumptions have been in progress since 1935; the present landlords are the local housing authority, and the entire farm has eventually been absorbed in a housing scheme.'

Having established that the proposed resumption falls within the literal meaning of the resumption clause, the next question is, 'Was it within the contemplation of the parties when they entered into this lease, that the landlord should be able to exercise the right of resumption in the manner which he proposes?'

The basis of an agricultural lease is that both the landlord and the tenant

1 1948 SLT 425.

contemplate that the property is to be used for the purpose of generating a profit. If the effect of the proposed resumption is to reduce the farm to such an extent that it is incapable of producing a profit, there will be more of a presumption that it was not within the contemplation of the parties that resumption to that extent would take place.

The leading case on this is *The Admiralty v Burns*.[2] The farms in question were Rosyth, Orchardhead and Hilton. The Admiralty were the landlords and the purpose of the resumption was the construction of the Rosyth Naval Dockyard. The resumption clauses in the three leases all provided:

> 'Reserving also full power at all times to take off land from any part or parts of the subjects hereby let for the purpose of planting, feuing or letting on building leases, or for making, altering or widening roads, or for making railroads or canals; or for any other purpose.'

Because of the very wide power of resumption 'for any other purpose', it was argued that the width of the purpose must be read as restricted by the operation of the *ejusdem generis* rule but this construction was rejected by the First Division purely as a matter of interpretation. Having so ruled, Lord Kinnear continued:

> 'I do not doubt that the generality of the power must be limited by reference to the purpose and scope of the contract, and therefore the landlord could not take ground to such an extent and for such purposes as would prevent the tenant from making a profitable use of the remainder for the purpose for which it was let.'

Lord Salvesen in a concurring judgment said:

> 'This clause must be construed with reference to the subject matter of the lease, and consistently with the farm continuing to be tenanted as an agricultural subject. To take an extreme case: it is obvious that Lord Hopetoun would not under this clause have resumed possession of the bulk of the agricultural land, leaving only the steading and its immediate surroundings in the possession of the tenant. A power so exercised would have defeated the purpose for which the lease was entered into. Apart from such an extreme case, it must be a question of circumstances whether the land sought to be resumed forms so material a part of the subjects let that it cannot be reasonably be regarded as within the contemplation of and would be against the good faith of the bargain embodied in the lease.'

From this it appears that one must look at the nature and extent of the proposed resumption. A budget will have to be prepared for the farm as it at present exists and another budget for the farm without the resumed area so that the effect on the viability of the farm can be demonstrated. If the effect of the resumption is to turn a farm with a reasonable prospect of generating profit into a farm with a certainty of loss it is easier to say that it would not have been within the contemplation of the parties that such a resumption would take place. Without such a budget it will be difficult for the arbiter to gauge the precise effect of the proposed resumption.

There have been various cases over the last few years in the Scottish Land Court which illustrate the approach taken. In *Secretary of State for Scotland v Campbell*[3] the landlords sought to resume 1,515 acres out of an 8,940-acre hill farm for tree planting. Having commented that the areas to be resumed were extensive, but so also was the farm itself, the court went on to decide that

2 1910 1 SLT 277.
3 1959 SLCR 49.

'the tenant is left with an extensive farming unit which in our opinion, should prove to be an economic farming unit. In these circumstances the notice of resumption is not invalid as being contrary to the good faith of the tenant's lease'.

A case in which the decision went the other way was *Glencruitten Trs v Love*.[4] In that case two adjoining farms were let to the tenant. Each farm had originally had a house and a steading but one house was excluded from the lease. The resumption clause in the lease allowed the landlord to resume any part of the land for any non-agricultural purpose. A question arose as to whether the landlords were entitled to resume the steading buildings and courtyard adjoining the excluded house for use in connection with that house. The Land Court decided that they were not so entitled. The ratio of the court's decision was:

'The steading forms so material a part of the subjects let that its resumption could not reasonably be regarded as within the contemplation of and would be against the good faith of the bargain embodied in the lease.'

The approach therefore is to look to the lease itself and then draw conclusions as to what must have been within the contemplation of the parties when that contract was made. The court sought to draw the inference that if the effect of the resumption is to make it impossible for the tenant to make a profit, this will not have been within the contemplation of the parties. But this is simply a legal presumption or inference, and it can be rebutted if the terms of the parties' contract or the circumstances in which it was to be performed demonstrate a contrary intention. There may be perfectly good commercial reasons why a tenant should enter into a contract anticipating that extensive resumption will take place. He may own or rent a nearby farm and may be quite happy to have some extra productive acres, if only for a few years and on a steadily diminishing basis, especially as the wide-ranging nature of the resumption clause will have the effect of depressing the rent which the landlord can command for the holding.

A paradox appears to arise from the approach taken by the courts. If the test of whether the good faith of the lease has been complied with is the ability of the tenant to continue farming profitably, then the more competent and efficient the farmer is, the more likely he is to be able to make a profit off the rump of the farm and the more at risk of resumption he is. The Land Court raised but did not answer this question in the case of *Fothringham v Fotheringham*,[5] pointing out that it meant that if a resumption was allowed down to the minimum viable size, in future circumstances a landlord could return for further resumptions as and when the tenant, by making further improvements, effectively constricted the area of viability. In practice, however, there may be no paradox, as the question of what was in the contemplation of the parties relates to the situation as it obtained at the point when the parties were making their bargain and surely the question of viability must be looked at as at that date and not at the date when the resumption took place.

The majority of cases referred to were decided before the introduction of full security of tenure. The Scottish Land Court suggested in *Fothringham* that the security of tenure has to be borne in mind when considering Lord

4 1966 SLT (Land Ct) 5.
5 1987 SLT (Land Ct) 10.

Cooper's dictum and the other passages referred to. The court said (at p 14):

'The earlier cases to which we were referred namely *The Admiralty v Burns* in 1910 and *Edinburgh Corporation v Gray* in 1948 were both decided prior to the passing of the 1949 Act which gave security of tenure for the first time to agricultural tenants. In those earlier cases the tenants therefore had no security beyond the contractual terms of their leases, whereas in this case the lease was entered into in 1954 after the passing of the 1949 Act when both parties must be assumed to have been aware of the new statutory position.'

The court then drew attention to subsections (1) and (2) of section 3 of the 1949 Act which, as reconsolidated in 1991, now read:

'3. Notwithstanding any agreement or any provision in the lease to the contrary, the tenancy of an agricultural holding shall not come to an end on the termination of the stipulated endurance of the lease, but shall be continued in force by tacit relocation for another year and thereafter from year to year, unless notice to quit has been given by the landlord or notice of intention to quit has been given by the tenant.'

The court then continued:

'Notice to quit would only be granted on stated grounds with the Secretary of State's [later this court's] consent to the operation of the notice other than where specifically provided by statute.'

They then referred to what is now section 21(1) in terms of which a tenancy of an agricultural holding shall not come to an end except by operation of a notice to quit or of a notice of intention to quit. The court went on to point out that in *Morrison's Exrs v Rendall*[6] the Second Division pointed out the overriding effect of these provisions.

From this the Scottish Land Court drew the conclusion that the dictum of Lord President Cooper about freedom of contract must be considered with the impact of security of tenure in mind. The court concluded:

'Consisting with the statutes now requires compliance with the security of tenure provisions of the 1949 Act and in particular section 3.'

In support of their argument the court relied on *Pigott v Robson*[7] where a landlord tried to resume the whole of a holding so that she could farm it herself. In doing so she relied on a clause in the lease permitting resumption for various agricultural purposes 'or for any other purposes that the landlord may desire'. Lord President Clyde said:

'It would be a very different thing to grant an agricultural lease for a period of years and to embody in it a clause entitling the landlord to resume the agricultural land or a part of it so that the landlord may himself farm it or let it to someone else. It may be that such a power could be incorporated in a lease, but that could only be done by clear and express terms, for such a provision would go far to negative the security of tenure which the lease is designed to give.'

The conclusion drawn by the Land Court was that here there is a recognition of the interrelation between a resumption clause and security of tenure. It is suggested that the security of tenure provisions in the statute do not bear on the question of the validity of a resumption and of what will have

6 1986 SC 69.
7 1958 SLT 49.

been in the contemplation of the parties when they made their bargain. Lord Clyde, in the passage quoted, made no reference to the security of tenure which the statute conferred. He was concerned with the security of tenure deriving from the terms of the lease itself. Equally, the argument disregards the provisions of section 21(7) of the 1991 Act which specifically disapplies the provisions about notice to quit to a notice given in pursuance of a stipulation in a lease entitling the landlord to resume land for building, planting, fencing or other purposes (not being agricultural purposes).

At common law there is no specific period of notice for exercise of a right of resumption. In *Edinburgh Corporation* the Lord President said:

> 'Though what is called in the case "notice" was actually given, the time allowance was so short as to be useless, being in one instance three days and in another one day. I cannot see that any valid objection can be taken to that.'

Although what is now the 1991 Act has had little impact on the law regarding the validity of the grounds on which a notice of resumption will operate it has effected very considerable changes on the financial consequences of a resumption. At common law, the measure of compensation for resumption was the lease itself. It was simply another facet of the freedom of contract to which Lord President Cooper referred in *Edinburgh Corporation*.

Section 49(1)(b) of the 1991 Act now provides that where the landlord of an agricultural holding resumes possession of part of the holding in pursuance of a provision in that behalf contained in the lease the provisions of the Act in respect of compensation shall apply as if that part of the holding were a separate holding which the tenant had quitted in consequence of a notice to quit. Although the 1991 Act does not specifically say so, the effect of assimilating a notice of resumption to a notice to quit for the purposes of compensation must be to increase the period of notice to two months or such longer period as the lease may specify. This is because the effect of section 49 is to give the dispossessed tenant a right to remove fixtures under section 18, a right to compensation for disturbance under section 43, a right to compensation for high farming under section 44 and a right to compensation for improvements. But the right to remove fixtures and the right to compensation for high farming only arise if the tenant has within one month before termination of the tenancy given the landlord notice of his intention to make the claim.

Accordingly, unless the notice of resumption is given in time to permit these notices by the tenant to be given the effect would be to deprive the tenant of these elements of compensation. There is English authority for the view that this is not competent (*Re Disraeli Agreement*)[8] and that authority would probably be followed in Scotland.

Section 31 of the 1991 Act provides that where the landlord of an agricultural holding resumes possession of part of the holding in pursuance of a provision in that behalf contained in the lease, the tenant shall be entitled to a reduction of rent proportionate to that part of the holding together with an amount in respect of any depreciation of the value to him of the residue of the holding caused by the severance or by the use to be made of the part severed. The arbiter who determines the amount of the reduction is directed

8 [1939] Ch 382.

to take into account any benefit or relief allowed to the tenant under the lease in respect of the part whose possession is being resumed. This means that the arbiter must look at the rental value of the area proposed to be resumed. He is not entitled simply to take an average rental per acre over the whole area of the farm and to apply that average to the area proposed to be renewed. He must analyse the whole rent payable for the farm and apply the appropriate rental per acre depending upon the productive quality of the type of land proposed to be resumed. He must then consider the impact of the severance on the rental value of the residue remaining in the hands of the tenant. Suppose, for example, that the original farm consisted of 500 acres of arable with sufficient buildings to store the crops produced by that acreage. The tenant will have pitched his rent on the basis that he has buildings which are sufficient, but no more than sufficient, for his productive acreage. Suppose then that the landlord is entitled to resume half the arable acreage, but no part of the buildings. Some of these buildings will now be redundant, and it is unreasonable that the tenant should be rented on them. Equally if the landlord is entitled to resume the buildings only the impact on the holding will be much greater than would be represented by the application of an acreage rate to the footprint of the buildings.

Chapter 11

COMPULSORY PURCHASE

It is not proposed to go into those rules which are common to all types of compulsory purchase but only to consider a few matters which are unique to the acquisition of tenanted farms. Special rules are required for these because of the long-term nature of farming and also because the original legislation, section 114 of the Lands Clauses Consolidation Act 1845, drew a distinction between the terms of compensation available to the holder of a lease for a year or from year to year and those with a greater interest whose rights were assimilated to those of owners. In 1845, no one could have conceived of the degree of security of tenure which would be available to the agricultural tenant. As a result instead of parties negotiating fresh terms for the renewal of their leases on the expiry of the contractual periods, the majority of leases now simply run from year to year by tacit relocation. The result of this is that while the norm is for the tenant to hold on what is nominally a lease for a year only, in practice his lease is capable of renewal for generations.

The applicable statutory provisions are sections 56 to 59 of and Schedule 8 to the Agricultural Holdings (Scotland) Act 1991 and the Land Compensation (Scotland) Act 1973. The purpose of the sections is to ensure that a tenant whose interest terminates in consequence of a compulsory acquisition will not be worse off than one who quits in consequence of having received a notice to quit from his landlord.

Any dispute with respect to any sum payable under these provisions is to be referred to and determined by the Lands Tribunal for Scotland (1991 Act, Schedule 8, paragraph 1).

The Schedule also contains provisions with a view to avoiding the situation where the landlord and tenant agree an artificially inflated rent in order to increase the tenant's compensation claim. Unless the rent has been fixed by arbitration or by the Scottish Land Court, if the acquiring authority consider the rent to be unduly high, the authority may refer the rent to the Lands Tribunal for consideration. The onus lies on the acquiring authority to displace the presumption that the rent payable is the proper rent by reference to which compensation falls to be assessed. The tribunal are directed to dismiss the application in two situations. The first is when the rent is 'substantially higher' than the rent which would be determined by arbitration under section 13 of the 1991 Act. The tribunal are given a broad measure of discretion to determine what margin of excess they will consider substantial. It must also be shown that the rent, even if substantially higher than appropriate, was not fixed by the parties with a view to increasing the amount of any compensation payable in consequence of the compulsory acquisition.

As the purpose of the statutory provisions is to recompense the working farmer who has to change his working practices, section 57 provides that no reorganisation payment is due to a tenant who has sub-leased his holding, unless the sub-lease is one to which section 2(1) applies, ie a seasonal grazing let.

The payment is also not due where the acquiring authority require the land comprised in the holding for the purposes of agricultural research or experiment or demonstrating agricultural methods or for forming small-holdings. Where a landlord gives notice to quit for the same reason and the Scottish Land Court gives its consent, the landlord is also absolved from liability for a reorganisation payment (1991 Act, ss 24(1)(c) and 55(1)(a)).

The provisions of the 1973 Act also innovate upon the original 1845 Act provisions. Section 114 of the 1845 Act provides that if lands are in the possession of any person having no greater interest than as tenant for a year or from year to year, and if such person be required to give up possession of any lands so occupied by him before the expiration of his term or interest therein, he shall be entitled to compensation for the value of his unexpired term or interest in such lands, and for any just allowance which ought to be made to him by any incoming tenant, and for any loss or injury he may sustain or, if a part only of such lands be required, compensation for severance or injurious affection.

Thus the compensation to be received would be the value of the remainder of the lease, and loss of profit for that period, together with a payment for tenant's improvements and unexhausted manures and similar items either under statute or at common law.

Section 22(2)(b) of the 1991 Act excludes from the protection of security of tenure a tenant who receives notice to quit on the ground that the land is required for a non-agricultural use for which planning permission is granted. Similarly section 24(1)(e) requires the Land Court to consent to a notice to quit if it is satisfied that the landlord proposes to terminate the tenancy for land being used for a non-agricultural use other than in terms of section 22(2)(b). Section 44 of the 1973 Act now provides that if the land is required or is to be used for such a non-agricultural purpose by an authority with compulsory purchase powers, the landlord's right to give notice to quit or notice of resumption is to be disregarded.

The effect of this provision is that in assessing the value of the unexpired term the tribunal are now to take into account the prospect of renewal afforded by security of tenure and to value the unexpired term accordingly. This provision is thus squarely within the rule that the valuation exercise is to be carried out in a 'no scheme' world. Section 44 of the 1973 Act requires a similar disregard of the landlord's right to serve notice to quit when the valuation of the landlord's interest is carried out. As a result the landlord's interest is valued subject to tenant's rights and not with the benefit of vacant possession. The operation of section 44 is illustrated by *Anderson v Moray District Council*.[1] In that case the Lands Tribunal held on the evidence that in the absence of the local authority's scheme of acquisition the ground was near ripe for private development. In these circumstances the landlord, having gained planning permission for private development, would have been able to serve notice to quit. Taking the evidence of a planning expert in conjunction with the notice requirements in the Agricultural Holdings Acts, they held that the tenant's possession would have ended after two years.

Section 55 of the 1973 Act also recognises security of tenure by giving a person having no greater interest than as a tenant for a year or from year to year access to 'notice of entry' compensation, ie the full range of compensation under the compulsory purchase code rather than the more restricted compensation under the Agricultural Holdings legislation. It

1 1978 SLT (Lands Tr) 37.

achieves this by requiring that a notice to quit must have been served on the tenant with no greater interest than from year to year. Before the notice is served the acquiring authority must either have served a notice to treat on the landlord or have agreed to acquire his interest in the holding. The land must be required for a non-agricultural use for which planning permission has been granted or the Land Court has consented to the operation of the notice for a non-agricultural purpose.

In order to qualify for compensation under the compulsory purchase code, the tenant must elect that the section is to apply to the notice and must give up possession of the holding to the acquiring authority on or before the date on which the tenancy terminates in accordance with the notice. By section 55(3), no election shall be made or, if already made, shall continue to have effect in relation to any land if, before the expiration of the notice, an acquiring authority take possession of that land in pursuance of an enactment providing for the taking of possession of land compulsorily. If such a taking of possession occurs, the tenant is brought within the scope of section 114 of the 1845 Act and section 44 of the 1973 Act as already discussed. Section 55(4) provides that any election is to be made by notice in writing and that written notice is to be served on the acquiring authority not later than the date on which possession of the holding is given up.

The provisions on notice of entry compensation also apply where the notice applies only to part of the tenant's holding. In that event if the tenant elects for notice of entry compensation section 55(6) provides that he cannot give notice under section 30 of the 1991 Act to treat a notice to quit part of the holding as a notice to quit the entire holding. The reason for this exclusion is that section 57 provides the tenant in that situation with a different mechanism by which the entire holding may be given up. Section 57 imposes a tighter time-limit on the tenant than section 55. Whereas section 55 allows an election at any time before possession is given up, section 57 is only brought into play if the election is made within two months of service of the notice to quit. In addition the tenant must, within the same two-month period, serve notice claiming that the remainder of the holding is not reasonably capable of being farmed, either by itself or in conjunction with other relevant land, as a separate agricultural unit.

After the notice has been served on them, the acquiring authority have two months in which to decide whether to accept the notice as valid. If the acquiring authority do not accept the validity of the notice within the two-month period, either the claimant or the acquiring authority may apply to the Lands Tribunal for a determination of the validity of the notice. Where a notice is accepted as or declared valid and within one year thereafter the tenant goes out, then notice of entry compensation is payable as if notice of entry had been given at the end of the year current of the tenancy during which the notice as accepted as valid either by the acquiring authority or the Lands Tribunal.

CHAPTER 12

ARBITRATION UNDER THE 1991 ACT

Practically all questions between landlord and tenant in relation to an agricultural holding (except as to liability for rent) are referred to arbitration under section 60.

The effect of what is now section 60 was considered in *Houison-Craufurd's Trs v Davies*[1] and by a court of seven judges in *Brodie v Ker; McCallum v McNair*,[2] where it was held that the section is imperative and that the parties cannot prorogate the jurisdiction of the courts. Even where there is no plea to that effect the court has held that such questions must be determined by arbitration as it is part of the judicial function to take notice of matters of competence.

The section applies only to questions and differences between landlord and tenant of an agricultural holding. The question whether the parties are in that relationship is primarily one for the court. It is competent for the matter to be determined by arbitration, but such an arbitration is a common law arbitration and not an arbitration under the 1991 Act. The award in such an arbitration would not be *res judicata* unless all parties interested were parties to the arbitration. The Secretary of State has no power to appoint an arbiter to determine such a matter.

An arbiter is entitled to explicate his own jurisdiction; but this is not a matter on which he has any exclusive jurisdiction. He may require to decide a preliminary question on this before dealing with the substantive matter referred to him but his decision on jurisdiction would be open to reduction and not binding. He has no jurisdiction to answer such a question which involves the rights of a third party and is not a necessary preliminary to any other matter which it is competent for him to decide. The Land Court acting in a joint reference under section 60(2) has only such jurisdiction as an arbiter could exercise and the parties cannot confer on it a jurisdiction not conferred by statute. It accordingly declined to deal with a question whether a tenancy of an agricultural holding had validly terminated. It may, however, explicate its own jurisdiction in a case where its substantive jurisdiction is otherwise involved. There is often a question whether the court should interdict an arbiter from acting or allow him to proceed with the prospect of reduction of his award.

Despite the wide terms of section 60 one matter which must be dealt with by the court is the landlord's remedy of interdict under section 7(3). Section 7(4) provides that an arbiter shall determine whether or not the tenant has exercised his rights in such a way as to deteriorate the holding and the ascertainment of damages for this will also be a matter for arbitration. Interdict is, however, a remedy competent only in the courts and where invoked for the purposes of section 7(3) it is probable that the judge would pronounce interim interdict where a prima facie case has been made, and allow a sist to enable an arbiter to decide the real question. This was the

1 1951 SC 1.
2 1952 SC 216.

course which the court would have followed in *Wildfowl and Wetlands Trust (Holdings) Ltd v Quinn.*[3] In that case the landlord applied to the Court of Session for interdict against a breach of contract allegedly being carried out by the tenant. The tenant denied that there was a breach of contract and argued that the court had no jurisdiction as the matter was a 'question or difference' falling within section 60. Although he refused interim interdict on the balance of convenience Lord Johnston held that the court retained jurisdiction to grant interdict to maintain the status quo pending the determination of the dispute. The alternative would be to have the arbitration before initiating any proceedings in the ordinary courts. It is not a 'question or difference' between the landlord and tenant, but an administrative act exercisable by the courts to preserve the landlord from loss.

Questions between an outgoing and incoming tenant are not dealt with under section 60 and fall to be settled by application to the courts or by arbitration at common law.

Certain questions – for example, with regard to the carrying out of improvements included in Schedule 5, Part II – are referred to the decision of the Land Court (section 39(2)).

By section 17 the awaygoing tenant is required to offer hay, straw, manure, etc to the landlord or incoming tenant at their market value, but it is thought that, even in that case, the right to enforce the obligation would lie solely with the landlord against the awaygoing tenant.

By virtue of section 60(2), parties may agree to refer their differences to the Land Court instead of to an arbiter. The Act further provides in section 64 for cases where the Secretary of State is the landlord in which circumstances the assistance of the Land Court is invoked in appointing an arbiter. In cases which go to the Land Court, attention must be paid to the rules of the Land Court. The normal statutory provisions as to arbitration procedure do not apply.

<h2 style="text-align:center">CLAIMS BY THE TENANT</h2>

In all cases notice of intention to claim just be given within two months from the termination of the tenancy. It is not necessary to quantify or specify the claim in detail; it is sufficient to refer to the section of the Act under which the claim is made and to state its nature in general terms.

A full statement of case and details of claim must be supplied to an arbiter within twenty-eight days of his appointment (Schedule 7, paragraph 5).

I Scheduled improvements

These are now divided into 'old improvements', ie those made before 1st November 1948 and 'new improvements', ie those made on or after that date. 'Old improvements' are further divided into '1923 Act improvements', ie those begun before 31st July 1931 and '1931 Act improvements', ie those made on or after 31st July 1931, and before 1st November 1948 (section 33). Reference should be made to Schedules 3, 4 and 5 which each detail the improvements under three separate headings.

3 1994; unreported.

Schedule 3: old improvements under the 1923 Act, ie those begun before 31st July 1931

Conditions

(1) A tenant under a lease dated before 1st January 1921, is not entitled to compensation for an improvement which he was bound by his lease to carry out (section 34 (2)).

(2) Compensation is not payable unless before carrying out an improvement under Part I of the Schedule the tenant obtained the landlord's consent in writing (agreed compensation may be substituted for compensation under the Act) (section 37).

(3) Compensation is not payable for an improvement under Part II unless the tenant, not more than three nor less than two months before he began to carry out the improvement, gave the landlord notice in writing of his intention and either (a) the parties agreed as to compensation; or (b) the landlord failed to carry out the improvement himself (section 38).

(4) In the case of repairs to buildings the tenant must have given notice in writing of intention to carry out the repairs and the landlord failed to carry them out himself within a reasonable time (section 34(8)).

Schedule 4: old improvements under the 1931 Act, ie those begun on or after 31st July 1931 and before 1st November 1948

Conditions

(1) The tenant is not entitled to compensation for improvements which he was bound by a lease entered into before 1st January 1921 to carry out (section 34(2)).

(2) Compensation is not payable unless before carrying out an improvement in Part I of the Schedule the tenant obtained the landlord's consent in writing. Agreed compensation may be substituted for compensation under the Act (section 37).

(3) In the case of an improvement under Part II of the Schedule the tenant must have given not more than six and not less than three months' notice in writing of his intention and either (a) the parties have agreed to the terms as to compensation; or (b) the landlord failed to carry out the improvement; or (c) the appropriate authority at the time (now the Land Court) determined that the improvement should be carried out (section 38).

(4) In the case of repairs to buildings the tenant must have given notice in writing to the landlord of his intention and the landlord failed to carry out repairs himself within a reasonable time (section 34(8)).

Schedule 5: new improvements, ie those carried out after 1st November 1948

Conditions

(1) The tenant is not entitled to compensation for improvements which he was bound to carry out by a lease entered into before 1st January 1921 (section 34(2)).

(2) Improvements under Part I. Landlord must consent in writing (section 37).

(3) Improvements under Part II. The parties may dispense with notice and provide also as to the terms of compensation. Otherwise the tenant must

have given written notice of his intention not less than three months before carrying out the improvement.

II Compensation for continuous good farming (section 44)

Conditions
(1) There must be a record of the fixed equipment on and cultivation of the holding, and only so far as the improvement is made after the date of that record is compensation payable.
(2) Notice of intention to claim, not later than one month before termination of tenancy.

III Compensation for disturbance (section 43)

Conditions
(1) Notice to quit by the landlord in ordinary form, or in the form required to exclude additional payments under section 54 or notice to quit part of the holding followed by a counter-notice by the tenant that he is to treat the notice as a notice to quit the whole (section 30) followed in each case by the tenant quitting (section 43).
(2) Landlord to be given one month's notice of sale of implements, stock, etc, and a reasonable opportunity of making a valuation of goods, implements, fixtures, product and stock (section 43(4)(b)), if claim exceeds one year's rent.
(3) Notice of intention to claim within two months after termination of tenancy (section 62(2)).

IV Additional payments under s 54

Conditions
(1) Entitlement to compensation for disturbance. See III above.
(2) Payment not excluded under section 55 of the Act (see Chapter 6 under 'Reorganisation of Tenant's Affairs').
(3) Notice of intention to claim within two months after termination of tenancy (section 68(2)).

V Compensation for early resumption (s 58)

Condition
Notice of intention to claim within two months after termination of tenancy (section 62(2)).

VI Claims (by the tenant) in respect of any matter arising out of the tenancy (s 74)

Condition
Notice of intention to claim must be given within two months after termination of tenancy in the event that the claim arises on or out of the termination of the tenancy.

VII Fixtures, machinery or buildings (s 18)

These are not, properly speaking, 'improvements' for which compensation may be claimed but where the landlord agrees to take them over, their value falls to be fixed by arbitration under the Act. It may be noted that the basis is the value to an incoming tenant, being the same basis as applies to permanent improvements to which the landlord consented in writing.

Conditions
(1) One month's notice in writing of intention to remove the fixtures.
(2) All rent must be paid and other obligations under the lease performed.
(3) Unless the landlord elects to take them over, they may be removed (subject to making good damage) before or within six months after the termination of tenancy.

VIII Damage by game (s 52)

Damage by game can form the subject of a claim, during, as well as at the termination of a tenancy.

Conditions
(1) Notice of the damage must be given in writing as soon as may be after its discovery, and a reasonable opportunity given to the proprietor to inspect the damage.
(2) The claim must be made within a month after the end of the calendar year in which it occurs, or such other period of twelve months as the parties shall agree to substitute for the calendar year.

IX Variation of rent (s 13)

Conditions
(1) Notice in writing demanding arbitration as to rent payable as from the next ensuing day on which the tenancy could have been terminated by notice to quit or notice of intention to quit given at the date of demanding the reference.
(2) Demand not effective if alteration in rent would take effect earlier than three years from (a) the commencement of the tenancy; (b) the date from which a previous alteration in rent took effect; or (c) the date from which a direction in an arbitration as to rent under the section took effect. Note that there are certain exceptions (section 13(9)).

Where a tenant quits part of a holding under section 29 or the landlord resumes possession of part of the holding under the provisions of a lease the reduction of rent is determined by arbitration (section 31).

Conditions
(1) The reduction is proportionate to the part given up and in respect of the depreciation of the remainder caused by the severance or the use to be made of the part severed.
(2) Where there is resumption under a lease any benefit or relief allowed to the tenant is taken into account.

Where a landlord has carried out any certain improvements specified in section 15, the rent may be increased by arbitration.

Condition
Landlord to serve notice in writing on the tenant within six months from the completion of the improvement.

X Adjustment of terms of leases

(a) Where land is let without the consent of the Secretary of State for less than one year the lease will be treated as one from year to year, if the circumstances are such that if the tenant were a tenant from year to year the tenancy would come under the Act. Any question falls to be decided by arbitration (section 2(3)); (b) where liability for the maintenance of any fixed equipment is transferred from the tenant to the landlord any claim by the tenant in respect of the landlord's previous failure is also settled by arbitration (section 5(5)); (c) an arbiter may be appointed to settle the terms of a lease (section 4).

Conditions
(1) Either: (a) there is no lease; or (b) a lease has been entered into after 1st November 1948, or the tenant is sitting under tacit relocation and the lease contains no provision for one or more of the matters contained in Schedule 1 or provisions inconsistent with that Schedule or section 5.
(2) One party must give to the other six months' notice requesting a lease to be entered into (section 4).
(3) Every new lease is held to have incorporated in it an undertaking by the landlord to put the fixed equipment in order (based on a record to be made in every case) the tenant's liability being to maintain it in as good a state as it is put in by the landlord. Any question arising is referred to arbitration (section 5).

XI Market garden 'direction' (s 41)

The Land Court may direct that a holding, or part thereof, be treated as market garden.

Conditions
(1) Intimation in writing by tenant of desire to carry out market gardening improvements.
(2) Tenant may not claim compensation if he is removed on account of apparent insolvency unless he provides a suitable tenant within one month of the notice to quit being served.

XII Payment for implements, fixtures, produce or stock agreed to be purchased by landlord on termination of tenancy (s 19)

Where payment is not made within one month after the tenant has quitted the holding or within one month after the issue of the award the outgoing tenant may sell or remove the goods and claim compensation equal to any loss or expense unavoidably incurred thereby, including the expense of preparing his claim.

XIII Restriction on operation of notices to quit (s 27)

The provision that a tenant on receipt of a notice to quit may serve a counter-notice requiring section 22(1) to apply, in which case the notice is subject to the consent of the Land Court, does not apply in certain circumstances – for example, where the court has already consented to the notice to quit.

I Compensation for deterioration of holding (section 45)

Conditions
(1) Tenant quitting holding.
(2) Notice in writing of intention to claim not less than three months before termination of tenancy (section 47(1)).
(3) Record of fixed equipment and cultivation to have been made if claim is under section 45 when the lease was entered into after 31st July 1931, or the claim is under a lease entered into after 1st November 1948 (section 42(2)).

II Any other matter arising between the landlord and the tenant arising out of the tenancy which is referred to arbitration by the lease or under the Act

Condition
Notice of intention to claim must be given within two months after termination of tenancy where the claims arise at the awaygoing (section 62(2)).

III Questions as to rent (s 13)

Condition
As under claims by tenant.

IV

Under section 15, landlord may demand arbitration by notice in writing as to rent to be paid in respect of improvements carried out by him as specified in that section.

Condition
Landlord must serve notice on tenant within six months of executing the improvements.

PARTICULARS OF CLAIMS

A party who is intending to proceed to an arbitration is entitled to invoke the procedure in section 1 of the Administration of Justice (Scotland) Act 1972 to recover documents and other evidence necessary to found his case: *Anderson v Gibb*.[4]

In general, claims arising out of the termination of the lease can be dealt with by arbitration under the 1991 Act only if notice of intention to claim in general terms (not full 'particulars') has been given by the claimant before the expiration of two months from the termination of the tenancy.

Within twenty-eight days of the appointment of an arbiter, however, each party must deliver to him 'a statement of that party's case with all necessary particulars' (Schedule 7, paragraph 5). A 'statement of case' amounts to a narrative of facts and averments corresponding to the condescendence in a

4 1991, per Lord Penrose; unreported.

case in court: it is usual to include pleas-in-law. No amendment or addition to the case can be made without the arbiter's consent.

COMPETENCY AND RELEVANCY OF CLAIMS

An explanatory statement under this heading may be desirable for the information of arbiters, especially as many of them are practical farmers and not lawyers.

An arbiter may be interdicted from proceeding where the claim is not competently founded, but the Secretary of State cannot be interdicted from appointing an arbiter – see section 21(1)(a) of the Crown Proceedings Act 1947, as applied to Scotland by section 43(a) of that Act. Where, however, it is thought that the Secretary of State is about to exceed his powers it is open to either party to seek an order in the courts declaratory of his rights. When such an order is asked for it should be formulated with precision. Such an application must be to the Court of Session and will proceed by way of judicial review.

A claim or question to be competent must be one which falls to be dealt with by arbitration under the 1991 Act and, accordingly, it must arise in connection with the tenancy of a holding as defined in the Act; further, it must be between the landlord and tenant of such a holding. This excludes questions and claims between awaygoing and incoming tenants, even for compensation of the kinds embraced under the Act. Where a tenant is bound to hand over his waygoing crops to the landlord or incoming tenant he, as the debtor in an alternative obligation, is entitled to elect with whom he will deal.

All claims between landlord and tenant in connection with the holding, whether arising out of the termination of the tenancy, or during its currency (except a difference as to liability for rent) are now referred to arbitration in terms of section 60.

Questions relating to the valuation of sheep stocks, dung, fallow, and general awaygoing valuations are excluded from the arbitration procedure of the Act under section 61(7).

The subject of relevancy frequently provides questions of difficulty. In litigation, the pursuer must state a relevant case, ie his averments of fact, as stated, must be such as, if established, would justify a decision in his favour. Assuming a relevant case for the pursuer, the defender would have decree given against him unless he states a relevant defence, ie a defence which, if established, would effectively answer the pursuer's claim.

Though arbitrations under the Act are not litigations, and need not be conducted with the same rigid adherence to form and procedure, nevertheless it is the duty of the arbiter to ascertain if there be a relevant claim, for, as soon as he is satisfied to the contrary, he ought to rule it out, and thus save parties the trouble and expense of needless proof and other procedure. For example, if a tenant were to claim for improvement by sowing wild, white clover (to which many farmers attach importance), the arbiter would have no difficulty in seeing at once that such an improvement is not specifically included as an improvement in the Schedule to the Act. He might, however, consider whether, consistently with the terms of the claim as stated, it could be taken into consideration under the provision for compensation for temporary pasture. If – but only if – the claim was well based on that provision, he would be entitled to hold it relevant, otherwise not (in the latter case for the reason that there would be no statutory authority for it).

Arbiters are entitled to satisfy themselves that they have jurisdiction to proceed. If an arbiter is inclined to decide that he has no jurisdiction, it is most important that he make a proposed finding to that effect in order that the point may be tested in court.

APPOINTMENT OF ARBITER

The parties are entitled to agree to the appointment of any person as arbiter. Agricultural questions are usually submitted to a practical person, but legal questions, such as the interpretation of a lease, are sometimes submitted to counsel or solicitors. Many arbitrations involve both types of questions when the usual course is to have a practical arbiter advised by a lawyer as clerk.

Where the parties are unable to agree with reference to claims and questions under the Act, or under the lease, there is provision for arbitration before an arbiter agreed on by them or appointed by the Secretary of State on application by either of them. The leading provisions are contained in Part VII of and Schedule 7 to the Act. These provisions also apply to other sections which deal with particular claims and questions. Where an application is made to the Secretary of State to appoint an arbiter, the appointment must be made from a panel of arbiters drawn up by the Lord President of the Court of Session in consultation with the Secretary of State in accordance with section 63. It has been held that in making such appointment the Secretary of State is acting in an administrative capacity and that his selection of an arbiter from the panel could not be challenged. Once the Secretary of State has made the appointment his functions end and he has no further duties other than the fixing of the arbiter's fee. The appointment of an arbiter by the Secretary of State does not imply either that the arbiter has jurisdiction to deal with all the possible disputes between the parties or that any claims made are valid.

It would be inequitable if the Secretary of State was entitled to appoint the arbiter to resolve disputes to which he is a party either as landlord or as tenant. In these cases the arbiter is appointed by the Land Court (section 64).

Appointments must be in writing. The document of appointment should be dated and forwarded to the arbiter. An agreement to appoint a named arbiter is not an appointment. An appointment determined by drawing one of several names by lot is not objectionable. In any case the arbiter must observe the rules laid down by the Act.

The Secretary of State has been more disposed to appoint than to decline to do so. It has been his custom to appoint on all bona fide applications and where there was *ex facie* a claim or question between landlord and tenant in connection with the holding. In this attitude he received encouragement from a dictum of Lord President Dunedin. Where the dispute is whether a person is in fact a tenant the determination of such a question would be for the courts. A landlord or tenant who was anxious not to have an arbiter appointed to deal with such a question might require to invoke section 21 of the Crown Proceedings Act 1947.

It would appear that the Secretary of State ought to satisfy himself whether the case falls under the exception set out in section 61(7) of the 1991 Act to valuations of sheep stocks, dung, fallow, straw, crops, fences and other specific things agreed to be taken over. It should be noted that subsection (7) does not apply where the stock belongs to the landlord.

In arbitration other than rent arbitration an arbiter appointed by the parties is, in all respects except two, in the same position, and must act in the same way as an arbiter appointed by the Secretary of State – that is to say, he must act conform to Schedule 7 to the Act. The exceptions are that the fee of an arbiter appointed by the Secretary of State must be fixed by him and that an arbiter appointed by the Secretary of State as a tribunal within the meaning of the Tribunals and Inquiries Act 1971 is subject to supervision by the Council on Tribunals and can be required to give reasons for his award.

In rent arbitrations there are three further differences in addition to the above:

(1) there may be an appeal to the Land Court;
(2) the arbiter's award must state his findings in fact and the reasons for his award in prescribed form; and
(3) any stated case is to the Land Court and not to the sheriff.

If the arbiter dies, or is incapable of acting, or for seven days after notice requiring him to act fails to do so, a new arbiter may be appointed to take his place, just as if no arbiter had been appointed (Schedule 7, paragraph 2).

The arbitration will subsist notwithstanding the death of one of the parties and his executors may become parties in his place.

Every appointment (whether by the parties or by the Secretary of State), notice, revocation, and consent must be in writing, and an appointment is irrevocable except of consent. The Secretary of State, having made an appointment, cannot revoke it, but the parties may jointly agree to do so.

The better practice is for an arbiter to accept in writing but this is not strictly necessary. Once he has accepted office he is not entitled to resign, and unless parties agree to revoke his appointment, he must apply to the court for leave to resign on cause shown – for example, ill-health, intention to go abroad for a long time, or emerging interest.

The Court of Session alone can compel an arbiter to proceed with his task. The proper course is by petition for judicial review in the Outer House. On the other hand, interdict is competent if the arbiter is clearly exercising or proposing to exercise powers that he does not properly possess.

DISQUALIFICATION AND REMOVAL OF ARBITER

An arbiter may be removed by the sheriff where he 'misconducts' himself – for example, by refusing to act on the opinion of the court. Misconduct here is evidently misconduct in the arbitration, but in extreme circumstances the court would remove an arbiter on personal grounds, such as conviction of grave crime.

An arbiter is not disqualified by having an interest in the subject in dispute if, where the interest existed previous to his appointment, the fact is known to both parties and neither takes objection. If his interest supervened at a subsequent date, he would be disqualified in the absence of the parties agreeing to his continuance in office. In any event the interest must be substantial.

Acting as adviser to one of the parties in a different matter is no disqualification. It is, however, not desirable for one of the parties' advisers to act as arbiter if he has already applied his mind to the particular dispute in issue. He must be in a position to approach questions submitted with an open mind. It would probably be held that an arbiter whose award had been reduced could not act again on the ground that he could not free his mind of his earlier experience. An arbiter has been interdicted from acting when he had previously made a record of the holding and improperly expressed therein an opinion on the subject of the dispute on which he was subsequently called on to arbitrate. On the other hand the mere making of a record is not in itself a disqualification.

An objection to the competency of an arbiter acting, or to his conduct in the arbitration, or to the competency or propriety of the proceedings must be timeously stated, otherwise it will be rejected.

MINUTE OF SUBMISSION

There is no provision in the statute for the execution of a formal minute of submission. Where the arbiter is appointed by the Secretary of State, the form of appointment constitutes the only submission that is necessary. That form always follows on and embodies the claim or question at issue as set forth in the application for the appointment of the arbiter.

Where the arbiter is appointed by the parties, it is necessary to have a joint minute of appointment, because the Schedule provides that the appointment of an arbiter must be in writing. No particular form is required. It is, however, necessary to state clearly what claims and questions are submitted to arbitration, and it should always be stated that the arbitration is one under the Act. The arbiter must confine himself to the questions and claims stated, unless the parties agree in writing to his going further. Without such agreement, an arbiter appointed to deal with a claim for compensation for improvements would not be entitled to deal with a claim for compensation for disturbance.

PROCEDURE IN ARBITRATION

The arbiter has a very wide discretion as to his procedure. He must decide what he considers are the subjects and questions submitted to him, but in the last resort it lies with the court to decide matters of jurisdiction. An arbiter may be interdicted if he proposes to deal with matters not referred to him, or if there is no question to try. Interdict would probably not be granted against findings unless the arbiter made it clear that, despite representations, he was to incorporate the findings in his award. The jurisdiction of the arbiter may be extended by the actings of parties when he has entered on the business of the submission, but writing is always preferable. As a rule, he should follow the order adopted in the courts – not that the courts will insist on anything like rigid adherence to such procedure. The arbiter should not overlook the fact that the arbitrations are statutory, and should be careful to adhere to the code of procedure laid down in Schedule 7. Over and above everything, he should be careful to be strictly impartial, to show that he is impartial and to do nothing which might be calculated to prejudice either party or to defeat the ends of justice.

APPOINTMENT OF CLERK

In terms of paragraph 19 of Schedule 7 an arbiter may not include a sum in respect of remuneration or expenses of a clerk in the arbitration unless the clerk was appointed (a) after submission to him of the claims and answers, and (b) with either the consent of the parties or the sanction of the sheriff. The reference to 'claims and answers' in this paragraph was carried over without amendment from earlier Acts and is inconsistent with the provisions of paragraph 5 relating to claims. The appointment of a clerk will be approved if there are questions of a legal character which would properly be referred to an assessor. If an application has to be made to the sheriff, the appointment and statements of case of the parties should be lodged and intimation of the application should be served on the parties to give them an opportunity to oppose it. The application should narrate the appointment, the lodging of the claims, and the reason, such as the complexity of the case or the legal questions involved, which necessitates the services of a clerk being retained. A style of initial writ is given in the Appendix.

RECEIVING CLAIMS AND OBJECTIONS

Paragraph 5 of Schedule 7 provides that each of the parties to an arbitration must, within twenty-eight days from the arbiter's appointment, deliver to him 'a statement of that party's case with all necessary particulars'. In the case of an appointment by the Secretary of State, the twenty-eight-day period runs from the date on which the Secretary of State's representative actually signs the appointment and not from any later date on which notice of the appointment is received by the parties. Similarly, where the appointment is made by the parties, the twenty-eight-day period runs from the date of the arbiter's acceptance of office.

If one of the parties fails to lodge a statement of case within the statutory period it is not competent for the arbiter to permit him to do so out of time. The consequence of this is that the party failing to lodge a statement, cannot subsequently at the hearing put his positive case forward. The reason for this is that paragraph 5(b) restricts a party to the matters alleged in his statement. It is, however, competent to the party who has omitted to lodge a statement to test his opponent's case by cross-examination, so long as that cross-examination is not intended to set up an alternative positive case. If both parties fail to lodge statements of case, the arbitration cannot proceed unless it relates to review of rent and the arbiter will require to dismiss the case. A rent arbitration would require to proceed because section 13(2) imposes a duty on the arbiter to determine the rent in accordance with the statutory criteria. If the parties and the arbiter all agree, a statement of case may be accepted out of time in spite of the peremptory terms of the statute. The reason for this is that the statutory time-limit was imposed for the protection of the parties by providing machinery intended to keep the arbitration moving. If the party intended to be protected by that machinery chooses to waive the protection he is at liberty to do so. Similarly, the interests of justice will be served if the parties are both able to state their contending points of view to the arbiter and for that reason he should be reluctant to refuse his consent to late lodging: *Suggett v Shaw*.[5]

5 1987 SLT (Land Ct) 5.

No amendment or addition to the statement of case is allowed after the period of twenty-eight days has elapsed without the arbiter's consent and parties are confined to the matters stated in the claim. With the statement of case and particulars of claim before him, the arbiter will be in a position to decide on further procedure. He will bear in mind in doing so that the purpose of written statements is to allow him to see precisely what is in dispute between the parties. As the parties are both constrained to lodge their statement of case within twenty-eight days of the appointment of the arbiter, each may do so in ignorance of the terms of the other's statement. A period of adjustment may therefore be necessary to allow each party to answer statements made by his opponent and with which he has not dealt in his original statement of case. It is competent at the stage of adjustment to add completely new statements of fact or pleas-in-law provided they do not go outside the questions or dispute submitted to arbitration. The arbiter may ask for production of documents (leases, records, etc) and may consider that answers to the claim are necessary. Formerly he could issue an order to that effect but there is no specific authority for this procedure under the present Act. If answers are allowed it should be of consent. It is obviously desirable in many cases to have the parties' respective averments of fact incorporated into a document like a court record but the co-operation of both parties is required for this, as there is no statutory warrant for it.

HEARING AND INSPECTION

The arbiter's next step will be probably to fix a hearing of the parties, and an inspection of the farm. In certain circumstances he is not even bound to hear parties, and an inspection may be dispensed with.

In many cases the first hearing may, with advantage, be at the farm and unless the parties are sharply in conflict on important facts and questions of law, a very informal hearing may suffice. After an informal hearing and an inspection (where necessary), the arbiter may in very simple cases be sufficiently informed to enable him to issue his award. There is, however, a danger in allowing proceedings to be too informal and if there are questions of fact in dispute it is better to proceed with a proof with opportunity for examination and cross-examination. The matters which fall within an arbiter's jurisdiction are now more important than ever before. In rent arbitrations a proof is desirable, having regard to the complexity of the calculation which the arbiter requires to make. He will probably also require to inspect any comparables.

If notice is issued for a hearing and inspection, the arbiter should not then take any evidence except with the consent of both parties, because one party might say he had had no intimation that evidence was to be taken, and that, therefore, he had not prepared for it. The inspection is for the purpose of enabling the arbiter to see the condition of the farm, its buildings, fences and drains, etc so far as necessary to enable him to deal with the claims. He should have the fields, and parts of buildings, fences, or drains, in respect of which claims are made, pointed out to him. The court has held that the mere fact that the tenant met the arbiters upon the ground and gave them information outwith the presence of the landlord was not sufficient reason for reducing an award, but that is a practice which should be avoided. So far as the arbiter can see anything with his own eyes, he is entitled to refuse to listen to evidence of or concerning it, but this step should rarely be taken. He cannot, however, refuse to receive evidence of previous condition (which he could not himself be aware of) if a comparison of past with present conditions is relevant.

As a rule, the arbiter should not proceed with the arbitration or even with the inspection in the presence of only one of the parties. If, however, due notice has been given a party cannot complain if the arbiter proceeds in his absence.

EVIDENCE

Although there are cases in which no proof is required or should be allowed – and the arbiter is generally entitled to decide whether and what proof should be taken – there are cases in which it would be wrong to refuse to hear evidence. Wherever relevant facts not within his knowledge are in question, proof should be allowed, and he may at any time before making his award permit or require the production of further evidence. In fact, the arbiter should never fail to follow such procedure as is essential to justice. In one case the court set aside an award on account of the arbiter taking into account evidence by one side only where he had decided no proof was necessary. In the sheriff court, an arbiter was held justified on the evidence of one witness and after an inspection of the farm, in holding that the tenant was justified in refusing to accept the landlord's offer to withdraw the notice to quit. No evidence should be taken except at a place, date and hour, of which both parties have had reasonable notice. If the arbiter has ruled out any question or claim as irrelevant, he should not hear evidence on it. He may, however, defer his decision on relevancy until after hearing evidence and, where he finds anything relevant, he must allow proof on it provided he has not all the necessary facts within his own knowledge as an expert. If proof is allowed, the parties must also have the opportunity of addressing the arbiter on the effect of the evidence and any matters of law arising from it, should they so desire. Questions of relevancy may come up at the proof if there is no preliminary hearing on the question and may either be disposed of or 'proof before answer' may be allowed.

The arbiter may rely on his personal knowledge of facts relevant to the question at issue. He is not bound to hear expert evidence on any matters on which he is able to judge without such evidence, but the better practice is to hear the evidence in case the arbiter's prima facie view is mistaken.

He may take the opinion or advice of a man of skill, such as an architect, builder or engineer. He is not, however, bound to act on such opinion or advice. He cannot bind himself in advance to adopt the report of any expert, for that would practically amount to substituting an expert for himself as arbiter. If he has appointed a layman as his clerk, the arbiter is entitled to call in the services of a law agent for his guidance on questions of law, and for framing a stated case, award, or other document. He is not bound by the views either of his clerk or of such agent. With the consent of parties, he can submit a question of law to counsel, but parties would not necessarily be bound by counsel's opinion.

The arbiter is not bound to have evidence taken down in shorthand or recorded, but where both parties request him to do so, he should have this done.

> 'The parties to the arbitration, and all persons claiming through them respectively, shall subject to any legal objection—
>> (a) submit to be examined by the arbiter on oath or affirmation in relation to the matters in dispute' (Schedule 7, paragraph 6).

'Persons claiming through them respectively' may possibly apply to cases where the incoming tenants take over the obligations of the landlord, or where assignees come in place of the landlord or the tenant.

'Subject to any legal objection' would appear to refer to confidentiality, mental competency, or the age of the witness. It is thought that, just as in ordinary judicial proceedings, agent and client are not bound to disclose communications between them in relation to the subject-matter of the arbitration.

'On oath or affirmation'. The parties and persons claiming through them 'shall ... submit to be examined ... on oath or affirmation' and it would appear that the arbiter should insist on their doing so.

As regards witnesses, there is no absolute obligation under the Schedule which reads: 'The arbiter shall have power to administer oaths, and to take the affirmation of parties and witnesses appearing, and witnesses shall, if the arbiter thinks fit, be examined on oath or affirmation', but better practice is to examine witnesses on oath or affirmation.

In both cases the party to give evidence may choose between oath and affirmation.

The usual form of oath is: 'I swear by Almighty God that I shall tell the truth, the whole truth, and nothing but the truth'.

The corresponding form of affirmation is: 'I solemnly, sincerely, and truly affirm and declare that I shall truly answer make to all questions as shall be asked of me touching the matters in difference in the arbitration.'

The Civil Evidence (Scotland) Act 1988 is specifically applied to arbitration, so that corroboration is no longer necessary.

The parties and witnesses must also produce all samples, books, deeds, papers, accounts, writings and documents within their possession or power respectively, which may be required or called for, or do all other things which, during the proceedings, the arbiter may require. This is all subject to any legal objection (already referred to) and to relevancy to the question at issue.

When a witness objects to produce documents on the ground of confidentiality, the party who has obtained an order from the arbiter for the recovery of documents may apply by summary application to the sheriff to compel production. The sheriff, in dealing with the application, will determine the question of confidentiality. An application may also be made to the sheriff to order a witness to produce documents for the recovery of which diligence had been granted.

It is thought that a formal specification of documents called for is not necessary, though it may be desirable to have one, especially where the production of numerous documents is required. In any case, an order by the arbiter for production must be obtained before applying to the sheriff.

If application for warrant to cite witnesses and havers (ie a person holding documents or other productions) is made to the sheriff court, it should be by initial writ; if to the Court of Session, by petition; and, in the latter case, where it is desired to obtain the evidence of witnesses in England, application should be made for the appointment of a commission for that purpose. The court will not grant warrant to cite a witness resident out of Scotland to attend before an arbiter in Scotland. Where the application is by either party, it should be made with the concurrence of the arbiter.

Parties are entitled to be present along with their agents and counsel during the whole proceedings, notwithstanding that they may intend to give evidence themselves. Unless the parties otherwise agree, the arbiter should follow the usual judicial course of excluding all witnesses (other than the parties or their agents) not examined while the evidence of other witnesses is being taken. A request is frequently made to allow expert witnesses to remain during the proof. This may shorten proceedings, but if there is opposition to the request it is better for the experts to withdraw. A witness who gives false evidence in an arbitration is guilty of perjury and may be prosecuted.

STATED CASE

The arbiter is, generally speaking, final on questions of fact, but on questions of law, or mixed law and fact, he may, either on his own initiative or at the request of either party, state a case for the opinion of the sheriff (Schedule 7, paragraph 20). This does not apply where the arbiter has been appointed by the Secretary of State or the Land Court in a rent arbitration. In that case the arbiter may at the request of either party or on his own initiative state a case on any question of law arising in the course of the arbitration for the opinion of the Land Court (Schedule 7, paragraph 22). There is no provision in paragraph 22 for the arbiter to be directed to state a case to the Land Court but the parties still have the opportunity to appeal to the Land Court against the arbiter's decision in terms of section 61(2). A case may be stated 'at any stage of the proceedings'. From this it follows that a case cannot be stated after the final award has been issued, as the act of issuing the award brings the proceedings to an end.

It is sometimes difficult to determine whether a question of law is involved. The interpretation of statute is a matter of law, but interpretation of a lease or agreement may involve questions of fact and law. It is a question of law whether facts found are sufficient to justify the arbiter in arriving at a particular decision – for example, whether a tenancy has been terminated. In general, the court will not interfere, even though the arbiter has erred, where a pure question of fact alone is involved. Where it is clear that the arbiter had facts before him on which he might competently arrive at his decision the court will not interfere, except in the case of appeal to the Land Court under section 61.

If the arbiter is of opinion that no question of law has arisen, he may decline to state a case, but (except where the arbiter has been appointed by the Secretary of State or Land Court in a rent arbitration) either party may apply to the sheriff to have him ordered to do so. It has been held that it is not the function of the court to entertain the kind of representations appropriate before an arbiter.

The duty is on the arbiter to state the case, which is generally drafted by his clerk, and should be submitted to the parties for revisal.

A case should be in three parts:

(1) a narrative containing a clear statement of the relevant facts found proved or admitted;
(2) the contentions of parties;
(3) the question or questions of law.

The facts found should be confined to such facts as are relevant to the question of law, and no superfluous narrative should be given. If either party requires a particular fact to be stated, and the fact has been proved or admitted, the arbiter should state it unless he is clearly satisfied that it is not relevant. If the arbiter should decline to state a material and relevant fact, which has been proved or admitted, he may be ordered to do so by the sheriff. It is important to note that to state the facts does not require an elaborate recital of the evidence. In fact a recital of the evidence is positively unhelpful unless the arbiter states clearly what facts he found to be proved as a result of hearing that evidence. The bare facts based on the evidence led, and on which the questions of law depend, should be stated by the arbiter as he finds them, but the arbiter should state enough to make it plain how the question of law arises.

The contentions of the parties should be set out as nearly as may be in their own words – or altered by the arbiter merely for the purpose of making them free from ambiguity.

The question or questions of law should generally be in the precise terms in which the question is put forward by the parties, though there may be variation or adjustment by the arbiter for the purpose of making the point at issue clear.

If the case, as stated, is ambiguous, or if it is not in terms to enable the question of law to be fairly dealt with, the sheriff may remit it back to the arbiter for amendment. In England a case was remitted back to enable one party to instruct counsel where the other party had done so. It may be open to doubt whether the courts in Scotland would follow this case.

It would be misconduct on the part of the arbiter if, when requested, he refused to state a case or to delay his award until an application could be made to the court, provided that his findings upon a question of fact did not render immaterial the question of law.

When the case had been adjusted and signed, it falls to be lodged in court by the arbiter's clerk and thereafter the arbiter need take no further steps regarding it until either party or the court itself informs him of the court's decision.

The stated case may be heard either by the sheriff or by the Sheriff Principal and practice varies from sheriffdom to sheriffdom. If it is heard by the sheriff there is no appeal to the Sheriff Principal (section 67). The sheriff or Sheriff Principal's decision is final, unless an appeal is taken by either party to the Inner House of the Court of Session as provided by the Rules of Court 267 to 273. There is no further appeal from the Court of Session to the House of Lords (Schedule 7, paragraph 21).

Where a case was stated and answered, it was held that a further case was incompetent regarding questions suggested by the decision on the first case arising out of other claims acquiesced in at the stating of the earlier case.

The arbiter must act in accordance with the opinion of the court.

As to expenses in a stated case, see under 'Expenses' below.

NOTE OF PROPOSED FINDINGS

It is usual for the arbiter to issue a note of his proposed findings, though he is not bound to do so. It is generally prudent to issue such a note, and, if desired, to hear parties or their agents thereon, or on the representations with reference thereto although the arbiter is not bound to do so.

A note of proposed findings is generally expedient where questions of law are involved, because it is desirable that parties should know how the arbiter proposes to answer such questions, in order that they may have an opportunity of applying for a stated case for the opinion of the court. The note of proposed findings, which may be in the form of a draft award, should be stated in clear language – preferably in numbered paragraphs arranged in logical order, and ought to cover all the questions included in the arbitration. It is sometimes convenient to include the arbiter's proposals regarding expenses. It is usual to allow a week to a fortnight for making representations.

The Tribunals and Inquiries Act 1971 applies to agricultural arbitrations where the appointment has been made by the Secretary of State. The effect of section 12 of the Act is that such an arbiter is bound to furnish a statement of the reasons for his decision, if requested to do so by a party to the arbitration.

There may, however, be questions as to the adequacy of reasons given. It has been held that reasons where given are to be treated as part of the award and must be adequate and substantial and that if they do not comply with the statutory provisions there is an error of law on the face of the award. On the other hand it has been pointed out that 'it must have been realised that certain tribunals could do no more than state that the case was not made or that the figure was certain sums' – Parker, L J in *ex parte Woodhouse* (*The Times*, 18th June 1960). In a case regarding an award which found that a tenant had failed to remedy a breach of his lease it was held that there was no need to detail the precise extent of the failure to remedy the breach or reasons for minor findings of fact. This was not, however, a case under what is now the 1991 Act, the arbiter having been appointed by agreement.

EXPENSES

The expenses of and incidental to the arbitration and award are in the discretion of the arbiter, who is entitled to direct to and by whom and in what manner the expenses or any part thereof shall be paid.

The arbiter must deal with the expenses in his award, otherwise it may be set aside. It is sufficient, however, if he does so in the usual way by setting forth the proportions of expenses payable to or by the respective parties.

In the general case, the expenses commence with the appointment of the arbiter, and do not include anything done prior to that, except (1) the procedure for making the appointment; and (2) the framing and lodging of the claim. It is unlawful to include in the expenses of a statutory arbitration any expenses to a clerk unless such appointment was made after submission of the claim and answers to the arbiter and with either the consent of the parties or the sanction of the sheriff. The expenses of preparing a claim for compensation for disturbance are expressly referred to in section 35(2) of the 1991 Act. It is thought that expenses do not extend to the preceding statutory procedure such as giving notice of intention to claim (where notice is required), nor to the making of the claim, because these are essential conditions of, and precedent to, a claim, and not expenses of, or incidental to, the arbitration. As such they correspond to extrajudicial expenses.

The arbiter has a general discretion in dealing with expenses and is not bound to follow the procedure of the courts regarding them. His discretion must be properly exercised. Where he departs from the settled practice of the courts, that of awarding expenses to the successful party, such an exercise of his discretion must be judicial and not capricious. He need not, however, state in terms the reason for his departure from the usual practice. The House of Lords held that it was not incompetent for the arbiter to find the successful party liable in expenses where he claimed £740 for dilapidations and was awarded only £71.

The arbiter is directed to take into consideration, in dealing with expenses, the reasonableness or unreasonableness of the claim of either party, either in respect of amount or otherwise and any unreasonable demand for, or refusal to supply, particulars and generally all the circumstances of the case, and he may disallow the expenses of any witness whom he considers unnecessarily called, and any expenses he may consider to have been unnecessarily incurred. This direction is a salutary one, and is obviously intended to put a check on the practice of making extravagant claims. Unfortunately, few arbiters appear to act on it effectively. The direction should, of course, be applied in a commonsense way. Parties cannot be expected to estimate their claims with exactitude, and, in some cases, these may be greatly in excess of the amount ultimately awarded. But it is thought that the arbiter is entitled to consider whether there was a reasonable ground for stating the claim as lodged. The arbiter in considering his award as to expenses must direct his mind to the most important element in the case.

The expenses are subject to taxation by the auditor of the sheriff court, on the application of either party, and the taxation is subject to review by the sheriff.

It is thought that an arbiter should not award expenses on the basis of agent and client.

The remuneration of an arbiter appointed by the Secretary of State is to be fixed by him, and if so fixed, it is thought that there can be no taxation of the amount by the auditor of the Court of Session or sheriff court. Otherwise, the arbiter's fees, as part of the expenses in the arbitration, are subject to taxation by the auditor of the sheriff court.

The fees, etc, of the clerk are held to be earned, though the arbiter died before issuing an award, and the parties cannot deny the clerk's right to his fee by delaying to take up the award.

The expenses of a stated case fall to be dealt with by the court, not by the arbiter. These expenses do not include the preparation of the stated case and work incidental thereto, which work is part of the expenses incidental to the arbitration, and ought to be covered by the arbiter's award of expenses apart from the expenses proper of the stated case. Generally, he should deal with the expenses of preparation of the case consistently with the court's decision regarding expenses.

In one case, where, contrary to general practice, a conclusion for expenses was sought against the arbiter, he offered not to appear if that conclusion was withdrawn. On this being refused he lodged defences confined entirely to the question of expenses, and was successful. An English case decided that if the arbiter takes part in proceedings to set aside his award, costs can be given against him.

THE AWARD

The arbiter is required to make and sign his award within three months after his appointment (whether by the parties or by the Secretary of State), or within such longer period as (either before or after the expiry of the period of three months) the parties may agree on, or the Secretary of State may direct (Schedule 7, paragraph 8).

The arbiter should be careful to cease acting after the period has expired and until an extension is granted.

A question may arise in the case where the arbiter has issued an interim award which has been acted on, and the arbitration lapses in consequence of the award not being made and signed within the statutory period. It is thought that the interim award would stand in that case as in the case where the arbitration lapses by the death of the arbiter after an interim award has been made.

A distinction has been drawn between interim and partial or part awards. It is thought that the provision for interim awards was mainly intended to allow the whole sum payable in respect of any particular head or item of claim to be awarded, and not merely so much to account thereof. If this course is followed, the interim award would be practically final as regards the heads or item of claim embraced in it and regarding which no difficulty need arise in the event of the arbitration lapsing from any cause and a new arbiter being appointed. In order to have this effect, it is well to state in the interim award that though otherwise it is intended to be final as regards the items with which it deals, it is issued under reservation of other items and all questions of expenses. An interim award, which would show clearly that it is interim, may be sustained even though the final award is reduced or invalid.

The award must be in the form prescribed by the Secretary of State in the Agricultural Holdings (Specification of Forms) (Scotland) Order 1991 (see Appendix 5), varied to meet the circumstances. The Order requires that when the award relates to variation of rent and the arbiter has been appointed by the Secretary of State or the Land Court, it should contain the following particulars:

(1) a summary of the statement of case submitted by or on behalf of the landlord;
(2) a summary of the statement of case submitted by or on behalf of the tenant;
(3) details of any evidence of the condition of the holding, including the state of the landlord's and tenant's fixed equipment, which emerged at the inspection of the holding and were taken into account;
(4) a summary of the relevant evidence considered at any hearing;
(5) an appraisal of the evidence submitted under (1) to (4);
(6) details of any other evidence of open market rents for comparable subjects introduced by the arbiter on which the parties had an opportunity to comment and which the arbiter took into account;
(7) the reasons for seeking evidence (in terms of the factors specifically

listed in section 13(4) of the 1991 Act) other than evidence of open market rents for comparable subjects in the surrounding area;

(8) details of the factors specified in section 13(4) of the 1991 Act which the arbiter considers it desirable to take into account;

(9) an indication of the weight attached by the arbiter to the various criteria taken into account;

(10) an explanation of any adjustment made by the arbiter to take account of differences in holdings used for comparative purpose;

(11) any other explanation necessary to clarify the arbiter's decision.

An award in a form materially different from the statutory form could probably be reduced. Awards must be tested.

Alternative awards – for example, awarding a certain sum in a particular event and a different sum in another event – are not competent under the statute.

The arbiter is bound (Schedule 7, paragraph 12(a)) to state separately in his award, the amounts awarded in respect of the several claims referred to him. This does not mean that he must give a detailed statement – for example, if there are long and detailed claims for manures and feeding-stuffs – it is thought that he need only give the amount awarded under (1) purchased artificial manures, and (2) feeding-stuffs. There are usually separate items for temporary pasture, for disturbance, manures, feeding-stuffs, etc, and each of these should be regarded as a separate claim, and the same course should be followed regarding the other claims respectively. In short, there should be an item in the award for each claim according to its class and character, and generally following the relative language of the Schedules. In an English case an award was set aside for not stating the amounts awarded for each item of claim.

The arbiter must also, if required by either party, specify the amounts awarded in respect of any particular improvement or any particular matter the subject of the award, and the award must fix a day, not later than one month after its delivery, for the payment of the sum or sums awarded as compensation, expenses or otherwise (paragraph 14).

An arbiter has power at common law to alter or cancel his award, even after it has been signed, so long as it has not been issued. It is thought that this power can be exercised by an arbiter under the 1991 Act, so long as the period for making the award has not expired. He is expressly given power to correct any clerical mistake or error arising from an accidental slip or omission. This is supplementary to the common law power already referred to, and is evidently intended to operate even after the award has been issued, but this may not be quite free from doubt. When the award is issued the arbiter is *functus officio*, and if his award does not embrace the matters really in issue, he cannot of his own motion treat it as no award and issue another. In England it was held that an arbiter could supplement his award after issue by a letter disposing of expenses with which he had omitted to deal. A report and valuation of a house was not probative and was held not to be an effective award and could not be sued on. In an arbitration under the 1991 Act, however, an award was not probative – ie signed before witnesses – but it was held that the claimant could sue on it on proof that the document was in fact the award of the arbiters and oversman.

An award or agreement under the Act as to compensation, expenses or otherwise, if any sum payable thereunder is not paid within a month after it becomes due, may (if it contains a consent to registration) be recorded in the Books of Council and Session or in the Sheriff Court Books, and is enforceable in like manner as a recorded decree-arbitral (section 65).

REDUCTION OF AWARD

There is no appeal in the ordinary sense, against an award under the 1991 Act, but there are grounds on which an award may be set aside or reduced. Paragraph 24 of Schedule 7 provides that where an arbiter has misconducted himself or an arbitration or award has been improperly procured the sheriff may set the award aside. Misconduct may be merely technical such as failure to issue the award within the time allowed under paragraph 8 of Schedule 7 or more serious misconduct which could result in reduction of an award in any arbitration.

An award may be challenged because:

(1) it is contrary to the Act of Regulations 1695;
(2) it is bad at common law:
(3) it does not provide details required in terms of section 68 with regard to sheep stock valuations.

Under (1) the grounds are corruption, bribery and falsehood. Corruption must be actual, the earlier cases which treated any failure in duty by the arbiter as constructive corruption having been overruled by the House of Lords.

As to bribery, it has been held improper for an arbiter to accept hospitality from one of the parties; and, if the hospitality is given with the object, or has the effect, of inducing the arbiter to act unfairly, the court will set aside the award; but the mere dining or lunching with one of the parties and the witnesses, in the absence of the other party, will not, of itself, necessarily invalidate the award. Treating the arbiter, where there was no evidence of corrupt intention to influence him, was not enough to reduce the award.

As to falsehood, it is thought that dishonesty or deceit on the arbiter's part, which affected the award, would afford ground of reduction. Despite its comprehensive terms the Act of Regulations does not preclude reduction at the common law.

The chief grounds on which reduction of an award may be granted at common law are:

(1) where the award is bad on the face of it, ambiguous, uncertain, or improperly executed according to what formalities are appropriate;
(2) misconduct or improper conduct of the arbiter – for example, examining a witness on one side in the absence of the other party or his agent, although in one case the award was not reduced because the pursuers had been successful on the point at issue;
(3) where there has been a mistake which the arbiter admits. An error of judgment is not a ground for reduction;
(4) where the arbiter has acted *ultra vires*, ie has exceeded his powers by, for example, including matters not referred to him;
(5) where the award does not exhaust the reference;
(6) an arbiter cannot make an order *ad factum praestandum*, ie an order to do some act. This is because a failure to carry out such an order is punishable as contempt of court and an arbiter has no power to inflict such punishment and thereby to make his order effective.

In the sheriff court two unsuccessful attempts to upset awards on the ground of misconduct may be mentioned. It was averred in one that the arbiter appointed to fix a new rent had not made an adequate inspection of the subjects. In the other the principal averments were that the arbiter had not called for claims or evidence or had a hearing, but the sheriff held that the submission was sufficiently specific to inform the arbiter what questions he had to decide and that otherwise his procedure was not open to challenge.

Although it is true that an arbiter has a wide latitude as to what procedure he follows and as to what proof he may allow, he will generally be well advised to call for detailed claims and to hesitate before he refuses any not unreasonable request by a party for proof or hearing. He may be competent to judge for himself in many cases, but if the parties are allowed the opportunity of stating their own case, they cannot be heard to make any effective complaint at a later stage.

The following dictum of Lord President Clyde is useful as a summary of one aspect of the law:

> 'If it could be proved that in arriving at his award an arbiter had invented the facts to suit some view of his own, or had fashioned the law to suit his own ideas then however innocent might be the eccentricity which had seduced him into such a travesty of judicial conduct, his behaviour would naturally imply that justice had not been done: he would be guilty of ... misconduct, and his award would be reduced' (*Mitchell-Gill v Buchan*).[6]

Moreover, the arbiter must observe certain understood rules of conduct to ensure that injustice is not done. He must act judiciously and not capriciously.

A general submission is limited by the claims of parties and cannot be held unexhausted, simply because a possible claim has not been dealt with. Where one of the parties reserved a competent claim, and the other party did not object, a plea that the award (which contained a reservation of the claim) did not exhaust the submission was repelled.

Where it is possible, from the award itself, to explain it to the effect that part is unobjectionable, that part may be upheld, and only what is objectionable reduced.

An award may be cut down where it is obtained by fraud by one of the parties. Irregularities in conducting the arbitration may be waived by the parties' consent, after the irregularities have been discovered; and parties may, either expressly or by their actings, so extend the limits of a submission as to bar the plea of *ultra vires*.

A refusal to make a reference to oath, the admission of incompetent evidence, oral or documentary, or the rejection of evidence which a court of law would have admitted, are not always sufficient grounds for reducing an award.

A refusal to state a case is not good ground for reduction because the proper remedy is an application to the sheriff to order a stated case, although it would be misconduct for the arbiter having refused to state a case forthwith to issue his award before application to the sheriff can be made.

Where it was contended that an arbiter had shown bias, Lord President Clyde held that the court ought not to decide a matter concerning the bona fides of an arbiter without giving him an opportunity to be heard in the process.

6 1921 SC 390.

CHAPTER 13

VALUATION OF BOUND SHEEP STOCKS

It has long been customary in leases of hill sheep farms to provide that the sheep stock is bound to the ground; ie that the tenant at his waygoing must leave the stock and the landlord or incoming tenant take it over at valuation. The main reasons for having a sheep stock bound are:

(1) to safeguard the incoming occupier from taking over the hill grazing without stock and then being faced with the many physical and economic problems of hefting strange sheep of perhaps unsuitable and irregular ages to an unaccustomed environment; and

(2) to ensure that there will be a sheep stock on a hill from when it is relet.

A hill sheep stock which has been built up over a period and is in regular ages, acclimatised and hefted has a value as a going concern greater than the stock would realise if removed to a market and sold. By 'acclimatisation' is meant not only being accustomed to the local climate but also the development of greater immunity to disease. 'Hefting' means getting the sheep used to the run of the hill or accustomed to remain on their own ground although there are no fences. Much difficulty has arisen from attempts to assess the additional value to be ascribed to these factors. It was at one time the custom to determine the likely values if stock were sold in the market and to make percentage additions. This practice was, however, disapproved in *Williamson v Stewart*[1] in which the court held that it was the duty of the arbiters (or oversman) to value the sheep upon the basis of their value to an occupant of the farm, in view of the arbiter's estimate of the return to be realised by such occupant from them in accordance with the course of prudent management, in lambs, wool, and price when ultimately sold, and not upon the basis either

(1) of market value only; or

(2) the cost and loss which would be involved in the restocking of the farm with a like stock if the present stock were removed.

The arbiter was entitled to take into account both current market prices and the special qualities of the sheep, both in themselves and in relation to the ground which in his opinion would tend either to enhance or to diminish the return to be realised from them by an occupant of the farm. The judges agreed that two meanings can be given to the expression 'market value'. There is the market value which an individual sheep will bring if it is exposed in the auction mart. On the other hand, if a sheep stock is sold on the ground and as a whole, it has a considerably greater 'market value' in the sense of the price an incoming tenant competing with others will be prepared to pay for the stock. The measure of the additional value should be the expenditure of the previous tenant in building up the stock at a time when it could not earn its full income qualified by conditions existing at the time which will determine what price it is economically possible for an incoming tenant to pay. A flock can only be said to be complete when the stock is not only healthy and acclimatised, but of regular ages and properly graded according

1 1912 SC 235.

to numbers. If a flock has to be built up by the gradual purchase of sheep in the markets, there is no doubt that a considerable period will elapse before it will produce the best results and it is this loss of income which an incoming tenant taking over a complete stock is saved and which he has properly to pay for. In an 'open valuation' (ie one to which the provisions of section 68 of the 1991 Act do not apply) the basis of valuation should be stated in the lease or submission. In a submission to value a sheep stock at 'the actual price and simple market value of the sheep without any deductions or additions of any kind' there was a clause that 'if the arbiter either intentionally or by error in judgment or by a clerical error or for any other cause whatsoever' included in his award anything beyond market value the award should be null and void. The valuation was made on the basis of its value to the incoming tenant without regard to the prices which would have been got in the ring and the award was reduced: *Williamson*.

Before they were regulated by statute sheep stock valuations were much criticised for being too high. It was said that arbiters, by making excessive allowances for hefting and acclimatisation, had been fixing the valuation of hill sheep stocks at wholly artificial figures far above market value. Although the court had decided that something more than ring price was justified when the value of a stock, as such, of regular ages and established on the farm, was to be fixed, some arbiters undoubtedly had made quite excessive allowances. The result had been detrimental to the industry by putting an excessive burden on the landlord or incoming tenant, who had to pay an uneconomic price for the sheep stock he took over at entry.

In an effort to minimise the effect of these practices the Sheep Stocks Valuation (Scotland) Act was passed in 1937. This was amended in 1946 and 1986 and all the provisions of the Hill Farming Acts relating to sheep stock valuation have now been consolidated in sections 68 to 72 of the 1991 Act.

Sections 68 to 72 of and Schedules 9 and 10 to the Act make special provision for sheep stock valuation, with definitions which vary from those generally applicable under the Act. For this purpose 'agricultural holding' is defined restrictively to mean a piece of land held by a tenant which is wholly or in part pastoral, and which is not let to the tenant during and in connection with his continuance in any office, appointment or employment held under the landlord.

Section 61(7) provides that the general arbitration provisions contained in sections 60 and 61 are not to apply to sheep stock valuations.

The word 'arbiter' is not defined for the purposes of the general provisions but for the purposes of sheep stock valuation is to include an oversman and any person required to determine the value or price of sheep stock in pursuance of any provision in the lease of an agricultural holding.

A 'sheep stock valuation' is where under a lease of an agricultural holding, the tenant is required at the termination of the tenancy to leave the stock of sheep on the holding to be taken over by the landlord or the incoming tenant at a price or valuation to be fixed by arbitration.

It will be seen that these provisions in the Act do not apply on the transfer of a bound stock between ingoing and outgoing owner occupiers where the basis of valuation must be fixed by contract.

The basis on which the arbiter must value the stock is determined by the date of commencement of the lease whose termination gives rise to the valuation. If the tenant has held under a succession of tenancies, the arbiter must look at the commencement date of the latest tenancy. The commencement date of the tenancy also has certain procedural consequences.

The relevant dates are:

(1) before or on 6th November 1946;
(2) after 6th November 1946 and before 1st December 1986; and
(3) on or after 1st December 1986.

Different criteria will also apply according to whether the termination is at Whitsunday or Martinmas.

LEASE COMMENCING BEFORE OR ON 6TH NOVEMBER 1946

The arbiter is directed to show the basis of valuation of each class of stock. He is also to state separately any amounts included in respect of acclimatisation or hefting or of any other consideration or factor for which he has made special allowance.

LEASE COMMENCING AFTER 6TH NOVEMBER 1946 AND BEFORE 1ST DECEMBER 1986 (SCH 9)

Whitsunday termination

The arbiter has to ascertain the '3-year average price' of ewes and of lambs sold off the farm, basing his figures on the sale prices and allowing for shotts as these are ascertained by him. Where, however, the number of ewes and lambs sold in the three preceding years has been less than half the total number sold, the '3-year average price' is determined by the Land Court on the application of the parties, the court basing its findings on the experience of similar farms in the same district. What happens if one party refuses to make an application is not stated, but if the statute is to be made to work, an application by one party must in these circumstances be competent. No form of application is provided. It is assumed that once it has established the '3-year average price' the court refers further procedure back to the arbiters – an extremely dilatory provision. Having arrived at the '3-year average price' the arbiters may adjust the figure by 20 per cent, more or less having regard to 'the general condition of the stock under valuation and to the profit which the purchaser may reasonably expect it to earn'. In the case of leases entered into before 15th May 1963 (the date of the passing of the Agriculture (Miscellaneous Provisions) Act 1963) the adjustment permitted is 50p. The resultant figure is the 'basic ewe value' and the 'basic lamb value'. The arbiter then makes the following further adjustments. He adds 30 per cent of basic ewe value per head in the case of ewes (or 75p for pre-15th May 1963 leases). He adjusts the price of twin lambs as he considers proper (single lambs being at 'basic lamb value'). Ewe hoggs are valued at two-thirds of the combined basic value of ewe and lamb, adjusted within a limit of 10 per cent (or 25p) up or down having regard to quality and condition. Tups are taken at the value put on them by the arbiter, allowing for acclimatisation or any other factor he thinks fit. Wool is not taken into account and no specific allowance can be made for acclimatisation (except for tups) or hefting or regular ages, although presumably these factors fall to be taken into account in adjusting the three-year average. Eild sheep are valued at the ewe value, subject to adjustment for quality and condition, and shotts at not more than two-thirds of the value of good sheep of the same age and class.

Martinmas termination

After fixing the 'basic ewe value' ewes (including gimmers) are taken at the value plus 30 per cent (or 75p) per head; and ewe lambs at basic ewe value subject to an adjustment of 10 per cent (or 25p) per head up or down, having regard to quality and condition.

These provisions are based on the assumption that reliable evidence of value will be available from sales of cast ewes each autumn through the markets and that fluctuations in value will be suitably corrected by taking an average over three years. The former assumption is no longer justified as it is not now the usual practice to sell stock from the hill at auction in the traditional way and the latter assumption has not been justified in times of high inflation. The Land Court has strongly criticised the operation of these provisions and drawn attention to the difficulty of operating its provisions and to the inequitable results which these may have. In *Secretary of State for Scotland v Anderson*[2] the court observed that it was probable that the provisions would become inoperable because stock was being sold privately and not by auction. In *Tuffnell and Nether Whitehaugh Co Ltd*[3] the court again referred to the lack of evidence. There having been sales of cast ewes in only two of the three relevant years the court had to supply figures from its own knowledge and experience. It also drew attention to the very low valuation which resulted from application of the 1946 Act provision being approximately two-fifths of the value the court would have fixed under the 1937 Act. After explaining the valuation the court's note states:

> 'We have valued the sheep, as explained in the note above, by the provisions laid down in the 1946 Act, although as a result of changes brought about by economic forces the whole foundation of the 1946 Act has been rendered inaccurate and unreliable, and as a method of achieving a fair valuation is now totally discredited and produces an inequitable award.'

LEASE COMMENCING ON OR AFTER 1ST DECEMBER 1986 (SCH 10)

Whitsunday termination

The arbiter is to ascertain the number of and the prices realised for the regular cast ewes and the lambs sold off the hill from the stock in each of the three preceding years. He is to inspect the stock to determine the number of shotts at the time of the valuation and calculates the proportion of shotts to the total number of ewes and lambs. He must then calculate an average price per ewe and an average price per lamb for each of these three years. The statute assumes that the percentage of shotts to the total flock will be constant. He must therefore disregard the lowest prices achieved of the same proportion of total sales as the number of shotts bears to the total flock. Having calculated the average price per ewe and the average price per lamb for each of the three years, the arbiter then takes the mean of the figures to produce the '3-year average price for regular cast ewes' and the '3-year

2 1967 SLCR App 117.
3 1977 SLT (Land Ct) 14.

average price for lambs'. Provision is made for the Land Court to fix the prices in the absence of evidence of sale prices. Applying the criteria of the general condition of the stock and the profit which the purchaser may reasonably expect it to earn, the arbiter may adjust the price within the limits of 30 per cent upwards or downwards to produce the 'basic ewe value'. The three-year average price for lambs is to be adjusted within the limits of 20 per cent upwards or downwards to produce the 'basic lamb value'. The Schedule then provides how each of these is to be applied to the various classes of sheep.

Martinmas termination

The basic ewe value is determined by ascertaining the average price during the current and the two preceding years, disregarding one-fifth of the total of regular cast ewes sold in each year being the ewes sold at the lowest price. The mean of the three prices so calculated may be adjusted within the limits of 30 per cent upwards or downwards to produce the basic ewe value which is then applied with various adjustments to different classes of stock, as specified in the Schedule.

PROCEDURAL MATTERS

As an alternative to the manner of determination referred to in the lease, the Land Court may determine any question which would fall to be decided by a sheep stock valuation. Where the lease was entered into before or on 6th November 1946 the Land Court only has jurisdiction on the joint application of the parties. Where the lease was entered into after that date, either party may apply to the Land Court. In determining any question, the Land Court is to apply the same basis of valuation as would an arbiter.

Section 71 provides that evidence of sales to enable the arbiter or the court to make the necessary calculations shall be provided to the arbiter and shall be open to inspection by the other party to the valuation. Not less than twenty-eight days before determination of the question, the outgoing tenant is to submit a statement of the sales from the stock for the three years which are relevant to enable the valuer to make his calculations. He also requires to submit such sale notes and other evidence as may be required by the valuer to vouch the accuracy of the statement of sales. It is considered that 'sale' means a genuine sale and that the arbiter is entitled to disregard any sales which he finds in fact to be collusive sales at an artificially high price intended to distort his calculation for the benefit of the outgoing tenant.

The arbiter is required to set out particulars in his award to enable his calculations to be checked. Under Schedule 9 he must show the three-year average prices for ewes and lambs or the mean average prices according to whether it is a Whitsunday or Martinmas valuation. He must show any adjustment to reach the basic ewe value. He must set out the numbers of each class of stock and the value, and any further adjustments made.

Similar particulars have to be shown under Schedule 10.

If an arbiter fails to set out the basis of his valuation, his award may be set aside by the sheriff.

If the lease was entered into after 10th June 1937, the arbiter may state a case to the sheriff on a question of law arising in the course of the arbitration.

A stated case is not competent after issue of the award. The arbiter has a discretion as to whether a case should be stated unless he is directed by the sheriff to state the case. Either party may apply to the sheriff for a direction. The decision of the sheriff may be appealed to the Court of Session but no further.

Because of the hardship to the outgoing tenant, which could be caused while a stated case is dealt with, the arbiter may order payment to the outgoing tenant of a sum to account of the sum that may ultimately be awarded. Before doing so the arbiter must be satisfied that the sum ultimately to be found due will be not less than the amount of the interim award.

CHAPTER 14

ARBITRATIONS AND VALUATIONS (OUTSIDE THE ACT) GENERALLY BETWEEN AWAYGOING AND INCOMING TENANTS

The usual awaygoing valuations are, by section 61(7) of the 1991 Act, excluded from the arbitration provisions of section 60 and Schedule 7 and fall to be dealt with as common law arbitrations. Accordingly it is competent for parties to have these valuations made by one arbiter or two arbiters and an oversman as they may decide. Prior to the passing of the Administration of Justice (Scotland) Act 1972 there was no appeal by way of stated case or otherwise in a common law arbitration. There is provision for a stated case on a question of law in a sheep stock valuation under section 69 of the 1991 Act but in all other waygoing valuations the parties had to accept the decision of the arbiters whether it was in accordance with the law or not. Section 3(1) of the 1972 Act provides:

'Subject to express provision to the contrary in an agreement to refer to arbitration, the arbiter or oversman may on the application of a party to the arbitration and shall if the Court of Session on such an application so directs at any stage in the arbitration state a case for the opinion of that court on any question of law arising in the arbitration.'

No appeal to the House of Lords is competent against the decision of the Court of Session on such a stated case.

The parties can still obtain finality in arbitration by expressly excluding section 3 in the submission. In terms of section 3(4) the section does not apply in relation to an agreement to refer to arbitration made before the commencement of the Act. The 'agreement to refer' means the arbitration clause in the lease and not the submission to the arbiter.

All claims arising out of the tenancy (either during the currency or at the termination of the lease) at the instance of the landlord or the tenant against the other must be dealt with by arbitration under sections 60 and 61 of the 1991 Act.

It was held by the House of Lords in *Stewart v Williamson*[1] that there is no essential distinction to be made between valuation and arbitration in Scots law and that accordingly the arbitration provisions in the Agricultural Holdings (Scotland) Act 1908 applied to sheep stock valuation. A distinction is commonly made and it is said that where arbiters are merely appointed as skilled men to put a value on such things as dung, crops, fallow or sheep stock, which they can inspect, though called arbiters they are really valuers. The distinction is perhaps in the subject-matter rather than the nature of the proceedings but in practice the courts will not require valuers to follow strictly the rules of arbitration, or reduce an award or valuation merely on the ground of irregularity of form of procedure. At the same time, it is generally

1 1910 SC (HL) 47.

desirable, where there is a formal minute of submission, to have a formal award (see forms in Appendix 1). As a rule, it is safe to act in accordance with long-established practice in these matters. A valuer is subject to an action for loss caused by his negligence whereas an arbiter is not.

It is frequently the case that, in connection with such valuations, questions arise which might appear to be appropriate for settlement in a proper and formal arbitration, but where these questions are incidental to the valuations and must be dealt with in order to enable the valuations to be made, it is generally in the power of the arbiter (or valuer) to decide them, and even to hear evidence to enable him to do so. Such incidental arbitration questions are expressly excluded from the arbitration provisions of the 1991 Act by section 61(7). That subsection not only excludes the valuations of sheep stocks, dung, fallow, straw, crops, fences and other specific things the property of an outgoing tenant, agreed to be taken over at the termination of a tenancy by the proprietor or incoming tenant, but also any questions which it may be necessary to determine in order to ascertain the sum to be paid in pursuance of such an agreement, and whether such valuations and questions are referred to arbitration under the lease or not. This exclusion has the effect of throwing these questions back on the common law.

An arbiter (or valuer) appointed to value sheep stock has been held to have jurisdiction for the purposes of the valuation to determine what is the bona fide sheep stock. So also, where there is a reference to arbiters to value dung made after the sowing of the last green crop, in the event of dispute on the point the arbiters or oversman may hear evidence as to when the dung was made, and base the valuation on the facts as they find them. In short, it is assumed that where arbiters are appointed to value a thing, they are entitled to decide such incidental questions as may be necessary in order to enable them to make the valuation. This is consistent with the principles laid down by the court.

A submission should specify clearly how much dung is to be taken over. All dung up to one year old should generally be taken over. Arbiters should state in their award (or in an explanatory note) if they are including the value of unexhausted feeding-stuffs in their valuation of the dung or if that value is excluded. Different arbiters may have to settle the two questions and the tenant should not receive payment on two counts.

THE SUBJECTS OF COMMON LAW ARBITRATION OR VALUATION

It was formerly common practice for the landlord to assign to his incoming tenant all his rights and claims against the awaygoing tenant, in respect of failure to maintain and leave buildings, fences, drains, etc, in tenantable repair, and in respect of failure to fulfil the terms of the lease regarding cultivation. Section 35(2) of the Act provides that an agreement between a landlord and an incoming tenant made after 1st November 1948 shall be null and void if it provides that the latter shall pay to the outgoing tenant compensation under the Act. The landlord and incoming tenant may, however, agree in writing that the incoming tenant shall pay up to a maximum specified sum in respect of compensation for improvements under Part III of Schedule 5, ie for the unexhausted value of manure and feeding-stuffs and similar claims. There appears to be nothing, however, to prevent the outgoing and incoming tenant making any arrangement they wish with the landlord's consent either tacit or otherwise. It has been customary to refer these matters to two arbiters and an oversman, in a submission between the awaygoing tenant and the incoming tenant. They are outside these sections which apply only to questions and claims between landlord and tenant.

An incoming tenant is not under an obligation to take over anything at valuation unless, as is usual, he is expressly taken bound to do so, with the exception of:

(1) grass seeds sown with the last white crop of the awaygoing tenant, and the cost of harrowing and rolling them. If the tenant fails to sow good seed or to hain the young grass he will be liable;

(2) land left in bare fallow for which the awaygoing tenant is entitled to receive payment;

(3) dung. Where a tenant on entry received, without payment, fallow ground prepared with a certain quantity of manure, he was bound to leave the same state of things at awaygoing, and was held entitled to payment for the surplus only.

An awaygoing tenant is only entitled to the value of such dung as is lawfully withheld from application to the land, and generally only for what is made after the sowing of the last green crop, but there may be variation according to the known custom of the district. In an old case a tenant was bound to consume the whole fodder, except hay and straw of the last crop, and the practice had been to reserve part of the dung to be laid on the wheat crop land in the autumn instead of applying it all in the preceding spring. The outgoing tenant was held entitled to compensation for (a) the reserved dung left on the farm unused at the outgoing Whitsunday, being no more than he had been in use to reserve; and (b) for straw, being no more than would have been required to fodder his bestial until separation of crop.

All these rules, which are largely based on equity, may be altered by contract.

If the entry is a Whitsunday one, the incoming tenant is sometimes bound to take over, at a valuation, first and second years' grass, fallow (rent and labour of ploughings), dung, straw (sometimes also grain), of the awaygoing crop, and occasionally subdivision fences. He may also have to pay for the potato or turnip crop based on the cost of seed, labour, and manure applied at the date of quitting. In some cases the straw of the awaygoing crop is steelbow, and must be left without payment, while in other cases, the incoming tenant must take the whole awaygoing crop.

If the entry is Martinmas, the incoming tenant has generally less to take over. In most cases he has to take at valuation

(1) dung made after the sowing of the last green crop;

(2) green crop, so far as remaining in the land;

(3) winter grain crops;

(4) grain drying and storage plant or other fixed machinery.

Here, again, there is variation, according to contract or the custom of the district.

With regard to sheep stocks, there is no obligation, apart from contract, to take these over at valuation, but such an obligation is often imposed.

Silage valuations depend on the nature and quantity of the nutrients it contains and its suitability in other respects as a food for livestock. The valuers will require to ascertain what crops were used in making the silage and when it was made. There can be considerable variation in protein and moisture content and analysis may be advisable.

The property in implements, stock, crop, etc, does not pass to the buyer (incoming tenant) until payment of the price which must be made within one month after quitting or within one month of the award (section 19). This applies in spite of any agreement to the contrary.

APPOINTMENT OF ARBITERS AND OVERSMAN

In all these cases, it is usual to have the valuations made by two arbiters mutually chosen, or by an oversman appointed by the arbiters in case of their differing in opinion.

Where there is difficulty concerning the appointment of arbiters or oversman, parties can fall back on the provisions of the Arbitration (Scotland) Act 1894, the leading sections of which are:

'2. Should one of the parties to an agreement to refer to a single arbiter refuse to concur in the nomination of such arbiter, and should no provision have been made for carrying out the reference in that event, or should such provision have failed, an arbiter may be appointed by the court on the application of any party to the agreement, and the arbiter so appointed shall have the same powers as if he had been appointed by all the parties.

3. Should one of the parties to an agreement to refer to two arbiters refuse to name an arbiter, in terms of the agreement, and should no provision have been made for carrying out the reference in that event, or should such provision have failed, an arbiter may be appointed by the court on the application of the other party, and the arbiter so appointed shall have the same powers as if he had only been duly nominated by the party so refusing.

4. Unless the agreement to refer shall otherwise provide, arbiters shall have power to name an oversman, on whom the reference shall be devolved in the event of their differing in opinion. Should the arbiters fail to agree on the nomination of an oversman, the court may, on the application of any party to the agreement, appoint an oversman. The decision of said oversman, whether he has been named by the arbiters or appointed by the court shall be final.'

If parties have agreed upon the appointment of arbiters, or arbiters have been appointed under the above statute, it is usual to enter into a minute of submission. It is important to refer to the lease for its terms. If the lease is not referred to the submission is final and regulates the basis on which the arbitration must proceed. But if the submission is not itself explicit on any question it should be competent for the arbiters to refer to the lease.

The minute should be drawn by the agent for the party who is to receive the money (generally the awaygoing tenant) and revised by the agent for the other party. This course should be followed even though, as is sometimes the case, there are counter-claims by the incoming tenant either on his own behalf or as coming in place of the proprietor.

The submission having been executed, the arbiters should sign a short minute (to be written on the submission) accepting office and appointing an oversman, who should also sign a short minute accepting office. This minute need not be tested.

The two arbiters and the oversman all have the same function, namely to determine in a judicial fashion the true value of the items with which they are required to deal. The arbiter appointed by each party is not a partisan for that party and should not behave as such.

Procedure and Principles of Valuation

Where no directions are given, in the minute of submission, or in the lease as to procedure to be followed, the arbiters and oversman should follow the course generally adopted in the district.

Where arbiters, as men of skill, were appointed to value awaygoing crops, it was observed that it would be incompetent to take evidence.

As regards the principle of valuation, in valuing manure and fences, the actual value at the time and place in question should be taken and not the cost. In the case of crops, market value is usually the basis of valuation. It may be, however, that a tenant bound by his lease to consume fodder such as turnips on the farm will only get consuming value. In order to arrive at market value, account must be taken of the expense of harvesting, marketing, etc, and to arrive at consuming value the manurial benefit of the crop will have to be kept in view. Generally, where the lease and submission are silent market value should rule, ie the market price the produce would have fetched on the farm at the time, less any expense which the awaygoing tenant would have had to bear, such as for reaping, harvesting, delivering, etc. Turnips left in terms of a lease, at its expiry, must be paid for at actual market value, and not merely consuming value.

Even if the crop to be valued at consuming value is not usually consumed (for example, white crop) it should be valued on the lower basis. Wholesale price is not the same as consuming value wholesale being sale in bulk as contrasted with sale by retail, ie the sale of individual articles. Crops consumed on the land benefit the land on account of the manurial value of the residue. Consuming value is the value to an occupant who gets the benefit of the crop without having to incur the expense of lifting, storage, transport and realisation. In the case of turnips fed on the land all expense is saved. Market value includes remuneration to the grower and all expense of cultivation, reaping, etc, down to the date of sale.

The Duties of Arbiters and Oversman

The oversman has an overriding jurisdiction, but it should not be exercised unless the arbiters have failed to agree. Frequently certain questions are devolved and others are not, and although the practice is not to be commended, it has been decided that an award signed by both arbiters and the oversman could not, on that ground, be reduced.

The arbiters, or where there has been a devolution, the oversman, having accepted office, must proceed and issue an award disposing of the matters submitted to them. They are not entitled capriciously to decline to do so. The only excuses the court would be likely to accept are ill-health, intention to go abroad for a long time, or emerging interest. The submission may bear that the award is to be issued within a stated time or 'between this ... and the ... day of ... next to come'. Where the date is thus left blank, the submission lasts for a year and a day. If no reference to endurance is made, there is no period except that imposed by the negative prescription. The parties can themselves agree on an extension and in certain circumstances their actings may be held to imply an agreed-on extension. An arbitration in the absence of special provisions in the submission comes to an end by the death of a party (not merely one of a body of trustees) of an arbiter or oversman.

The Court of Session alone can compel an arbiter to proceed with his task. The proper procedure is by way of application for judicial review in the Outer House. Where one arbiter is obstructive, and will neither proceed nor devolve, the court may order him to devolve; and where there is a difference of opinion between the arbiters, even on a point of procedure only, the oversman is entitled to act, at the request of one of the arbiters, notwithstanding the dissent of the other. An arbiter has power, by implication, to award expenses. He has, however, no power to assess damages or to award interest from any date prior to his award unless expressly empowered to do so. He is entitled to require and obtain assistance from men of skill – for example, engineers or valuers – or to consult a law agent or counsel. He is not affected by the provisions of the Act with regard to the appointment of a clerk.

Procedure in Making Valuations

The arbiters and oversman generally go together to make the valuation, but the oversman should not act unless and until the arbiters differ and devolve upon him. In a reference to two arbiters named and an oversman to be named by them, the arbiters appointed the oversman before entering on the reference and the oversman accompanied them at their inspection of the subjects. The oversman died before the arbiters issued their award. The award was valid as the reference did not devolve on the oversman except in the event of the arbiters differing. The court allows very wide latitude as regards procedure, and will not interfere merely because the oversman settles points in dispute as they arise, and thereafter the arbiters sign a general award.

Awaygoing Crop Valuations

Where the submission does not specify the precise procedure to be adopted in making the valuations, the arbiters and oversman can follow any course they think best suited to the case. They will generally proceed in the manner usual in the district. There is a common practice in valuing such things as manure, fences, and grass, but it is different with the corn crop, regarding which methods vary. The arbiters must, of course, follow the method (if any) provided in the submission.

CHAPTER 15

QUOTAS AND SET ASIDE

INTRODUCTION

This chapter aims to deal with milk and livestock quotas and the arable areas payment scheme in the context of landlord and tenant, but does not cover the whole subject.

MILK QUOTAS

Milk quotas were introduced into the UK with effect from 1st April 1984.[1] Quotas were continued in 1992 and the regime is now governed by Council Regulation (EEC) 3950/92[2] and the Dairy Produce Quotas Regulations 1994.[3]

Milk quotas were introduced to deal with the long-term surplus of milk which was being produced within the community.[4] Only about three-quarters of the milk being produced was used within the community. The balance had to be purchased at intervention prices by the community, which then incurred long-term storage costs. As the Milk Producers Outgoers Schemes had not proved sufficient to reduce production, milk quota was introduced to deal with the crisis.

Milk quota operates by way of a super levy imposed upon producers whose production in any year exceeds their quota. It has been defined as 'a form of licence to produce a given quantity of a commodity at more or less guaranteed price without incurring a penalty'.[5]

The holding

In general, milk quota was allocated to existing 'holdings' as at 1st April 1984 based on the milk production of the holding in the calendar year 1983, less a 9 per cent deduction.

'Holding' is defined as 'all the production units operated by the single producer and located within the geographical territory of the Community'. 'Production unit' is not defined, but a ' "producer" means a natural or legal person or a group of natural or legal persons farming a holding within the geographical territory of the Community'.[6]

---

1 Council Regulation (EEC) 804/68, as amended by Council Regulation (EEC) 856/84 and the Dairy Produce Quotas Regulations 1984 (SI 1984/1047). The current regulations are the Diary Produce Quotas Regulations 1994 (SI 1994/672), as amended by SIs 1994/2448, 1994/2919, 1995/254.
2 Amended by Council Regulations (EEC) 748/93 and 1560/93 and Commission Regulation (EEC) 536/93, amended by Commission Regulation (EEC) 1756/93 and Commission Regulation (EC) 470/94.
3 SI 1994/672, amended by SIs 1994/2448, 1994/2919, 1995/254.
4 See Wood *et al*, *Milk Quotas, Law and Practice* (1st edn), Ch 1.
5 The Advocate General's opinion in *Wachauf v Bundesamt für Ernährung und Forstwirtschaft* [1991] 1 CMLR 328.
6 Dairy Produce Quotas Regulations 1994, reg 2(1); Council Regulation (EEC) 3950/92, art 9(d).

A milk quota holding is the whole production unit or aggregate of land occupied by the producer, whether or not that land is part owner-occupied and part tenanted or held on some other agreement. Where a holding is held under different titles or leases it may be described as a 'composite EEC holding', which is not a statutory definition.

It should be noted that the definition of 'holding' for milk quota purposes is different from the definition of 'agricultural holding' in section 1(1) of the 1991 Act.

In relation to any region, which are the regions of the UK, means the division of that holding in the region. The Scottish regions are mainland Scotland less Kintyre and the Scottish islands area, which includes Kintyre.[7]

This definition of 'holding' for milk quota purposes raises a difficulty where a holding is part tenanted or where part of a holding is disposed of. In those circumstances the milk quota will have to be apportioned between the different units of land within the holding.

Apart from the initial allocation of milk quota, usually in 1984, further allocation may have been made by the Secretary of State for Scotland or by the Dairy Produce Quota Tribunal after that date – for example, a development claim allocation. The producer may have had additional quota transferred to the holding by purchase after the initial allocation date. There have been subsequent allocations – for example, special quota; additional milk products quota, etc.[8]

Types of quota

The types of milk quota which may be registered in respect of the holding include 'direct sales quota' and 'wholesale quota'.[9]

A number of terms are used to describe different categories of milk quota which may have been acquired by a holding. These include:

Allocated quota. This describes the quota that was allocated in respect of a holding in 1984 or was allocated subsequently. For the purposes of compensation at the termination of a lease, it is defined by paragraph 2(1) of Schedule 2 to the Agriculture Act 1986 as quota allocated to a tenant in respect of the holding.

Transferred quota. This describes quota which has been acquired by way of purchase or other means, where quota has been transferred from one holding to the holding to which it now relates. In relation to a tenant for the purposes of compensation at the termination of a lease, it is defined by paragraph 2(2) of Schedule 2 to the 1986 Act as quota transferred to the tenant by virtue of the transfer to him of the whole or part of a holding.

Special quota. Special quota allocated in terms of article 3a of Council Regulation (EEC) 857/84 (introduced by Council Regulations (EEC) 764/89 and 2055/93) to producers who had participated in the Non-Marketing of Milk or Dairy Herd Conversion Schemes and whose

7 Dairy Produce Quotas Regulations 1994, reg 2(1).
8 Council Regulation (EEC) 763/89; Dairy Produce Quotas Regulations 1991, Sch 9.
9 Defined by the Dairy Produce Quotas Regulations 1994, reg 2(1).

undertaking expired after 31st December 1983, may have been allocated to eligible producers after June 1989.[10]

Additional milk products quota. Additional milk products[11] were brought within the quota regime by Council Regulation (EEC) 306/91. Additional milk quota was allocated in terms of Schedule 9 to the Dairy Produce Quotas Regulations 1991.

Apportionments or prospective apportionments of milk quota

The requirement to apportion milk quota between parts of a holding may arise on three occasions: where there is a transfer of part of a holding;[12] in a rent review, where the tenancy is only part of the holding;[13] and in regard to compensation on the termination of a tenancy where the tenancy is only part of the holding.[14]

Regulation 7(1)[15] provides for an apportionment in terms of regulation 10, where there is or has been a transfer of part of the holding.

Regulation 11 provides for a prospective apportionment where there is a future intention that there should be a change of occupation of part of the holding provided the request is made within six months preceding the change of occupation. A prospective apportionment may be revoked.[16]

Where part of a holding, in respect of which the producer has special quota registered as his, is transferred, otherwise than by an exempt transfer[17] the proportion of the special quota which has to be returned to the national reserve is the same proportion which the agricultural area of the holding sold or leased bears to the total agricultural area farmed by the producer.[18] Where the transfer is an exempt transfer then an apportionment requires to be carried out in terms of regulation 10.

Milk quota including exempt special quota may be apportioned between parts of a holding by agreement between the parties intimated to the Secretary of State for Scotland[19] apportioning the milk quota 'taking account of areas used for milk production as specified in the statement'.[20]

The milk quota cannot be arbitrarily apportioned by the parties, but has to be apportioned by taking account of the areas used for milk production.[21] The apportionment has to be agreed by all parties having an interest in the holding.[22]

There is an important distinction between an agreed apportionment and one effected by arbitration. An apportionment by arbitration requires the

10 Ibid, reg 2(1) 'special quota'.
11 Dairy Produce Quotas Regulations 1991, reg 2(1) 'means dairy produce other than milk, butter, cream or cheese'.
12 Dairy Produce Quotas Regulations 1994, reg 7.
13 Agriculture Act 1986, s 16.
14 Ibid, Sch 2, para 2(2).
15 Dairy Produce Quotas Regulations 1994.
16 Ibid, reg 11(2).
17 Ibid, reg 8(5); ie exempt from the requirement to return the quota to the national reserve.
18 Ibid, reg 8(4).
19 Ibid, regs 7(1)(a), and 10.
20 NB: 'taking account of ... ': see below re arbitration where the apportionment is 'on the basis of findings made as to areas used for milk production ... '.
21 Dairy Produce Quotas Regulations 1994, reg 7(2)(a).
22 Ibid, reg 7(2)(b); eg, standard security holder, landlord, etc.

arbiter to 'decide the apportionment on the basis of findings made as to areas used for milk production in the preceding five-year period during which production took place before the change of occupation',[23] whereas an agreed apportionment is not required to take into consideration the preceding five years.[24]

If the Intervention Board has reasonable grounds for believing that the areas used for milk production are not as specified in the notice or were not as agreed by the parties it may refer the apportionment to arbitration under Schedule 3.[25]

Where parties cannot agree on the apportionment, then the apportionment has to be carried out by arbitration under Schedule 3.[26]

The arbiter can be appointed by agreement between the parties reached within twenty-eight days of the change of occupation.[27] Where an arbiter is appointed by agreement the transferee requires to notify the appointment to the Secretary of State in writing within fourteen days of the appointment.[28]

During that period any party may apply to the Secretary of State to appoint an arbiter.[29] If no arbiter has been appointed by agreement or by the Secretary of State within the twenty-eight days, then the Secretary of State may appoint the arbiter.[30]

The Land Court may carry out the apportionment if all parties interested in the holding make a joint application to the court within twenty-eight days of the change of occupation.[31]

Where the Intervention Board has given notice under regulation 12, the Board is required to apply to the Land Court for the appointment of an arbiter.

Any party having an interest in the holding is entitled to make representations to the arbiter or be a party to the proceedings in the Scottish Land Court.[32] Interested persons would include the landlords if one of the parties were tenants and the standard security holder as having an interest in the value of his security subject, which will be affected by the quantum of the milk quota registered in respect of the holding.

An arbiter or the Land Court is required to

'decide the apportionment on the basis of findings made as to areas used for milk production in the last five-year period during which production took place before the change of occupation or, in the case of a prospective apportionment, in the last five-year period during which production took place before the appointment of the arbiter or the application to the Scottish Land Court'.[33]

---

23 Ibid, Sch 3, para 2(1).
24 Wood et al, *Milk Quotas, Law and Practice* (1st edn), para 4.07.
25 Dairy Produce Quotas Regulations 1994, reg 12.
26 Ibid, reg 10(b)(ii).
27 Ibid, Sch 3, para 3(1).
28 Ibid, Sch 3, para 3(1).
29 Ibid, Sch 3, para 3(2).
30 Ibid, Sch 3, para 3(3).
31 Ibid, Sch 3 para 1(3).
32 Ibid, Sch 3, paras 12, 28.
33 Ibid, Sch 3, para 2(1). Prior to the coming into force of the Dairy Produce Quotas Regulations 1993 the earlier regulations referred to the five-year period prior to the change of occupation. This led to difficulties if milk production had ceased some years before there was a change of occupation, which is why the regulation was amended.

There is no difficulty where the whole holding has been used for milk production in the preceding five years.

The arbiter will have to determine which areas of that holding or each part of that holding have been used for milk production. Thus it is not possible to apportion milk quota to an area of the holding which has not been and cannot be used for milk production.

The 'area used for milk production' has been defined in *Puncknowle Farms Ltd v Kane*[34] to mean

'not merely the farm area used for current production but includes land which, taking the annual cycle of agriculture, is used for the support of the dairy herd and to provide for future milk production, and therefore includes land used for dry cows and heifers, land used for buildings and yards of a dairy unit and land used for dairy or dual-purpose bulls, which have been bred to enter the production herd rather than for sale'.

The arbiter's definition, which was approved with the additions noted above, was that areas used for milk production

'are the forage areas used by the dairy herd and to support the dairy herd by the growing of grass and any fodder crop for the milking dairy herd, dry cows and all dairy following female youngstock (and home bred dairy and dual purpose bulls for use on the premises if applicable) if bred to enter the production herd and not for sale. In this case maize, silage, hay and grass were fodder crops, but consideration would have been given to corn crops or part of corn crops grown for consumption by the dairy herd or youngstock, including the use of straw'.

In *Posthumus v Oosterward*[35] the Advocate General expressed the view that areas used in milk production should include the yards, buildings and roads provided they make a significant contribution to the production of milk.

It is now settled by *Posthumus* that 'areas used for milk production' are to be established by the arithmetical approach, without regard to the productivity or otherwise of the holding, even if this arrives at an inequitable result. Where there is a dual use of land, such as summer grazing of dairy cows and overwintering of sheep, the dairy and non-dairy use requires to be apportioned out.

Paragraphs 3 to 19 of Schedule 3 deal with the appointment and remuneration of the arbiter, statements of case, conduct of proceedings, time-limits, the clerk, witnesses, the award, and expenses. The procedural provisions of the Schedule are very similar to those applying to an agricultural arbitration under Schedule 7 to the 1991 Act.[36]

There is no appeal against an arbiter's decision. At any stage of the proceedings the arbiter may or if so directed by the sheriff shall state a case for the opinion of the sheriff on any question of law arising in the course of the arbitration.[37] It is important to ask the arbiter to produce a draft award, so that consideration can be given to asking for a stated case, because it is not competent to ask for a stated case after the award has been delivered.[38] The sheriff's decision is final.

34 [1985] 3 All ER 790; (1985) 275 EG 1283.
35 [1992] CMLR 336.
36 See the 1991 Act, Sch 7, notes.
37 Dairy Produce Quotas Regulations 1994, Sch 3, para 20.
38 *Johnson v Gill* 1978 SC 74; *Johnston v Glasgow Corporation* 1912 SC 300; *Hendry v Fordyce* (1953) 69 Sh Ct Rep 191; *Fairlie Yacht Slip Ltd v Lumsden* 1977 SLT (Notes) 41.

Where the apportionment is being carried out by the Land Court a party may ask for a special case to be stated for the opinion of the Court of Session on any question of law within one month after the date of intimation of the decision.[39]

Where the arbiter has misconducted himself or an arbitration or the award has been improperly procured, the sheriff may set the award aside.[40]

Milk quota and rent review

Section 16 of the 1986 Act makes provision for dealing with milk quota allocated to the subjects of the tenancy in a rent review arbitration under section 13 of the 1991 Act.

The section only applies where the tenant is the person who has milk quota 'registered as his in relation to a holding' (section 16(2)). This means that the landlord, where the tenant is farming through the medium of a partnership and where the milk quota is registered in the name of the partnership, is probably not entitled to the benefits of this section in any rent review. This restriction is similar to that which applies to a tenant's right to compensation or for milk quota at outgo.[41]

A preliminary matter, which may have to be determined by the arbiter of the Scottish Land Court, is the proportion of the milk quota allocated to the holding, which is attributable to the subjects of the tenancy, if they are only part of the holding.[42] This will be determined in accordance with the criteria of regulation 10 and paragraph 2(1) of Schedule 3,[43] as it might apply at the date of the rent review. Unless the parties can agree on the apportionment for the purposes of the rent review, the arbiter will have to undertake the apportionment on the basis of finding as to areas used for milk production in the preceding five years. Such a determination, being an incidental to the rent review, will not be binding on the parties or other interested parties on a transfer of part of the milk quota holding, which in any event will be taking place at a different date.

The milk quota which was allocated to the holding or which was transferred to the holding, where the tenant did not bear the cost of that transfer transaction, is taken into account in determining the rent of the holding, because quantum of milk quota attached to the holding increases the rental value. Where milk quota has been allocated to a holding only because the tenant's improvements have made dairy farming possible and in consequence milk quota has been allocated, the milk quota still falls to be taken into account in a rent arbitration.[44] It is only transferred quota, where the tenant has borne all or part of the cost of the transaction, which falls to be disregarded in a rent review. The 'tenant' includes successors.[45]

---

39 Rules of the Scottish Land Court, rule 88. Cf Dairy Produce Quotas Regulations 1994, Sch 3, para 25.
40 Ibid, Sch 3, paras 21, 22. For a review of the legal grounds upon which an arbiter's award may be set aside, see the 1991 Act, Sch 7, note 33 and *Stair Memorial Encyclopaedia*, vol 2, para 472.
41 See the Agriculture Act 1986, Sch 2, para 2, note.
42 Ibid, s 16(3)(b).
43 See above. 'Apportionments or prospective apportionments of milk quota'.
44 *Broadland Properties Estates Ltd v Mann* 1994 SLT (Land Ct) 7.
45 As defined in the Agriculture Act 1986, Sch 2, para 3.

In terms of section 16(3) the arbiter or the Scottish Land Court is required to disregard any increase in rental value of the tenancy, which is due to the proportion of transferred quota the cost of which has been borne by the tenant and the proportion of which relates to the tenancy.

It should be noted that section 16(4) provides that any payment by a tenant, when he was granted the lease or when the lease was assigned to him, shall be disregarded. For the purposes of the subsection it does not amount to the cost of a transfer transaction being borne by the tenant. This means that where a tenant pays the landlord the value of the compensation that the landlord has had to pay the outgoing tenant, this is not to be taken into account in subsequent rent reviews.

The section also applies in rental questions between the tenant and sub-tenant (1986 Act, section 16(6)).

Problems arise where either inadequate or excess quota was allocated to an agricultural holding. As the allocation of quota in 1984 was based on the efficiency of the tenant in the production base year, usually 1983, the quota allocated will depend on the efficiency of the tenant in occupation at that date. It has been suggested that where there is an inadequate quota allocated to the holding that the landlord will fall to be penalised by a reduced rental assessment in future years, because the rent has to be assessed by reference to the lawful productive capacity of the holding. The holding may only produce milk up to the allocated quota (and any transferred quota, although the latter falls to be disregarded in the rent review if the tenant paid for the transfer) and that therefore is its lawful productive capacity.[46]

The converse does not necessarily apply because the tenant in 1984 might have been employing a system of farming more beneficial to the holding or more productive (ie feeding high concentrates or milking three times daily) than it is reasonable to expect a hypothetical tenant to adopt. In those circumstances, the arbiter might require to disregard the excess quota, on the basis that a reasonable competent tenant may not be able to produce milk to that capacity.

Milk quota compensation on termination of the lease

A tenant who has milk quota registered as his in relation to a holding which consists of or includes the tenancy, is entitled to compensation from the landlord or termination of the lease in terms of Schedule 2 to the 1986 Act.[47]

It should be noted that a claim for compensation for milk quota has to be intimated in writing within two months of the termination of the lease. If negotiations fail within eight months of the termination then the matter has to be referred to arbitration, but the arbiter must be appointed before the expiry of the eight months.[48]

Tenants who obtain a new lease after milk quota was allocated to the holding do not qualify for compensation in terms of Schedule 2 to the 1986

---

46 Scammell and Densham, *Law of Agricultural Holdings* (7th edn), p 98.
47 See annotations to Sch 2 to the Agriculture Act 1986 for a more detailed consideration of the statutory provisions.
48 See ibid, Sch 2, para 11.

Act (see below). They should negotiate a private compensation arrangement before entering into the lease.[49]

Qualifying interest to claim compensation

Of particular relevance is the qualifying requirement in paragraph 2 of Schedule 2 to the 1986 Act, before compensation may be claimed. It is only where the 'tenant has milk quota registered as his', that the tenant has a right to claim compensation. This excludes tenants, where the milk quota is registered in the name of, for example, a partnership, from claiming compensation on termination of the lease, because the milk quota is not registered as the tenant's.

Paragraphs (a) and (b) of section 2(1) impose other requirements on the tenant, who has milk quota registered as his, before he qualifies for compensation. The tenant requires to have had milk quota allocated to him, so milk quota transferred from, say, a partnership name to the tenant's name at a later date, is not allocated quota.[50]

Further, a tenant only qualifies for compensation in respect of transferred quota under paragraph 2(1)(b) if he either had quota allocated to him or was in occupation of the tenancy as tenant at 2nd April 1984 and he has borne the cost of the transaction of transferring quota. If the quota is transferred gratuitously from the partnership to the tenant, then, even if he had quota allocated to the holding or was in occupation on the qualifying date, he will still not have borne the cost of the transfer.

In 1984 when milk quota was first allocated, it did not particularly matter in whose name the quota was registered as producer. There are many examples of quota registered to partnerships, where the tenant was an individual and vice versa. This may well lead to problems when the tenancy terminates.

It may be that an arbiter or the courts could be persuaded to approach the construction of these provisions on a broad or teleological approach so as to include the partnership that has in fact operated the tenant's interest in the milk quota. Alternatively it can be argued that the provisions are illegal under EC law, because they discriminate in a common farming situation for no good reason.

Similarly, care should be taken in considering whether or not to transfer quota from the tenant as registered holder to a partnership that may have been formed after the initial allocations.

Whether or not milk quota or the right to compensation for it is a partnership asset will depend on the rights of the partnership in the tenancy or in the land. If the partnership has no rights in the tenancy – for example, the tenant holds the lease in trust for the partnership – or land, then it will probably have no rights in the quota or compensation.[51]

As the arbiter does not have power to award interest from a date earlier than the date of his decree, a tenant would be well advised to set the arbitration procedure in motion in early course if a quick settlement is unlikely.[52]

49 See ibid, Sch 2, para 3, note 3.
50 Ibid, Sch 2, para 2(1)(a).
51 *Faulks v Faulks* [1992] 1 EGLR 9.
52 See *Farrans (Construction) Ltd v Dunfermline District Council* 1988 SLT 466; *John McGregor (Contractors) Ltd v Grampian Regional Council* 1991 SLT 136.

Valuation of quota

Paragraph 9 of Schedule 2 to the 1986 Act recognised that milk quota has a value. In determining the value 'there shall be taken into account such evidence as is available' including sales of land with and without milk quota.

Where farms with milk quota are sold, the milk quota is often valued separately, usually at the price it would obtain on a sale by transfer at the date of entry. Such evidence would comply with paragraph 9.

It should be noted that in *Carson v Cornwall County Council*[53] the arbiter valued the quota on a capitalisation over ten years of the rental value of leasing quota. This was upheld on appeal. The reasoning was that farmers in urgent need of quota paid over the odds for a transfer of quota, whereas what the landlord was receiving back was quota which could be leased out to another tenant for an appropriate rental value.

Quota leasing

Member states were first authorised to introduce a temporary leasing scheme for milk quota in 1987.[54] This allows dairy farmers to lease out part of their unused milk quota on a temporary basis. A scheme requires to be approved annually.

A producer may agree with another producer to make a temporary transfer of all or part of any unused quota registered as his for a period of one quota year to the other producer.[55] The transferee requires to submit notice of the temporary transfer to the Intervention Board with the prescribed fee.[56] A temporary transfer cannot be agreed which results in an increase or reduction of quota available within the Scottish islands area.[57]

In order to be able to lease out the quota it must be unused quota registered in the name of the lessor before the date specified in the scheme.[58]

A tenant is empowered both to lease in and lease out quota. To be safe a tenant should obtain his landlord's permission to lease out quota on a temporary basis.[59] Quota, which a tenant has leased in, is registered in his name on a temporary basis only. It does not qualify for compensation under Schedule 2 to the 1986 Act.

Where quota has been permanently transferred without land it cannot be leased in or leased out during the same or the following quota year.[60]

Tenants who are about to terminate their lease or to have their lease terminated, would be well advised to consider the terms of the lease before leasing out their quota at the end of the lease, if the lease of the quota is to continue beyond the end of the lease. Such an arrangement might leave them open to a claim for damages, because it is probably an implied term of any

53 [1993] 1 EGLR 21.
54 Council Regulation (EEC) 2998/87; now governed by Council Regulation (EEC) 3950/92, art 6.
55 Dairy Produce Quotas Regulations 1994, reg 15(1).
56 Ibid, reg 15(3). Forms MQ/3 and MQ/4.
57 Ibid, reg 15(4).
58 15th December 1995 for 1995.
59 Form MQ/3, note 4.
60 Dairy Produce Quotas Regulations 1994, reg 13(2).

lease of a dairy farm that the quota will be available to the incoming tenant at the outgo.

It should be noted that in *Cambusmore Estate v Little*[61] the Land Court held that the leasing out of milk quota on a more or less permanent basis was not a practice which amounted to farming the farm, which could be relied upon as a defence, in a landlord's application for a certificate of bad husbandry.

SHEEP AND SUCKLER COW ANNUAL PREMIUM QUOTAS[62]

Sheep annual premium quotas (SAP) were first allocated to producers in February 1993 based on premium received in respect of the 1991 scheme and a claim submitted under the 1992 scheme. Provision was made for the allocation of quota to additional categories of producer, including those who had not claimed in 1991 or 1992, new producers, developers, newcomers to farming and others.

Suckler cow premium quota (SCP) was allocated in respect of 1992 claims.

Quota is ring fenced in sensitive areas. The areas relevant to Scotland are the Highlands and Islands area, the rest of the Scottish Less Favoured Area (LFA) and Great Britain non-LFA. With some specific exceptions a producer shall not transfer or lease quota to a producer whose holding is not situated within the same ring fence.[63]

Ownership of quota

Differing from milk quota, which attaches to the land of the holding in respect of which it was allocated, sheep and suckler cow annual premium quota is personal to the producer to whom it was allocated and leased out or transferred by him to another producer.

As SAP and SCP quotas are personal to the producer, unless there is any provision to the contrary in a lease, a tenant producer may deal in his quota without reference to the landlord. On termination of the lease he may transfer the quota to another holding in his own name or to another producer under the regulations.

If there is a provision in the lease binding the quota to the holding, the landlord will have to ensure that quota is not lost by the tenant underusing his quota.

Transfer of quota with holding

Deadlines for the transfer of quota have relevance to the termination of leases and the inputting of tenants, so as to avoid siphon where quota is not transferred.

The deadline for notification of a transfer or lease of SAP and SCP quota, if the producer receiving the quota lodges his premium application form, is the date of lodgement of the application form or if no such application is lodged, the end of the period in which such application forms may be

61 1991 SLT (Land Ct) 33.
62 See the Sheep Annual Premium and Suckler Cow Premium Quotas Regulations 1993 (SI 1993/1626), amended by SIs 1993/3036, 1994/2894.
63 SI 1993/1626, regs 8, 9.

lodged.[64] The lodgement date is set annually in terms of the SAP and SCP schemes. The current deadline allows for the common situation of a tenant taking entry at Martinmas (28th November).

With effect from 1996 one application and retention period was introduced. The claim for SAP was combined with that for HLCA (Sheep). The 1996 application period was from 4th December 1995 to 4th February 1996, with the retention period from midnight 4th February 1996 to end at midnight on 14th May 1996.[65]

Where quota is transferred without a transfer of the holding 15 per cent of the transferred quota is siphoned to the national reserve.[66] Where quota is transferred with the holding, there is no siphon to the national reserve provided the transfer is notified timeously.[67]

Leasing of quota

Although both schemes allow for a tenant to lease in and lease out quota, a tenant who leases out quota without the agreement of his landlord may be vulnerable to a claim that he is not farming in accordance with the rules of good husbandry.[68]

Quota and rent

The payment and amount of SAP and SCP will be a relevant consideration in determining the rent of a holding.[69]

In determining the open market rent that a willing tenant might be prepared to tender to a willing landlord, the availability of quota to the incoming tenant and the price that might have to be paid will be material considerations.

It is not clear whether an arbiter will have to consider the hypothetical tenant as a person already in possession of quota, or whether he will have to be considered as a person who will require to acquire quota in respect of the proposed tenancy. Probably the latter view is correct. In that case the availability of quota from the national reserves for nothing may be a consideration in contrast to the situation where the tenant will have to buy in the quota as part of his capital contribution to the tenancy.

ARABLE AREAS PAYMENT SCHEME

A voluntary five-year set-aside scheme for arable land was introduced in 1988,[70] the last date of entry being in 1992. The scheme will expire in 1997.

This voluntary scheme was extended under the CAP reform in 1992 by

64 SI 1993/3036, reg 5(2), as amended. The original deadline was two months before the first date for submitting SAP applications (ie in mid-September), which made it impossible to effect a transfer of quota, where a holding changed hands at Martinmas (28th November).
65 SOAEFD, SAPS 1996 etc, Explanatory Leaflet SAP 1996/HLCA 1996 (Sheep) 2.
66 SI 1993/1626, reg 6(1).
67 Ibid, reg 7.
68 *Cambusmore Estate v Little* 1991 SLT (Land Ct) 33.
69 1991 Act, s 13.
70 Set-Aside Regulations 1988 (SI 1988/1352), amended by SI 1990/1716.

the introduction of the arable area payment scheme,[71] which applies to land used for the production of particular cereal, oil seed and protein crops.[72]

Participants may elect to set aside land under a number of options.[73] It is also possible to set aside land for woodland or access.[74]

This chapter is not concerned with the detailed rules for set-aside which must be observed by the participant, but with the impact of the schemes on the landlord/tenant relationship.

The set-aside rules or participation in the varying schemes does not necessarily vary or alter the contractual arrangements between the landlord and tenant. A tenant will still require to farm in accordance with the rules of good husbandry, which in many cases will conflict with set-aside obligations and be bound by any other obligations in the lease.

In respect that participation in the arable area payment scheme is no longer voluntary, as it was under the 1988 scheme, the requirement to set aside land overrides any provision in the lease to the contrary. However, participation in voluntary schemes within the set-aside regime which conflict with contractual obligations under the lease may well be in breach of the lease. Entry into a guaranteed scheme where a particular part of a holding is set aside or in the set-aside access scheme may breach lease obligations.[75]

A particular difficulty may arise if a landlord gives notice to quit while a tenant is participating in a guaranteed scheme. First, the tenant's freedom to crop terminates during the last year of the lease[76] and his cropping obligations under the lease may be incompatible with the set-aside obligations. Secondly, the tenant is at risk that a landlord will withdraw from any guaranteed scheme entered into, leaving the tenant vulnerable to penalty, which might be exigible on premature withdrawal from any scheme.[77]

A tenant would therefore be wise to try to agree with his landlord any particular set-aside regime that he wishes to enter.[78] It may be possible to avoid penalties if the obligation is transferred under the transfer scheme to another farm, prior to the termination of the tenancy.[79]

The income available to a holding under one of the arable area payment schemes will be a relevant consideration in rental assessments, because the level of payment and the prospects for the future will affect tenders for open market rentals of farms.

---

71 Council Regulation (EEC) 1765/92; Commission Regulations (EEC) 2293/92 and 334/93; Arable Area Payment Regulations 1994 (SI 1994/947), amended by SI 1994/2287; Arable Area Payments 1995, Explanatory Booklets Pts 1 and 2, AAP 1 and AAP 2.

72 Annex 1 to Council Regulation (EEC) 1765/92.

73 Basic set-aside; six-year rotational set-aside (RSA); flexible set-aside; guaranteed set-aside for five years; voluntary set-aside or additional voluntary set-aside: see Arable Area Payments 1995, AAP 1, Section D.

74 Set-Aside Access (Scotland) Regulations 1994 (SI 1994/3085); Set-Aside Access Scheme, Explanatory Booklet, SAA1 – 1995.

75 A tenant is required to notify his landlord if he intends to participate in the scheme: Set-Aside Access Scheme, Explanatory Booklet, SAA1 – 1995, para 32.

76 1991 Act, s 7(5)(a).

77 Arable Area Payments 1995, Explanatory Booklet Pt 1, para 75.

78 Ibid, Explanatory Booklet Pt 1, AAP 1, para 77.

79 Transfers of Set-aside Obligations between Producers, AAPL 3 (Rev) March 1995.

ANNOTATED TEXT OF THE AGRICULTURAL HOLDINGS (SCOTLAND) ACT 1991

(1991, c 55)

ARRANGEMENT OF SECTIONS

PART I

AGRICULTURAL HOLDINGS

SECT.
1. Meaning of 'agricultural holding' and 'agricultural land'.
2. Leases for less than year to year.
3. Leases to be continued by tacit relocation

PART II

TERMS OF LEASES AND VARIATIONS THEREOF

4. Written leases and the revision of certain leases.
5. Fixed equipment and insurance premiums.
6. Sums recovered under fire insurance policy.
7. Freedom of cropping and disposal of produce.
8. Record of condition, etc, of holding.
9. Arbitration as to permanent pasture.
10. Power of landlord to enter on holding.
11. Bequest of lease.
12. Right of landlord to object to acquirer of lease.

Variation of rent

13. Variation of rent.
14. Arbitrations under sections 4 and 5.
15. Increase of rent for certain improvements by landlord.

Termination of tenancy

16. Leases not terminated by variation of terms, etc.
17. Prohibition of removal of manure, etc, after notice to quit, etc.
18. Tenant's right to remove fixtures and buildings.
19. Payment for implements, etc, sold on quitting holding.
20. Removal of tenant for non-payment of rent.

Part III

Notice to Quit and Notice of Intention to Quit

21. Notice to quit and notice of intention to quit.
22. Restrictions on operation of notices to quit.
23. Consent by Land Court or arbitration on notices to quit.
24. Consents for purposes of section 22.
25. Termination of tenancies acquired by succession.
26. Certificates of bad husbandry.
27. Penalty for breach of condition.
28. Effect on notice to quit of sale of holding.
29. Notice to quit part of holding to be valid in certain cases.
30. Tenant's right to treat notice to quit part as notice to quit entire holding.
31. Reduction of rent where tenant dispossessed of part of holding.
32. Further restrictions on operation of certain notices to quit.

Part IV

Compensation for Improvements

33. Improvements.
34. Right to compensation for improvements.
35. Payment of compensation by incoming tenant.
36. Amount of compensation under this Part.
37. Consents necessary for compensation for some improvements.
38. Notice required of certain improvements.
39. Compensation for Sch 5, Pt II, improvements conditional on approval of Land Court in certain cases.

Part V

Other Provisions Regarding Compensation

Market gardens

40. Market gardens.
41. Direction by Land Court that holding be treated as market garden.
42. Agreements as to compensation relating to market gardens.

Miscellaneous

43. Compensation for disturbance.
44. Compensation for continuous adoption of special standard of farming.
45. Compensation to landlord for deterioration etc of holding.
46. Compensation for failure to repair or maintain fixed equipment.
47. Provisions supplementary to ss 45 and 46.
48. Landlord not to have right to penal rent or liquidated damages.
49. Compensation provisions to apply to parts of holdings in certain cases.
50. Determination of claims for compensation where holding is divided.

51. Compensation not to be payable for things done in compliance with this Act.
52. Compensation for damage by game.
53. Extent to which compensation recoverable under agreements.

Part VI

Additional Payments

54. Additional payments to tenants quitting holdings.
55. Provisions supplementary to s 54.
56. Additional payments in consequence of compulsory acquisition etc of agricultural holdings.
57. Provisions supplementary to s 56.
58. Effect of early resumption clauses on compensation.
59. Interpretation etc of Part VI.

Part VII

Arbitration and Other Proceedings

60. Questions between landlord and tenant.
61. Arbitrations.
62. Claims on termination of tenancy.
63. Panel of arbiters, and remuneration of arbiter.
64. Appointment of arbiter in cases where Secretary of State is a party.
65. Recovery of compensation and other sums due.
66. Power to enable demand to remedy a breach to be modified on arbitration.
67. Prohibition of appeal to sheriff principal.

Sheep stock valuation

68. Sheep stock valuation.
69. Submission of questions of law for decision of sheriff.
70. Determination by Land Court of questions as to value of sheep stock.
71. Statement of sales of stock.
72. Interpretation of sections 68 to 71.

Part VIII

Miscellaneous

73. Power of Secretary of State to vary Schedules 5 and 6.
74. Power of limited owners to give consents, etc.
75. Power of tenant and landlord to obtain charge on holding.
76. Power of land improvement companies to advance money.
77. Appointment of guardian to landlord or tenant.
78. Validity of consents, etc.

CONTENTS OF THE 1991 ACT

PART IX

SUPPLEMENTARY

Crown and Secretary of State

79. Application to Crown land.
80. Determination of matters where Secretary of State is landlord or tenant.
81. Expenses and receipts.
82. Powers of entry and inspection.

Land Court

83. Proceedings of the Land Court.

Service of notices

84. Service of notices, etc.

Interpretation

85. Interpretation.
86. Construction of references in other Acts to holdings as defined by earlier Acts.
87. Savings.

Consequential amendments and repeals

88. Consequential amendments and repeals.

Citation, commencement and extent

89. Citation, commencement and extent.

SCHEDULES:
  Schedule 1—Provisions Required in Leases.
  Schedule 2—Grounds for Consent to Operation of Notices to Quit a Tenancy Where Section 25(3) Applies
    Part I—Grounds for Consent to Operation of Notice to Quit a Tenancy Let Before January 1, 1984.
    Part II—Grounds for Consent to Operation of Notice to Quit a Tenancy Let on or After January 1, 1984.
    Part III—Supplementary.
  Schedule 3—1923 Act Improvements For Which Compensation May Be Payable.
    Part I—Improvements For Which Consents Required.
    Part II—Improvements For Which Notice Required.
    Part III—Improvements For Which No Consents Or Notice Required.
  Schedule 4—1931 Act Improvements For Which Compensation May Be Payable.
    Part I—Improvements For Which Consent Required.
    Part II—Improvements Of Which Notice Required.
    Part III—Improvements For Which No Consent Or Notice Required.

Schedule 5—New Improvements For Which Compensation May Be Payable.
    Part I—Improvements For Which Consent Is Required.
    Part II—Improvements For Which Notice Is Required.
    Part III—Improvements For Which No Consent Or Notice Required.
Schedule 6—Market Garden Improvements.
Schedule 7—Arbitrations.
Schedule 8—Supplementary Provisions with Respect to Payments Under Section 56.
Schedule 9—Valuation of Sheep Stock in Scotland in Respect of Old Leases.
    Part I—Valuation Made in Respect of a Tenancy Terminating at Whitsunday.
    Part II—Valuation Made in Respect of a Tenancy Terminating at Martinmas.
    Part III—Particulars to be Shown in an Arbiter's Award.
    Part IV—Interpretation.
Schedule 10—Valuation of Sheep Stock in Scotland in Respect of Leases Entered into after December 1, 1986.
    Part I—Valuation Made in Respect of a Tenancy Terminating at Whitsunday.
    Part II—Valuation Made in Respect of a Tenancy Terminating at Martinmas.
    Part III—Particulars to be Shown in an Arbiter's Award.
    Part IV—Interpretation.
Schedule 11—Consequential Amendments of Enactments.
Schedule 12—Transitionals and Savings.
Schedule 13—Repeals and Revocations.
    Part I—Repeals.
    Part II—Revocations of Subordinate Legislation.

PART 1

AGRICULTURAL HOLDINGS

Meaning of 'agricultural holding' and 'agricultural land'

1.—(1) In this Act (except sections 68 to 72)[1] 'agricultural holding' means the aggregate of the agricultural[2] land comprised in a lease,[3] not being a lease under which the land is let to the tenant during his continuance in any office, appointment or employment held under the landlord.[4]

(2) In this section and in section 2 of this Act, 'agricultural land' means land used for agriculture[5] for the purposes of a trade or business,[6] and includes any other land which, by virtue of a designation of the Secretary of State under section 86(1) of the Agriculture (Scotland) Act 1948, is agricultural land within the meaning of that Act.

---

1 Sections 68 to 72 relate to the valuation of sheep stocks and are excepted because those sections relate to holdings which are wholly or mainly pastoral.
2 See pp 3–4. **'Agriculture'**, as defined in s 85(1), has a very wide meaning: see *Dunn v Fidoe* [1950] 2 All ER 685 (CA); *Howkins v Jardine* [1951] 1 KB 614; [1951] 1 All ER 320 (CA) (considered in *Short v Greeves* [1988] 08 EG 109 (CA); *R v Agricultural Land Tribunal (South*

128

Eastern Province), ex parte Palmer [1954] JPL 181. Land which contains some agricultural and some non-agricultural subjects must be either wholly an agricultural holding or not at all: *Howkins v Jardine; Gold v Jacques Amand Ltd* [1992] 2 EGLR 1. The principle of excision applied by the Land Court in *McGhie v Lang and Anr* 1953 SLCR 22 (following *McNeill v Duke of Hamilton's Trs* 1918 SC 221) was rejected in *Cameron v Duke of Argyll's Trs* 1981 SLT (Land Ct) 2. The predominant use decides whether the holding is subject to the Act or not. In terms of s 49(3), (4) compensation may be payable for the part of a non-agricultural holding, which is used for agriculture. The extent of the subjects is not material: *Stevens v Sedgeman* [1951] 2 KB 434; *Malcolm v McDougall* 1916 SC 283 (holding of quarter of an acre). An agricultural holding may cease to be an agricultural holding if the tenant ceases to use it for agriculture: *Weatherall v Smith* [1980] 1 WLR 1290; [1980] 2 All ER 530.

3 **'Lease'**: see definition of 'agricultural holding' in s 85(1) and note 1 thereto.
4 **'Continuance in any office, appointment or employment'.** In *Budge v Gunn* 1925 SLCR 74, in construing the same words in s 33 of the Crofters' Holdings (Scotland) Act 1886, the Land Court said that the point of the exclusion 'is that the letting of the holding to the tenant shall have been limited to, or conditional on, his continuance in the employment of the landlord'. Whether or not the exclusion applies is a question of proof: *Budge v Gunn; Dunbar's Trs v Bruce* (1900) 3 F 137; *MacGregor v Dunnett* 1949 SC 510. An arrangement for tenancy for a trial period was held not to be an appointment: *Verall v Farnes* [1966] 1 WLR 1254.
5 See note 2 above.
6 **'Trade or business'**: not necessarily agricultural. See *Rutherford v Maurer* [1962] 1 QB 16 (let for grazing to owner of a riding school), followed in *Crawford v Dun* 1981 SLT (Sh Ct) 66. For a case where the scale of the tenant's livestock breeding and dealing were not enough to constitute the carrying on of a trade or business, see *Hickson and Welch v Cann* (1977) 40 P & CR 218 (CA).

Leases for less than year to year

2.—(1) Subject to subsection (2) below, where, under a lease[1] entered into on or after November 1, 1948, land is let for use as agricultural land for a shorter period than from year to year,[2] and the circumstances are such that if the lease were from year to year the land would be an agricultural holding, then, unless the letting was approved by the Secretary of State before the lease was entered into,[3] the lease shall take effect, with the necessary modifications,[4] as if it were a lease of the land from year to year.

(2) Subsection (1) above shall not apply to—
(a) a lease entered into (whether or not the lease expressly so provides) in contemplation[5] of the use of the land only for grazing or mowing[6] during some specified period of the year;[7]
(b) a lease granted by a person whose interest in the land is that of a tenant under a lease for a shorter period than from year to year which has not by virtue of that subsection taken effect as a lease from year to year.[8]

(3) Any question arising as to the operation of this section in relation to any lease shall be determined by arbitration.[9]

1 **'Lease'.** *Hollings v Swindell* (1950) 155 EG 269 held that an award of an arbitrator amounted to an agreement between the parties for a tenancy from year to year.
2 **'A shorter period than from year to year'.** It has been held in England that a tenancy of eighteen months is greater than from year to year: *Gladstone v Bower* [1960] 2 QB 384. Whether subjects in Scotland let for more than one year and less than two would be an agricultural holding depends on whether such a let is for a term of years. A tenancy for one year was held to be for a shorter period than from year to year: *Rutherford v Maurer* [1962] 1 QB 16; *Bernays v Prosser* [1963] 2 QB 592; *Lower v Sorrell* [1963] 1 QB 959.
3 The Secretary of State's approval, obtained from the Department of Agriculture, must be granted prior to the lease, which itself must be entered into before the expiry of approval. The approval has to apply to the whole subjects let, although it has not yet been determined whether the whole subjects for which approval has been obtained have to be the subject of the

lease: *NCB v Drysdale* 1989 SLT 825. *NCB* also suggested *obiter* (but commented on by Gill, *The Law of Agricultural Holdings in Scotland* (2nd edn), on this point at para 83) that it is for an arbiter to determine whether or not the Secretary of State's approval was obtained prior to the grant of the lease. The terms of the Secretary of State's consent are a matter of construction: *Pahl v Trevor* [1992] 1 EGLR 22; cf *Ashdale Land & Property Co Ltd v Manners* [1992] 2 EGLR 5.

4 **'The necessary modifications'.** If the modifications necessary would radically alter the nature of the agreement it will not be converted into a lease from year to year by s 2(1): see *Goldsack v Shore* [1950] 1 KB 708 at p 713; *Harrison-Broadley v Smith* [1964] 1 WLR 465 at p 467; and Court of Appeal decision in *Bahamas International Trust Co Ltd v Threadgold* [1974] 1 WLR 1514; [1974] 3 All ER 428 (not commented on by House of Lords: [1974] 3 All ER 881).

5 **'Contemplation':** see *Scene Estate v Amos* [1957] 2 All ER 325.

6 **'Grazing or mowing'.** Where an agreement for a grazing let stipulated that the tenant was not to plough except 'in the interests of good husbandry on a crop rotation basis' and there was an obligation to comply with the rules of good husbandry, it was held that the ploughing and cropping although subsidiary excluded use for grazing during a specified period of the year and so the let took effect on a lease from year to year: *Lory v London Borough of Brent* [1971] 1 All ER 1042, *per contra* where ploughing operations were treated as ancillary to the grazings use see *Sanson v Chalmers* 1965 SLCR 135. Where use was substantially for grazing a gratuitous licence to use buildings for stabling was held ancillary and did not exclude the application of the proviso: *Avon County Council v Clothier* (1977) 242 EG 1048. A shared grazing agreement may not amount to a tenancy: *Evans v Tompkins* [1994] 2 EGLR 6; cf *Brown v Tiernan* [1993] 1 EGLR 11.

7 **'Period of the year'** may be adequately specified without definite dates being laid down as *termini*, eg 'grazing season': *Mackenzie v Laird* 1959 SC 266; *Gairneybridge Farm and King Applicants* 1974 SLT (Land Ct) 8; *Stone v Whitcombe* (1980) 40 P & CR 296 (CA); *Watts v Yeend* [1987] 1 WLR 323. Let for 364 days: *Reid v Dawson* [1954] 3 All ER 498. Let for 'six months' periods' was held to be for at least one year and so not within the proviso: *Rutherford v Maurer* [1962] 1 QB 16. A contract for a series of lets of less than a year can fall within the proviso (*Mackenzie v Laird*), but a series of lets of less than a year, where occupation is continuous, although theoretically within the proviso, can give rise to difficulties as to the nature of the agreement: *Rutherford v Maurer; Scene Estate v Amos* [1957] 2 All ER 325.

8 A lease under this subsection which has not yet taken effect as a lease from year to year is disregarded in a question of additional payments on compulsory acquisition: see ss 56 and 57.

9 It was held in a question arising out of s 2 of the Agricultural Holdings Act 1948 that the applicability of the Act as distinct from its operation is a matter for the courts: *Goldsack v Shore* [1950] 1 KB 708 (CA). This has been followed in Scotland: see *Craig and Anr Applicants* 1981 SLT (Land Ct) 12; *Love v Montgomerie and Logan* 1982 SLT (Sh Ct) 60 (overruling *Maclean v Galloway* 1979 SLT (Sh Ct) 32); see p 7. See also *Houison-Craufurd's Trs v Davies* 1951 SC 1; *Cormack v McIldowie's Exrs* 1974 SLT 178; *Donaldson's Hospital v Esslemont* 1925 SLT 92; 1925 SC 199; *Allan-Fraser's Trs v Macpherson* 1981 SLT (Land Ct) 17.

Leases to be continued by tacit relocation

3. Notwithstanding any agreement or any provision in the lease[1] to the contrary,[2] the tenancy of an agricultural holding shall not come to an end on the termination of the stipulated[3] endurance of the lease, but shall be continued in force by tacit relocation for another year and thereafter from year to year, unless notice to quit[4] has been given by the landlord or notice of intention to quit has been given by the tenant.[5]

1 **Lease:** see definition in s 85(1) and notes. This section does not apply to leases for less than year to year subject to s 2.

2 **Contracting out.** It is not competent to contract out of this section: *Duguid v Muirhead* 1926 SC 1078; *Morrison v Rendall* 1986 SC 69. It is doubtful whether personal bar could be pled against this statutory provision: *Kok Hoong v Leong Cheong Kweng Mines Ltd* [1964] AC 993.

3 **'Stipulated'.** If no period is 'stipulated' and possession is given the period would be implied as for a year and thereafter from year to year: *Gray v Edinburgh University* 1962 SC 157. The 'termination' of the stipulated endurance may be at a 'break' in the lease.

4 **'Notice to quit'** or 'notice of intention to quit' requires to be given in terms of s 21.

5 **'Tenant'.** Notice by one of two joint tenants is sufficient to terminate the tenancy of both: *Smith v Grayton Estates Ltd* 1960 SC 349; see also *Graham v Stirling* 1922 SC 90; *Combey v Gumbrill* [1990] 2 EGLR 7.

Part II

Terms of Leases and Variations Thereof

Written leases and the revision of certain leases

4.—(1) Where in respect of the tenancy of an agricultural holding—

(a) there is not in force a lease in writing;[1] or

(b) there is in force a lease in writing, being either—

(i) a lease entered into on or after November 1, 1948, or

(ii) a lease entered into before that date, the stipulated period of which has expired and which is being continued in force by tacit relocation,[2]

but such lease contains no provision for one or more of the matters specified in Schedule 1 of this Act or contains a provision inconsistent with that Schedule or with section 5 of this Act,

either party may give notice in writing to the other requesting him to enter into a lease in writing containing, as the case may be, provision for all of the matters specified in Schedule 1 to this Act, or a provision which is consistent with that Schedule or with section 5 of this Act; and if within the period of 6 months after the giving of such notice no such lease has been concluded, the terms of the tenancy shall be referred to arbitration.[3]

(2) On a reference under subsection (1) above, the arbiter shall by his award specify the terms of the existing tenancy and, in so far as those terms do not make provision for all the matters specified in Schedule 1 to this Act or make provision inconsistent with[4] that Schedule or with section 5 of this Act, make such provision for those matters as appears to the arbiter to be reasonable.

(3) On a reference under subsection (1) above, the arbiter may include in his award any further provisions relating to the tenancy which may be agreed between the landlord and the tenant, and which are not inconsistent with this Act.[5]

(4) The award of an arbiter under this section or section 5 of this Act shall have effect as if the terms and provisions specified and made therein were contained in an agreement in writing between the landlord and the tenant, having effect as from the making of the award or from such later date as the award may specify.[6]

---

1 **'Lease in writing'** is not limited to tested leases, and informal writings can exclude the provisions of this section, provided that the writings meet the statutory requirements: *Grieve & Sons v Barr* 1954 SC 414; Requirements of Writing (Scotland) Act 1995.

2 The important question which arises under this section is to determine what effect it may have on existing leases. Reference may be made to s 16, which provides that a lease is not to be

regarded as brought to an end only by reason of some new term being added to it or it has been varied or revised in pursuance of the Act. For tacit relocation, see s 3.

3 The desirability of having a written lease cannot be too strongly emphasised as it enables both parties at any given time to determine their rights.

4 **'Inconsistent with'** in this context is thought to involve a positive and contradictory provision. If the lease does not contain provisions inconsistent with Sch 1 and s 5 the arbiter does not have power to make provision for including its terms.

5 Subsection (3) gives arbiters powers to include matters which may have been outwith the consideration of the parties at the time of making a reference to arbitration, provided the matters are agreed. For arbiters' powers to vary rent, upon varying the terms of the lease, see s 14.

6 The object of postponing the operation of an award in certain cases to a specified date may be to obviate hardship in these cases. Where no hardship would result and no other reason for postponing is apparent, the arbiter will usually cause the award to have immediate effect.

Fixed equipment and insurance premiums

5.—(1) When a lease of an agricultural holding to which this section applies is entered into, a record of the condition of the fixed equipment on the holding shall be made forthwith,[1] and on being so made shall be deemed to form part of the lease; and section 8 of this Act shall apply to the making of such a record and to the cost thereof as it applies to a record made under that section.

(2)[2] There shall be deemed to be incorporated in every lease of an agricultural holding to which this section applies—

(a) an undertaking by the landlord that, at the commencement of the tenancy or as soon as is reasonably practicable thereafter,[3] he will put the fixed equipment on the holding into a thorough state of repair,[4] and will provide such buildings and other fixed equipment as will enable an occupier reasonably skilled in husbandry to maintain efficient production as respects both—

(i) the kind of produce specified in the lease, or (failing such specification) in use to be produced on the holding,[5] and

(ii) the quality and quantity thereof,

and that he will during the tenancy effect such replacement or renewal of the buildings or other fixed equipment as may be rendered necessary by natural decay or by fair wear and tear;[6] and

(b) a provision that the liability of the tenant in relation to the maintenance of fixed equipment shall extend only to a liability to maintain the fixed equipment on the holding in as good a state of repair (natural decay and fair wear and tear excepted) as it was in—

(i) immediately after it was put in repair[7] as aforesaid, or

(ii) in the case of equipment provided, improved, replaced or renewed during the tenancy, immediately after it was so provided, improved, replaced or renewed.

(3)[8] Nothing in subsection (2) above shall prohibit any agreement made between the landlord and the tenant after the lease has been entered into whereby one party undertakes to execute on behalf of the other, whether wholly at his own expense or wholly or partly at the expense of the other, any work which the other party is required to execute in order to fulfil his obligations under the lease.[9]

(4) Any provision in a lease to which this section applies requiring the tenant to pay the whole or any part of the premium due under a fire

insurance policy over any fixed equipment on the holding shall be null and void.[10]

(5)[11] Any question arising as to the liability of a landlord or tenant under this section shall be determined by arbitration.[12]

(6) This section applies to any lease of an agricultural holding entered into on or after November 1, 1948.

1 **'Record'**. The obligation to make a record only applies to post-November 1948 leases: subsection (6). There is no provision as to the responsibility for having the record made and no penalty except that the parties lose their rights under ss 44 and 45 respectively. Although it is desirable that a comprehensive record as to the condition of the holding is made, it is only in respect of fixed equipment that it is obligatory. The record requires to be made in terms of s 8(3), (4), (6)–(9) and the Agricultural Records (Scotland) Regulations 1948 (SI 1948/2817).

2 Subsections (2), (3) and (5) apply also to works of the nature of fixed equipment required under the Agriculture (Safety, Health and Welfare Provisions) Act 1956: see s 25(4) of that Act. Replacement of electrical wiring may fall within the tenant's repair and maintenance obligation: *Roper v Prudential Assurance Co Ltd* [1992] 1 EGLR 5.

3 **'As soon as is reasonably practicable thereafter'**. It is impossible to give guidance as to what length of time may be reasonably practical in any set of circumstances. It will clearly depend on the condition of the fixed equipment at date of entry, on the availability of labour and materials in the district and the prevailing legislation or regulations as to building, etc. There may be other local circumstances which can assist in determination of what is reasonable and comparison with like cases will obviously be helpful.

4 **'A thorough state of repair'** suggests a higher standard than is required at common law where the obligation is to put buildings in a proper state of repair sufficient for the stipulated endurance of the lease.

5 The words **'in use to be produced on the holding'** are very important and limit the arbiter's discretion. For example, it is not contemplated that a stock farm should be equipped for dairy purposes, unless the lease is silent on the kind of produce to be produced on the holding. See *Taylor v Burnett's Trs* 1966 SLCR App 139 where the farm was let as 'an ordinary holding or general purpose farm' and the lease stipulated that the landlords were not to be liable for improvements necessary for any other type of farm. It was held that, although dairying was carried on, the landlords were bound to provide fixed equipment only for the type of farming stipulated in the lease, and not that required for dairying. See also *Spencer-Nairn v IRC* 1985 SLT (Lands Tr) 46.

6 This is a peremptory provision: see *Secretary of State for Scotland v Sinclair* 1960 SLCR 10. The obligation is a continuing one for the duration of the lease including the period when the lease is running on tacit relocation: *Macnab v Willison* 1960 SLT (Notes) 25 (1960 SC 83 on different points, but the facts are more fully set out).

7 **'After it was put in repair'**. If the landlord fails to put items of fixed equipment into a thorough state of repair the tenant cannot be required to repair them: *Austin v Gibson* 1979 SLT (Land Ct) 12; *Pentland v Hart* 1967 SLT (Land Ct) 2. If the tenant fails in his obligations he renders himself liable to a demand to remedy (s 22(2)(d)), or a notice to quit under s 22(2)(e) and a claim for the cost of restoring the items to the required condition.

8 See note 2 above.

9 *Murray v Fane*, Perth Sh Ct, 22nd April 1996. NB 'made after'. It is not provided that such an agreement must be in writing.

10 See s 6 for the application of sums recovered under fire insurance policy in the case of earlier leases where the tenant is liable in payment of part of the premium. Provision is sometimes made in agreements under s 5(3) for the tenant to pay the fire insurance premium on fixed equipment. This is not covered by s 5(3) which relates only to undertakings to execute work. It is thought that a provision on insurance in such an agreement would be treated as a provision in the lease for the purpose of subsection (4) and so null and void.

11 See note 2 above.

12 The scope of the arbiter's remit in proceedings for specific implement (and possibly damages, but cf *Hill v Wildfowl Trust (Holdings) Ltd* 1995 SCLR 778, where the sheriff held that the arbiter has power to assess damages) is to establish the obligation incumbent upon the party and the extent of the breach of the obligation: *Tustian v Johnston* [1993] 2 All ER 673; *Hammond v Allen* [1994] 1 All ER 307. Where an arbitration follows upon a demand to

remedy or a notice to quit based on breaches of obligations in relation to fixed equipment the arbiter has powers under s 66 to modify the demand.

See s 14 which gives an arbiter power to vary the rent on a reference under s 5.

Sums recovered under fire insurance policy

6. Where the tenant of an agricultural holding is responsible for payment of the whole or part of the premium due under a fire insurance policy in the name of the landlord over any buildings or other subjects included in the lease of the holding and the landlord recovers any sum under such policy in respect of the destruction of, or damage to, the buildings or other subjects by fire, the landlord shall be bound, unless the tenant otherwise agrees, to expend such sum on the rebuilding, repair, or restoration of the buildings or subjects so destroyed or damaged in such manner as may be agreed or, failing agreement, as may be determined by the Secretary of State.[1]

1 This section can only affect leases entered into before 1st November 1948. Disputes fall to be determined by the Secretary of State, whose decision could only be reviewed by judicial review, and not by arbitration.

Freedom of cropping and disposal of produce

7.[1]—(1) Subject to subsections (2) and (5) below, the tenant of an agricultural holding shall, notwithstanding any custom of the country or the provisions of any lease or of any agreement respecting the disposal of crops or the method of cropping of arable lands,[2] have full right, without incurring any penalty, forfeiture or liability,[3]—

(a) to dispose of the produce of the holding,[4] other than manure produced thereon;

(b) to practise any system of cropping[5] of the arable land on the holding.

(2) Subsection (1) above shall not have effect unless, before exercising his rights thereunder or as soon as is practicable after exercising them, the tenant makes[6] suitable and adequate provision[7]—

(a) in the case of an exercise of the right to dispose of crops, to return to the holding the full equivalent manurial value to the holding of all crops sold off or removed from the holding in contravention of any such custom, lease or agreement;[8] and

(b) in the case of an exercise of the right to practise any system of cropping, to protect the holding from injury or deterioration.

(3) If the tenant of an agricultural holding exercises his rights under subsection (1) above so as to injure or deteriorate, or to be likely to injure or deteriorate, the holding,[9] the landlord shall have the following remedies, but no other—

(a) should the case so require, he shall be entitled to obtain an interdict restraining the exercise of the tenant's rights under that subsection in that manner;

(b) in any case, on the tenant quitting the holding on the termination of the tenancy the landlord shall be entitled to recover damages[10] for any injury to or deterioration of the holding attributable to the exercise by the tenant of his rights under that subsection.

(4) For the purposes of any proceedings for an interdict brought under subsection (3)(a) above, the question whether a tenant is exercising, or has

exercised, his rights under subsection (1) above in such a manner as to injure or deteriorate, or to be likely to injure or deteriorate the holding, shall be determined by arbitration; and a certificate of the arbiter as to his determination of any such question shall, for the purposes of any proceedings (including an arbitration) brought under this section, be conclusive proof of the facts stated in the certificate.

(5) Subsection (1) above shall not apply—

(a) in the case of a tenancy from year to year, as respects the year before the tenant quits the holding or any period after he has received notice to quit or given notice of intention to quit which results in his quitting the holding;[11] or

(b) in any other case, as respects the year before the expiry of the lease.[12]

(6)—

(a) In this section 'arable land' does not include land in grass which, by the terms of a lease, is to be retained in the same condition throughout the tenancy;[13]

(b) the reference in paragraph (a) above to the terms of a lease shall, where the Secretary of State has directed under section 9 of the 1949 Act or an arbiter has directed under that section or under section 9 of this Act that the lease shall have effect subject to modifications, be construed as a reference to the terms of the lease as so modified.

---

1 **'Cropping'** etc: see p 57. Where there is no written lease, and where the lease is silent as to cropping, the tenant must leave the land in the rotation customary in the district.

2 **'Arable lands':** see definition in subsection (6). Land may be considered arable which is being or had been cultivated, and has not returned to its natural state. Rough hill pasture is not 'arable'. Nor is market garden ground: *Taylor v Steel Maitland* 1913 SC 562.

3 **'Any penalty, forfeiture or liability'.** Any attempt to impose such by lease would be invalid: see *Gore-Browne-Henderson's Trs v Grenfell* 1968 SLT 237. A stipulation, for example, that a tenant who sold off turnips should bring back, say, twice their manurial value could not be enforced to the full extent. To the extent of one-half, it would be a penalty.

4 **'Produce of the holding'** is very general, and would cover crops which according to usual contract and even according to what were wont to be considered the rules of good husbandry, had to be consumed on the holding – eg, turnips, straw, hay, etc. Reference should be made to s 85(1), which defines 'produce' as including anything (whether live or dead) produced in the course of agriculture. It would include manure but this is excluded in s 7(1)(a). It would not be right for an arbiter to hold that a tenant should pay compensation for removing such produce off the farm in respect merely that he was thereby infringing the rules of good husbandry. It would, however, be competent and right to hold a tenant liable in compensation, not for removing the crops but, after having removed the crops, for failing to satisfy the requirements of this section by bringing back equivalent manurial value. It is not for taking away, but for failing to bring back, that compensation is due. There is a difference here in principle which should not be overlooked. A tenant has the right to keep all kinds of farming livestock in accordance with normal practice and cannot be prevented by his lease from doing so.

5 **'System of cropping'.** The tenant is free to grow any crops he may think proper, and that with or without following a regular rotation. An express contract to follow a particular rotation can be ignored except insofar as it applies to the last year: subsection (5). It is in doubt whether the tenant may cease cropping or lay down grass on a large scale over practically the whole of a holding.

6 Where practicable, this provision should be made before departing from contract or custom, although the tenant is entitled to make an infringement provided that 'as soon as is practicable', he makes provisions in the nature of restoration. **'As soon as is practicable'** would be interpreted with reference to usual agricultural conditions and practice.

7 **'Suitable and adequate provision'** will, of course, vary according to circumstances. Sometimes it is attempted, in leases, to specify what would be suitable and adequate provision, but apart from the removal of crops the conditions are so varied that it is scarcely

possible to meet them all by specification, and it is generally safer not to attempt to do so. In the case of removal of crops the case is different.

8 Here we have a standard imposed, and so long as that standard is followed the landlord would not be entitled to find fault with the tenant for failure to protect the holding from injury or deterioration arising from the disposal of crops contrary to custom or contract: *Stark v Edmonstone* (1826) 5 S 45. As to 'full equivalent manurial value', see p 58. It is thought that this includes mechanical as well as chemical properties.

'**In contravention of any such custom, lease or agreement'.** In order to secure that full and adequate provision is made, the wise course would be to adhere, in leases, to the usual clauses prohibiting the removal of crops which are commonly consumed on the land, and especially straw and turnips. Where potatoes are grown, it is generally necessary that they be sold for removal off the farm, and that would not be prevented by a prohibitory clause which would merely have the effect of requiring the full manurial value of the potatoes to be applied to the land. Such a provision is not at all unreasonable in view of the fact that the potato crop is very exhaustive of the fertility of the soil.

With reference to 'custom', it may be pointed out that it is not the custom of the particular estate that is referred to, unless in some way that custom had been imported into the contract of tenancy: *Allan v Thomson* (1829)7 S 784; *Officer v Nicolson* 1807 Hume 827; *Anderson v Tod* 1809 Hume 842. It is the custom of the country or district that is meant. This custom to be effective must be general or, if local, must be known to and relied on by both parties: *Armstrong & Co v McGregor & Co* (1875) 2 R 339; *Anderson v McCall* (1866) 4 M 765; *Holman v Peruvian Nitrate Co* (1878) 5 R 657.

9 The Act assumes the right of the tenant to injure or deteriorate the holding temporarily, because it contemplates the making of 'adequate provision' after the event. Further, it allows 'the return' to the holding of 'equivalent manurial value' of crops sold off. Accordingly, it is thought that interdict would only be granted against gross acts, and especially such as could not readily be made good. See Rankine on Leases (3rd edn), p 418.

10 Failing agreement, the amount of damages should probably be settled by arbitration; *Hill v Wildfowl Trust (Holdings) Ltd* 1995 SCLR 778; cf Gill, *The Law of Agricultural Holdings in Scotland* (2nd edn), who suggests that it is an open question and *McDiarmid v Secretary of State for Scotland* 1970 SLT (Land Ct) 17, where the court refused to remit a delictual claim for damages to arbitration. The measure of damages is the injury to the reversion on the determination of the tenancy, ie the diminution of the rent which the landlord can obtain on reletting: *Williams v Lewis* [1915] 3 KB 493.

11 As, in order to terminate all tenancies, including those renewed from year to year on tacit relocation, notice for not less than one nor more than two years is required, there will be very few cases in which the quitting tenant will neither receive nor give such notice. He will generally know what is the last year of the tenancy before beginning to lay down the last crop. Do the tenant's powers under this section cease the moment notice to quit is given in the case where the landlord gives longer than one year's notice? It may seem unreasonable to suppose that the rights of the tenant under (a) were less than under (b) and the latter extends only to the 'year before expiration of the lease' but this appears to be the effect of this subsection. It is difficult to give a meaning to (a) in the context of a notice to quit which must be at least one year. There appears to have been an inappropriate repetition of the provisions of the Agricultural Holdings (Scotland) Act 1923 under which only six months' notice to quit was required in the case of certain leases from year to year.

See also s 17, which prevents sale or removal of hay, straw, roots, etc, grown in the last year. It should be noted, however, that the present section prohibits the sale or removal of any crops in the last year, whether grown in that year or not: *Gale v Bates* (1864) 33 LJ Ex 235; *Meggeson v Groves* [1917] 1 Ch 158.

12 See preceding note. What is the year before the expiry of the lease? It is thought that, in the case of an arable farm, if a lease provides for entry at Whitsunday as to houses and grass and at separation of crop thereafter as regards land under crop, the expiry 'of the lease' would be the Martinmas in the last year of the tenancy. The doubt arises from the different expressions '**the year before the tenant quits, etc'** and '**the year before the expiry of the lease'**, but this section is concerned with cropping, and it would be strange indeed if the period of restriction were terminated prior to reaping. '**Expiry of the lease'** may be at a '**break'**: see *Edell v Dulieu* [1924] AC 38; *Alston's Trs v Muir* 1919 2 SLT 8.

In respect of (a) and (b) the tenant should be careful to see that, towards the natural termination of his lease, whether at a break or not, he has his cropping arrangements in such order that they would permit of his leaving the land in rotation prescribed by his lease or, if there is none prescribed, in the rotation customary in the district: *Carron Co v Donaldson*

(1858) 20 D 681; *Hunter v Miller* (1862) 24 D 1011; *Marquis of Tweeddale v Brown* (1821) 2
Mur 563; *Meggeson v Groves* [1917] 1 Ch 158; see also the rules of good husbandry in the
Agriculture (Scotland) Act 1948, Sch 6. It is not, however, clear whether a tenant is bound
to do this or only to take such steps as he reasonably can after giving or receiving notice to
quit. He cannot say when the tenancy will end until such notice is given.
13 See note 2 above.

Record of condition, etc, of holding

8.[1]—(1) The landlord or the tenant of an agricultural holding[2] may, at any
time during the tenancy, require the making of a record[3] of the condition of
the fixed equipment on, and of the cultivation of, the holding.

(2) The tenant may, at any time during the tenancy, require the making of
a record of—

(a) existing improvements carried out by him or in respect of the carrying
out of which he has, with the consent in writing of his landlord, paid
compensation to an outgoing tenant;[4]

(b) any fixtures or buildings which, under section 18 of this Act, he is
entitled to remove.

(3) A record under this section shall be made by a person[5] to be appointed
by the Secretary of State, and shall be in such form as may be prescribed.

(4) A record made under this section shall show any consideration or
allowances which have been given by either party to the other.

(5) Subject to section 5 of this Act, a record may, if the landlord or the
tenant so requires, be made under this section relating to a part only of the
holding or to the fixed equipment only.

(6) Any question or difference between the landlord and the tenant arising
out of the making of a record under this section shall, on the application of
the landlord or the tenant, be referred to the Land Court for determination
by them.[6]

(7) The cost of making a record under this section shall, in default of
agreement between the landlord and the tenant, be borne by them in equal
shares.

(8) The remuneration of the person appointed by the Secretary of State to
make a record under this section shall be such amount as the Secretary of
State may fix, and any other expenses of and incidental to the making of the
record shall be subject to taxation by the auditor of the sheriff court, and that
taxation shall be subject to review by the sheriff.

(9) The remuneration of the person appointed by the Secretary of State to
make a record under this section shall be recoverable by that person from
either the landlord or the tenant, but any amount paid by either of those
parties in respect of—

(a) that remuneration, or

(b) any other expenses of and incidental to the making of the record, in
excess of the share payable by him under subsection (7) above of the
cost of making the record, shall be recoverable by him from the other
party.

1 See p 59 and note 1 to s 5. The section is wider than s 5, allowing a record to be made at any
  time during the currency of a lease. Only a record made under s 5(1) forms part of the lease.
2 See definitions in s 85(1) and notes to s 5.
3 Such records are essential to claims for high farming (s 44) and to statutory claims for
  deterioration (ss 45, 46). In any new lease there must be a record of the fixed equipment

(s 5(1)). It is suggested that photographs of defects in the condition of buildings, fences, etc, could be held part of a record. Such records are useful as evidence, especially in arbitrations at awaygoing.
4 See s 35.
5 Not necessarily a member of the panel of arbiters.
6 Disputes under this section are referred to the Land Court and not to arbitration.

Arbitration as to permanent pasture

9.[1]—(1) Where under the lease of an agricultural holding, whether entered into before or after the commencement of this Act, provision is made for the maintenance of specified land, or a specified proportion of the holding, as permanent pasture,[2] the landlord or the tenant may, by notice in writing served on the other party, demand a reference to arbitration under this Act of the question whether it is expedient in order to secure the full and efficient farming[3] of the holding that the amount of land required to be maintained as permanent pasture should be reduced.

(2) On a reference under subsection (1) above the arbiter may by his award direct that the lease shall have effect subject to such modifications of its provisions as to land which is to be maintained as permanent pasture or is to be treated as arable land, and as to cropping, as may be specified in the direction.

(3) If the arbiter gives a direction under subsection (2) above reducing the area of land which is to be maintained as permanent pasture, he may also by his award direct that the lease shall have effect as if it provided that on quitting the holding on the termination of the tenancy the tenant should leave—

(a) as permanent pasture, or
(b) as temporary pasture sown with seeds mixture of such kind as may be specified in that direction,

(in addition to the area of land required by the lease, as modified by the direction, to be maintained as permanent pasture) a specified area of land not exceeding the area by which the land required to be maintained as permanent pasture has been reduced by the direction under subsection (2) above.[4]

1 Formerly questions arising under this section were dealt with by the Secretary of State but from 1958 they had to be referred to arbitration.
2 There is no statutory definition of 'permanent pasture'.
3 **'Full and efficient farming'**: see *Secretary of State v Maclean* 1950 SLCR 33 for a consideration of the phrase 'full and efficient use for agriculture', where it was held that the phrase meant 'use of land as a commercial unit, ie use of land in the normal course of good farming by an active intelligent farmer'.
4 See s 51(1)(a) which excludes compensation for restoration of pasture in accordance with a direction under s 9(3) and which requires averaging of the value of pasture.

Power of landlord to enter on holding

10. The landlord of an agricultural holding or any person authorised by him may at all reasonable times enter on the holding for any of the following purposes—

(a) viewing the state of the holding;[1]

(b) fulfilling the landlord's responsibilities to manage the holding in accordance with the rules of good estate management;[2]

(c) providing, improving, replacing or renewing fixed equipment on the holding otherwise than in fulfilment of such responsibilities.

1 Under common law, a landlord in Scotland can enter a holding for inspection or similar purposes. See also the Agriculture (Safety, Health and Welfare Provisions) Act 1956, s 25(4). In *Luss Estates Co v Firkin Farm Co* 1985 SLT (Land Ct) 17 the court admitted evidence of stock numbers gained at landlord's gatherings, but commented that 'the court doubt whether the landlord's right to inspect these holdings entitled them to handle the tenant's own sheep stock'.

2 These rules are defined in Sch 5 to the Agriculture (Scotland) Act 1948. See Appendix 4.

Bequest of lease

11.[1]—(1) Subject to subsections (2) to (8) below, the tenant of an agricultural holding[2] may, by will or other testamentary writing, bequeath[3] his lease of the holding to his son-in-law or daughter-in-law or to any one of the persons who would be, or would in any circumstances have been, entitled to succeed to the estate on intestacy by virtue of the Succession (Scotland) Act 1964.[4]

(2) A person to whom the lease of a holding is so bequeathed (in this section referred to as 'the legatee') shall, if he accepts the bequest,[5] give notice[6] of the bequest to the landlord of the holding within 21 days[7] after the death of the tenant, or, if he is prevented by some unavoidable cause[8] from giving such notice within that period, as soon as practicable thereafter.

(3) The giving of a notice under subsection (2) above shall import acceptance of the lease and, unless the landlord gives a counter-notice under subsection (4) below, the lease shall be binding on the landlord and on the legatee, as landlord and tenant respectively, as from the date of the death of the deceased tenant.

(4) Where notice has been given under subsection (2) above, the landlord may within one month thereafter give to the legatee a counter-notice intimating that he objects to receiving him as tenant under the lease.

(5) If the landlord gives a counter-notice under subsection (4) above, the legatee may make application[9] to the Land Court for an order declaring him to be tenant under the lease as from the date of the death of the deceased tenant.

(6) If, on the hearing of such an application, any reasonable ground of objection[10] stated by the landlord is established to the satisfaction of the Land Court, they shall declare the bequest to be null and void, but in any other case they shall make an order in terms of the application.

(7) Pending any proceedings under this section, the legatee, with the consent of the executor in whom the lease is vested under section 14 of the Succession (Scotland) Act 1964, shall, unless the Land Court on cause shown otherwise direct, have possession of the holding.

(8)[11] If the legatee does not accept the bequest, or if the bequest is declared null and void under subsection (6) above, the right to the lease shall be treated as intestate estate of the deceased tenant in accordance with Part I of the Succession (Scotland) Act 1964.[12]

1 Parties can contract out of this section. It has been held that where there was an express exclusion of the tenant's legatee in a lease, s 11 could not be invoked: *Kennedy v Johnstone*

1956 SC 39. This decision is not affected by s 29(2) of the Succession (Scotland) Act 1964, which provides that an *implied* condition prohibiting assignation does not render a bequest of a lease invalid. Are testamentary trustees legatees within the meaning of this section? This was the view taken by the Land Court: *Andrew Linton's Trs v Wemyss Landed Estates Co Ltd* 1953 SLCR 14, *per contra* in *Kennedy v Johnstone* the Lord President said *obiter* that it was inappropriate to describe trustees as legatees. Executors may, in certain circumstances, become the tenants under a lease: *Morrison-Low v Paterson* 1985 SC (HL) 49.

2 **'Agricultural holding'**: see definition in s 85(1) and notes to s 1.

3 It is prudent to make specific reference in the will to the lease. It has been held that a general bequest of residue did not carry a lease which contained an exclusion of assignees: *Reid's Trs v Macpherson* 1975 SLT 101. Where there is power of bequest it may be a question of construction of the will whether the lease is carried by a general bequest: see Rankine on Leases (3rd edn), p 162.

4 In the Agricultural Holdings (Scotland) Act 1949 the tenant's right of bequest extended to 'any person'. Section 6(1) of the Agriculture Act 1958 limited this right of bequest to 'any member of his family', as defined in s 6(2). The present wording was introduced by s 16 of the Succession (Scotland) Act 1964. A bequest may only be made to an individual within the class.

5 **'Accepts the bequest'**. Where a legatee gave notice after the twenty-one-day period had elapsed (see note 7 below) and he was not prevented by unavoidable cause from giving notice within that period, he was held to have no right to the tenancy but, since he had accepted a valid bequest, s 11(7) did not apply and so the right to the lease was not to be treated as intestate estate which would be transferred by the executor. The tenancy accordingly terminated: *Coats v Logan* 1985 SLT 221.

6 **'Notice'**. The notice of acceptance must be by the legatee personally: see, eg, *Garvie's Trs v Garvie's Tutors* 1975 SLT 94. Although this is not expressly required to be in writing, it is clearly advisable that it be in writing and sent by recorded delivery, in order to avoid questions both as to the fact and the date of the intimation. For intimation by telephone see *Irving v Church of Scotland General Trs* 1960 SLCR 16.

7 **'Within 21 days'** means that the intimation has to arrive before midnight on the twenty-first day after the date of the death, ie twenty-one days excluding the date of death: see *Stair Memorial Encyclopedia*, vol 22, para 826(9). Intimation posted before the time-limit but received after the twenty-first day is not timeous intimation.

8 **'Unavoidable cause'**. For example, the legatee might be abroad and he might not hear of the bequest in time to permit of the intimation being made within the twenty-one days: but see *Wight v Marquis of Lothian's Trs* 1952 SLCR 22. Where a will was not found within twenty-one days of the testator's death the legatee was held prevented by unavoidable cause: *MacKinnon v Martin* 1958 SLCR 19. For circumstances where a widow's exhaustion and inability to give instructions were held not to be an unavoidable cause, see *Thomson v Lyall* 1966 SLCR 136. Following the Court of Session decision in *Garvie's Trs v Still* 1972 SLT 29 it is doubtful that the Land Court has jurisdiction to determine whether or not there has been 'unavoidable cause'.

9 **'Application'**. No time-limit is specified for the application nor is any time-limit introduced by s 16 of the Succession (Scotland) Act 1964, but the courts might well construe the provision to mean 'within a reasonable time': per Lord Allanbridge in *Gladstone v Halliday* Outer House, 1981; unreported. In the absence of counter-notice under subsection (3) application is incompetent: *Andrew v Smith* (1983) Strathclyde RN 242. If the tenant's legatee neglects to follow procedure in this section the landlord may ask the Land Court to direct under s 20(6) that the landlord or his nominee has possession of the holding instead of the legatee. In *Wight v Marquis of Lothian's Trs* 1952 SLCR 22 at p 25 the Land Court expressed the opinion that where the legatee was dilatory in making application under s 20(4) of the Agricultural Holdings (Scotland) Act 1949 (now s 11) the landlord might competently apply to the Land Court to have the bequest declared null and void. The court recognised that the section did not specifically give the landlord the right to make such an application but took the view that where a legatee has been dilatory such an application by the landlord 'becomes necessary and is not inconsistent with the provisions of the section'. It does not follow, however, that the application should be to the Land Court. Gill, *The Law of Agricultural Holdings in Scotland* (2nd edn), paras 605, 662, indicates that this would not be competent and that the landlord in such circumstances must raise proceedings in the civil court, and that is probably correct.

10 **'Objection'**. The Land Court is given a wide discretion as to these objections. Objections must be on personal grounds: *Marquis of Lothian's Trs v Johnston* 1952 SLCR App 233;

Howie v David Lowe & Sons Ltd 1952 SLCR 14 (in the latter it was held that the tenant's ability, character and resources were the only relevant considerations). A landlord may not found on his own needs or requirements: *Fraser v Murray's Trs* 1954 SLCR 10. A person who has not a great amount of agricultural knowledge and skill would not necessarily be rejected, because he may be able to employ a thoroughly experienced grieve. Such a person might, however, be removed by notice to quit. Section 25(2)(c) and Sch 2, Cases 1 and 5, direct that the Land Court shall consent to the operation of notice to quit given to a 'near relative' successor if it is satisfied that he 'has neither sufficient training in agriculture nor sufficient experience in the farming of land to enable him to farm the holding with reasonable efficiency'. If the legatee were a person of disreputable habits, or had insufficient capital, objection on such grounds should succeed. In *Sloss v Agnew* 1923 SLT (Sh Ct) 33, objection was sustained to a bequest to a daughter who did not possess sufficient skill, capital or equipment. For cases where landlords' objections on grounds of, *inter alia,* tenants' lack of experience failed when skilled assistance was available, see *Service v Forestry Commission of Argyll* 1951 SLT (Sh Ct) 2; *Fraser v Murray's Trs; Dunsinnan Estate Trs v Alexander* 1978 SLCR App 146; *Bell v Forestry Commission* 1980 SLCR App 116. See also *Reid v Duffus Estate Ltd* 1955 SLCR 13 (tenant's financial resources and experience held sufficient). For cases concerning personal qualities and character see *Marquis of Lothian's Trs v Johnston* and *Luss Estate Co v Campbell* 1973 SLCR App 96 (where one conviction for poaching did not prevent the legatee from succeeding).

11 Where the landlord attacks the validity of the bequest, that question falls to be dealt with by proceedings in the civil court: *Mackenzie v Cameron* (1894) 21 R 427; *Garvie's Trs v Still* 1972 SLT 29. If the landlord has objected to the legatee and the lease is vested in the executor under s 14 of the Succession (Scotland) Act 1964 the legatee may have possession only with the executor's consent. In this situation the executor and not the legatee is the tenant as defined in s 85(1), ie 'the holder of land under a lease'. If the legatee intimates the bequest within twenty-one days of the death and the landlord does not object the legatee will usually have become the tenant before the lease vests in the executor. In terms of s 16(8) of the 1964 Act the fact that the interest is vested in the executor is not to prevent the operation of subsections (2) to (7) of s 11.

12 If a legatee or the acquirer on intestacy succeeds to the tenancy a new lease is not thereby constituted.

Right of landlord to object to acquirer of lease

12.[1]—(1) A person to whom the lease of an agricultural holding is transferred under section 16 of the Succession (Scotland) Act 1964 (referred to in this section as 'the acquirer')[2] shall give notice of the acquisition to the landlord of the holding within twenty-one days[3] after the date of the acquisition, or, if he is prevented by some unavoidable cause[4] from giving such notice within that period, as soon as is practicable thereafter and, unless the landlord gives a counter-notice under subsection (2) below, the lease shall be binding on the landlord and on the acquirer, as landlord and tenant respectively, as from the date of the acquisition.[5]

(2) Within one month after receipt of a notice given under subsection (1) above the landlord may give a counter-notice to the acquirer intimating that the landlord objects to receive him as tenant under the lease; and not before the expiry of one month from the giving of the counter-notice the landlord may make application to the Land Court for an order terminating the lease.

(3) On an application under subsection (2) above, the Land Court shall, if they are satisfied that the landlord has established a reasonable ground of objection,[6] make an order terminating the lease, to take effect as from such term of Whitsunday or Martinmas[7] as they may specify.

(4) Pending any proceedings under this section, the acquirer, with the consent of the executor in whom the lease is vested under section 14 of the

Succession (Scotland) Act 1964 shall, unless the Land Court on cause shown otherwise direct, have possession of the holding.[8]

(5) Termination of the lease under this section shall be treated, for the purposes of Parts IV and V of this Act (compensation), as termination of the acquirer's's tenancy of the holding; but nothing in this section shall entitle him to compensation for disturbance.[9]

1 This section was substituted by para 22 of Sch 2 to the Succession (Scotland) Act 1964 for the original s 21 of the Agricultural Holdings (Scotland) Act 1949, which dealt with the landlord's right to object to the succession to the holding of the tenant's heir-at-law.

2 'Acquirer'. This section provides for notice to be given by the 'acquirer' as defined in the subsection in the same way as a legatee gives notice under s 11. Where notice was given by the transferors of a lease instead of the transferee but this resulted in no prejudice to the landlords, the notice was held to be effective: *Garvie's Trs v Garvie's Tutors* 1975 SLT 94. The practice is, however, dangerous and should not be followed.

3 'Within 21 days': see note 7 to s 11.

4 'Some unavoidable cause': see note 8 to s 11.

5 'Date of the acquisition'. This may be up to one year after the date of death of the tenant: see the Succession (Scotland) Act 1964, s 16. Delay by the deceased tenant's executor in transferring the lease to one of the persons entitled to succeed to the tenant's estate may thus have the effect of precluding the landlord from giving the statutory notice to quit against a break in the lease or the conventional ish.

6 'Reasonable ground of objection': see note 9 to s 11.

7 Whitsun and Martinmas are defined by the Term and Quarter Days (Scotland) Act 1990 to be 28th May and 28th November.

8 An acquirer to whom the landlord objects may have possession but only with consent of the executor in whom the lease is vested. The acquirer is not the tenant as defined in s 85(1), ie 'the holder of land under a lease', although he is treated as such for some purposes of the Act – eg, compensation for improvements at termination. The acquirer becomes tenant if he gives notice within twenty-one days of the acquisition (see note 3 above) and the landlord does not object or fails in his objection: *Coats v Logan* 1985 SLT 221. The executor requires to make a formal transfer of the lease to the acquirer. A docket in the form (suitably modified) of Sch 1 to the Succession (Scotland) Act 1964 is suggested.

9 He will be entitled to all usual waygoing rights under the Act, except a disturbance claim, but difficulties may arise if the occupation is terminated at other than the usual terms.

Variation of rent

Variation of rent

13.[1]—(1) Subject to subsection (8) below, the landlord[2] or the tenant of an agricultural holding may, whether the tenancy was created before or after the commencement of this Act, by notice in writing served on the other party, demand a reference to arbitration of the question what rent should be payable in respect of the holding as from the next day after the date of the notice on which the tenancy could have been terminated by notice to quit (or notice of intention to quit) given on that date,[3] and the matter shall be referred[4] accordingly.

(2) On a reference under subsection (1) above, the arbiter shall determine, in accordance with subsections (3) to (7) below the rent properly payable in respect of the holding as from the 'next day' mentioned in subsection (1) above.

(3) For the purposes of this section the rent properly payable in respect of a holding shall normally[5] be the rent at which, having regard to the terms of the tenancy (other than those relating to rent),[6] the holding might reasonably be expected to be let in the open market[7] by a willing landlord to a willing

tenant,[8] there being disregarded (in addition to the matters referred to in subsection (5) below) any effect on rent of the fact that the tenant is in occupation of the holding.[9]

(4)[10] Where the evidence available to the arbiter is in his opinion insufficient to enable him to determine the rent properly payable or he is of the view that the open market for rents of comparable subjects in the surrounding area is distorted by scarcity of lets or by other factors, the rent properly payable for the purposes of this section shall be the rent which he would expect to be paid, in a market which was not affected by such distortion, having particular regard to the following—

(a) information about open market rents of comparable subjects outside the surrounding area;

(b) the entire range of offers made as regards any lease of subjects which are comparable after regard is had to the terms of that lease;

(c) sitting tenants' rents fixed by agreement for subjects in the surrounding area which are comparable after regard is had to any element attributable to goodwill between landlord and tenant or to similar considerations; and

(d) the current economic conditions in the relevant sector of agriculture.

(5) The arbiter shall not take into account any increase in the rental value of the holding which is due to improvements[11]—

(a) so far as—

(i) they have been executed wholly or partly at the expense of the tenant (whether or not that expense has been or will be reimbursed by a grant out of moneys provided by Parliament) without equivalent allowance or benefit[12] having been made or given by the landlord in consideration of their execution; and

(ii) they have not been executed under an obligation imposed on the tenant by the terms of his lease;[13]

(b) which have been executed by the landlord, in so far as the landlord has received or will receive grants out of moneys provided by Parliament in respect of the execution thereof,

nor fix the rent at a higher amount than would have been properly payable if those improvements had not been so executed.

(6) The continuous adoption by the tenant of a standard of farming or a system of farming more beneficial to the holding than the standard or system required by the lease or, in so far as no system of farming is so required, than the system of farming normally practised on comparable holdings in the district, shall be deemed, for the purposes of subsection (5) above, to be an improvement executed at his expense.[14]

(7) The arbiter shall not fix the rent at a lower amount by reason of any dilapidation or deterioration of, or damage to, fixed equipment or land caused or permitted by the tenant.[15]

(8) Subject to subsection (9) below, a reference to arbitration under subsection (1) above shall not be demanded in circumstances which are such that any increase or reduction of rent made in consequence thereof would take effect as from a date earlier than the expiry of 3[16] years from the latest in time of the following—

(a) the commencement of the tenancy;[17]

(b) the date as from which there took effect[18] a previous variation of rent (under this section or otherwise);

143

(c) the date as from which there took effect a previous direction under this section that the rent should continue unchanged.[19]

(9) There shall be disregarded for the purposes of subsection (8) above—

(a) a variation of rent under section 14 of this Act;

(b) an increase of rent under section 15(1) of this Act;

(c) a reduction of rent under section 31 of this Act.[20]

1 This section does not apply to rent review provisions in a lease, which apply before the date at which a lease can be terminated. Thus leases for twenty-one years with five-yearly rent review provisions in line with the retail prices index, do not fall within the terms of the section until the first date at which the lease could be brought to an end: *Duncan v Anderson* 1985 SLCR 1. It is not competent to contract out of the provisions of s 13(2) while the lease is running on tacit relocation and any agreement to vary those statutory provisions would be unenforceable: *Moll v Macgregor* 1990 SLT (Land Ct) 59 (*sub nom Wallace v Moll* 1989 SLCR 21). While *Moll* appears to decide *obiter* that it is not competent to contract out of s 13 during the stipulated endurance of the lease this would appear to be wrong: *Duncan supra.* The parties may agree a variation of rent outwith the statutory periods of revision: *Boyd v McDonald* 1958 SLCR 10. If the farm is a dairy farm, the arbiter will have to take into account the terms of s 16 of the Agriculture Act 1986 in fixing the rent, even if the milk quota was only brought to the holding by reason of the tenant's improvements: *Broadland Properties Estates Ltd v Mann* 1994 SLT (Land Ct) 7. If opencast coal mining is taking place on the farm, see the Opencast Coal Act 1958, s 14A. Where the arbiter has been appointed by the Secretary of State (but not where the appointment is by agreement) (1) the arbiter may, at any stage of the proceedings state a case for the opinion of the Land Court (Sch 7, para 22); and (2) the parties may appeal to the Land Court against the final award on any question of law or fact, including the amount of the award (see 61(2): cf *Maciver v Broadland Properties Estates Ltd* 1994 SLCR 18).

2 'Landlord'. The landlord need not be infeft: *Alexander Black & Sons v Paterson* 1968 SLT (Sh Ct) 64. Where there is a change of landlord between the date of serving the demand and the review date it is thought that no further demand is required, although it would be wise for the outgoing landlord to assign his rights under the demand to the incoming landlord.

3 The application for the appointment of an arbiter has to be given more than one year and less than two years before the review date: ie the same period of notice as is required to terminate a tenancy under s 21(3).

4 'The matter shall be referred'. The arbiter must be appointed before the date when the alteration of rent is to take effect: *Graham v Gardner* 1966 SLT (Land Ct) 12, following *Sclater v Horton* [1954] 2 QB 1; cf *Dundee Corporation v Guthrie* 1969 SLT 93.

5 'Normally'. Added by the Agricultural Holdings (Amendment)(Scotland) Act 1983, s 2. The basis of open market rent is still the norm and the provisions of subsection (4) apply where evidence of open market rents is insufficient or the rents are distorted by scarcity or otherwise. Paradoxically the latter may be the more usual situation as was observed by the Land Court in *Dunbar's Trs v Anderson* 1985 SLCR 1.

6 'Having regard to the terms of the tenancy (other than those relating to rent)'. The arbiter or the Land Court must have regard to all the terms of the lease even if they are not enforced: *Secretary of State for Scotland v Davidson* 1960 SLT (Land Ct) 7; *Strathclyde Regional Council v Arneil* 1987 SLCR 44; *British Alcan Aluminium Co v Shaw* 1987 SLCR 1. Disregarding the terms relating to rent would require the arbiter to disregard factors such as whether or not the rent is forehand or backhand, whether interest is payable on arrears of rent, etc: cf Scammell and Densham, *Law of Agricultural Holdings* (7th edn, p 96).

7 'Open market'. The discretion of the arbiter or the Land Court is strictly limited: see *Secretary of State for Scotland v Sinclair* 1962 SLCR 6.

8 'Willing landlord', 'willing tenant': see *Kilmarnock Estates Ltd v Barr* 1969 SLT (Land Ct) 10; *F R Evans (Leeds) Ltd v English Electric Co Ltd* (1977) 36 P & CR 185.

9 This paragraph was added by s 2 of the Agriculture Act 1958, and amended by the Agricultural Holdings (Amendment)(Scotland) Act 1983. Subsection (3) provides as the normal criterion for arbiters fixing rents, the open market rent. It is important that proof as to market rent be adduced: *Secretary of State for Scotland v Sinclair* 1962 SLCR 6; *Witham v Stockdale* 1981 SLT (Land Ct) 27.

10 This subsection was introduced by the Agricultural Holdings (Amendment)(Scotland) Act 1983. The purpose of the subsection is to discount in a hypothetical open market rent any

unfair distortion in favour of the landlord caused by scarcity or competition. For its application by the Land Court, see *Dunbar's Trs v Anderson* 1985 SLCR 1; *Earl of Seafield v Stewart* 1985 SLT (Land Ct) 35; *Kinnaird Trust v Boyne* 1985 SLCR 19; *Aberdeen Endowment Trust v Will* 1985 SLT (Land Ct) 23; *Buccleuch v Kennedy* 1986 SLCR App 1; *British Alcan Aluminium Co v Shaw* 1987 SLCR 1; *Shand v Christie's Trs* 1987 SLCR 29; and *Towns v Anderson* 1989 SLT (Land Ct) 17, where comment was made that account could be taken of rent fixed in other arbitrations provided proper reasons had been given by the arbiter. In *Moll v McGregor* 1991 SLCR 1 the Land Court reserved the question of whether or not the phrase 'in the surrounding area' in subsection (4)(c) restricted the arbiter or court to a consideration only of rents fixed by agreement of those subjects 'in the surrounding area' or whether they might also take into account rents fixed by agreement outwith the surrounding area. In reserving the question the court opined that it appeared that only locally agreed rents could be taken into account.

11 **'Improvements'.** Even if a sitting tenant is not entitled to compensation for improvements at outgo, he is not to have his rent increased in consequence of these improvements: *Towns v Anderson* 1989 SLT (Land Ct) 17. It is thought that this provision is not confined to improvements scheduled under the Act. Improvements made by a former tenant are not to be disregarded: *Kilmarnock Estates Ltd v Barr* 1969 SLT (Land Ct) 10.

12 Questions may arise as to what is **'equivalent allowance or benefit'**: see note 2 to s 36. Apparently the improvements referred to are such as the tenant voluntarily effected, and for which, by the contract of tenancy or otherwise, he received no concession or benefit. A tenant's fixtures are not improvements.

13 It is generally understood that, when a new lease is entered into, all common law claims by the landlord or by the tenant against each other, under the expired lease, are extinguished except such as are maintained in force by statute, or by agreement in the new lease. The same rule applied in the case of a renunciation: *Lyons v Anderson* (1886) 13 R 1020; *Walker's Trs v Manson* (1886) 13 R 1198. But where a tenancy has been renewed by tacit relocation the case is different: per Lord President Clyde in *Cowe v Millar* 1923; unreported. Where rent has been fixed in an arbitration under the Act the other provisions of the lease continue to apply; the arbiter has no power to vary them: see *Grant v Broadland Properties Estates Ltd* 1995 SLCR 39.

14 Cf s 44. It is essential for a claim under s 44 that there be a record of fixed equipment and cultivation. There is no such requirement here.

15 This, it is thought, applies only to deterioration or dilapidation during the currency of the lease last entered into, including renewals thereof by tacit relocation: see *Findlay v Munro* 1917 SC 419; *Kilmarnock Estates Ltd v Barr* 1969 SLT (Land Ct) 10. Deterioration made or permitted by the tenant appears to be confined to deterioration in breach of contract. Dilapidations for which the landlord is responsible do not fall to be disregarded even though the tenant may have a remedy: see *Strathclyde Regional Council v Arneil* 1987 SLCR 44; *Metropolitan Properties Co Ltd v Woolridge* (1968) 20 P & CR 64.

16 **'3'.** Formerly five years; this was altered by the Agricultural Holdings (Amendment)(Scotland) Act 1983.

17 **'Commencement of the tenancy'.** It was suggested in previous editions that this referred to the term when the tenant first entered the holding and not the current lease. Gill, *The Law of Agricultural Holdings in Scotland* (2nd edn), para 200, persuasively indicates the contrary view. The question is likely to remain academic.

18 **'Took effect'.** Assuming that a reduction had been granted on the rent of the year from Martinmas 1989 to Martinmas 1990, it is thought that the reduction took effect as at Martinmas 1989, irrespective of the date at which the rent was payable or the reduction agreed or decreed, and that the three years would be counted from that term and not from Martinmas following. Note the three years run from any 'previous variation' whether under s 13 'or otherwise', so any variation affects the start point for the next three years. The provision is wider than the English equivalent under the Agricultural Holdings Act 1986, Sch 2, para 4.

19 This applies to a direction in an arbitration or Land Court reference, but may not apply to a voluntary agreement to leave the rent unchanged: see *Moll v Macgregor* 1990 SLT (Land Ct) 59.

20 A voluntary variation of rent in respect of any of these events, as opposed to a variation by an arbiter under the sections, is not covered: cf *Mann v Gardner* (1991) 61 P & CR 1.

Arbitrations under sections 4 and 5

14.[1] Where it appears to an arbiter—

(a) on a reference under section 4 of this Act that, by reason of any provision which he is required by that section to include in his award, or

(b) on a reference under section 5 of this Act that, by reason of any provision included in his award,

it is equitable that the rent of the holding should be varied, he may vary the rent accordingly.

1 This confers a wide discretion on the arbiter who should exercise it with great care. It would seem that he should determine the annual value of the changes made to the party benefited by them and vary the rent by a similar amount. The provisions of s 13 are not expressly applicable and Gill, *The Law of Agricultural Holdings in Scotland* (2nd edn), para 223, suggests that the arbiter's pre-1958 discretion may still apply. It is thought, however, that the object of the subsection is to allow adjustment of rent to take account of the changes made. This might not be achieved if a different basis were applicable from that in s 13. The provisions of s 61(2), appeal to the Land Court, and para 10 and 22 of Sch 7, regarding reasons to be given in the arbiter's award and the provision for stated case to the Land Court, respectively apply only when the arbiter is appointed by the Secretary of State or the Land Court 'in an arbitration under section 13(1)'. The arbiter can still be required to state a case for the sheriff under paras 20 and 21 of Sch 7.

Increase of rent for certain improvements by landlord

15.[1]—(1) Where the landlord of an agricultural holding has, whether before or after the commencement of this Act, carried out on the holding an improvement (whether or not one for the carrying out of which compensation is provided for under Part IV of this Act)—

(a) at the request of, or in agreement with, the tenant,

(b) in pursuance of an undertaking given by the landlord under section 39(3) of this Act,[2] or

(c) in compliance with a direction given by the Secretary of State under powers conferred on him by or under any enactment,

subject to subsections (2) and (3) below, the rent of the holding shall, if the landlord by notice in writing served on the tenant within 6 months from the completion of the improvement so requires, be increased as from the completion of the improvement by an amount equal to the increase in the rental value of the holding[3] attributable to the carrying out of the improvement.

(2) Where any grant has been made to the landlord out of moneys provided by Parliament, in respect of an improvement to which subsection (1) above applies, the increase in rent provided for by that subsection shall be reduced proportionately.[4]

(3) Any question arising between the landlord and the tenant in the application of this section shall be determined by arbitration.

1 Section 25(5) of the Agriculture (Safety, Health and Welfare Provisions) Act 1956 provides: 'Where the landlord of an agricultural holding has executed thereon works of the nature of fixed equipment which are required to be executed ... or has executed similar works at the request of, or in agreement with, the tenant, section 15 of the Agricultural Holdings (Scotland) Act 1991 (which provides for increases of rent in respect of improvements carried out by the landlord) shall have effect as if the works so executed were such an improvement as is mentioned in subsection (1) of that section.' Similar provisions are contained in s 256 of the

Housing (Scotland) Act 1987 in regard to improvements carried out in compliance with notices or undertakings given under that Act. The landlord may not obtain a rent increase during the five years following improvements effected with a grant obtained under the 1987 Act. Provision is made by subsection (2) for proportionate reduction of the increase in rent if the tenant has contributed to the cost of the improvement. See also the Opencast Coal Act 1958, s 14A(1), (9) as amended by the Housing and Planning Act 1986, Sch A, para 5, Sch 11, para 12.

2 This refers to an undertaking to execute the improvements given after receipt of notice from the Land Court under s 39(3) that the tenant may execute certain improvements and the landlord undertakes to execute them.

3 **'Rental value of the holding'** must be assessed in accordance with s 13(1) and (2). The provisions of s 61(2), appeal to the Land Court, and paras 10 and 22 of Sch 7 regarding reasons to be given for the arbiter's award and the provisions for a stated case to the Land Court respectively, do not apply as they only apply to an arbiter appointed by the Secretary of State or the Land Court 'in an arbitration under section 13(1)'. A stated case to the sheriff under paras 20 and 21 can still be requested.

4 A rent reduction can be obtained under this subsection where an improvement has been effected under a livestock rearing land improvement scheme under the Hill Farming Act 1946 (as amended), where the Secretary of State has reduced the grant under s 7(3).

Termination of tenancy

Leases not terminated by variation of terms, etc

16.[1] The lease of an agricultural holding shall not be brought to an end, and accordingly neither party shall be entitled to bring proceedings to terminate the lease or, except with the consent of the other party, to treat it as at an end, by reason only that any new term has been added to the lease or that any terms of the lease (including the rent payable) have been varied or revised in pursuance of this Act.

1 The effect of this section is not clear: see *Tuffnell and Nether Whitehaugh Co* 1977 SLT (Land Ct) 14 and *Mackie v Gardner* 1973 SLT (Land Ct) 11. It appears to be that, if the terms of a lease are varied under any of ss 2(1), 4, 5(2), (3), 9, 13, 14, 15 – eg, with regard to rent, or with regard to the respective liabilities of landlord and tenant for the maintenance of fixed equipment – the existing lease is continued and there is no new lease. If the lease is varied in any other way it may constitute a new contract, which has significant effects when the commencement of the lease is of importance under the Act; see, eg, ss 5 and 68 to 70 and the valuation of sheep stock: *Tuffnell and Nether Whitehaugh Co*. The provisions of s 5 are not held to be incorporated in the lease. They would be, however, if the lease, as varied, was regarded as a new lease. In view of the terms of s 4 these last-mentioned provisions could be incorporated in any lease containing provisions inconsistent with s 5 and continued by tacit relocation, but, if they are, an arbiter would require to vary the rent payable in order to take into account any transfer of liability.

Prohibition of removal of manure, etc, after notice to quit, etc

17. Where, in respect of an agricultural holding, notice to quit is given by the landlord or notice of intention to quit is given by the tenant, the tenant shall not, subject to any agreement to the contrary, at any time after the date of the notice, sell or remove from the holding any manure or compost, or any hay, straw or roots[1] grown in the last year[2] of the tenancy, unless and until he has given the landlord or the incoming tenant a reasonable opportunity[3] of agreeing to purchase them on the termination of the tenancy at their fair market value, or at such other value as is provided by the lease.

1 **'Roots'** includes mangolds, swedes, turnips, and cabbage, but not potatoes. The Agriculture Act 1986, s 15(3), (7) defines roots to mean 'the produce of any root crop of a kind normally grown for consumption on the holdings': see 'Procedure and Principles of Valuation', p 110.
2 As hitherto, this will generally be regulated by the conditions of the lease but, insofar as that is not done, this section will operate, unless there is contracting out. In the case of a Whitsunday and separation of crop entry, the last year would, it is thought, be Martinmas to Martinmas, just as in the case of a Martinmas entry, because separation of the last crop must be included.
3 What is a reasonable opportunity? In *Barbour v M'Douall* 1914 SC 844, it was held, in connection with a claim for compensation for unreasonable disturbance under the Agricultural Holdings (Scotland) Act 1908, that the tenant had no duty to give any intimation to the landlord before advertising his stock for sale. Nevertheless, it would be prudent for the tenant to write to the landlord and incoming tenant, offering to sell at a fair market value or at the value provided by the contract of tenancy. Where the lease provides for a valuation any arbitration will be non-statutory (s 61(7)). Where there is no provision in the lease for valuation this would apparently be covered by s 61, in a question between landlord and tenant, but not in a question between tenant and incoming tenant, because the scheme of the Act is generally confined to questions and claims between landlord and tenant, and s 61 is expressly so confined: see *Roger v Hutcheson* 1922 SC (HL) 140, where it was held that it was not illegal for the outgoing and incoming tenants to agree a non-statutory arbitration. The point is not, however, clear, especially where the incoming tenant agrees to take over from awaygoing tenant.

Tenant's right to remove fixtures and buildings

18.[1]—(1) Subject to subsections (2) to (4) below, and to section 40(4)(a) of this Act—

(a) any engine, machinery, fencing or other fixture[2] affixed to an agricultural holding by the tenant thereof; and
(b) any building (other than one in respect of which the tenant is entitled to compensation under this Act or otherwise) erected by him on the holding,

not being a fixture affixed or a building erected in pursuance of some obligation in that behalf, or instead of some fixture or building belonging to the landlord, shall be removable by the tenant at any time during the continuance of the tenancy or before the expiry of 6 months, or such longer period as may be agreed, after the termination of the tenancy[4] and shall remain his property[5] so long as he may remove it by virtue of this subsection.

(2) The right conferred by subsection (1) above shall not be exercisable in relation to a fixture or building unless the tenant—

(a) has paid all rent owing by him and has performed or satisfied all his other obligations to the landlord in respect of the holding,[6] and
(b) has, at least one month before whichever is the earlier of the exercise of the right and the termination of the tenancy, given to the landlord notice in writing of his intention to remove the fixture or building.[7]

(3) If, before the expiry of the period of notice specified in subsection (2)(b) above, the landlord gives to the tenant a counter-notice in writing electing to purchase a fixture or building comprised in the notice, subsection (1) above shall cease to apply to that fixture or building, but the landlord shall be liable to pay to the tenant the fair value thereof to an incoming tenant of the holding.[8]

(4) In the removal of a fixture or building by virtue of subsection (1) above, the tenant shall not do to any other building or other part of the holding any avoidable damage, and immediately after the removal shall make good all damage so occasioned.

1 See 'Record of Holding', p 59, and s 8. It was held competent to contract out this section (*Premier Dairies v Garlick* [1920] 2 Ch 17), but see *Johnson v Moreton* [1980] AC 37; [1978] 3 All ER 37, where Lord Hailsham observes that at the time of the decision 'the statutory scheme was different in some important respects'. See also the Opencast Coal Act 1958, s 27.

2 **'Fixture'.** The Act gives no definition of 'fixture'. The definition of 'fixed equipment' is now much wider (s 85(1)) as it includes buildings, fences, drains, etc. It must be assumed, therefore, that this provision only applies to things which are of the nature of landlord's fixtures; items such as shelving grates, etc, which can be removed entire, and are only slightly fixed do not come under this section. But 'fixtures' erected for the purpose of trade, though they would be removable if the trade were other than farming, did not apply to agricultural fixtures. The Scots courts were more favourable to the tenant, not by treating agricultural fixtures in the same way as other trade fixtures but by applying more leniently the test of whether something was a fixture. See Marshall on *Agricultural Outgoing Claims*, p 39. The words 'engine, machinery, fencing' appear to be qualified by the words 'or other fixture'. Again 'any building' applies, it is thought, only to structures of a permanent nature. Glasshouses on market gardens were held to be 'buildings' (*Smith v Richmond* [1899] AC 448; *Meux v Cobley* [1892] 2 Ch 253) but in *Mears v Callender* [1901] 2 Ch 388 it was held that glass-houses erected by a tenant could be removed under his common law rights. It is thought that any engine, machinery, fencing, or temporary structure, which the tenant could remove at common law as not being in its nature a 'fixture' can be removed without regard to the provisions of this section. Section 100 of the Agricultural Holdings (Scotland) Act 1949 seemed to reserve the tenant's common law rights sufficiently in this connection. That section is not repeated in the 1991 Act.

It is sometimes difficult to determine whether a thing falls within the category of fixture or not, and, where there is doubt, it will generally be safer to follow the procedure prescribed by this section. In determining, at common law, whether a thing is a fixture or not, the points for consideration are (1) whether the thing can be moved without injury to itself or to the subjects; and (2) the object for which the thing was attached to the soil, whether as a permanent improvement or for a merely temporary purpose.

There is a distinction in the case of things which are not fixtures; they can generally only be removed before, or at least, at the termination of the tenancy (*Brand's Trs v Brand's Trs* (1876) 3 R (HL) 16; *Miller v Muirhead* (1894) 21 R 658), whereas in the case of 'fixtures' they may be removed within six months thereafter: see *Scottish Discount Co Ltd v Blin* 1985 SC 216.

3 **'Entitled to compensation'.** The tenant's right will be significant in the not uncommon case where the tenant has omitted to give notice of intention to carry out an improvement of the kind listed in Pt II of Schs 3, 4 and 5. Muir Watt, *Agricultural Holdings* (13th edn), p 263, suggests that a tenant is 'not entitled to compensation' and may remove a building if it has been written off over a period of years which has expired. To avoid this such agreements commonly provide for nominal compensation rather than a complete write-off.

4 **'Termination of the tenancy'**: see definition in s 85(1) and notes thereto.

5 **'Shall remain his property'.** If the landlord should refuse to allow the removal of fixtures, this would confer a right of action by the tenant for their value: *Thomas v Jennings* (1896) 66 LJ QB 5. A renunciation of a lease prima facie includes all fixtures on the holding (*Leschallas v Woolf* [1908] 1 Ch 641), but there seems no reason why the terms of this section should not apply in that case.

6 Generally all claims at the landlord's instance must be settled before the removal of the fixtures, but this implied that the landlord does not unreasonably hold back his claims. In a case where a tenant was in arrears with his rent at the time of giving notice, it was held that this deferred his right to compensation but did not extinguish it: *Roberts v Magor* (1953) 103 LJ 703 CC.

7 See note 10 to s 21(7).

8 **'Fair value thereof to an incoming tenant'** seems to accord with the basis on which compensation is payable for permanent and other improvements. Any difference as to the value could be settled by arbitration under s 60. It will be noted that the fixtures become the property of the landlord.

Payment for implements, etc, sold on quitting holding

19.—(1) Where a tenant of an agricultural holding has entered into an agreement or it is a term of the lease of the holding that the tenant will on quitting the holding, sell to the landlord or to the incoming[1] tenant any implements of husbandry, fixtures, farm produce or farm stock on or used in connection with the holding, notwithstanding anything in the agreement or lease to the contrary, it shall be deemed to be a term of the agreement or of the lease, as the case may be, that the property in the goods shall not pass to the buyer until the price is paid and that payment of the price shall be made within one month after the tenant has quitted the holding or, if the price of the goods is to be ascertained by a valuation, within one month after the delivery of the award in the valuation.[2]

(2) Where payment of the price is not made within one month as aforesaid the outgoing tenant shall be entitled to sell or remove the goods and to receive from the landlord or the incoming tenant, as the case may be, by whom the price was payable, compensation of an amount equal to any loss or expense unavoidably incurred by the outgoing tenant upon or in connection with such sale or removal, together with any expenses reasonably incurred by him in the preparation of his claim for compensation.[3]

(3) Any question arising as to the amount of compensation payable under subsection (2) above shall be determined by arbitration.[4]

1 The outgoing tenant can elect with whom he will deal unless the terms of the lease are specified to the contrary. As a rule, he should deal with the landlord, whose interest is permanent.
2 It is to the interest of the outgoing tenant that the valuation should be carried out and the award issued as soon as possible after the awaygoing and in the submission a date for the issue of the award might with advantage be fixed.
3 This provision is difficult of application in the case of sheep stocks bound to the ground; cf *Keswick v Wright* 1924 SC 776.
4 If the arbitration is between landlord and tenant it will be under s 60, but if between ingoing and outgoing tenants, it will have to be at common law.

Removal of tenant for non-payment of rent

20.[1]—(1) When 6 months' rent of an agricultural holding is due and unpaid, the landlord[2] shall be entitled to raise an action of removing[3] in the sheriff court against the tenant, concluding for his removal from the holding at the term of Whitsunday or Martinmas[4] next ensuing after the action is raised.

(2) In an action raised under subsection (1) above, the sheriff may, unless the arrears of rent then due are paid or caution is found to his satisfaction for them, and for one year's rent further, decern the tenant to remove, and may eject him at the said term in like manner as if the lease were determined and the tenant had been legally warned to remove.

(3) A tenant of a holding removed under this section shall have the rights of an outgoing tenant[5] to which he would have been entitled if his tenancy had terminated by operation of notice to quit or notice of intention to quit at the term when he is removed.

(4) Section 5 of Chapter XV of Book L of the Codifying Act of Sederunt of June 14, 1913, anent removings, shall not apply in any case where the procedure under this section is competent.

150

1 As the tenant can purge these provisions, it is better to rely on a conventional irritancy in the lease, which cannot be purged (*British Rail Pension Trustee Co Ltd v Wilson* 1989 SLT 340) or on a written demand for payment of arrears of rent leading to an incontestable notice to quit under s 22(2)(d).

2 **'Landlord'**: see definition in s 85(1). The landlord in possession is entitled to take proceedings to recover rent although he may have to account therefor to his predecessors' representatives: *Lennox v Reid* (1893) 21 R 77; *Lord Elibank v Hay* (1780) M 13869; Hailes 847.

3 **'Action of removing'**. This action need not be raised forty days before the term of removal: *Ballantyne v Brechin* (1893) 1 SLT 306. The action was formerly for immediate removal. An action was raised in the sheriff court for payment of arrears which failing for decree of removing. Held that the action was incompetent in respect that the Act gave the tenant right to prevent ejection by making payment of arrears at any time prior to extract of decree of removing, and the decree sought would deprive him of that right: *Fletcher v Fletcher* 1932 SLT (Sh Ct) 10. Such an action can, of course, be met by a defence which will force both parties to arbitration: see *Brodie v Ker* 1952 SC 216. Held that an irritancy, being a conventional irritancy, eg, for payment of rent, could not be purged: *McDouall's Trs v MacLeod* 1949 SC 593.

4 **'Whitsunday'** and **'Martinmas'** are now defined by the Term and Quarter Days (Scotland) Act 1990. Care will have to be taken in lodging the writ not to seek removing at a term, which may be reached before the action is concluded.

5 **'Rights of an outgoing tenant'**. This entitled the tenant to the usual common law awaygoing rights, implied or expressed by the terms of the lease, and including, it is thought, compensation for improvements under this Act, provided the provisions of the Act are complied with. Questions may arise with reference to the term of removal. Suppose a tenancy runs from Whitsunday as to houses and grass and separation of crop thereafter as regards land under crop, would the tenancy nevertheless expire as regards the whole at the one term, say Whitsunday, or would the sheriff follow the awaygoing in terms of the lease? If he were not to do so the rights of the tenant would be prejudiced, apparently contrary to the intention of the statute. Under the Hypothec Abolition (Scotland) Act 1880, the rights reserved to the tenant were such as he could have had at the term preceding his ejection, where he was ejected between terms.

PART III

NOTICE TO QUIT AND NOTICE OF INTENTION TO QUIT

Notice to quit and notice of intention to quit

21.[1]—(1) Subject to section 20 of this Act and to subsections (6) and (7) below a tenancy[2] of an agricultural holding shall not come to an end except by operation of a notice which complies with this subsection notwithstanding any agreement or any provision in the lease to the contrary.[3]

(2) In this Act, a notice which complies with subsection (1) above is referred to as a 'notice to quit' if it is given by the landlord to the tenant and as a 'notice of intention to quit' if it is given by the tenant to the landlord.[4]

(3) A notice complies with subsection (1) above if—

(a) it is in writing;

(b) it is a notice of intention to bring the tenancy to an end;

(c) where the notice is to take effect at the termination of the stipulated endurance of the lease, it is given not less than one year nor more than 2 years before that date;[5]

(d) in the case of a lease continued in force by tacit relocation, it gives not less than one year nor more than 2 years' notice.[6]

(4) The provisions of the Sheriff Courts (Scotland) Act 1907 relating to removings shall, in the case of an agricultural holding, have effect subject to this section.[7]

(5) Notice to quit shall be given either—

(a) in the same manner as notice of removal under section 6 of the Removal Terms (Scotland) Act 1886; or

(b) in the form and manner prescribed by the Sheriff Courts (Scotland) Act 1907,[8]

and such notice shall come in place of the notice required by the said Act of 1907.

(6) Nothing in this section shall affect the right of the landlord of an agricultural holding to remove a tenant whose estate has been sequestrated under the Bankruptcy (Scotland) Act 1985 or the Bankruptcy (Scotland) Act 1913, or who by failure to pay rent or otherwise has incurred irritancy of his lease or other liability to be removed.[9]

(7) This section shall not apply—

(a) to a notice given in pursuance of a stipulation in a lease entitling the landlord to resume land for building, planting, feuing or other purposes (not being agricultural purposes);[10] or

(b) in relation to subjects let under a lease for any period less than a year, not being a lease which by virtue of section 2 of this Act takes effect as a lease from year to year.[11]

1 See Chapter 4. The wording of parts of this section is substantially different from that used in s 24 of the Agricultural Holdings (Scotland) Act 1949, although the effect of the section should be the same. It should be noted that this section applies to the case where notice is given to quit part of a holding held from year to year for the purposes specified in s 29: *Hamilton v Lorimer* 1959 SLCR 7. The full statutory notice is required. It is not competent to contract out of the requirements of this subsection: see *Morrison's Exrs v Rendall* 1986 SC 69 where it was held (1) that verbal renunciation of a lease was not effective without *rei interventus*; (2) that an agreement to terminate an agricultural tenancy was unenforceable if the procedures of s 24(1) of the 1949 Act were not followed; and (3) that a party relying on a waiver of the requirements of the subsection had to aver that he acted on the basis of the waiver: see also *Johnson v Moreton* [1980] AC 37; *Duguid v Muirhead* 1926 SC 1078. Although personal bar and waiver were argued in *Morrison's Exrs* no issue was taken on whether or not personal bar could be pled in the face of this statutory provision, which implements a social policy. There must be some doubt as to whether or not personal bar can be properly pled in the face of this statute: see *Kok Hoong v Leong Cheong Kweng Mines Ltd* [1964] AC 993 and some of the dicta in *Johnson v Moreton*. It is competent to compromise a Land Court application following upon a notice to quit and reach an agreement to surrender the tenancy: *Kildrummy (Jersey) Ltd v Calder* 1994 SLT 888. In serving a notice under this section considerations should be given as to whether or not a statement is required in terms of s 55 so as to avoid payment of an additional payment under s 54. A notice to quit which contains a fraudulent misrepresentation in its terms is null and will not be enforced by the courts: *Rous v Mitchell* [1991] 1 WLR 469; cf *Luttenberger v North Thoresby Farms Ltd* [1993] 1 EGLR 3.

2 **'Tenancy'.** The word 'tenancy' must be construed under reference to the definitions of 'tenant' and 'lease' in s 85(1) and s 3 relating to tacit relocation.

3 **'Notwithstanding any agreement or any provision in the lease to the contrary'.** These words fall to be read disjunctively and make it clear that parties cannot contract out of the provisions either before or after entering into the lease. *Morrison's Exrs v Rendall* 1986 SC 69 suggests that a tenant can unilaterally renounce a tenancy, but such a renunciation may be difficult to enforce, if the tenant changes his mind. Question reserved whether letter of removal is an agreement within the meaning of this section: *Cushnie v Thomson* 1954 SLCR 33.

4 This subsection introduces the new term 'notice of intention to quit'. Although the landlord's notice has to be in the statutory form (see subsections (4) and (5)) the tenant's notice can be in any form provided it makes his intention clear and gives the statutory notice. Notice by one of two joint tenants may bring the lease to an end: *Smith v Grayton Estates Ltd* 1960 SC 349; *Graham v Stirling* 1922 SC 90; *Combey v Gumbrill* [1990] 2 EGLR 7; see also *Montgomerie v Wilson* 1924 SLT (Sh Ct) 48; *Wight v Earl of Hopetoun* (1864) 2 M (HL) 35. In terms of s 85(5) notice may be given by or to an agent of either party. Where a holding has

been divided among two or more proprietors all must be parties to a notice to quit either the entire holding or (under s 32) the part owned by any one of them: *Secretary of State for Scotland v Prentice* 1963 SLT (Sh Ct) 48; *Stewart v Moir* 1965 SLT (Land Ct) 11. Where there were two *pro indiviso* proprietors (husband and wife) and the notice was served by the solicitors of the husband as 'proprietor of the farm' it was held that the notice was good, subject to proof of the wife's authority. There was no infeftment when the notice was served: *Walker v Hendry* 1925 SC 855. Where there are joint tenants all of them together are 'the tenant' in terms of s 85(1) and all must join in giving or authorising counter-notice or intimation to a landlord: *Newman v Keedwell* (1977) 33 P & CR 333; but see *Graham v Stirling* 1922 SC 90 where notice given by one joint tenant with authority of the other. Notice of termination of the tenancy given by one of two joint tenants is sufficient to stop tacit relocation and terminate the whole tenancy: *Smith v Grayton Estates* 1960 SC 349. A landlord who sold part of the holding after serving notice to quit ceased to be 'the landlord' and could not proceed on his own with an application for the Land Court's consent to operation of the notice: *Gordon v Rankin* 1972 SLT (Land Ct) 7. Where a farm was held at first by one owner, who sold part, and the proprietors of the two parts gave notice to quit the whole farm, and the tenant bought the part which belonged to one of the owners, and refused to give up possession of the other part, contending that under s 27 of the Agricultural Holdings (Scotland) Act 1923 the contract of sale rendered the notice to quit void, it was held that, as the contract to sell was not made by the persons who gave the notice to quit, that section did not apply, and that the notice to quit was valid: *Rochester and Chatham Joint Sewerage Board v Clinch* [1925] Ch 753.

5 It is crucial that the notice is served against the correct ish. In an informal let for less than one year extended into a lease from year to year under s 2 and continued by tacit relocation it was held that the ish date was 28th February, where the date of entry was 1st March: *Morrison's Exrs v Rendall* 1989 SLT (Land Ct) 89; *McGill v Bichan* 1970 SLCR App 122. It is probably safer to serve against the anniversary date, ie 1st March. In *Callander v Watherston* 1970 SLT (Land Ct) 13 and *Austin v Gibson* 1979 SLT (Land Ct) 12, the court accepted notices to the wrong ish (Martinmas 28th November in error for 11th November) as valid because there was no prejudice. Where there are several dates for ish, the notice must be given for the earliest of them: *Earl of Hopetoun v Wright* (1864) 2 M (HL) 35. A distinction falls to be made, however, between a genuine multiple ish as in *Black v Clay* (1894) 21 R (HL) 72 or *Montgomerie v Wilson* 1924 SLT (Sh Ct) 48, and a single ish with different dates for possession such as is referred to in *Waldie v Mungall* (1896) 23 R 792 per Lord McLaren at p 801, and *Milne v Earl of Seafield* 1981 SLT (Sh Ct) 37. In the former case the lease ends by stages. In the latter there is a single date of termination but as a matter of convenience provision is made for an incomer to have access at different dates. Thus in *Montgomerie v Wilson* where termination was Martinmas from arable lands and Whitsunday following from grass lands a notice a year before Whitsunday was held bad. In *Milne v Earl of Seafield* the lease bore to run from Whitsunday which was declared to be the term of entry but there was provision for the incomer to have earlier access to parts of the holding at various dates. The tenant was obliged to remove from these parts at dates prior to Whitsunday. Notice to quit was served a year before Whitsunday but less than a year prior to the earlier dates. It was held valid on the ground that there was a single ish and not several separate ishes. See also *Millar v McRobbie* 1949 SLT 2; 1949 SC 1. The section applies at a break as well as at the natural termination of the lease: *Alston's Trs v Muir* 1919 2 SLT 8; see also *Strachan v Hunter* 1916 SC 901 (correspondence held not equivalent to notice); *Edell v Dulieu* [1924] AC 38.

6 See preceding note.

7 This subsection alters the period of notice required by the Sheriff Courts (Scotland) Act 1907 in a notice to quit an agricultural holding: *Houison-Craufurd's Trs v Davies* 1951 SC 1; *Brodie v Ker* 1952 SC 216. The effect of the subsection as decided in *Milne v Earl of Seafield* 1981 SLT (St Ct) 37 is that s 34 of the 1907 Act and rule 103 of the Ordinary Cause Rules 1993 must be taken as requiring not less than one nor more than two years' notice against the termination of the lease.

8 The Removal Terms (Scotland) Act 1886 dealt only with the *manner* of sending notice and required service by registered post. The Sheriff Courts (Scotland) Act 1907, Ordinary Cause Rules 1993, rule 34.8 provides for service by messenger at arms, sheriff officer or registered letter. A letter sent by recorded delivery in terms of the Recorded Delivery Service Act 1962, is equivalent to a registered letter but if this method is used the receipt issued by the post office must be initialled. It has been decided that notice sent by ordinary post is ineffective: *Department of Agriculture for Scotland v Goodfellow* 1931 SLT 388. A tenant refused to sign a receipt for a registered letter which contained the notice which he therefore did not see. The

letter was returned to the post office. The court granted an order for ejectment: *Van Grutten v Trevenen* [1902] 2 KB 82. In England it has been held that a notice was effective if in fact delivered although not sent by registered post: *Re Poyser and Mills Arbitration* [1964] 2 QB 467. A notice to quit is valid though given on a Sunday: *Sangster v Noy* (1867) 16 LT 157. A notice given on a Monday would not be in time if Sunday was the last day: *Scott v Scott* 1927 SLT (Sh Ct) 6. The form of notice must be in Form H2 annexed to the 1907 Act: see Appendix 1, Form 1. It is vital to adhere to the statutory form of notice: *Rae & Cooper v Davidson* 1954 SC 361; *Watters v Hunter* 1927 SC 310; *Morrison's Exrs v Rendall* 1989 SLT (Land Ct) 89. The notice must contain a description of the subjects, state the term or terms of ish and refer to the lease. If any of these is omitted the notice is invalid: *Rae & Cooper v Davidson; Taylor v Brick* 1982 SLT 25; *Watters v Hunter; Mackie v Gardner* 1973 SLT (Land Ct) 11. The description of the subjects should be stated as in the lease or if there is no written lease there must be sufficient description to identify the subjects. Where lands were described as 'The village lands at Strichen extending to approximately twenty acres or thereby' and the holding comprised various fields making up considerably more than twenty acres, uncertainty as to what was covered rendered the notice invalid: *Taylor v Brick*. A tenant of a cottage, garden, byre, and a five-acre field holding from year to year received notice to quit as follows: 'I beg to serve formal notice to quit at 28th May 1918, as I shall be requiring the cottage for an employee'. This was held invalid for insufficient description of the subjects: *Scott v Livingstone* 1919 SC 1; see also *Watters v Hunter*. The notice to quit must specify the date of the termination of the lease 'or the anniversary thereof' in accordance with s 21(3)(c) or (d). This means the date or dates of the contractual ish and not the date when occupation may be finally relinquished. In a written lease the ish is usually clearly stated. In an improbative lease where no term of entry was specified it was held that any legal presumption there might be as to the implied term of entry might be displaced by evidence and proof as to when the actual entry to and possession of the subjects was allowed: *Watters v Hunter*. As to common law presumption, see Rankine on Leases (3rd edn), p 339. As to the meaning of 'Whitsunday' and 'Martinmas', see the Term and Quarter Days (Scotland) Act 1990. Where a notice to quit was served against the 28th instead of the 11th but the tenant was not prejudiced the notice was held valid: *Callander v Watherston* 1970 SLT (Land Ct) 13. Where there was no written lease a removal notice sent by a sheriff officer was held not to be invalid in respect that it did not state that it was given on behalf of the landlord: *Seggie v Haggart* 1926 SLT (Sh Ct) 104. A notice not referring to or specifying subjects as 'presently possessed and leased by you' and signed by a solicitor 'agent for WW, by whom the said land and houses are sub-let to you', was held sufficient: *Watters v Hunter*. Correspondence was not held to be a valid notice of intention to take advantage of a break: *Strachan v Hunter* 1916 SC 901. As to the arbiter's jurisdiction to decide whether a notice to quit was valid, see *Hoth v Cowan* 1926 SC 58, where it was held that he did not have jurisdiction to determine the validity of a notice to quit, but reserved the question of whether the arbiter might have jurisdiction to decide if an old lease had been continued by tacit relocation.

9 This subsection preserves the valuable remedy to a landlord of irritancy, and emphasises the importance of including a conventional irritancy clause in every agricultural lease. Section 4 of the Law Reform (Miscellaneous Provisions) (Scotland) Act 1985 (requiring a warning notice demanding payment to be served before an irritancy) does not apply to an agricultural holding: 1985 Act, s 7(1)(b). See *British Rail Pension Trustee Co Ltd v Wilson* 1989 SLT 340 at p 380 regarding the irritancy of an agricultural lease, where it was made clear that a conventional irritancy cannot be purged, while a legal irritancy may be, thus emphasising the importance of the drafting of the irritancy clause, so that the clause is not a repetition of a legal irritancy, which is purgeable. As regards a landlord's rights after irritating a lease on the tenant's bankruptcy, see *Chalmers' Tr v Dick's Tr* 1909 SC 761; *McKinley v Hutchison's Trs* 1935 SLT 62. Where a lease was irritated for failure to pay the rent and there was an obligation to take over sheep stock at the expiry of the lease, it was held that there was no awaygoing within the meaning of the lease: *Marquis of Breadalbane v Stewart* (1904) 6 F (HL) 23; *McDouall's Trs v MacLeod* 1949 SC 593. As a lease is a mutual contract a landlord who is in breach of his own obligations thereunder cannot enforce an irritancy unless the lease expressly so provides: *Macnab of Macnab v Willison* 1960 SLT (Notes) 25. In the event of an irritancy being incurred the landlord can only remove the tenant by action of declarator of irritancy and removing. If the action is defended, the merits of any defence may have to be determined by statutory arbitration.

10 The words 'not being agricultural purposes' were added by the Agriculture Act 1958. Subject to the *de minimis* rule purposes are not non-agricultural although mainly so if they

also include agricultural purposes: *Crawford v Dun* 1981 SLT (Sh Ct) 66. The words 'other purposes' in the Agricultural Holdings (Scotland) Act 1949 and in leases have given rise to difficulties of construction; cf *Admiralty v Burns* 1910 SC 531; *Crichton-Stuart v Ogilvie* 1914 SC 888; *Turner v Wilson* 1954 SC 296; *Pigott v Robson* 1958 SLT 49. The argument is still open that too large a resumption for a non-agricultural purpose may be fraud on the lease: see the dicta of Lord Macintosh in *Turner v Wilson*; *Edinburgh Corporation v Gray* 1948 SC 538; *Glencruitten Trs v Love* 1966 SLT (Land Ct) 5 (resumption of buildings held to be contrary to good faith of lease – following *Trotter v Torrance* (1891) 18 R 848); *Fothringham v Fotheringham* 1987 SLT (Land Ct) 10. On resumption the tenant should be given such notice as will enable him to comply with the time-limits in ss 14 and 56: see *Re Disraeli Agreement* [1939] Ch 382; *Coates v Diment* [1951] 1 All ER 890. There is authority to the effect that if the lease so provides the landlord may resume without any period of notice (*Kininmonth v British Aluminium Co* 1915 SC 271) but the safer course would be to give, say, two months' notice, thus enabling the tenant to give the one month's notice required by ss 18 and 44. Additional compensation may be payable in terms of s 58. The principle of mutuality does not prevent the landlord from exercising a power of resumption when he himself is in breach of his obligations: *Edmonstone v Lamont* 1975 SLT (Sh Ct) 57.

11 Where a tenant refuses to remove at the end of a grazing tenancy under s 2, an action of removing or declarator and removing should be raised in the civil courts: see notes to s 2.

Restrictions on operation of notices to quit

22.[1]—(1) Where not later than one month from the giving of a notice to quit an agricultural holding (or, in a case where section 23(3) of this Act applies, within the extended period therein mentioned) the tenant serves on the landlord a counter-notice in writing requiring that this subsection shall apply to the notice to quit, subject to subsection (2) below and to section 25 of this Act, the notice to quit shall not have effect unless the Land Court consent to the operation thereof.

(2)[2] Subsection (1) above shall not apply where—

(a) the notice to quit relates to land being permanent pasture which the landlord has been in the habit of letting annually for seasonal grazing or of keeping in his own occupation and which has been let to the tenant for a definite and limited period[3] for cultivation as arable land on the condition that he shall, along with the last or waygoing crop, sow permanent grass seeds;

(b)[4] the notice to quit is given on the ground that the land is required for use, other than agriculture, for which permission has been granted on an application made under the enactments relating to town and country planning, or for which (otherwise than by virtue of any provision of those enactments) such permission is not required;

(c) the Land Court, on an application[5] in that behalf made not more than 9 months before the giving of the notice to quit, were satisfied that the tenant was not fulfilling his responsibilities to farm the holding in accordance with the rules of good husbandry, and certified that they were so satisfied;

(d) at the date of the giving of the notice[6] to quit the tenant had failed to comply with a demand in writing served on him by the landlord requiring him within 2 months from the service thereof to pay any rent due in respect of the holding,[7] or within a reasonable time to[8] remedy any breach[9] by the tenant, which was capable of being remedied,[10] of any term or condition of his tenancy[11] which was not inconsistent[12] with the fulfilment of his responsibilities to farm in accordance with the rules of good husbandry;[13]

(e) at the date of the giving of the notice to quit the interest of the landlord in the holding had been materially prejudiced by a breach by the tenant, which was not capable of being remedied in reasonable time and at economic cost, of any term or condition of the tenancy which was not inconsistent with the fulfilment by the tenant of his responsibilities to farm in accordance with the rules of good husbandry;

(f) [14]at the date of the giving of the notice to quit the tenant's apparent insolvency had been constituted in accordance with section 7 of the Bankruptcy (Scotland) Act 1985;

(g) [15]section 25(1) of this Act applies, and the relevant notice complies with section 25(2)(a), (b) and (d) of this Act;

and, where any of paragraphs (a) to (f) above applies, the ground under the appropriate paragraph on which the notice to quit proceeds is stated in the notice.[16]

1 This section must be read together with s 23 which was introduced to the Agricultural Holdings (Scotland) Act 1949 by the Agriculture Act 1958. It is not competent for joint tenants (where one of the joint tenants is under the landlord's control) to contract out of the right to serve a counter-notice: *Featherstone v Staples* [1986] 2 All ER 461 (CA). It is essential that the counter-notice is served timeously and received by the landlord within the month. The tenant's counter-notice should state simply that 'the tenant requires that section 22(1) of the Agricultural Holdings (Scotland) Act 1991 shall apply to the notice to quit, dated .... served upon him by .... in respect of [description of holding]. [The tenant reserves all rights competent to him to challenge the validity or competence of the notice in any proceedings.]' The counter-notice has to make clear that s 22(1) is being invoked: *Mountford v Hodkinson* [1956] 1 WLR 422; *Taylor v Brick* 1982 SLT 25; *Luss Estates Co v Colquhoun* 1982 SLCR 1. If there is doubt as to the validity of the notice to quit, the tenant's right to contest it should be expressly reserved, although this is not strictly necessary. If there is no valid counter-notice, application to the Land Court under s 24 is unnecessary: see *Luss Estates Co v Colquhoun*. An angry letter is not a counter-notice (*Mountford v Hodkinson*) nor is a letter indicating refusal to remove: *Taylor v Brick*. Where a counter-notice referred to a repealed statute it was held as referring to the corresponding sections in force: *Ward v Scott* [1950] 66 TLR (Pt 1) 340; but cf *Secretary of State for Scotland v Fraser* 1954 SLCR 24. The counter-notice may be served upon the landlord's agents, provided the agent has authority to receive the notice (s 85(5)): see also *Hemington v Walter* (1949) 100 LJ 51; *Hewson v Matthews* (1950) 100 LJ 654. For suspension of the operation of a notice to quit pending an arbitration, or decision of the Land Court, see s 23(4).

See also s 29(4) of the Agriculture Act 1967, which provides that s 22 of the 1991 Act is not to apply to a notice to quit given by the Secretary of State to enable him to use or dispose of land to effect amalgamation or reshaping of uncommercial agricultural units, the tenant having agreed in the lease that the land might be so used. The Land Court is empowered to permit the serving of a counter-notice under this subsection on behalf of a non-regular serviceman who is abroad: Reserve and Auxiliary Forces (Protection of Civil Interests) Acts 1951; Agricultural Holdings (Servicemen) (Scotland) Regulations 1952 (SI 1952/1338).

2 A notice to quit can be construed by reference to the surrounding facts and circumstances known to the landlord and tenant: *Land v Sykes* [1992] 1 EGLR 1; *Cayzer v Hamilton (No 2)* 1995 SLCR 13.

A notice to quit which contains a statement that is false and made fraudulently by the landlord knowing that the statement was false or recklessly whether it was true or false is invalid and unenforceable: *Rous v Mitchell* [1991] 1 WLR 469; cf *Luttenberger v North Thoresby Farms Ltd* [1993] 1 EGLR 3.

3 **'A definite and limited period'**: see discussion of this phrase in *Stirrat and Anr v Whyte* 1968 SLT 157, per Lord Cameron at p 163; see also *Roberts v Simpson* (1954) 70 Sh Ct Rep 159. The expression may be contrasted with the phrase 'specified period of the year' in the proviso to s 2(1). For that purpose a grazing season is a specified period although it may be indefinite: *Mackenzie v Laird* 1959 SC 266. In this case dates of commencement and termination must be stated. A let for 'a rotation of cropping' was held to be outwith the definition of 'lease' in s 85(1): *Stirrat and Anr v Whyte*. As well as stating a definite and

limited period the lease must require that tenant to sow grass seeds along with his last or waygoing crop. This should be stipulated expressly. A requirement that the tenant leave the land 'in grass' would not be sufficient. Whether the tenant in fact undersows the waygoing crop is irrelevant. It is the stipulation in the lease that matters. The paragraph is designed to allow rotation of pasture through cropping without creating security of tenure. There is, however, no requirement that the period of let correspond with one of the usual rotations nor is any maximum period stated.

4 See Chapter 4. A future requirement does not satisfy the section: *Paddock Investments v Lory* (1975) 236 EG 803; *Jones v Gates* [1954] 1 WLR 222. The requirement can be by a party other than the landlord: *Rugby Joint Water Board v Shaw Fox* [1973] AC 202. Planning permission or outline planning permission must have been granted unless it is not required otherwise than by virtue of the planning Acts: cf *Minister of Agriculture v Jenkins* [1963] 2 QB 317. If planning permission is not required by virtue of the planning Acts, the Land Court's consent must be obtained under s 24(1)(e).

'**Other than agriculture**'. The use of land for growing crops and weeds in order to test agricultural chemicals in a use other than for agriculture: *Dow Agrochemicals Ltd v E A Lane (North Lynn) Ltd* (1965) 192 EG 737. '**Permission has been granted on an application**' does not include the general permission under a General Development Order (*Minister of Agriculture v Jenkins*) nor deemed planning permission under s 2 of the Opencast Coal Act 1958: see the 1958 Act, s 14A(6). As to notice of planning application to be given to tenants, see s 24 of the Town and Country Planning (Scotland) Act 1972. In *Teignmouth UDC v Elliott* (1958) 108 LJ 204 it was held under the corresponding subsection of the Agricultural Holdings Act 1948 that merely throwing land open to the public was a material change of use and required planning permission. For a consideration of 'otherwise than by virtue of any provision of those enactments', see *Bell v McCubbin* [1989] EG 100 (CA).

5 '**Application**', ie an application under s 26: see 'Certificate of Bad Husbandry', p 61. For rules of good husbandry see, the Agriculture (Scotland) Act 1948, Sch 6. The certificate has to be served after the grant of the certificate and not more than nine months after the application was made.

6 '**At the date of the giving of the notice**' is evidently not confined to acts in process of execution at precisely that date. It includes such acts and also prior acts, so far as these prior acts had results which were at the date of the notice contrary to the rules of good husbandry, and especially if the results were so serious that the tenant could not remedy them before the determination of the tenancy. That this is the intention seems to be obvious from the fact that it is a breach if there be failure to *maintain* the land clean and in a good state of cultivation and fertility, to have drains and ditches properly *maintained* and clear, and to have fences, etc, in a proper state of repair. On the other hand, acts done subsequent to the date of the notice cannot afford justification for serving the notice. The tenant cannot comply with the demand if he fails to carry out his obligation within the time specified. An attempt to pay arrears of rent after the expiry of the two-month period is of no effect. In that event the landlord has in effect a vested right to serve notice to quit: *Price v Romilly* [1960] 1 WLR 1360; *Stoneman v Brown* [1973] 1 WLR 459; [1973] 2 All ER 225. Failure to exercise the right to serve notice promptly may amount to a waiver: *Cayzer v Hamilton (No 2)* 1995 SLCR 13. In the case of notices to do work of provision, repair, maintenance or replacement of fixed equipment, this is subject to the arbiter's powers under s 66 and to a possible reference to the Land Court under s 32. No particular form of notice is required. Notice may be given by the agent of the landlord: s 85(5). A demand for payment of rent must clearly require payment within two months: *Morrison-Low v Howison* 1961 SLT (Sh Ct) 53. An ordinary rent notice will not suffice. The rent must be due at the date when the demand is served: *Magdalen College Oxford v Heritage* [1974] 1 WLR 441; *Pickford v Bishop* (1975) 119 SJ 407; *Urwick v Taylor* [1969] EGD 1106.

Where the landlord reserves power in the lease to carry out maintenance at the expense of the tenant it was held he can nevertheless found on the tenant's failure: *Halliday v William Fergusson & Sons and Ors* 1961 SC 24, overruling *Forbes-Sempill's Trs v Brown* 1954 SLCR 36; see also *Allan's Trs v Allan & Son* (1891) 19 R 215; Gloag on Contract (2nd edn), p 669.

7 The demand must contain a statement that the rent is due within two months: *Magdalen College Oxford v Heritage* [1974] 1 WLR 441; *Official Solicitor v Thomas* [1986] 2 EGLR 1. The amount due must be accurately stated and due at the date, although the *de minimis* rule applies: *Dickson v Boucher* (1984) 269 EG 1159; *Luttenberger v North Thoresby Farms Ltd* [1993] 1 EGLR 3. Payment by cheque made before the expiry of the two months is timeous payment, provided the cheque is subsequently honoured: *Beevers v Manson* (1978) 37 P & CR 452; *Luttenberger v North Thoresby Farms Ltd*; *Hannaford v Smallacombe* [1994] 1 EGLR

9. It is too late to pay the rent after the two-month period, whether or not the notice to quit has been served: *Brown v Stoneman* [1973] 1 WLR 459; *Price v Romilly* [1960] 1 WLR 1360; *Hannaford v Smallacombe*.

8 **'Reasonable time'.** It is obviously convenient if the landlord can specify what he regards as reasonable time, but he need not so specify: *Morrison-Low v Howison* 1961 SLT (Sh Ct) 53; *Stewart v Brims* 1969 SLT (Sh Ct) 2. Where the demand requires work of 'provision, repair, maintenance or replacement of fixed equipment' the tenant may have the period fixed or extended by an arbiter (s 66). The arbiter's powers under s 66 may be invoked either in an arbitration on the demand to remedy or in an arbitration under s 23(2) following upon the notice to quit: *Fane v Murray* 1995 SLT 567. For circumstances where two months was not a reasonable time, see *Pentland v Hart* 1967 SLT (Land Ct) 2; see also *Nicholl's Trs v Maclarty* 1971 SLCR 85. See McBryde on Contract, Index, *sub nom* 'Reasonable Time' for examples of 'reasonable time' in contracts.

9 **'Remedy any breach'.** Failure to comply with one of the requirements of a notice to remedy breaches is sufficient to found a notice to quit unless the breach is such that the rule *de minimis non curat lex* applies: *Price v Romilly* [1960] 3 All ER 429; *Edmunds v Woollacott* (1958) 109 LJ 204. Where certain breaches were not remedied because the landlord failed to supply materials the landlord was still entitled to rely on other failures by the tenant to remedy breaches where no materials had to be supplied: *Shepherd and Anr v Lomas* [1963] 1 WLR 962. It has been held that a notice to quit under (now) s 22(2)(d) was not invalid because the landlord was in breach of his obligations under the lease: *Wilson-Clarke v Graham* 1963 SLT (Sh Ct) 2. The position is different where the landlord seeks to operate an irritancy clause. See note 9 to s 21.

The notice to remedy breaches must state clearly which provision of the lease, including any common law provision or provision implied by the 1991 Act, has been breached and what is required of the tenant, otherwise a subsequent notice to quit may be invalid: *Morris v Muirhead* 1969 SLT 70. The observation by Lord Robertson at 74 that (now) s 22(2)(d) is intended to apply to works of repair, maintenance and replacement rather than to general complaints or failure in husbandry, must be regarded with reservation. The provision has been held to apply to (1) residence clauses: *Morrison-Low v Howison* 1961 SLT (Sh Ct) 53 and *Sumnall v Statt* (1985) 49 P & CR 367 (tenant in prison, held entitled to have length of sentence and likely release date taken into account); (2) stocking provisions: *Pentland v Hart* 1967 SLT (Land Ct) 2; and (3) an obligation to pay interest on a landlord's expenditure: *Official Solicitor v Thomas* (1986) 279 EG 407. See also Muir Watt, *Agricultural Holdings* (13th edn) p 57 where he deals with notices to remedy other than notices to do work.

Demands to remedy in relation to maintenance or repair of fixed equipment are subject to the provisions of s 32 and 66: see *Fane v Murray* 1995 SLT 567.

10 **'Capable of being remedied'.** This is unlikely to be a matter of contention as any breach not capable of being remedied will found a notice to quit under s 22(2)(e). It is essential to distinguish in a demand to remedy and following notice to quit, whether the demand and the notice are founded on a remedial breach under s 22(2)(d) or an irremedial breach under s 22(2)(e). If the demand and notice relate to both they must be distinguished: *Macnabb v Anderson* 1957 SC 213.

11 **'Any term or condition of his tenancy'** is clearly not limited to terms of written lease. A verbal lease will contain terms implied at common law and by the 1991 Act.

12 **'Not inconsistent'.** It would be unusual for a lease to contain provisions inconsistent with the tenant's responsibilities to farm in accordance with the rules of good husbandry but requirements which have become obsolete or stipulations in the interests of game rather than agriculture may be encountered. For rules of good husbandry see the Agriculture (Scotland) Act 1948, Sch 6.

13 Where a notice to quit is founded upon a failure to remedy a breach of a condition of the lease in relation to a failure to do any work of provision, repair, maintenance or replacement of fixed equipment, see s 32 in respect that the Land Court's consent is required in certain circumstances to such a notice.

14 This section would apply when the tenant was apparently insolvent at the commencement of the tenancy and subsequently received notice to quit bearing that it was given because of his bankruptcy: *Hart v Cameron* (1935) Sh Ct Rep 166. Apparent insolvency is defined by s 7 of the Bankruptcy (Scotland) Act 1985. It includes practical insolvency as well as absolute insolvency: *Murray v Nisbet* 1967 SLT (Land Ct) 14. The 1985 Act provides in s 75(9) that reference to a person being notour bankrupt shall be construed, unless the context otherwise requires, to a person being apparently insolvent within the meaning of s 7 of the 1985 Act.

15 This subsection, first introduced by the Agriculture Act 1958, relates to the removal of a

successor to the tenant who is not a near relative. It is essential that the requirements of s 25 are complied with. Unlike paras (a) to (f), which require the reason to be stated, there is no requirement to state in the notice that the notice to quit has been given under s 25.

16 **'Stated in the notice'.** This provision is of vital importance. Failure to state the reason in the notice to quit renders the notice invalid. Where possible the words should follow the wording of the subsection. Such an omission might be rectified by withdrawing the notice and serving a new one and stating therein the reason, provided the second notice is otherwise in order and timeous. See, however, *Tayleur v Wildin* [1868] LR 3 Ex 303, followed in *Lower v Sorrell* [1963] 1 QB 959. It cannot be withdrawn after it has been accepted: *Gilmour v Cook* 1975 SLT (Land Ct) 10; *Edell v Dulieu* [1924] AC 38. It was held under now- superseded legislation in England that the reasons for a notice to quit might be stated in an accompanying letter: *Turton v Turnbull* [1934] 2 KB 197; *Sellick v Hellens* [1928] LJ KB 214. It is understood that this is not now (following the English Agricultural Holdings (Notices to Quit) Act 1977) sufficient under the English Agricultural Holdings Act 1986 (Scammell and Densham, *Law of Agricultural Holdings* (7th edn), p 167), but *Turton v Turnbull* was followed in *Barns-Graham v Lamont* 1971 SLT 341 where an accompanying letter was held to be part of a notice to quit. See also *Copeland v McQuaker* 1973 SLT 186 where the court had regard to the terms of an accompanying letter. A statement of the reasons in a letter subsequent to the date of the notice to quit will not suffice. The notice to quit must identify the paragraph relied on and the reason should be stated by quoting in full from the paragraph (*Macnabb v Anderson* 1957 SC 213), although it has been held sufficient in England to refer to the paragraphs without setting out the reasons themselves: *In re Digby and Penny* [1932] 2 KB 491; see also *Budge v Hicks* [1951] 2 KB 335; *Cowan v Wrayford* [1953] 2 All ER 1138; *Jones v Gates* [1954] 1 All ER 158; *Hammon v Fairbrother* [1956] 2 All ER 108. Paragraphs (d) and (f) are mutually exclusive: *Macnabb v Anderson*. Where two reasons are given, or where two concurrent notices are given, see *French v Elliott* [1960] 1 WLR 40. Note that subsection (2) read in conjunction with s 21(3) does not authorise a landlord to serve notice to quit during the currency of a lease otherwise than against a break or the conventional ish: see *Macnabb v Anderson* 1955 SC 38, per Lord Patrick at p 44.

Consent by Land Court or arbitration on notices to quit

23.—(1) An application by a landlord for the consent of the Land Court under section 22 of this Act to the operation of a notice to quit shall be made within one month after service on the landlord by the tenant of a counter-notice requiring that subsection (1) of that section shall apply to the notice to quit.[1]

(2) A tenant who has been given a notice to quit in connection with which any question arises under section 22(2) of this Act shall, if he requires such question to be determined by arbitration under this Act, give notice to the landlord to that effect within one month after the notice to quit has been served on him.[2]

(3) Where the award of the arbiter in an arbitration required under subsection (2) above is such that section 22(1) of this Act would have applied[3] to the notice to quit if a counter-notice had been served within the period provided for in that subsection, that period shall be extended up to the expiry of one month from the issue of the arbiter's award.

(4) Where such an arbitration as is referred to in subsection (2) above has been required by the tenant, or where an application has been made to the Land Court for their consent to the operation of a notice to quit, the operation of the notice to quit shall be suspended until the issue of the arbiter's award or of the decision of the Land Court, as the case may be.

(5) Where the decision of the Land Court giving their consent to the operation of a notice to quit, or the award of the arbiter in such an arbitration as is referred to in subsection (2) above, is issued at a date later than 6 months before the date on which the notice to quit is expressed to take effect,

the Land Court, on application made to them in that behalf at any time not later than one month after the issue of the decision or award[4] aforesaid, may postpone the operation of the notice to quit for a period not exceeding 12 months.[5]

(6) If the tenant of an agricultural holding receives from the landlord notice to quit the holding or a part thereof and in consequence thereof gives to a sub-tenant notice to quit that holding or part, section 22(1) of this Act shall not apply to the notice given to the sub-tenant; but if the notice to quit given to the tenant by the landlord does not have effect, then the notice to quit given by the tenant to the sub-tenant shall not have effect.[6]

(7) For the purposes of subsection (6) above, a notice to quit part of the holding which under section 30 of this Act is accepted by the tenant as notice to quit the entire holding shall be treated as a notice to quit the holding.[7]

(8) Where notice is served on the tenant of an agricultural holding to quit the holding or a part thereof, being a holding or part which is subject to a sub-tenancy, and the tenant serves on the landlord a counter-notice in accordance with section 22(1) of this Act, the tenant shall also serve on the sub-tenant notice in writing that he has served such counter-notice on the landlord and the sub-tenant shall be entitled to be a party to any proceedings before the Land Court for their consent to the notice to quit.[8]

1 In its present form this section was first introduced by the Agriculture Act 1958, Sch 1, para 37, in place of the Agricultural Holdings (Scotland) Act 1949 provision. The time-limits are imperative: *Gemmell v Hodge* 1974 SLT (Land Ct) 2. The application must be made on the appropriate Land Court form and specify the ground of the application: *O'Donnell v Heath* 1995 SLT (Land Ct) 15.
2 The time-limit within which to demand arbitration is imperative. Where the arbitration relates to a notice to quit following upon a demand to remedy fixed equipment, the arbiter may exercise the powers conferred upon him by s 66: *Fane v Murray* 1995 SLT 567.
3 **'Would have applied'.** This would be the case if a notice to quit were given in alternative form, ie either under s 25(2) or as a plain notice to quit and the arbiter found in the tenant's favour in the arbitration on the section 25(2) notice. Whether it would be so if the notice were not expressly given in alternative form is arguable but the tenant's only safe course is to assume that it would and serve counter-notice within one month after the arbiter's award.
4 **'At any time not later than one month after the issue of the decision or award'.** Application may be made before the issue of the decision (*Moffat v Young* 1975 SLCR App 98) or after the date when the notice to quit was expressed to take effect (*Allan Fraser's Trs v Macpherson* 1981 SLT (Land Ct) 17), but must be made within one month after issue.
5 See *Graham v Wilson-Clarke* 1962 SLCR 35.
6 Where the sub-tenancy is a sham the sub-tenant may be treated as the tenant and accordingly this provision will not apply: *Gisbourne v Burton* [1988] 3 WLR 921. This provision will not effect a sub-tenancy created by the later interposition of an interposed lease under s 17 of the Land Tenure Reform (Scotland) Act 1974: *Kildrummy (Jersey) Ltd v Calder (No 2)* 1996 GWD 8–458.
7 This subsection refers to the tenant's right under s 30 to treat a notice to quit part of the holding as a notice to quit the whole holding.
8 The tenant is required to intimate a counter-notice to his sub-tenant so that the sub-tenant may be a party to any proceedings before the Land Court. This provision will not affect a sub-tenancy created by the later interposition of an interposed lease under s 17 of the Land Tenure Reform (Scotland) Act 1974.

Consents for purposes of section 22

24.[1]—(1) Subject to subsection (2) below and to section 25(3) of this Act, the Land Court shall consent under section 22 of this Act to the operation of a notice to quit an agricultural holding or part of an agricultural holding if, but only if, they are satisfied[2] as to one or more of the following matters, being a matter or matters specified by the landlord in his application for their consent[3]—

(a) that the carrying out of the purpose for which the landlord proposes to terminate the tenancy is desirable in the interests of good husbandry[5] as respects the land to which the notice relates, treated as a separate unit;[6]

(b) that the carrying out thereof is desirable in the interests of sound management[7] of the estate of which that land consists or forms part;

(c) that the carrying out thereof is desirable for the purposes of agricultural research,[8] education, experiment or demonstration, or for the purposes of the enactments relating to allotments, smallholdings or such holdings as are referred to in section 64 of the Agriculture (Scotland) Act 1948;

(d) that greater hardship[9] would be caused by withholding than by giving consent to the operation of the notice;

(e) that the landlord proposes to terminate the tenancy for the purpose of the land being used for a use, other than for agriculture,[10] not falling within section 22(2)(b) of this Act.[11]

(2) Notwithstanding that they are satisfied as aforesaid, the Land Court shall withhold consent to the operation of the notice to quit if in all the circumstances it appears to them that a fair and reasonable landlord would not insist on possession.[12]

(3) Where the Land Court consent to the operation of a notice to quit they may (subject to section 25(4) of this Act) impose such conditions as appear to them requisite for securing that the land to which the notice relates will be used for the purpose for which the landlord proposes to terminate the tenancy.[13]

(4) Where, on an application by the landlord in that behalf the Land Court are satisfied that by reason of any change of circumstances or otherwise any condition imposed under subsection (3) above ought to be varied or revoked, they shall vary or revoke the condition accordingly.[14]

1 This subsection was enacted by the Agriculture Act 1958 in substitution for the subsection of the Agricultural Holdings (Scotland) Act 1949 and has been amended by the Agricultural Holdings (Amendment) (Scotland) Act 1983. See also the Opencast Coal Act 1958, s 14A(6).

2 'Satisfied'. The landlord must satisfy the court that there are grounds for its consent even if the tenant does not answer the application: *McLellan v McGregor* 1952 SLCR 3; *Buchanan v Buchanan* 1983 SLT (Land Ct) 31. If no valid counter-notice is served application is unnecessary: *Luss Estates Co v Colquhoun* 1982 SLCR 1.

3 Note that it is necessary to specify in the application the reasons in respect of which consent is sought. The application should refer specifically to particular paragraphs of s 24(1): *Benington Wood's Trs v Mackay* 1969 SLT (Land Ct) 9; *O'Donnell v Heath* 1995 SLT (Land Ct) 160. If there is a question whether there is in fact a tenancy this is not a matter for the Land Court but for the ordinary courts. The application may be sisted pending their decision: *Allan Fraser's Trs v Macpherson* 1981 SLT (Land Ct) 17; *Eagle Star Insurance Co Ltd v Simpson* 1984 SLT (Land Ct) 37. The Land Court has of consent dealt with an application subject to the landlord's observation of right to dispute the existence of a tenancy: *Prior v J & A Henderson Ltd* 1984 SLT (Land Ct) 51; *O'Donnell v Heath*.

4 The onus is on the landlord to show that he intends to use the holding by himself or by another tenant which will effect a substantial improvement in the operation of the holding: *Clark v Smith* 1981 SLCR 84; *Prior v J & A Henderson Ltd* 1984 SLT (Land Ct) 51.

5 'Good husbandry' – distinguished from 'rules of good husbandry': see *Mackenzie v Tait* 1951 SLCR 3; *Fenton v Howie* 1951 SLCR 7; *Young v Steven* 1951 SLCR 10.

6 **'Treated as a separate unit'**: see *Yuill v Semple* 1954 SLCR 3; *Turner v Wilson* 1954 SC 296; *Clarke v Smith* 1981 SLCR App 84; *R v Agricultural Land Tribunal for Wales, ex parte Davies* [1953] 1 All ER 1182. This phrase distinguishes an application under subs (1)(a) from an application under subs (1)(b), where the management of the whole estate can be considered.

7 **'Sound management'**: see note 6 above. This is not the same as good estate management; see the Agriculture (Scotland) Act 1948, Sch 5. The effect on the whole estate is to be considered but not whether the tenant will suffer. This may be relevant under the proviso: *Evans v Roper* [1960] 1 WLR 814; *Leask v Grains* 1981 SLT (Land Ct) 11. 'The interests of sound management' connotes the furtherance or improvement of the actual management: see *J & A Peace v Peace* 1984 SLT (Land Ct) 6.

8 **'Agricultural research'**: see *University of Edinburgh v Craik* 1954 SC 190.

9 **'Greater hardship'**. This is a practical question to be determined on the facts and circumstances of each case and a wide discretion is given to the Land Court: see p 34. The onus of proof of greater hardship is on the landlord: *McLaren v Lawrie* 1964 SLT (Land Ct) 10; *Somerville v Watson* 1980 SLT (Land Ct) 14; *McBay v Birse* 1965 SLT (Land Ct) 10. Incidental proof of the tenant's hardship has to come from the tenant: *Hutchison v Buchanan* 1980 SLT (Land Ct) 17. The personal circumstances of both parties must be carefully considered: see *Mackenzie v Tait* 1951 SLCR 3; *Grant v Murray* 1950 SLCR 3; *Eastern Angus Properties Ltd v Chivers & Sons Ltd* 1960 SLCR 3; *Loganair v Reid* 1960 SLCR 34; *Gibson v McKenzie* 1961 SLCR 11; *Mackenzie v Mackenzie* 1969 SLCR App 86; *Graham v Lamont* 1970 SLT (Land Ct) 10; *Lovie v Davidson* 1988 SLCR 13 (authorities reviewed). The court will take into account the financial consequences on the landlord (ie the liability to pay waygoing claims including compensation, etc) if the consent is granted. These liabilities may mean that a landlord would in fact be worse off if the consent were granted. Consent has been granted in a number of cases to enable landlords to sell holdings: see *McBay v Birse; Moffat v Young* 1975 SLCR App 98; *Forbes v Darling* 1965 SLCR App 139; *Skinner v Cooper* 1971 SLCR App 83; *Purser v Bailey* [1967] 2 QB 500; *McRobie v Halley* 1984 SLCR 10. Consent has been granted in some cases to enable the landlord to take the holding in hand: see *Mackenzie v Mackenzie; Gordon Lennox Estate Co v Christie* 1969 SLCR App 84; *Clarke v Smith* 1981 SLCR App 84. For cases of hardship not primarily financial, see *Graham v Lamont* (possible frustration of plans for farming by son who had undertaken training for this); *Skinner v Cooper* (possible effect on champion sheep breeding); *Davies v Barber* 1965 SLCR App 133 (solely effect on agricultural operations of whether ground available or not); *Geddes v Mackay* 1971 SLCR App 94 (land sought for slurry disposal fully used by tenant and important as access); *Lindsay-MacDougall v Peterson* 1987 SLCR 59 (landlord living in squat in London wanted house and the two acres for accommodation for self and family, where tenant had neighbouring new house and sixty acres). Business hardship and hardship to a company are relevant: *Gordon Lennox Estate Co v Christie; Eastern Angus Properties Ltd v Chivers & Sons Ltd.*

Hardship to a person other than the landlord or the tenant may be relevant: *Graham v Lamont* (landlord's son); *Mackenzie v Tait* (landlord's son); *Skinner v Cooper* (tenant's daughter); *Purser v Bailey* (widow and son of deceased owner); *Forbes v Darling* (tenant's employees); cf *Somerville v Watson; Patrons of Cowane's Hospital v Rennie* 1966 SLCR App 147 (beneficiaries of charitable trust); *Edmonston v Smith* 1986 SLCR 97 (hardship to son of landlord who wanted to farm). A bad investment is not hardship in this sense: *Crawford v McKinlay* 1954 SLCR 39; *Patrons of Cowane's Hospital v Rennie; Benington-Wood's Trs v Mackay* 1969 SLT (Land Ct) 9; *McGill v Bichan* 1970 SLCR App 122.

The ordinary operation of security of tenure is not hardship: *Hutchison v Buchanan* 1980 SLT (Land Ct) 17; nor is mere inconvenience: *Geddes v Mackay.*

10 **'Other than for agriculture'**. This use of land for growing crops and weeds in order to test agricultural chemicals is a use other than for agriculture: *Dow Agrochemicals Ltd v E A Lane (North Lynn) Ltd* (1965) 192 EG 737; see also *Carnegie v Davidson* 1966 SLT (Land Ct) 3; *Arbroath Town Council v Carrie* 1972 SLCR App 114. This provision differs from s 22(2)(b), where planning permissions have been granted and relates to applications where planning permission is not required because of a provision in the planning Acts, eg, forestry.

11 It is to be noted that any one of the conditions is sufficient: see the Opencast Coal Act, s 14A(6).

12 **'A fair and reasonable landlord'**: see p 38. Questions of hardship on the tenant may be relevant to the proviso although not relevant to the principal section: see *Evans v Roper* [1960] 1 WLR 814. For Scottish cases where the proviso has been applied, see *Carnegie v Davidson* 1966 SLT (Land Ct) 3. For land sought for experimental forestry with doubtful commercial prospects, landlord having other suitable land, see *Altyre Estate Trs v McLay*

1975 SLT (Land Ct) 12 (land sought for amalgamation; tenant had other two-man holding; future use by landlord problematical).

See also cases where the Land Court would have applied proviso if consent had not been refused on main ground: *Sykes v Edgar* 1974 SLCR App 95 (land sought for shelter-belt scheme which would have caused difficulties to tenants); *Earl of Seafield v Currie* 1980 SLT (Land Ct) 10 (land sought for amalgamation; hardship to tenant). For a case defended on the proviso alone see *Earl of Morton v Hamilton* 1977 SLCR App 136; cf *Mackenzie v Lyon* 1984 SLT (Land Ct) 30. See *Trs of the Main Calthorpe Settlement v Calder* 1988 SLT (Land Ct) 30, where the proviso was considered in relation to a near relative successor tenant under (now) Case 3 of Sch 2.

13 See *Robertson v Lindsay* 1957 SLCR 3; *Shaw-Mackenzie v Forbes* 1957 SLCR 34; *Graham v Lamont* 1970 SLT (Land Ct) 10 for examples of conditions. See s 27 for the penalties for breach of conditions.

14 See *Burnett v Gordon* 1950 SLCR 9; *Cooper v Muirden* 1950 SLCR 45. Note that there is no corresponding power to vary conditions imposed under s 25(4).

The Land court making an order continuing an appeal to allow landlords to provide another holding was held competent: *University of Edinburgh v Craik* 1954 SC 190. See s 11 of the Agriculture (Miscellaneous Provisions) Act 1968 for circumstances in which additional payments may be due under s 9 of that Act if the Land Court consents under this section to operation of notice to quit. See Chapter 4 and forms of notice to quit in Appendix 1.

Termination of tenancies acquired by succession

25.[1]—(1) This section applies where notice to quit is duly given to the tenant of an agricultural holding who acquired right to the lease of the holding—

(a) under section 16 of the Succession (Scotland) Act 1964; or

(b) as a legatee, under section 11 of this Act.

(2) Notice to quit[2] is duly given to a tenant whom this section applies if—

(a) it complies with section 21 of this Act; and

(b) it specifies as its effective date[3]—

(i) where, when he acquired right to the lease, the unexpired period of the lease exceeded 2 years, the term of outgo stipulated in the lease;

(ii) where, when he acquired[4] right to the lease, the unexpired period was 2 years or less, the term of outgo stipulated in the lease of the corresponding date in any subsequent year, being a date not less than one nor more than 3 years after the said acquisition;

(c) where he was a near relative of the deceased tenant from whom he acquired right, it specifies the Case set out in Schedule 2 of this Act under which it is given; and

(d) where he was not a near relative of the deceased tenant from whom he acquired right, he acquired right to the lease after August 1, 1958.

(3)[5] Section 22(1) of this Act shall apply and section 24 of this Act shall not apply where subsection (2)(c) above applies and notice to quit is duly given in accordance with subsection (2)(a) to (c) above; and in such a case the Land Court shall consent to the operation of a notice duly given—

(a) where the holding was let before January 1, 1984, if they are satisfied that the circumstances are as specified in any Case set out in Part I of Schedule 2 to this Act;

(b) where the holding was let on or after that date and the notice specifies any of Cases 4, 5 or 7 in that Schedule, unless the tenant satisfies them that the circumstances are not as specified in that Case (provided that, for the purposes of Case 7, the tenant shall not be required to prove that he is not the owner of any land);

(c) where the holding was let on or after that date, if they are satisfied that
the circumstances are as specified in Case 6 in that Schedule;

except that where any of Cases 1, 2, 3, 6 or 7 in that Schedule is specified, the
Court shall withhold consent on that ground if it appears to them that a fair
and reasonable landlord would not insist on possession.

(4) Where consent is given because the circumstances are as specified in
Case 2 or 6 in Schedule 2 to this Act, the Land Court shall impose such
conditions as appear to them necessary to secure that the holding to which
the notice relates will, within 2 years after the termination of the tenancy, be
amalgamated with the land specified in the notice; and section 27 of this Act
shall, with any necessary modifications, apply to a condition imposed under
this subsection as that section applies to a condition imposed under section
24 of this Act.[6]

(5) Part III of Schedule 2 to this Act shall have effect for the purposes of
interpretation of this section and that Schedule.

1 This section was added by the Agricultural Holdings (Amendment) (Scotland) Act 1983.
 This section removes the security of tenure of a successor to a lease, who succeeded after 1st
 August 1958, whether by bequest or under s 16 of the Succession (Scotland) Act 1964, unless
 he is a near relative successor, in which case the lease may be liable to termination if one of the
 cases in Sch 2 applies. Where the tenant is not a near relative successor the Land Court's
 consent to a notice to quit is not required (s 22(2)(g)). Near relative is defined by Sch 2, Pt
 III, para 1.
2 The notice to quit must comply with s 21. It must specify the effective date. If the notice is
 given to a near relative successor it must specify the case in Sch 2 founded on (subsection
 (2)(c)). If served on a successor, who is not a near relative, he must have succeeded to the
 lease after 1st August 1958.
3 'Effective date'. Note the provisions of the subsection as to the effective date. Where the
 lease has more than two years to run from the date of acquisition then the date is the
 stipulated ish. A break in the lease can be an effective date. If the period of the lease left to run
 is two years or less, which will probably be the norm with leases running on tacit relocation,
 then the date has to be not less than one year or more than three years from the date of
 acquisition.
4 'Acquired'. This is the date at which the successor acquired the lease, which in a bequest will
 probably be the date of death, but if acquired from executors it will be the date of transfer of
 the lease to the successor.
5 This subsection protects the position of the near relative successor and gives him security of
 tenure, unless one of the cases in Sch 2 can be proved to apply. The dividing date of 1st
 January 1984 relates to the fact that this provision was first introduced on that date and it
 protects the position of successors, whose lease predates the introduction of this provision. A
 notice to quit served on a near relative successor requires the Land Court's consent and
 requires to specify the effective date and the case upon which it is founded. A separate notice
 to quit can be served founded on any of the provisions of s 24(1). For a detailed consideration
 of the cases, see the footnotes to Sch 2. For the 'fair and reasonable landlord' defence, see
 note 12 to s 24 and p 38.
6 This subsection obliges the Land Court to attach conditions to its consent under Cases 2 and
 6 (amalgamation): see note 13 to s 24. Unlike s 24, there is no power to vary the conditions.
 The penalties for breach of conditions are prescribed by s 27.

Certificates of bad husbandry

26.[1]—(1) For the purposes of section 22 (2)(c) of this Act, the landlord of
an agricultural holding may apply[2] to the Land Court for a certificate that the
tenant is not fulfilling his responsibilities to farm in accordance with the rules
of good husbandry,[3] and the Land Court, if satisfied that the tenant is not
fulfilling his said responsibilities, shall grant such a certificate.[4]

(2) In determining whether to grant a certificate under this section, the Land Court shall disregard any practice adopted by the tenant in compliance with any obligation imposed on him by or accepted by him under section 31B of the Control of Pollution Act 1974.

1 This section was substituted for the former section by the Agriculture Act 1958, Sch 1, para 38. Under the former section application was made to the Secretary of State who had delegated his powers to the Agricultural Executive Committees. Application went first to the Agricultural Executive Committees and then to the Land Court by way of appeal.
2 The application must specify the breaches of the rules of good husbandry founded upon. It is important to have the Land Court inspect the holding as soon as practicable after the certificate is requested: *Rae v Pringle* 1990 Borders RN 27. The onus is on the landlord to prove the breach even if the application is not opposed: *McGill v Bichan* 1982 SLCR 33. If the certificate is obtained the notice to quit must be served within nine months: see s 22(2)(c). A notice given on the same day as the application is invalid: *Gilmour v Osborne's Trs* 1951 SLCR 30. A landlord is not barred from invoking this section merely because he has the rights under the lease to remedy the breach: *Halliday v Fergusson* 1961 SC 24.
3 **'Rules of good husbandry':** see the Agriculture (Scotland) Act 1948, Sch 6. Rule 2 of the rules of good husbandry is subsidiary to rule 1. The main test is whether a reasonable standard of efficient production has been maintained and the holding kept in condition to maintain such a standard: see *Austin v Gibson* 1979 SLT (Land Ct) 12; *Ross v Donaldson* 1983 SLT (Land Ct) 26; *Cambusmore Estate Trust v Little* 1991 SLT (Land Ct) 33. The rules of good husbandry are to be regarded in the light of the rules of good estate management: 1948 Act, Sch 5. The court refused to grant a certificate of bad husbandry in a situation primarily caused by the landlord: *Sinclair v Mackintosh* 1983 SLT (Land Ct) 29; 1982 SLCR 43. Failure to follow a more intensive system of farming regarding substantial expenditure and capital not available to the tenant did not amount to a failure to observe the rules of good husbandry: *McGill v Bichan* 1982 SLCR 33. In *Cambusmore Estate Trust v Little* the court commented that leasing out milk quota could not be regarded as the equivalent of 'a farming operation or a "kind of produce"' and further that the tenant's state of health could not be pled as a mitigating factor if he was in breach of the rules. Once bad husbandry has been established the court has no discretion to refuse a certificate.
4 For circumstances where a certificate was granted, see *Buchanan v Buchanan* 1983 SLT (Land Ct) 31; *Luss Estates v Firkin Farm Co* 1985 SLT (Land Ct) 17; *Cambusmore Estate Trust v Little* 1991 SLT (Land Ct) 33.

Penalty for breach of condition

27.[1]—(1) Where, on giving consent under section 22 of this Act to the operation of a notice to quit an agricultural holding or part of an agricultural holding, the Land Court imposes a condition under section 24(3) of this Act, and it is proved, on an application to the Land Court on behalf of the Crown that the landlord—

(a) has failed to comply with the condition within the period allowed, or

(b) has acted in breach of the condition,

the Land Court may impose on the landlord a penalty of an amount not exceeding 2 years' rent of the holding at the rate at which rent was payable immediately before the termination of the tenancy, or, where the notice to quit related to a part only of the holding, of an amount not exceeding the proportion of the said 2 years' rent which it appears to the Land Court is attributable to that part.

(2) A penalty imposed under this section shall be a debt due to the Crown and shall, when recovered, be paid into the Consolidated Fund.

1 This section was substituted by the Agriculture Act 1958, Sch 1, Pt II. The Secretary of State had power under the original s 30 of the Agricultural Holdings (Scotland) Act 1949 to take possession of land where a condition imposed under s 26 had not been complied with. The

power was seldom exercised and is now abolished. The sum is a civil penalty payable to the Crown, and not to the tenant. Whether or not a tenant, who has been unjustly deprived of a tenancy where the conditions have not been complied with, has a civil remedy raises difficult questions. This section applies conditions imposed under ss 22 and 24(3).

Effect on notice to quit of sale of holding

28.[1]—(1) This section shall apply where a contract for the sale[2] of the landlord's interest in land which comprises or forms part of an agricultural holding is made after the giving of a notice to quit and before its expiry.

(2) Unless, within the period of 3 months ending with the date on which a contract to which this section applies is made, the landlord and the tenant have agreed in writing whether or not the notice to quit shall continue to have effect[3]—

    (a) the landlord shall—

        (i) within 14 days after the making of the contract; or

        (ii) before the expiry of the notice to quit,

    whichever is the earlier, give notice to the tenant of the making of the contract; and

    (b) the tenant may, before the expiry of the notice to quit and not later than one month after he has received notice under paragraph (a) above, give notice in writing to the landlord that he elects that the notice to quit shall continue to have effect.

(3) Where this section applies, unless

    (a) the landlord and tenant have agreed that the notice to quit shall continue to have effect;

    (b) the tenant has so elected, under subsection (2)(b) above; or

    (c) the landlord having failed to give notice of the making of the contract in accordance with subsection (2)(a) above, the tenant quits the holding in consequence of the notice to quit,

the notice to quit shall cease to have effect.

(4) Where this section applies and there is an agreement between the landlord and the tenant that the notice to quit shall continue to have effect, the notice shall not be invalid by reason only that the agreement is conditional.

---

1 In general, the conclusion of missives to sell the subjects after a notice to quit has been served invalidates the notice, unless the provisions of this section are followed. If the landlord and tenant agree in writing three months before the missives are concluded that the notice to quit shall continue to have effect, it remains effective. Such an agreement can be conditional (subsection (4)). This section does not apply to notices to quit served, by the selling landlord, after missives have been concluded.

    On the corresponding section of the Agricultural Holdings Act 1948 (provision now repealed by the Agricultural Holdings Act 1986), see *Blay v Dadswell* [1922] 1 KB 632; *Rochester v Chatham Joint Sewerage Board and Clinch* [1925] Ch 753; *Purser v Bailey* [1967] 2 QB 500.

2 'Contract for the sale' is the conclusion of missives not the granting of a subsequent disposition: *Gordon v Rankin* 1972 SLT (Land Ct) 7.

3 The landlord and tenant may come to an agreement but this will not be effective if it is entered into more than three months before the contract for sale. The section does not apply where missives are concluded before notice to quit is served: *Gordon v Rankin* 1972 SLT (Land Ct) 7.

Notice to quit part of holding to be valid in certain cases

29.[1]—(1) A notice to quit part of an agricultural holding held on a tenancy from year to year shall not be invalid on the ground that it relates to part only of the holding if it is given—

(a) for the purpose of adjusting the boundaries between agricultural units or of amalgamating agricultural units or parts thereof, or

(b) with a view to the use of the land to which the notice relates for any of the purposes mentioned in subsection (2) below,[2]

and the notice states that it is given for that purpose or with a view to such use, as the case may be.

(2) The purposes referred to in subsection (1)(b) above are—

(a) the erection of farm labourers' cottages or other houses[3] with or without gardens;

(b) the provision of gardens for farm labourers' cottages or other houses;

(c) the provision of allotments;[4]

(d) the provision of small holdings under the Small Landholders (Scotland) Acts 1886 to 1931, or of such holdings as are referred to in section 64 of the Agriculture (Scotland) Act 1948;

(e) the planting of trees;

(f) the opening or working of coal, ironstone, limestone, brickearth, or other minerals, or of a stone quarry, clay, sand, or gravel pit, or the construction of works or buildings to be used in connection therewith;

(g) the making of a watercourse or reservoir;

(h) the making of a road, railway, tramroad, siding, canal or basin, wharf, or pier, or work connected therewith.

1 This section legalises a notice to quit part of a farm where such notice is not competent apart from this section. Notice to quit part of a holding is invalid at common law: *Gates v Blair* 1923 SC 430. Section 21 and notices under the Act must generally apply to the whole holding. No special provision is made concerning the awaygoing tenant's rights apart from the statute. Apparently they would be enforced in full. See s 31 on abatement of rent and s 49 on dealing with rights to compensation. The tenant will be entitled to his usual waygoing claim including compensation for disturbance. He will thus also be able to claim a reorganisation payment under s 54.

2 The notice to quit here is that required under s 21 and must include a statement in accordance with s 29(1). The section gives no power to break the tenancy during its currency. The tenant may give counter-notice under s 22(1): see *Hamilton v Lorimer* 1959 SLCR 7. Shortly, the section provides that a landlord of a holding let from year to year (including a tenant sitting from year to year after renewal of the tenancy on tacit relocation) may give notice to the tenant to quit part only of the holding, when the object is to use the land for any of the purposes specified; but the tenant may, within twenty-eight days after service of the notice to quit, intimate to the landlord that he accepts the notice to quit the part as notice to quit the entire holding (s 30).

Where part of an agricultural holding is purchased, the purchaser cannot serve a valid notice to quit without the collaboration of the landlord of the remainder of the holding: *Secretary of State for Scotland v Prentice* 1963 SLT (Sh Ct) 48; *Stewart v Moir* 1965 SLT (Land Ct) 11.

3 **'Other houses'.** In *Paddock Investments v Lory* (1975) 236 EG 803 it was held by the Court of Appeal that 'other houses' were confined to farm labourers' houses (with which Gill agrees: *The Law of Agricultural Holdings in Scotland* (2nd edn), para 418, although earlier editions of *Connell* suggested that this provision would not be confined to houses for purposes connected with agriculture), as power was given to terminate the tenancy for wider purposes.

4 Not necessarily allotments under any statute.

Tenant's right to treat notice to quit part as notice to quit entire holding

30.[1] Where a notice to quit part of an agricultural holding is given to a tenant, being a notice which is rendered valid by section 29 of this Act, and the tenant within 28 days after—

(a) the giving of the notice, or

(b) where the operation of the notice depends on any proceedings under the foregoing provisions of this Act, the time when it is determined that the notice has effect,

whichever is later, gives to the landlord a counter-notice in writing that he accepts the notice as a notice to quit the entire holding, to take effect at the same time as the original notice, the notice to quit shall have effect accordingly.

1 This section gives the tenant the right to terminate the whole tenancy, following that notice, by giving counter-notice to the landlord within twenty-eight days of either the receipt of the notice under s 29 or upon determination of the Land Court proceedings, that he accepts the notice to quit as a notice to quit the entire holding.

The tenant will be entitled to his usual waygoing claims, including compensation for disturbance and consequently to a payment under s 54. In terms of s 43(7), however, if the part of the holding affected by notice or notices to quit is less than a quarter by area or rental value and the residue is reasonably capable of being farmed as a separate holding the compensation for disturbance is payable only for the part for which the notice to quit relates and the section 54 payment will be likewise restricted.

In a compulsory purchase situation, a tenant served with notice to quit part of an agricultural holding under s 29 is not entitled to give counter-notice under s 30 if he has elected for notice of entry compensation under s 55(2) of the Land Compensation (Scotland) Act 1973: see Chapter 11.

Reduction of rent where tenant dispossessed of part of holding

31.—(1) Where—

(a) the tenancy of part of an agricultural holding[1] terminates by reason of a notice to quit which is rendered valid by section 29 of this Act; or

(b) the landlord of an agricultural holding resumes possession of part of the holding in pursuance of a provision in that behalf contained in the lease,[2]

the tenant shall be entitled to a reduction of rent of an amount, to be determined by arbitration, proportionate to that part of the holding, together with an amount in respect of any depreciation of the value to him of the residue of the holding caused by the severance or by the use to be made of the part severed.

(2) Where subsection (1)(b) above applies, the arbiter, in determining the amount of the reduction, shall take into account any benefit or relief[3] allowed to the tenant under the lease in respect of the part whose possession is being resumed.

1 **'Agricultural holding'.** See the definition in s 85(1).

2 This relates to cases where there is a provision in a lease, reserving right to the landlord to resume part of a holding for certain specific purposes, and generally on certain specific terms as to compensation or abatement of rent. This notice of resumption need not be in any particular form so long as it complies with the provisions of the lease. Resumption cannot be of such an amount of the land as to amount to a fraud on the lease: *Fothringham v Fotheringham* 1987 SLT (Land Ct) 10.

3 **'Benefit or relief'.** In some cases there is provision in the lease, by which the landlord undertakes to give the tenant an abatement of rent in respect of the land resumed, together with surface damages. Where there was power to resume on condition that the tenant should receive an abatement, he was held not entitled to claim for severance damages: *Robertson v Ross & Co* (1892) 19 R 967. 'Surface damages' includes damage to crops and plantations: *Galbraith's Trs v Eglinton Iron Co* (1868) 7 M 167. For basis of a claim for loss of profits, see *McIntyre v Board of Agriculture* 1916 SC 983; *Fleming v Middle Ward of Lanark* (1895) 23 R 98. Loss of profits is only claimable when there is compulsory acquisition or a provision in the lease. The arbiter is directed to 'take into account any benefit or relief' allowed under the contract: see 'Ascertaining the Value of Improvements', p 52. The arbiter is bound to take into account the rental value of the area taken back and not the average rental value of the holding per acre: *Hoile v Sheriffs* 1948 SLCR 24 and s 43(7). It is thought that the arbiter must award in terms of this section and that in doing so he must have in view the terms of a contractual arrangement entered into between the parties. The intention is not to have two awards, one under the lease and one under the statute. The tenant may, if he thinks proper (usually when they are more beneficial), confine his claims to those in the lease. If he does so, he is not restricted by procedure under the 1991 Act, except that the arbitration must be under Sch 7: see s 49 re compensation rights; also ss 29, 30 and 43(7).

Further restrictions on operation of certain notices to quit

32.[1]—(1) Subsections (2) to (5) below shall apply where—

(a) notice to quit an agricultural holding or part of an agricultural holding is given to a tenant; and

(b) the notice includes a statement in accordance with section 22(2) of this Act and paragraph (d) thereof to the effect that it is given by reason of the tenant's failure to remedy a breach of a kind referred to in section 66(1) of this Act.[2]

(2) If not later than one month from the giving of the notice to quit the tenant serves on the landlord a counter-notice in writing requiring that this subsection shall apply to the notice to quit, subject to subsection (3) below, the notice to quit shall not have effect (whether as a notice to which section 22(1) of this Act does or does not apply) unless the Land Court consent to the operation thereof.

(3) A counter-notice under subsection (2) above shall be of no effect if within one month after the giving of the notice to quit the tenant serves on the landlord an effective notice under section 23(2) of this Act requiring the validity of the reason stated in the notice to quit to be determined by arbitration.

(4) Where—

(a) the tenant has served on the landlord a notice of the kind referred to in subsection (3) above;

(b) the notice to quit would, apart from this subsection, have effect in consequence of the arbitration; and

(c) not later than one month from the date on which the arbiter's award is delivered to the tenant the tenant serves on the landlord a counter-notice in writing requiring that this subsection shall apply to the notice to quit;

the notice to quit shall not have effect (whether as a notice to which section 22(1) of this Act does or does not apply) unless the Land Court consent to the operation thereof.

(5) On an application made in that behalf by the landlord, the Land Court shall consent under subsection (2) or (4) above or (6) below to the operation

of the notice to quit unless in all the circumstances it appears to them that a fair and reasonable landlord would not insist on possession.[3]

(6) Where a notice to quit is given in accordance with section 66(3) of this Act in a case where the arbitration under that section followed an earlier notice to quit to which subsection (1) above applied, if the tenant serves on the landlord a counter-notice in writing within one month after the giving of the subsequent notice to quit (or, if the date specified in that notice for the termination of the tenancy is earlier, before that date), the notice to quit given under section 66(3) of this Act shall not have effect unless the Land Court consent to the operation thereof.[4]

1 This section requires that the Land Court's consent is obtained in respect of certain notices to quit served under s 22(2)(d), which would otherwise be incontestable. It should be read along with s 66. These sections were introduced by the Agriculture (Miscellaneous Provisions) Act 1976 to alleviate the rigours of a demand to remedy a breach of the lease by doing any work of provision, repair or maintenance or replacement of fixed equipment, where the tenant disputed either his liability to do the work in question or the reasonableness of the time allowed, which could not be effectively done prior to the introduction of these provisions: see Gill, *The Law of Agricultural Holdings in Scotland* (2nd edn), para 342.

2 The tenant has two options open to him after receipt of a notice to quit founded upon s 22(2)(d) (failure to remedy a breach of lease by doing work) under subsections (2) and (3). Within one month of receipt of the notice to quit, he can either serve a counter-notice requiring the Land Court's consent to be obtained or demand a reference to arbitration of the validity of the reason stated in the notice. In the event that the arbiter finds against the tenant under a reference, the tenant can, not later than one month after the arbiter's award is delivered, serve a counter-notice requiring a reference to the Land Court: see subsection (4).

3 **'Fair and reasonable landlord would not insist on possession'**: see p 38. This is the only ground upon which the Land Court may refuse consent to the notice to quit. As the section provides 'shall consent . . . unless' the onus, unlike the onus in the similar provision in s 24(2), is firmly on the tenant to establish that a fair and reasonable landlord would not insist upon repossession. The tenant who relies on this provision faces formidable difficulties: Gill, *The Law of Agricultural Holdings in Scotland* (2nd edn), para 350.

4 This subsection deals with the situation where the initial notice to quit was rendered invalid by a reference to arbitration under s 66, but a subsequent notice to quit is served under the provisions of section 66(3). If the tenant serves a counter-notice within one month of receipt of the notice to quit, under subsection (3), then the notice to quit shall not have effect unless the Land Court consents, which can only be refused on the 'fair and reasonable' provision: see note 3 above.

Part IV

Compensation for Improvements

Improvements

33.[1] In this Part the following are referred to as 'improvements'—

'1923 Act improvement' means an improvement carried out on an agricultural holding,[2] being an improvement specified in Schedule 3 to this Act, and begun before July 31, 1931;

'1931 Act improvement' means an improvement so carried out, being an improvement specified in Schedule 4 to this Act and begun on or after July 31, 1931 and before November 1, 1948;

'old improvement' means a 1923 Act improvement or a 1931 Act improvement;

'new improvement' means an improvement carried out on an agricultural holding,[3] being an improvement specified in Schedule 5 to this Act begun on or after November 1, 1948.

1 This section defines the type of improvements by reference to the dates at which they were made, which might be found on an agricultural holding. The purpose of the definitions, as linked to the compensation provisions of the following sections, is that the tenant should be compensated for an improvement upon the basis of law applicable at the time that the improvement was made. Unlike the Agricultural Holdings (Scotland) Act 1949, which dealt with each type of improvement separately, the provisions of the 1991 Act deal with improvements generally, where improvements are dealt with compositely in each section.
2. **'On an agricultural holding'.** It will have to be confirmed, by reference to the Acts applicable at the time, that the holding was an agricultural holding at the date the improvement was made. In 1923 it was not uncommon for a holding to be let to a person during his continuance in an office, appointment or employment of the landlord, thus excluding it from the provisions of the Act, which in the following years became a normal tenancy. Claims for 1923 Act or old improvements are probably now rare, but those that exist are likely to be substantial, eg houses or farm buildings.
3 See preceding note.

Right to compensation for improvements

34.[1]—(1) Subject to subsections (2) to (4), (7) and (8) below, and to sections 36 and 39 to 42 of this Act, a tenant of an agricultural holding shall be entitled, on quitting[2] the holding at the termination of the tenancy,[3] to compensation from the landlord[4] in respect of improvements carried out by the tenant.

(2) A tenant whose lease was entered into before January 1, 1921 shall not be entitled to compensation under this section for an improvement which he was required to carry out by the terms of his tenancy.[5]

(3) A tenant shall not be entitled to compensation under this section for an old improvement carried out on land which, at the time the improvement was begun, was not a holding within the meaning of the Agricultural Holdings (Scotland) Act 1923 as originally enacted, or land to which provisions of that Act relating to compensation for improvements and disturbance were applied by section 33 of that Act.

(4) Nothing in this section shall prejudice the right of a tenant to any compensation to which he is entitled—
(a) in the case of an old improvement, under custom,[6] agreement[7] or otherwise;
(b) in the case of a new improvement, under an agreement in writing[8] between the landlord and the tenant;
in lieu of any compensation provided by this section.

(5) Where a tenant has remained in an agricultural holding during two or more tenancies, he shall not be deprived of his right to compensation under subsection (1) above by reason only that the improvements were not carried out during the tenancy on the termination of which he quits the holding.[9]

(6) Subject to section 36(4) of this Act, a tenant shall be entitled to compensation under this section in respect of the 1931 Act improvement specified in paragraph 28 of Schedule 4 to this Act, or the new improvement specified in paragraph 32 of Schedule 5 to this Act (laying down of temporary pasture), notwithstanding that the laying down or the leaving at the termination of the tenancy of temporary pasture was in contravention of the terms of the lease or of any agreement made by the tenant respecting the

method of cropping the arable lands; but, in ascertaining the amount of the compensation, the arbiter shall take into account any injury to or deterioration of the holding due to the contravention (except insofar as the landlord may have recovered damages therefor).[10]

(7) Where under an agreement in writing entered into before January 1, 1921 a tenant is entitled to compensation which is fair and reasonable having regard to the circumstances existing at the time of the making of the agreement, for an old improvement specified in Part III of Schedule 3 to this Act or in Part III of Schedule 4 to this Act, such compensation shall, as respects that improvement, be substituted for compensation under subsection (1) above.[11]

(8) Compensation shall not be payable under this Part of this Act in respect of repairs of the kind specified in paragraph 29 of Schedule 3 to this Act or in paragraph 29 of Schedule 4 to this Act unless, before beginning to execute any such repairs, the tenant gave to the landlord notice in writing under paragraph (29) of Schedule 1 to the Agricultural Holdings (Scotland) Act 1923, or under paragraph (30) of Schedule 1 to the Small Landholders and Agricultural Holdings (Scotland) Act 1931, of his intention to execute the repairs, together with particulars thereof, and the landlord failed to exercise the right conferred on him by the said paragraph (29) or, as the case may be, the said paragraph (30) to execute the repairs himself within a reasonable time after receiving the notice.

1 Unlike the Agricultural Holdings (Scotland) Act 1949, the section now deals with the right to compensation in respect of both old and new improvements: see Chapter 5.
2 **Quitting.** If the tenant does not go out on the expiry of a notice to quit but stays on in spite of the notice, he is generally not entitled to compensation: *Cave v Page* (1923) 67 SJ 659; *Hendry v Walker* 1927 SLT 333. A case in which the tenant left the holding but not the farmhouse (owing to the illness of his wife) held that, if the tenant was ejected, the ejectment was in consequence of the landlord's notice to quit, and that therefore the tenant had quitted the farm in consequence of the notice to quit, and that he was entitled to compensation for disturbance: *Mills v Rose* (1923) 68 SJ 420.
3 'Termination of the tenancy': see definition in s 85(1) and note 9 thereto.
4 'Landlord': see definition in s 85(1). The seller, and not the purchaser with entry at the same time as the tenant quits, is the person against whom a claim for compensation falls to be made in spite of the fact that the tenant may claim within two months after the termination of the tenancy: *Waddell v Howat* 1925 SC 484; *Tombs v Turvey* (1923) 68 SJ 385.
5 This includes compensation for improvements which the tenant contracted to execute under a lease entered into prior to 1st January 1921, whenever the improvement was carried out. But where a lease permitted alternative methods of cropping, one of which would result in an improvement and the other would not, and the tenant chose the former method, it was held that, as the tenant was not contractually bound to choose that method, he was entitled to compensation: *Gibson v Sherret* 1928 SC 493.
6 'Custom'. Customary compensation has been more in vogue in England than in Scotland, but the effect of liability may be seen in *Stewart v Maclaine* (1899) 37 SLR 623. This subsection reserves the right of a tenant to claim compensation for improvements where, apart from the Act, he is entitled to claim under local custom or custom of the country: see s 85(4). But in any case such a claim must be dealt with by arbitration under the Act. If the arbiter awards under custom, he cannot, of course, also award 'under the Act' for the same improvement.
7 'Agreement'. The use of the word 'agreement' in contrast to 'agreement in writing' in subsection (4)(b) implies that the agreement can be verbal.
8 'Agreement in writing' need not be formal or probative: see s 78. It will generally be a lease, but in any case it is thought that the agreement would fall to be interpreted in accordance with this subsection and 'custom of the country' would accordingly have effect so far as applicable, and the section would apply alike to compensation payable under

agreement and 'custom of the country'. There remains, however, the difference regarding local custom. It is doubtful if local custom is reserved under this subsection, which depends on whether it is included in the words 'or otherwise'.

9 Under s 85(1) 'tenant' is defined as including 'executors, administrators, etc', accordingly this subsection may enable a tenant's successors to antedate their claims by a considerable number of years.

Where a tenant has sat on under successive leases or for a period from year to year, he may claim compensation when he actually quits even for the unexhausted value of improvements effected during the lease or years preceding those at the expiry of which he quits. As to whether a tenancy continued on tacit relocation in a new tenancy or a continuation of the old one, see *Mackenzie v McGillivray* 1921 SC 722. The sitting tenant constructively takes over improvements from himself each time the tenancy is renewed: *Earl of Galloway v McClelland* 1915 SC 1062; see also s 3.

It is thought that the subsection would not apply where there was a material reduction in the area of the subjects let, but it probably would so far as the improvements related to the part remaining. Can it be said that a tenant remains in his holding if he only remains in, say, half of it? Section 50 does not apply to the case. Again, if there is any change in the personnel of the 'tenant' the section would not apply: eg, the original tenant may have been 'A' and he, along with 'B', becomes a joint tenant. A mere change in the rent or conditions of the tenancy would probably make no difference, nor would the fact that part of the farm had been resumed under the Act or under the lease.

10 It is to be noted that the subsection is affected by the terms of s 40 of the Small Landholders and Agricultural Holdings (Scotland) Act 1931 and accordingly only applies to pasture laid down after the passing of that Act: see *Blair v Meikle* (1934) Sh Ct Rep 224. It applies whether the lease was entered into before or after the passing of the Act. The onus of showing the extent of the pasture at his ingoing probably lies on the outgoing tenant making a claim. See s 36(4) regarding deductions for deteriorations.

11 This subsection is confined, in its effect, to the temporary improvements comprised in Pt III of Schs 3 and 4. It applies to all agricultural holdings within the meaning of the Act, including market gardens, regarding which see the special provisions of ss 40 to 42.

'**Agreement in writing**': see note 8 above. Where an arbiter is required to assess compensation in terms of an agreement in writing, if the agreement is objected to as not providing 'fair and reasonable compensation' as under this section, the arbiter has the duty to determine the point. But his determination may not be final and may be set aside by the court: *Bell v Graham* 1908 SC 1060. What is 'fair and reasonable [compensation] having regard to the circumstances existing at the time of the making of the agreement' is, of course, a question of fact, but there may also be involved a question of law. It may be suggested that the landlord should be entitled to object to the agreement where it gives more than fair and reasonable compensation. It is thought, however, that the court would hold that the section means that the agreement must have effect so long as it secures at least fair and reasonable compensation, the Act not aiming at interfering with contracts except to the extent of ensuring that the minimum compensation, namely what is fair and reasonable, shall be secured. It has hitherto been usual to embody such agreement in leases, the agreements referring to a scale or scales annexed thereto. In *Bell v Graham* it was laid down by Lord Dunedin that the agreement being signed by both parties, it is necessary for the party seeking to repudiate it to condescend specifically on the provisions objected to, and to the reasons for maintaining that the provisions are not fair and reasonable.

Payment of compensation by incoming tenant

35.[1]—(1) This section applies to compensation which is payable or has been paid to an outgoing tenant of an agricultural holding by the landlord under or in pursuance of this Act or the Agricultural Holdings (Scotland) Act 1923, the Small Landholders and Agricultural Holdings (Scotland) Act 1931, the Agriculture (Scotland) Act 1948 or the 1949 Act.

(2) Subject to subsection (3) below, any agreement made after November 1, 1948 between an incoming tenant and his landlord whereby the tenant undertakes to pay to the outgoing tenant or to refund to the landlord any compensation to which this section applies shall be null and void.[2]

(3) Subsection (2) above shall not apply in the case of an improvement of a kind referred to in Part III of Schedule 5 to this Act, where the agreement is in writing and states a maximum amount which may be payable thereunder by the incoming tenant.[3]

(4)[4] Where, on entering into occupation of an agricultural holding, a tenant, with the consent in writing of the landlord pays to the outgoing tenant compensation to which this section applies—

(a) in respect of an old improvement, in pursuance of an agreement in writing made before November 1, 1948; or

(b) where subsection (3) above applies,[5]

the incoming tenant shall be entitled, on quitting the holding, to claim compensation for the improvement or part in like manner, if at all, as the outgoing tenant would have been entitled if the outgoing tenant had remained tenant of the holding and quitted it at the time at which the tenant quits its.

(5) Where, in a case not falling within subsection (2) or (3) above, a tenant, on entering into occupation of an agricultural holding, paid to his landlord any amount in respect of the whole or part of a new improvement, he shall, subject to any agreement in writing between the landlord and the tenant, be entitled on quitting the holding to claim compensation in respect of the improvement or part in like manner, if at all, as he would have been entitled if he had been tenant of the holding at the time when the improvement was carried out and the improvement or part thereof had been carried out by him.[6]

---

1 This specifies that the section only applies to improvements, whether new or old. It does not cover agreements in relation to, eg, payment of milk quota compensation due under Sch 2 to the Agriculture Act 1986.

2 This subsection refers only to agreements between landlord and incoming tenant. Probably the incoming and outgoing tenants are free to make such bargains as they think fit with the landlord's consent. If such a consent was formal the agreement might be regarded as void under the subsection.

3 This refers to temporary improvements such as compensation for feeding-stuffs and manures.

4 The consent in writing need not be tested (s 78). It is necessary, however, if this subsection is to be founded on, that the written evidence of consent and the vouchers for the sum paid are carefully preserved. Vouchers are useful as evidence not to enable the value of the improvement to be determined, but to prove that the consent was actually obtained. If the consent were given in general terms, the incoming tenant would not be in safety to agree with the awaygoing tenant regarding the amount of compensation payable to the latter. In such circumstances, the safe course is to let an arbiter fix the amount, and to preserve his award. A common arrangement has been to bind the incoming tenant in the lease to relieve the landlord of any claim by the awaygoing tenant for compensation for improvements. In this connection see subsection (2) above which, with exceptions, makes such agreements invalid. It is not clear whether this would base a claim for the improvements at the termination of the tenancy. It may be argued that the obligation imposed on the tenant implies the landlord's consent. The obligation may, however, be imposed by the landlord without his being aware of what improvements had in fact been claimed. In any event, the cases to which the section may apply will mainly refer to temporary improvements which will be exhausted before a claim arises. In respect of improvements upon land agreed to be let or treated as a market garden, the consent of the landlord to the purchase by the incoming tenant is not necessary. See also the Opencast Coal Act 1958, s 24.

5 Evidently this includes all substituted compensation as is recognised under the Act.

6 Improvements, for which a tenant has paid in terms of this section, may be included in a record of the holding under s 8. It is important to preserve evidence of the amount paid on entry of the tenant with details – arbiter's award, receipts, etc.

Amount of compensation under this Part

36.—(1) Subject to subsections (2) to (4) below, the amount of any compensation payable to a tenant under this Part of this Act shall be such sum as fairly represents the value of the improvement to an incoming tenant.[1]

(2) In the ascertainment of the amount of compensation payable in respect of an old improvement, there shall be taken into account[2] any benefit[3] which the landlord has given or allowed to the tenant (under the lease or otherwise) in consideration of the tenant carrying out the improvement.[4]

(3) In the ascertainment of the amount of compensation payable under this section for a new improvement, there shall be taken into account—

(a) any benefit which the landlord has agreed in writing to give the tenant in consideration of the tenant carrying out the improvement; and

(b) any grant[5] out of moneys provided by Parliament which has been or will be made to the tenant in respect of the improvement.

(4) In ascertaining the amount of any compensation payable under section 34(6) of this Act, the arbiter shall take into account any injury to or deterioration of the holding due to the contravention of the lease or agreement referred to in that subsection, except in so far as the landlord has recovered damages in respect of such injury or deterioration.[6]

1 **'Value of the improvement to an incoming tenant'.** The indefinite, not the definite article is deliberately used. *'An'* incoming tenant is not necessarily *'the'* incoming tenant. There may be no incoming tenant, or the particular incoming tenant may intend to use the farm in such a way that the 'improvements', eg, certain buildings, would be of little or no value to him. These special conditions cannot affect the right of the quitting tenant to compensation, nor the measure of compensation. In the event of dispute, the arbiter would be entitled to fix the compensation value to a hypothetical new tenant on the supposition that the tenant had been bound to carry on the farm on the same lines substantially as his predecessor had done: see *MacMaster v Esson* 1921 SLCR 18; *Strachan's Tr v Harding* 1990 SLT (Land Ct) 6 at p 8B. An improvement, however costly, if of no value to a hypothetical incoming tenant, does not fall to be valued. In *Mackenzie v McGillivray* 1921 SC 722 it was suggested that the improvement should be valued on the basis of the value added to the whole holding. The Land Court has given useful guidance on the valuer's approach to the test in *MacEwen and Law* 1986 SLCR 109 and *Strachan's Tr v Harding*. The court recognised that there was no one proper approach to valuation. In *McEwan and Law* at pp 120–121, the court favoured an approach of valuing the improvement on the basis of the cost to the incoming tenant of erecting the improvement, taking into account grants, under a deduction for the age of the actual improvement.

2 **'Shall be taken into account'.** This is imperative – not optional – and throws on the arbiter the duty to inquire into the relevant facts and apply this provision to them.

3 **'Any benefit'**: see pp 43, 47, 53. This is very wide, and would embrace not money payments only, but also anything given or allowed which has a value to the tenant, eg, agreeing to accept a low rent, providing drainpipes for drainage to be executed by the tenant, or the providing of timber or other material for permanent improvements, or fencing. Clearly 'benefit' cannot take the form of a relaxation of cropping conditions which, in respect of the statutory right to freedom of cropping, the tenant is entitled to ignore, subject to maintaining fertility. A 'benefit' could, however, be conferred by allowing the tenant to break up permanent pasture which by contract was to remain unbroken up, or to exercise freedom of cropping or sale of crops during the last year of the tenancy. The mere non-termination of a tenancy by the landlord is not a 'benefit' under the Act: *Mackenzie v McGillivray* 1921 SC 722.

The question of 'benefit' has been raised with reference to claims for compensation for unexhausted manures and temporary pasture: *McQuater v Fergusson* 1911 SC 640; *Mackenzie v McGillivray.*

It does not matter whether the benefit is mentioned in the lease or not. In order that 'benefit' may be taken into account, the arbiter must be satisfied that (1) benefit or actual value to the tenant was actually given; and (2) that it was given or allowed in consideration of the tenant making the improvement in question. No writing is required. Proof that a benefit was given is not enough of itself. There must be a clear connection between the benefit and the improvement, namely agreement between the parties of intention to set the former against the latter: *McQuater v Fergusson*; *Mackenzie v McGillivray*; *Earl of Galloway v McClelland* 1915 SC 1062. There must be a bilateral agreement of which the benefit is a counterpart for the improvement.

4 Although this subsection makes no reference to taking into account grant moneys (see subsection (3)(b) for new improvements), there are dicta in *Strachan's Tr v Harding* 1990 SLT (Land Ct) 6, which suggest that even in valuing old improvements, the availability of grants should be taken into account if the improvement is to be valued on the basis of the cost of erecting the improvement at the date of valuation.

5 See *Strachan's Tr v Harding* 1990 SLT (Land Ct) 6 regarding grants. See the Housing (Scotland) Act 1987, ss 246 and 256 regarding deduction of housing improvement and repair grants so long as grant conditions remain in force.

6 See note 10 to s 34. The landlord might have recovered damages for deterioration under s 7 (3)(b).

Consents necessary for compensation for some improvements

37.[1]—(1) Compensation under this Part of this Act shall not be payable for—

(a) a 1923 Act improvement specified in Part I of Schedule 3 to this Act;

(b) a 1931 Act improvement specified in Part I of Schedule 4 to this Act; or

(c) a new improvement specified in Part I of Schedule 5 to this Act;

unless, before the improvement was carried out, the landlord consented to it in writing[2] (whether unconditionally[3] or upon terms as to compensation or otherwise agreed on between the parties).

(2) Where such consent was given on terms agreed as to compensation, the compensation payable under the agreement shall be substituted for compensation under section 34 of this Act.

1 See p 43. This section relates to both old and new permanent (or landlord's) improvements specified in Pt 1 of Schs 3 to 5, which are affected generally by the provisions of the immediately preceding sections. Being so affected, is compensation payable for improvements under this section, even when the tenant contracted to make the improvements, where the lease was entered into on or after 1st January 1921? It is thought not, because otherwise the landlord could derive no advantage by binding his tenant to effect such improvements except that he would get the improvements effected without having to pay for it immediately. If the landlord gives his consent – the tenant being free to make or not to make the improvements – the tenant would have to be satisfied with what compensation he had agreed to accept as a condition of the consent.

2 The consent in writing may be embodied in the lease or separately. If there is no written consent the tenant has no claim, although he may have a remedy under s 18 – tenant's right to remove fixtures and buildings. Agreements giving a conditional right to compensation and giving no right were both held legal in *Turnbull v Millar* 1942 SC 521. The English case of *Mears v Callender* [1901] 2 Ch 388 was not followed. An estate factor would probably be held impliedly to have authority to consent on behalf of his principal. It was held to be within the power of a factor to consent to the conversion of a farm into a market garden: *Re Pearson and I'Anson* [1899] 2 QB 618; *Turner v Hutchinson* (1860) 2 F & F 185.

The consent need not be expressed in a formal deed (s 78).

The question whether consent had been granted or not is a dispute which must go to arbitration, under s 60 of the Agricultural Holdings (Scotland) Act 1991. *Sinclair v Clyne's Tr* (1887) 15 R 185 has in effect been superseded.

The landlord may give consent on such terms as to compensation or otherwise as may be agreed. It may be argued that 'or otherwise' would allow the landlord to attach the condition that no compensation should be paid. That is at least doubtful, and in *Mears v Callender* compensation was found to be due, though consent was given to the tenant to make the improvement 'at his own cost'. It is thought that an agreement for compensation, though small, if not illusory, would be competent.

3 If consent is given unconditionally, the compensation would be the value to an incoming tenant. If a definite sum is agreed on and the improvement destroyed, say, by fire, before the termination of the tenancy, a question may arise whether the sum is nevertheless payable: *Duke of Hamilton's Trs v Fleming* (1870) 9 M 329; where the lease terminated by renunciation, see *Walker's Trs v Manson* (1886) 13 R 1198.

Notice required of certain improvements

38.[1]—(1) Subject to subsections (2) to (6) below, compensation under this Act shall not be payable for—
   (a) a 1923 Act improvement specified in Part II of Schedule 3 to this Act;
   (b) a 1931 Act improvement specified in Part II of Schedule 4 to this Act;
   (c) a new improvement specified in Part II of Schedule 5 to this Act;
unless the tenant gave notice to the landlord in accordance with subsection (3) below of his intention to carry it out[2] and of the manner in which he proposed to do so.

(2) Subsection (1) above shall not apply in the case of an improvement mentioned in subsection (1)(a) or (b) above, if the parties agreed by the lease or otherwise to dispense with the requirement for notice under subsection (3).[3]

(3) Notice shall be in accordance with this subsection if it is in writing and—
   (a) in the case of an improvement mentioned in subsection (1)(a) above, it was notice under section 3 of the Agricultural Holdings (Scotland) Act 1923, given not more than 3 nor less than 2 months,
   (b) in the case of an improvement mentioned in subsection (1)(b) above, it was notice under the said section 3, given not more than 6 nor less than 3 months,
   (c) in the case of an improvement mentioned in subsection (1)(c) above, it was given not less than 3 months,
before the tenant began to carry out the improvement.

(4) In the case of an improvement mentioned in subsection (1)(a) or (b) above, compensation shall not be payable unless—
   (a) the parties agreed on the terms as to compensation or otherwise on which the improvement was to be carried out;[4]
   (b) where no such agreement was made and the tenant did not withdraw the notice, the landlord failed to exercise his right under the said section 3 to carry out the improvement himself within a reasonable time,[5] or
   (c) in the case of an improvement mentioned in subsection (1)(b) above, where the landlord gave notice of objection and the matter was referred under section 28(2) of the Small Landholders and Agricultural Holdings (Scotland) Act 1931 for determination by the appropriate authority,[6] that authority was satisfied that the improvement should be carried out and the improvement was carried out in accordance with any directions given by that authority as to the manner of so doing.

(5) If the parties agreed (either after notice was given under this section or by an agreement to dispense with it) on terms as to compensation, the compensation payable under the agreement shall be substituted for compensation under this Part of this Act.[7]

(6) In subsection (4) above, 'the appropriate authority' means—
(a) in relation to the period before September 4, 1939, the Department of Agriculture for Scotland;
(b) in relation to the period starting on that day, the Secretary of State.

1 See p 43. This section now combines the requirements for both old and new improvements, which were dealt with separately under the Agricultural Holdings (Scotland) Act 1949. The category of old improvements under the Agricultural Holdings (Scotland) Act 1923 was confined to 'drainage': see Sch 3, para 19. It is thought that the section would apply to the substantially complete renewal of worn-out drains of considerable extent, but not to mere repairs. It applies to all kinds of agricultural drainage. A test to be applied on all improvements proposed to be executed under this section will be whether they are those which the tenant himself should carry out in terms of the obligations of his lease.

2 The time-limits provided for in subsection (3) must be complied with. The notice must contain a statement of the manner in which the tenant proposes to do the work: *Hamilton Ogilvy v Elliot* (1905) 7 F 1115. In the case of drainage this can generally be done most effectively by giving a reference to the field, with a statement of the direction, length, and depth of the proposed drains and particulars of the kind and diameter of pipes to be used. A simple tracing plan showing the direction of the drains is an advantage. Knowledge on the part of the landlord or his factor, or the fact that either agreed to the tenant's scheme of drainage, would not be held to imply that the landlord had dispensed with notice: *Barbour v M'Douall* 1914 SC 844.

3 It is not expressly provided that this agreement must be in writing. Lord Kincairney held the contrary in *Hamilton Ogilvy v Elliot* (1905) 7 F 1115. Although writing may not be essential under the proviso to this subsection it is in the interests of both parties that an agreement to dispense with notice should be in writing.

4 The agreement here contemplated may provide much less than full compensation and could not be repudiated on that ground.

5 If the landlord failed to do the work within a reasonable time, the tenant could do so and claim compensation. What is a reasonable time is a question of fact for the arbiter to decide.

6 See subsection (6) below.

7 See s 34(7) regarding substituted compensation. It would appear that parties cannot contract out of right to some compensation, as can be done with improvements to which s 37 applies. This subsection is differently worded from s 51(2) of the Agricultural Holdings (Scotland) Act 1949, permitting agreement 'as to compensation or otherwise', which was construed to mean that agreement could be reached as to no compensation. Accordingly there would appear to be 'pre-1991 new improvements', for which no compensation could be agreed and 'post-1991 new improvements', where the parties have to agree at least some compensation as substitute compensation.

Compensation for Sch 5, Pt II, improvements conditional on approval of Land Court in certain cases

39.[1]—(1) Subject to subsections (2) to (4) below, compensation under this Part of this Act shall not be payable in respect of a new improvement specified in Part II of Schedule 5 to this Act if, within one month after receiving notice under section 38(3) of this Act from the tenant of his intention to carry out the improvement, the landlord gives notice in writing to the tenant that he objects to the carrying out of the improvement or to the manner in which the tenant proposes to carry it out.

(2) Where notice of objection has been given under subsection (1) above, the tenant may apply to the Land Court for approval of the carrying out of the improvement, and on such application the Land Court may approve the carrying out of the improvement either—
(a) unconditionally, or
(b) upon such terms, as to reduction of the compensation which would

otherwise be payable or as to other matters, as appears to them to be just,

or may withhold their approval.

(3) If, on an application under subsection (2) above, the Land Court grant their approval, the landlord may, within one month after receiving notice of the decision of the Land Court, serve notice in writing on the tenant undertaking to carry out the improvement himself.

(4) Where, on an application under subsection (2) above the Land Court grant their approval, then if either—

(a) no notice is served by the landlord under subsection (3) above, or

(b) such a notice is served but, on an application made by the tenant in that behalf, the Land Court determines that the landlord has failed to carry out the improvement within a reasonable time,

the tenant may carry out the improvement and shall be entitled to compensation under this Part of this Act in respect thereof as if notice of objection had not been given by the landlord, and any terms subject to which the approval was given shall have effect as if they were contained in an agreement in writing between the landlord and the tenant.

1 This section was considerably amended by the Agriculture Act 1958, Sch 1, Pt II. Under the Agricultural Holdings (Scotland) Act 1949 application for approval of the carrying out of an improvement was made to the Secretary of State who delegated his functions under the section to the Agricultural Executive Committees.

Approval by the Land Court under this section must be limited to such improvements as are required to enable the tenant to carry on the type of farming specified in the lease. For examples of the exercise of the Land Court's jurisdiction see *Taylor v Burnett's Trs* 1966 SLCR App 139; *Hutcheson v Wolfe-Murray* 1980 SLCR 12; *Fothringham v Fotheringham* 1987 SLT (Land Ct) 10; *Renwick v Rodger* 1988 SLT (Land Ct) 23; *Mackinnon v Arran Estate Trust* 1988 SLT 32.

See also the Housing (Scotland) Act 1987, s 256.

Part V

Other Provisions Regarding Compensation

Market gardens

Market gardens

40.[1]—(1) This section applies to any agricultural holding which, by virtue of an agreement in writing made on or after January 1, 1898, is let or is to be treated as a market garden.[2]

(2) This section also applies where—

(a) a holding was, on January 1, 1898 under a lease then current, in use or cultivation as a market garden with the knowledge of the landlord; and

(b) an improvement of a kind specified in Schedule 6 to this Act (other than such an alteration of a building as did not constitute an enlargement thereof) has been carried out on the holding; and

(c) the landlord did not, before the improvement was carried out, serve on the tenant a written notice dissenting from the carrying out of the improvement;

in relation to improvements whether carried out before or after January 1, 1898.[3]

(3) In the application of Part IV of this Act to an agricultural holding to which this section applies, subject to subsections (5) and (7) below, the improvements specified in Schedule 6 to this Act shall be included in the improvements specified in Part III of each of Schedules 3, 4 and 5 to this Act.[4]

(4) In the case of an agricultural holding to which this section applies—

(a) section 18 of this Act shall apply to every fixture or building affixed or erected by the tenant to or upon the holding or acquired by him since December 31, 1990 for the purposes of his trade or business as a market gardener;[5]

(b) it shall be lawful for the tenant to remove all fruit trees and fruit bushes planted by him on the holding and not permanently set out, but if the tenant does not remove such fruit trees and fruit bushes before the termination of his tenancy they shall remain the property of the landlord and the tenant shall not be entitled to any compensation in respect thereof;[6] and

(c) the right of an incoming tenant to claim compensation in respect of the whole or part of an improvement which he has purchased may be exercised although the landlord has not consented in writing to the purchase.[7]

(5) Where a tenancy of a kind described in subsection (2) above was a tenancy from year to year, the compensation payable in respect of an improvement of a kind referred to in that subsection shall be such (if any) as could have been claimed if the 1949 Act had not been passed.[8]

(6) Where the land to which this section applies consists of part only of an agricultural holding this section shall apply as if that part were a separate holding.

(7) Nothing in this section shall confer a right to compensation for the alteration of a building (not being an alteration constituting an enlargement of the building) where the alteration was begun before November 1, 1948.

---

1 See Chapter 9 and s 41.

2 For definition, see s 85(1): *Watters v Hunter* 1927 SC 310; *Twygen v Assessor for Tayside* 1991 GWD 4–226. Under subsection (3), part of a farm may be a market garden as regards compensation (*Callander v Smith* (1890) 2 F 1140; *Taylor v Steel Maitland* 1913 SC 562), and under s 41 there is provision whereby the tenant of a farm may, with the authority of the Land Court, use part thereof as a market garden. An estate factor has implied authority to bind the landlord by an agreement with the tenant authorising the latter to change the cultivation of the land from ordinary agriculture to market gardening: *Re Pearson and I'Anson* [1899] 2 QB 618. Where there was a lease for twenty-eight years of a residence, garden, pleasure ground, and twenty-seven acres, and the tenant was bound not to use the subjects for any trade except that of nurseryman, market gardener or florist, it was held that there was an agreement within the section although there was no other reference to market garden cultivation: *Saunders-Jacobs v Yates* [1933] 2 KB 240. Where a holding was let on condition that it would not be deemed 'to be or treated as a market garden' within the meaning of the Agricultural Holdings (Scotland) Act 1908 it was decided that the tenant could not claim compensation: *Masters v Duveen* [1923] 2 KB 729. Land used as an orchard, with rhubarb and other crops grown underneath the trees, the fruit and crops being sold, is a 'market garden': *Lowther v Clifford* [1927] 1 KB 130; see also *Grewer v Moncur's Curator Bonis* 1916 SC 764; *Bickerdike v Lucy* [1920] 1 KB 707.

3 This subsection, because of the Market Gardeners' Compensation (Scotland) Act 1897, places land which, under lease current on 1st January 1898, was being used as a market garden with the knowledge of the landlord, and on which the tenant had 'then' (interpreted by

the decision as 'thereafter') executed thereon without previous notice of dissent from the landlord, any improvement comprised in Sch 6, in the same position as land agreed in writing, on or after that date, to be treated as a market garden. See also *Morse v Dixon* (1917) 87 LJ KB 1, in which it was held that a term in a lease under which the tenant who planted fruit trees was entitled to remove them, was not an agreement within the meaning of the subsection.

4 This is intended to enable the tenant of a market garden to effect the improvements comprised in Schs 3, 4 and 5 without the consent of, or notice to, the landlord. As these improvements include the erection or enlargement of buildings for the purpose of the trade or business of a market gardener, the compensation payable by a landlord at the termination of a tenancy might be large in amount. This consideration operated to deter some landlords from freely letting land for market gardens, and to increase the rents of market garden land, a fact which led to the passing of s 10(3) of the Agriculture Act 1920 (later s 66 of the Agricultural Holdings (Scotland) Act 1949 and now s 41), which aimed at introducing the Evesham custom into Scotland: see p 66.

Tenants of market gardens should be careful not to erect expensive buildings without first coming to an arrangement with the landlord as to the amount of the compensation which would be paid therefor at quitting. Compensation is only payable for buildings required for the purpose of the trade or business of a market gardener, and is limited to such sum as 'fairly represents the value of the improvement to an incoming tenant'. As an incoming tenant can only, at best, have a temporary interest, it would appear that the compensation would be on a lower scale than if it had been based on the more permanent interest of the landlord. Thus there is some risk of an improving tenant failing to recover what he may consider to be adequate compensation.

5 See Chapter 9 and s 18, relating to fixtures and buildings. It is thought that the tenant is entitled to treat buildings erected under Schs 3, 4 and 5 either as fixtures subject to the conditions under s 18, or as improvements for which he would be entitled to claim compensation provided he complies with the provisions of the Act for claiming such compensation. As, however, there may be doubts on this point, the latter alternative should be preferred. A lease of a market garden contained a reservation in favour of the landlord of right to work minerals. Glass-houses, which were the tenant's fixtures, and were in existence at the commencement of the lease, were destroyed by mineral workings sanctioned by the landlord. Held that the landlord was bound to compensate the tenant: *Gibson v Farie* 1918 1 SLT 404.

6 As this relates to fruit trees and fruit bushes *not* permanently set out, this part of the subsection seems merely to state the common law: *Wardell v Usher* (1841) 3 Scott (NR) 508. Generally, trees are held to be permanently set out when they are in a position from which it is not intended to transplant them.

7 This refers to s 35(4).

8 This differentiates a year-to-year market garden tenancy from a year-to-year farm tenancy. In the former case the compensation in respect of an improvement comprised in Schs 3, 4 and 5 is such (if any) as could have been claimed had this Act not been passed; that is to say, it is necessary to fall back on the provisions of the previous statutes (s 96 of the Agricultural Holdings (Scotland) Act 1949). Section 42 of the Agricultural Holdings (Scotland) Act had the effect of interrupting the currency of the lease when neither party had right to terminate the tenancy after 1st January 1898: *In re Kedwell v Flint & Co* [1911] 1 KB 797. In the case, therefore, of a year-to-year tenancy, a new lease would be held to have commenced at the end of each year, with the result that an agreement in writing would be required under subsection (1) to entitle the tenant to compensation.

9 See note 2 above.

Direction by Land Court that holding be treated as market garden

41.[1]—(1) Where—

(a) the tenant of an agricultural holding intimates to the landlord in writing his desire to carry out on the holding or any part thereof an improvement specified in Schedule 6 to this Act;

(b) the landlord refuses, or within a reasonable time fails, to agree in writing that the holding, or that part thereof, shall be treated as a market garden;

(c) the tenant applies to the Land Court for a direction under this subsection; and

(d) the Land Court is satisfied that the holding or that part thereof is suitable for the purposes of market gardening;

the Land Court may direct that section 40 of this Act shall apply to the holding or, as the case may be, part of a holding, either—

(i) in respect of all the improvements specified in Schedule 6 to this Act, or

(ii) in respect of some only of those improvements,

and that section shall apply accordingly as respects any improvement carried out after the date on which the direction is given.[2]

(2) A direction under subsection (1) above may be given subject to such conditions, if any, for the protection of the landlord[3] as the Land Court may think fit and, in particular, where the direction relates to part only of the holding, the direction may, on the application of the landlord, be given subject to the condition that the tenant shall consent to the division of the holding into two parts (one such part being the part to which the direction relates) to be held at rents agreed by the landlord and tenant or in default of agreement determined by arbitration, but otherwise on the same terms and conditions (so far as applicable) as those on which the holding is held.[4]

(3) Where a direction is given under subsection (1) above, if the tenancy is terminated—

(a) by notice of intention to quit given by the tenant, or

(b) by reason of the tenant's apparent insolvency being constituted under section 7 of the Bankruptcy (Scotland) Act 1985,

the tenant shall not be entitled to compensation in respect of improvements specified in the direction unless he produces an offer which complies with months after the production thereof.[5]

(4) An offer complies with this subsection if—

(a) it is in writing;

(b) it is made by a substantial and otherwise suitable person;[6]

(c) it is produced by the tenant to the landlord not later than one month after the date of the notice of intention to quit or constitution of apparent insolvency[7] as the case may be, or at such later date as may be agreed;

(d) it is an offer to accept a tenancy of the holding from the termination of the existing tenancy on the terms and conditions of the existing tenancy so far as applicable;

(e) it includes an offer, subject to subsection (5) below, to pay to the outgoing tenant all compensation payable under this Act or under the lease;[8]

(f) it is open for acceptance for a period of 3 months from the date on which it is produced.

(5) If the landlord accepts an offer which complies with subsection (4) above the incoming tenant shall pay to the landlord on demand all sums payable to him by the outgoing tenant on the termination of the tenancy in respect of rent or breach of contract or otherwise in respect of the holding.

(6) Any amount paid by the incoming tenant under subsection (5) above may, subject to any agreement between the outgoing tenant and incoming tenant, be deducted by the incoming tenant from any compensation payable by him to the outgoing tenant.

(7) A tenancy created by the acceptance of an offer which complies with subsection (4) above shall be deemed for the purposes of section 13 of this Act not to be a new tenancy.[9]

1 See Chapter 9. This important provision is substantially based on the Evesham custom: see p 66. But this section goes further by putting it in the power of any farmer, with the approval of the Land Court, to have part of his land treated as a market garden subject to conditions for the protection of the landlord.

2 It may be directed that all or only certain of the improvements in Sch 6 shall apply to the holding or to the part, and, of course, any claim for compensation would be confined to these particular improvements effected after the date of the direction. For example, 'Erection or enlargement of buildings for the purpose of the trade or business of a market gardener' might be excluded. What is 'a reasonable time' is a question of fact.

3 **'For the protection of the landlord'.** One can imagine that the effect of putting this section into operation would be prejudicial to the landlord, and that the only or the main way of protecting him might be to require payment of an increased rent. It might not be fair to other market gardeners who generally pay higher than the ordinary agricultural rent to let the tenant who converts the whole or part of his land into a market garden, under the Act, escape with an abnormally low rent. The conditions would doubtless include such obligations for cultivation, cleaning, manuring, etc, as are usual on market garden land.

4 The effect of this clause is simply to make the one holding into two separate holdings – separate as regards improvements, compensation for disturbance, etc. One of them will remain under the same conditions as the original lease (subject, possibly, to an alteration in rent). The other will also remain under these conditions, plus the conditions attached by the Land Court and by this section. The apportionment of rent falls to be settled by arbitration failing mutual agreement. It seems to be in the power of an arbiter to increase the rent so that joint rents of the two holdings would exceed the rent of the holding as undivided. Further, it could be stipulated that the use of the buildings would be available for both holdings, and that, should the tenant give up one of the holdings, the landlord would be entitled to insist on his giving up the other at the same time. In some cases it would, evidently, be very awkward if two different tenants had joint use of the same buildings for separate holdings.

5 There does not appear to be any express reference to arbitration regarding the question which may rise under this subsection. It is thought, however, that in view of the wide terms of s 60, that these questions would fall to be determined by an arbiter.

6 **'A substantial and otherwise suitable person'.** Apparently this person must have sufficient capital, and he must be otherwise capable from experience and character of undertaking the obligations of the tenancy. Probably objections similar to those that may be stated against a legatee under s 11 relating to bequest of a lease may be taken here. A dispute as to whether a 'substantial and otherwise suitable person' has been put forward would be settled by arbitration under the Act. Where the holding is not divided, as provided for under subsection (2) the provisions of subsection (4) appear to apply to the whole farm, including the part which has been turned into a market garden as a result of a 'direction' under the section.

7 **'Constitution of apparent insolvency'.** See the Bankruptcy (Scotland) Act 1985, s 7.

8 **'All compensation'**, ie in respect of the whole subject where it is undivided, or in respect of the part in question, where it is divided. The compensation embraces all the compensation payable under the Act and not merely the compensation for market garden improvements, as 'directed' by the Land Court.

9 Section 13 *inter alia* prevents an increase of rent (under demand) from having effect until the lapse of three years from 'the commencement of the tenancy'. In a case to which this subsection applies the three years would apparently be counted as if the original tenant has sat on under tacit relocation, and there had been no change of rent.

Agreements as to compensation relating to market gardens

42.—(1) Where under an agreement in writing a tenant of an agricultural holding is entitled to compensation which is fair and reasonable having regard to the circumstances existing at the time of making the agreement, for an improvement for which compensation is payable by virtue of section 40 of this Act, such compensation shall, as respects that improvement, be substituted for compensation under this Act.[1]

(2) The landlord and the tenant of an agricultural holding who have agreed that the holding shall be let or treated as a market garden may by agreement in writing substitute, for the provisions as to compensation which would otherwise be applicable to the holding, the provisions as to compensation in section 41(3) to (6) of this Act.[2]

1 The effect of this subsection is that, in regard to market garden improvements (in Sch 6), substituted compensation may be provided as hitherto. In other cases substituted compensation according to an agreed scale can only be provided now for the other improvements embraced in Pt III of Schs 3 and 4 where the lease was entered into prior to 1st January 1921.
2 The provisions of this subsection are only available, where the parties have agreed (as opposed to the Land Court directing) that the holding become a market garden.

Compensation for disturbance

43.[1]—(1) Where the tenancy of an agricultural holding[2] terminates by reason of—

(a) a notice to quit[3] given by the landlord; or
(b) a counter-notice given by the tenant under section 30 of this Act,

and in consequence the tenant quits the holding, subject to subsections (2) to (8) below, compensation for the disturbance shall be payable by the landlord to the tenant.

(2) Compensation shall not be payable under this section where the application of section 22(1) of this Act to the notice to quit is excluded by any of paragraphs (a) or (c) to (f) of subsection (2) of that section.[4]

(3) Subject to subsection (4) below, the amount of the compensation payable under this section shall be the amount of the loss or expense directly attributable to the quitting of the holding which is unavoidably incurred by the tenant upon or in connection with the sale or removal of his household goods, implements of husbandry, fixtures, farm produce or farm stock on or used in connection with the holding, and shall include any expenses reasonably incurred by him in the preparation of his claim for compensation (not being expenses of an arbitration to determine any question arising under this section).[5]

(4) Where compensation is payable under this section—

(a) the compensation shall be an amount equal to one year's rent[6] of the holding at the rate at which rent was payable immediately before the termination of the tenancy without proof by the tenant of any such loss or expense as aforesaid;
(b) the tenant shall not be entitled to claim any greater amount than one year's rent of the holding unless he has given to the landlord not less than one month's notice of the sale of any such goods, implements, fixtures, produce or stock as aforesaid and has afforded him a reasonable opportunity of making a valuation thereof;[7]
(c) the tenant shall not in any case be entitled to compensation in excess of 2 years' rent of the holding.[8]

(5) In subsection (4) above 'rent' means the rent after deduction of such an amount as, failing agreement, the arbiter finds to be the amount payable by the landlord in respect of the holding for the year in which the tenancy was

terminated by way of any public rates, taxes or assessments or other public burdens, the charging of which on the landlord would entitle him to relief in respect of tax under Part II of the Income and Corporation Taxes 1988.

(6) Where the tenant of an agricultural holding has lawfully sub-let the whole or part of the holding, and in consequence of a notice to quit given by his landlord becomes liable to pay compensation under this section to the sub-tenant, the tenant shall not be debarred from recovering compensation under this section by reason only that, owing to not being in occupation of the holding or part of the holding, on the termination of his tenancy he does not quit the holding or that part.[9]

(7) Where the tenancy of an agricultural holding terminates by virtue of a counter-notice given by the tenant under section 30 of this Act and—

(a) the part of the holding affected by the notice to quit given by the landlord, together with any part of the holding affected by any previous notice to quit given by the landlord which is rendered valid by section 29 of this Act, is either less than a quarter of the area of the original holding or of a rental value less than one quarter of the rental value of the original holding, and

(b) the holding as proposed to be diminished is reasonably capable of being farmed as a separate holding,

compensation shall not be payable under this section except in respect of the part of the holding to which the notice to quit relates.[10]

(8) Compensation under this section shall be in addition to any compensation to which the tenant may be entitled apart from this section.[11]

---

1 See Chapter 6. The tenant must have quitted at the time required by the notice. See note 2 to s 34: *Roberts v Magor* (1953) 103 LJ 703. The court has held that quit 'in consequence of the notice' means quit at the time specified in the notice: *Hendry v Walker* 1927 SLT 333. In that case a claim for compensation was rejected in respect that the tenant who quitted in July 1925 (while he should have done so at Martinmas 1923 and Whitsunday 1924, in terms of the notice to quit), on being compelled to quit by order of the court, did not quit in consequence of the notice to quit. The Lord Ordinary said that for more than a year prior to the quitting there had neither been a holding within the meaning of the Agricultural Holdings (Scotland) Act 1923 nor a tenant thereof nor could it reasonably be said that the loss and expense then incurred was directly attributable to the quitting: 'I think that the Act plainly implies that the quitting of possession shall take place at or immediately after the termination of the tenancy.' In a sheriff court case a tenant was held to have left in consequence of a notice to quit and not in consequence of an obligation in his lease to grant a letter of removal and that the arbiter was entitled to award damages for breach of contract relying on the cases of *Webster & Co v Cramond Iron Co* (1872) 2 R 752; *Beveridge and Ors v McAdam* (1925) Sh Ct Rep 288. See also s 54, regarding additional payments for reorganisation of the tenant's affairs. (Where payable the additional sum is of four years' rent which together with compensation for disturbance gives a minimum of five years' and a maximum of six years' rent.) The additional payment is due only where the tenant is entitled to compensation for disturbance (s 54). It is not otherwise related to disturbance payments and is due irrespective of the actual loss or expense incurred by the tenant.

An unsuccessful defence to an action of removing probably does extinguish a claim for a disturbance payment, if a protective claim has been intimated under s 62: *Preston v Norfolk County Council* [1947] 1 KB 233.

2 **'Agricultural holding'.** See s 1 for definition.

3 **'Notice to quit'.** Case in which it was questioned whether due notice to quit was given: *Forbes v Pratt* 1923 SLT (Sh Ct) 91. 'Notice to quit' is not defined, and it does not follow that the notice must be such as is required under s 21. Sheriff Brown (in *Earl of Galloway v Elliot* 1926 SLT (Sh Ct) 123) decided that it did, in a case where the landlord gave notice more than two years before the termination of tenancy, but against that view there are the cases of *Tinball v Marshall* [1922] EGD 396, to which he was referred (where six months' notice instead of twelve months' notice was given), and *Westlake v Page* [1926] 1 KB 298, in

which Lord Justice Banks, who gave the leading opinion, said: 'The first point taken by the landlord is a technical one, that the notice to quit was in law a bad notice, because it was conditional, etc, and in these circumstances the case does not come within the section at all, for that section, when speaking of a holding being terminated by a notice to quit, presumably refers to a termination by a valid notice. I cannot accept that contention. It seems to me that if a notice to quit is given, *whether it be a good or bad one*, and it is accepted as a good notice by the tenant who quits the holding in consequence of it, the case comes within the language of the section. The technical point therefore fails.' See also *Kestell v Langmaid* [1950] 1 KB 233, which reached the same decision. In *Farrow v Orttewell* [1933] Ch 480 it was held that the notice to quit was invalid but that the landlord was estopped by his actings from denying the validity of the notice.

A tenant who, in expectation of receiving a notice to quit, but before receiving such notice, made inquiries after another farm and left after getting a statutory notice was held to have quitted in consequence of that notice: *Johnston v Malcolm* 1923 SLT (Sh Ct) 81.

The notice to quit may be at a break or at the natural termination of the lease.

Notice of intention to quit by the tenant is not notice to quit. Nor is notice under s 16 of the Succession (Scotland) Act 1964. Nor is a termination of the tenancy by a legal irritancy. In all these cases disturbance compensation is not payable and nor is an additional payment under s 54.

4 Compensation is payable if the Land Court consents to the notice or if s 22(2)(b) is applicable: see *Kestell v Langmaid* [1950] 1 KB 233; *Dean v Secretary of State for War* [1950] 1 All ER 344.

5 **'Directly attributable'** and **'unavoidably incurred'** are restrictive terms. No indirect or avoidable loss or expense will be allowed. This would exclude loss or expense arising from the sale of stock, insofar as the stock might and should have been sold in the ordinary course, apart from the quitting. Again, if the tenant is going a long distance – say, to Canada – he would not be allowed to claim for the expense of removing his furniture, etc, when it might be more economical to sell here and buy new in Canada. The loss or expense of removal must not be too remote. As regards selling implements of husbandry, produce, and farm stock, it will sometimes be found that the chief item of expense is that attending the sale, because, in the general case, a tenant will get the market value of what he sells. At the same time, there may be loss on the sale of immature stock, and on the dispersal of pedigree herds, and dairy and sheep stocks. It may no doubt be contended that the difference between going-concern value and break-up value is considerable, and that this difference represents the amount of the tenant's loss. Each case must, however, stand on its own merits. Where a sheep stock was sold by public roup, it was averred that it was sold at break-up value, whereas the claimant was entitled to going-concern value. The court held that there was a relevant claim: *Keswick v Wright* 1924 SC 766. Where grain threshed and delivered showed less quantity than on valuation, it was held that the difference was not 'a loss directly attributable to the quitting of the holding': *Macgregor v Board of Agriculture* 1925 SC 613.

Loss or expense unavoidably incurred in connection with the sale of the tenant's stock was held to include loss sustained in selling by public roup as against a sale under ordinary circumstances, and also the cost of supplying refreshments, but not a fee paid for valuing stock before the sale: *Evans v Glamorgan County Council* (1912) 28 TLR 517. The compensation may include loss through deterioration of the stock on a sale: *Barbour v M'Douall* 1914 SC 844. A tenant cannot claim loss and expense through the removal of a fixture or building where he omits to give the notice required under the section relating to fixtures: *Harvey and Manns' Arbitration* (1920) 89 LJ KB 687.

'Any expenses reasonably incurred by him in the preparation of his claim'. This is confined to a claim for compensation for disturbance. Though expenses of the arbitration are not included, it is still in the discretion of the arbiter to determine all questions as to such expenses and by whom and in what proportion they shall be paid.

6 **'Rent'** here referred to is the net rent as defined. The rent current for the last year of the tenancy should be taken on the basis both in the case of one year's rent and in the case of two years' rent: see *Copeland v McQuaker* 1973 SLT 186. Where a tenant has been receiving abatements of rent, possibly only the sum actually paid can be considered, but the point is not free from doubt. There may arise questions as to whether for the purposes of this subsection 'rent' should be held to include other payments by the tenant, such as insurance premiums on the farm buildings, interest on drainage, and other improvements: see *Callander v Smith* (1900) 8 SLT 109 as to interest being rent. In *Marquis of Breadalbane v Robertson* 1914 SC 215 the court held that fire insurance premium, payable by the tenant on a policy effected by the landlord, was not 'present rent' within the meaning of the Small

Landholders (Scotland) Act 1911. But in *Duke of Hamilton's Trs v Fleming* (1870) 9 M 329; *Bennie v Mack* (1832) 10 S 255; *Clark v Hume* (1902) 5 F 252 there is a good deal to suggest that such premiums are 'rent' and even more can be said in favour of the inclusion of interest on improvement expenditure. On the other hand, where a landlord, in implement of an obligation in a lease, repaid the tenant half the cost of lime put upon the land, the court held that, in entering the farm in the valuation roll, the assessor was bound to allow a deduction from the rent specified in the lease of the sum so repaid. The deduction amounted to £29 5s: *Miller's Trs v Berwickshire Assessor* 1911 SC 908. It is unfortunate that the statute does not give a definition of 'rent' apart from the deductions to be made from gross rent for the purposes of this subsection. Either landlord or tenant may make a demand for arbitration as to 'rent' to be paid for the holding. In fixing the rent, the arbiter would require to take into account the landlord's improvements in respect of which interest was being paid; in other words, he would have to fix a rent for the holding in its then improved state (subject, however, to s 13(2)). That being so, practically the same result is reached as by including interest as part of the rent. Although the word 'taxes' is used, this cannot be held to include imperial taxes, which are levied on the same basis in England as in Scotland and it is thought that the word is used in the popular sense, as we frequently use 'local taxation' for 'local rating': *Lord Provost, etc, Edinburgh v The Lord Advocate* 1923 SLT 14.

Shortly stated the 'year's rent' was subject to deduction of such of the local rates and perhaps council tax as are paid by owners. No deduction falls to be made in respect of stipend.

7 This does not have effect where the tenant restricts his claim to a year's rent, as clearly it would serve no purpose in that case. What is a reasonable opportunity? Where a tenant gave notice in May 1912 that he intended to claim compensation, and, without further notice, proceeded to sell stock and implements by public roup, which the factor knew about, it was held that he had given the landlord the reasonable opportunity here required, there being no duty on the tenant to give notice of such opportunity: *Barbour v M'Douall* 1914 SC 844. See also *Dale v Hatfield Chase Corporation* [1922] 2 KB 282 in which it was held that it was a question of fact for the arbiter to decide whether a reasonable opportunity had been given. A tenant may not know whether or not he will desire to make a claim in excess of one year's rent, but where he is likely to do so it is a good precaution to have a valuation of stock made by an independent valuer and there should also be removal of any doubt if the landlord is notified of an opportunity of valuation.

8 **'2 years' rent of the holding'** would be twice the net rent for the last year: see *Copeland v McQuaker* 1973 SLT 186.

9 This preserves the position of the tenant, who has sub-let the holding, because, but for this provision, he would not be entitled to compensation as he would not be quitting the holding, although he would still be liable to make a payment to the sub-tenant: see s 55(5).

10 This sentence means that compensation for disturbance is confined to the part to which the notice to quit applied, except where the area included in that notice, and in any previous notice to quit, amounts to or exceeds one-fourth part of the area of the original holding or has a rental value more than a fourth of that of the original holding or where the holding, as proposed to be diminished, is not reasonably capable of being cultivated as a separate holding. In such cases compensation for disturbance may be claimed in respect of the entire holding, as it was at the time when the last notice to quit was served.

11 This subsection makes it clear that a disturbance payment is in addition to any other waygoing or compensation claims.

Compensation for continuous adoption of special standard of farming

44.[1]—(1) Where the tenant of an agricultural holding proves that the value of the holding[2] to an incoming tenant has been increased during the tenancy[3] by the continuous adoption of a standard of farming or a system of farming[4] which has been more beneficial to the holding than—

(a) the standard or system required by the lease,[5] or

(b) in so far as no system of farming is so required, the system of farming normally practised on comparable holdings in the district,

the tenant shall be entitled, on quitting the holding, to obtain from the landlord such compensation as represents the value to an incoming tenant of the adoption of that more beneficial standard or system.[6]

(2) Compensation shall not be recoverable under subsection (1) above unless—

(a) the tenant has, not less than one month before the termination of the tenancy, given to the landlord notice in writing of his intention to claim such compensation,[7] and

(b) a record of the condition of the fixed equipment on, and the cultivation of, the holding has been made under section 8 of this Act;[8]

and shall not be so recoverable in respect of any matter arising before the date of the record so made or, where more than one such record has been made during the tenancy, before the date of the first such record.

(3) In assessing the compensation to be paid under subsection (1) above, due allowance shall be made for any compensation agreed or awarded to be paid to the tenant under Part IV of this Act for any improvement which has caused or contributed to the benefit.[9]

(4) Nothing in this section shall entitle the tenant to recover, in respect of any improvement, any compensation which he would not be entitled to recover apart from this section.[10]

1 See p 52.

For convenience and brevity the continuous adoption of a special standard of farming or system of farming is commonly referred to as 'high farming'. In some respects it resembles the improvement which has sometimes been claimed under the name of 'cumulative or accumulated fertility'. A tenant would probably not be safe to confine himself to the name 'high farming' or to the name 'cumulative fertility', in claiming under this section.

2 Here it will be noted that the increase in the value 'of the holding' is referred to. In the case of compensation for improvements under s 36 it is the 'value of the improvement'.

3 **'During the tenancy'.** There is no provision for this section corresponding to that in s 34(5) for compensation for improvements effected by the same tenant during a previous tenancy. High farming is not 'an old improvement' or 'a new improvement' as defined in s 33.

4 **'Standard of farming or a system of farming'.** The interpretation of these terms is left to the arbiter, but his interpretation might be subject to review by the court on a stated case. Standard or system required by the lease does not necessarily refer to a specific standard or system in a written lease, for under the definition of lease in 85(1) a lease may be verbal. One essential is that the substituted standard or system must have been more beneficial to the holding than the standard or system required by the contract of tenancy. If the tenant were continuously to have land much longer in grass than his contract requires, if he were continuously to follow a five-course shift while he was at liberty to follow a four-course, if he were greatly to improve his pastures by sowing down and specially nurturing wild white clover, if, by the bringing in of exceptionally large quantities of dung, he were to improve the mechanical quality of the soil as well as its fertility – in any of these cases it is thought a valid claim might be made under this section, always keeping in view the provisos.

5 Here we find the arbiter is directed to award compensation representing the value to an incoming tenant 'of the adoption of that more beneficial standard or system'. What appears to be intended is that the arbiter is to fix the value to an incoming tenant of the improvement which has resulted from the adoption by the awaygoing tenant of the standard or system.

6 See preceding note.

7 Notice has to be given not later than one month before the termination of the tenancy. This, as regards notice, differs from compensation for other improvements which may be claimed, so long as intimation of intention to claim in terms of s 62 is given within two months after the termination of the tenancy. On a resumption sufficient notice should be given to enable the tenant to give the notice required by this section. See note 6 to s 22.

8 Presumably the record may have been made under the Agriculture Act 1920, or under the Agricultural Holdings (Scotland) Acts 1923 to 1949.

9 This is intended to prevent the tenant from receiving payment twice for the same improvement. A claim might be made under this section for special treatment of pastures

(say, by liberal sowing of wild white clover) which had been improved by the liberal consumption on them of purchased feeding-stuffs which may be claimed for separately. The arbiter must be careful to discriminate between the improvement resulting from the respective operations so as to ensure that double compensation is not allowed: see note 4 above.

10 This seems to mean that, so far as regards the improvements in Schs 3, 4, 5 and 6, the arbiter shall award no more compensation than he would and could have awarded had this section not been passed.
  See the Opencast Coal Act 1958, s 25.

Compensation to landlord for deterioration etc of holding

45.[1]—(1) The landlord of an agricultural holding shall be entitled to recover from the tenant, on his quitting the holding on termination of the land tenancy compensation—
  (a) where the landlord shows that the value of the holding has been reduced by dilapidation, deterioration or damage caused by;[2]
  (b) where dilapidation, deterioration[3] or damage has been caused to any part of the holding or to anything in or on the holding by;
non-fulfilment by the tenant of his responsibilities to farm in accordance with the rules of good husbandry.[4]
  (2) The amount of compensation payable under subsection (1) above shall be—
  (a) where paragraph (a) of that subsection applies, (insofar as the landlord is not compensated for the dilapidation, deterioration or damage under paragraph (b) thereof) an amount equal to the reduction in the value of the holding;[5]
  (b) when paragraph (b) of that subsection applies, the cost, as at the date of the tenant's quitting the holding, of making good the dilapidation, deterioration or damage.[6]
  (3) Notwithstanding anything in this Act, the landlord may, in lieu of claiming compensation under subsection (1)(b) above, claim compensation in respect of matters specified therein, under and in accordance with a lease in writing,[7] so however that—
  (a) compensation shall be so claimed only on the tenant's quitting the holding on the termination of the tenancy;
  (b) subject to section 46(4) of this Act compensation shall not be claimed in respect of any one holding both under such a lease and under subsection (1) above;[8]
and compensation under this subsection shall be treated, for the purposes of subsection (2)(a) above and of section 46(2) of this Act as compensation under subsection (1)(b) above.

1 A record made under s 8 is essential to a claim under this section. Three months' notice before the termination of the tenancy has to be given in respect of a claim under this section. See s 47.
2 As to the scope of this subsection, see *Evans v Jones* [1955] 2 QB 58.
3 **'Dilapidation, deterioration'.** Scammell and Densham, *Law of Agricultural Holdings* (7th edn), pp 34 ff defines 'dilapidation' as a failure to repair gates, fences, drains, etc, and 'deterioration' as applying to conditions not readily curable, such as loss of soil fertility from lack of fertilisation.
4 See p 42. The English equivalent of this section, under reference to the equivalent of s 100 of the Agricultural Holdings (Scotland) Act 1949 has been held not to bar action for damages for breach of covenant to repair during the currency of the tenancy: *Gulliver v Catt* [1952] 2 QB 308; *Kent v Conniff* [1953] 1 QB 361. As s 100 of the 1949 Act has not been repeated in

the 1991 Act, it may be that the landlord cannot now claim damages during the currency of the tenancy.

5 It will be noted that here the reference is to the value of the holding. The damage will depend on the expenditure required to bring the land, etc, back to proper condition and the loss incurred during the period when the subjects are not earning full rent.

6 For matters to be considered by an arbiter in determining a claim under this subsection, see *Barrow Green Estate Co v Walker's Exrs* [1954] 1 All ER 204. Claims for rehabilitation of fields have been held to fall within the English equivalent of this provision: *Evans v Jones* [1955] 2 QB 58. A claim for damages during the currency of tenancy if made under the lease is competent: *Kent v Conniff* [1953] 1 QB 361.

7 It should be borne in mind that a tenant has freedom of cropping, except perhaps in the last year of his tenancy.

8 This refers to rights and not to methods of enforcing them. A landlord who gave notice of claims both under the lease and under the Act could abandon one and validly pursue the other: *Boyd v Wilton* [1957] 2 QB 277. The landlord cannot elect to claim for some items under the statutory head and others under a contractual head; he has to elect, prior to the claims being determined.

See the Opencast Coal Act 1958, s 25.

Compensation for failure to repair or maintain fixed equipment

46.[1]—(1) This section applies where, by virtue of section 4 of this Act, the liability for the maintenance or repair of an item of fixed equipment is transferred from the tenant to the landlord.

(2) Where this section applies, the landlord may within the period of one month beginning with the date on which the transfer takes effect[2] require that there shall be determined by arbitration, and paid by the tenant, the amount of any compensation which would have been payable under section 45(1)(b) of this Act in respect of any previous failure by the tenant to discharge the said liability, if the tenant had quitted the holding on the termination of his tenancy at the date on which the transfer takes effect.

(3) Where this section applies, any claim by the tenant in respect of any previous failure by the landlord to discharge the said liability shall, if the tenant within the period of one month referred to in subsection (2) above so requires, be determined by arbitration, and any amount directed by the award to be paid by the landlord shall be paid by him to the tenant.[3]

(4) For the purposes of section 45(3)(b) of this Act any compensation under this section shall be disregarded.[4]

1 This section deals with the situation where liability for repair and maintenance of fixed equipment is transferred from the tenant to the landlord under s 4. The object is to have the tenant make good any failures by paying compensation to the landlord at the date of transfer of liability, so that the 'slate is clean' from that date.

2 **'Date on which the transfer takes effect'.** In terms of s 4(4) the transfer has 'effect as from the making of the award or from such later date as the award may specify'. A claim has to be made within one month from the date on which the transfer takes effect.

3 This subsection, which derives from s 6(2) of the Agricultural Holdings (Scotland) Act 1949, does not include the transfer provisions of that subsection dealing with transfers from landlord to tenant. Without those transfer provisions this subsection appears to be otiose.

4 This subsection provides that the landlord can choose to make his claim for dilapidations at outgo.

Provisions supplementary to ss 45 and 46

47.[1]—(1) Compensation shall not be recoverable under section 45 of this Act, unless the landlord has, not later than 3 months before the termination of the tenancy, given notice in writing to the tenant of his intention to claim compensation thereunder.

(2) Subsection (3) below shall apply to compensation—

(a) under section 45 of this Act, where the lease was entered into after July 31, 1931; or[2]

(b) where the lease was entered into on or after November 1, 1948.

(3) When this subsection applies, no compensation shall be recoverable—

(a) unless during the occupancy of the tenant a record of the condition of the fixed equipment on, and cultivation of, the holding has been made under section 8 of this Act;

(b) in respect of any matter arising before the date of the record referred to in paragraph (a) above; or

(c) where more than one such record has been made during the tenant's occupancy, in respect of any matter arising before the date of the first such record.[3]

(4) If the landlord and the tenant so agree in writing a record of the condition of the holding shall, notwithstanding that it was made during the occupancy of a previous tenant, be deemed, for the purposes of subsection (3) above, to have been made during the occupancy of the tenant and on such date as may be specified in the agreement and shall have effect subject to such modifications (if any) as may be so specified.[4]

(5) Where the tenant has remained in his holding during 2 or more tenancies, his landlord shall not be deprived of his right to compensation under section 45 of this Act in respect of any dilapidation, deterioration or damage by reason only that the tenancy during which the relevant act or omission occurred was a tenancy other than the tenancy at the termination of which the tenant quit the holding.[5]

1 Note the landlord has to give notice in writing three months before the termination of the lease of a claim under this section. In practice this means that no claim under the Act is available for any dilapidations, deteriorations or damage occurring in the last three months of the tenancy, which is perhaps the period when the tenant is most likely to lose interest in the farm and so cause such problems. If deterioration, etc, is being caused during that period the landlord will have to consider a common law remedy of interdict, etc.

2 The requirement to have a record of the holding before a claim is eligible does not apply to pre-1931 leases, which must be a rarity, but see subsection (5).

3 This subsection makes it an essential requirement that a record of the holding should have been made during the currency of the lease (see note 4 below) before a claim can be made. A claim cannot be made in respect of any dilapidations, etc, occurring before the record was made.

4 Parties may agree in writing to adopt a record made by the previous tenant, with or without modification.

5 See note 9 to s 34 regarding 'two or more tenancies'.

Landlord not to have right to penal rent or liquidated damages

48.[1] Notwithstanding any provision to the contrary in a lease of an agricultural holding,[2] the landlord shall not be entitled to recover any sum, by way of higher rent, liquidated damages or otherwise, in consequence of any breach or non-fulfilment of a term or condition of the lease, which is in excess of the damage actually suffered by him in consequence of the breach or non-fulfilment.[3]

1 See p 59.
2 **'Agricultural holding'.** See the definition in s 85(1).
3 This strikes at those clauses in leases which require the tenant to pay a penalty on the basis of one, two, or more rents in cases where he infringes the conditions of his lease generally with reference to cultivation and cropping. A tenant who is bound not to sell hay or straw under a penalty of £3 a ton for every ton sold off was found liable only for the actual manurial value of the hay sold off: *Wilson v Love* [1896] 1 QB 626.

Compensation provisions to apply to parts of holdings in certain cases

49.—(1) Where—
  (a) the tenancy of part of an agricultural holding terminates by reason of a notice to quit which is rendered valid by section 29 of this Act; or
  (b) the landlord of an agricultural holding resumes possession of part of the holding in pursuance of a provision in that behalf contained in the lease;
the provisions of this Act with respect to compensation shall apply as if that part of the holding were a separate holding which the tenant had quitted in consequence of a notice to quit.

(2) In a case falling within subsection (1)(b) above, the arbiter, in assessing the amount of compensation payable to the tenant, shall take into account any benefit or relief[1] allowed to the tenant under the lease in respect of the land possession of which is resumed by the landlord.

(3)[2] Where any land comprised in a lease is not an agricultural holding[3] within the meaning of this Act by reason only that the land so comprised includes land to which subsection (4) below applies, the provisions of this Act with respect to compensation for improvements and for disturbance shall, unless it is otherwise agreed in writing, apply to the part of the land exclusive of the land to which subsection (4) below applies as if that part were a separate agricultural holding.

(4) This subsection applies to land which, owing to the nature of the building thereon or the use to which it is put, would not, if it had been separately let, be an agricultural holding.

1 **'Benefit or relief'.** See note 3 to s 31.
2 Gill, *The Law of Agricultural Holdings in Scotland* (2nd edn), para 20, gives the historical background to this section which was introduced to take account of the different definition of 'holding' in the pre-1949 Acts. It could give rise to compensation claims if the parties do not contract out. If subjects let are not, on the test of predominant use (see note 2 to s 1), an agricultural holding but contain agricultural subjects then, in the absence of agreement to the contrary, there will be a liability to pay compensation for improvements and disturbance as if the agricultural part were a separate agricultural holding.
3 See definition of 'agricultural holding' in s 85(1).

Determination of claims for compensation where holding is divided

50.[1] Where the interest of the landlord in an agricultural holding has become vested in several parts in more than one person and the rent payable by the tenant of the holding has not been apportioned with his consent or under any statute, the tenant shall be entitled to require that any compensation payable to him under this Act shall be determined as if the holding had not been divided; and the arbiter shall, where necessary, apportion the amount awarded between the persons who for the purposes of this Act together constitute the landlord of the holding, and any additional expenses of the award caused by the apportionment shall be directed by the arbiter to be paid by those persons in such proportions as he shall determine.

1 This provision should be useful in cases where estates have been put on the market for sale, and it has been found expedient to sell part of a particular farm to one purchaser and part to another. Where that occurs it is necessary for the tenant to comply with the provisions of the statute in relation to both proprietors. In the case of two purchasers of separate parts of the same farm, and where there has been no apportionment of rent, the tenant should duplicate all his notices, claims, etc, and send, in proper time, one to each of the owners. He should make no attempt to allocate between them, but leave the arbiter to deal with the claim under this section. A part owner is not the 'landlord' as defined in s 85(1). All the part owners must join in giving notice to quit or a demand for arbitration. See *Secretary of State for Scotland v Prentice* 1963 SLT (Sh Ct) 48; *Stewart v Moir* 1965 SLT (Land Ct) 11. In an English case two purchasers individually gave notice to the tenant to quit; both notices were served timeously, so as to expire at the same time. They were independent notices, which made no reference to each other; they were served at different dates, and each was limited to a particular part of the farm. The court held that the notices were bad: *Bebington v Wildman* [1921] 1 Ch 559. It has also been decided in England that the liability is not joint and several: *Weston v Duke of Devonshire* [1923] 12 LJCCR 74.

This section applies to sums payable for reorganisation under s 55(5) and to compensation for milk quota under Sch 2, the Agriculture Act 1986, para 11(5).

The compensation under this section would include compensation for disturbance where applicable. The arbiter would be entitled to apportion rent in order to ascertain the proportion of compensation for disturbance payable by each proprietor.

Compensation not to be payable for things done in compliance with this Act

51.[1]—(1) Notwithstanding anything in the foregoing provisions of this Act or any custom or agreement—

(a) no compensation shall be payable to the tenant of an agricultural holding in respect of anything done in pursuance of a direction under section 9(2) of this Act;

(b) in assessing compensation to an outgoing tenant of an agricultural holding where land has been ploughed up in pursuance of a direction under section 9(2) of this Act, the value per hectare of any tenant's pasture comprised in the holding shall be taken not to exceed the average value per hectare of the whole of the tenant's pasture comprised in the holding on the termination of the tenancy.[2]

(2) In subsection (1)(b) above, 'tenant's pasture' means pasture laid down at the expense of the tenant or paid for by the tenant on entering the holding.

(3) The tenant of an agricultural holding shall not be entitled to compensation for an improvement specified in Part III of any of Schedules 3 to 5 to this Act, being an improvement carried out for the purposes of—

(a) the proviso to section 35(1) of the Agricultural Holdings (Scotland) Act 1923;

(b) the proviso to section 12(1) of the 1949 Act;[3] or

(c) section 9 of this Act.

1 This section makes provision for the ploughing up of permanent pasture, but restricts the tenant's right to compensation if a direction was made under s 9(2) that he should leave a specified area under permanent pasture at outgo.

193

2 See s 9(3).
3 Providing for restoration of fertility.

Compensation for damage by game

52.[1]—(1) Subject to subsection (2) below, where the tenant of an agricultural holding has sustained damage to his crops from game,[2] the right to kill and take which is vested neither in him nor in anyone claiming under him other than the landlord,[3] and which the tenant has not permission in writing to kill,[4] he shall be entitled to compensation from his landlord for the damage it extends.[5]

(2) Compensation shall not be recoverable under subsection (1) above, unless—

(a) notice in writing is given to the landlord as soon as is practicable after the damage was first observed by the tenant, and a reasonable opportunity is given to the landlord to inspect the damage[6]—

    (i) in the case of damage to a growing crop, before the crop is begun to be reaped, raised or consumed;[7]

    (ii) in the case of damage to a crop reaped or raised, before the crop is begun to be removed from the land;[8] and

(b) notice in writing of the claim, together with the particulars thereof, is given to the landlord within one month after the expiry of the calendar year, or such other period of 12 months as by agreement between the landlord and the tenant may be substituted therefor, in respect of which the claim is made.[9]

(3) The amount of compensation payable under subsection (1) above shall, in default of agreement made after the damage has been suffered, be determined by arbitration.[10]

(4) Where the right to kill and take the game is vested in some person other than the landlord, the landlord shall be entitled to be indemnified by that other person against all claims for compensation under this section; and any question arising under this subsection shall be determined by arbitration.

(5) In this section 'game' means deer, pheasants, partridges, grouse and black game.

1 See p 54.
2 **'Game'.** For definition, see subsection (5). Ground game is not included, because the tenant has statutory right to protect himself against damage by such game under the Ground Game Acts. Compensation was, however, payable under this section despite the tenant's right to kill deer under s 43(1) of the Agriculture (Scotland) Act 1948 (now repealed by the Deer (Amendment) (Scotland) Act 1982): *Lady Auckland v Dowie* 1964 SLT (Land Ct) 20; 1965 SLT 76.
3 These words prevent the landlord avoiding the provisions by using the device of having the tenant sub-let the shootings to him.
4 In England an agricultural tenant is vested under common law in the right to kill 'game' unless the right is expressly excluded. The damage referred to in this section includes damage by game coming from an adjacent estate, and even during close time: *Thomson v Earl of Galloway* 1919 SC 611. It has been suggested that the permission to kill would require to be co-extensive with the entire holding; at all events if the holding is in one 'unit'. But, on the contrary, it may be argued that, if the permission was confined to certain fields, that would bar a claim for damage in these fields. It is difficult to decide between these views, but the latter appears sounder, and would simply place the tenant in the same position, in relation to the excluded fields, as if they were in the occupation of another tenant. Obviously, the permission must be given in sufficient time to enable the tenant to have an opportunity of preventing the damage. The permission may be restricted to one or more of the five kinds of

game specified. In that event the tenant could claim only for damage by the other kinds: *Ross v Watson* 1943 SC 406.

5 Here the question is, does the damage over the area damaged (not over the whole field or over the farm) exceed 12p per hectare of that area? If it does not, no compensation is due; if it does, the full compensation is due, without deduction of the 12p per hectare. The compensation is due, even though the landlord can prove that he took all reasonable steps to keep down the game.

6 What is 'a reasonable opportunity' will be a matter of opinion, and will depend on the circumstances. If for any reason the time is limited, the fact should be stated in the notice. For example, the tenant may desire to get on with his harvesting, and, if he were to delay long, he might thereby suffer greater loss than the amount of the game damage.

7 This evidently means that the crop must be left growing, and it is a question whether it only applies to the area of the actual damage. It would be safer to leave the whole field uncut.

8 This applies only to the case where the damage has been done after the crop was cut but before it was begun to be removed. In such a case the crop must be left standing on the ground. To remove it, say, into the stockyard, would be removing it from the land. It is a question whether this applies only to the area of the actual damage. It would be safer to leave the whole crop in the particular field.

9 Note in particular that the tenant has to give (a) a notice of damage, and separately (b) a notice of claim. The calendar year is from 1st January to 31st December. This proviso might result in a claim being made after the tenant has quitted possession, which is why it is normal to alter these dates to the rental year under the lease. The particulars here required need only consist of a statement of the fact of the damage by the game as defined in this section, of the approximate date when the damage was caused, of the crop damaged, of the locality (field), approximately the area of the damage, and the amount claimed. Probably only one claim can be made in each one year period: *Earl of Morton's Trs v Macdougall* 1944 SC 410.

10 It seems strange that the game tenant should be liable, but there is nothing in this section to prevent him from contracting out with the landlord. Where the damage is caused not by game reared by the landlord but by game from covers on an adjoining property, no right of indemnity is conferred by the Act, but it is thought that at common law the landlord would have a right of indemnity against the neighbouring proprietor who reared the game which caused the damage: *Farrer v Nelson* (1860) 15 QBD 258. The sporting tenant cannot be a party in his own name to an arbitration for game damage at the instance of the agricultural tenant against the landlord, nor can the agricultural tenant claim against the game tenant (*Inglis v Moir's Tutors* (1871) 10 M 204) although the landlord has relief against the game tenant: *Kidd v Byrne* (1875) 3 R 255. His right of relief is now to be determined by arbitration, probably under this Act.

Extent to which compensation recoverable under agreements

53.—(1) Unless this Act makes express provision to the contrary,[1] where provision is made in this Act for compensation to be paid to a landlord or tenant—

(a) he shall be so entitled notwithstanding any agreement,[2] and

(b) he shall not be entitled to compensation except under that provision.

(2) Where the landlord and the tenant of an agricultural holding enter into an agreement in writing for such a variation of the terms of the lease as could be made by direction under section 9 of this Act, the agreement may provide for the exclusion of compensation in the same manner as under section 51(1) of this Act.[3]

(3) A claim for compensation by a landlord or tenant of an agricultural holding in a case for which this Act does not provide for compensation shall not be enforceable except under an agreement in writing.[4]

1 **'Express provision to the contrary'.** Eg, the provisions of ss 34(4), (7), 37(2), 38(5), 42, 45(3), and subsection (2) below.

2 Held that a limitation in a lease of the right to compensation for disturbance was void: *Coates v Diment* [1951] 1 All ER 890.

195

3 This subsection provides another exception in relation to agreements anent permanent pasture, which are made between the parties in lieu of having the matter referred to arbitration, provided the agreement excludes compensation in the same manner as under s 51(1). An agreement excluding compensation in a manner not consistent with s 51(1) would probably be void.

4 **'Agreement in writing'.** This need not be probative: see s 78.

PART VI

ADDITIONAL PAYMENTS

Additional payments to tenants quitting holdings

54.[1]—(1) Where compensation for disturbance in respect of an agricultural holding or part of such a holding becomes payable—

(a) to a tenant, under this Act; or

(b) to a statutory small tenant,[2] under section 13 of the 1931 Act;

subject to this Part of this Act, there shall be payable by the landlord to the tenant, in addition to the compensation, a sum to assist in the reorganisation of the tenant's affairs[3] of the amount referred to in subsection (2) below.

(2) The sum payable under subsection (1) above shall be equal to 4 times the annual rent[4] of the holding or, in the case of part of a holding, times the appropriate portion of that rent, at the rate at which the rent was payable immediately before the termination of the tenancy.

1 It is only where compensation for disturbance is payable under s 43 that a right to an additional payment under this section arises. If the landlord seeks to avoid a payment under this section, he has to take such steps as are available to him to avoid a claim for a disturbance payment under s 43 or to invoke the provisions of s 55.

2 **'Statutory small tenant'** is defined by s 2 (1)(iii) proviso (b) of the Small Landholders (Scotland) Act 1911. A statutory small tenant is entitled to a disturbance payment under s 13 of the Small Landholders and Agricultural Holdings (Scotland) Act 1931 if the Land Court authorises resumption in whole or in part of the holding. In those circumstances the statutory small tenant becomes entitled to an additional payment under this section.

3 **'To assist in the reorganisation of the tenant's affairs'.** Where the entitlement arises the additional payment is due without proof of loss or need: *Copeland* v *McQuaker* 1973 SLT 186 at 191.

4 **'Rent'.** It is the rent payable immediately before the termination of the tenancy, irrespective of any earlier abatements: see note 8 to s 43.

Provisions supplementary to s 54

55.[1]—(1) Subject to subsection (2) below no sum shall be payable under section 54 of this Act in consequence of the termination of the tenancy of an agricultural holding or part of such a holding by virtue of a notice to quit where—

(a) the notice contains a statement[2] that the carrying out of the purpose for which the landlord proposes to terminate the tenancy is desirable on any grounds referred to in section 24(1)(a) to (c)[3] of this Act and, if an application for consent in respect of the notice is made to the Land Court in pursuance of section 22(1) of this Act, the Court consent to its operation and state in the reasons for their decision[4] that they are satisfied that termination of the tenancy is desirable on that ground;

(b) the notice contains a statement[5] that the landlord will suffer hardship unless the notice has effect and, if an application for consent in respect of the notice is made to the Land Court in pursuance of section 22(1) of this Act, the Court consent to its operation and state in the reasons for their decision[6] that they are satisfied that greater hardship[7] would be caused by withholding consent than by giving it;

    (c) [8]the notice is one to which section 22(1) of this Act applies by virtue of section 25(3) of this Act and the Land Court consent to its operation and specify in the reasons for their decision the Case in Schedule 2 to this Act as regards which they are satisfied; or

    (d) [9]section 22(1) of this Act does not apply to the notice by virtue of section 29(4) of the Agriculture Act 1967 (which relates to notices to quit given by the Secretary of State or a Rural Development Board with a view to boundary adjustments or an amalgamation).

(2)[10] Subsection (1) above shall not apply in relation to a notice to quit where—

    (a) the reasons given by the Land Court for their decision to consent to the operation of the notice include[11] the reason that they are satisfied as to the matter referred to in section 24(1)(e) of this Act; or

    (b) the reasons so given include[12] the reason that the Court are satisfied as to the matter referred to in section 24(1)(b) of this Act or, where the tenant has succeeded to the tenancy as the near relative of a deceased tenant, as to the matter referred to in any of Cases 1, 3, 5 and 7 in Schedule 2 to this Act; but the Court state in their decision that they would have been satisfied also as to the matter referred to in section 24(1)(e) of this Act if it had been specified in the application for consent.

(3) In assessing the compensation payable to the tenant of an agricultural holding in consequence of the compulsory acquisition of his interest in the holding or part of it or the compulsory taking of possession of the holding or part of it, no account shall be taken of any benefit which might accrue to the tenant by virtue of section 54 of this Act.[13]

(4) Any sum payable in pursuance of section 54 of this Act shall be so payable notwithstanding any agreement to the contrary.[14]

(5)[15] The following provisions of this Act shall apply to sums claimed or payable in pursuance of section 54 of this Act as they apply to compensation claimed or payable under section 43 of this Act—

    section 43(6);
    section 50;
    section 74;

(6)[16] No sum shall be payable in pursuance of section 54 of this Act in consequence of the termination of the tenancy of an agricultural holding or part of such a holding by virtue of a notice to quit where—

    (a) the relevant notice is given in pursuance of section 25(2)(a), (b) and (d) of this Act;

    (b) the landlord is terminating the tenancy for the purpose of using the land for agriculture only; and

    (c) the notice contains a statement that the tenancy is being terminated for the said purpose.

(7) If any question arises between the landlord and the tenant as to the purpose for which a tenancy is being terminated, the tenant shall, notwithstanding section 61(1) of this Act, refer the question to the Land Court for determination.[17]

(8)[18] In this section—

(a) references to section 54 of this Act do not include references to it as applied by section 56 of this Act; and

(b) for the purposes of subsection (1)(a) above, the reference in section 24(1)(c) of this Act to the purposes of the enactments relating to allotments shall be ignored.

1 This subsection provides circumstances in which compensation for reorganisation can be avoided, provided the provisions of the subsection as to notice are complied with.

2 **'Notice contains a statement'.** The notice should contain the statement: see note 16 to s 22.

3 These subsections relate to 'good husbandry', 'sound estate management' and 'desirable for the purposes of agricultural research': see notes 5, 7 and 8 to s 24. In terms of s 55 (2) if the Land Court finds that it is satisfied that the reason is one of good estate management, then subsection (1) is excluded. It is difficult to see why s 24 (1)(b) was included here, when it appears to be excluded by subsection (2).

4 Note that the Land Court has to 'state in the reasons for their decision' that it is satisfied the ground is established. In any application before the Land Court the applicant should remind the court of this provision in final submissions.

5 See note 2 above.

6 See note 4 above.

7 **'Hardship'.** See note 9 to s 24. The notice should specify 'greater hardship' although in *Barnes Graham v Lamont* 1971 SLT 341 the Court of Session held that reference to a prior agreement to vacate the farm on the son completing his agricultural training was sufficient from which hardship could be inferred: *per contra* see also *Copeland v McQuaker* 1973 SLT 186.

8 See notes to s 25. This subsection excludes the right of a near relative successor, whose succession is objected to, from obtaining a reorganisation payment, provided the Schedule 2 case is made out and the Land Court so specifies. It is subject to the restrictions contained in s 55(2), which provides a defence to the application where a case is laid under Cases 1, 3, 5 and 7 and the near relative successor can establish that the real reason is that the landlord requires the land for a non-agricultural purpose: see note 10 below. The Land Court has to specify in the reasons for its decision the case in Sch 2: see note 4 above.

9 This deals with the special case under s 29(4) of the Agriculture Act 1967 where the Secretary of State terminates a terminable tenancy. No statement is required in the notice and no counter-notice can be served.

10 This subsection restricts the scope of subsection (1): (a) where the Land Court is satisfied that the landlord is terminating the tenancy for the purpose of using the land for non-agricultural use, or (b) the landlord claims that the notice is founded on one of the cases in Sch 2, but the Land Court is satisfied and it so states, that reason relates to an intention to use for non-agricultural purposes under s 24(1)(e). This near relative successor under Cases 1, 3, 5 and 7 should therefore state as a defence to any application, if the defence is available, that the real reason for termination of the tenancy is that the landlord wants the land for non-agricultural purposes, thus preserving the right to reorganisation payment.

11 **'Include'.** Note it is 'include', so a decision consenting to the notice on other grounds, but including this particular ground, is sufficient to exclude the provisions of s 55(1).

12 See preceding note.

13 See s 56 regarding compensation in compulsory purchase situations.

14 This excludes contracting out.

15 This subsection extends claims for reorganisation payments to sub-letting (s 43(6)), divided holdings (s 50) and the situation where limited owners are the landlords (s 74).

16 This subsection extends the exemptions to notices to quit served on successors who are not near relatives under s 25(2). The notice has to contain a statement that the tenancy is being terminated for the purpose of using land for agriculture only.

17 This section provides that questions arising between landlord and tenant as to the purpose for which the tenancy is being terminated shall be referred to the Land Court rather than to arbitration. The subsection does not require to be invoked in cases under subsections (1) and (2), where the Land Court's decision follows upon counter-notices. The subsection would appear to apply to the case where the tenant does not intend to challenge notice to quit by serving a counter-notice or where statutorily he cannot serve a counter-notice, but nevertheless wishes to challenge the reason in the notice to quit with a view to maintaining a

claim for reorganisation compensation. There are difficulties posed by this subsection, which Gill, *The Law of Agricultural Holdings in Scotland* (2nd edn), para 510, described as a lacuna in the Agricultural Holdings (Scotland) Act 1949: see 1973 SLT (News) 41.

18 Section 56 relates to compulsory purchase and so reference to s 54 does not include reference to compulsory purchase. The section does not apply if the reason stated under subsection (1)(a) above is, in terms of s 24 (1)(c), for the purpose of the establishment of allotments.

Additional payments in consequence of compulsory acquisition etc of agricultural holdings

56.[1]—(1) This section applies where, in pursuance of any enactment providing for the acquisition or taking of possession of land compulsorily, any person (referred to in this section and in sections 57 and 58 of and Schedule 8 to this Act as 'an acquiring authority') acquires the interest of the tenant in, or takes possession of, an agricultural holding or any part of an agricultural holding or the holding of a statutory small tenant.

(2)[2] Subject to subsection (3) below and sections 57 and 58 of this Act, where this section applies section 54 of this Act shall apply as if the acquiring authority were the landlord of the holding and compensation for disturbance in respect of the holding or part in question had become payable to the tenant on the date of the acquisition or taking of possession.

(3)[3] No compensation shall be payable by virtue of this section in respect of an agricultural holding held under a tenancy for a term of 2 years or more unless the amount of such compensation is less than the aggregate of the amounts which would have been payable by virtue of this section if the tenancy had been from year to year: and in such a case the amount of compensation payable by virtue of this section shall (subject to section 57(4) of this Act) be equal to the difference.

1 This provides that the section is to apply to all cases of compulsory acquisition of either the interest in the agricultural tenancy or the whole interest in the land including an agricultural tenancy.

2 The tenant's claim under s 54 is against the acquiring authority. Compensation paid by an acquiring authority under compulsory purchase provisions is tax free.

3 This subsection derives from s 12(2) of the Agriculture (Miscellaneous Provisions) Act 1968, but appears to contain a drafting error in that 'by way of compensation and' has been omitted after the second 'payable'. The error should not affect the intention of the section. A tenant for more than two years should be compensated for the longer tenancy including disturbance payments under the Land Compensation (Scotland) Act 1963, etc, which should more than compensate him for the cost of reorganisation. This will not apply to a yearly tenant, who is accordingly entitled to a reorganisation payment. This subsection covers the unlikely situation where a tenant for more than two years might find himself entitled to less than a tenant from year to year, in which case under this subsection he is entitled to payment of the difference by the acquiring authority.

Provisions supplementary to s 56

57.—(1) For the purposes of section 56 of this Act, a tenant of an agricultural holding shall be deemed not to be a tenant of it in so far as, immediately before the acquiring of the interest or taking of possession referred to in that section, he was neither in possession,[1] nor entitled to take possession, of any land comprised in the holding: and in determining, for those purposes, whether a tenant was so entitled, any lease relating to the land of a kind referred to in section 2(1)[2] of this Act which has not taken effect as a lease of the land from year to year shall be ignored.

(2)[3] Section 56(1) of this Act shall not apply—

(a) where the acquiring authority require the land comprised in the holding or part in question for the purposes of agricultural research or experiment or of demonstrating agricultural methods or for the purposes of the enactments relating to smallholdings;

(b) where the Secretary of State acquires the land under section 57(1)(c) or 64 of the Agriculture (Scotland) Act 1948.

(3)[4] Where an acquiring authority exercise, in relation to any land, power to acquire or take possession of land compulsorily which is conferred on the authority by virtue of section 102 or 110 of the Town and Country Planning (Scotland) Act 1972 or section 7 of the New Towns (Scotland) Act 1968, the authority shall be deemed for the purposes of subsection (2) above not to require the land for any of the purposes mentioned in that subsection.

(4) Schedule 8 to this Act shall have effect in relation to payments under section 56 of this Act.[5]

---

1 **'Possession'.** This means actual possession, although not so defined in this Act as it was by s 17 of the Agriculture (Miscellaneous Provisions) Act 1968.

2 **'Any lease relating to the land of a kind referred to in section 2(1)'** excludes grazing sub-lets by the tenant, so a tenant who has sub-let for grazing under s 2(1), although not in actual possession for the duration of the sub-let, still has a claim.

3 This excludes the right to compensation where the land is acquired for agricultural research or creation of smallholdings (see s 55(1)(a)), or where the Secretary of State acquires the land under s 57(1)(c) or 64 of the Agriculture (Scotland) Act 1948.

4 Where the power is exercised for development purposes, subsection (2) is excluded and a reorganisation payment can be claimed. This provision is similar in effect to the exemption in s 55(2); ie where the landlord is to use the land for non-agricultural purposes, probably development.

5 Claims are assessed in accordance with Sch 8. Claims are determined by the Lands Tribunal for Scotland.

Effect of early resumption clauses on compensation

58.[1]—(1) Where—

(a) the landlord of an agricultural holding resumes land under a provision in the lease entitling him to resume land for building, planting, feuing or other purposes (not being agricultural purposes); or

(b) the landlord of the holding of a statutory small tenant resumes the holding or part thereof on being authorised to do so by the Land Court under section 32(15) of the 1911 Act; and

(c) in either case, the tenant has not elected that section 55(2) of the Land Compensation (Scotland) Act 1973 (right to opt for notice of entry compensation) should apply to the notice;

compensation shall be payable by the landlord to the tenant (in addition to any other compensation so payable apart from this subsection) in respect of the land.

(2) The amount of compensation payable under subsection (1) above shall be equal to the value of the additional benefit (if any) which would have accrued to the tenant if the land had, instead of being resumed at the date of

resumption, been resumed at the expiry of 12 months from the end of the current year of the tenancy.[2]

(3)[3] Section 55(4) and (5) of this Act shall apply to compensation claimed or payable under subsection (1) above with the substitution for references to section 54 of this Act of references to this section.

(4)[4] In the assessment of the compensation payable by an acquiring authority to a statutory small tenant in the circumstances referred to in section 56(1) of this Act, any authorisation of resumption of the holding or part thereof by the Land Court under section 32(15) of the 1911 Act for any purpose (not being an agricultural purpose) specified therein shall—

(a) in the case of an acquisition, be treated as if it became operative only on the expiry of 12 months from the end of the year of the tenancy current when notice to treat in respect of the acquisition was served or treated as served on the tenant; and

(b) in the case of a taking of possession, be disregarded;

unless compensation assessed in accordance with paragraph (a) or (b) above would be less than would be payable but for this subsection.

(5) For the purposes of subsection (1) above, the current year of a tenancy for a term of 2 years or more is the year beginning with such day in the period of 12 months ending with a date 2 months before the resumption mentioned in that subsection as corresponds to the day on which the term would expire by the effluxion of time.[2]

---

1 Where land is resumed the tenant is entitled to compensation under this section. Where a resumption is made or authorised in respect of a compulsory acquisition scheme the tenant is entitled to compensation either under this Act or under the compulsory purchase code if he so opts under s 55(8) of the Land Compensation (Scotland) Act 1973, but not both.

2 See 'Early Resumption', p 51. See subsection (5).

3 Contracting out is excluded. This section applies the provisions to divided holdings, sub-lets and holdings with limited owners as landlords.

4 This subsection relates to statutory small tenants under the Small Landholders (Scotland) Act 1911.

5 See note 2 above.

Interpretation etc of Part VI

59. In sections 54 to 58 of and Schedule 8 to this Act—

'acquiring authority' has the meaning assigned to it by section 56(1) of this Act;

'statutory small tenant' and 'holding' in relation to a statutory small tenant have the meanings given in section 32(1) of the 1911 Act; and

references to the acquisition[1] of any property are references to the vesting of the property in the person acquiring it.

---

1 'Acquisition' means infeftment as opposed to the date of taking possession. This may have consequences in determining the valuation date and the date from which interest is due on a compulsory acquisition, because the normal rule is that the valuation date from which interest runs is either the date of taking actual possession or the date of infeftment, whichever is the earlier: see *Stair Memorial Encyclopaedia*, vol 5, para 119, and *Birmingham Corporation v West Midland Baptist (Trust) Association* [1970] AC 874.

PART VII

Arbitration and Other Proceedings

Questions between landlord and tenant

60.[1]—(1) Subject to subsection (2) below and except where this Act makes express provision to the contrary, any question or difference[2] between the landlord and the tenant of an agricultural holding arising out of the tenancy or in connection with the holding (not being a question or difference as to liability for rent)[3] shall, whether such question or difference arises during the currency or on the termination of the tenancy, be determined by arbitration.

(2)[4] Any question or difference between the landlord and the tenant of an agricultural holding which by or under this Act or under the lease is required to be determined by arbitration may, if the landlord and the tenant so agree, in lieu of being determined by arbitration be determined by the Land Court, and the Land Court shall, on the joint application of the landlord and the tenant, determine such question or difference accordingly.

1 See 'Arbitration under the Act', Chapter 12. Arbitration cannot be invoked to determine whether or not a tenancy exists as that is a matter for the courts. Arbitration can only be invoked where the landlord/tenant relationship exists. In *Houison-Craufurd's Trs v Davies* 1951 SC 1, landlords served on a tenant a notice under a resumption clause in a lease of their intention to resume certain parts of land and called upon the tenant to remove. The tenant refused and the landlords raised an action of removing in the sheriff court. The sheriff held the defences irrelevant and granted decree to the landlords. The tenant appealed to the Court of Session and took the plea, which he had not taken in the inferior court, that the question was one for arbitration in terms of s 74 of the 1949 Act (now s 60). It was held (Lord Patrick dissenting) that the question fell to be determined by arbitration under s [60] and that as s [60] was imperative parties cannot prorogate the jurisdiction of the courts. The decision in *Houison-Craufurd's Trs v Davies* was affirmed by a court of seven judges in *Brodie v Ker* 1952 SC 216.
2 **'Question or difference'** covers both questions of arbitration and valuation except in relation to the specific valuations excluded by s 61(7). It includes assessment of damages: *Hill v Wildfowl Trust (Holdings) Ltd* 1995 SCLR 778.
3 **'Not being a question or difference as to liability for rent'**: see *Budge v Mackenzie* (1934) Sh Ct Rep 168; *Ross v Macdonald* (1934) Sh Ct Rep 201. Note the exception is of a question or difference as to *liability* for rent and not any question as to rent: see *Boyd v McDonald* 1958 SLCR 10. Arbitration applies where the tenant claims to be entitled to withhold rent, because the liability for rent is not in dispute: *Brodie v Ker* 1952 SC 216 at p 226.
   See *Goldsack v Shore* [1950] 1 KB 708; *Davidson v Chiskan Estate Co Ltd* 1952 SLCR 41; *Galbraith and Ors v Ardnacross Farming Co* 1953 SLT (Notes) 30; *Gulliver v Catt* [1952] 2 QB 308.
4 The Land Court acting under this subsection has no higher jurisdiction than that of the arbiter: *Craig* 1981 SLT (Land Ct) 12. This procedure is now being invoked to some extent. In disputes sent to the Land Court, the decision of that court is not subject to a stated case to the sheriff or an appeal to the Court of Session. There is, however, provision in the Land Court Rules for a special case stated on any question of law 'for the opinion of a Division of the Court of Session': rules 84 to 90.
   See the Agriculture Act 1967, Sch 3, para 7(5).

Arbitrations

61.—(1) Any matter which by or under this Act, or by regulations made thereunder, or under the lease of an agricultural holding is required to be determined by arbitration[1] shall, whether the matter arose before or after the passing of this Act, be determined, notwithstanding any agreement under the lease or otherwise providing for a different method of arbitration, by a single arbiter in accordance with the provisions of Schedule 7 to this Act,[2] and the Arbitration (Scotland) Act 1894 shall not apply to any such arbitration.

(2) An appeal by application to the Land Court by any party to an arbitration under section 13(1) of this Act (variation of rent) against the award of an arbiter appointed by the Secretary of State or the Land Court on any question of law or fact (including the amount of the award) shall be competent.[3]

(3) An appeal under subsection (2) above must be brought within 2 months of the date of issue of the award.

(4) The Secretary of State may by regulations made by statutory instrument subject to annulment in pursuance of a resolution of either House of Parliament make such provision as he thinks desirable for expediting, or reducing the expenses of, proceedings on arbitrations under this Act.[4]

(5) The Secretary of State shall not make regulations under subsection (4) above which are inconsistent with the provisions of Schedule 7 to this Act.

(6) Section 62 of this Act shall apply to the determination by arbitration of any claims which arise—

(a) under this Act or any custom or agreement, and

(b) on or out of the termination of the tenancy of an agricultural holding or part thereof.

(7) This section and section 60 of this Act shall not apply to valuations of sheep stocks, dung, fallow, straw, crops, fences and other specific things the property of an outgoing tenant, agreed under a lease to be taken over from him at the termination of a tenancy by the landlord or the incoming tenant, or to any questions which it may be necessary to determine in order to ascertain the sum to be paid in pursuance of such an agreement, whether such valuations and questions are referred to arbitration under the lease or not.[5]

(8) Any valuation or question mentioned in subsection (7) above falling to be decided by reference to a date after May 16, 1975, which would, if it had fallen to be decided by reference to a date immediately before that day, have been decided by reference to fiars prices, shall be decided in such manner as the parties may by agreement determine or, failing such agreement, shall, notwithstanding the provisions of that subsection, be decided by arbitration under this Act.[6]

1 See 'Arbitration under the Act', Chapter 12. Practically every question arising between landlord and tenant in relation to the holding comes under the arbitration procedure of the Act. It is not competent to contract out of this provision and conditions in older leases for reference to two arbiters and an oversman are now superseded by this provision: see also the Agriculture Act 1967, Sch 3, para 7(5). These arbitration provisions also apply to milk quota compensation on termination of the tenancy: see the Agriculture Act 1986, Sch 2, paras 10(1), 11(4).

2 The arbiter has no exclusive jurisdiction to determine whether a tenancy has terminated. It was held that the question whether a tenancy had terminated was a question precedent to the existence of a statutory claim: *Donaldson's Hospital v Esslemont* 1926 SC (HL) 68. See also *Hendry v Walker* 1927 SLT 333; *Cormack v McIldowie's Exrs* 1974 SLT 178; and see *Cowdray v Ferries* 1919 SC (HL) 27, where it was held that the arbiter had jurisdiction to decide whether notice to quit was valid.

3 This subsection was added by the Agricultural Holdings (Amendment) (Scotland) Act 1983. The appeal may be on any question of fact or law including the amount of the award. It is for the appellant to identify in the award the errors into which it is said that the arbiter has fallen and to explain and show to what extent the award should be altered. It is not enough to say the award is 'too high' or 'too low': *Maciver v Broadland Properties Estates Ltd* 1994 SLCR 18.

Even if the appeal is unopposed the burden is on the appellant to show why the award should be altered: *Maciver v Broadland Properties Estates Ltd*. Appeal may be on grounds of failure to comply with the specified form of award or because of failure to assess the rent properly: see *Aberdeen Endowment Trust v Will* 1985 SLT (Land Ct) 23; *Earl of Seafield v Stewart* 1985 SLT (Land Ct) 35. As the arbiter is *functus*, if the Land Court is persuaded that an appeal is appropriate, then the matter is usually heard *de novo*. See Gill, *The Law of Agricultural Holdings in Scotland* (2nd edn), para 219.

4 No such directions have yet been issued. For forms of award and applications to the Secretary of State see the Agricultural Holdings (Specification of Forms) (Scotland) Order 1991 (SI 1991/2154).

5 See note 2 above and Chapter 14. It is unfortunate that 'outgoing tenant' is not stated to include the landlord where the landlord is also the occupier. A landlord who was in possession agreed with an incoming tenant for valuation of the crops, the property of the landlord, by two arbiters and an oversman. The tenant refused to pay, as the valuation had been by more than one arbiter, and it was held that s 1 of the Agricultural Holdings (Scotland) Amendment Act 1910 did not apply to a reference between a landlord in personal occupation and the tenant ingoing: *Methven v Burn* 1923 SLT (Sh Ct) 25. These excluded items fall to be determined by a common law arbitration which is subject to the Arbitration (Scotland) Act 1894 and to an application for a stated case under s 3 of the Administration of Justice (Scotland) Act 1972.

6 The Local Government (Scotland) Act 1973 abolished fiars prices. By s 228 (4) it provided that any valuation or question which was to have been fixed by reference to fiars prices was in future to be fixed, failing agreement, by a statutory arbitration. This section gives effect to that provision for the purposes of an agricultural holding.

Claims on termination of tenancy

62.—(1) Without prejudice to any other provision of this Act, any claim by a tenant of an agricultural holding against his landlord or by a landlord of an agricultural holding against his tenant, being a claim which arises, under this Act or under any custom or agreement, on or out[1] of the termination of the tenancy (or of part thereof) shall, subject to subsections (2) to (5) below, be determined by arbitration.[2]

(2) Without prejudice to any other provision of this Act, no claim to which this section applies shall be enforceable unless before the expiry of 2 months after the termination of the tenancy the claimant has given notice in writing to his landlord or his tenant, as the case may be, of his intention to make the claim.[3]

(3) A notice under subsection (2) above shall specify the nature of the claim, and it shall be a sufficient specification thereof if the notice refers to the statutory provision, custom, or term of an agreement under which the claim is made.[4]

(4) The landlord and the tenant may within 4 months after the termination of the tenancy by agreement in writing settle any such claim[5] and the Secretary of State may upon the application of the landlord or the tenant made within that period extend the said period by 2 months and, on a second such application made during these 2 months, by a further 2 months.[6]

(5) Where before the expiry of the period referred to in subsection (4) above and any extension thereof under that subsection any such claim has not been settled, the claim shall cease to be enforceable unless before the expiry of one month after the end of the said period and any such extension, or such longer time as the Secretary of State may in special circumstances allow, an arbiter has been appointed[7] by agreement between the landlord and the tenant under this Act or an application for the appointment of an arbiter under those provisions has been made by the landlord or the tenant.[8]

(6) Where a tenant lawfully remains in occupation of part of an agricul-

tural holding after the termination of a tenancy, references in subsections (2) and (4) above to the termination of the tenancy thereof shall be construed as references to the termination of the occupation.[9]

1 Both conditions must be fulfilled, namely a claim under the Act or under custom and on the termination of the tenancy. See s 85(1) for definition of 'termination' of tenancy.

2 See also the notes to the general arbitration section, s 60. This section appears to apply to common law waygoing valuations (see s 61(7)), although this results in inconsistencies in that the Secretary of State does not appoint two arbiters.

3 At this stage only a general intimation is required, but it must be in writing. Note that some claims have to be intimated earlier – eg, high farming (s 44(2)) and landlord's claims for dilapidations (s 47(1)). Notice may be given before the termination of the tenancy. Where land is resumed the claim should be intimated two months from the date of resumption. The provisions appear to apply when the tenancy is renounced. In a notice under the corresponding section of the Agricultural Holdings Act 1948 the landlord's son's name was inserted in place of the landlord's in error. The notice was held valid as it was received by the landlord and he could not reasonably mistake its intentions: *Frankland v Capstick* [1959] 1 All ER 209. It would be unwise to assume that this decision would be followed in Scotland.

4 At this stage only a general intimation is required, but it must be in writing. The notice should at least refer to the statutory provision, custom or term of the lease under which the claim is made: *E D & A D Cooke Bourne (Farms) Ltd v Mellows* [1983] QB 104; *Walker v Crocker* [1992] 1 EGLR 29.

5 This envisages settlement without detailed particulars.

6 Note it is 'within that period'. Extensions cannot be sought after the period has expired. These provisions give scope for delaying tactics which the general scheme of the Act seeks to prevent. In general, an arbiter has no power to award interest from a date earlier than his award and accordingly a delay can only benefit the landlord.

7 Mere agreement to appoint is not enough: *Chalmers Property Investment Co Ltd v MacColl* 1951 SC 24. Paragraph 5 of Sch 7 to the Act lays down the manner in which the parties must present their claims to the arbiter and failure to comply therewith renders the claim invalid: *Robertson's Trs v Cunningham* 1951 SLT (Sh Ct) 89. For the purposes of lodging claims the twenty-eight days run from the date of appointment and not from the date that the appointment was intimated to the parties: *Suggett v Shaw* 1987 SLT (Land Ct) 5.

8 It is important to note that the provision is one month or longer.

9 Note 'lawfully'. Any tenant remaining in occupation under a challenge to the validity of a notice to quit would be well advised to make the appropriate claims on a 'without prejudice' basis, have an arbiter appointed and then sist the arbitration pending the outcome of the challenge to the notice to quit. It has been judicially observed that this section applies only to the case where the landlord permitted the tenant to retain possession of part of the holding after the ish in terms of a new agreement: *Coutts v Barclay-Harvey* 1956 SLT (Sh Ct) 54.
 See the Opencast Coal Act 1958, s 24.

Panel of arbiters, and remuneration of arbiter

63.[1]—(1) Such number of persons as may be appointed by the Lord President of the Court of Session, after consultation with the Secretary of State, shall form a panel of persons from whom any arbiter appointed, otherwise than by agreement, for the purposes of this Act shall be selected.

(2) The panel of arbiters constituted under subsection (1) above shall be subject to revision by the Lord President of the Court of Session, after consultation with the Secretary of State, at such intervals not exceeding 5 years, as the Lord President and the Secretary of State may from time to time agree.

(3)—

(a) the remuneration of an arbiter appointed by the Secretary of State under Schedule 7 to this Act shall be such amount as is fixed by the Secretary of State;

(b) the remuneration of an arbiter appointed by the parties to an arbitration under this Act shall, in default of agreement between those parties and the arbiter, be such amount as, on the application of the arbiter or of either of the parties, is fixed by the auditor of the sheriff court, subject to appeal to the sheriff;

(c) the remuneration of an arbiter, when agreed or fixed under this subsection, shall be recoverable by the arbiter as a debt due from either of the parties;

(d) any amount paid in respect of the remuneration of the arbiter by either of the parties in excess of the amount (if any) directed by the award to be paid by that party in respect of the expenses of the award shall be recoverable from the other party.

1 It is for the arbiter to apply to the Secretary of State to fix his fee, which is over and above his out-of-pocket expenses. The application should be accompanied by a detailed note of all the work done and time occupied by the arbiter in connection with the arbitration. In important cases the process may with advantage be placed before the Secretary of State.

Appointment of arbiter in cases where Secretary of State is a party

64.[1] Where the Secretary of State is a party to any question or difference which under this Act is to be determined by arbitration or by an arbiter appointed in accordance with this Act, the arbiter shall, in lieu of being appointed by the Secretary of State, be appointed by the Land Court, and the remuneration of the arbiter so appointed shall be such amount as may be fixed by the Land Court.

1 *Secretary of State v John Jaffray and Ors* 1957 SLCR 27 (rent fixed by Land Court in lieu of arbiter); *Commissioners of Crown Lands v Grant* 1955 SLCR 25 (where it was observed that it was inappropriate for an arbiter from the official panel to be appointed to decide on matters where a government department had an interest); *Secretary of State for Scotland v Brown* 1993 SLCR 41 (where the Land Court fixed the arbiter's remuneration); see also s 80.
  See the Agriculture Act 1967, Sch 3, para 7(5).

Recovery of compensation and other sums

65.[1] Any award or agreement under this Act as to compensation, expenses or otherwise may, if any sum payable thereunder is not paid within one month after the date on which it becomes payable, be recorded for execution in the Books of Council and Session or in the sheriff court books, and shall be enforceable in like manner as a recorded decree arbitral.

1 It is thought that the submission or award would not require to contain a warrant of registration for execution, although it would be advisable in any agreement to include a consent for registration for execution. This section also applies to compensation for milk quotas under the Agriculture Act 1986, Sch 2.

Power to enable demand to remedy a breach to be modified on arbitration

66.[1]—(1) Where a question or difference required by section 60 of this Act to be determined by arbitration relates to a demand in writing served on a tenant by a landlord requiring the tenant to remedy a breach of any term or condition of his tenancy by the doing of any work of provision, repair, maintenance or replacement of fixed equipment,[2] the arbiter may—

(a) in relation to all or any of the items specified in the demand, whether or not any period is specified as the period within which the breach should be remedied, specify such period for that purpose as appears in all the circumstances to the arbiter to be reasonable;

(b) delete from the demand any item or part of an item which, having due regard to the interests of good husbandry as respects the holding and of sound-management of the estate of which the holding forms part or which the holding constitutes, the arbiter is satisfied is unnecessary or unjustified;

(c) substitute, in the case of any item or part of an item specified in the demand, a different method or material for the method or material which the demand would otherwise require to be followed or used where, having regard to the purpose which that item or part is intended to achieve, the arbiter is satisfied that—

    (i) the latter method or material would involve undue difficulty or expense,

    (ii) the first-mentioned method or material would be substantially as effective for the purpose, and

    (iii) in all the circumstances the substitution is justified.[3]

(2) Where under subsection (1)(a) above an arbiter specifies a period within which a breach should be remedied or the period for remedying a breach is extended by virtue of subsection (4) below, the Land Court may, on the application of the arbiter or the landlord, specify a date for the termination of the tenancy by notice to quit in the event of the tenant's failure to remedy the breach within that period, being a date not earlier than whichever of the two following dates is the later, that is to say—

(a) the date on which the tenancy could have been terminated by notice to quit served on the expiry of the period originally specified in the demand, or if no such period is so specified, on the date of the giving of the demand, or

(b) 6 months after the expiry of the period specified by the arbiter or, as the case may be, of the extended period.[4]

(3) A notice to quit on a date specified in accordance with subsection (2) above shall be served on the tenant within one month after the expiry of the period specified by the arbiter or the extended time, and shall be valid notwithstanding that it is served less than 12 months before the date on which the tenancy is to be terminated or that that date is not the end of a year of the tenancy.[5]

(4) Where—

(a) notice to quit to which 22(2)(d) of this Act applies is stated to be given by reason of the tenant's failure to remedy within the period specified in the demand a breach of any term or condition of his tenancy by the doing of any work of provision, repair, maintenance or replacement of fixed equipment, or within that period as extended by the landlord or the arbiter; and

(b) it appears to the arbiter on an arbitration required by notice under section 23(2) of this Act that, notwithstanding that the period originally specified or extended was reasonable, it would, in consequence of any happening before the expiry of that period, have been unreasonable to require the tenant to remedy the breach within that period;

the arbiter may treat the period as having been extended or further extended and make his award as if the period had not expired; and where the breach has not been remedied at the date of the award, the arbiter may extend the period as he considers reasonable, having regard to the length of period which has elapsed since the service of the demand.[6]

1 These provisions were introduced by s 13 of the Agriculture (Miscellaneous Provisions) Act 1976. Prior to that date there was no means whereby an unreasonable demand to remedy served as a prelude to a notice to quit under s 22(2)(d) could be moderated. A tenant risked losing his tenancy if he did not comply with such a demand. See Gill, *The Law of Agricultural Holdings in Scotland* (2nd edn), paras 342–352. The arbiter's powers may be invoked in an arbitration either in response to the demand to remedy or in an arbitration under s 23(2) following the notice to quit: *Fane v Murray* 1995 SLT 567.

2 See s 32.

3 The arbiter's powers are widely stated for modifying the terms of a demand to remedy, fixing a reasonable period for completion of the works and deleting such works as are considered unreasonable or not falling within the terms of the lease and by modifying the method by which the works are to be completed.

4 This provision is designed to prevent a tenant who fails to comply with the arbiter's revised time-limits obtaining a further year's occupation. The Land Court may on the application of the arbiter or the landlord specify the date for the termination of the tenancy by notice to quit if the tenant fails to implement the obligations to remedy within the new time-limits. The date must not be earlier than the later of (a) the date at which the tenancy could have been terminated by notice to quit serviced on the expiry of period originally specified, or (b) six months after the expiry of the period specified by the arbiter.

5 This provides new time-limits for the service of a second notice to quit, where the tenant has failed to remedy within the new time-limits set by the arbiter. Section 32(6) allows a counter-notice to be served against this new notice to quit.

6 This provision covers the situation where the failure to comply with the demand to remedy within the original period or any extended period can be attributed to any happening before (note 'before') the expiry of the period; then in an arbitration required by notice under s 23(2) the arbiter can extend the period. The 'any happening' would appear to cover events both personal to the tenant (eg, sickness, etc) and those outwith his control (eg, weather, strikes, failures by contractor, etc). Where the remedial action has been completed, but late, then the arbiter can retrospectively extend the time-limit. The provision has some similarities to the position of an architect or an arbiter in a building contract, where retrospective extensions of time can be granted even after the contract has been completed. The arbiter may grant further extensions. Where the arbiter extends the time the notice to quit will be invalidated, but if the tenant fails to comply with the further extension of time, a second notice to quit can be served based on this failure.

Prohibition of appeal to sheriff principal

67.[1] Where jurisdiction is conferred by this Act on the sheriff, there shall be no appeal to the sheriff principal.

1 **'Sheriff'**, **'Sheriff principal'**: see the Sheriff Courts (Scotland) Act 1971, s 49 and the Interpretation Act 1978, Sch 1. The section applies only to jurisdiction conferred by the Act, not to the common law jurisdiction, when the normal appeals are available: *Cameron v Ferrier* (1912) Sh Ct Rep 220.

Sheep stock valuation[1]

Sheep stock valuation

68.—(1) This section and sections 69 to 72 of this Act shall apply where under a lease of an agricultural holding,[2] the tenant is required at the termination of the tenancy to leave the stock of sheep on the holding[3] to be taken over by the landlord or by the incoming tenant at a price or valuation to be fixed by arbitration,[4] referred to in this section and sections 69 to 72 of this Act as a 'sheep stock valuation.'

(2) In a sheep stock valuation where the lease was entered into before or on November 6, 1946, the arbiter shall in his award show the basis of valuation of each class of stock and state separately any amounts included in respect of acclimatisation or hefting or of any other consideration or factor for which he has made special allowance.

(3) In a sheep stock valuation where the lease was entered into after November 6, 1946,[5] the arbiter shall fix the value of the sheep stock in accordance—

(a) in the case of a valuation made in respect of a tenancy terminating at Whitsunday in any year, with Part I of Schedule 9 to this Act if the lease was entered into before December 1, 1986, otherwise with Part I of Schedule 10 to this Act; or

(b) in the case of a valuation made in respect of a tenancy terminating at Martinmas in any year, with the provisions of Part II of Schedule 9 to this Act, if the lease was entered into before December 1, 1986, otherwise with Part II of Schedule 10 to this Act,

and subsection (2) above shall apply in such a case as if for the words from 'show the basis' to the end of the subsection there were substituted the words 'state separately the particulars set forth in Part III of Schedule 9 (or, as the case may be, Schedule 10) to this Act.'[6]

(4) Where an arbiter fails to comply with any requirement of subsection (2) or (3) above, his award may be set aside by the sheriff.[7]

(5) The Secretary of State may, by order made by statutory instrument subject to annulment in pursuance of a resolution of either House of Parliament, vary the provisions of Schedule 10 to this Act, in relation to sheep stock valuations under leases entered into on or after the date of commencement of the order.

1 See Chapter 13. These sections are taken from the Sheep Stocks Valuation (Scotland) Act 1937, the Hill Farming Act 1946 and the Hill Farming Act 1946 (Variation of Second Schedule) (Scotland) Order 1986 (SI 1986/1823) and now incorporate sheep stock valuations into the Act.

2 'Agricultural holding'. Note the different definition in s 72 for the purposes of these sections.

3 'Required at the termination of the tenancy to leave the stock of sheep on the holding'. For 'termination' see s 85(1). This is the provision which invokes the statutory valuation procedures. Any other arrangement between the landlord and tenant to take over the sheep stock by arbitration falls to be determined by a common law arbitration and not under these sections: see *Bell v Simpson* 1965 SLT (Sh Ct) 9; *Toms v Parnell* 1948 SLCR 8. Similarly any arrangement between a landlord in occupation and an incoming tenant will be subject to a common law arbitration. The parties may agree that the statutory provisions should apply: *Secretary of State v White* 1967 SLCR App 133.

4 'Arbitration': see s 72 for definition of 'arbiter', 'arbitration' and note 3 thereto.

5 Note that the provisions are not retrospective and so the specific provisions apply depending on the date at which the lease was entered into: see *Pott's Judicial Factor v Rutherford* 1940 SLT (Sh Ct) 18.

6 The provisions of the Hill Farming Act 1946 severely restrict the arbiter's discretion. It was inconsistent with modern practice where only cast ewes were sold. It was held not competent to make a valuation by reference to similar stocks in the district: *Macpherson v Secretary of State for Scotland* 1967 SLT (Land Ct) 9. Valuations under these provisions can be unfair: see *Pott's Judicial Factor v Johnston* 1952 SLCR 22; *Garrow and Anr* 1958 SLCR 13; *Secretary of State for Scotland v Anderson* 1967 SLCR App 117; *Tuffnell and Nether Whitehaugh Co* 1977

SLT (Land Ct) 14; and 'Valuations of Bound Sheep Stocks' 1978 SLT (News) 37. The Hill Farming Act 1946 (Variation of Second Schedule) (Scotland) Order 1986 (SI 1986/1823) was issued to alleviate these problems, but it is not retrospective.
7 Failure to show basis of valuation is a good ground for reduction of award: *Dunlop v Mundell* 1943 SLT 286; see also *Paynter v Rutherford and Ors* 1940 SLT (Sh Ct) 18.

Submission of questions of law for decision of sheriff

69.—(1) In a sheep stock valuation where the lease was entered into after June 10, 1937[1] the arbiter may, at any stage of the proceedings, and shall, if so directed by the sheriff (which direction may be given on the application of either party) submit, in the form of a stated case for the decision of the sheriff, any question of law arising in the course of the arbitration.

(2) The decision of the sheriff on questions submitted under subsection (1) above shall be final unless, within such time and in accordance with such conditions as may be prescribed by Act of Sederunt, either party appeals to the Court of Session, from whose decision no appeal shall lie.

(3) Where a question is submitted under subsection (1) above for the decision of the sheriff, and the arbiter is satisfied that, whatever the decision on the question may be, the sum ultimately to be found due will be not less than a particular amount, it shall be lawful for the arbiter, pending the decision of such question, to make an order directing payment to the outgoing tenant of such sum, not exceeding that amount, as the arbiter may think fit, to account of the sum that may ultimately be awarded.[2]

1 The Sheep Stocks Valuation (Scotland) Act 1937 did not make appeals available prior to the date on which it came into force. Appeals lie from the sheriff to the Court of Session, whose decision is final.
2 The arbiter has the power to award an interim payment of a sum, which he finds 'will be not less than a particular amount'.

Determination by Land Court of questions as to value of sheep stock

70.[1]—(1) Any question which would fall to be decided by a sheep stock valuation—
   (a) where the lease was entered into before or on November 6, 1946 may, on the joint application of the parties; and
   (b) where the lease was entered into after that date shall, on the application of either party,
in lieu of being determined in the manner provided in the lease, be determined by the Land Court.

(2) The Land Court shall determine any question or difference which they are required to determine, in a case where subsection (1)(b) above applies, in accordance with the appropriate provisions—
   (a) where the lease was entered into before December 1, 1986, of Schedule 9 to this Act;
   (b) where the lease was entered into on or after that date, of Schedule 10 to this Act.

1 Note that in leases entered into on or before 6th November 1946 a joint application to the Land Court is required, but for leases after that date either party may apply. The Land Court is required to apply the same Schedules as an arbiter.

Statement of sales of stock

71.—(1) Where any question as to the value of any sheep stock has been submitted for determination to the Land Court or to an arbiter, the outgoing tenant shall, not less than 28 days[1] before the determination of the question, submit to the Court or to the arbiter, as the case may be—

(a) a statement of the sales of sheep from such stock—

(i) in the case of a valuation made in respect of a tenancy terminating at Whitsunday during the preceding three years; or

(ii) in the case of a valuation made in respect of a tenancy terminating at Martinmas during the current year and in each of the two preceding years;[2] and

(b) such sale-notes and other evidence as may be required by the Court or the arbiter to vouch the accuracy of such statement.

(2) Any document submitted by the outgoing tenant in pursuance of this section shall be open to inspection by the other party to the valuation proceedings.

1 **'Not less than 28 days'** falls to be construed strictly. There would appear to be no discretion to allow a late lodging of the statement, unless, perhaps, the other party agrees: see eg, *Suggett v Shaw* 1987 SLT (Land Ct) 5, which deals with the late lodgment of a statement of claim to an arbiter under para 5 of now Sch 7. The same principles probably apply.
2 Now generally 28th May or November: Term and Quarter Days (Scotland) Act 1990.

Interpretation of sections 68 to 71

72. In sections 68 to 71 of this Act—

(a) 'agricultural holding'[1] means a piece of land held by a tenant which is wholly or in part pastoral, and which is not let to the tenant during and in connection with his continuance in any office, appointment, or employment[2] held under the landlord;

(b) 'arbiter'[3] includes an oversman and any person required to determine the value or price of sheep stock in pursuance of any provision in the lease of an agricultural holding, and 'arbitration' shall be construed accordingly; and

(c) 'sheep stock valuation' shall be construed in accordance with section 68(1) of this Act.

1 **'Agricultural holding'**. Note that the definition is different from that in s 1(1). This definition is required because there cannot be a bound sheep stock holding which is wholly arable.
2 **'Continuance in any office, appointment, or employment':** see note 4 to s 1.
3 **'Arbiter'**. Note that 'arbiter' is not confined to a single arbiter as required for other statutory arbitrations under this Act: see s 61.

PART VIII

MISCELLANEOUS

Power of Secretary of State to vary Schedules 5 and 6

73.[1]—(1) The Secretary of State may, after consultation with persons appearing to him to represent the interests of landlords and tenants of agricultural holdings, by order vary the provisions of Schedules 5 and 6 to this Act.

(2) An order under this section may make such provision as to the operation of this Act in relation to tenancies current when the order takes effect as appears to the Secretary of State to be just having regard to the variation of the said Schedules effected by the order.

(3) Nothing in any order made under this section shall affect the right of a tenant to claim, in respect of an improvement made or begun before the date on which such order comes into force, any compensation to which, but for the making of the order, he would have been entitled.

(4) Orders under this section shall be made by statutory instrument which shall be of no effect unless approved by resolution of each House of Parliament.

1 The Schedules relate to new improvements defined in s 33(1) and market garden improvements referred to in s 40(3).
   See the Opencast Coal Act 1958, ss 26, 28.

Power of limited owners to give consents, etc

74.[1] The landlord of an agricultural holding, whatever may be his estate or interest in the holding, may for the purposes of this Act give any consent, make any agreement, or do or have done to him any act which he might give or make or do or have done to him if he were the owner of the dominium utile[2] of the holding.

1 See s 85(1) for definitions. A limited owner includes a liferenter. A difficult question arises as to whether or not a liferenter can grant a lease of an agricultural holding, which might extend beyond his lifetime.
2 'Owner of the dominium utile'. As mentioned above, s 80 of the Agricultural Holdings (Scotland) Act 1949 used the words 'absolute owner'.

Power of tenant and landlord to obtain charge on holding

75.[1]—(1) Where any sum has become payable to the tenant of an agricultural holding in respect of compensation by the landlord and the landlord has failed to discharge his liability therefor within one month after the date on which the sum became payable, the Secretary of State may, on the application of the tenant and after giving not less than 14 days' notice of his intention so to do to the landlord, create, where the landlord is the owner of the dominium utile of the holding, a charge on the holding, or where the landlord is the lessee of the holding under a lease recorded under the Registration of Leases (Scotland) Act 1857 a charge on the lease for the payment of the sum due.

(2) For the purpose of creating a charge of a kind referred to in subsection (1) above, the Secretary of State may make in favour of the tenant a charging order charging and burdening the holding or the lease, as the case may be, with an annuity to repay the sum due together with the expenses of obtaining the charging order and recording it in the General Register of Sasines or registering it in the Land Register of Scotland.

(3)[2] Where the landlord of an agricultural holding, not being the owner of the dominium utile[3] of the holding, has paid to the tenant of the holding the amount due to him under this Act, or under custom or agreement, or otherwise, in respect of compensation for an improvement or in respect of compensation for disturbance, or has himself defrayed the cost of an improvement proposed to be executed by the tenant, the Secretary of State may, on the application of the landlord and after giving not less than 14 days notice to the absolute owner of the holding, make in favour of the landlord a charging order charging and burdening the holding with an annuity to repay the amount of the compensation or of the cost of the improvement, as the case may be, together with the expenses of obtaining the charging order and recording it in the General Register of Sasines or registering it in the Land Register of Scotland.

(4) Section 65(2), (4) and (6) to (10) of the Water (Scotland) Act 1980 shall, with the following and any other necessary modifications, apply to any such charging order as is mentioned in subsection (2) or (3) above, that is to say—

(a) for any reference to an islands or district council there shall be substituted a reference to the Secretary of State;

(b) for any reference to the period of 30 years there shall be substituted—

(i) where subsection (1) above applies, a reference to such period (not exceeding 30 years) as the Secretary of State may determine;

(ii) in the case of a charging order made in respect of compensation for, or of the cost of, an improvement, a reference to the period within which the improvement will, in the opinion of the Secretary of State, have become exhausted;

(c) for references to Part V of the said Act of 1980 there shall be substituted references to this Act.

(5) Where subsection (3) above applies, an annuity constituted a charge by a charging order recorded in the General Register of Sasines or registered in the Land Register of Scotland shall be a charge on the holding specified in the order and shall rank after all prior charges heritably secured thereon.

(6) The creation of a charge on a holding under this section shall not be deemed to be a contravention of any prohibition against charging or burdening contained in the deed or instrument under which the holding is held.

1 See p 61. This remedy is additional to the remedy under s 65. It extends to compensation for milk quota under para 12 of Sch 2 to the Agriculture Act 1986. An incoming landlord taking over at the date of the tenant's outgo must ensure that the compensation due has been paid otherwise the holding can be charged, even though the obligation to make payment rests with the selling landlord.
2 This provision can give a limited owner such as a liferenter security for any payments of compensation that might have been made.
3 'Owner of the dominium utile'. As mentioned above, s 80 of the Agricultural Holdings (Scotland) Act 1949 used the words 'absolute owner'. In rare cases where the land is not held on a feudal title this may cause difficulties.

Power of land improvement companies to advance money

76.[1] Any company incorporated by Parliament or incorporated under the Companies Act 1985 or under the former Companies Acts within the meaning of that Act and having power to advance money for the improvement of land, or for the cultivation and farming of land, may make an advance of money upon a charging order duly made and recorded or registered under this Act, on such terms and conditions as may be agreed upon between the company and the person entitled to the order.

1 Such a charging order is rare as a lender will normally insist upon a standard security.

Appointment of guardian to landlord or tenant

77.[1] Where the landlord or the tenant of an agricultural holding is a pupil or a minor or is of unsound mind, not having a tutor, curator or other guardian, the sheriff, on the application of any person interested, may appoint to him, for the purposes of this Act, a tutor or a curator, and may recall the appointment and appoint another tutor or curator if and as occasion requires.

1 See s 85(1) for definitions. A tutor or curator falls within the statutory definitions of 'landlord' and 'tenant'. A tutor or curator as landlord will have the powers conferred by s 74.

Validity of consents, etc

78.[1] It shall be no objection to any consent in writing or agreement in writing under this Act signed by the parties thereto or by any persons authorised by them that the consent or agreement has not been executed in accordance with the enactments regulating the execution of deeds in Scotland.

1 This practically places 'consent in writing', under the Act, among the class of privileged writing such as those in *re mercatoria*, which 'are effectual although neither attested (by witnesses) nor holograph', on account of the rapidity which may be necessary in preparing them. Cf the Requirements of Writing (Scotland) Act 1995.

PART IX

SUPPLEMENTARY

Crown and Secretary of State

Application to Crown Land

79.[1]—(1) This Act shall apply to land belonging to Her Majesty in right of the Crown, with such modifications as may be prescribed; and for the purposes of this Act the Crown Estate Commissioners or other proper officer or body having charge of the land for the time being, or if there is no such officer or body, such person as Her Majesty may appoint in writing under the Royal Sign Manual, shall represent Her Majesty and shall be deemed to be the landlord.

(2) This Act shall apply to land notwithstanding that the interest of the landlord or the tenant thereof belongs to a government department or is held on behalf of Her Majesty for the purposes of any government department with such modifications as may be prescribed.

1 These provisions apply to rent arbitrations where milk quota is involved: see s 16(7) of the Agriculture Act 1986. No modifications have been prescribed by the Secretary of State.

Determination of matters where Secretary of State is landlord or tenant

80.[1]—(1) This section applies where the Secretary of State is the landlord or the tenant of an agricultural holding.

(2) Where this section applies, any provision of this Act—

(a) under which any matter relating to the holding is referred to the decision of the Secretary of State; or

(b) relating to an arbitration concerning the holding,

shall have effect with the substitution for every reference to 'the Secretary of State' of a reference to 'the Land Court', and any provision referred to in paragraph (a) above which provides for an appeal to an arbiter from the decision of the Secretary of State shall not apply.

1 This section is designed to prevent the Secretary of State being held to have acted *auctor in rem suam*: see s 64. See observations in *Commissioners for Crown Lands v Grant* 1955 SLCR 25. The Land Court's jurisdiction is extended under this section to milk quota arbitrations in terms of paras 10 and 11 of Sch 2 to the Agriculture Act 1986.
    See the Agriculture Act 1967, Sch 3, para 5.

Expenses and receipts

81.—(1) All expenses incurred by the Secretary of State under this Act shall be paid out of moneys provided by Parliament.

(2) All sums received by the Secretary of State under this Act shall be paid into the Consolidated Fund.

Powers of entry and inspection

82.[1]—(1) Any person authorised by the Secretary of State in that behalf shall have power at all reasonable times to enter on and inspect any land for the purpose of determining whether, and if so in what manner, any of the powers conferred on the Secretary of State by this Act are to be exercised in relation to the land, or whether, and if so in what manner, any direction given under any such power has been complied with.

(2) Any person authorised by the Secretary of State who proposes to exercise any power of entry or inspection conferred by this Act shall, if so required, produce some duly authenticated document showing his authority to exercise the power.

(3) Admission to any land used for residential purposes shall not be demanded as of right in the exercise of any such power unless 24 hours' notice of the intended entry has been given to the occupier of the land.

(4) Save as provided by subsection (3) above, admission to any land shall not be demanded as of right in the exercise of any such power unless notice has been given to the occupier of the land that it is proposed to enter during a period, specified in the notice, not exceeding 14 days and beginning at least 24 hours after the giving of the notice and the entry is made on the land during the period specified in the notice.

(5) Any person who obstructs a person authorised by the Secretary of State exercising any such power shall be guilty of an offence and shall be liable on summary conviction to a fine not exceeding level 2 on the standard scale.

1 Note the purpose for which the powers may be exercised. The powers granted are similar to those of a landlord under s 10. The powers are conferred so that the Secretary of State can carry out inspections to determine whether any of the powers conferred on him are to be exercised: eg, making charging orders under s 75 or approving insurance arrangements under para 5 of Sch 1.

Land Court

Proceedings of the Land Court

83. [Repealed by the Scottish Land Court Act 1993]

Service of notices

Service of notices, etc

84.[1]—(1) Any notice or other document required or authorised by or under this Act to be given to or served on any person shall be duly given or served if it is delivered to him, or left at his proper address, or sent to him by registered post or recorded delivery.[2]

(2) Any such document required or authorised to be given to or served on an incorporated company or body shall be duly given or served if it is delivered to or sent by registered post or recorded delivery to the registered office of the company or body.

(3) For the purposes of this section and of section 7 of the Interpretation Act 1978, the proper address of any person to or on whom any such document as aforesaid is to be given or served shall, in the case of the secretary or clerk of any incorporated company or body, be that of the registered or principal office of the company or body, and in any other case be the last known address of the person in question.

(4) Unless or until the tenant of an agricultural holding shall have received notice that the person previously entitled to receive the rents and profits of the holding (hereinafter referred to as 'the original landlord') has ceased to be so entitled, and also notice of the name and address of the person who has become so entitled, any notice or other document served on or delivered to the original landlord by the tenant shall be deemed to have been served on or delivered to the landlord of the holding.[3]

1 This section relates to general notices. Notices to quit have to be served in terms of s 21(5) by recorded or registered mail – delivery to or leaving at the address is not sufficient.
2 This subsection is concerned with proof of service, and may raise questions of corroboration. Service by recorded delivery is accepted as proof, unless the contrary is proved: *Lady Hallinan v Jones & Jones* [1985] CLY 38. The notice must actually be received to be effective. Service by ordinary post is competent but may be difficult to prove: *Sharpley v Manby* [1942] 1 KB 217. Service on person in occupation held valid: *Wilbraham v Colclough and Ors* [1952] 1 All ER 979. Notice sent by recorded delivery before the passing of the Recorded Delivery Service Act 1962 was held duly served: *Re Poyser and Mills Arbitration* [1964] 2 QB 467. A notice put through the back door of the farmhouse and not received by the tenant was held effective service: *Datnow v Jones* [1985] 2 EGLR 1.
3 Note that this subsection relates to 'the tenant'. A legatee under s 11 or an acquirer on intestacy giving notice under the Act is not yet 'the tenant' for the purposes of this section. He must ascertain the correct identity and address of the landlord.

Interpretation

85.—(1) In this Act, unless the context otherwise requires—
'the 1911 Act' means the Small Landholders (Scotland) Act 1911;
'the 1949 Act' means the Agricultural Holdings (Scotland) Act 1949;
'agricultural holding'[1] (except in sections 68 to 72 of this Act) and 'agricultural land' have the meanings assigned to them by section 1 of this Act;
'agricultural unit'[2] means land which is an agricultural unit for the purposes of the Agriculture (Scotland) Act 1948;
'agriculture'[3] includes horticulture, fruit growing; seed growing; dairy farming; livestock breeding and keeping; the use of land as grazing land, meadow land, osier land, market gardens and nursery grounds; and the use of land for woodlands where that use is ancillary to the farming of land for other agricultural purposes: and 'agricultural' shall be construed accordingly;
'building' includes any part of a building;
'fixed equipment' includes any building or structure affixed to land and any works on, in, over or under land, and also includes anything grown on land for a purpose other than use after severance from the land, consumption of the thing grown or of produce thereof, or amenity, and, without prejudice to the foregoing generality, includes the following things, that is to say—

(a) all permanent buildings, including farm houses and farm cottages, necessary for the proper conduct of the agricultural holding;

(b) all permanent fences, including hedges, stone dykes, gate posts and gates;

(c) all ditches, open drains and tile drains, conduits and culverts, ponds, sluices, flood banks and main water courses;

(d) stells, fanks, folds, dippers, pens and bughts necessary for the proper conduct of the holding;

(e) farm access or service roads, bridges and fords;

(f) water and sewerage systems;

(g) electrical installations including generating plant, fixed motors, wiring systems, switches and plug sockets;

(h) shelter belts,

and references to fixed equipment on land shall be construed accordingly;
'improvement' shall be construed in accordance with section 33 of this Act, and 'new improvement,' 'old improvement,' '1923 Act improvement' and '1931 Act improvement' have the meanings there assigned to them;
'Land Court' means the Scottish Land Court;
'Lands Tribunal' means the Lands Tribunal for Scotland;
'landlord'[4] means any person for the time being entitled to receive the rents and profits or to take possession of an agricultural holding, and includes the executor, assignee, legatee, disponee, guardian, curator bonis, tutor, or permanent or interim trustee (within the meaning of the Bankruptcy (Scotland) Act 1985), of a landlord;

'lease' means a letting of land for a term of years, or for lives, or for lives and years, or from year to year;

'livestock'[5] includes any creature kept for the production of food, wool, skins or fur, or for the purpose of its use in the farming of land;

'market garden'[6] means a holding, cultivated, wholly or mainly, for the purpose of the trade or business of market gardening;

'prescribed' means prescribed by the Secretary of State by regulations made by statutory instrument which shall be subject to annulment in pursuance of a resolution of either House of Parliament;

'produce'[7] includes anything (whether live or dead) produced in the course of agriculture;

'tenant'[8] means the holder of land under a lease of an agricultural holding and includes the executor, assignee, legatee, disponee, guardian, tutor, curator bonis, or permanent or interim trustee (within the meaning of the Bankruptcy (Scotland) Act 1985), of a tenant;

'termination'[9] in relation to a tenancy, means the termination of the lease by reason of effluxion of time or from any other cause;

(2) Schedules 5 and 6 to the Agriculture (Scotland) Act 1948 (which have effect respectively for the purpose of determining for the purposes of that Act whether the owner of agricultural land is fulfilling his responsibilities to manage it in accordance with the rules of good estate management and whether the occupier of such land is fulfilling his responsibilities to farm it in accordance with the rules of good husbandry) shall have effect for the purposes of this Act as they have effect for the purposes of that Act.

(3) References in this Act to the farming of land include references to the carrying on in relation to the land of any agricultural activity.

(4) References to the terms, conditions, or requirements of a lease of or of an agreement relating to, an agricultural holding shall be construed as including references to any obligations, conditions or liabilities implied by the custom of the country in respect of the holding.[10]

(5) Anything which by or under this Act is required or authorised to be done by, to or in respect of the landlord or the tenant of an agricultural holding may be done by, to or in respect of any agent of the landlord or of the tenant.[11]

---

1 **'Agricultural holding':** see notes to s 1. The lease of an agricultural holding only has security of tenure under this Act if it complies with the statutory requirements of ss 1, 2 and 3. It has to comprise mainly 'agricultural land' let on a lease, not being a lease to a tenant during his continuance in any office, appointment or employment of the landlord.

The first essential is to establish that there is a lease. In *Morrison-Low v Paterson* 1985 SC (HL) 49 it was held that admitting a person into possession and accepting rent gives rise to an inference that a tenancy has been brought into existence. In contrast, in *Strachan v Robertson-Coupar* 1989 SLT 488, it was held that where no direct evidence of a contract of lease existed the court should look to the whole circumstances to see if they could only be explained on the basis that the parties must have agreed to create a tenancy. *Strachan v Robertson-Coupar* appears to exclude licences to occupy for limited purposes such as to take one crop from a field from the creation of a tenancy. It would be unwise to rely on such a 'licence' as excluding a tenancy. Tenancies, particularly of partnership, can be brought to an end on the termination of the partnership, eg, at death, thus excluding a continuance of the lease: see *IRC v Graham's Trs* 1971 SC (HL) 1.

It is only a tenancy from year to year, or which is to take effect under s 2 from year to year, which is a secure tenancy under the Act. In England it has been held that a tenancy for one year certain was an interest less than a tenancy from year to year: *Bernays v Prosser* [1963] 2 QB 592.

A let of land 'for a course of cropping for four years' comes under the Act (*McKenzie v Buchan* (1889) 5 Sh Ct Rep 40), as does a let for 'four years and crops' (*Stonehaven v Adam* 1970 SLT (Sh Ct) 43), but a let for a 'rotation of cropping' subject to termination in the event of sale was not within the Act: *Stirrat and Anr v Whyte* 1968 SLT 157. A let of four fields on a farm each year for cropping, where four different fields were let each year and the crop to be grown had to conform to the landlord's rotation system, was held not to be a lease: *Strachan v Robertson-Coupar*.

Notice served under the Act must generally apply to the entire 'holding' (but see ss 29, 30, 31, 49 and 50): *Gates v Blair* 1923 SC 430.

The mere fact that a farmhouse on a large farm has been let to a sub-tenant, with approval of the landlord, for the purpose of taking in paying guests does not prevent the farm from being a 'holding' as defined in this section: *In re Russell & Harding's Arbitration* (1922) 67 SJ 123. In *Salmon v Eastern Regional Hospital Board*, Forfar Sheriff Court, 1960; unreported, it was held by Sheriff Ford that although the defenders used an agricultural unit to grow produce for consumption in the hospital and had substantial sales the unit was not a holding to which the Act applied.

A 'holding' may be even quarter of an acre in extent: *Malcolm v McDougall* 1916 SC 283. The following decisions under earlier Acts may still be relevant but regard should be had to the different definitions involved.

House and grounds principal subjects, and land accessory: *Taylor v Earl of Moray* (1892) 19 R 399. A farmhouse, outbuildings and garden ground held not to be a holding: *Barr v Strang and Gardner* 1935 SLT (Sh Ct) 10. Where dwellinghouse of greater value than holding: *Hamilton v Duke of Hamilton's Trs* 1918 SC 282. Inclusion of non-agricultural subjects in holding: *Stormonth-Darling v Young* 1915 SC 44 – blacksmith's shop; *Yool v Shepherd* 1914 SC 689 – spinning mill. Small non-agricultural element immaterial: *Taylor v Fordyce* 1918 SC 824 – porter and ale licence; *In re Russell & Harding's Arbitration* – dwellinghouse sub-let. Hotel and about thirty acres of land: *Mackintosh v Lord Lovat* (1886) 14 R 282. See also *In re Lancaster & Macnamara* [1918] 2 KB 472; a 'stud-farm' is not a holding: *Berwick v Baird* [1930] 2 Ch 359. Poultry farm: *Lean v Inland Revenue* 1926 SC 15; *Robinson v Rowbottom* 1942 SLT (Sh Ct) 43. Piggery: *Inland Revenue v Assessor for Lanarkshire* 1930 SLT 164.

Exclusions from the tenancy were considered in *Thomson v Murray* 1990 SLT (Land Ct) 45, where the court determined that an area of woodland was not excluded from the ground leased under a reservation of 'all natural and planted woods'. It was held that the exclusion reserved to the landlord the timber, but not the solum of the area.

For cases in which subjects were let in part remuneration for services: see note 4 to s 1 and *Dunbar's Trs v Bruce* (1900) 3 F 137. See *Budge v Gunn* 1925 SLCR 74 for a consideration of the words 'continuance in any office, appointment or employment'.

2 **'Agricultural unit'.** In *Jenners Princes Street Edinburgh v Howe* 1990 SLT (Land Ct) 26 it was held that the unit included land actually occupied for agricultural purposes: see s 86(2) of the Agriculture (Scotland) Act 1948.

3 **'Agriculture'**: see note 2 to s 1.

4 **'Landlord'.** The definition is in the alternative so that there can be a different person in right of the rent and in right of possession: *Alexander Black & Sons v Paterson* 1968 SLT (Sh Ct) 64: see note 8 below. 'The primary object of this definition was to extend the meaning of the word "landlord" so as to include heritable creditors in possession, liferenters, &c': *Waddell v Howat* 1925 SLT 403. A purchaser having given notice of termination of a tenancy is impliedly liable to pay compensation to the tenant. The vendor has no duty to disclose a sale to the tenant (*Re Lord Derby and Fergusson's Contract* [1912] 1 Ch 479), but in terms of s 84(4) if the tenant is not informed of the change of landlord any notice or document served by him on the original landlord is deemed to have been served on the landlord. The provisions referred to protect the tenant but do not interfere with the liability of seller and purchaser *inter se*. A tenant who sub-lets stands in the relation of proprietor to his sub-tenant. For the meaning of 'assignee', see *Cunningham v Fife County Council* 1948 SC 439. 'Landlord' includes an uninfeft proprietor although infeftment is necessary to an action of removing: *Alexander Black & Sons v Paterson*; *Walker v Hendry* 1925 SC 855. A part owner is not a landlord and all part owners must join in serving notices to quit or demands for arbitration: *Secretary of State for Scotland v Prentice* 1963 SLT (Sh Ct) 48; *Stewart v Moir* 1965 SLT (Land Ct) 11. If a landlord sells part of the holding after serving notice to quit he ceases to be the landlord and so has no title to seek the Land Court's consent to the operation of the notice: *Gordon v Rankin* 1972 SLT (Land Ct) 7.

5 **'Livestock'.** The definition of 'livestock' is very wide and could include birds, fish or bees:

see Scammell and Densham, *Law of Agricultural Holdings* (7th edn), p 23 which indicates that a trout farm may be an agricultural holding. Gill, *The Law of Agricultural Holdings in Scotland* (1st edn), para 9 indicated that fish farming is excluded but gives as authority a rating case where the court was concerned with the ordinary meaning of 'agricultural'. It was held in *Wallace v Perth & Kinross Assessor* 1975 SLT 118 that a fish farm was not agricultural but that was a case under the Rating Act 1971 which defined livestock as including any mammal or bird kept for the production of food or wool or for the purpose of its use in the farming of the land.

6 **'Market garden'.** A farmer, who was in the habit of growing, in open fields, a quantity of peas and young potatoes as a fallow crop, and sending them to London for sale, was held not to be a market gardener, within the meaning of s 10 of the Bankruptcy Act 1842: *Hammond, ex parte* [1844] De G 93; cf *In re Wallis ex parte Sully* (1885) 14 QBD 950.

As to definition of 'market gardens', see *Cooper v Pearce* [1896] 1 QB 562; *Purser v Worthing Local Board* (1887) 18 QB 818 (whole under glass). Holding held a market garden where wholly under raspberries: *Grewar v Moncur's Curator Bonis* 1916 SC 764. Lease of buildings and ground for two years for the purpose of growing bulbs held not a 'holding': *Watters v Hunter* 1927 SC 310. Where under flowers only: *Drummond v Thomson* (1921) 37 Sh Ct Rep 180. Where occupier of a residence sold surplus of his requirements – not a market garden: *Bickerdike v Lucy* [1920] 1 KB 707; a piece of ground for growing raspberries for jam held not to be a market garden, but a fruit farm is probably a market garden. Market garden described as supplying a market for buying and selling of produce for consumption: *Twygen v Assessor for Tayside* 1991 GWD 4–226, a rating case.

7 **'Produce':** see s 7 regarding freedom of cropping. Manure is not covered by the definition because it cannot be disposed of by the tenant.

8 **'Tenant'** includes sub-tenants, and as below. Where a tenancy is assigned, with the consent of the landlord, by one tenant to himself and another as joint tenants, this does not amount to the creation of a new lease: *Saunders, Trs of v Ralph* (1993) 66 P & CR 335.

A sub-tenant cannot impugn the title of the principal tenant: *Dunlop & Co v Meiklem* (1876) 4 R 11. A sub-tenant falls within the definition of a 'tenant'. The principal tenant is the landlord in relation to the sub-tenant. Where there is a sub-tenant, and the principal tenant has no property on the holding, the latter would not be entitled to claim compensation for disturbance: *Ministry of Agriculture v Dean* [1924] 1 KB 851.

A general bequest of residue was held not to carry an agricultural lease which expressly excluded assignees: *Reid's Trs v Macpherson* 1975 SLT 101 at p 109. In the absence of such exclusion a general bequest may carry the lease: Rankine on Leases, p 164.

Bankruptcy does not in the absence of a condition in the lease terminate a tenancy; the trustee in bankruptcy is entitled to carry on the lease in virtue of the effect of the Act and warrant as an assignation in his favour, assuming he is not barred from doing so by the lease. Any landlord is likely to terminate the lease of a bankrupt under s 21(6) or 22(2)(f).

So also in the case of all the other successors of a tenant; if they are entitled to take up and do take up the lease, they become tenants, subject to all a tenant's rights and liabilities, and may be entitled to claim compensation under the Act.

A trustee in bankruptcy, who had taken up a tenancy, was held entitled to claim under the Agricultural Holdings (Scotland) Act 1883: *Sinclair v Clyne's Tr* (1887) 15 R 185. On the other hand, it was held that the bankrupt could not claim where the lease was prematurely terminated by bankruptcy: *Walker &c v M'Knight* (1886) 13 R 599; *Scott's Exrs v Hepburn* (1876) 3 R 816; *Ex parte Dyke, in re Morrish* (1882) 22 Ch 410; *Schofield v Hincks* 58 LJ QB 147. Held that a trustee for creditors was not entitled to claim: *Christison's Trs v Callender Brodie* (1905) 8 F 928. See also *Egerton v Rutter* [1951] 1 KB 472.

Where there is an express exclusion of the tenant's legatee in the lease, s 11 cannot be invoked: *Kennedy v Johnstone* 1956 SC 39 and see notes to s 11. Waiving right to exclude assignees: *Lord Elphinstone v Monkland Iron Co* (1886) 13 R (HL) 98. Abandonment of lease by tenant's heir: *Forbes v Ure* (1856) 18 D 577; *Duff v Keith* (1857) 19 D 713. Heir's failure to vindicate right: *Gray v Low* (1859) 21 D 293; *Wilson v Stewart* (1853) 16 D 106; *M'Iver v M'Iver* 1909 SC 639. Cases in which trustee in bankruptcy not held to have taken over lease, notwithstanding that he cut and harvested crops, etc: *McGavin v Sturrock's Tr* (1891) 18 R 576; *Taylor's Tr v Paul* (1888) 15 R 313; *Imrie's Tr v Calder* (1897) 25 R 15. Cases *contra* to above: *Ross v Monteith* (1786) M 15290; *Kirkland v Gibson* (1831) 9 S 596; *Dundas v Morison* (1875) 20 D 225; *M'Lean's Tr v M'Lean* (1850) 13 D 90; *Moncrieffe v Ferguson* (1890) 24 R 47; *Mackessack & Son v Molleson* (1886) 13 R 445.

9 The termination of the tenancy is the termination of the contractual relationship and not the date or dates on which the tenant ceases to occupy the subjects. In the case of a genuine

multiple ish the termination takes place at more than one date. Notice to quit must be served against the earliest date but for notice of claims the latest date may be the termination. See *Black v Clay* (1894) 21 R (HL) 72. In England where a lease terminates on different dates the latest of these is the termination of the tenancy: *Swinborne v Andrews* [1923] 2 KB 483.

Whitsunday and separation of crop waygoing: see *Coutts v Barclay-Harvey* 1956 SLT (Sh Ct) 54.

In *Breadalbane v Stewart* (1904) 6 F (HL) 23 the expression 'at my away-going' meant the expiry of the lease through the effluxion of time, and did not apply where the landlord had irritated the lease on the tenant being in arrears with his rent: see also *Pendreigh's Tr v Dewar* (1871) 9 M 1037. Where a tenant took advantage of a break at the end of fourteen years (in a twenty-one-year lease), the landlord agreeing to pay the tenant compensation for seeds, gooseberry and currant bushes, 'at the end of the term', it was held that the tenant was entitled to compensation for improvements: *Bevan v Chambers* (1896) 12 TLR 417.

Termination of the tenancy by voluntary renunciation of lease does not bar a claim for compensation: *Strang v Stuart* (1887) 14 R 637; *Gardiner v Lord Abercromby* (1893) 9 Sh Ct Rep 33; and *Osler v Lansdowne* (1885) 1 Sh Ct Rep 48. In the last of these cases, not only the lease but also all claims in the tenancy were expressly discharged in the renunciation. In the case of abandonment by the tenant there was no determination of the tenancy in the sense of s 42 of the Agricultural Holdings (Scotland) Act 1883: *Todd v Bowie* (1902) 4 F 435.

A tenant under an agreement for a lease for fourteen years was to receive compensation on a valuation basis for the tillages and improvements he might leave on the farm. A dispute arose between landlord and tenant. The tenant said he would quit at the end of the year and the landlord agreed. He left accordingly, and on his claiming compensation the court held that such a quitting was not a quitting under the terms of the tenancy, but in reality a running away and, therefore, it rejected the claim: *Whittaker v Barker* (1832) 1 C & M 113.

The person who is owner at the quitting terms must meet the claim even though the notice to quit was given to or by a previous owner. The reason is that the Act bears that the tenant shall be entitled to compensation from the landlord on *quitting*. Apparently it is the person who is then the owner who must pay: *Bradshaw v Bird* [1920] 3 KB 144. This was decided mainly on the definition of landlord as the person for the time being entitled to receive the rents, etc. This decision was followed in the case of *Dale v Hatfield Chase Corporation* [1922] 2 KB 282. In *Bennett v Stone* [1920] 1 Ch 226, where a tenant gave notice after the date of an agreement to sell by the landlord, and where the notice expired before the completion of the purchase, the vendor was obliged to pay compensation for improvements to the tenant, but it was held that he was entitled to recover the compensation from the purchaser: see also *Re Lord Derby and Fergusson's Contract* [1912] 1 Ch 479. In *Bradshaw v Bird* [1920] 3 KB 144 the seller gave notice in 1917 to terminate the tenancy at 29th September 1918. In October 1917 the purchaser agreed to purchase the farm 'and from that date became the person entitled to the rents and profits of the land'. The conveyance in his favour was dated 18th July 1918. Claim for compensation was made on 10th December 1918, against the purchaser, and the tenants quitted at Michaelmas 1918, in accordance with the notice to quit. It was held that he was liable, in respect that he was the person who was entitled to the rents and profits of the land for the time being. Scrutton LJ said: 'So that the purchaser of the land at the termination of the tenancy, *when the tenant has* quitted the holding, is the person to pay compensation'. Atkin LJ said: 'The person entitled to receive the rents and profits of the land at the termination of the tenancy, or when payment is to be made, is the person to pay compensation.' Where the landlord sold the farm with entry at the same term as the tenant quitted, the Board of Agriculture appointed an arbiter to deal with a claim for compensation for improvements by the tenant. Lord Constable interdicted the arbiter from proceeding, as he found that the purchaser was the party liable. The First Division reversed the decision, holding that the seller was liable: *Waddell v Howat* 1925 SC 484.

It was held in England that the purchaser who got entry after the date when he contracted to get entry, which was also the date of termination of tenancy, was not, at the material time (namely, 'the expiration of the tenancy') the landlord within the meaning of the Act: *Tombs v Turvey* (1923) 93 LJ KB 785.

Note. Most tenancies terminate at Whitsunday and Martinmas. For the meaning of these words, which are no longer defined in the Act, see the Term and Quarter Days (Scotland) Act 1990, which confirms the date at the 28th of each month, unless the context otherwise requires or the parties have had the 15th or 11th set upon summary application to the sheriff within the twelve months: see s 1(5) of the 1990 Act. In *Austin v Gibson* 1979 SLT (Land Ct) 12 the definition in s 93 of the Agricultural Holdings (Scotland) Act 1949 was held to apply to the interpretation of leases and not only to the use of 'Whitsunday' or 'Martinmas' in the

Act. This may be doubted: see Gill, *The Law of Agricultural Holdings in Scotland* (2nd edn), para 149; see also *Hunter v Barron's Trs* (1886) 13 R 883; *Fraser's Trs v Maule & Son* (1904) 6 F 819. In an improbative lease, where no term of entry was specified, it was held that any legal presumption which there might be as to the implied term of entry might be displaced by evidence and proof as to the actual entry to, and possession of, the subjects allowed: *Watters v Hunter* 1927 SLT 232; *Macleod v Urquhart* 1808 Hume 840; *Russell v Freen* (1835) 13 S 752.

10 Always insofar as the 'custom of the country' is not inconsistent with the express terms of the contract of tenancy. See *Mackenzie v McGillivray* 1921 SC 722, per the Lord President at p 731 regarding a consideration to the principles of good husbandry in relation *inter alia* to the custom of the district.
11 Notice to landlord's agent is prima facie notice to the landlord: *Ingham v Fenton* (1893) 10 TLR 113; *Hemington v Walter* (1949) 100 LJ 51. Any notice should disclose the agency.

Construction of references in other Acts to holdings as defined by earlier Acts

86. References, in whatever terms, in any enactment, other than an enactment contained in—

this Act,

the Agricultural Holdings (Scotland) Acts 1923 and 1931, or,

Part I of the Agriculture (Scotland) Act 1948

to a holding within the meaning of the Agricultural Holdings (Scotland) Act 1923 or of the Agricultural Holdings (Scotland) Acts 1923 to 1948 shall be construed as references to an agricultural holding within the meaning of this Act.

Savings

87. Schedule 12 to this Act, which exempts from the operation of this Act certain cases current at the commencement of this Act and contains other transitional provisions and savings shall have effect.

Consequential amendments and repeals

Consequential amendments and repeals

88.—(1) The enactments specified in Schedule 11 to this Act shall be amended in accordance with that Schedule.

(2) The enactment specified in Schedule 13 to this Act are repealed to the extent there specified.

Citation, commencement and extent

Citation, commencement and extent

89.[1]—(1) This Act may be cited as the Agricultural Holdings (Scotland) Act 1991.

(2) This Act shall come into force at the end of the period of 2 months beginning with the date on which it is passed.

(3) This Act shall extend to Scotland only, except for those provisions in Schedule 11 which amend enactments which extend to England and Wales or to Northern Ireland.

1 The Act received the Royal Assent on 25th July 1991 and came into force on 25th September 1991.

SCHEDULES

Section 4   SCHEDULE 1

PROVISIONS REQUIRED IN LEASES[1]

1. The names of the parties.

2. Particulars of the holding with sufficient description, by reference to a map or plan, of the fields and other parcels of land comprised therein to identify the extent of the holding.

3. The term or terms for which the holding or different parts thereof is or are agreed to be let.

4. The rent and the dates on which it is payable.

5. An undertaking by the landlord in the event of damage by fire to any building comprised in the holding to reinstate or replace the building if its reinstatement or replacement is required for the fulfilment of his responsibilities to manage the holding in accordance with the rules of good estate management, and (except where the interest of the landlord is held for the purposes of a government department or a person representing Her Majesty under section 79 of this Act is deemed to be the landlord, or where the landlord has made provision approved by the Secretary of State for defraying the cost of any such reinstatement or replacement) an undertaking by the landlord to insure to their full value all such buildings against damage by fire.

6. An undertaking by the tenant, in the event of the destruction by fire of harvested crops grown on the holding for consumption thereon, to return to the holding the full equivalent manurial value of the crops destroyed, in so far as the return thereof is required for the fulfilment of his responsibilities to farm in accordance with the rules of good husbandry, and (except where the interest of the tenant is held for the purposes of a government department or where the tenant has made provision approved by the Secretary of State in lieu of such insurance) an undertaking by the tenant to insure to their full value all dead stock on the holding and all such harvested crops against damage by fire.

1 See 'Provision for Written Leases', p 8, and notes to s 4.

Section 25   SCHEDULE 2[1]

GROUNDS FOR CONSENT TO OPERATION OF NOTICES TO QUIT A
TENANCY WHERE SECTION 25(3) APPLIES

PART I

GROUNDS FOR CONSENT TO OPERATION OF NOTICE TO QUIT A
TENANCY LET BEFORE JANUARY 1, 1984

Case 1[2]

The tenant has neither sufficient training in agriculture nor sufficient experience in the farming of land to enable him to farm the holding with reasonable efficiency.

Case 2[3]

(a) The holding or any agricultural unit of which it forms part is not a two-man unit;
  (b) the landlord intends to use the holding for the purpose of effecting an amalgamation within 2 years after the termination of the tenancy; and
  (c) the notice specifies the land with which the holding is to be amalgamated.

Case 3[4]

The tenant is the occupier (either as owner or tenant) of agricultural land which—
(a) is a two-man unit;
  (b) is distinct from the holding and from any agricultural unit of which the holding forms part; and
  (c) has been occupied by him since before the death of the person from whom he acquired right to the lease of the holding;
and the notice specifies the agricultural land.

PART II

GROUNDS FOR CONSENT TO OPERATION OF NOTICE TO QUIT A
TENANCY LET ON OR AFTER JANUARY 1, 1984

Case 4[5]

The tenant does not have sufficient financial resources to enable him to farm the holding with reasonable efficiency:

Case 5[6]

The tenant has neither sufficient training in agriculture nor sufficient experience in the farming of land to enable him to farm the holding with reasonable efficiency:
Provided that this Case shall not apply where the tenant has been engaged, throughout the period from the date of death of the person from whom he acquired right to the lease, in a course of relevant training in agriculture

which he is expected to complete satisfactorily within 4 years from the said date, and has made arrangements to secure that the holding will be farmed with reasonable efficiency until he completes that course.

Case 6[7]

(a) The holding or any agricultural unit of which it forms part is not a two-man unit;

(b) the landlord intends to use the holding for the purpose of effecting an amalgamation within 2 years after the termination of the tenancy; and

(c) the notice specifies the land with which the holding is to be amalgamated.

Case 7[8]

The tenant is the occupier (either as owner or tenant) of agricultural land which—

(a) is a two-man unit;

(b) is distinct from the holding; and

(c) has been occupied by him throughout the period from the date of giving of the notice;

and the notice specifies the land.

PART III

SUPPLEMENTARY

1. For the purposes of section 25 of this Act and this Schedule—

'amalgamation'[9] means a transaction for securing that agricultural land which is comprised in a holding to which a notice to quit relates and which together with other agricultural land could form an agricultural unit, shall be owned and occupied in conjunction with that other land (and cognate expressions shall be construed accordingly);

'near relative' in relation to a deceased tenant of an agricultural holding means a surviving spouse or child of that tenant, including a child adopted by him in pursuance of an adoption order (as defined in section 23(5) of the Succession (Scotland) Act 1964);[10] and

'two-man unit' means an agricultural unit which in the opinion of the Land Court is capable of providing full-time employment for an individual occupying it and at least one other man.

2. For the purposes of determining whether land is a two-man unit, in assessing the capability of the unit of providing employment it shall be assumed that the unit is farmed under reasonably skilled management, that a system of husbandry suitable for the district is followed and that the greater part of the feeding stuffs required by any livestock kept on the unit is grown there.

3. [11]For the purposes of Case 7 of this Schedule, occupation of agricultural land—

(a) by a company which is controlled by the tenant shall be treated as occupation by the tenant; and

(b) by a Scottish partnership shall, notwithstanding section 4(2) of the Partnership Act 1890, be treated as occupation by each of its partners.

1 See s 25 and notes. Cases 1 to 3 were introduced by the Agriculture (Miscellaneous Provisions) Act 1968 and Cases 4 to 7 by the Agricultural Holdings (Amendment) (Scotland) Act 1983. With regard to the defence of a 'fair and reasonable landlord', see note 12 to s 24 and p 38.

2 *Case 1:* it is the tenant's personal qualities which are in issue. Access to skilled advice is of no avail. The landlord has to prove inadequacy in both respects: see *Macdonald v Macrae* 1987 SLCR 72.

3 *Case 2:* note the differences from Case 3. **'Agricultural unit'** includes land occupied formally and informally at the date of the hearing and not the date of the notice; **'two-man unit'** means a unit capable of employing two men and does not relate to the actual regime being employed by the tenant: see definition in Pt III, paras 1, 2; *Jenners Princes Street Edinburgh v Howe* 1990 SLT (Land Ct) 26. The landlord must have a specific proposal for amalgamation: see *Mackenzie v Lyon* 1984 SLT (Land Ct) 30; *Earl of Seafield v Currie* 1980 SLT (Land Ct) 10. The 'fair and reasonable landlord' defence is available under s 25(3): see *Altyre Estate Trs v McLay* 1975 SLT (Land Ct) 12; *Earl of Seafield v Currie.*

4 *Case 3:* contrast with Case 7. **'Agricultural unit':** see note 3 above. The two-man unit must be distinct from both the holding subject to the notice and from the agricultural unit of which it is part. The tenant must be proved to be the 'occupier' as 'owner or tenant'. Unlike Case 2 informal occupation is not enough. Occupation by a partnership of which the tenant is a partner is not occupation under this case: *Haddo House Estate Trs v Davidson* 1982 SLT (Land Ct) 17 – *per contra* Case 7, see Pt III, para 3. In England under a similar provision it was held that sole occupancy was not required (*Jackson v Hall* [1980] AC 854), but then in England a partnership does not have a separate persona. Gill, *The Law of Agricultural Holdings in Scotland* (2nd edn), para 395, raises, without answering, the questions of whether the tenant's occupation must be of land in Scotland alone (relevant in cases concerning cross-border farming) and whether the tenancy has to be a secure tenancy under the Act or under any tenancy. The 'fair and reasonable landlord' defence under s 25(3) is available. The provision that the occupation must have been 'since before the date of the death' fixes the relevant date. It takes no account of land inherited by the tenant at the previous tenant's death – *per contra* see wording to Case 7.

5 *Case 4:* see *Reid v Duffus Estate* 1955 SLCR 13 for an objection to a tenant on the ground that he would have to farm with an overdraft. In terms of s 25(3)(b) the tenant has to satisfy the Land Court that he has the resources. The 'fair and reasonable landlord' defence is not available.

6 *Case 5:* see note 1. The onus in terms of s 25(3)(b) is on the tenant to prove that he has sufficient training, etc. Note the proviso. It is not clear whether 'from the date of death' will be construed to mean starting a course as soon as reasonably practicable after the death, but before the acquisition of the tenancy (which on intestacy could be up to a year after the death) or whether the tenant will in fact have had to have been on a course at the time of the death. The latter appears to comply with a strict construction, although the former could be said to comply with the intention, which is to allow a young person unexpectedly inheriting the tenancy to take up the necessary training. The 'fair and reasonable landlord' defence is not available.

7 *Case 6:* see note 2. Under s 25(3)(b) the onus of proof is on the tenant. The 'fair and reasonable landlord' defence is available.

8 *Case 7:* see note 3. See Pt III, para 3. In terms of s 25(3)(b) the onus of proof is on the tenant. Unlike Case 3, land inherited by reason of the death or taking into occupancy as owner or tenant after succession, but before the notice is given, can be taken into account. The two-man unit need only be distinct from the holding, but not from any agricultural unit as required by Case 3. The 'fair and reasonable landlord' defence is available.

9 **'Amalgamation':** see *Mackenzie v Lyon* 1984 SLT (Land Ct) 12.

10 See *Poett v Henderson* [1979] Central RN 11; *Earl of Seafield v Currie* 1980 SLT (Land Ct) 10; *Jenners Princes Street Edinburgh v Howe* 1990 SLT (Land Ct) 26.

11 This provision was introduced in 1983 to reverse with effect from after that date the decision in *Haddo House Estate Trs v Davidson* 1982 SLT (Land Ct) 17.

Section 33 SCHEDULE 3[1]

1923 ACT IMPROVEMENTS FOR WHICH COMPENSATION MAY BE PAYABLE

PART I

IMPROVEMENTS FOR WHICH CONSENTS REQUIRED

1. Erection, alteration, or enlargement of buildings.
2. Formation of silos.
3. Laying down of permanent pasture.
4. Making and planting of osier beds.
5. Making of water meadows or works of irrigation.
6. Making of gardens.
7. Making or improvement of roads or bridges.
8. Making or improvement of watercourses, ponds, wells, or reservoirs, or of works for the application of water power or for supply of water for agricultural or domestic purposes.
9. Making or removal of permanent fences.
10. Planting of hops.
11. Planting of orchards or fruit bushes.
12. Protecting young fruit trees.
13. Reclaiming of waste land.
14. Warping or weiring of land.
15. Embankments and sluices against floods.
16. Erection of wirework in hop gardens.
17. Provision of permanent sheep dipping accommodation.
18. In the case of arable land, the removal of bracken, gorse, tree roots, boulders, or other like obstructions to cultivation.

PART II

IMPROVEMENTS FOR WHICH NOTICE REQUIRED

19. Drainage.

PART III

IMPROVEMENTS FOR WHICH NO CONSENTS OR NOTICE REQUIRED

20. Chalking of land.
21. Clay-burning.
22. Claying of land or spreading blaes upon land.
23. Liming of land.
24. Marling of land.
25. Application to land of purchased artificial or other manure.
26. Consumption on the holding by cattle, sheep, or pigs, or by horses other than those regularly employed on the holding, of corn, cake, or other feeding stuff not produced on the holding.
27. Consumption on the holding by cattle, sheep, or pigs, or by horses

other than those regularly employed on the holding, of corn proved by satisfactory evidence to have been produced and consumed on the holding.

28. Laying down temporary pasture with clover, grass, lucerne, sainfoin, or other seeds, sown more than 2 years prior to the termination of the tenancy, in so far as the value of the temporary pasture on the holding at the time of quitting exceeds the value of the temporary pasture on the holding at the commencement of the tenancy for which the tenant did not pay compensation.

29. Repairs to buildings, being buildings necessary for the proper cultivation or working of the holding, other than repairs which the tenant is himself under an obligation to execute.

1 See notes to Sch 5.

Section 33   SCHEDULE 4[1]

1931 ACT IMPROVEMENTS FOR WHICH COMPENSATION MAY BE PAYABLE

PART I

IMPROVEMENTS FOR WHICH CONSENT REQUIRED

1. Erection, alteration, or enlargement of buildings.
2. Laying down of permanent pasture.
3. Making and planting of osier beds.
4. Making of water meadows or works of irrigation.
5. Making of gardens.
6. Planting of orchards or fruit bushes.
7. Protecting young fruit trees.
8. Warping or weiring of land.
9. Making of embankments and sluices against floods.

PART II

IMPROVEMENTS OF WHICH NOTICE REQUIRED

10. Drainage.
11. Formation of silos.
12. Making or improvement of roads or bridges.
13. Making or improvement of watercourses, ponds or wells, or of works for the application of water power or for the supply of water for agricultural or domestic purposes.
14. Making or removal of permanent fences.
15. Reclaiming of waste land.
16. Repairing or renewal of embankments and sluices against floods.
17. Provision of sheep dipping accommodation.
18. Provision of electrical equipment other than moveable fittings and appliances.

PART III

IMPROVEMENTS FOR WHICH NO CONSENT OR NOTICE REQUIRED

19. Chalking of land.
20. Clay-burning.
21. Claying of land or spreading blaes upon land.
22. Liming of land.
23. Marling of land.
24. Eradication of bracken, whins, or gorse growing on the holding at the commencement of a tenancy and in the case of arable land the removal of tree roots, boulders, stones or other like obstacles to cultivation.
25. Application to land of purchased artificial or other manure.
26. Consumption on the holding by cattle, sheep, or pigs, or by horses other than those regularly employed on the holding, of corn, cake, or other feeding stuff not produced on the holding.
27. Consumption on the holding by cattle, sheep, or pigs, or by horses other than those regularly employed on the holding, of corn proved by satisfactory evidence to have been produced and consumed on the holding.
28. Laying down temporary pasture with clover, grass, lucerne, sainfoin, or other seeds, sown more than 2 years prior to the termination of the tenancy, in so far as the value of the temporary pasture on the holding at the time of quitting exceeds the value of the temporary pasture on the holding at the commencement of the tenancy for which the tenant did not pay compensation.
29. Repairs to buildings, being buildings necessary for the proper cultivation or working of the holding, other than repairs which the tenant is himself under an obligation to execute.

1 See notes to Sch 5.

Section 33   SCHEDULE 5[1]

NEW IMPROVEMENTS FOR WHICH COMPENSATION MAY BE PAYABLE

PART I[2]

IMPROVEMENTS FOR WHICH CONSENT IS REQUIRED

1. Laying down of permanent pasture.
2. Making of water-meadows or works of irrigation.[3]
3. Making of gardens.
4. Planting of orchards or fruit bushes.[4]
5. Warping or weiring of land.[5]
6. Making of embankments and sluices against floods.
7. Making or planting of osier beds.
8. Haulage or other work done by the tenant in aid of the carrying out of any improvement made by the landlord for which the tenant is liable to pay increased rent.

PART II

IMPROVEMENTS FOR WHICH NOTICE IS REQUIRED[6]

9. Land drainage.

10. Construction of silos.

11. Making or improvement of farm access or service roads, bridges and fords.

12. Making or improvement of watercourses, ponds or wells, or of works for the application of water power for agricultural or domestic purposes or for the supply of water for such purposes.

13. Making or removal of permanent fences, including hedges, stone dykes and gates.

14. Reclaiming of waste land.

15. Renewal of embankments and sluices against floods.

16. Provision of stells, fanks, folds, dippers, pens and bughts necessary for the proper conduct of the holding.

17. Provision or laying on of electric light or power, including the provision of generating plant, fixed motors, wiring systems, switches and plug sockets.[7]

18. Erection, alteration or enlargement of buildings, making or improvement of permanent yards, loading banks and stocks and works of a kind referred to in paragraph 13(2) of Schedule 8 to the Housing (Scotland) Act 1987 (subject to the restrictions mentioned in that subsection).[8]

19. Erection of hay or sheaf sheds, sheaf or grain drying racks,[9] and implement sheds.

20. Provision of fixed threshing mills, barn machinery and fixed dairying plant.

21. Improvement of permanent pasture by cultivation and re-seeding.

22. Provision of means of sewage disposal.

23. Repairs to fixed equipment, being equipment reasonably required for the efficient farming of the holding, other than repairs which the tenant is under an obligation to carry out.[10]

PART III[11]

IMPROVEMENTS FOR WHICH NO CONSENT OR NOTICE REQUIRED

24. Protecting fruit trees against animals.

25. Clay burning.

26. Claying of land.

27. Liming (including chalking) of land.

28. Marling of land.

29. Eradication of bracken, whins or broom growing on the holding at the commencement of the tenancy and, in the case of arable land, removal of tree roots, boulders, stones or other like obstacles to cultivation.[12]

30. Application to land of purchased manure and fertiliser, whether organic or inorganic.[13]

31. Consumption on the holding of corn (whether produced on the holding or not) or of cake or other feeding stuff not produced on the holding by horses, cattle, sheep, pigs or poultry.

32. Laying down temporary pasture with clover, grass, lucerne, sainfoin, or other seeds, sown more than 2 years prior to the termination of the tenancy, in so far as the value of the temporary pasture on the holding at the time of quitting exceeds the value of the temporary pasture on the holding at the time of quitting exceeds the value of the temporary pasture on the holding at the commencement of the tenancy for which the tenant did not pay compensation.[14]

1 See Chapter 5. This Schedule sets forth the statutory improvements for which compensation may be claimed.

Where a tenant was required under the Defence of the Realm Regulations to plough up parts of his farm (which he was under covenant not to convert from permanent pasture to tillage), it was held he had a good claim for temporary pasture: *Ware v Davies* (1932) 146 LT 130.

2 See the Opencast Coal Act 1958, s 24.

3 **'Making of water-meadows or works of irrigation'.** It is unlikely that tenants in Scotland would seek to make water-meadows but spray irrigation installations may require to be dealt with under this paragraph.

4 **'Planting of orchards or fruit bushes'.** For provisions relating to fruit trees and bushes in market gardens, see s 40 and Sch 6.

5 **'Warping or weiring of land'.** This is a method of improving land by flooding it with muddy water. It is not known to have been practised in Scotland: the paragraph derives from the English Acts.

6 As to notice required for Part II improvements, see s 38. As to Land Court consent, see s 39.

7 **'Provision or laying on of electric light or power'.** The valuation of improvements under this paragraph commonly causes difficulty. The basis of valuation being 'the value to an incoming tenant' (s 36), the original cost is not usually relevant but an estimate of the cost of installation as the date of termination of the tenancy would require not only to be discounted in respect of the time since installation but to be further reduced if the installation is of a type which is obsolescent or inferior to the newer kinds.

8 In the case of new leases an obligation is imposed on the landlord to provide buildings necessary for the proper equipment of the farm. See also the Housing Act 1964, s 38(2) and the Housing (Scotland) Act 1966, s 80(2), as amended by the Housing (Scotland) Act 1974 (now all repealed) and the Housing (Scotland) Act 1987, s 256.

9 Grain handling plant and storage bins are not specifically mentioned but would come within paras 20 and 10 respectively.

10 As a tenant is bound, at common law or by s 5, to keep the farm buildings in a state of tenantable repair, ordinary wear and tear and natural decay excepted, the right to make this improvement would appear to be useful mainly in connection with repairs rendered necessary by causes for which the tenant is not responsible such as, eg, extraordinary hurricane or snowstorm or accidental fire. What is here referred to is 'repair' not reconstruction. New building is covered by para 18 or 19.

11 See the Opencast Coal Act 1958, s 26.

12 **'Arable land'** presumably means arable *before* the improvement but containing obstacles to cultivation. Otherwise the paragraph could overlap with para 14 in Pt II – 'reclaiming waste ground'.

13 See 'Artificial Manure and Feeding Stuffs', p 45. Purchased straw made into manure is not a 'manure': *Brunskill v Atkinson* 1884 Sol J 29. If it were consumed by stock, compensation could be claimed for it as a feeding-stuff. For calculation of values see the annual report of the Scottish Standing Committee for the calculation of residual values of fertilisers and feeding-stuffs.

14 See 'Temporary Pasture', p 47, and *Mackenzie v McGillivray* (1921) 58 SLR 488. Second year's grass is generally sown more than two years before the termination of the tenancy and is 'temporary pasture' within this definition: *Earl of Galloway v McClelland* 1915 SC 1062, per Lord Johnston: see notes to s 34.

Section 40   SCHEDULE 6

Market Garden Improvements[1]

1. Planting of fruit trees or bushes permanently set out.
2. Planting of strawberry plants.
3. Planting of asparagus, rhubarb, and other vegetable crops which continue productive for 2 or more years.
4. Erection, alteration or enlargement of buildings for the purpose of the trade or business of a market gardener.

1 Chapter 9.

Section 61   SCHEDULE 7

Arbitrations[1]

Appointment of Arbiters

1. A person agreed upon between the parties or, in default of agreement,[2] appointed on the application in writing of either of the parties by the Secretary of State from among the members of the panel constituted under this Act for the purpose, shall be appointed arbiter.[3]

2. If a person appointed arbiter dies, or is incapable of acting,[4] or for 7 days after notice from either party requiring him to act fails to act, a new arbiter may be appointed as if no arbiter had been appointed.[5]

3. Neither party shall have the power to revoke the appointment of the arbiter without the consent of the other party.[6]

4. An appointment, notice, revocation and consent of a kind referred to in any of paragraphs 1 to 3 of this Schedule must be in writing.[7]

Particulars of Claim[8]

5. Each of the parties to the arbitration shall, within 28 days from the appointment of the arbiter,[9] deliver to him a statement of that party's case with all necessary particulars; and—

(a) no amendment or addition to the statement or particulars delivered shall be allowed after the expiration of the said 28 days except with the consent of the arbiter;[10]

(b) a party to the arbitration shall be confined at the hearing to the matters alleged in the statement and particulars so delivered and any amendment thereof or addition thereto duly made.[11]

Evidence

6. The parties to the arbitration, and all persons claiming through them respectively,[12] shall, subject to any legal objection—

(a) submit to be examined by the arbiter on oath or affirmation in relation to the matters in dispute; and

(b) produce before the arbiter;

all samples, books, deeds, papers, accounts, writings, and documents, within their possession or power respectively which may be required or called for, and do all other things which during the proceedings the arbiter may require.

7. The arbiter shall have power to administer oaths, and to take the affirmation of parties and witnesses appearing, and witnesses shall, if the arbiter thinks fit, be examined on oath or affirmation.

AWARD

8. The arbiter shall make and sign his award within 3 months of his appointment or within such longer period as may, either before or after the expiry of the aforesaid period be agreed to in writing by the parties, or be fixed by the Secretary of State.[13]

9. The arbiter may, if he thinks fit, make an interim award for the payment of any sum[14] on account of the sum to be finally awarded.

10. An arbiter appointed by the Secretary of State or the Land Court in an arbitration under section 13(1) of this Act shall, in making his award, state in writing his findings of fact and the reasons for his decision and shall make that statement available to the Secretary of State and to the parties.[15]

11. The award and any statement made under paragraph 10 of this Schedule shall be in such form as may be specified by statutory instrument made by the Secretary of State.[16]

12. The arbiter shall—

(a) state separately in his award the amounts awarded in respect of the several claims referred to him; and

(b) on the application of either party,[17] specify the amount awarded in respect of any particular improvement or any particular matter which is the subject of the award.[18]

13. Where by virtue of this Act compensation under an agreement is to be substituted for compensation under this Act for improvements, the arbiter shall award compensation in accordance with the agreement instead of in accordance with this Act.

14. The award shall fix a day[19] not later than one month after delivery[20] of the award for the payment of the money awarded as compensation, expenses or otherwise.

15. Subject to section 61(2) of this Act, the award shall be final and binding on the parties and the persons claiming under them respectively.[21]

16. The arbiter may correct in an award any clerical mistake or error arising from any accidental slip or omission.[22]

EXPENSES[23]

17. The expenses of and incidental to the arbitration and award shall be in the discretion of the arbiter, who may direct to and by whom and in what manner those expenses or any part thereof are to be paid, and the expenses shall be subject to taxation by the auditor of the sheriff court on the application of either party, but that taxation shall be subject to review by the sheriff.[24]

18. The arbiter shall, in awarding expenses, take into consideration the reasonableness or unreasonableness of the claim of either party whether in

respect of amount or otherwise, and any unreasonable demand for particulars or refusal to supply particulars, and generally all the circumstances of the case, and may disallow the expenses of any witness whom he considers to have been called unnecessarily and any other expenses which he considers to have been incurred unnecessarily.[25]

19. It shall not be lawful to include in the expenses of and incidental to the arbitration and award, or to charge against any of the parties, any sum payable in respect of remuneration or expenses to any person appointed by the arbiter to act as clerk or otherwise to assist him in the arbitration unless such appointment was made after submission of the claim and answers to the arbiter and with either the consent of the parties to the arbitration or the sanction of the sheriff.[26]

STATEMENT OF CASE[27]

20. Subject to paragraph 22 of this Schedule, the arbiter may at any stage of the proceedings,[28] and shall, if so directed by the sheriff (which direction may be given on the application of either party),[29] state a case for the opinion of the sheriff on any question of law arising in the course of the arbitration.[30]

21. Subject to paragraph 22 of this Schedule, the opinion of the sheriff on any case stated under the last foregoing paragraph shall be final unless, within such time and in accordance with such conditions as may be specified by act of sederunt, either party appeals to the Court of Session, from whose decision no appeal shall lie.[31]

22. Where the arbiter in any arbitration under section 13(1) of this Act has been appointed by the Secretary of State or by the Land Court, paragraphs 20 and 21 of this Schedule shall not apply, and instead the arbiter may at any stage of the proceedings state a case (whether at the request of either party or on his own initiative) on any question of law arising in the course of the arbitration, for the opinion of the Land Court, whose decision shall be final.

REMOVAL OF ARBITER AND SETTING ASIDE OF AWARD[32]

23. Where an arbiter has misconducted[33] himself the sheriff may remove him.

24. When an arbiter has misconducted himself, or an arbitration or award has been improperly procured, the sheriff may set the award aside.[34]

FORMS

25. Any forms for proceedings in arbitrations under this Act which may be specified by statutory instrument made by the Secretary of State shall, if used, be sufficient.[35]

---

1 See 'Review of Rent', p 11, and 'Arbitration under the 1991 Act', p 77.
2 **'In default of agreement'.** These words in the corresponding para 1 of Sch 6 to the

Agriculture Holdings Act 1948 were held to mean only that the parties have not agreed. It is not necessary that they should attempt to agree and fail to do so: *Chalmers Property Investment Co Ltd v MacColl* 1951 SC 24, per Lord President Cooper at p 30; *F R Evans (Leeds) Ltd v Webster* (1962) LJ 703.

3 In an action of reduction of letter of appointment on the ground that material facts were withheld from the knowledge of the Department of Agriculture for Scotland, and that the arbiter was an interested party, it was held that the Department in appointing arbiters acted in an administrative capacity and that its selection of an arbiter from the panel could not be challenged: *Ramsay v McLaren and Ors* 1936 SLT 35.

4 **'Incapable of acting'.** This is not limited to incapacity by reason of physical or mental disability but includes incapacity from any cause: *Dundee Corporation v Guthrie* 1969 SLT 93 in which an arbiter had been removed and his award reduced and it was held competent to appoint a second arbiter.

5 The second arbiter to be appointed acts as if his date of appointment was the same date as the date of appointment of the first arbiter: *Dundee Corporation v Guthrie* 1969 SLT 93; *Pennington-Ramsden v McWilliam* [1982] CLY 28.

6 An appointment by the Secretary of State may be revoked of consent: *Dundee Corporation v Guthrie* 1969 SLT 93.

7 Not necessarily tested (s 78).

8 Each party must lodge not only particulars but a statement of his case. The period of twenty-eight days is from 'the date of appointment' (see note 9 below) and cannot be extended by the arbiter (*Stewart v Brims* 1969 SLT (Sh Ct) 2), but may be extended with the parties' agreement: *Suggett v Shaw* 1987 SLT (Land Ct) 5. No provision is made for answers to such statements but possibly the arbiter has authority to order answers if they appear to him necessary. If he does so he should get the consent of the parties. If one party alone lodges a claim and particulars the other may lead evidence in rebuttal but may not set up a case of his own: *Collett v Deeley* (1949) 100 LJ 108; *Jamieson v Clark* (1951) 67 Sh Ct Rep 17; *Re Bennion and National Provincial Banks' Arbitration* (1965) 115 LJ 302. As to form of claim, see *Robertson's Trs v Cunningham* 1951 SLT (Sh Ct) 89; *Simpson v Henderson* 1944 SC 365; *Adam v Smythe* 1948 SC 445.

9 **'Appointment of the arbiter'.** The date of appointment and the date from which the twenty-eight-day period runs is the date of the submission in an agreed appointment or the date of the letter of appointment by the Secretary of State: see *Suggett v Shaw* 1987 SLT (Land Ct) 5. This differs from the position under the corresponding provision of the Agricultural Holdings Act 1948, where it was said *obiter* that time ran from the date when the appointment was notified to the parties: see *University College Oxford v Durdy* [1982] Ch 413 (CA). In *Hannaford v Smallacombe* [1994] 1 EGLR 9 it was held that the date of appointment of an agreed arbiter, who had indicated that he was to accept the appointment, was the date on which the arbiter received the deed of appointment. It is incompetent for an arbiter to accept a statement of case after the time-limit, unless the other party consents: *Suggett v Shaw*.

10 **'Except with the consent of the arbiter'.** An arbiter should not refuse to allow such amendment or addition if there is no prejudice to the other party: see *Cooke Bourne (Farms) v Mellows* [1983] QB 104; *Strang v Abercairney Estates* 1992 SLT (Land Ct) 32. If the document originally lodged was not a 'statement of case' that defect cannot be cured by amendment under this paragraph: *Robertson's Trs v Cunningham* 1951 SLT (Sh Ct) 89.

11 Matters not included in the statement are inadmissible even if raised in evidence by the other party: *Stewart v Brims* 1969 SLT (Sh Ct) 2; *Murray v Fane*, Perth Sh Ct, 22nd April 1996.

12 Where, for example, the landlord has assigned his rights to the incoming tenant, who, on the other hand had undertaken to satisfy the landlord's objections to the awaygoing tenant.

13 The period runs from the date of appointment: see note 9 above. An application for an extension of time can be made after the expiry of the statutory period: *Dundee Corporation v Guthrie* 1969 SLT 93. See the form of application for extension in Appendix 1. An award made after the expiry of the permitted period may be set aside for misconduct: *Halliday v Semple* 1960 SLT (Sh Ct) 22.

14 The provision here is apparently restricted to an award for money payment, and does not provide for an interim award with declaratory or other findings. See s 69(3) for special provisions regarding interim awards in sheep stock valuations.

15 This applies only to rent arbitrations under s 13. An arbiter appointed by agreement is not statutorily obliged to follow this paragraph, but would be well advised to do so.

16 See the form of award in Appendix 1. Failure to comply with the specific form of award will be grounds for appeal under s 61(2): see *Aberdeen Endowments Trust v Will* 1985 SLT (Land

Ct) 23; *Earl of Seafield v Stewart* 1985 SLT (Land Ct) 35. An arbiter may not make an award *ad factum praestandum*.

17 By landlord or tenant respectively. This application need not be in writing.

18 Here there must be a figure put down in respect of any particular 'improvement or matter', the subject of the award. Thus either party could request the arbiter to state how much he had awarded in respect of any of the items of claim under the different items in the Schedules.

19 It is not practicable to fix the particular day, because it is rarely, if ever, known at the time the award is signed on what date it will be delivered. It is sufficient to state that payment shall be made on (say) the fifteenth day after delivery of the award. The arbiter or his clerk should always endorse on the back of the award the date of delivery. In general an arbiter has no power to award interest except from the date from which he directs payment to be made. In milk quota compensation arbitrations the period is three months after delivery: Agriculture Act 1986, Sch 2, para 11(4).

20 **'Delivery'.** It has been held that actual delivery to the parties is not essential to completion of the award, and that the award is validly issued if signed and put into the clerk's hands for the purpose of being delivered: *McQuaker v Phoenix Assurance Co* (1859) 21 D 794. Circumstances determine whether the award is held for the arbiter or the parties: *Johnson v Gill* 1978 SC 74.

21 This is, of course, subject to the right to have the award reduced at common law (by way of judicial review) or set aside under rule 24 or because the arbiter has improperly dealt with an agreement purporting to provide fair and reasonable compensation: *Bell v Graham* 1908 SC 1060. The exception relates to rental arbitrations where s 61(2) provides for an appeal to the Land Court.

22 This may be done even after delivery of the award.

23 See 'Expenses', p 94.

24 The expenses of a stated case fall to be dealt with by the sheriff and not by the arbiter: *McQuater v Fergusson* 1911 SC 640.

The fees of arbiters appointed by the Secretary of State fall to be fixed by him.

25 The arbiter should, in general, follow the same course as regards expenses as that adopted by the court although what he awards is always in his discretion. In general, expenses should follow success, unless there is divided success (eg, in valuations where the arbiter awards somewhere between the parties' contentions), when no expenses due to or by might be appropriate. As expenses are taxed at sheriff court scales the arbiter may have to consider whether certification of counsel is appropriate.

26 This rule is copied from the earlier Acts and is inconsistent in that the present rule (para 5) makes no provision for answers. The purpose of the rule is to prevent arbiters making appointments of a clerk when the questions at issue are trivial, and to avoid unnecessary expense in the earlier stages of the proceedings.

27 See 'Stated Case', p 92.

28 Not after the award has been issued.

29 In *Edmund Nuttall Ltd v Amec Projects Ltd* 1993 SLT 255 it was observed (not in an agricultural arbitration, but the principle appears to apply) that although a stated case could be obtained at any stage in an arbitration it did not mean that it would be appropriate for an arbiter to be directed to state a case at every stage, particularly where an arbiter considered the application premature as he intended to deal with the question of law after ascertaining the facts.

30 The court will not deal with a case until the arbiter has made such findings of fact as are necessary for its decision: *Ferguson v Norman* (1837) 4 Bing NC 52. There may be an appeal from the sheriff to the Court of Session (para 21). Arbiter held right in refusing to state a case (a) as to competency of arbitration, and (b) as to conduct of the arbitration procedure: *Broxburn Oil Co Ltd v Earl of Buchan* (1926) 42 Sh Ct Rep 300. The terms in which the case is stated are for the arbiter to decide: *Forsyth-Grant v Salmon* 1961 SC 54.

31 For procedure on appeal, see Rules of Court of Session 267–273.

32 See 'Reduction of Award', p 98.

33 **'Misconduct'**: see *Mitchell-Gill v Buchan* 1921 SC 390 and *Stair Memorial Encyclopaedia*, vol 2, para 483. Where an arbiter visited the farm with an architect in the absence of the parties it was assumed that evidence was received and the award was set aside: *Ellis v Lewin* (1963) 107 SJ 851.

34 Reduction in the Court of Session by judicial review is probably also competent: *Dunlop v Mundell* 1943 SLT 286.
35 See the forms in Appendix 1.

Section 57   SCHEDULE 8

SUPPLEMENTARY PROVISIONS WITH RESPECT TO PAYMENTS UNDER SECTION 56

1. Subject to paragraph 4 of this Schedule, any dispute with respect to any sum which may be or become payable by virtue of section 56(1) of this Act shall be referred to and determined by the Lands Tribunal for Scotland.

2. If in any case the sum to be paid by virtue of the said section 56(1) to the tenant of an agricultural holding or to a statutory small tenant by an acquiring authority would, apart from this paragraph and paragraph 3 of this Schedule, fall to be ascertained in pursuance of section 54(2) of this Act by reference to the rent of the holding at a rate which was not—

(a) determined by arbitration under section 13 or 15 of this Act;

(b) determined by the Land Court in pursuance of section 61(2) of this Act; or

(c) in the case of a statutory small tenant, fixed by the Scottish Land Court in pursuance of section 32(7) and (8) of the 1911 Act;

and which the authority consider is unduly high, the authority may make an application to the Lands Tribunal for Scotland for the rent to be considered by the tribunal.

3. Where, on an application under paragraph 2 above, the tribunal are satisfied that—

(a) the rent to which the application relates is not substantially higher than the rent which in their opinion would be determined for the holding in question on a reference to arbitration duly made in pursuance of—

(i) section 13 of this Act; or

(ii) in the case of a statutory small tenancy, the equitable rent which in their opinion would be fixed by the Land Court under section 32(7) and (8) of the 1911 Act; (hereafter in this paragraph referred to as 'the appropriate rent'); or

(b) the rent to which the application relates is substantially higher than the appropriate rent but was not fixed by the parties to the relevant lease with a view to increasing the amount of any compensation payable, or of any sum to be paid by virtue of section 56(1) of this Act, in consequence of the compulsory acquisition or taking of possession of any land included in the holding,

they shall dismiss the application; and if the tribunal do not dismiss the application in pursuance of the foregoing provisions of this paragraph they shall determine that, in the case to which the application relates, the sum to be paid by virtue of section 56(1) of this Act shall be ascertained in pursuance of the said section 13 by reference to the appropriate rent instead of by reference to the rent to which the application relates.

4. For the purposes of paragraph 3(a) above, section 13(1) of this Act shall have effect as if for the reference therein to the next ensuing day there were substituted a reference to the date of the application referred to in paragraph 3(a) above.

5. The enactments mentioned in paragraph 6 of this Schedule shall, subject to any necessary modifications, have effect in their application to such an acquiring of an interest or taking of possession as is referred in section 56(1) of this Act (hereafter in this paragraph referred to as 'the relevant event')—

(a) in so far as those enactments make provision for the doing, before the relevant event, of any thing connected with compensation (including in particular provision for determining the amount of the liability to pay compensation or for the deposit of it in a Scottish bank or otherwise), as if references to compensation, except compensation for damage or injurious affection, included references to any sum which will become payable by virtue of section 56 of this Act in consequence of the relevant event; and

(b) subject to sub-paragraph (a) above, as if references to compensation (except compensation for damage or injurious affection) included references to sums payable or, as the context may require, to sums paid by virtue of section 56 of this Act in the consequence of the relevant event.

6. The enactments aforesaid are—

(a) sections 56 to 60, 62 to 65, 67 to 70, 72, 74 to 79, 83 to 87, 114, 115 and 117 of the Lands Clauses Consolidation (Scotland) Act 1845;

(b) paragraph 3 of Schedule 2 to the Acquisition of Land (Authorisation Procedure) (Scotland) Act 1947;

(c) Parts I and II and section 40 of the Land Compensation (Scotland) Act 1963;

(d) paragraph 4 of Schedule 6 to the New Towns (Scotland) Act 1968;

(e) any provision in any local or private Act, in any instrument having effect by virtue of an enactment, or in any order or scheme confirmed by Parliament or brought into operation in accordance with special parliamentary procedure, corresponding to a provision mentioned in sub-paragraph (a), (b) or (d) above.

Section 70   SCHEDULE 9

VALUATION OF SHEEP STOCK IN SCOTLAND IN RESPECT OF OLD LEASES[1]

PART I

VALUATION MADE IN RESPECT OF A TENANCY TERMINATING AT WHITSUNDAY

1. The Land Court or the arbiter (in Part I and Part II of this Schedule referred to as 'the valuer') shall ascertain the number of, and the prices realised for, the ewes and the lambs sold off the hill from the stock under valuation at the autumn sales in each of the 3 preceding years, and shall determine by inspection the number of shotts present in the stock at that time of the valuation.

2. The valuer shall calculate an average price per ewe, and an average price per lamb, for the ewes and lambs sold as aforesaid for each of the 3 preceding

years. In calculating the average price for any year the valuer shall disregard such number of ewes and lambs so sold in that year, being the ewes or lambs sold at the lowest prices, as bears the same proportion to the total number of ewes or lambs so sold in that year as the number of shotts as determined bears to the total number of ewes or lambs in the stock under valuation.

3. The valuer shall then ascertain the mean of the average prices so calculated for the 3 preceding years for ewes and for lambs, respectively. The figures so ascertained or ascertained, in a case to which paragraph 4 below applies, in accordance with that paragraph, are in this Part of this Schedule referred to as the '3-year average price for ewes' and the '3-year average price for lambs.'

4. In the case of any sheep stock in which the number of ewes or the number of lambs sold off the hill at the autumn sales during the preceding 3 years has been less than half the total number of ewes or of lambs sold, the 3-year average price for ewes or the 3-year average price for lambs, as the case may be, shall, in lieu of being ascertained by the valuer as aforesaid, be determined by the Land Court on the application of the parties; and the Land Court shall determine such prices by reference to the prices realised at such sales for ewes and for lambs respectively from similar stocks kept in the same district and under similar conditions.

5. The 3-year average price for ewes shall be subject to adjustment by the valuer within the limits of 20 per cent (in the case of leases entered into before May 15, 1963, 50 pence) upwards or downwards as he may think proper having regard to the general condition of the stock under valuation and to the profit which the purchaser may reasonably expect it to earn. The resultant figure shall be the basis of the valuation of the ewes, and is in this Part of this Schedule referred to as the 'basic ewe value.'

The valuer shall similarly adjust the 3-year average price for lambs, and the resultant figure shall be the basis for the valuation of the lambs and is in this Part of this Schedule referred to as the 'basic lamb value.'

6. In making his award the valuer shall value the respective classes of stock in accordance with the following rules, that is to say—

(a) ewes of all ages (including gimmers) shall be valued at the basic ewe value with the addition of 30 per cent (in the case of leases entered into before May 15, 1963, 75 pence) of such value per head;

(b) lambs shall be valued at the basic lamb value; so however that twin lambs shall be valued at such price as the valuer thinks proper;

(c) ewe hoggs shall be valued at two-thirds of the combined basic values of a ewe and a lamb subject to adjustment by the valuer within the limits of 10 per cent (in the case of leases entered into before May 15, 1963, 25 pence) per head upwards or downwards as he may think proper, having regard to their quality and condition;

(d) tups shall be valued at such price as in the opinion of the valuer represents their value on the farm having regard to acclimatisation or any other factor for which he thinks it proper to make allowance;

(e) eild sheep shall be valued at the value put upon the ewes subject to such adjustment as the valuer may think proper having regard to their quality and condition; and

(f) shotts shall be valued at such value not exceeding two-thirds of the value put upon good sheep of the like age and class on the farm as the valuer may think proper.

Part II

Valuation Made in Respect of a Tenancy Terminating at Martinmas

7. The valuer shall ascertain the number of, and the prices realised for, the ewes sold off the hill from the stock under valuation at the autumn sales in the current year and in each of the 2 preceding years, and shall calculate an average price per ewe so sold for each of the said years. In calculating the average price for any year the valuer shall disregard one-tenth of the total number of ewes so sold in that year being the ewes sold at the lowest price.

8. The mean of the average prices so calculated shall be subject to adjustment by the valuer within the limits of 10 per cent (in the case of leases entered into before May 15, 1963, 25 pence) upward or downwards as he may think proper having regard to the general condition of the stock under valuation and to the profit which the purchaser may reasonably expect it to earn. The resultant figure shall be the basis of the valuation of the ewes and is in this Part of this Schedule referred to as the 'basic ewe value.'

9. In making his award the valuer shall assess the respective classes of stock in accordance with the following rules, that is to say—
   (a) ewes of all ages (including gimmers) shall be valued at the basic ewe value with the addition of 30 per cent (in the case of leases entered into before May 15, 1963, 75 pence) of such value per head;
   (b) ewe lambs shall be valued at the basic ewe value subject to adjustment by the valuer within the limits of 10 per cent (in the case of leases entered into before May 15, 1963, 25 pence) per head upwards or downwards as he may think proper having regard to their quality and condition; and
   (c) tups shall be valued at such price as in the opinion of the valuer represents their value on the farm having regard to acclimatisation or any other factor for which he thinks it proper to make allowance.

Part III

Particulars to be Shown in an Arbiter's Award

10. The 3-year average price for ewes and the 3-year average price for lambs ascertained under Part I, or the mean of the average prices calculated under Part II, of this Schedule, as the case may be.

11. Any amount added or taken away by way of adjustment for the purpose of fixing the basic ewe value or the basic lamb value, and the grounds on which such adjustment was made.

12. The number of each class of stock valued (ewes and gimmers of all ages with lambs being taken as one class, and eild ewes and eild gimmers being taken as separate classes at a Whitsunday valuation, and ewes and gimmers of all ages being taken as one class at a Martinmas valuation) and the value placed on each class.

13. Any amount added to or taken away by way of adjustment in fixing the value of ewe hoggs at a Whitsunday valuation, or the value of ewe lambs at a Martinmas valuation, and the grounds on which such adjustment was made.

SCHEDULE 10

PART IV

INTERPRETATION

14. In this Schedule the expressions 'ewe,' 'gimmer,' 'eild ewe,' 'eild gimmer,' 'lamb,' 'ewe hogg,' 'eild sheep' and 'tup' shall be construed as meaning respectively sheep of the classes customarily known by those designations in the locality in which the flock under valuation is maintained.

1 See Chapter 13.

Section 70   SCHEDULE 10

VALUATION OF SHEEP STOCK IN SCOTLAND IN RESPECT OF LEASES
ENTERED INTO AFTER DECEMBER 1 1986[1]

PART I

VALUATION MADE IN RESPECT OF A TENANCY TERMINATING AT
WHITSUNDAY

1. The Land Court or the arbiter (in Part I and Part II of this Schedule referred to as 'the valuer') shall ascertain the number of, and the prices realised for, the regular cast ewes and the lambs sold off the hill from the stock under valuation at the autumn sales in each of the 3 preceding years, and shall determine by inspection the number of shotts present in the stock at that time of the valuation.

2. The valuer shall calculate an average price per ewe, and an average price per lamb, for the regular cast ewes and lambs sold as aforesaid for each of the 3 preceding years. In calculating the average price for any year the valuer shall disregard such number of regular cast ewes and lambs so sold in that year, being the ewes or lambs sold at the lowest prices, as bears the same proportion to the total number of regular cast ewes or lambs so sold in that year as the number of shotts as determined bears to the total number of ewes or lambs in the stock under valuation.

3. The valuer shall then ascertain the mean of the average prices so calculated for the 3 preceding years for regular cast ewes and for lambs, respectively. The figures so ascertained or ascertained, in a case to which paragraph 4 below applies, in accordance with that paragraph, are in this Part of this Schedule referred to as the '3-year average price for regular cast ewes' and the '3-year average price for lambs.'

4. In the case of any sheep stock in which the number of regular cast ewes or the number of lambs sold off the hill at the autumn sales during the preceding 3 years has been less than half the total number of regular cast ewes or of lambs sold, the 3-year average price for regular cast ewes or the 3-year average price for lambs, as the case may be shall, in lieu of being ascertained by the valuer as aforesaid, be determined by the Land Court on the application of the parties; and the Land Court shall determine such prices by reference to the prices realised at such sales for regular cast ewes

and for lambs respectively from similar stocks kept in the same district and under similar conditions.

5. The 3-year average price for regular cast ewes shall be subject to adjustment by the valuer within the limits of 30 per cent upwards or downwards as he may think proper having regard to the general condition of the stock under valuation and to the profit which the purchaser may reasonably expect it to earn. The resultant figure shall be the basis of the valuation of the ewes, and is in this Part of this Schedule referred to as the 'basic ewe value.'

The valuer shall adjust the 3-year average price for lambs within the limits of 20 per cent upwards or downwards as he may think proper having regard to their quality and condition. The resultant figure shall be the basis for the valuation of the lambs and is in this Part of this Schedule referred to as the 'basic lamb value.'

6. In making his award the valuer shall value the respective classes of stock in accordance with the following rules, that is to say—

(a) ewes of all ages (including gimmers) shall be valued at the basic ewe value with the addition of 30 per cent of such value per head;

(b) lambs shall be valued at the basic lamb value but twin lambs shall be valued at such price as the valuer thinks proper;

(c) ewe hoggs shall be valued at three quarters of the combined basic values of a ewe and a lamb subject to adjustment by the valuer within the limits of 25 per cent per head upwards or downwards as he may think proper, having regard to their quality and condition;

(d) tups shall be valued at such price as in the opinion of the valuer represents their value on the farm having regard to acclimatisation or any other factor for which he thinks it proper to make allowance;

(e) eild sheep shall be valued at the value put upon the ewes subject to such adjustment as the valuer may think proper having regard to their quality and condition; and

(f) shotts shall be valued at such value not exceeding two-thirds of the value put upon good sheep of the like age and class on the farm as the valuer may think proper.

Part II

Valuation Made in Respect of a Tenancy Terminating at Martinmas

7. The valuer shall ascertain the number of, and the prices realised for, the regular cast ewes sold off the hill from the stock under valuation at the autumn sales in the current year and in each of the 2 preceding years, and shall calculate an average price per ewe so sold for each of the said years. In calculating the average price for any year the valuer shall disregard one-fifth of the total number of regular cast ewes so sold in that year being the ewes sold at the lowest price.

8. The mean of the average prices so calculated shall be subject to adjustment by the valuer within the limits of 30 per cent upwards or downwards as he may think proper having regard to the general condition of the stock under valuation and to the profit which the purchaser may

reasonably expect it to earn. The resultant figure shall be the basis of the valuation of the ewes and is in this Part of this Schedule referred to as the 'basic ewe value.'

9. In making his award the valuer shall assess the respective classes of stock in accordance with the following rules, that is to say—

(a) ewes of all ages (including gimmers) shall be valued at the basic ewe value with the addition of 30 per cent of such value per head;

(b) ewe lambs shall be valued at the basic ewe value subject to adjustment by the valuer within the limits of 20 per cent per head upwards or downwards as he may think proper having regard to their quality and condition; and

(c) tups shall be valued at such price as in the opinion of the valuer represents their value on the farm having regard to acclimatisation or any other factor for which he thinks it proper to make allowance.

Part III

Particulars to be Shown in an Arbiter's Award

10. The 3-year average price for regular cast ewes and the 3-year average price for lambs ascertained under Part I, or the mean of the average prices calculated under Part II, of this Schedule, as the case may be.

11. Any amount added or taken away by way of adjustment for the purpose of fixing the basic ewe value or the basic lamb value, and the grounds on which such adjustment was made.

12. The number of each class of stock valued (ewes and gimmers of all ages with lambs being taken as one class, and eild ewes and eild gimmers being taken as separate classes at a Whitsunday valuation, and ewes and gimmers of all ages being taken as one class at a Martinmas valuation) and the value placed on each class.

13. Any amount added to or taken away by way of adjustment in fixing the value of ewe hoggs at a Whitsunday valuation, or the value of ewe lambs at a Martinmas valuation, and the grounds on which such adjustment was made.

Part IV

Interpretation

14. In this Schedule the expressions 'regular cast ewes,' 'ewe,' 'gimmer,' 'eild ewe,' 'eild gimmer,' 'lamb,' 'ewe hogg,' 'eild sheep' and 'tup' shall be construed as meaning respectively sheep of the classes customarily known by those designations in the locality in which the flock under valuation is maintained.

1 See Chapter 13.

CONSEQUENTIAL AMENDMENTS OF ENACTMENTS

Hill Farming Act 1946 (c 73)

1. In section 9, as substituted by the Seventh Schedule to the 1949 Act—
(a) in subsection (1), for 'Agricultural Holdings (Scotland) Act 1949' substitute 'Agricultural Holdings (Scotland) Act 1991', referred to in subsections (2) and (4) below as 'the 1991 Act';
(b) in subsections (2) and (4), for 'the said Act of 1949' substitute 'the 1991 Act';
(c) in subsection (2)—
> (i) for 'Part I or Part II of the First Schedule' substitute 'Part I or II of Schedule 5,';
> (ii) in paragraph (a), for 'section fifty of that Act' substitute 'section 37 of the 1991 Act';
> (iii) in paragraph (b), for 'section fifty-one of that Act' substitute 'section 38 of the 1991 Act';
> (iv) in paragraph (b), for 'section fifty-two of that Act' substitute 'section 39 of the 1991 Act,';
> (v) for 'the said section fifty or the said fifty-one' substitute 'section 37 or 38 of the 1991 Act';
(d) in subsection (3), for 'section eight of the Agricultural Holdings (Scotland) Act 1949' substitute 'section 15 of the 1991 Act.'

Reserve and Auxiliary Forces (Protection of Civil Interests) Act 1951 (c 65)

2. In section 21—
(a) in subsection (2) for 'Subsection (1) of section twenty-five of the Agricultural Holdings (Scotland) Act 1949' substitute 'section 22 of the Agricultural Holdings (Scotland) Act 1991,' and for 'section twenty-six of that Act' substitute 'section 24 of that Act,';
(b) in subsection (3) for 'section twenty-five' in both places where it occurs substitute 'section 22,' and for 'section twenty-six' substitute 'section 24';
(c) in subsection (8) for 'the said Act of 1949' substitute 'the Agricultural Holdings (Scotland) Act 1991.'
3. In section 22(4)(a), for 'subsection (1) of section twenty-five of the Agricultural Holdings (Scotland) Act 1949' substitute 'section 22(1) of the Agricultural Holdings (Scotland) Act 1991.'
4. In section 38(6)(a)(i), for 'Agricultural Holdings (Scotland) Act 1949' substitute 'Agricultural Holdings (Scotland) Act 1991.'

Crofters (Scotland) Act 1955 (c 21)

5. In section 14(10), for 'Agricultural Holdings (Scotland) Act 1949' substitute 'Agricultural Holdings (Scotland) Act 1991.'
6. In section 37(1), in the definition of 'fixed equipment,' for 'Agricultural Holdings (Scotland) Act 1949' substitute 'Agricultural Holdings (Scotland) Act 1991.'
7. In Schedule 2, paragraph 10, for 'section 15 of the Agricultural

Holdings (Scotland) Act 1949' substitute 'section 52 of the Agricultural Holdings (Scotland) Act 1991.'

Agriculture (Safety, Health and Welfare Provisions) Act 1956 (c 49)

8. In section 25(4), for the words from 'the provisions' to 'section eighteen' substitute 'section 5(2), (3) and (5) of the Agricultural Holdings (Scotland) Act 1991 (liabilities of landlord and tenant of agricultural holding regarding fixed equipment) and section 10.'

9. In section 25(5), for 'section eight of the Agricultural Holdings (Scotland) Act 1949' substitute 'section 15 of the Agricultural Holdings (Scotland) Act 1991.'

10. In section 25(10), in the definition of 'agricultural holding,' 'fixed equipment' and 'landlord,' for 'the Agricultural Holdings (Scotland) Act, 1949' substitute 'the Agricultural Holdings (Scotland) Act 1991.'

Coal Mining (Subsidence) Act 1957 (c 59)

11. In section 10(1)(a), for 'Agricultural Holdings (Scotland) Act 1949' substitute 'Agricultural Holdings (Scotland) Act 1991.'

Opencast Coal Act 1958 (c 69)

12. In section 14A—
(a) in subsection (3), for the words 'Agricultural Holdings (Scotland) Act 1949 in this Act referred to as the Scottish Act of 1949' substitute 'the Scottish Act of 1991,';
(b) in subsection (4), for 'the Scottish Act of 1949' substitute 'the Scottish Act of 1991';
(c) in subsection (5), for 'the Scottish Act of 1949' substitute 'the Scottish Act of 1991';
(d) in subsection (6)—
    (i) for 'section 25(2) of the Scottish Act of 1949' substitute 'section 22(2) of the Scottish Act of 1991'; and
    (ii) for '(c)' substitute '(b)';
(e) in subsection (7), for the words from 'For the purposes' to 'paragraph (e) of subsection (1)' substitute 'The condition specified in section 24(1)(e) of the Scottish Act of 1991 (consent of Land Court to notice to quit where land to be used for purposes other than agriculture)';
(f) in subsection (8), for 'section 7 of the Scottish Act of 1949' substitute 'section 13 of the Scottish Act of 1991';
(g) in subsection (9), for 'section 8 of the Scottish Act of 1949' substitute 'section 15 of the Scottish Act of 1991.'

13. For section 24(10) substitute—
    '(10) In the application of this section to Scotland, for references—
    (a) to the Act of 1986 and to sections 70 and 83(4) of that Act there shall be substituted respectively references to the Scottish Act of 1991 and to sections 44 and 62(3) of that Act;
    (b) to subsections (1), (2) and (3) of section 69 of the Act of 1986 there shall be substituted respectively references to sections 34(5) and 35(4) and (5) of the Scottish Act of 1991 (as they apply to new improvements);
    (c) to Parts I and II of Schedule 7 to the Act of 1986 and to the first day

of March 1948 there shall be substituted respectively references to Parts I and II of Schedule 5 to the Scottish Act of 1991 and to the first day of November 1948; and

(d) to sub-paragraphs (1) and (2) of paragraph 5 of Part I of Schedule 9 to the 1986 Act there shall be substituted respectively references to sections 34(5) and 35(4) of the Scottish Act of 1991 (as they apply to old improvements).'

14. For section 25(3) substitute—

'(3) In the application of this section to Scotland, for paragraphs (a) and (b) of subsection (1) above there shall be substituted the words 'under section 45 of the Scottish Act of 1991' (which relates to compensation for deterioration of a holding or part thereof for which a tenant is responsible).'

15. In section 26(6) after 'Scotland' insert '(a)' and for the words from 'in subsection (3)' to the end substitute—

'(b) in subsection (3) of this section for the reference to the Act of 1986 there shall be substituted a reference to the Scottish Act of 1991; and

(c) in subsection (5) of this section there shall be substituted—

(i) for the reference to section 91 of the Act of 1986 a reference to section 73 of the Scottish Act of 1991;

(ii) for the reference to Schedule 8 to the Act of 1986 a reference to Part III of Schedule 5 to the Scottish Act of 1991;

(iii) for the reference to Parts I, II and III of the Fourth Schedule to this Act a reference to Parts IV and V of that Schedule.'

16. In section 27(4), for 'section fourteen of the Scottish Act of 1949' substitute 'section 18 of the Scottish Act of 1991.'

17. In section 28(6)—

(a) for 'to section sixty-five of the Scottish Act of 1949 and to paragraph (b) of subsection (1) of that section' substitute 'section 40 of the Scottish Act of 1991 and to subsection (4)(a) of that section';

(b) for 'to subsection (1) of section sixty-six of the Scottish Act of 1949 and to section 14 of that Act' substitute 'to section 41(1) and to section 18 of the Scottish Act of 1991';

(c) for 'to section seventy-nine of the Scottish Act of 1949 and to the Fourth Schedule to that Act' substitute 'to section 73 of the Scottish Act of 1991 and to Schedule 6 thereto.'

18. In section 52(2)—

(a) in the definition of 'agricultural holding,' for '1949' substitute '1991';

(b) for the definition of 'the Scottish Act of 1949' substitute ' "the Scottish Act of 1991" means the Agricultural Holdings (Scotland) Act 1991;'.

19. In section 52(5)(a)—

(a) for 'the Scottish Act of 1949' where it first occurs substitute 'the Scottish Act of 1991'; and

(b) for 'sections fifty-seven and fifty-eight of the Scottish Act of 1949' substitute 'section 45 of the Scottish Act of 1991.'

20. In Schedule 6, paragraph 31, for 'section 2(1) of the Scottish Act of 1949' substitute 'section 2 of the Scottish Act of 1991.'

21. For Schedule 7, paragraph 25(a) substitute—

'(a) for references—

(i) to the Act of 1986 and to sections 12, 13, 23 and 84 of that Act there shall be substituted respectively references to the Scottish Act of 1991 and to sections 13, 15, 10 and 61 of that Act;

(ii) to section 10 of the Act of 1986 and to subsections (3) and (4) of that section there shall be substituted respectively references to section 18 of the Scottish Act of 1991 and to subsections (2) and (3) of that section; and

(iii) to subsection (3) of section 79 of the Act of 1986 there shall be substituted references to section 40(4)(a) of the Scottish Act of 1991.'.

Horticulture Act 1960 (c 22)

22. In section 1(1)(b), for 'Agricultural Holdings (Scotland) Act 1949' substitute 'Agricultural Holdings (Scotland) Act 1991.'

Crofters (Scotland) Act 1961 (c 58)

23. In section 13(1), for 'Agricultural Holdings (Scotland) Act 1949' substitute 'the Agricultural Holdings (Scotland) Act 1991.'

Succession (Scotland) Act 1964 (c 41)

24. In section 16—
(a) in subsections (2)(c) and (3)(b)(i), for 'section 20 of the Act of 1949' substitute 'section 11 of the 1991 Act';
(b) in subsection (6)(b), for 'section 27(2) of the Act of 1949' substitute 'section 23(2) and (3) of the 1991 Act' and for 'section 25(2)(f)' substitute 'section 22(2)(e)';
(c) in subsection (8), for 'subsections (2) to (7) of section 20 of the Act of 1949' substitute 'section 11(2) to (8) of the 1991 Act';
(d) in subsection 9—
    (i) in the definition of 'agricultural lease,' for 'the Act of 1949' substitute 'the 1991 Act';
    (ii) for the definition of 'the Act of 1949' substitute ' "the 1991 Act" means the Agricultural Holdings (Scotland) Act 1991;'.

25. In section 29(2), for 'section 20 of the Agricultural Holdings (Scotland) Act 1949' substitute 'section 11 of the Agricultural Holdings (Scotland) Act 1991.'

Agriculture Act 1967 (c 22)

26. In section 26(1) for 'the Agricultural Holdings (Scotland) Act 1949' substitute 'the Agricultural Holdings (Scotland) Act 1991.'

27. In section 27(5B), for 'the Agricultural Holdings (Scotland) Act 1949' substitute 'the Agricultural Holdings (Scotland) Act 1991.'

28. In section 28(1)(a), for 'section 35 of the Agricultural Holdings (Scotland) Act 1949' substitute 'section 43 of the Agricultural Holdings (Scotland) Act 1991.'

29. In section 29—
(a) in subsection (3)(a), for 'section 35 of the Agricultural Holdings (Scotland) Act 1949' substitute 'section 43 of the Agricultural Holdings (Scotland) Act 1991'; and
(b) in subsection (4), for 'section 25(1) of the Agricultural Holdings

(Scotland) Act 1949' substitute 'section 22(1) of the Agricultural Holdings (Scotland) Act 1991.'

30. In section 48(2)(a), for 'section 35 of the Agricultural Holdings (Scotland) Act 1949' substitute 'section 43 of the Agricultural Holdings (Scotland) Act 1991.'

31. In Schedule 3, paragraph 7(5)—
(a) for 'sections 75 and 77 of the Agricultural Holdings (Scotland) Act 1949' substitute 'sections 61 and 64 of the Agricultural Holdings (Scotland) Act 1991'; and
(b) for 'sections 78 and 87(2)' substitute 'sections 60(2) and 80(2).'

Conveyancing and Feudal Reform (Scotland) Act 1970 (c 35)

32. In Schedule 1 in paragraph 5(a), for 'Agricultural Holdings (Scotland) Act 1949' substitute 'Agricultural Holdings (Scotland) Act 1991.'

Land Compensation (Scotland) Act 1973 (c 56)

33. In section 31(3)(c) for 'Agricultural Holdings (Scotland) Act 1949' substitute 'Agricultural Holdings (Scotland) Act 1991.'

34. In section 44—
(a) in subsection 2(a)(i) for 'section 25(2)(c) of the Agricultural Holdings (Scotland) Act 1949' substitute 'section 22(2)(b) of the Agricultural Holdings (Scotland) Act 1991';
(b) in subsection (2)(a)(ii)—
    (i) for 'section 26(1)(e)' substitute 'section 24(1)(e)'; and
    (ii) for 'section 25(2)(c)' substitute 'section 22(2)(b)';
(c) in subsection (3)(a) for 'sections 25(2)(c) and 26(1)(e)' substitute 'sections 22(2)(b) and 24(1)(e)';
(d) in subsection (4), for 'section 12 of the Agriculture (Miscellaneous Provisions) Act 1968' substitute 'section 56 of the Agricultural Holdings (Scotland) Act 1991.'

35. In section 52—
(a) in subsection (3)(d) for 'Agricultural Holdings (Scotland) Act 1949' substitute 'Agricultural Holdings (Scotland) Act 1991'; and
(b) in subsection (4) for 'section 59(1) of the Agricultural Holdings (Scotland) Act 1949' substitute 'section 47(1) of the Agricultural Holdings (Scotland) Act 1991' and for 'the said section 59(1)' substitute 'the said section 47(1).'

36. In section 55—
(a) for subsection (1)(b) substitute—
    '(b) either—
        (i) section 22(1) of the Agricultural Holdings (Scotland) Act 1991 does not apply by virtue of subsection (2)(b) of that section; or
        (ii) the Scottish Land Court have consented to the notice on the ground set out in section 24(1)(e) of that Act.';
(b) in subsection (2)(a), for 'section 12 of the Agriculture (Miscellaneous Provisions) Act 1968' substitute 'section 56 of the Agricultural Holdings (Scotland) Act 1991';
(c) in subsection (2)(b) for 'Agricultural Holdings (Scotland) Act 1949' substitute 'Agricultural Holdings (Scotland) Act 1991,' and for 'sec-

tions 9 and 15(3) of the Agriculture (Miscellaneous Provisions) Act 1968' substitute 'sections 54 and 58(1) and (2) of that Act';
  (d) in subsection (6) for 'section 33 of the Agricultural Holdings (Scotland) Act 1949' substitute 'section 30 of the Agricultural Holdings (Scotland) Act 1991.'
37. In section 80(1), in the definitions of 'agricultural holding' and 'holding' for 'Agricultural Holdings (Scotland) Act 1949' substitute 'Agricultural Holdings (Scotland) Act 1991.'

Land Tenure Reform (Scotland) Act 1974 (c 38)

38. In section 8(5)(a), for 'Agricultural Holdings (Scotland) Act 1949' substitute 'Agricultural Holdings (Scotland) Act 1991.'

Control of Pollution Act 1974 (c 40)

39. In section 31(B)(2)(a), for the words 'an absolute owner (within the meaning of section 93 of the Agricultural Holdings (Scotland) Act 1949)' substitute 'the owner of the dominium utile.'

Matrimonial Homes (Family Protection) (Scotland) Act 1981 (c 59)

40. In section 13(8), in the definition of 'agricultural holding,' for 'Agricultural Holdings (Scotland) Act 1949' substitute 'Agricultural Holdings (Scotland) Act 1991.'

Rent (Scotland) Act 1984 (c 58)

41. For section 25(1)(iii) substitute—
  '(iii) the Agricultural Holdings (Scotland) Act 1991.'

Law Reform (Miscellaneous Provisions) (Scotland) Act 1985 (c 73)

42. In section 7(2), in the definition of 'agricultural holding,' for 'section 1 of the Agricultural Holdings (Scotland) Act 1949' substitute 'the Agricultural Holdings (Scotland) Act 1991.'

Agriculture Act 1986 (c 49)

43. In section 14(a) for 'the Agricultural Holdings (Scotland) Act 1949' substitute 'the 1991 Act.'
44. In section 16—
  (a) in subsection (2), for 'section 7 of the 1949 Act' substitute 'section 13 of the 1991 Act'; and
  (b) in subsection (7), for 'section 86 of the 1949 Act' substitute 'section 79 of the 1991 Act.'
45. In section 18(6) for the words from 'the absolute owner' to '1949' substitute 'the owner of the dominium utile.'
46. In section 19(4) for 'the Crofters (Scotland) Act 1955' substitute 'the 1955 Act.'
47. After section 23 insert—
'23A. In this Act—
  'the 1886 Act' means the Crofters Holdings (Scotland) Act 1886;
  'the 1911 Act' means the Small Landholders (Scotland) Act 1911;
  'the 1955 Act' means the Crofters (Scotland) Act 1955; and

'the 1991 Act' means the Agricultural Holdings (Scotland) Act 1991.'
48. In Schedule 2, paragraph 1(1)—
(a) in the definition of 'landlord'—
      (i) in sub-paragraph (a), for 'the 1949 Act' substitute 'the 1991 Act' and for 'section 93(1)' substitute 'section 85(1)'; and
      (ii) in sub-paragraph (c), for 'the 1949 Act' substitute 'the 1991 Act';
(b) in the definition of 'tenancy,' for 'the 1949 Act' substitute 'the 1991 Act'; and
(c) in the definition of 'tenant'—
      (i) in sub-paragraph (a), for 'the 1949 Act' substitute 'the 1991 Act' and for 'section 93(1)' substitute 'section 85(1)'; and
      (ii) in sub-paragraph (c), for 'the 1949 Act' substitute 'the 1991 Act.'
49. In Schedule 2, paragraph 3(1)(b), for 'section 20 of the 1949 Act' substitute 'section 11 of the 1991 Act.'
50. In Schedule 2, paragraph 7—
(a) in sub-paragraph (2), for 'the 1949 Act' where it first occurs substitute 'the 1991 Act' and for 'section 7 of the 1949 Act' substitute 'section 13 of the 1991 Act'; and
(b) in sub-paragraph (4)—
      (i) in sub-paragraph (a)(i), for 'section 93 of the 1949 Act' substitute 'section 85 of the 1991 Act';
      (ii) in sub-paragraph (a)(iii), for 'the 1949 Act' substitute 'the 1991 Act'; and
      (iii) in sub-paragraph (b), for 'section 93 of the 1949 Act' substitute 'section 85 of the 1991 Act.'
51. In Schedule 2, paragraph 10(1)—
(a) in sub-paragraph (a), for 'the 1949 Act' substitute 'the 1991 Act' and for 'section 78' substitute 'section 60(2)'; and
(b) for 'section 75 (or, where the circumstances require, sections 77 and 87) of the 1949 Act' substitute 'section 60(1) (or, where the circumstances require, sections 64 and 80) of the 1991 Act.'
52. In Schedule 2, paragraph 11—
(a) in sub-paragraph (1)(a), for 'the 1949 Act' substitute 'the 1991 Act' and for 'section 78' substitute 'section 60(2)';
(b) in sub-paragraph (4)—
      (i) for 'section 75 (or, where the circumstances require, sections 77 and 87) of the 1949 Act' substitute 'section 60(1) (or, where the circumstances require, sections 64 and 80) of the 1991 Act'; and
      (ii) for 'paragraph 13 of the Sixth Schedule' substitute 'paragraph 14 of Schedule 7'; and
(c) in sub-paragraph (5), for 'section 61 of the 1949 Act' substitute 'section 50 of the 1991 Act.'
53. In Schedule 2, for paragraph 12 substitute—
'Sections 65 and 75(1), (2), (4) and (6) of the 1991 Act (recovery of sums due and power of tenant to obtain charge on holding) shall apply in relation to any sum payable to the tenant under this Schedule as they apply to sums payable under that section.'

Housing (Scotland) Act 1987 (c 26)

54. In section 256(1) and (3) for 'Agricultural Holdings (Scotland) Act 1949' substitute 'Agricultural Holdings (Scotland) Act 1991.'

55. In section 338(1), in the definition of 'agricultural holding,' for 'Agricultural Holdings (Scotland) Act 1949' substitute 'Agricultural Holdings (Scotland) Act 1991.'

56. In Schedule 8, Part IV, paragraph 13—

(a) in sub-paragraph (1)—

    (i) for 'Section 8 of the Agricultural Holdings (Scotland) Act 1949' substitute 'Section 15 of the Agricultural Holdings (Scotland) Act 1991';

    (ii) for 'the said section 8' substitute 'the said section 15';

(b) in sub-paragraph (2)—

    (i) for 'paragraph 18 of Schedule 1 to the said Act of 1949' substitute 'paragraph 18 of Schedule 5 to the Agricultural Holdings (Scotland) Act 1991';

    (ii) for 'section 79' substitute 'section 73';

    (iii) for 'the said Schedule 1' substitute 'the said Schedule 5';

    (iv) for 'sections 51 and 52' substitute 'sections 38 and 39';

    (v) for 'section 49 of the said Act of 1949' substitute 'section 36 of that Act.'

Housing (Scotland) Act 1988 (c 43)

57. In Schedule 4 in paragraph 6(a), for 'Agricultural Holdings (Scotland) Act 1949' substitute 'Agricultural Holdings (Scotland) Act 1991.'

Section 87   SCHEDULE 12

TRANSITIONALS AND SAVINGS

Continuation of savings

1. The repeal by this Act of an enactment which repealed a previous enactment subject to a saving shall not affect the continued operation of that saving.

Construction of references to old and new law

2.—(1) Where an enactment contained in this Act repeals and re-enacts an earlier enactment—

(a) for the purpose of giving effect to any instrument or other document it shall be competent, so far as the context permits, to construe a reference to either enactment as a reference to the other;

(b) anything done or required to be done for the purposes of either enactment may, so far as the context permits, be treated as having been done or as something required to be done for the purposes of the other.

(2) In this paragraph, a reference to an enactment re-enacted in this Act includes a reference to any such enactment repealed by the Agricultural Holdings (Scotland) Act 1923, the 1949 Act or the Agricultural Holdings (Amendment) (Scotland) Act 1983.

Savings for specific enactments

3. Nothing in this Act shall affect any provision of the Allotments (Scotland) Act 1922.

4. Section 21 of the Reserve and Auxiliary Forces (Protection of Civil Interests) Act 1951 (as read with section 24 of that Act) shall continue to have effect—

(a) in subsections (2) and (3) with the substitution for references to the Secretary of State of references to the Land Court; and

(b) with the reference in subsection (6) to section 27 of the 1949 Act being construed as a reference to that section as originally enacted.

Compensation

5. Notwithstanding section 16 of the Interpretation Act 1978, rights to compensation conferred by this Act shall be in lieu of rights to compensation conferred by any enactment repealed by this Act.

Section 88   SCHEDULE 13

REPEALS AND REVOCATIONS

PART I

REPEALS

Chapter	Short title	Extent of repeal
1 Edw 8 & 1 Geo 6 c 34.	Sheep Stocks Valuation (Scotland) Act 1937.	The whole Act.
9 & 10 Geo 6 c 73.	Hill Farming Act 1946.	Sections 28 to 31. Second Schedule.
11 & 12 Geo 6 c 45.	Agriculture (Scotland) Act 1948.	Section 52. In section 54, the definitions of 'deer', 'occupier of an agricultural holding' and 'woodlands'.
12, 13 and 14 Geo 6 c 75.	Agricultural Holdings (Scotland) Act 1949.	The whole Act.
14 & 15 Geo 6 c 18.	Livestock Rearing Act 1951.	In section 1(2)(b) the words 'in paragraph (d) of subsection (1) of section 8 of the Agricultural Holdings (Scotland) Act 1949'.
14 & 15 Geo 6 c 65.	Reserve and Auxiliary Forces (Protection of Civil Interests) Act 1951.	In section 24(b), the words from 'for references' to 'twenty-seven thereof'.
6 & 7 Eliz 2 c 71.	Agriculture Act 1958.	Section 3. Schedule 1.

SCHEDULE 13

Chapter	Short title	Extent of repeal
1963 c 11.	Agriculture (Miscellaneous Provisions) Act 1963.	Section 21.
1964 c 41.	Succession (Scotland) Act 1964.	In Schedule 2, paragraphs 19 to 23.
1968 c 34.	Agriculture (Miscellaneous Provisions) Act 1968.	Part II. Schedules 4 and 5.
1973 c 65.	Local Government (Scotland) Act 1973.	Section 228(5).
1976 c 21.	Crofting Reform (Scotland) Act 1976.	Schedule 2, para 25.
1976 c 55.	Agriculture (Miscellaneous Provisions) Act 1976.	Sections 13 and 14.
1980 c 45.	Water (Scotland) Act 1980.	In Schedule 10, Part II, the entry relating to the 1949 Act.
1983 c 46.	Agricultural Holdings (Amendment) (Scotland) Act 1983.	The whole Act.
1985 c 73.	Law Reform (Miscellaneous Provisions) (Scotland) Act 1985.	Section 32.
1986 c 5.	Agricultural Holdings Act 1986.	In Schedule 14, paras 25(8), 26(11) and 33(8).
1986 c 49.	Agriculture Act 1986.	In Schedule 2, para 1, the definitions of 'the 1986 Act', 'the 1911 Act', 'the 1949 Act' and 'the 1955 Act'.

PART II

REVOCATIONS OF SUBORDINATE LEGISLATION

Number	Citation	Extent of revocation
SI 1950/1553.	The Agricultural Holdings (Scotland) Regulations 1950.	The whole Instrument.
SI 1978/798.	The Agricultural Holdings (Scotland) Act 1949 (Variation of First Schedule) Order 1978.	The whole Order.
SI 1986/1823.	The Hill Farming Act 1946 (Variation of Second Schedule) (Scotland) Order 1986.	The whole Order.

TABLE OF DERIVATIONS

Note: The following abbreviations are used in this Table—

1937	= The Sheep Stocks Valuation (Scotland) Act 1937 (1 Edw 8 & 1 Geo 6 c 34).
1946	= The Hill Farming Act 1946 (9 & 10 Geo 6 c 73).
1948	= The Agriculture (Scotland) Act 1948 (11 & 12 Geo 6 c 45).
1949	= The Agricultural Holdings (Scotland) Act 1949 (12, 13 & 14 Geo 6 c 75).
1958	= The Agriculture Act 1958 (c 71).
1963	= The Agriculture (Miscellaneous Provisions) Act 1963 (c 11).
1964	= The Succession (Scotland) Act 1964 (c 41).
1968	= The Agriculture (Miscellaneous Provisions) Act 1968 (c 34).
1973	= The Local Government (Scotland) Act 1973 (c 65).
1976	= The Agriculture (Miscellaneous Provisions) Act 1976 (c 55).
1983	= The Agricultural Holdings (Amendment) (Scotland) Act 1983 (c 46).
1986	= The Agricultural Holdings Act 1986 (c 5).
SI 1950/1553	= The Agricultural Holdings (Scotland) Regulations 1950 (SI 1950/1553).
SI 1977/2007	= The Agriculture (Adaptation of Enactments) (Scotland) Regulations 1977 (SI 1977/2007).
SI 1978/798	= The Agricultural Holdings (Scotland) Act 1949 (Variation of First Schedule) Order 1978 (SI 1978/798).
SI 1986/1823	= The Hill Farming Act 1946 (Variation of Second Schedule) (Scotland) Order 1986.

Provision of Act	Derivation
1	1949 s 1; 1958 s 9(1).
2	1949 s 2.
3	1949 s 3; 1949 s 24(1).
4	1949 s 4, s 6(4).
5	1949 s 5.
6	1949 s 23.
7	1949 s 12; 1958 Sch 1, Pt II, para 33.
8	1949 s 17.
9	1949 s 9; 1958 Sch 1, Pt II, para 32.
10	1949 s 18.
11	1949 s 20; 1964 s 34(1), Sch 2, paras 19, 20 and 21.
12	1949 s 21; 1964 s 34(1), Sch 2, para 22.
13	1949 s 7; 1983 s 2.
14	1949 s 6(3).
15	1949 s 8.
16	1949 s 10.
17	1949 s 13.

Provision of Act	Derivation
18	1949 s 14.
19	1949 s 22.
20	1949 s 19.
21	1949 s 24; 1958 Sch 1, Pt II, para 34.
22	1949 s 25; 1958 s 3(1), (3), Sch 1, Pt II, para 35.
23	1949 s 27; 1958 Sch 1, Pt II, para 37.
24	1949 s 26; 1958 s 3(2), (3), Sch 1, Pt II, para 36; 1983 s 4(1).
25	1949 s 26A; 1983 s 3, s 4(2).
26	1949 s 28; 1958 Sch 1, Pt II, para 38; 1989 (c 15) Sch 25, para 12.
27	1949 s 30; 1958 Sch 1, Pt II, para 40.
28	1949 s 31.
29	1949 s 32.
30	1949 s 33.
31	1949 s 34.
32	1976 s 14.
33	1949 s 36; s 47.
34	1949 s 37, s 41, s 42, s 43, s 44(4), s 45, s 48, s 53, s 54.
35	1949 s 11, s 46, s 55.
36	1949 s 38, s 43, s 44(1), s 49, s 53.
37	1949 s 39, s 50.
38	1949 s 40, s 51.
39	1949 s 52; 1958 Sch 1, Pt II, para 41.
40	1949 s 65.
41	1949 s 66; 1958 Sch 1, Pt II, para 43.
42	1949 s 67.
43	1949 s 35.
44	1949 s 56.
45	1949 s 57, s 58.
46	1949 s 6(1), (2); s 57(3); SI 1950/1553.
47	1949 s 59.
48	1949 s 16.
49	1949 s 60.
50	1949 s 61.
51	1949 s 63; 1958 Sch 1, Pt II, para 42; SI 1977/2007.
52	1949 s 15; SI 1977/2007.
53	1949 s 64.
54	1968 s 9, s 16, Sch 5, para 1.
55	1968 s 11.
56	1968 s 12, s 16.
57	1968 s 14; 1972 (c 52) Sch 21, Pt II.
58	1968 s 15, s 16, Sch 5, para 5.
59	1968 s 16, s 17.
60	1949 s 74, s 78.
61	1949 s 68, s 75; 1973 s 228(5); 1983 s 5(1).
62	1949 s 68.
63	1949 s 76; 1971 (c 58) s 4.

Provision of Act	Derivation
64	1949 s 77, s 87(2); 1986 s 17(3).
65	1949 s 69.
66	1976 s 13.
67	1949 s 91; 1971 (c 58) s 4.
68	1937 s 1; 1946 s 28; 1985 (c 73) s 32; SI 1986/1823.
69	1937 s 2.
70	1937 s 3; 1946 s 29; SI 1986/1823.
71	1946 s 30.
72	1937 s 4.
73	1949 s 79.
74	1949 s 80.
75	1949 s 70, s 82; 1980 (c 45) Sch 10.
76	1949 s 83.
77	1949 s 84.
78	1949 s 85.
79	1949 s 86; 1968 s 17(3).
80	1949 s 87(1).
81	1949 s 88.
82	1949 s 89; 1975 (c 21) s 289; 1977 (c 45) s 31.
83	1949 s 73; 1976 s 14(6); 1976 (c 21) Sch 2, para 25.
84	1949 s 90; 1985 (c 6) s 725(1).
85	1949 s 93.
86	1949 s 95.
87	1949 s 99(2).
88	1949 s 97.
89	1949 s 101.
Schedule 1	1949 Sch 5.
Schedule 2	1983 Sch 1.
Schedule 3	1949 Sch 2.
Schedule 4	1949 Sch 3.
Schedule 5	1949 Sch 1; SI 1978/798.
Schedule 6	1949 Sch 4.
Schedule 7	1949 Sch 6; 1983 s 5(2).
Schedule 8	1968 Sch 4, Sch 5, para 6, para 7.
Schedule 9	1946 Sch 2; 1963 s 21.
Schedule 10	1946 Sch 2; 1963 s 21.

TABLE OF DESTINATIONS

1937	1991
s 1	s 68
s 2	s 69
s 3	s 70
s 4	s 72

1946	1991
s 28	s 68
s 29; SI 1986/1823	s 70
s 30	s 71
Sch 2	Sch 9
Sch 2	Sch 10

1949	1991
s 1	s 1
s 2	s 2
s 3	s 3
s 4	s 4
s 5	s 5
s 6(1)	s 46
s 6(2)	s 46
s 6(3)	s 14
s 6(4)	s 44
s 7	s 13
s 8	s 15
s 9	s 9
s 10	s 16
s 11	s 35
s 12	s 7
s 13	s 17
s 14	s 18
s 15; SI 1977/2007	s 52
s 16	s 48
s 17	s 8
s 18	s 10
s 19	s 20
s 20	s 11
s 21	s 12
s 22	s 19
s 24	s 21
s 24(1)	s 3
s 25	s 22
s 26	s 24
s 26A	s 25
s 27	s 23
s 28	s 26
s 30	s 27

1949	1991
s 31	s 28
s 32	s 29
s 33	s 30
s 34	s 31
s 35	s 43
s 36	s 33
s 37	s 34
s 38	s 36
s 39	s 37
s 40	s 38
s 41	s 34
s 43	s 34
s 44(1)	s 36
s 44(4)	s 34
s 45	s 34
s 46	s 35
s 47	s 33
s 48	s 34
s 49	s 36
s 50	s 37
s 51	s 38
s 52	s 39
s 53	ss 34, 36
s 54	s 34
s 55	s 35
s 56	s 44
s 57	s 45
s 57(3); SI 1950/1553	s 46
s 58	s 45
s 59	s 47
s 60	s 49
s 61	s 50
s 63	s 51
s 64	s 53
s 65	s 40
s 66	s 41
s 67	s 42
s 68	ss 61, 62
s 69	s 65
s 70	s 75
s 73	s 83
s 74	s 60
s 75	s 61
s 76	s 63
s 77	s 64
s 79	s 73
s 80	s 74
s 82	s 75

1949	1991
s 83	s 76
s 84	s 77
s 85	s 78
s 86	s 79
s 87(1)	s 80
s 87(2)	s 64
s 78	s 60
s 88	s 81
s 89	s 82
s 90	s 84
s 91	s 67
s 93	s 85
s 95	s 86
s 99(2)	s 87
s 97	s 88
s 101	s 89
Sch 5	Sch 1
Sch 1; SI 1978/798	Sch 5
Sch 2	Sch 3
Sch 3	Sch 4
Sch 4	Sch 6
Sch 6	Sch 7

1958	1991
s 3(1), (3)	s 22
s 3(2), (3)	s 24
s 9(1)	s 1
Sch 1, Pt II, para 33	s 7
Sch 1, Pt II, para 31	s 9
Sch 1, Pt II, para 34	s 21
Sch 1, Pt II, para 35	s 22
Sch 1, Pt II, para 36	s 24
Sch 1, Pt II, para 37	s 23
Sch 1, Pt II, para 38	s 26
Sch 1, Pt II, para 40	s 27
Sch 1, Pt II, para 41	s 39
Sch 1, Pt II, para 42; SI 1977/2007	s 51
Sch 1, Pt II, para 43	s 41

1963	1991
s 21	Sch 9
s 21	Sch 10

1964	1991
s 34(1)	s 11
Sch 2, paras 19, 20, 21	s 11
Sch 2, para 22	s 12

1968	1991
s 9	s 54
s 11	s 55
s 12	s 56
s 14	s 57
s 15	s 58
s 16	ss 54, 56, 58, 59
s 17	s 59
s 17(3)	s 79
Sch 4	Sch 8
Sch 5, para 1	s 54
Sch 5, para 5	s 58
Sch 5, para 6	Sch 8

1971	1991
(c 58) s 4	s 63
(c 58) s 4	s 67

1972	1991
(c 52) Sch 21, Pt II	s 57

1973	1991
s 228(5)	s 61

1975	1991
(c 21) s 289	s 82

1976	1991
s 13	s 66
s 14	s 32
s 14(6)	s 83
(c 21) Sch 2, para 25	s 83

1977	1991
(c 45) s 31	s 82

1980	1991
(c 45) Sch 10	s 75

1983	1991
s 2	s 13
s 3	s 25
s 4(1)	s 24
s 4(2)	s 25
s 5(1)	s 61
s 5(2)	Sch 7

1983	1991
Sch 1	Sch 2

1985	1991
(c 6) s 725(1)	s 84
(c 73) s 32; SI 1986/1823	s 68

1986	1991
s 17(3)	s 64

1989	1991
(c 15) Sch 25, para 12	s 26

FORMS FOR USE IN CONNECTION WITH THE 1991 ACT

A. NOTICES TO QUIT AND MISCELLANEOUS

		PAGE
1.	Notice to Quit by Landlord to Tenant (ss 21, 22).	265
2.	Notice to Quit by Landlord to Legatee or 'acquirer' of Lease but not 'near relative' of deceased Tenant (ss 22(2)(g), 25(2)).	266
3.	Notice to Quit by Landlord to exclude additional payment under s 54.	266
4.	Counter-Notice under s 22(1) by Tenant to Notice to Quit by Landlord.	268
5.	Notice by Tenant to Landlord requiring questions arising out of Notice to Quit to be referred to Arbitration (s 23).	268
6.	Notice to Tenant to pay rent within two months (s 22(2)(d)).	269
7.	Notice by Landlord to Tenant to remedy Breach of Conditions of Tenancy capable of being remedied (s 22(2)(d)).	269
8.	Notice by Landlord to Tenant to Remove from Part of Farm (s 29).	270
9.	Counter-Notice by Tenant accepting Notice to Remove from Part as Notice to Remove from Entire Holding (s 30).	270
10.	Notice by Landlord to Tenant of Contract for Sale of Holding (s 28(2)).	271
11.	Agreement between Landlord and Tenant as to Notice to Quit being valid on sale of holding (s 28(2)).	271
12.	Notification by Tenant to Landlord that he elects that Notice to Quit shall remain in force following on sale of holding (s 28(2)).	272
13.	Demand for execution of Tenancy Agreement (ss 4,5).	272
14.	Reference to arbitration by Landlord as to amount of compensation payable by Tenant on transfer of liability for maintenance of fixed equipment (s 46).	273
15.	Requirement by Tenant for Arbitration as to claim against Landlord on transfer of liability for maintenance of fixed equipment (s 46(3)).	274
16.	Demand by Landlord for Arbitration as to Rent (s 13).	274
17.	Notice by Landlord requiring Increase of Rent on completion of Improvements (s 15).	275
18.	Agreement between Landlord and Incoming Tenant with regard to the latter paying Outgoing Tenant's Claims for Compensation (s 35(3)).	276
19.	Notice to Landlord that Tenant intends to Remove Fixtures, etc (s 18).	276
20.	Notice to Tenant by Landlord that he Elects to Purchase Fixtures, etc (s 18).	277

21. Notice of Damage by Game (s 52). 277
22. Claim for Damage by Game (s 52). 278
23. Notification by Landlord or Tenant requiring a Record to be made (s 8). 278
24. Intimation to Landlord of Bequest of Lease (s 11). 279
25. Intimation by Landlord Declining to accept Legatee as Tenant (s 11(3)). 279
26. Intimation to Landlord of acquisition of Lease from Executor (s 12). 280
27. Intimation by Landlord Declining to accept Acquirer as Tenant (s 12(2)). 280
28. Application by Tenant to Landlord for written consent to Improvements (s 37, Sch 5, Pt I). 281
29. Landlord's Consent in Writing to Execution of Improvements (s 37, Sch 5, Pt I). 281
30. Notice by Tenant of Intention to make Improvements (s 38, Sch 5, Pt II). 282
31. Notice by Landlord to Tenant of objection to carrying out of Improvements (s 39(1), Sch 5, Pt II). 283
32. Notice by Landlord that he intends to execute the Improvements himself (s 39(3), Sch 5, Pt II). 283
33. Notice of Intention by Tenant to Claim Compensation for Continuous Special System of Farming (s 44). 284
34. Notice by Landlord of Intention to Claim Compensation from Tenant for Deterioration of Holding (s 45). 284
35. Notice of Intention to Claim Compensation by Waygoing Tenant (s 62(2)). 285
36. Notice by Landlord to Tenant of change of Landlord (s 84(4)). 286
37. Statement of Case and Particulars of Claim (s 61, Sch 7, paras 5, 20). 287

B. APPLICATIONS TO THE SECRETARY OF STATE FOR SCOTLAND

See also C below for applications to the Secretary of State for the appointment of arbiters and for extension of time for making award. These must be in the forms specified.

Application by landlord or tenant to extend the time for settling claims at termination of tenancy (s 62(4)).

C. ARBITRATION PROCEDURE

PAGE
1. Joint Appointment of Arbiter by Landlord and Outgoing Tenant (Sch 7). 290
2. Joint Intimation to Arbiter of his Appointment where he has been appointed by the Parties. 291
3. Joint Minute of Revocation of Arbiter's Appointment. 291
4. Extension by Parties of Time for Award. 292
5. Minute of Devolution by Arbiters on Oversman. 292

6. Incidental Orders by Arbiter   293
    (a) Order by Arbiter for Claims.   293
    (b) Order to Produce Documents.   293
    (c) Intimation to Parties of Inspection.   294
    (d) Extension of Time.   294
    (e) Revisal.   294
    (f) Appointment of Clerk.   295
    (g) To Answer Statement of Facts.   295
    (h) For Closing Record.   295
    (i) Closing and Proof.   295
    (j) Avizandum.   296
    (k) Proposed Findings.   296
    (l) Representations Repelled.   297
7. Application by an Arbiter to the Sheriff for the appointment of a Clerk in the Arbitration.   297
8. Stated Case for Opinion of the Sheriff.   298
9. Application to Sheriff for Order on Arbiter to State a Case.   299
10. Application to Sheriff to have Arbiter Removed.   300
11. Common Law Submission between Outgoing and Incoming Tenants.   300
12. Award in Common Law Submission.   303
13. Minute of Acceptance by Arbiters and Nomination of Oversman and Clerk.   304
14. Minute of Acceptance by Oversman following thereon.   304
15. Minute of Prorogation by Parties.   304
16. Minute of Prorogation when Submission has expired.   305
17. Minute of Prorogation by Arbiters.   305

D. ADDITIONAL FORMS

                                               PAGE
1. Claim by Outgoing Tenant against Incoming Tenant.   306
2. Abbreviated Form of Lease.   306
3. Supplementary Agreement in terms of s 5(3).   309

(See also the Agricultural Holdings (Specification of Forms) (Scotland) Order 1991 in Appendix 5, p 333, below.)

A. NOTICES TO QUIT AND MISCELLANEOUS

NOTICES AND INTIMATIONS BY LANDLORD AND TENANT AND AGREEMENTS, ETC

Unless otherwise indicated the following styles are not statutory and are suggestions only, capable of modification to suit particular cases.

1.
                                      Notice to Quit by Landlord to Tenant (ss 21, 22).

Place................................

Date ....

To [name, designation and address of the party in possession]

You are required to remove from [describe subjects] at the term of [or, if different terms, state them and the subjects to which they apply], in terms of lease [describe it] [or in terms of your letter of removal of date   ] [or otherwise as the case may be].

The reason [or reasons] for giving this notice is [are] [quote from s 22, so far as applicable].

                                        (Signed) A B [landlord]

Notes:

1 This is a statutory form and is taken from Form H in the First Schedule to the Sheriff Courts (Scotland) Act 1907. It should be sent by recorded delivery. There are unlikely to be many cases in which a notice to quit without reasons should be given. See Chapter 4.

2 If the landlord does not agree that the tenant is entitled to compensation for disturbance, he must add to this notice the reason for which it is given, as above. To exclude payment under s 54 reasons must be given as in Form 3.

3 This form is obligatory (s 21(5)).

4 Where two concurrent notices are sent or two reasons given in one notice, see *French v Elliott* [1960] 1 WLR 40.

5 See also Forms 2 and 3.

2.   Notice to Quit by Landlord
                                            to Legatee or 'acquirer' of
                                            Lease but not 'near relative'
                                            of deceased Tenant (ss
                                            22(2)(g), 25(2)).

                                            _____

                                            Place...............................

                                            Date ....

To [name, designation and address of the party in possession]
    You are required to remove from [describe subjects] at the term of [or, if
different terms, state them and the subjects to which they apply], in terms of
lease [describe it] [or in terms of your letter of removal of date   ] [or
otherwise as the case may be].
    This notice is given in pursuance of s 22(2)(g) of the Agricultural Holdings
(Scotland) Act 1991. [The tenancy is being terminated for the purpose of my
using the land for agriculture only.][3]

                                            (Signed) A B [landlord]

Notes:
1 For dates when such notice may be given see s 25(2)(b).
2 Unlike the other paragraphs of s 22(2) para (b) does not require that a notice to quit given in
   terms thereof must state that it is so given. It may be unnecessary but it is suggested that it is
   preferable to give the tenant notice of the reason for the notice to quit so that he knows he
   must require arbitration within one month under s 23(2) if he has any ground for challenging
   the application of s 22(2)(g).
3 If these words are not included compensation will be payable under s 54. The question
   whether the tenancy is being terminated for the purpose stated may be referred by the tenant
   to the Land Court.
      If notice is given in this form and either the tenant does not contest the statement or the
   Land Court finds that the subjects are to be used for agriculture only compensation for
   disturbance will be payable but not the additional sum under s 54.
4 For suggested form of notice to quit to 'near relative' successor see Form 3.

3.   Notice to Quit by Landlord
                                            to exclude additional pay-
                                            ment under s 54.

                                            _____

                                            Place...............................

                                            Date ....

To [name, designation and address of the party in possession].
    You are required to remove from [describe subjects] at the term of [or, if
different terms, state them and the subjects to which they apply], in terms of
lease [describe it] [or in terms of your letter of removal of date   ] [or
otherwise as the case may be].
    The carrying out of the purpose for which I propose to terminate the
tenancy is desirable on the following grounds:
    [Quote from paras (a), (b) or (c) of s 24(1).][1]

[or] I hereby intimate that unless this notice has effect I shall suffer hardship[2] [or if the tenant is 'near relative' successor to deceased tenant].[3]

(a) This notice is given under Case 1 [or Case 5] of Schedule 2 to the Agricultural Holdings (Scotland) Act 1991 by reason of the fact that you have neither sufficient training in agriculture nor sufficient experience of farming to enable you to farm the said holding with reasonable efficiency; or

(b) This notice is given under Case 2 [or Case 6] of Schedule 2 to the Agricultural Holdings (Scotland) Act 1991 in order to enable me to use the said holding for the purpose of effecting an amalgamation with [specify land with which holding is to be amalgamated]; or

(c) This notice is given under Case 3 [or Case 7] of Schedule 2 to the Agricultural Holdings (Scotland) Act 1949 by reason of the fact that you are the occupier of [specify land occupied] which has been occupied by you since before the date of death of [name and designation of deceased tenant] and is a two-man unit as defined in Part III of said Schedule; or

(d) This notice is given under Case 4 of Schedule 2 to the Agricultural Holdings (Scotland) Act 1991 by reason of the fact that you do not have sufficient financial resources to enable you to farm the holding with reasonable efficiency.

(Signed) A B [landlord]

Notes:
1 See s 55(1)(a).
2 See s 55(1)(b).
3 See ss 22(2)(g), 25(2)(c), 55(1)(c), Sch 2. Note that if Land Court consents to application under s 24(1)(e) (use of land for non-agricultural purposes) or under s 24(1)(b) (sound estate management) or on one of the grounds in Sch 2 but certifies that it would also have been satisfied under s 24(1)(e) the additional sum under s 54 will be payable.

If notice is given in this form and the tenant omits to serve counter-notice under s 22(1), compensation for disturbance will be payable but not the additional sum under s 54.

If the tenant serves counter-notice and the landlord succeeds in an application to the Land Court under s 24(1) compensation for disturbance will be payable but the additional sum under s 54 will not be payable unless either (a) the reasons for the court's decision include that it is satisfied as to the matter mentioned s 24(1)(e) (use of land for non-agricultural purposes), or (b) the reasons for the decision include that it is satisfied as to the matter mentioned in s 24(1)(b) (sound management of estates) or under Case 1 or 5 (lack of training or experience), or Case 3 or 7 (tenant having other agricultural land) of Sch 2 but would have been satisfied also as to the matter mentioned in s 24(1)(e) if it had been specified in the application.

4.   Counter-Notice   under
                                      s 22(1) by Tenant to Notice
                                      to Quit by Landlord.

                                      _____

                                      Place...............................
                                      Date ....

To A B [design landlord]

Agricultural Holdings (Scotland) Act 1991
Holding of

With reference to your notice dated   19   , to quit the
above holding at the term of   , I hereby require that subsection
(1) of section 22 of the Agricultural Holdings (Scotland) Act 1991, shall
apply to the said notice.

                                      (Signed) C D [tenant]

Notes:
1 It is recommended that this notice be sent by first-class recorded delivery and a copy
  retained.
2 It may be advisable to reserve right to object to the validity of the notice to quit.
3 Where the notice to quit states that it is given for any of the reasons stated in s 22(2), the
  tenant must within one month serve a notice requiring the question to be determined by
  arbitration (s 23).

5.   Notice by Tenant to Land-
                                      lord   requiring   questions
                                      arising out of Notice to
                                      Quit to be referred to Arbi-
                                      tration (s 23).

                                      _____

                                      Place...............................
                                      Date ....

To A B [design landlord]

Agricultural Holdings (Scotland) Act 1991
Holding of

With reference to your notice to quit the above holding, dated
            19   , I hereby intimate to you that I require all questions
arising out of the reasons stated in the said notice to quit to be determined by
arbitration under the above Act.

                                      (Signed) C D [tenant]

Notes:
1 This notice must be given within one month of the date of the notice to quit (s 23).
2 Where the notice to quit states one or more of the reasons in s 22(2) the tenant should require

arbitration and not serve a counter-notice requiring the operation of s 22(1). On the award of the arbiter being issued the tenant may then serve a notice under s 22(1) within one month of the date of the award (s 23(3)).
3 See *French v Elliott* [1960] 1 WLR 40 where two reasons given or two notices sent.

6.

Notice to Tenant to pay rent within two months (s 22(2)(d)).

_____

Place................................

Date ....

To C D [design tenant]

AGRICULTURAL HOLDINGS (SCOTLAND) ACT 1991
HOLDING OF

I hereby give you notice that you are required to pay the rent amounting to £ due at 19 , in respect of the above holding within two months of this intimation.

(Signed) A B [landlord]

Note:
The service of this notice, which should be sent by recorded delivery letter, is essential if the landlord is to found on the tenant's failure to pay in a notice to quit.

7.

Notice by Landlord to Tenant to remedy Breach of Conditions of Tenancy capable of being remedied (s 22(2)(d)).

_____

Place................................

Date ....

To C D [design tenant]

AGRICULTURAL HOLDINGS (SCOTLAND) ACT 1991
HOLDING OF

I hereby intimate to you as tenant of the above holding that you are required to remedy within [state time considered to be reasonable or say 'a reasonable time'] from the date of this intimation the following breaches of the conditions of your tenancy, which are capable of being remedied and which are not inconsistent with your responsibilities to farm in accordance with the rules of good husbandry, namely [here specify the breach of conditions in detail with reference to the conditions of the tenancy].

(Signed) A B [landlord]

Notes:
1 This notice should be sent by recorded delivery letter and is essential if the landlord is to found on the tenant's failure in a notice to quit.
2 Where it is desired to give two notices or two reasons see *French v Elliott* [1960] 1 WLR 40.
3 The time need not be stated: *Morrison-Low v Howison* 1961 SLT (Sh Ct) 53; *Stewart v Brims* 1969 SLT (Sh Ct)2.

8.   Notice by Landlord to Tenant to Remove from Part of Farm (s 29).

                                                    Place................................
                                                    Date ....

To C D [tenant]

AGRICULTURAL HOLDINGS (SCOTLAND) ACT 1991
HOLDING OF

In terms of the Agricultural Holdings (Scotland) Act 1949, section 32, I hereby give notice that you are required to remove at [specify date] from that area of land, part of the above holding of which you are the tenant [describe the part or preferably refer to a plan drawn to scale, so as clearly to identify the part]. The said ground is required for the following purpose[s], namely [set out the purpose in terms of s 29(2)].

                                                    (Signed) A B [landlord]

Note:
This notice should be sent by recorded delivery.

9.   Counter-Notice by Tenant accepting Notice to Remove from Part as Notice to Remove from Entire Holding (s 30).

                                                    Place................................
                                                    Date ....

To A B [design landlord]

AGRICULTURAL HOLDINGS (SCOTLAND) ACT 1991
HOLDING OF

Having received your notice dated   to remove at [insert date] from part of the above holding, I hereby accept said notice as a notice to remove from the entire holding occupied by me in terms of section 30 of the Agricultural Holdings (Scotland) Act 1991, to take effect at the same time as the original notice.

(Signed) C D [tenant]

Note:
This notice must be served within twenty-eight days of the service of the landlord's notice to quit or within twenty-eight days of it being determined by arbitration that the notice is effective.

10.

Notice by Landlord to Tenant of Contract for Sale of Holding (s 28 (2)).

Place...............................

Date ....

To C D [design tenant]

AGRICULTURAL HOLDINGS (SCOTLAND) ACT 1991
HOLDING OF

I hereby give you notice that on   19 , I entered into a contract for the sale of E F [design purchaser] of the above-mentioned holding of which you are tenant.

This notice is given to you in terms of s 28(2) of the Agricultural Holdings (Scotland) Act 1991.

(Signed) A B [landlord]

Note:
This notice must be given within fourteen days of the making of the contract for sale.

11.

Agreement between Landlord and Tenant as to Notice to Quit being valid on sale of holding (s 28(2)).

Place...............................

Date ....

AGRICULTURAL HOLDINGS (SCOTLAND) ACT 1991
HOLDING OF

We, A B [design], the landlord, and C D [design], the tenant, of the holding of   in the Parish of   and the County of   , hereby agree that the notice to quit dated   19 , served by the landlord on the tenant shall [continue in force] [be of no effect] if a contract for the sale of the said holding is entered into by the landlord within three months of the date of this agreement: In witness whereof

12.

Notification by Tenant to Landlord that he elects that Notice to Quit shall remain in force following on sale of holding (s 28(2)).

Place.................................

Date ....

To A B [design landlord]

AGRICULTURAL HOLDINGS (SCOTLAND) ACT 1991
HOLDING OF

With reference to your intimation to me dated   19   , of the sale of the above holding of which I am tenant, I hereby notify you that I elect that the notice to quit served on me and dated   19   , shall remain in force.

(Signed) C D [tenant]

Note:
This notice must be given before the expiry of one month from the receipt by the tenant of the notice of the making of the contract.

13.

Demand for execution of Tenancy Agreement (ss 4, 5).

Place.................................

Date ....

To C D [tenant]

AGRICULTURAL HOLDINGS (SCOTLAND) ACT 1991
HOLDING OF

I hereby give you notice to enter into a written lease containing provisions as to the terms of your tenancy of the above holding, in terms of section 4 of the Agricultural Holdings (Scotland) Act 1991 [or agree to additions or revised terms of your existing lease in accordance with ss 4, 5, etc].

I enclose draft of the proposed agreement [or note of proposed provisions] and shall be obliged by your returning same approved or intimating any adjustments you propose. In the event of agreement not being reached within six months from this date the terms of the lease will be referred to arbitration under the Act.

(Signed) A B [landlord]

APPENDIX 1: FORMS

Notes:
1 At the expiry of six months, if no agreement is reached, the landlord or tenant should send notice requiring the other party to arbitrate under the section, and, if this is not agreed, application should be made to the Secretary of State to appoint an arbiter.
2 The form should be adjusted when it is to be served by the tenant.

14.

Reference to arbitration by Landlord as to amount of compensation payable by Tenant on transfer of liability for maintenance of fixed equipment (s 46).

Place...............................

Date ....

To C D [design tenant]

AGRICULTURAL HOLDINGS (SCOTLAND) ACT 1991
HOLDING OF

Whereas in virtue of section 4 of the above Act liability for the maintenance or repair of certain fixed equipment, as specified in the list annexed hereto, has been transferred by the arbiter from you to me as from   19 , in terms of award dated   19 , I hereby require that the compensation to be paid by you to me in respect of said transfer of liability up to the said date of transfer shall be settled by arbitration under the Act in terms of section 46.

(Signed) A B [landlord]

List of Equipment

Note:
The reference must be made within one month from the date on which the transfer of liability takes effect.

15.

Requirement by Tenant for Arbitration as to claim against Landlord on transfer of liability for maintenance of fixed equipment (s 46(3)).

Place..............................

Date ....

To A B [design landlord]

Agricultural Holdings (Scotland) Act 1991
Holding of

Whereas in virtue of section 4 of the above Act the liability for the maintenance or repair of certain fixed equipment as specified in the list annexed hereto, has been transferred as from   19 , from you to me in terms of agreement between us dated   19 , [or award by E F, the arbiter, dated   19], I hereby require that my claim in respect of your previous failure to discharge your liability for such maintenance or repair shall be settled by arbitration under section 46.

(Signed) C D [tenant]

List of Equipment

Note:
This notice must be given within one month from the date on which the transfer liability takes effect.

16.

Demand by Landlord for Arbitration as to Rent (s 13).

Place..............................

Date ....

To C D [design tenant]

Agricultural Holdings (Scotland) Act 1991
Holding of

I hereby, in terms of the Agricultural Holdings (Scotland) Act 1991, section 13, demand arbitration as to the rent to be paid for the above holding from and after the term of   being the next ensuing term at which I could terminate the tenancy by notice to quit, given at this date [or, as to the additional rent to be paid in respect of the following improvements (specify, and refer to s 15)].

Please acknowledge receipt of this demand [and suggest the names of two or three arbiters whom you would agree to appoint. Failing agreement, I shall apply to the Secretary of State to make an appointment].

(Signed) A B [landlord]

Notes:

1 Although not essential, it is well to send this notice by recorded delivery letter.

2 This form may be adapted to the case of a tenant demanding arbitration as to the rent under the same sections. The part of the first paragraph in brackets is appropriate to s 15.

3 When there is more than one ish the notice should refer to the first in time.

4 The part of the second paragraph in brackets should be omitted if it is desired to have the appointment made by the Secretary of State. An arbiter so appointed in an arbitration under s 13(1) must give reasons for his award and there may be an appeal to the Land Court. A stated case on a question of law would also go to the Land Court if the arbiter were so appointed in an arbitration under s 13(1). There is also the consideration that an arbiter approved by the Secretary of State is subject to the provisions of the Tribunals and Inquiries Act 1971 and that his fee falls to be fixed by the Secretary of State.

17.

Notice by Landlord requiring Increase of Rent on completion of Improvements (s 15).

Place.................................

Date ....

To C D [design tenant]

AGRICULTURAL HOLDINGS (SCOTLAND) ACT 1991
HOLDING OF

I hereby intimate to you as tenant of the above holding that I require the rent thereof to be increased by an amount equal to the increase in the rental value of the improvements carried out by me as from   19   , the date of their completion.

I annex a note of the improvements and consider that the rent should be increased by £   per annum. Failing agreement, I require the increase in rent to be determined by arbitration.

This notice is given in terms of section 15 of the above Act.

(Signed) A B [landlord]

Statement of Improvements
[Detail the improvements and their cost]

Note:
This notice requires to be served within six months of the completion of the improvements.

18.   Agreement between Landlord and Incoming Tenant with regard to the latter paying Outgoing Tenant's Claims for Compensation (s 35(3)).

AGRICULTURAL HOLDINGS (SCOTLAND) ACT 1991
HOLDING OF

Whereas I, A B [design], the landlord of the holding of   ,
have let the said holding to me C D [design] as incoming tenant at the term
of   , it is hereby agreed between us that I the said C D will
settle [or refund to the said A B the amount of] the claim of E F, the outgoing
tenant, in respect of compensation for improvements on the holding in
respect of [specify the particular improvements in terms of Pt III of Sch 5 to
the Act] and that up to a maximum of £   : In witness whereof

19.   Notice to Landlord that Tenant intends to Remove Fixtures, etc (s 18).

Place..............................

Date ....

To A B [design landlord]

AGRICULTURAL HOLDINGS (SCOTLAND) ACT 1991
HOLDING OF

In terms of the above Act (s 18), I hereby give you notice that I intend at
Whitsunday [or Martinmas, as the case may be] next, or within six months
thereafter, to remove the following fixtures [and/or buildings, as the case may
be] erected by me [or acquired by me from   on
    ] on the above holding, namely [specify the fixtures and/or
buildings in such manner that they can be identified, and, if necessary, where
and when and from whom any of the buildings or fixtures were acquired].

(Signed) C D [tenant]

Note:

This notice must be served at least one month before both the exercise of the right to remove the
fixtures or buildings and the termination of the tenancy. The landlord may give counter-notice:
see Form 20.

20.

Notice to Tenant by Land-
lord that he Elects to Purchase Fixtures, etc (s 18).

——————————

Place................................

Date ....

To C D [design tenant]

AGRICULTURAL HOLDINGS (SCOTLAND) ACT 1991
HOLDING OF

With reference to your notice dated   intimating that you
intend to remove certain fixtures [and/or buildings] from the above holding,
of which you are [were] my tenant, at Whitsunday [or Martinmas] next, or
within six months thereafter, I hereby give you notice in terms of the
Agricultural Holdings (Scotland) Act 1991, section 18(3) that I elect to
purchase the same [or the following (specify)] at a price, failing agreement,
which will be determined by arbitration. Please acknowledge receipt of this
notice.

(Signed) A B [landlord]

Note:
See note to Form 19. This counter-notice must be given before the expiration of the tenant's
notice.

21.

Notice of Damage by Game
(s 52).

——————————

Place................................

Date ....

To A B [design landlord]

AGRICULTURAL HOLDINGS (SCOTLAND) ACT 1991
HOLDING OF

TAKE NOTICE that the field [describe by name or reference to Ordnance
Survey] now in oats [or as the case may be] on the above holding, of which I
am tenant, has been and is being damaged by game other than ground game,
and that it is my intention to claim compensation therefor under the
Agricultural Holdings (Scotland) Act 1991, section 52. You may inspect the
damage within [state a reasonable time] before the crop is removed. Please
acknowledge receipt of this notice.

(Signed) C D [tenant].

22.   Claim for Damage by
                                             Game (s 52).

                                             ———————

                                 Place.............................

                                 Date ....

To A B [design landlord]

Agricultural Holdings (Scotland) Act 1991
Holding of

Referring to my notice to you dated   [or as the case may
be] in terms of the Agricultural Holdings (Scotland) Act 1991, section 52, I
hereby claim the sum of £   for damage to oats [or as the case may be] on
the above holding of which I am tenant, by game in or about [specify date]. I
am prepared to refer the matter to arbitration under the Acts if you do not
agree to the amount claimed.

                                 (Signed) C D [tenant]

Note:
This notice requires to be given within one month after the end of the calendar year, or such
other period of twelve months as the parties may agree (s 52(2)(b)).

23.   Notification by Landlord or
                                             Tenant requiring a Record
                                             to be made (s 8).

                                             ———————

                                 Place.............................

                                 Date ....

To C D [design tenant]

Agricultural Holdings (Scotland) Act 1991
Holding of

In terms of section 8 of the Agricultural Holdings (Scotland) Act 1991, I
hereby require a record to be made of the fixed equipment on, and of the
cultivation of, the above holding, of which you are tenant. I suggest the
following persons whom I am prepared to accept for the purpose of making
the record, namely [names]. Failing agreement on a person to make the
record I shall apply to the Secretary of State to make an appointment.

                                 (Signed) A B [landlord]

Notes:
1 Adapt this form when it is to be sent to the tenant, who may also require the record to refer
to improvements he has carried out or to fixtures and buildings he is entitled to remove
(s 17(1)(a),(b).

2 The record is to be made by a person appointed by the Secretary of State and shall be in such
form as may be prescribed (s 8(3)), but the prescribed form does not make provision for the
parties to agree a nomination. If a nomination is agreed, this will require to be drawn to the
Secretary of State's attention in a covering letter accompanying the application. The person

nominated by the Secretary of State does not require to be a member of the panel of arbiters.

24.   Intimation to Landlord of
                                                 Bequest of Lease (s 11).

                                                 _____

                                                 Place...............................
                                                 Date ....

To A B [design landlord]

AGRICULTURAL HOLDINGS (SCOTLAND) ACT 1991
HOLDING OF

In terms of section 12 of the Agricultural Holdings (Scotland) Act 1991, I hereby intimate to you as landlord of the above holding that C D, tenant of said holding, who died on   by his last will and testament, dated   [of which a copy is herewith enclosed], bequeathed to me the current lease of said holding, and I hereby intimate that it is my intention to take up the lease.

I shall be glad to supply you with any information which you may reasonably require in connection with my resources or capacity.

Please acknowledge receipt and confirm that you accept me as tenant.

                                                 (Signed) J H [legatee]

Notes:
1 This intimation must, if possible, be made within twenty-one days of the tenant's death.
2 Notice must be given by the acquirer.

25.   Intimation by Landlord
                                                 Declining to accept Legatee
                                                 as Tenant (s 11(3)).

                                                 _____

                                                 Place...............................
                                                 Date ....

To J H [design legatee]

AGRICULTURAL HOLDINGS (SCOTLAND) ACT 1991
HOLDING OF

With reference to your letter of   intimating that the late C D, tenant of the above holding, by his last will and testament bequeathed to you the current lease of said holding, I hereby intimate in terms of the Agricultural Holdings (Scotland) Act 1991, s 11(3), that I object to receive you as tenant under the said lease. [The reasons for my objection are   .]

                                                 (Signed) A B [landlord]

Notes:
1 This notice must be given within one month of receipt of the notice from the legatee.
2 The reasons for the objection do not require to be stated in the notice but it is preferable to do so.

26.   Intimation to Landlord of
                                                       acquisition of Lease from
                                                       Executor (s 12).

                                                       _____

                                                       Place...............................
                                                       Date ....

To A B [design landlord]

AGRICULTURAL HOLDINGS (SCOTLAND) ACT 1991
HOLDING OF

In terms of section 12 of the Agricultural Holdings (Scotland) Act 1991, I hereby intimate to you as landlord of the above holding that XY [design] as executor of C D, tenant of said holding, who died on
transferred to me on [insert date of transfer] the current lease of said holding, and I hereby intimate that it is my intention to take up the lease.

I shall be glad to supply you with any information which you may reasonably require in connection with my resources or capacity.

Please acknowledge receipt and confirm that you accept me as tenant.

                                                       (Signed) J H [legatee]

Notes:
1 This intimation must be made within twenty-one days of the date of transfer or if prevented by unavoidable cause as soon as possible thereafter.
2 This notice must be given by the acquirer and *not* by the executors.

27.   Intimation by Landlord
                                                       Declining to accept Ac-
                                                       quirer as Tenant (s 12(2)).

                                                       _____

                                                       Place...............................
                                                       Date ....

To J H [design acquirer]

AGRICULTURAL HOLDINGS (SCOTLAND) ACT 1991
HOLDING OF

With reference to your letter of   intimating that the current lease of the above holding has been transferred to you I hereby intimate in terms of the Agricultural Holdings (Scotland) Act 1991, section

12(2), that I object to receive you as tenant under said lease. [The reasons for my objections are   .]

(Signed) A B [landlord]

Notes:
1 This notice must be given within one month of receipt of the notice from the acquirer.
2 The reasons for the objection do not require to be stated in the notice but it is preferable to do so.

28.   Application by Tenant to Landlord for written consent to Improvements (s 37, Sch 5, Pt I).

Place...............................

Date ....

To A B [design landlord]

AGRICULTURAL HOLDINGS (SCOTLAND) ACT 1991
HOLDING OF

I hereby intimate that I propose to carry out on the above holding the following improvements referred to in Part I of Schedule 5 to the above Act and I request you to give your written consent thereto [unconditionally] [or on such other terms as to compensation or otherwise as may be agreed or between us in writing], namely [specify the proposed improvements in detail, using the appropriate words in the Schedule].

(Signed) C D [tenant]

Note:
If certain conditions are proposed they should be mentioned.

29.   Landlord's Consent in Writing to Execution of Improvements (s 37, Sch 5, Pt I).

Place...............................

Date ....

To C D [design tenant]

AGRICULTURAL HOLDINGS (SCOTLAND) ACT 1991
HOLDING OF

I hereby consent to your executing on the above holding the following improvements embraced in Schedule 5, Part I of the above Act, namely [here specify the improvements mentioned in the Schedule so far as applicable and the conditions as to compensation, etc, on which the consent is given]. Please notify me when they have been completed.

(Signed) A B [landlord]

Note:

If the landlord proposes conditions additional to those proposed by the tenant the whole conditions acceptable to the landlord should be detailed. See *Turnbull v Millar* 1942 SC 521.

30.

Notice by Tenant of Intention to make Improvements (s 38, Sch 5, Pt II).

Place.................................

Date ....

To A B [design landlord]

AGRICULTURAL HOLDINGS (SCOTLAND) ACT 1991
HOLDING OF

In terms of section 38 of the Agricultural Holdings (Scotland) Act 1991, I hereby intimate that it is my intention, on the expiry of three months from this date, to execute the improvements embraced under Part II, Schedule 5 to the Act, on the above holding as specified in the statement annexed hereto. Please acknowledge receipt of this notice.

(Signed) C D [tenant]

Annexed Statement

Specify the several improvements particularly under the heads detailed in Nos 9–23 of the Schedule and amplify where necessary.

Notes:

1 In order to entitle the tenant to compensation for improvements embraced in Pt II of Sch 5 to the Act, it is necessary for him to give such notice not less than three months before beginning to execute the improvements.
2 It is necessary to follow the different heads in the Schedule and to state before beginning to work with some particularity the improvement proposed, its situation, and the manner in which the work is to be carried out. The landlord must not be left in doubt as to what is intended. It is generally desirable to supply an estimate of cost, with specification made up by a practical man, and a plan where necessary.
3 Landlords are referred to the provisions of s 39.

31.   Notice by Landlord to Ten-
                                         ant of objection to carrying
                                         out of Improvements
                                         (s 39(1), Sch 5, Pt II).

                                         _____

                                         Place...............................
                                         Date ....

To C D [tenant]

AGRICULTURAL HOLDINGS (SCOTLAND) ACT 1991
HOLDING OF

With reference to your letter dated   intimating your
intention to make (in accordance with the Agricultural Holdings (Scotland)
Act 1991, section 38) on the above holding the improvements therein
specified. I hereby intimate in terms of section 39(1) that I object to the
carrying out of those improvements [or to the manner in which you propose
to carry out those improvements].

                                         (Signed) A B [landlord]

Notes:
1 This notice must be given within one month after receiving notice from the tenant of his
  intention to make improvements.
2 On receipt of this notice the tenant may, without further notice, apply to the Land Court for
  approval of the carrying out of the proposed improvements.

32.   Notice by Landlord that
                                         he intends to execute
                                         the Improvements himself
                                         (s 39(3), Sch 5, Pt II).

                                         _____

                                         Place...............................
                                         Date ....

To C D [tenant]

AGRICULTURAL HOLDINGS (SCOTLAND) ACT 1991
HOLDING OF

With reference to your letter dated   , intimating your
intention to make (in accordance with the Agricultural Holdings (Scotland)
Act 1991, section 38) on the above holding the improvements therein
specified and the approval of the Scottish Land Court having now been
obtained thereto, such approval being dated   , I hereby
intimate, in terms of section 39(3), that I undertake to execute those
improvements myself. Please acknowledge receipt of this intimation. The

amount of increased rent payable in respect of these improvements will be settled, in the absence of agreement, by arbitration under the Act.

(Signed) A B [landlord]

Notes:
1 After giving this intimation the landlord may, unless the tenant's notice is previously withdrawn, proceed to do the work himself in any reasonable and proper manner.
2 This notice must be given within one month of the date of the decision of the Scottish Land Court.

33.
            Notice of Intention by Tenant to Claim Compensation for Continuous Special System of Farming (s 44).

Place...............................

Date ....

To A B [design landlord]

AGRICULTURAL HOLDINGS (SCOTLAND) ACT 1991
HOLDING OF

I hereby give you notice (in accordance with the Agricultural Holdings (Scotland) Act 1991, section 44) that I intend to claim from you compensation under that Act in respect of the continuous adoption by me (in the years) of a special standard or system of farming on the above holding.

(Signed) C D [tenant]

Note:
This notice must be given one month before termination of the tenancy; the existence of a record is prerequisite.

34.
            Notice by Landlord of Intention to Claim Compensation from Tenant for Deterioration of Holding (s 45).

Place...............................

Date ....

To C D [design tenant]

AGRICULTURAL HOLDINGS (SCOTLAND) ACT 1991
HOLDING OF

I hereby give you notice that (in accordance with the Agricultural Holdings (Scotland) Act 1991, section 45) I intend to claim compensation from you (under that section) at the termination of your tenancy of the above holding, in respect of the undernoted dilapidation [or deterioration or damage], the value of the farm having been deteriorated during the said tenancy by your failure.

(Signed) A B [landlord]

Notes:
1 This notice must be given not later than three months before the termination of the tenancy.
2 In the case of a lease entered into after 31st July 1931 such claim is competent only where the failure has occurred after the date of a record.
3 The above form may be adjusted to meet the case of a claim for general deterioration or at common law.
4 In the case of a lease entered into after 1st November 1948, all claims including one under the lease, are competent only if there is a record (s 47(3)).

35.

Notice of Intention to Claim Compensation by Waygoing Tenant (s 62(2)).

Place..............................

Date ....

To A B [design landlord]

AGRICULTURAL HOLDINGS (SCOTLAND) ACT 1991
HOLDING OF

I hereby intimate to you as landlord of the above holding my intention to make the following claims, under and in accordance with the above Act, on the termination of my tenancy of the said holding at [state date or dates of termination of tenancy], namely:

(1) claims for compensation under the said Acts for improvements embraced in the Schedules to the Act; and

(2) additional claims, all as set forth in the annexed statement.

Please acknowledge receipt.

(Signed) C D [tenant]

Annexed Statement

1. Claims for improvements under the Agricultural Holdings (Scotland) Act 1991 [specify using the words of the Schedules to the Act].

    I.   CLAIMS UNDER PART I, SCHEDULE 5
        State the nature of each improvement for which prior consent in writing was given by the landlord.

    II. CLAIMS UNDER PART II, SCHEDULE 5
        State each improvement under the heads contained in the statute so far as applicable.

    III. CLAIMS UNDER PART III, SCHEDULE 5
        State the particulars under the heads in the statute.

2. Additional claims by the tenant:
  (a) *Statutory Claims*
      (i) Claim for value of buildings or fixtures taken over by landlord (s 8).
         [Specify the buildings or fixtures.]
      (ii) Claim for compensation for disturbance (s 43).
      (iii) Claim for additional sum for reorganisation of tenant's affairs (s 54).
      (iv) In respect of increased value of holding (s 44).

Note:
When the claim for disturbance is more than one year's rent (maximum two years' rent) one month's notice must be given to the landlord of the sale of implements, etc, which form the basis of the claim, and an opportunity of making a valuation must also be afforded (s 35).

  (b) *Claiming under Lease or Agreement*
      The particulars of claim need not be given very fully but should be sufficient to indicate the nature of the claim and the relevant provision of the lease or agreement.

36.   Notice by Landlord to Tenant of change of Landlord (s 84(4)).

                                        Place...............................

                                        Date ....

To C D [design tenant]

AGRICULTURAL HOLDINGS (SCOTLAND) ACT 1991
HOLDING OF

I hereby give you notice in terms of section 84(4) of the above Act that as from   19   , I cease to be entitled to receive the rents and profits of the above holding and E F [design] is now entitled to receive the same. All notices or other documents requiring to be served on the landlord of the holding should be served on the said E F as from the said date.

                                        (Signed) A B [landlord].

37.   Statement of Case and Par-
                                       ticulars of Claim (s 61, Sch
                                       7, paras 5, 20).

AGRICULTURAL HOLDINGS (SCOTLAND) ACT 1991
HOLDING OF
A B [design], Landlord.
C D [design], Tenant.

Statement of Case – Landlord's Claim

1. The claimant is landlord of the holding of   in the
Parish of   and the County of   and C D
is [was] tenant of the said holding in terms of lease between the parties
dated   a copy of which is produced herewith and referred
to.

2. The lease expired at Whitsunday, and separation of crop, 19   [or
otherwise as the case may be], since when the tenant has been sitting on tacit
relocation. The tenant quitted the farm at Whitsunday, and separation of
crop, 19 , in consequence of notice to quit by the landlord, dated
            , copy of which is produced herewith.

3. In terms of the said lease the tenant was bound to maintain the
buildings, fences, etc, in good and tenantable repair during the period of his
tenancy, his obligations being defined as follows: [take in from lease].

4. No repairs have been carried out by the tenant during his occupancy of
the holding. In addition, the tenant has allowed the farm generally
to deteriorate, has failed to keep the ground clean and in a good state of
fertility and he has not left it in the rotation prescribed in the lease [give
details].

5. The landlord has frequently called on the tenant to implement his
obligations under the lease [or at common law], which he has failed to do. In
particular, reference is made to letters addressed to the tenant, dated
            , which are produced.

6. The tenant being bound under his lease to maintain the said subjects
and at common law cultivate the farm in accordance with the rules of good
husbandry and having failed to do so is liable to the landlord in damages,
which are reasonably estimated at a sum of £ . Particulars are annexed
hereto.

7. On   19 , the landlord gave notice to the tenant of his
intention to claim for deterioration of the holding in terms of section 45 of
the Agricultural Holdings (Scotland) Act 1991.

8. A record of the farm was made by   on
            a copy of which is produced herewith, the date of the
record being earlier than the date of the tenant's failure to perform his
obligations as condescended on.

9. The tenant by letter dated   admitted liability in
respect of the repairs to buildings but disputed the amount as excessive and
denied liability for the other claim. This arbitration is therefore necessary.

Particulars of Claims

*Amount
claimed*

1. Dilapidations to buildings [specify these in detail with reference to particular buildings].
2. Dilapidation of fences [specify with reference to fields or number in record].
3. Dilapidation of drains [do].
4. Cost of restoration of fertility in respect of the tenant's failure to restore fertility in respect of crops sold off the farm in exercise of his rights under section 7.
5. Failure to leave the farm in the rotation prescribed in the lease in the following respects: [detail].
6. General deterioration in respect of failure to leave the land clean and in good condition of fertility (s 45).

Statement of Case re Tenant's Claims

1. Reference is made to the foregoing statement of the landlord's case.

2. With regard to the tenant's claim for the unexhausted value of manures and feeding-stuffs, the claim is excessive and should be reduced.

3. Reference is made to the tenant's claim for compensation for disturbance. The landlord by letter dated   (copy herewith produced) called on the tenant to remedy within two months breaches of the condition of his tenancy with regard to repairs as above condescended on. The tenant at the date of the notice to quit had failed to remedy these breaches and that fact was stated in the notice to quit.

4. The breaches in question being capable of being remedied and being within the meaning of s 22 (2)(d) of the Agricultural Holdings (Scotland) Act 1991, the tenant is not entitled to compensation for disturbance and the landlord is not liable accordingly.

Notes:
1 Adapt this form in the case of a tenant's claim.
2 The statement of case and particulars must be lodged with the arbiter within twenty-eight days of his appointment. There is no provision that a copy must be sent to the other party to the arbitration, but in practice this should be done. See note to Arbitration Form 6(a).
3 The lodgment must be timeous to entitle the arbiter to proceed but if the parties and the arbiter agree, statements of case may be lodged out of time. Where a party fails to lodge timeously he cannot set up an affirmative case: *Collett v Deeley* (1949) 100 LJ 108; *Jamieson v Clark* (1951) 67 Sh Ct Rep 17.
4 There is no provision in the Act for answers being lodged and this does not appear to be competent, as parties are confined at the hearing to what is alleged in the statement of case and particulars lodged. If they are allowed, the formal consent of parties should be obtained.
5 Where at the end of a tenancy parties have been in negotiation for four months or more (s 62(4)), it is assumed with justification that each knows the other's case and can answer it in the original statement of case.
6 It is envisaged by Sch 7, para 5(a) that amendments or additions may be made to the original statement of case compared with the adjustment of record in civil actions in the courts.

B. APPLICATIONS TO THE SECRETARY OF STATE FOR SCOTLAND

Application by Landlord or Tenant to extend the time for settling claims at termination of tenancy (s 62(4)).

To the Secretary of State for Scotland.

AGRICULTURAL HOLDINGS (SCOTLAND) ACT 1991
HOLDING OF

I, A B [landlord]/C D [tenant] of the above holding in the Parish of
and County of   the tenancy of which
terminated at [specify term or terms], hereby apply under section 62(4) of
the above Act for an extension of two months [or a further extension of two
months] of the period within which claims between the parties may be settled
by agreement.

(Signed) A B [landlord]
or
(Signed) C D [tenant]

Notes:

1 The application may be signed by one or both parties.
2 It must be made before the lapse of the initial period of four months, or, in the case of a
   second application, before the lapse of six months, from the termination of the tenancy.

C. ARBITRATION PROCEDURE

1.

Joint Appointment of Arbiter by Landlord and Outgoing Tenant (Sch 7)

AGRICULTURAL HOLDINGS (SCOTLAND) ACT 1991
HOLDING OF

We, A B [designation and address] landlord of the farm of
in the Parish of   and County of   , and
C D [designation and address], outgoing tenant of the said farm at the term
of   19   , hereby appoint E F [designation and address]
arbiter under the Agricultural Holdings (Scotland) Act 1991, to determine
what sum or sums, if any, are payable by either of us to the other in respect of
the questions and claims detailed in the annexed Schedule[s] or the
compensation (if any) payable under the Agricultural Holdings (Scotland)
Act 1991, by me, the said A B to me, the said C D, in respect of damage by
game to the crops of the latter on said farm during the year ending the
                          day of   19   .
   In witness whereof

[Date]

To be witnessed

(Signed) A B [landlord]
(Signed) C D [tenant]

Notes:
1 The Tribunals and Inquiries Act 1971 does not apply to arbiters appointed by agreement. If
  either party desires the arbiter to be bound to give reasons for his decision, his better course is
  to apply to the Secretary of State for Scotland for the appointment of an arbiter. It is not
  necessary for parties to try to agree upon the person to be appointed.
2 It is important to state the questions and claims as clearly and fully as possible.
3 An appointment by agreement of parties need not be made from the panel of arbiters
  appointed under the Act.
4 An appointment may be made by the Secretary of State on the application of either party.
5 An appointment by the parties is not complete until it is delivered.

APPENDIX 1: FORMS

2.

Joint Intimation to Arbiter
of his Appointment where
he has been appointed by
the Parties.

Place...............................

Date ....

To R W [design arbiter]

AGRICULTURAL HOLDINGS (SCOTLAND) ACT 1991
HOLDING OF

We enclose minute of your appointment by us as arbiter under the above Act
to deal with the claims therein referred to, and we have to request that you
will commence to act thereunder forthwith.

Copies of our respective statements of case and particulars of claims are
enclosed [or will follow].

We consent to the appointment of a clerk in the reference under submission of the statements of claim of the parties.

Please acknowledge receipt and confirm your acceptance of the appointment.

(Signed) A B [landlord]
(Signed) C D [tenant]

Notes:
1 Statements of case and full particulars must be lodged with the arbiter within twenty-eight
days of his appointment.
2 The award must be made within three months after the appointment unless the time is
extended by the parties jointly or by the Secretary of State for Scotland (Sch 7, para 8).

3.

Joint Minute of Revocation
of Arbiter's Appointment.

AGRICULTURAL HOLDINGS (SCOTLAND) ACT 1991
HOLDING OF

We hereby revoke the appointment of E F as arbiter, in the arbitration
between us under the Agricultural Holdings (Scotland) Act 1991 with
reference to the above holding.

Dated at   , the   day of   19 .

(Signed) A B [landlord]
(Signed) C D [tenant]

Note:
The Secretary of State for Scotland does not have power to revoke the appointment of an
arbiter. Paragraph 3 of Sch 7 provides that neither party can revoke the appointment of the

arbiter without the consent of another. Clearly both parties can revoke a joint appointment and both jointly can revoke an appointment made by the Secretary of State on the application of one or both of them.

4.   Extension by Parties of
                                           Time for Award.

                                           _____

                                           Place..............................
                                           Date ....

To R W [design arbiter]

ARBITRATION–HOLDING OF

We extend the time for the issue of your award in the arbitration between us
until the   day of   19 .
                                           (Signed) A B [landlord]
                                           (Signed) C D [tenant]

5.   Minute of Devolution by
                                           Arbiters on Oversman.

                                           _____

We, A B and C D, the arbiters under the foregoing submission having differed in opinion regarding the determination of the matters submitted to us, hereby devolve the said reference and submission and whole matters therein contained upon G H the oversman: IN WITNESS WHEREOF

Notes:
1 It is competent to devolve part only of the question or claim.
2 This style has no application to the single arbiter procedure laid down in the 1949 Act.

6.   Incidental Orders by Arbiter.

(Some of these orders may not be appropriate in statutory arbitrations.)

———————

(a) Order by Arbiter for Claims.

———————

Place...............................

Date ....

AGRICULTURAL HOLDINGS (SCOTLAND) ACT 1991
ARBITRATION–HOLDING OF

Having, on   19 , been appointed by the Secretary of State for Scotland [or by the parties] as arbiter in the arbitration between A B and C D relating to the above holding, I require the parties to lodge with me [or the clerk] their claims and also allow them to see and answer the claim of the other party within   days from this date.

(Signed) R W [arbiter]

Note:
If his expenses are to be recovered, a clerk can only be appointed after the claims and answers are lodged with the consent of the parties or the sheriff (Sch 7, para 18). Rule 5 makes no reference to the lodging of answers and it is doubtful if the arbiter can make an order for answers unless they come within the scope of the words 'amendment or addition' in that rule. It is thought that 'amendment or addition' should be by way of adjustment on the original document for each party. If parties consent to the lodging of answers they would be personally barred from objecting to the procedure. The rule only applies to arbitrations under the Act and not at common law.

(b) Order to Produce Documents.

———————

Place...............................

Date ....

ARBITRATION–HOLDING OF

I require you to attend at [place] on the   day of   , 19   at   o'clock, and to bring with you and produce the documents, receipts, etc, mentioned in the annexed list, so far as the same may be in your possession or within your power.

(Signed) R W [arbiter]

To C D [design]

[Subjoin List of Documents referred to.]

Note:
Where parties refuse to produce documents, etc, in response to an order as above, or where a necessary witness declines to attend and give evidence, application may be made to the sheriff for an order to compel him to attend, give evidence and produce documents.

(c) Intimation to Parties of Inspection.

Place................................

Date ....

To A B [design]

ARBITRATION–HOLDING OF

I hereby notify you that I require parties to meet me at the above holding on the   day of   19   at   o'clock, when I propose to inspect the farm buildings, fences, etc, [and hear parties on their respective claims] [and objections] [or as the case may be].

(Signed) R W [arbiter]

(d) Extension of Time.

The arbiter on cause shown extends the time for the first parties lodging their claim to and for the second parties lodging answers thereto to.

Notes:
1 This order is not competent in a statutory arbitration.
2 See note above as to the competency of answers in a statutory arbitration.

(e) Revisal.

The arbiter allows parties to adjust their statements of case and claims (and answers) respectively and to intimate their adjustments to the other party within fourteen days of the date hereof.

(f) Appointment of Clerk.

_____

The arbiter appoints E F [design] to be clerk and legal adviser in the arbitration.

Notes:
1 In a statutory arbitration this order may only be pronounced after the arbiter has received the statements of case for the parties and either with their consent or with the approval of the sheriff.
2 In a common law arbitration the arbiter may pronounce the order at any time, subject to any provision in the submission.

(g) To Answer Statement of Facts.

_____

The arbiter allows the first parties to answer the statement of facts for the second parties by [date].

(h) For Closing Record.

_____

The arbiter having considered the revised statement of case and claim No of process and the revised answers No of process with the productions and whole process closes the record, and appoints parties to be heard on the preliminary pleas [or otherwise] at on the   day of   .

(i) Closing and Proof.

_____

The arbiter closes the record on the revised statement of case and answers Nos   and   of process; allows the parties a proof of their respective averments, the claimant A B to lead in the proof. Appoints the proof to commence in   on [date] at [hour]. Further the arbiter respectfully recommends to the Lords of Council and Session [or the sheriff of   ]to grant warrant for citing witnesses and havers on the application of either party.

(j) Avizandum.

——————

The arbiter having heard the proof adduced for both parties and their agents thereon and on the whole cause makes avizandum.

(k) Proposed Findings.

———————— Arbitration.

————

The arbiter, having inspected the lands of   and buildings let therewith in presence of the parties and their agents, and having thereafter heard the evidence adduced and the statements of parties' agents thereon, and having carefully considered the respective claims, now proposes to find and determine as follows:

1. **Tenant's Claim**
   To allow the following tenant's claims:

	Amount claimed	*Amount allowed*
(a) For disturbance		
(b) For additional sum to assist in reorganisation of tenant's affairs		
(c) For unexhausted manures		
(d) For feeding-stuffs [or otherwise according to claim]		

2. **Landlord's Claims**
   To allow the following claims [as above]

	Amount claimed	*Amount allowed*

The arbiter further proposes that the sum of £   , being the difference between the said respective claims, shall be payable by the said   to the said   on or before the twenty-first day after the issue of the award following on these proposed findings.

The arbiter further proposes that his and the clerk's fees and expenses shall be payable by the parties equally and that, otherwise, each party shall pay his own expenses [or otherwise as the case may be].

The arbiter allows the parties or either of them until the   day of   19   , to lodge written representations against these proposed findings, if so advised.

(Signed) R W [arbiter]

Note:
It is usual to add a note on any points of law or fact which appear to require explanation. An arbiter appointed by the Secretary of State must, if required to do so, give reasons for his decision. See the Tribunals and Inquiries Act 1971.

(l) Representations Repelled.

The arbiter having considered the representations lodged for the [landlord or tenant] adheres to his proposed findings and will issue his award accordingly.

Note:
It is not desirable to make proposed findings final without issuing an award.

---

7.   Application by an Arbiter to the Sheriff for the appointment of a Clerk in the Arbitration (Sch 7, Para 19)

SHERIFFDOM OF   AT

A B [design arbiter] (Pursuer)

against

C D [design tenant] and E F [design landlord] (Defenders)

The pursuer craves the court –
To grant authority to him to appoint a clerk in the arbitration under the Agricultural Holdings (Scotland) Act 1991, between the said defenders, and to find the defenders jointly and severally [or the defender C D or as the case may be] liable in expenses.

Condescendence

1. The pursuer was appointed by the Secretary of State for Scotland [or by the defenders jointly] as arbiter to deal with certain claims or questions between the defenders under the Agricultural Holdings (Scotland) Act 1949.

2. The present proceedings have as their object a tenancy of heritable property at   . This court has jurisdiction. To the knowledge of the pursuer, no proceedings are pending before any other court involving the present cause of action and the parties thereto. To the knowledge of the pursuer no agreement exists among the parties prorogating jurisdiction over the subject-matter of the present cause to another court.

3. Statements of case and particulars of the claims have been duly lodged with the pursuer and are produced herewith and he is of opinion that, on account of the magnitude and importance of the arbitration [and/or on account of the fact that questions of law have arisen in the arbitration] it is expedient that he should have the advice and assistance of a properly qualified clerk.

4. The pursuer having requested the defenders and they [or the defender C D or as the case may be] having refused to consent to the appointment of a

clerk he finds it necessary to make this application to the court for sanction to make the appointment.

Plea-in-law

In the circumstances condescended on, the court should grant authority to appoint a clerk as craved.

8.   Stated Case for Opinion of
                                                       the Sheriff.

SHERIFFDOM OF   AT

Case stated by

R S [design], arbiter in the arbitration under the Agricultural Holdings (Scotland) 1991,

between

A B [design], landlord of the holding of M, in the Parish of T and County of X,

and

C D [design], outgoing [or present] tenant of said farm.

1. This is an arbitration under the Agricultural Holdings (Scotland) Act 1949 [or as the case may be] brought before me as arbiter acting under joint appointment by the said A B and C D [or appointment by the Secretary of State for Scotland] to determine the following claims and questions in terms of the said statute [set forth]. The appointment was dated
and the period for issuing my award was extended by the parties [or by the Secretary of State] to   .

2. The present proceedings have as their object a tenancy of heritable property at   . This court has jurisdiction. To the knowledge of the pursuer no proceedings are pending before any other court involving the present cause of action and the parties thereto. To the knowledge of the pursuer no agreement exists among the parties prorogating jurisdiction over the subject-matter of the present cause to another court.

3. After certain procedure, in the course of which I inspected the farm, proof was led and the parties were heard on their respective claims and objections, I found *inter alia*, the following facts proved or admitted:
[Narrate the facts bearing on the question of law on which the opinion of the court is required.]

4. The said A B on those facts contends that [landlord's contentions].

5. The said C D, on the other hand, contends that [tenant's contentions].

6. After I issued notes of my proposed findings [or as the case may be] the said C D [or the said A B] requested me to state a case for the opinion of the court on the following.

Questions of Law

[State the question or questions in such form that the court may answer them by a simple affirmative or negative.]

This case is stated by me,

R S, Arbiter

Notes:
1 The draft stated case should be submitted to the parties' agents for revisal and the insertion of their contentions. The terms of the stated case are, however, for the arbiter to decide: *Forsyth-Grant v Salmon* 1961 SC 54.
2 This form may be adapted for a Stated Case to the Scottish Land Court in a statutory rent arbitration under s 13.

9.   **Application to Sheriff for Order on Arbiter to State a Case.**

SHERIFFDOM OF   AT

INITIAL WRIT

in causa

A B [design], recently tenant of the farm of   in the County
of   (Pursuer)

against

C D [design], the landlord of said farm, and E F [design arbiter] (Defenders)

The pursuer craves the court –
To ordain the defender, E F, as arbiter in the arbitration under the Agricultural Holdings (Scotland) Act 1949, between the pursuer and defender C D, to state a case for the opinion of the sheriff upon the following question [or questions] of law which has [have] arisen in the course of the said arbitration, namely [specify the question(s) of law referred to]; and in the meantime to interdict the said E F from pronouncing or issuing any award and for interim interdict and to find the defenders jointly and severally [or the defender E F or as the case may be] liable in expenses.

Condescendence

[Set out the facts of the case, insofar as relevant to the legal question, and particularly aver that the question (or questions) of law have arisen in the course of the arbitration.]

Plea-in-law

The said question[s] of law having arisen in the course of the arbitration, and the same being proper question[s] for the determination of the court, the defender, the said E F, ought to be ordained to state a case for the opinion of the sheriff thereon in terms of paragraph 20 of Schedule 7 to the Agricultural Holdings (Scotland) Act 1991.

299

10.   Application to Sheriff to
                                           have Arbiter removed.

SHERIFFDOM OF   AT

INITIAL WRIT

in causa

A B [design] (Pursuer)

against

C D [design] and E F [design] (Defenders)

The pursuer craves the court –
To remove the defender E F from the office of arbiter in the arbitration
between the pursuer and the defender C D; to find the pursuer entitled to
expenses against the said E F in any event and against the said C D in the
event of his defending this action.

Condescendence

[Here set out the facts in numbered paragraphs narrating the course of the
arbitration and setting forth in detail the misconduct alleged.]

Plea-in-law

The arbiter, having been guilty of misconduct as condescended on, should
be removed as craved.

11.   Common Law Submission
                                           between Outgoing and In-
                                           coming Tenants.

Submission

between

A B [design]

and

A C [design]

1. In this submission the following definitions shall apply:
   (a) 'The Act' means the Agricultural Holdings (Scotland) Act 1991.
   (b) 'The outgoing tenant' means the said A B.
   (c) 'The incoming tenant' means the said C D.
   (d) 'The landlord' means [name and design].
   (e) 'The farm' means [describe by reference to the lease].
   (f) 'The arbiters' mean [name and design].
   (g)'The lease' means [describe it].

2. Whereas the landlord undertook that he, or the incoming tenant, at the termination of the said lease, would take over from the outgoing tenant, on the terms therein set forth, various claims under the lease; further considering that the outgoing tenant's awaygoing takes place at [insert term or terms and date of the month and year], and that the incoming tenant will then enter as tenant of the said farm; Further considering that the outgoing tenant has agreed with the incoming tenant that the latter, in place of the landlord [where that is the case] should take over from the former at the termination of lease by arbitration the various items specified in the First Schedule annexed hereto; and to settle the claims of the outgoing tenant against the landlord for the improvements alleged to have been made by the outgoing tenant under Part III of Schedule 5 to the Act, as specified in Part III of the First Schedule hereto annexed, it being agreed that the landlord has received timeous and sufficient particulars of the claims to meet the requirements under the Act, and that the compensation for the said improvements shall be determined by arbitration, and shall be on the same basis as could have been claimed against the landlord under the Act; Further considering that the outgoing tenant has undertaken to pay to the incoming tenant, by agreement with the landlord, all sums [if any] due in respect of the claims competent to the landlord under the Act, and/or the lease for failure of the outgoing tenant to implement the conditions of his tenancy insofar as specified in the Second Schedule hereto annexed.

Therefore, the parties submit to the amicable decision, final sentence and decree arbitral to be pronounced by the arbiters, or in the case of their differing in opinion, then, insofar as they may differ, by an oversman to be named by them before entering on the business of the reference, to ascertain, fix and determine the sums payable by the outgoing and incoming tenants to each other, in respect of the several claims or matters embraced in the Schedules hereto annexed, with power to the arbiters and/or the oversman to call for and receive the claims of parties, to decide any question of ownership or other incidental question which it may be necessary to decide in order to enable the submission to be carried out, to hear parties, to take such probation, order such measurements and take such advice or assistance from solicitors, engineers, wrights, men of skill and others (without, however, being bound to do so), as they or he shall think proper, fix the time of payment of the sum found to be due under the submission, to prorogate the submission from time to time; and whatever the arbiters or oversman shall determine in the premises by any award or decree arbitral, interim or part or final, to be pronounced by them or him, both parties bind and oblige themselves, their executors and successors respectively to implement and fulfil to each other; Declaring (1) that the arbiters and/or oversman shall proceed with the reference and issue their awards in the manner and at the times usual in the district or otherwise as may be directed hereby; (2) that the death of either or both of the parties shall not be allowed to interrupt or terminate the reference, the representatives of any deceased party being bound to proceed and to implement the award or awards; (3) in the event of either arbiter dying during the subsistence of the reference the party who nominated him shall forthwith appoint a successor in the reference, and the oversman shall continue in office, and, in the event of the death of the oversman, a successor to him shall be appointed by the arbiters; (4) any interim or part award shall remain operative notwithstanding any change of arbiters or oversman, and any new arbiter or oversman shall give effect to the same in any subsequent interim or part final award in the same way as if such new arbiter or oversman had been in office from the outset; (5) the arbiters shall, if called on by either party, furnish along with any award, interim or final, full details showing in detail the manner in which each of the sums which may be found payable to or by either party to the other is arrived at including separate valuations of the various items in the Schedules; (6) in the event of the arbiters differing on certain matters but not on others, they may devolve on the oversman only the matter or matters of difference; (7) the fees and expenses of and incidental to the arbitration shall be borne by the parties equally (or as may be directed by the arbiters or oversman); (8) the arbiters or oversman shall have no power to state a case for the opinion of the Court of Session in terms of the Administration of Justice (Scotland) Act 1972; (9) and the parties consent to the registration hereof and of any prorogations or devolutions and interim or part or final decrees-arbitral to follow hereon for preservation and execution: IN WITNESS WHEREOF

FIRST SCHEDULE

PART I

Claims by the Outgoing Tenant
(1) Grass seeds sown with the awaygoing white crop.
(2) Dung made after sowing the last or awaygoing green crop.
(3) The turnip crop [if at consuming value, state the fact].
(4) The awaygoing white crop [with straw unless it is steelbow].
(5) Grain drying plant and bins.
(6) Sheep stock.

PART II

Further Claims by the Outgoing Tenant
The following buildings, fixtures, fences, etc [as the case may be], agreed to be taken over by the incoming tenant from the outgoing tenant [identify buildings, etc].

PART III

Further Claims by the Outgoing Tenant
Improvements to be valued on the same basis as under the Agricultural Holdings (Scotland) Act 1991. Specify the different improvements in terms of Schedule 5 to the Act of 1991, so far as applicable.

SECOND SCHEDULE

Claims as by the Landlord agreed by him to be credited to the Incoming Tenant
Claims for failure by the outgoing tenant to implement the conditions of the lease in respect of
[Dilapidations to farmhouse, steading, farm workers' cottages].
[Failure to leave the ditches and drains in tenantable order and not properly scoured and clear].
[Failure to leave the fences in reasonable repair].
[Failure to cultivate the farm and/or to leave the same conform to the rules

of good husbandry, and, in particular, to leave the farm in the prescribed rotation and/or in a clean and in a fertile condition, the following fields particularly being left in a dirty condition with wrack, knot-grass, thistles, and other noxious weeds].

[Refer to clauses of the lease so far as relevant.]

THIRD SCHEDULE

Any other question or claim connected with the outgoing or ingoing of the parties respectively that may with the consent of the parties in writing be remitted to the arbiters in the course of the arbitration.

12.   Award in Common Law
                                 Submission.

                           _____

We, E F and G H [design], the arbiters appointed by deed of submission dated   , between A B [design], the outgoing tenant of the farm of   in the Parish of   and County of   at the term of   , and C D [design], the incoming tenant of the said farm at the said term, whereby they submitted and referred to the decree-arbitral to be pronounced by us as arbiters mutually chosen or, in the event of difference, by an oversman to be named by us before entering on the submission, the claims therein referred to and specified in the Schedules thereto and hereto annexed; Having accepted the said submission (conform to acceptance dated   endorsed on the deed of submission), and having appointed an oversman (and having prorogated the submission conform to minute of prorogation dated   also endorsed on the submission); And having received and considered the respective claims of parties, together with the lease and all other documents produced, and inspected the farm, allowed and taken proof, and heard parties or their solicitors [issued proposed findings and considered the representations thereon] do hereby pronounce our final decree arbitral as follows, namely:

(In the First Place) We award and determine that the said C D shall pay to the said A B the following sums: (a) the sum of £   in respect of the matters specified in Part I of the First Schedule hereto annexed; (b) the sum of £   in respect of the claims specified in Part II of the First Schedule hereto annexed; and (c) the sum of £   in respect of the claims specified in Part III of the First Schedule hereto annexed;

(In the Second Place) We award and determine that the said A B shall pay to the said C D the sum of £   in respect of the matters specified in the Second Schedule hereto, with interest on the said sums due respectively to the said A B and C D at the rate of   per cent per annum from the date of payment hereinafter mentioned until paid; And we hereby fix the [date] as the date for payment of the foregoing sums; and

(In the Third Place) We direct that the said A B and C D shall be jointly and severally liable for our own and the oversman's [and the clerk's] fees and expenses, with equal liability and mutual relief *inter se*, and that otherwise the parties shall pay their own expenses [or as may be directed in terms of the submission]; [And we appoint the said deed of submission and this decree-arbitral to be recorded in the books of Council and Session, all in terms and to the effect of the consent to registration contained in the deed of submission]: IN WITNESS WHEREOF

Notes:
1 The Schedules will repeat the Schedules to the submission, the amount awarded in respect of the claims in each Schedule, or part of a Schedule, being stated, or 'nil' as the case may be, and the total being shown as due by each party.
2 Where, as is usual in the case of crops, any sums are awarded and paid on account, these will be stated and deducted from the sum finally awarded.
3 For particulars which require to be stated in sheep stock valuations see Schedules 9 and 10 to the 1991 Act.

13.

Minute of Acceptance by Arbiters and Nomination of Oversman and Clerk.

We, A B and C D, both designed in the foregoing minute of reference hereby accept office as arbiters and we appoint E F [design] to be oversman and G H [design] to be clerk [and legal assessor]: IN WITNESS WHEREOF

Note:
This minute is usually endorsed on the deed of submission.

14.

Minute of Acceptance by Oversman following thereon.

I, E F, designed in the foregoing minute, hereby accept office as oversman: IN WITNESS WHEREOF

Note:
To be endorsed on the minute of submission.

15.

Minute of Prorogation by Parties

We, the parties to the foregoing deed of submission hereby prorogate the same to the   day of   next to come and of new appoint the arbiters therein named and confer on them the whole powers therein mentioned, all in terms of the said deed of submission: And we agree and declare that the orders already pronounced by the said arbiters and the nomination of an oversman by them and the whole procedure which has already taken place under the submission shall remain effectual: IN WITNESS WHEREOF

Note:
This minute is usually endorsed on the deed of submission.

16.   Minute of Prorogation when Submission has expired.

We, A B and C D, the parties to the foregoing submission, considering that the arbiters therein named by minute dated   appointed E F [design] to be oversman and that the time for making an award has expired without any award having been made and that we have agreed to adopt and homologate the whole proceedings in the submission and to renew the submission to the said arbiters and to the said E F as oversman. Therefore we hereby adopt and homologate the whole proceedings in the submission and renew the submission in terms of the foregoing deed of submission to the said arbiters and to the said E F as oversman appointed by them whom failing before giving forth a final award to any other oversman whom the said arbiters may appoint and we hereby prorogate and extend the time within which they and he may determine the question thereby and hereby referred till the lapse of   from the last date of this minute: IN WITNESS WHEREOF

17.   Minute of Prorogation by Arbiters.

We, the arbiters appointed by the foregoing deed of submission, hereby prorogate the submission to [date]: IN WITNESS WHEREOF

Note:
Power of prorogation is generally conferred in deeds of submission. It is exercised by means of a minute of prorogation, which is usually endorsed on the submission. It does not require to be tested, but it is advisable that it should be.

D. ADDITIONAL FORMS

1.

Claim by Outgoing Tenant
against Incoming Tenant.

_____
Place................................
Date ....

To E F [design, incoming tenant]

AGRICULTURAL HOLDINGS (SCOTLAND) ACT 1991
HOLDING OF

I, C D, outgoing tenant of the above holding, have seen a letter dated addressed to you by A B [design] the landlord of the said farm consenting to the payment by you of compensation due to me for improvements under the Agricultural Holdings (Scotland) Act as the same shall be ascertained, failing agreement, by arbitration, but limited to the sum of £   , and having accepted as I hereby accept your obligation to make payment of the said compensation, now claim to be paid on quitting said farm at the term of Whitsunday, 19   , the following, namely:

The sum of £   being the value of the improvements effected by me on said farm by the application thereto of purchased artificial or other purchased manures all as detailed in the Schedule annexed [or otherwise as the case may be].

(Signed) A B [outgoing tenant]

2.

Abbreviated Form of Lease
incorporating provisions re-
quired by the Agricultural
Holdings (Scotland) Act
1991.

_____

LEASE

BETWEEN

A B [design], landlord of the farm of   in the Parish of
           and County of   (hereinafter called 'the
landlord').

AND

C D [design], tenant of the said farm (hereinafter called 'the tenant').

306

1. The landlord lets to the tenant excluding all assignees and sub-tenants, legal or voluntary, the farm of   in the Parish of   and County of   , extending to   acres or thereby, which measurement is not guaranteed, all as previously occupied by E F [design former tenant] and all as delineated and coloured red on the plan annexed and signed as relative hereto.

2. The lease will be for a period of fifteen years from and after Whitsunday (28th May 19   ), and separation of crop in that year, with mutual breaks at Whitsunday and separation of crop in the years 19   and 19   .

3. The rent will be £   per annum, payable at Whitsunday (28th May) and Martinmas (28th November) in each year, commencing the payment of the first half-year's rent at the term of Martinmas, 19   , and thereafter at Whitsunday and Martinmas each year, with 5 per cent interest on each term's payment until paid.

4. There are reserved to the landlord (a) all shootings and fishings on the subjects let, with the exclusive right of taking and killing game, subject to the tenant's right under the Ground Game (Scotland) Acts; (b) all woods, timber and plantations; (c) all minerals, sand, gravel and clay with right to work and remove the same, subject to payment of surface damages and an appropriate adjustment of rent as the same may be fixed by arbitration; (d) power to alter marches and excamb land with neighbouring proprietors; (e) power to resume at any time on giving two months' notice any part or parts of the farm for any purpose (other than agricultural or pastoral) including without prejudice to the foresaid generality, fencing, planting, the erection of houses or other buildings, working mineral quarries or sandpits, making ditches or drains, etc; (f) all existing wayleaves with power to grant further wayleaves, subject to payment for surface damages; (g) all common roads and means of access to other parts of the estate; (h) right to terminate the lease forthwith if the tenant becomes bankrupt or is sequestrated, grants a trust deed for behoof of his creditors or allows one-half year's rent to remain unpaid when the next half-year's rent falls due [or fails to implement other specific obligations].

5. The tenant shall be bound always to reside on the farm and to keep the same fully stocked and equipped with his own *bona fide* property. He shall cultivate and manage the farm according to the rules of good husbandry, shall not break up any permanent pasture (being the fields Nos   of the Ordnance Survey) and shall not add to or alter any buildings or the fixed equipment without the written authority of the landlord. At the termination of the lease, whether at its natural expiry or at a break, he shall leave the arable land in the following rotation, namely: [specify].

6. The landlord undertakes that, at the commencement of the tenancy or as soon as is reasonably possible thereafter, he will put the fixed equipment on the holding, as defined in section 85 of the Agricultural Holdings (Scotland) Act 1991, into a thorough state of repair and will provide such buildings and other fixed equipment as will enable the tenant (assuming he is reasonably skilled in husbandry) to maintain efficient production as respects both the kind of produce in use to be produced on the holding and the quantity thereof, and the landlord will further, during the tenancy, effect such replacement or renewal of the buildings or other fixed equipment as may be rendered necessary by natural decay or by fair wear and tear; [the tenant agrees that the landlord's undertaking to put the fixed equipment on

the holding in a thorough state of repair at the commencement of the tenancy has been duly implemented;] the liability of the tenant in relation to the maintenance of fixed equipment on the holding shall extend only to a liability to maintain the same on the holding in as good a state of repair (natural decay and fair wear and tear excepted) as it was in immediately after it was put in repair as aforesaid or, in the case of equipment provided, improved, replaced or renewed during the tenancy, as it was in immediately after it was so provided, improved, replaced or renewed. The march fences shall be the sole responsibility of the landlord [or otherwise as the case may be]. The tenant shall keep all hedges properly trimmed and cut and in good order, and shall paint all iron work at least every four years, during the currency of the lease. The tenant shall, free of charge, carry out all cartages required in connection with the repair, replacement or renewal of fixed equipment.

7. The landlord and tenant agree that a record of the condition of the fixed equipment [or a record of the fixed equipment on and of the cultivation of the holding] shall be made forthwith in compliance with the provisions of section 5 of the Agricultural Holdings (Scotland) Act 1991.

8. The landlord undertakes and binds himself and his executors and representatives (1) in the event of damage by fire to any building comprised in the holding to reinstate or replace the building if its reinstatement or replacement is required for the fulfilment of his responsibilities to manage the holding in accordance with the rules of good estate management; and (2) to insure to their full value all such buildings against damage by fire.

9. The tenant undertakes and binds himself and his executors and representatives (1) in the event of the destruction by fire of harvested crops grown on the holding for consumption thereon, to return to the holding the full equivalent manurial value of the crops destroyed, insofar as the return thereof is required for the fulfilment of his responsibilities to farm in accordance with the rules of good husbandry; and (2) to insure to their value all dead stock on the holding and all such harvested crops as aforesaid against damage by fire.

10. The tenant shall take over the waygoing tenant's white crop at mutual valuation and shall pay to the outgoing tenant the amount of his claim for improvements under Part III of Schedule 5 to the Agricultural Holdings (Scotland) Act 1991, limited to a maximum sum of £   . At his waygoing the tenant shall make over to the landlord or the incoming tenant the whole of the waygoing white crop at mutual valuation [or specify the basis of valuation].

11. The parties certify that this lease is not a lease which gives effect to an agreement for a lease as interpreted by the Inland Revenue in terms of the guidance note dated 30th June 1994, referring to section 240 of the Finance Act 1994.

12. Both parties consent to the registration of this lease for preservation and execution: IN WITNESS WHEREOF

Note:
This form includes the provision required by the Act but in almost all cases a fuller form will be appropriate. For a style of agricultural lease prepared by the Law Society of Scotland Styles Committee, see *Aspects of Agricultural Law* published by the Law Society of Scotland in 1981.

3.   Supplementary Agreement
   ·   in terms of s 5(3).

                                              _____

AGREEMENT
BETWEEN

A B [design], landlord of the holding of   in the Parish of
                 and County of   (hereinafter called 'the
landlord')

AND

C D [design], tenant of the said holding (hereinafter called 'the tenant').

WHEREAS by lease dated   the landlord let to the tenant the
holding of   in the Parish of   and County
of   and the parties have agreed that their obligations under
said lease be varied in manner underwritten THEREFORE they hereby agree as
follows, namely:

1. Notwithstanding the terms of said lease the tenant hereby accepts the
fixed equipment on the holding as being in a thorough state of repair and
sufficient in all respects to enable him to maintain efficient production and
further the tenant undertakes that he will during the tenancy effect at his own
expense on behalf of the landlord such replacement or renewal of the
buildings or other fixed equipment on the holding as may be rendered
necessary by natural decay or by fair wear and tear.

2. Except insofar as varied hereby, the parties confirm the terms of the said
lease: IN WITNESS WHEREOF

Note:
An agreement of this kind may be entered into immediately after the lease has been signed: see
Secretary of State for Scotland v Sinclair 1960 SLCR 10 and *Murray v Fane*, Perth Sh Ct, 22nd
April 1996.

FORM OF DOCKET TO CONFIRMATION FOR TRANSFER OF LEASE

I, A B, being by virtue of the within confirmation the executor on the estate
of the deceased C D so far as specified in confirmation (*or other document*),
hereby transfer to E F [design] as one of the persons entitled to succeed to
the said C D's intestate estate/or to claim legal rights/to claim the prior rights
of a surviving spouse from the estate of the deceased, the following item of
estate, that is to say the lease between W X as tenant and Y Z as landlord
dated [date] of All and Whole the farm of   , being number   of
the items of the estate specified in the said confirmation.

                                              (Signed) A B [executor]
                                              (Signed) [witness]

EXTRACTS FROM THE AGRICULTURE ACT 1986

(1986, c 49)

ARRANGEMENT OF SECTIONS

Compensation to tenants for milk quotas

14. Compensation to outgoing tenants for milk quota: Scotland.
16. Rent arbitrations: milk quotas, Scotland.

Schedule 2—Tenant's compensation for milk quota: Scotland.

An Act to make further provision relating to agriculture and agricultural and other food products, horticulture and the countryside; and for connected matters.   [25th July 1986]

14.[1]—Schedule 2 to this Act shall have effect in connection with the payment to outgoing tenants who are—

(a) tenants of agricultural holdings within the meaning of the Agricultural Holdings (Scotland) Act 1991;

(b) landholders within the meaning of section 2 of the Small Landholders (Scotland) Act 1911;

(c) statutory small tenants within the meaning of section 32(1) of that Act;

(d) crofters within the meaning of section 3(2) of the Crofters (Scotland) Act 1955,

of compensation in respect of milk quotas.

1 This section provides that milk quota compensation may be claimed by outgoing tenants in terms of Sch 2 to the Act, of agricultural holdings under the 1991 Act, landholders and small statutory tenants under the Small Landholders (Scotland) Act 1911 and crofters under the Crofters (Scotland) Act 1993.

16.[1]—(1) Paragraph 1 and the other provisions of Schedule 2 to this Act referred to therein shall have effect for the interpretation of this section, as they do in relation to that Schedule.

(2) This section applies where an arbiter or the Scottish Land Court is dealing with a reference under—

(a) section 6 of the 1886 Act;

(b) section 32(7) of the 1911 Act;

(c) section 13 of the 1991 Act; or

(d) section 5(3) of the 1955 Act,

(determination of rent) and the tenant has milk quota, including transferred quota[2] by virtue of a transaction the cost of which was borne wholly or partly by him, registered as his[3] in relation to a holding consisting of or including the tenancy.[4]

(3) Where this section applies, the arbiter or, as the case may be, the Land Court shall disregard any increase in the rental value of the tenancy which is due to—

(a) where the tenancy comprises the holding, the proportion of the transferred quota which reflects the proportion of the cost of the transaction borne by the tenant;

(b) where such transferred quota affects part only of the tenancy, that proportion of so much of the transferred quota as would fall to be apportioned to the tenancy under the [1994] Regulations on a change of occupation of the tenancy.[5]

(4) For the purposes of determining whether transferred quota has been acquired by virtue of a transaction the cost of which was borne wholly or partly by the tenant any payment by a tenant when he was granted a lease, or when a lease was assigned to him, shall be disregarded.[6]

(5) Paragraph 3 of Schedule 2 to this Act (in so far as it relates to transferred quota) shall apply in relation to the operation of this section as it applies in relation to the operation of that Schedule.[7]

(6) This section shall apply where paragraph 4 of Schedule 2 to this Act applies, and in any question between the original landlord and the head tenant, this section shall apply as if any transferred quota acquired by the sub-tenant by virtue of any transaction during the subsistence of the sub-lease had been acquired by the head tenant by virtue of that transaction.[8]

(7) Section 79 of the 1991 Act (Crown land) shall have effect in relation to this section as it does in relation to that Act.

1 This section makes provisions for dealing with the value of milk quota in rent reviews by arbitration or by the Scottish Land Court related to agricultural holdings under the 1991 Act, landholdings, statutory small tenancies and crofts, where the tenant has milk quota allocated to him or transferred to him by virtue of a transaction the cost of which was borne wholly or partly by him. In *Broadland Properties Estates v Mann* 1994 SLT (Land Ct) 7, the Land Court held that in determining the rent properly payable for the holding an allocated quota required to be taken into account. The court overturned the arbiter's decision that the allocated quota did not fall to be taken into account as it had only been brought to the holding by virtue of the tenant's improvements. Throughout the section there is reference to 'the tenant', where in reality the holding is often farmed through the medium of a partnership. It is not clear how the section should operate where it is the partnership in whose name the milk quota is registered or it is the partnership that has borne the cost of the transactions.

2 'Transferred quota'. Defined by Sch 2, para 2(2).

3 'Registered as his'. For 'registered', see Sch 2, para 1. If the milk quota is not registered in the name of the tenant (eg, registered in the name of a partnership, which is actually farming the lands), then the parties may not be able to invoke the provisions of this section: see Chap 15, p 119 'Qualifying interest to claim compensation' and note 2 to Sch 2, para 2.

4 If the tenancy comprises only part of the holding there may have to be an apportionment of the milk quota according to areas used for milk production, between the tenancy and the rest of the holding, at the date for the rent review for the purpose of the rent review.

5 The subsection is stated in the negative in that there are certain disregards, otherwise the milk quota allocated to the holding has to be taken into account. The arbiter (subsection (3)) is bound to disregard the increase in rental value of the tenancy, which is due to all or part of the milk quota transferred to the holding where all or part of the cost has been borne by the tenant. Provision is made to deal with proportions of transferred quota, where the landlord has borne part of the cost or where part of the quota affects only part of the holding. In the latter case the arbiter may have to do an apportionment of the milk quota for the purposes of the rent review, before he can carry out the rental arbitration. Any milk quota allocated to the holding in April 1984 or subsequently allocated as a hardship case or special quota, etc, for

which no payment was made, falls to be taken into account in assessing rent. Scammell and Densham *Law of Agricultural Holdings* (7th edn), p 99 suggest that where an excess of quota was allocated in 1984 because the then tenant was 'high farming' the excess may fall to be disregarded in a rent arbitration on the basis that in the open market a competent tenant would disregard the excess to which he could not normally produce. Where less than a reasonable amount of quota was allocated in 1984 because the tenant was dairying poorly, the arbiter can only have regard to the actual amount of quota allocated to the holding and cannot rent the holding on the basis of what should have been allocated. Where milk quota has been allocated to the holding only because the tenant's improvements have made dairy farming possible and in consequence milk quota allocated, the allocated milk quota still has to be taken into a counter-arbitration: see *Broadland Properties Estates Ltd v Mann* 1994 SLT (Land Ct) 7. Suspended quota will probably have to be apportioned between allocated quota and transferred quota in determining what quota falls to be taken into account for the rent review: cf *Broadland Properties Estates Ltd v Mann* Highland RN 449, 5th May 1995 (sequel to 1994 SLT (Land Ct) 7) for a consideration of the proper approach to the renting of allocated quota.

6 Subsection (4) provides that any payment made by the tenant to the landlord (ie a grassum) when granted the lease in respect of the milk quota is to be disregarded. This means that the tenant, who has had to pay the landlord the amount of the payment that the landlord had to make to the outgoing tenant as compensation for milk quota, is at a substantial disadvantage in rent arbitrations.

7 Successors in a lease, in terms of Sch 2, para 3, are entitled to have the milk quota element paid for by their predecessors disregarded as successors of the original tenants. In general they will be persons who will be entitled to payment on termination of the tenancy as successors.

8 The provisions are extended to a sub-tenant.

SCHEDULE 2

TENANTS' COMPENSATION FOR MILK QUOTA: SCOTLAND

Interpretation

1.—(1) In this Schedule, except where the context otherwise requires or provision is made to the contrary—

'allocated quota' has the meaning given in paragraph 2(1) below;[1]
'holding' has the same meaning as in the 1986 Regulations;[2]
'landlord' means—

      (*a*) in the case of an agricultural holding to which the 1991 Act applies, the landlord within the meaning of section 85(1) of that Act;

      (*b*) in the case of a croft within the meaning of the 1955 Act, the landlord within the meaning of section 37(1) of that Act;

      (*c*) in the case of a holding within the meaning of the 1911 Act to which the 1991 Act does not apply, the same as it means in the 1911 Act;

'milk quota' means—

      (*a*) in the case of a tenant registered in the direct sales register maintained under the 1986 Regulations, a direct sales quota within the meaning of those Regulations; and

      (*b*) in the case of a tenant registered in the wholesale register maintained under those Regulations, a wholesale quota within the meaning of those Regulations;[3]

'registered', in relation to milk quota, means—

      (*a*) in the case of direct sales quota within the meaning of the 1986 Regulations, registered in the direct sales register maintained under those Regulations; and

(b) in the case of a wholesale quota within the meaning of those Regulations, registered in a wholesale register maintained under those Regulations;

'relevant quota' has the meaning given in paragraph 2(2) below;

'standard quota' means standard quota as calculated under paragraph 6 below;

'tenancy' means, as the case may be—

(a) the agricultural holding, within the meaning of section 1 of the 1991 Act;

(b) the croft within the meaning of section 3(1) of the 1955 Act;

(c) the holding within the meaning of section 2 of the 1911 Act;

(d) the holding of a statutory small tenant under section 32 of the 1911 Act;

(e) any part of a tenancy which is treated as a separate entity for purposes of succession, assignation or sub-letting;

'tenant' means—

(a) in the case of an agricultural holding to which the 1991 Act applies, the tenant within the meaning of section 85(1) of that Act;

(b) in the case of a croft within the meaning of the 1955 Act, the crofter within the meaning of section 3(2) of that Act;

(c) in the case of a holding within the meaning of the 1911 Act to which the 1991 Act does not apply, the landholder within the meaning of section 2(2) of the 1911 Act;

'tenant's fraction' has the meaning given in paragraph 7 below;

'termination'[4] means the resumption of possession of the whole or part of the tenancy by the landlord by virtue of any enactment, rule of law or term of the lease which makes provision for removal of or renunciation by a tenant, or resumption of possession by a landlord, and in particular includes resumption of possession following—

(a) vacancy arising under section 11(5) of the 1955 Act;

(b) termination of a lease in pursuance of section 16(3) of the Succession (Scotland) Act 1964;

'transferred quota' has the meaning given in paragraph 2(2) below;

'the 1886 Act' means the Crofters Holdings (Scotland) Act 1886;

'the 1911 Act' means the Small Landholders (Scotland) Act 1911;

'the 1949 Act' means the Agricultural Holdings (Scotland) Act 1949;

'the [1993] Act' means the Crofters (Scotland) Act [1993];

'the 1986 Regulations' means the Dairy Produce Quotas Regulations 1986.[5]

(2) For the purposes of this Schedule, the designations of landlord and tenant shall continue to apply to the parties to any proceedings taken under or in pursuance of it until the conclusion of those proceedings.

---

1 Although allocated quota is defined in para 2(1)(a), a difficulty can arise in a claim for compensation as to whether or not suspended quota is part of 'allocated quota' or 'transferred quota'. Suspended quota probably falls to be disregarded, because 'milk quota' is defined by reference to the 1991 Regulations definition in para 2 of 'direct sales/wholesale quota', which is defined as the amount of milk which may be sold without becoming liable to pay a levy. If

suspended quota was delivered to a purchaser, a levy would be payable on that over-production, so suspended quota cannot be part of the 'direct sales/wholesale quota'. For the purposes of compensation, 'allocated quota' must mean the volume of quota attached to the farm at the date of termination of the lease, which the tenant may produce and deliver to the purchaser or sell by direct sales.

2 A milk quota 'holding' is defined by the 1994 Regulations, under reference to art 9(c) of Council Regulation (EEC) 3950/92, as 'all production units operated by the single producer' within the EEC. Often called a 'Euro holding', it consists of all the land occupied by the milk producer (art 9(d) of Council Regulation (EEC) 3950/92, 'producer means a natural or legal person or a group of natural or legal persons farming a holding within the geographical territory of the Community': cf *Stubbs v Hunt & Wrigley* [1992] 1 EGLR 17, where it was held that the partnership rather than the individual was the producer). It is not just the land used for dairying, even though the milk producer may hold different parts of the holding under different titles. The holding can consist of land owned by the producer, land leased by the producer including both agricultural tenancies under the 1991 Act, crofts and smallholdings and grazing lets over eight months in duration (Dairy Produce Quotas Regulations 1994, reg 7(6)(iii)).

3 See preceding note.

4 **'Termination'.** Note this definition is different from 'termination' as defined by s 85(1) of the 1991 Act. It relates to resumption of possession and includes resumption of only a part of the holding. Thus if a landlord resumes part of a holding under a resumption clause in the lease he will have to compensate the tenant for the milk quota relating to that area.

5 Now Dairy Produce Quotas Regulations 1994 (SI 1994/672), as amended by the Dairy Produce Quotas (Amendment) Regulations 1994 (SI 1994/2448, SI 1994/2919) and the Dairy Produce Quotas (Amendment) Regulations 1995 (SI 1995/254).

Tenant's right to compensation

2.—(1)[1] Subject to this Schedule, where, on the termination of the lease, the tenant has milk quota registered as his[2] in relation to a holding consisting of or including the tenancy, he shall be entitled, on quitting the tenancy[3] to obtain from his landlord a payment—

(a) if the tenant had milk quota allocated to him in relation to a holding consisting of or including the tenancy ('allocated quota'), in respect of so much of the relevant quota as consists of allocated quota and

(b) if the tenant had quota allocated to him as aforesaid or was in occupation of the tenancy as a tenant on 2nd April 1984 (whether or not under the lease which is terminating), in respect of so much of the relevant quota as consists of transferred quota by virtue of a transaction the cost of which was borne wholly or partly by him.[4]

(2) In sub-paragraph (1) above—

'the relevant quota' means—

(a) where the holding consists only of the tenancy, the milk quota registered in relation to the holding; and

(b) otherwise, such part of that milk quota as falls to be apportioned to the tenancy on the termination of the lease;[5]

'transferred quota' means milk quota transferred to the tenant by virtue of the transfer to him of the whole or part of a holding.

(3) A tenant shall not be entitled to more than one payment under this paragraph in respect of the same tenancy.

(4) Nothing in this paragraph shall prejudice the right of a tenant to claim any compensation to which he may be entitled under an agreement in writing, in lieu of any payment provided by this paragraph.[6]

1 The right arises 'on the termination of the lease' (defined in para 1) and should include termination for any reason including irritancy or the purchase of the holding or croft (under the Crofting Reform (Scotland) Act 1976) by the sitting tenant. See note 9 to s 85 of the 1991

Act. As 'termination' is defined in para 1(1) to include resumption of possession of part of the holding, the phrase must include termination of the lease as it relates to part of the holding, even if the lease continues as regards the remainder of the holding.

2 **'The tenant has milk quota registered as his'.** For 'registered', see para 1(1). Only the 'tenant' of the holding under the 1991 Act, a smallholding under the Small Landholders (Scotland) Act 1911 or a crofter under the Crofters (Scotland) Act 1993 is entitled to a payment; see definition of 'tenant' in para 1. Therefore a milk producer, who is the tenant of a holding, which is not an agricultural holding, smallholding or croft is not entitled to compensation; eg, a milk producer on a tenancy let 'during his continuance in any office, appointment or employment held under the landlord' (1991 Act, s 1(1)). Further persons occupying the land in some other capacity, who have had milk quota allocated or transferred to them, such as licensees, contractors, share-farmers, etc, will have no right to compensation for quota under this Schedule.

Note that the milk quota has to be registered 'as his' before the right to a payment arises. If the milk quota is registered to a person other than the tenant (eg, a farming partnership or limited company, which is not the tenant), then neither the tenant nor the registered producer of the milk quota have any right to a payment from the landlord. In Scammell and Densham, *Law of Agricultural Holdings* (7th edn), p 320, note 4, it is suggested that where the tenant is one of the partners of a partnership which is the registered producer, that the tenant is entitled to a percentage payment based on his percentage of the partnership. While this might be the position in England, where a partnership does not have a separate legal persona, in Scotland the tenant probably has no claim, because the partnership is a different legal persona: Partnership Act 1890, s 4(2). It may be possible to circumvent this difficulty if it can be proved that the partnership was the sub-tenant of the holding, in which case the sub-tenant can claim compensation under para 4.

There is a distinction made between paras 2(1)(a) and 2(1)(b) where para 2(1)(b) refers to a tenant in occupation. It might be argued that the now tenant under para 2(1)(a) qualifies if he had quota allocated to him in respect of the holding even if it was allocated in another capacity, such as licensee, because there is no occupation requirement in relation to the allocation, which there is in relation to a transfer of quota.

3 **'On quitting the tenancy'.** The entitlement arises on quitting the tenancy, rather than on the termination of the lease. The provisions must also relate to quitting part of the tenancy; see note 1 above. In para 11(3) provision is made for the position where a tenant continues in lawful occupation of the tenancy after the termination of the lease and the right to a payment arises only on his quitting the tenancy. See note 2 to s 34 in the 1991 Act.

4 Note that paras (a) and (b) are cumulative and give rise to a right to a payment for a share in the allocated quota and for any transferred quota, where the tenant has borne all or part of the cost of the transfer. Transferred quota is quota that has been lawfully transferred in terms of the appropriate Dairy Produce Quotas Regulations, applicable at the time of transfer. If a transfer arrangement was a sham transaction and no actual change of occupation took place, the landlord would be entitled to challenge that transfer in a claim for compensation under this schedule: *R v Ministry of Agriculture, Fisheries and Food, ex parte Cox* [1993] 1 EGLR 17. Paragraph (a) relates to quota 'allocated' to the tenant and will include quota allocated in 1984 and subsequently such as hardship quota or special quota. An occupier, who was a tenant on 2nd April 1984 will have had quota allocated to him, but a tenant who acquires a tenancy after that date is not a person who 'had quota allocated to him' unless he has had additional quota (eg, special quota) allocated to him at a later date. Therefore it is unlikely that a tenant of a tenancy, which is entered into after milk quota was first allocated in 1984, will have any right to a payment under para 2, unless he had quota allocated; eg, special quota.

Paragraph (b) is conditional upon a tenant either having milk quota allocated to him or upon him being in occupation of the tenancy on 2nd April 1984. It is only if he fulfils one or other of those two conditions, that a tenant will be entitled to a payment in respect of transferred quota the cost of which he has borne in whole or in part: see note 1 above.

Paragraph 3 makes provision for deemed allocations of quota, where there has been a succession to or assignation of a lease.

A tenant who has obtained a lease of a dairy farm with quota attached to it after April 1984, is not entitled to a payment under this paragraph, even if he has had to pay to the landlord a grassum for the milk quota; eg, the amount of compensation that the landlord has had to pay to the outgoing tenant under para 2. Further, he is not entitled to any compensation for quota transferred to the tenancy at his own cost, because he will not have qualified in regard to one or other of the conditions applicable to para 2(1)(b). A tenant in this position should stipulate

315

for a private compensation agreement in relation to the allocated milk quota and make provision in respect of any possible transferred quota, before taking on the tenancy, or he should sell his transferred quota before terminating the lease.

5 An arbiter appointed to determine compensation under this Schedule will not have power to apportion the milk quota between the tenancy holding and the rest of the holding. An apportionment will have to be agreed between the parties under the Dairy Produce Quotas Regulations 1994, reg 10(a) or made by an arbiter: see the Dairy Produce Quotas Regulations 1994, Sch 3, reg 10(b)(ii).

6 This sub-paragraph makes it competent to contract out of the provisions of the Schedule, provided that the agreement is in writing. The court cannot infer any agreement from actings where there is no writing: *Barbour v M'Douall* 1914 SC 844. The writing probably need not be probative, although there is no equivalent provision to s 78 of the 1991 Act.

Succession to lease of tenancy

3.[1]—(1) This paragraph applies where a person (the successor) has acquired right to the lease of the tenancy after 2nd April 1984—

(a) under section 16 of the Succession (Scotland) Act 1964;

(b) as a legatee, under section 11 of the 1991 Act or under section 16 of the 1886 Act;

(c) under a bequest of a croft under section 10 of the 1955 Act, or following nomination under section 11 of that Act;

(d) under a lawful assignation of the lease,

and the person whom he succeeded or, as the case may be, who assigned the lease to him is described in this paragraph as his 'predecessor'.

(2) Where this paragraph applies—

(a) any milk quota allocated or transferred to the predecessor (or treated as having been allocated or transferred to him) in respect of the tenancy shall be treated as if it had been allocated or transferred to his successor;

(b) where, under (a) above, milk quota is treated as having been transferred to the successor, he shall be treated as if he had paid so much of the cost of the transaction by virtue of which the milk quota was transferred as his predecessor bore (or is treated as having borne).

1 This paragraph makes provisions for the 'successor' in a lease, who has acquired the lease either on the death of the tenant or by valid assignation to enjoy and succeed to the rights of his 'predecessor' to obtain the payment from the landlord on termination of the tenancy. Where there is likely to be a long-continuing succession under this paragraph the parties would be well advised to have the standard quota and tenant's fraction determined under para 10 while matters are reasonably fresh in the parties' minds.

Where parties are considering an assignation of a lease, consideration will have to be given as to the compensation that the assignee should give to the assignor, bearing in mind that the assignee is not entitled to have his payment taken into account in rent reviews so as to make originally allocated quota into transferred quota: see note 6 to s 16.

Sub-tenants

4.[1] In the case of a tenancy which is sub-let, if the sub-tenant quits the tenancy—

(a) paragraph 2 above shall apply so as to entitle the sub-tenant to obtain payment from the head tenant, and for that purpose, references to the landlord and the tenant in this Schedule shall be respectively construed as references to the head tenant and the sub-tenant; and

(b) for the purposes of the application of paragraph 2 above as between the original landlord and the head tenant—

(i) the head tenant shall be deemed to have had the relevant quota allocated to him, and to have been in occupation of the tenancy as a tenant on 2nd April 1984; and

(ii) if the head tenant does not take up occupation of the tenancy when the sub-tenant quits, the head tenant shall be treated as if he had quitted the tenancy when the sub-tenant quitted it.

1 This paragraph makes provision for payment to be made to a sub-tenant by the head-tenant and gives the head-tenant, who may not have had any milk quota allocated to him, a right to compensation in his turn. The paragraph will be of limited application as sub-tenancies on agricultural holdings are a rarity, unless perhaps interposed lease in terms of s 17 of the Land Tenure Reform (Scotland) Act 1974.

Calculation of payment

5.[1]—(1) The amount of the payment to which a tenant is entitled under paragraph 2 above on the termination of the lease shall be determined in accordance with this paragraph.

(2) The amount of the payment in respect of allocated quota shall be equal to the value of—

(a) where the allocated quota exceeds the standard quota for the tenancy—

(i) the tenant's fraction of so much of the allocated quota as does not exceed the standard quota; together with

(ii) the amount of the excess;

(b) where the allocated quota is equal to the standard quota, the tenant's fraction of the allocated quota;

(c) where the allocated quota is less than the standard quota, such proportion of the tenant's fraction of the allocated quota as the allocated quota bears to the standard quota.

(3) The amount of the payment in respect of transferred quota shall be equal to the value of—

(a) where the tenant bore the whole of the cost of the transaction by virtue of which the transferred quota was transferred to him, the transferred quota; and

(b) where the tenant bore only part of that cost, the corresponding part of the transferred quota.

1 This paragraph defines the method by which the payment will be determined. The tenant is entitled to compensation for: (1) the tenant's fraction (defined in para 7) of so much of the allocated quota, ie the quota actually allocated to the holding (see note 1 to para 1 as to the amount of quota applying under the definition 'allocated quota') as does not exceed the standard quota, or where the allocated quota is less than the standard quota a proportion calculated in terms of sub-para (2)(c). Standard quota, which is the hypothetical quota, which should have been reasonably allocated to a holding, is calculated in terms of para 6; (2) as the amount of allocated quota in excess of the standard quota, if there is any excess; and (3) the value of the transferred quota if the tenant bore the whole cost, or a proportion of the value of the transferred quota, where he only bore part of the cost of transfer. Note that it is the value of the transferred quota at the time of the termination of the tenancy and not the value of the quota at the date at which it was transferred.

Standard quota

6.—(1) Subject to this paragraph, the 'standard quota' for any tenancy for the purposes of this Schedule shall be calculated by multiplying the relevant number of hectares by the standard yield per hectare.[1]

(2) Where by virtue of the quality of the land in question or of climatic conditions in the area the amount of milk which could reasonably be expected to have been produced from one hectare of the tenancy during the relevant period ('the reasonable amount') is greater or less than the average yield per hectare then sub-paragraph (1) above shall not apply and the standard quota shall be calculated by multiplying the relevant number of hectares by such proportion of the standard yield per hectare as the reasonable amount bears to the average yield per hectare; and the Secretary of State shall by order prescribe the amount of milk to be taken as the average yield per hectare for the purposes of this sub-paragraph.[2]

(3) Where the relevant quota includes milk quota allocated in pursuance of an award of quota made by the Dairy Produce Quota Tribunal for Scotland which has not been allocated in full, the standard quota shall be reduced by the amount by which the milk quota allocated in pursuance of the award falls short of the amount awarded (or, in the case where only part of the milk quota allocated in pursuance of the award is included in the relevant quota, by the corresponding proportion of that shortfall.[3]

(4) In sub-paragraph (3) above the references to milk quota allocated in pursuance of an award of quota include references to quota allocated by virtue of the amount awarded not originally having been allocated in full.

(5) For the purposes of this paragraph—
(a) 'the relevant number of hectares'[4] means the average number of hectares of the tenancy used during the relevant period for the feeding of dairy cows kept on the tenancy or, if different, the average number of hectares of the tenancy which could reasonably be expected to have been so used (having regard to the number of grazing animals other than dairy cows kept on the tenancy during that period); and
(b) 'the standard yield per hectare' means such number of litres as the Secretary of State may from time to time by order prescribe for the purposes of this sub-paragraph.
(6) In this and in paragraph 7 below—
(a) references to the area of a tenancy used for the feeding of dairy cows kept on the tenancy do not include references to land used for growing cereal crops for feeding to dairy cows in the form of loose grain; and[5]
(b) 'dairy cows' means milking cows and calved heifers.[6]
(7) An order under this paragraph may make different provision for different cases.
(8) The powers to make an order under this paragraph shall be exercisable by statutory instrument and any statutory instrument containing such an order shall be subject to annulment in pursuance of a resolution of either House of Parliament.

---

1 This sub-paragraph introduces two crucial terms: (1) 'relevant number of hectares'; and (2) 'standard yield'. The standard yield is prescribed by the Milk Quota (Calculation of Standard Quota) (Scotland) Order 1986 (SI 1986/1475), as amended from time to time in terms of sub-para (5)(b). In any calculation it is important to use the amendment applicable at the time of the termination of the tenancy and to determine which classification of land applies to the farm. There was some regrading of land in 1984/85. The 1986 Order at para 2 refers to the expressions 'disadvantaged land' etc to mean 'land which has been determined to be ...'; ie determined before the SI came into force. It would appear that the classification applicable as at 25th September 1986 is the classification that should be used, rather than the classification at April 1984.
 The amendments are: Milk Quota (Calculation of Standard Quota) (Scotland) Order 1986

(SI 1986/1475), amended by SI 1987/870, SI 1988/714, SI 1990/943, SI 1991/2309 and SI 1992/1152.

2 This sub-paragraph introduces a variable which can substantially affect the quantum of the tenant's claim.

'By virtue of' means 'by reason of' or 'because of'; *Surrey County Council v Carson* [1992] 1 EGLR 26.

Where 'the quality of land' *or* (and note it is 'or' and not both criteria) the 'climatic conditions' have an effect on the amount of milk, which could reasonably be expected to be produced, then the standard yield is recalculated in terms of the sub-paragraph and the prescribed standard yield is not used. These are inherent conditions of land and climate and have nothing to do with the quality of the farming by the tenant or the improvements that he may or may not have made to the land.

The test relates to the greater or lesser amount of milk which could reasonably have been produced during the relevant period (defined by para 8) than the average yield, because of the quality of the land or the climatic conditions. The average yield, which is prescribed by the same SIs, which define standard yield, is different from the standard yield. The onus will be on the party invoking this sub-paragraph to prove that the quality of the land or the climatic conditions have the effect of producing a greater or lesser quantity of milk than the average yield.

It is a matter of fact for determination by the arbiter whether the matter has been proved. If either of the criteria set out in the sub-paragraph can be established, then the arbiter is bound to do the calculation in terms of the sub-paragraph: *Surrey County Council v Carson*.

The English equivalent of this sub-paragraph (Sch 1, para 6(2)) was considered in *Grounds v AG of the Duchy of Lancaster* [1989] 1 EGLR 6, where it was said that the paragraph means 'if, by reason of the quality or the land or the particular climatic conditions, the land is more than averagely productive for dairy farming purposes and if as a result the amount of milk which could reasonably be expected to have been produced from one hectare during the relevant period ... was greater than the Minister prescribes as being the average yield', then the standard yield is to be recalculated. In that case the tenant had argued that the calculation of what milk could reasonably be produced from one hectare should be calculated by reference to the milk yield from grass and forage and should exclude concentrates. The Court of Appeal held that the arbiter was right to take into account the food-stuffs, which a reasonably successful and skilful farmer in the locality would have fed his cows at the time, in determining the amount of milk which could reasonably be produced from one hectare.

3 This sub-paragraph and sub-para (4) deal with the situation where the milk quota allocated falls short of the amount of quota awarded by a Dairy Produce Quota Tribunal.

4 **'Relevant number of hectares'** is the average number used, so if fields are used in part for feeding dairy cows (see note 6 below) and in part for feeding non-dairy cows, then over the whole holding the arbiter has to arrive at an average number of hectares used over the relevant period.

The test is in the alternative and if the alternative test is different from the first test, then the alternative has to be applied. The reason for this is to allow for exceptional uses in the base year, which might otherwise distort the year used. The relevant number of hectares falls to be determined during the relevant period (ie the year on which the milk quota allocation was based) and not the year in which the compensation is claimed. The 'relevant number of hectares' is either the average number used for feeding dairy cows 'or, if different' the average number of hectares, which could reasonably be expected to have been used. The area relates to the area used for 'feeding' dairy cows, which would include areas used for hay and silage making (but not land used for growing cereal crops for feeding – see note 5 below) and is not just the area used for grazing dairy cows. The reference to the number of grazing animals other than dairy cows suggests that regard should be had to the actual grazing system used, so that if other grazing animals are grazed, which makes the number of hectares used for dairy cows different from the number which could reasonably be used, then the second test is not applied. Scammell and Densham, *Law of Agricultural Holdings* (7th edn), p 324, note 4, suggests that this distinction is arbitrary.

In any arbitration, therefore, either parties will have to accept that the second test should be applied, or they will have to show that the first test is the same as the second test or, if different, it is only different because of other grazing animals.

5 The exclusion from areas used for feeding dairy cows of land used for growing cereal crops for feeding to dairy cows in the form of loose grain, means that definition of that area is narrower than the definition used in the apportionment of milk quota for holding under para 2 of Sch 3 to the Dairy Produce Quotas Regulations 1994, which relates to 'areas used for milk

production' as defined in *Puncknowle Farms v Kane* [1985] 3 All ER 790 at p 749. The effect of this distinction may be that on an apportionment, milk quota might be allocated to the tenancy part of the holding, but no compensation will be due as the area was used for dairy young stock alone and not milk production. Note that the only area excluded is the area used for growing cereal, which is fed as loose grain. It does not exclude areas used for growing grain, which is then turned into concentrates for feeding to the dairy cows.

6 The definition of 'dairy cows' which is different from the definition in the English provisions (Sch 1, para 6(5)(b)) where dairy cows are defined as 'cows kept for milk production (other than uncalved heifers)', probably includes all dairy cows, whether lactating or dry, which are kept in the milk production cycle. It can be argued, although this is improbable, that the difference between the two definitions is intentional and that the Scottish definition excludes dry cows, even if in the milk production cycle. The definition excludes bulls, followers and calves kept for sale, etc.

Tenant's fraction

7.—(1) For the purposes of this Schedule 'the tenant's fraction'[1] means the fraction of which—

(a) the numerator is the annual rental value at the end of the relevant period of the tenant's dairy improvements and fixed equipment; and[2]

(b) the denominator is the sum of that value and such part of the rent payable by the tenant in respect of the relevant period as is attributable to the land used in that period for the feeding, accommodation or milking of dairy cows kept on the tenancy.[3]

(2) For the purposes of sub-paragraph (1)(a) above, in the case of an agricultural holding within the meaning of the 1991 Act, the annual rental value of the tenant's dairy improvements and fixed equipment shall be taken to be the amount which would be disregarded, on a reference to arbitration made in respect of the tenancy under section 13 of the 1991 Act (variation of rent), as being—

(a) an increase in annual rental value due to dairy improvements at the tenant's expense (in terms of subsection (2)(a) of that section); or

(b) the value of tenant's fixed equipment and therefore not relevant to the fixing of rent under that section,

so far as that amount is attributable to tenant's dairy improvements and fixed equipment which are relevant to the feeding, accommodation or milking of dairy cows kept on the tenancy.[4]

(3) Where—

(a) the relevant period is less than or greater than 12 months; or

(b) rent was payable by the tenant in respect of only part of the relevant period,

the average rent payable in respect of one month in the relevant period or, as the case may be, in that part shall be determined and the rent referred to in sub-paragraph (1)(b) above shall be taken to be the corresponding annual amount.

(4) For the purposes of this paragraph—

(a) 'dairy improvement'—

(i) in the case of an agricultural holding or a statutory small tenancy, means a 'new improvement' or an 'old improvement' within the meaning of section 85 of the 1991 Act;

(ii) in the case of a croft, means a 'permanent improvement' within the meaning of section 37 of the 1955 Act;

(iii) in the case of a holding under the 1911 Act to which the 1991

Act does not apply, means a 'permanent improvement' within the meaning of section 34 of the 1886 Act,

so far as relevant to the feeding, accommodation or milking of dairy cows kept on the tenancy;

(b) 'fixed equipment' means fixed equipment, within the meaning of section 85 of the 1991 Act, so far as relevant to the feeding, accommodation or milking of dairy cows kept on the tenancy;

(c) all dairy improvements and fixed equipment provided by the tenant shall be taken into account for the purposes of sub-paragraph (1)(a) above, except for such improvements and fixed equipment in respect of which he has, before the end of the relevant period, received full compensation directly related to their value.[5]

(5) For the purposes of this paragraph—

(a) any allowance made or benefit given by the landlord after the end of the relevant period in consideration of the execution of dairy improvements or fixed equipment wholly or partly at the expense of the tenant shall be disregarded;

(b) any compensation received by the tenant after the end of the relevant period in respect of any dairy improvement or fixed equipment shall be disregarded; and

(c) where paragraph 3 above applies, dairy improvements or fixed equipment which would be regarded as tenant's dairy improvements or fixed equipment on the termination of a former tenant's lease (if he were entitled to a payment under this Schedule in respect of the land) shall be regarded as the new tenant's dairy improvements or fixed equipment.

---

1 The fraction can be expressed as:

$$\frac{\text{Numerator}}{\text{Numerator} + \text{Rent}} \times 100 = \text{xx.xx} \%$$

This percentage is then taken as a percentage of the standard quota to give the tenant's fraction of the standard quota, for which the tenant is entitled to compensation. The tenant is also entitled to compensation for any allocated quota in excess of the standard quota, the 'excess'.

2 The numerator is the annual rental value of the tenant's dairy improvements (defined in sub-para (4)(a)) which are to be determined at the end of the relevant period (para 8), using the criteria set out in sub-para (2) for an agricultural holding. The rental value is 'historic'; ie at the end of the relevant period. Although no statutory procedure is provided for calculating the annual rental value of dairy improvements in relation to smallholdings under the 1911 Act or crofts, hypothetically the same criteria might be an appropriate way to reach the same value. If good records are not kept, it might be difficult to reach a proper valuation of the improvements at a date which could be many years in the past. The rental value is basically the amount of rent that those dairy improvements would add to the rent of the farm if the farm was rented with those improvements as landlord's fixtures and improvements. A way in which to deal with this value is to take the actual rent of the farm and then to lead evidence of the rent the farm would have achieved if those were the landlord's fixtures and improvements.

As the sub-paragraph relates to the annual rental value of the tenant's dairy improvements at the end of the relevant period, and the rest of the Schedule deals with compensation on a historic basis, the dairy improvements affected after the end of the relevant period should be excluded from the calculation.

In terms of sub-para (2) the rental amount relates to the tenant's dairy improvements and fixed equipment so far as relevant to the feeding, accommodation or milking of dairy cows kept on the tenancy. Therefore if a farmer has built a large shed, which is used in part for accommodation of dairy cows and in part for accommodation of calves for sale, then there will have to be an apportionment of the rental value of that dairy improvement between the proportion used for dairy cows and the proportion used for other purposes.

3 The denominator is the sum of the annual rental value of the tenant's dairy improvements (the numerator) and 'such part of the rent' payable during the relevant period in relation to land used for 'feeding, accommodation or milking of dairy cows'. The area used for feeding in this paragraph also excludes the area used for growing grain for feeding loose to the dairy cows: see note 5 to para 6. The area to which the rental relates will be different from the 'relevant number of hectares' determined in para 6(5)(a), because that area related only to the area used for 'feeding', although it will include that area. If there was a rent increase during the relevant period, the rent will have to be apportioned over the year.

4 This sub-paragraph applies only to agricultural holdings, but hypothetically the same criteria might be relevant in working out the annual rental value of a tenant's improvements on a croft or smallholding.

See note 2 above regarding apportionment of the value of an improvement used in part for dairying.

5 Dairy improvements and fixtures are not taken into account if the tenant has received full compensation directly related to their value, before the end of the relevant period. This should not exclude improvements whose value has been written off over a number of years under an agreement with the landlord, for which he might not have to pay compensation under the 1991 Act, because they are not improvements for which he has received 'full compensation directly related to their value'. It would not include improvements, where there has been a rent reduction to compensate for the cost of the improvements: see sub-para (5)(a). Where the tenant is compensated for an improvement after the end of the relevant period, that improvement still has to be taken into account in a milk quota compensation calculation: sub-para (5)(b). Note it is 'compensation received', which implies that compensation agreed but not paid by the end of the relevant period falls to be disregarded.

Relevant period

8. In this Schedule 'the relevant period' means—

(*a*) the period in relation to which the allocated quota was determined; or

(*b*) where it was determined in relation to more than one period, the period in relation to which the majority was determined or, if equal amounts were determined in relation to different periods, the later of those periods.[1]

1 This paragraph defines the 'relevant period', which is the period in relation to which the allocated quota was determined. For those holdings allocated quota to take effect from 2nd April 1984, the relevant period is usually the calendar year 1983. Where special quota has been allocated the relevant period may well be different. Sub-paragraph (b) deals with the situation where quota was allocated in relation to different periods.

Valuation of milk quota

9. The value of milk quota to be taken into account for the purposes of paragraph 5 above is the value of the milk quota at the time of the termination of the lease and in determining that value there shall be taken into account such evidence as is available including evidence as to the sums being paid for interests in land—

(*a*) in cases where milk quota is registered in relation to land; and

(*b*) in cases where no milk quota is so registered.[1]

1 The value of the milk quota at the termination of the tenancy is a matter for an expert, who should be instructed at an early stage. Unless values are agreed, value has to be proved by competent evidence. If a particular sale or lease is to be relied upon, then witnesses will be required to speak to the sale and the values achieved. Although the paragraph provides that such evidence as is available shall be taken into account including evidence of the sums being paid for interests in land where milk quota is and is not registered, such evidence is generally

not available. More readily available is evidence of the value at which milk quota was being sold or transferred by way of a grazings lease under reg 7 of the Dairy Produce Quotas Regulations 1994, at about the date of the termination of lease. Caution is required in dealing with such evidence, because the price paid for a litre of milk quota depends on a number of factors, including the amount of unused quota left for the year in which the quota was purchased and the butter fat content in relation to the quota. Thus a price of 35p per litre on a neighbouring farm may not be applicable to the value of the milk quota on the farm in question, where for example the neighbouring farm had delivered only half its quota to date of sale, whereas the farm in question had delivered three-quarters of its quota at the same date. The value of the latter quota would be less than the former.

In *Carson v Cornwall County Council* [1993] 1 EGLR 21, the arbiter valued quota on the basis of a capitalisation over ten years of the rental value of leasing quota for a year or part year. He rejected a valuation based on the sale value of quota. This approach was upheld on appeal as the proper approach to valuation, because the tenant, it was said, was being compensated for the value by which he has built up the landlord's holding; ie the value by which the landlord is better off. It is questionable whether this is the correct approach as the compensation scheme is designed as an alternative to providing the tenant with quota that he can take with him on quitting the holding: cf Council Regulation (EEC) 590/85. It can be argued that the compensation is designed so that the tenant can buy quota for a new holding, in lieu of taking quota with him. On such an approach, the tenant would require to be compensated at open market value for purchasing quota on a short lease transfer.

Determination of standard quota and tenant's fraction before end of lease

10.—(1) Where it appears that on the termination of a lease, the tenant may be entitled to a payment under paragraph 2 above, the landlord or tenant may at any time before the termination of the lease by notice in writing served on the other demand that the determination of the standard quota for the land or the tenant's fraction shall be referred—

(a) in the case of an agricultural holding within the meaning of the 1991 Act to arbitration under that Act or, under section 60(2) of that Act, to the Scottish Land Court;

(b) in any other case, to the Scottish Land Court, for determination by that court,

and where (a) above applies, section 60 (or, where the circumstances require, sections 64 and 80) of the 1991 Act shall apply, as if the matters mentioned in sub-paragraph (1) above were required by that Act to be determined by arbitration.

(2) On a reference under this paragraph the arbiter or, as the case may be, the Scottish Land Court shall determine the standard quota for the land or, as the case may be, the tenant's fraction (as nearly as is practicable at the end of the relevant period).[1]

1 A demand for a reference under this paragraph must be made in writing and the determination be referred either to arbitration under the 1991 Act or to the Scottish Land Court. As to valid methods of service, see para 14.

As the determination of the standard quota and the tenant's fraction are the issues which involve the most difficulty under this Schedule, the Act makes provision for determining those factors, at any time before the lease is terminated. Once they are determined it should be possible to negotiate a settlement of the claim with the landlord.

As the 'relevant period', on which the claim to compensation depends, slips further into the past and evidence is harder to come by, it becomes more and more important that parties determine these two variables now, rather than at the termination of a tenancy, which might be years or generations into the future.

Paragraph 11(6) provides that the arbiter or Land Court has to award payment in terms of the agreement or findings under this paragraph unless (para 11(7)) the circumstances are materially different at the time of termination of the lease from those at the time of the determination under this paragraph.

Settlement of tenant's claim on termination of lease

11.—(1) Subject to this paragraph, any claim arising under paragraph 2 above shall be determined—

(*a*) in the case of an agricultural holding within the meaning of the 1991 Act by arbitration under that Act or, under section 60(2) of that Act, by the Scottish Land Court;

(*b*) in any other case, by the Scottish Land Court,

and no such claim shall be enforceable unless before the expiry of the period of 2 months from the termination of the lease the tenant has served notice in writing on the landlord of his intention to make the claim, specifying the nature of the claim.[1]

(2) The landlord and tenant may within the period of 8 months from the termination of the lease by agreement in writing settle the claim but where the claim has not been settled during that period it shall be determined as provided in sub-paragraph (1) above.[2]

(3) Where a tenant lawfully remains in occupation of part of the tenancy after the termination of the lease, the references in sub-paragraphs (1) and (2) above to the termination of the lease shall be construed as references to the termination of the occupation.[3]

(4) In the case of an arbitration under this paragraph, section 60(1) (or, where the circumstances require, sections 64 and 80) of the 1991 Act (arbitrations) shall apply as if the requirements of this paragraph were requirements of that Act, but paragraph 14 of Schedule 7 to that Act (arbitration awards to fix day for payment not later than one month after award) shall have effect for the purposes of this paragraph with the substitution for the words 'one month' of the words 'three months'.[4]

(5) In the case of an arbitration under this paragraph, section 50 of the 1991 Act (determination of claims for compensation where landlord's interest is divided) shall apply, where the circumstances require, as if compensation payable under paragraph 2 above were compensation payable under that Act.

(6) Where—

(*a*) before the termination of the lease of any land the landlord and tenant have agreed in writing the amount of the standard quota for the land or the tenant's fraction or the value of milk quota which is to be used for the purpose of calculating the payment to which the tenant will be entitled under this Schedule on the termination of the lease; or

(*b*) the standard quota or the tenant's fraction has been determined by arbitration in pursuance of paragraph 10 above,

the arbiter or, as the case may be, the Scottish Land Court in determining the claim under this paragraph shall, subject to sub-paragraph (7) below, award payment in accordance with that agreement or determination.[5]

(7) Where it appears to the arbiter or, as the case may be, the Scottish Land Court that any circumstances relevant to the agreement or determination mentioned in sub-paragraph (6) above were materially different at the time of the termination of the lease from those at the time the agreement or determination was made, he shall disregard so much of the agreement or

determination as appears to him to be affected by the change in circumstances.[5]

1 A claim for compensation has to be determined by arbitration or by the Scottish Land Court. The appointment of the arbiter has to be applied for within the time-limits of the 1991 Act and sub-paras (1) and (2): see below.

    The tenant has to serve notice in writing on the landlord within two months of the termination of the lease of his intention to make his claim specifying the nature of the claim: see *Walker v Crocker* [1992] 1 EGLR 29 for a consideration of what is sufficient specification. Failure to serve notice in writing within the time-limit renders the claim unenforceable. A claim may be competently made before the termination date (*Lady Hallinan v Jones & Jones* [1985] CLY 38), but probably only where a valid notice of intention to quit has been given. To avoid difficulties, the claim should be specified in fair detail noting that the claim is for the tenant's fraction, excess and transferred quota, as appropriate: see *Walker v Crocker* for a consideration of what is minimum for sufficient specification. Note that the two months runs from the date of termination of occupancy, where this has been lawfully continued after the termination of the lease and is then not the date of termination of the lease: sub-para (3). As to valid methods of service see para 14.

2 The landlord and the tenant have eight months from the termination of the lease, or termination of lawful occupation (see note 3 below) (and note that this is not eight months after service of the notice under sub-para (1)) during which time they may reach agreement in writing to settle the claim. As the sub-section uses 'may' it means that the parties do not have to wait out the eight months before invoking arbitration, if it is clear that they cannot reach agreement. The settlement has to be reached 'during that period', which means that arbitration has to be invoked before the end of the eight-month period, where agreement has not been reached, otherwise the application for arbitration will be time-barred.

    As no interest is payable on the sum until decree arbitral it is in the tenant's interest to invoke arbitration as soon as possible if the landlord is dilatory in reaching agreement.

3 The time-limits in sub-paras (1) and (2) run from the termination of the lease or from the date of termination of lawful occupation, if the landlord and tenant agreed that occupation of the holding should continue beyond the termination of the lease.

4 This sub-paragraph provides that the provisions for arbitration under ss 60(1), 64 and 80 of the 1991 Act shall apply to arbitrations under this Schedule, except that the time for payment fixed in para 14 of Sch 7 to the 1991 Act is extended to three months.

5 See note 1 to para 10.

Enforcement

12. Section 69 of the 1949 Act (enforcement) and section 70 of that Act (power of tenant to obtain charge on holding) shall apply to any sum which becomes due to a tenant by virtue of this Schedule as they apply to the sums mentioned in those sections.[1]

1 The enforcement provisions of ss 65 and 75(1), (2), (4), (6) of the 1991 Act are incorporated by this paragraph into this Schedule.

Powers of limited owners

13. Whatever his interest in the tenancy, the landlord may, for the purposes of this Schedule, do or have done to him anything which might be so done if he were absolute owner of the tenancy.[1]

1 This paragraph makes provision for the Schedule to apply to limited owners such as liferenters: see note 1 to s 74 of the 1991 Act. There is no provision equivalent to s 75(3) of the 1991 Act to allow the limited owner to charge the holding in respect of any payment he is required to make for recovery from the absolute owner.

Notices

14.—(1) Any notice or other document required or authorised by this Schedule to be served on any person shall be duly served if it is delivered to him, or left at his proper address, or sent to him by post in a recorded delivery letter or a registered letter.

(2) In the case of an incorporated company or body, any such document shall be duly served if served on the secretary or clerk of the company or body.

(3) Any such document to be served by or on a landlord or tenant shall be duly served if served by or on any agent of the landlord or tenant.

(4) For the purposes of this paragraph and of section 7 of the Interpretation Act 1978, the proper address of a person is—

(a) in the case of a secretary or clerk to a company or body, that of the registered or principal office of the company or body;

(b) in any other case, the person's last known address.

(5) Unless and until the tenant receives notice of a change of landlord, any document served by him on the person previously known to him as landlord shall be deemed to be duly served on the landlord under the tenancy.[1]

1 This paragraph, which echoes s 84 of the 1991 Act, provides for service of notices: see note thereto. A notice is duly served if it is delivered to the person (ie personally handed to him), left at the person's proper address, or posted by recorded or registered letter. Service by ordinary post is competent but may be difficult to prove: *Sharpley v Manby* [1942] 1 KB 217. Provision is made for service on incorporated companies and other bodies, by service on the Secretary or Clerk. Sub-paragraph (4) defines 'proper address', which is in the case of a company defined as the registered or principal office of the company or body. Sub-paragraph (5) provides for service on the last-known landlord, where a change of landlord has not been properly intimated; this provision is only available to the 'tenant', which does not include a legatee or acquirer of the lease under s 16 of the Succession (Scotland) Act 1964, who might wish to terminate the lease before his acquisition has been accepted by the landlord.

Crown Land

15.—(1) This Schedule shall apply to land belonging to Her Majesty in right of the Crown, subject to such modifications as may be prescribed; and for the purposes of this Schedule the Crown Estates Commissioners or other proper officer or body having charge of the land for the time being or, if there is no such officer or body, such person as Her Majesty may appoint in writing under the Royal Sign Manual, shall represent Her Majesty and shall be deemed to be the landlord.

(2) Without prejudice to sub-paragraph (1) above, subject to such modifications as may be prescribed, section 14 of this Act and this Schedule shall apply to land where the interest of the landlord or of the tenant belongs to a government department or is held on behalf of Her Majesty for the purposes of a government department.[1]

1 The paragraph applies the Schedule to Crown lands, which would otherwise not be bound by this statute.

EXTRACT FROM THE SUCCESSION (SCOTLAND) ACT 1964

(1964, c 41)

Provisions relating to leases

16.[1]—(1) This section applies to any interest,[2] being the interest of a tenant under a lease, which is comprised in the estate of a deceased person and has accordingly vested in the deceased's executor[3] by virtue of section 14 of this Act; and in the following provisions of this section 'interest' means an interest to which this section applies.

(2)[4] Where an interest—

(a) is not the subject of a valid bequest[5] by the deceased, or

(b) is the subject of such a bequest, but the bequest is not accepted by the legatee, or

(c) being an interest under an agricultural lease, is the subject of such a bequest, but the bequest is declared null and void in pursuance of section 16 of the Act of 1886 or section 11 of the Act of 1991, or becomes null and void under section 10 of the Act of 1955,

and there is among the conditions of the lease (whether expressly or by implication) a condition prohibiting assignation[6] of the interest, the executor shall be entitled, notwithstanding that condition, to transfer the interest to any one of the persons[7] entitled to succeed to the deceased's intestate estate, or to claim legal rights or the prior rights of a surviving spouse out of the estate, in or towards satisfaction of that person's entitlement or claim,[8] but shall not be entitled to transfer the interest to any other person without the consent—

(i) in the case of an interest under an agricultural lease, being a lease of a croft within the meaning of section 3(1) of the Act of 1955, of the Crofters Commission;

(ii) in any other case, of the landlord.

(3) If in the case of any interest—

(a) at any time the executor is satisfied that the interest cannot be disposed of according to law and so informs the landlord, or

(b) the interest is not so disposed of within a period of one year or such longer period as may be fixed by agreement between the landlord and the executor or, failing agreement, by the sheriff on summary application by the executor—[9]

(i) in the case of an interest under an agricultural lease which is the subject of a petition to the Land Court under section 16 of the Act of 1886 or an application to that court under section 11 of the Act of 1991, from the date of the determination or withdrawal of the petition or, as the case may be, the application,

(ia) [relates to crofts]

(ib) [relates to crofts]

(ii) in any other case, from the date of death of the deceased,

either the landlord or the executor may, on giving notice in accordance with the next following subsection to the other, terminate the lease[10] (in so far as it relates to the interest) notwithstanding any provision therein, or any enactment or rule of law, to the contrary effect.

(4) The period of notice[11] given under the last foregoing subsection shall be—

(a) in the case of an agricultural lease, such period as may be agreed, or, failing agreement, a period of not less than one year and not more than two years ending with such term of Whitsunday or Martinmas as may be specified in the notice; and

(b) [relates to non-agricultural leases]

Provided that paragraph (b) of this subsection shall be without prejudice to any enactment prescribing a shorter period of notice in relation to the lease in question.

(5)[12] Subsection (3) of this section shall not prejudice any claim by any party to the lease for compensation or damages in respect of the termination of the lease (or any rights under it) in pursuance of that subsection; but any award of compensation or damages in respect of such termination at the instance of the executor shall be enforceable only against the estate of the deceased and not against the executor personally.

(6)[13] Where an interest is an interest under an agricultural lease, and—

(a) [relates to crofts] or

(b) a reference is made under section 23(2) and (3) of the Act of 1991 to an arbiter to determine any question which has arisen under section 22 (2)(e) of that Act in connection with a notice to quit,

the Land Court shall not make the order, or, as the case may be, the arbiter shall not make an award in favour of the landlord, unless the court or the arbiter is satisfied that it is reasonable having regard to the fact that the interest is vested in the executor in his capacity as executor, that it should be made.

(7) [relates to non-agricultural leases]

(8)[14] Where an interest is an interest under an agricultural lease and is the subject of a valid bequest by the deceased, the fact that the interest is vested in the executor under the said section 14 shall not prevent the operation, in relation to the legatee, of paragraphs (a) to (h) of section 16 of the Act of 1886, or, as the case may be section 11(2) to (8) of the 1991 Act, or, as the case may be, subsections (2) to (6) of section 10 of the Act of [1993].

(9) In this section—

'agricultural lease' means a lease of a holding within the meaning of the Small Landholders (Scotland) Acts 1886 to 1931 or of the Act of 1991 or a lease of a croft within the meaning of section 3(1) of the Act of [1993];

'the Act of 1886' means the Crofters Holdings (Scotland) Act 1886;

'the Act of 1931' means the Small Landholders and Agricultural Holdings (Scotland) Act 1931;

'the Act of 1991' means the Agricultural Holdings (Scotland) Act 1991;

'the Act of [1993]' means the Crofters (Scotland) Act [1993];

'lease' includes tenancy.

1 See Chapter 3. The notes to this section should be read along with the notes to s 12 of the 1991 Act. An executor has no right to transfer the lease until he has confirmed to it:

Rotherwick's Trs v Hope 1975 SLT 187; *Morrison-Low v Paterson* 1985 SC (HL) 49. The lease should appear as a specific item 'sufficient to identify it' in the inventory: see the Act of Sederunt (Confirmation of Executors Amendment) 1966. It is essential that confirmation is obtained within one year so that the interest can be transferred timeously under subsection (3). The lease should be transferred after confirmation has been obtained, although in exceptional circumstances a transfer before confirmation was held valid: *Garvie's Trs v Garvie's Tutors* 1975 SLT 94.

2 **'Applies to any interest'.** The section only applies to the interest of a tenant under a lease, which is comprised in the estate of a deceased person. Section 32(2) provides that 'the interest of a tenant under a tenancy or lease which was not expressed to expire on his death' is included in the estate of the deceased. The normal agricultural lease to a tenant and his heirs or to a tenant and his successors is included. A destination 'to heirs' is implied at common law: Rankine on Leases (3rd edn), p 161. A lease subject to a special destination, unless it has been evacuated, cannot be transferred by the executor: proviso to s 36(2). A lease to 'A and his heirs excluding assignees and sub-tenants' or 'to A and B and to the survivor of them as sole tenant, and to the heirs of the survivor, but excluding heirs portioners (the eldest heir-female always succeeding without division), sub-tenants and assignees legal or voluntary' are not special destinations: *Reid's Trs v Macpherson* 1975 SLT 101; *Cormack v McIldowie's Exrs* 1975 SLT 212; but cf Halliday, *Conveyancing Law and Practice in Scotland*, vol 4, para 14–04, where those decisions are criticised. A lease subject to a valid bequest is excluded: see note 3 below. A liferent lease may be excluded: see Gill, *The Law of Agricultural Holdings in Scotland* (2nd edn), para 585.

3 **'Executor'.** The executor's title is administrative. He is the tenant for the purposes of s 16 and the 1991 Act, s 85(1). Payment of rent by the executor during his administration does not create a new tenancy (*Jardine-Paterson v Fraser* 1974 SLT 93 at 98), but an executor allowed to remain in occupation beyond the administration may become a tenant: *Morrison-Low v Paterson* 1985 SC (HL) 49. It is therefore essential to terminate an executor's occupation of the holding in terms of subsections (3) and (4) if the lease has not been validly transferred.

4 This subsection gives the executor power to transfer a lease which is comprised in the estate of the deceased provided the lease is not subject to a valid bequest (see notes to s 11 of the 1991 Act) or the valid bequest is not accepted or the bequest is declared null and void under s 11(6) of the 1991 Act, because the landlord has established, under that section, a reasonable ground of objection to the beneficiary. A modification of the docket at Sch 1 to the 1964 Act is probably an appropriate form for transferring the lease.

5 **'A valid bequest'.** See 'Bequest of Lease', p 19, and notes to s 11 of the 1991 Act. Where there is a valid bequest of the lease, but the beneficiary fails to intimate the bequest timeously, the executor does not have a right subsequently to transfer the lease: *Coats v Logan* 1985 SLT 221. Where a right of bequest is excluded by the lease, the deceased can still provide in his will for the person to whom he would like the executor to transfer the lease and make provision for the value at which that transfer is to be made.

6 **'A condition prohibiting assignation'.** At common law there is a prohibition against assignation of a lease, even if there is no specific provision excluding assignees in the lease. If the lease allows assignation, then the executor can transfer without reliance on this section.

7 **'Any one of the persons'.** The class of person to whom the lease may be transferred is limited by this subsection to one of the persons entitled to succeed on intestacy, or to claim legal rights or prior rights of a surviving spouse. With the consent of the landlord (subsection (2)(ii)) the lease may be transferred to other persons. The executor's discretion as to the selection of the transferee is unfettered, where there is more than one eligible person. It is competent for the deceased to provide in his will for a direction to the executor as to whom he would wish the lease transferred. The executor should be careful to transfer the lease to a suitable nominee, who will have reasonable prospects of overcoming any objection by the landlord under s 12 or a notice to quit under s 25 of the 1991 Act. If the executor is one of the class of persons entitled to have the lease transferred to himself and he wishes to have it so transferred then he must either resign office or obtain the consent of all other eligible persons. Otherwise he might be *auctor in rem suam* and held liable to account for his acquisition of the lease (see *Inglis v Inglis* 1983 SC 8) unless the deceased has specifically or by implication authorised the executor in the will to transfer the lease to himself (*Sarris v Clark* 1995 SLT 44). Once the executor has effected a transfer he is *functus* and cannot effect a subsequent transfer if the first fails: *Coats v Logan* 1985 SLT 221.

8 **'Towards satisfaction of that person's entitlement or claim'.** The proper basis for valuing the interest under the lease has not been judicially determined: but cf *Baird's Exr v*

IRC 1991 SLT (Lands Tr) 9 where the valuation turned on the special provisions of the Finance Act 1975 for valuing interests upon a transfer. Gill, *The Law of Agricultural Holdings in Scotland* (2nd edn), para 592 suggests that as it is 'the interest of a tenant *under* the lease' which is transferred, that the lease itself does not fall to be valued, but only the claims for compensation for improvements, etc. However, one of the interests under the lease can be said to be the right to occupy and use the land, which itself has a value.

9 The lease has to be transferred within one year of the death (subsection (3)(b)(ii)) or within one year of the Land Court declaring a bequest to be null and void under s 11 of the 1991 Act (subsection (3)(b)(i)). If the interest is not transferred within the time-limits the executor loses the right to transfer, unless, perhaps, the landlord consents. The period may be extended by agreement or upon a summary application to the sheriff, but the application for an extension to the sheriff must be applied for before the expiry of the year: *Gifford v Buchanan* 1983 SLT 613.

10 **'Terminate the lease'.** The lease has to be terminated otherwise the executor or whoever acquires possession and pays the rent may acquire the benefit of the lease or a new lease: *Morrison-Low v Paterson* 1985 SC (HL) 49.

11 The notice is not a notice to quit and there is no statutory form. The notice in respect of an agricultural lease is not related to the ish of the lease as it is in respect of a notice to quit under s 21 of the 1991 Act, but must be more than one year or less than two ending with a term of Whitsun (28th May) or Martinmas (28th November).

12 The subsection preserves the landlord's and the executor's claims: eg, for dilapidations or compensation for improvements and high farming. As the lease is not being terminated by a notice to quit the executor has no claim for disturbance (1991 Act, s 43) or for an additional payment (1991 Act, s 54). It should be noted that such claims have to be intimated timeously under ss 44, 45 and 68 of the 1991 Act. Unless the lease is running on tacit relocation, the executor runs the risk of a claim for damages (unlikely with an agricultural lease) for an early termination. All claims by the landlord are restricted to claims against the executory estate.

13 Some protection is provided by this subsection in respect of an arbitration under s 22(2)(e) of the 1991 Act in that the arbiter has to be satisfied that it is reasonable 'having regard to the fact that the interest is vested in the executor in his capacity as executor'. The onus should be on the landlord to satisfy the arbiter.

14 This subsection makes it clear that the deceased's interest under the lease vests in the executor even if subject to a valid bequest. Even though so vested the provisions of s 11(2) to (8) operate. Once the legatee has been accepted as the tenant, the executor should transfer his interests under the lease to the legatee.

EXTRACTS FROM THE AGRICULTURE (SCOTLAND) ACT 1948

(1948, c 45)

FIFTH SCHEDULE

RULES OF GOOD ESTATE MANAGEMENT

1. For the purposes of this Act, the owner of agricultural land shall be deemed to fulfil his responsibilities to manage it in accordance with the rules of good estate management in so far as his management of the land and (so far as it affects the management of that land) of other land managed by him is such as to be reasonably adequate, having regard to the character and situation of the land and other relevant circumstances, to enable an occupier of the land reasonably skilled in husbandry to maintain efficient production as respects both the kind of produce and the quality and quantity thereof.

2. In determining whether the management of land is such as aforesaid regard shall be had, but without prejudice to the generality of the provisions of the last foregoing paragraph, to the extent to which the owner is making regular muirburn in the interests of sheep stock, exercising systematic control of vermin on land not in the control of a tenant, and undertaking the eradication of bracken, whins and broom so far as is reasonably practicable, and to the extent to which the owner is fulfilling his responsibilities in relation to the provision, improvement, replacement and renewal of the fixed equipment on the land in so far as is necessary to enable an occupier reasonably skilled in husbandry to maintain efficient production as aforesaid.

SIXTH SCHEDULE

RULES OF GOOD HUSBANDRY

1. For the purposes of this Act, the occupier of an agricultural unit shall be deemed to fulfil his responsibilities to farm it in accordance with the rules of good husbandry in so far as the extent to which and the manner in which the unit is being farmed (as respects both the kind of operations carried out and the way in which they are carried out) are such that, having regard to the character and situation of the unit, the standard of management thereof by the owner and other relevant circumstances, the occupier is maintaining a reasonable standard of efficient production, as respects both the kind of produce and the quality and quantity thereof, while keeping the unit in a condition to enable such a standard to be maintained in the future.

2. In determining whether the manner in which a unit is being farmed is such as aforesaid regard shall be had, but without prejudice to the generality of the provisions of the last foregoing paragraph, to the following:

(*a*) the maintenance of permanent grassland (whether meadow or pasture) properly mown or grazed and in a good state of cultivation and fertility;

(*b*) the handling or cropping of the arable land, including the treatment of temporary grass, so as to maintain it clean and in a good state of cultivation and fertility;

(*c*) where the system of farming practised requires the keeping of livestock, the proper stocking of the holding;

(*d*) the maintenance of an efficient standard of management of livestock;

(*e*) as regards hill sheep farming in particular—

(i) the maintenance of a sheep stock of a suitable breed and type in regular ages (so far as is reasonably possible) and the keeping and management thereof in accordance with the recognised practices of hill sheep farming;

(ii) the use of lug, horn or other stock marks for the purpose of determining ownership of stock sheep;

(iii) the regular selection and retention of the best female stock for breeding;

(iv) the regular selection and use of tups possessing the qualities most suitable and desirable for the flock;

(v) the extent to which regular muirburn is made;

(*f*) the extent to which the necessary steps are being taken—

(i) to secure and maintain the freedom of crops and livestock from disease and from infestation by insects and other pests;

(ii) to exercise systematic control of vermin and of bracken, whins, broom and injurious weeds;

(iii) to protect and preserve crops harvested or in course of being harvested;

(iv) to carry out necessary work of maintenance and repair of the fixed and other equipment.

THE AGRICULTURAL HOLDINGS (SPECIFICATION OF FORMS) (SCOTLAND) ORDER 1991

(SI 1991/2154 (S 178))

The Secretary of State in exercise of the powers conferred on him by paragraphs 11 and 25 of Schedule 7 to the Agricultural Holdings (Scotland) Act 1991, and of all other powers enabling him in that behalf, and after consultation with the Council on Tribunals as provided in section 10 of the Tribunals and Inquiries Act 1971, hereby makes the following Order:

1.—(1) This Order may be cited as the Agricultural Holdings (Specification of Forms) (Scotland) Order 1991, and shall come into force on 25th September 1991.

(2) In this Order 'the Act' means the Agricultural Holdings (Scotland) Act 1991.

2. The form specified in Schedule 1 to this Order shall, modified as circumstances may require, be the form of an award in an arbitration under the Act.

3. The forms specified in Schedule 2 to this Order, or forms as near thereto as circumstances may require, may be used for proceedings in arbitrations under the Act as follows:

(a) for the making of an application for appointment by the Secretary of State of an arbiter to determine claims, questions or differences (except as to determination of rent) arising between the landlord and tenant of an agricultural holding – Form A;

(b) for the making of an application for appointment by the Secretary of State of an arbiter to determine the rent of an agricultural holding – Form B;

(c) for the making of an application to the Secretary of State by an arbiter for extension of time for making his award in an arbitration – Form C.

4.—(1) The Agricultural Holdings (Specification of Forms) (Scotland) Order 1983 is hereby revoked.

(2) Anything whatsoever done under or by virtue of the instrument revoked by this Order shall be deemed to have been done under or by virtue of the corresponding provision of this Order and anything whatsoever begun under any article of the said instrument may be continued under this Order as if begun under this Order.

Strathclyde
St Andrew's House, Edinburgh   Parliamentary Under Secretary of State
24th September 1991   Scottish Office

SCHEDULE 1

FORM OF AWARD

Agricultural Holdings (Scotland) Act 1991

Award in Arbitration between A B (name and address), the [outgoing] tenant, and C D (name and address), the landlord, with regard to the holding known as (insert name of holding, district and region), [lately] in the occupation of the said tenant.

Whereas under the Agricultural Holdings (Scotland) Act 1991, the claims, questions or differences set forth in the Schedule to this Award are referred to arbitration in accordance with the provisions set out in Schedule 7 to the said Act:

And whereas the appointment dated the   day of   19 , signed by (on behalf of) the said tenant and landlord [or, as the case may be – given under the seal of the Secretary of State], I, (insert name and address), was duly appointed under the said Act to be the arbiter for the purpose of
[1] settling the said claims

settling the said questions or differences

determining the rent to be paid in respect of the said holding as from[2]

in accordance with the provisions set out in Schedule 7 to the said Act:
[And whereas the time for making my Award has been extended by
[1] the written agreement of the said tenant and landlord, dated the day of   19 , order of the Secretary of State, dated the   day of   19 , to the   day of   19 .]
And whereas I, the said (insert name)   , having accepted the appointment as arbiter, and having heard the parties (agents for the parties) and examined the documents and other productions lodged and the evidence led and having fully considered the whole matters referred to me, do hereby make my final Award as follows:[3]

I award and determine that the said landlord shall pay to the said tenant the sum of   pounds and   pence, as compensation in respect of the claims set forth in the [first part of the] Schedule to this Award, the amount awarded in respect of each claim being as there stated.

I award and determine that the said tenant shall pay to the said landlord the sum of   pounds and   pence, in respect of the claims set forth in the [second part of the] Schedule of this Award, the amount awarded in respect of each claim being as there stated.

I determine the questions or differences set forth in the [third part of the] Schedule to this Award, as follows, namely:

[1]I fix and determine the rent to be paid by the said tenant to the said landlord, as from   to be the sum of   per annum. [My findings in fact and the reasons for my decision are set forth in the [fourth part of the] Schedule to this award.]

I award and direct that each party shall bear his own expenses and one half of the other expenses of and incidental to the arbitration and Award, including my remuneration [and that of the clerk].

(or otherwise as the arbiter shall see fit to direct in light of the provisions of section 63(3) of, and paragraphs 17 to 19 of Schedule 7 to, the said Act) and that, subject to the provisions of the said Act, all sums including any expenses, payable under or by virtue of this Award shall be so paid not later than[4]

In witness whereof I have signed this Award this   day of
19   , in the presence of the following witnesses.

Signature ....

Designation ....

Address ....

....

(Arbiter)

Signature ....

Designation ....

Address ....

Schedule to the above Award

In the case of appointment by the Secretary of State or by the Scottish Land Court of an arbiter to determine claims questions or differences (except as to rent) the arbiter must, if either party so requests, state the reasons for any determination arrived at (section 12 of the Tribunals and Inquiries Act 1971).

In the case of appointment by the Secretary of State or by the Scottish Land Court of an arbiter to determine the rent of an agricultural holding under section 13 of the 1991 Act, the arbiter shall, in every case, and regardless of whether or not he is requested to do so, state in writing his findings of fact and the reasons for his decisions under the headings set forth in Part IV of this Schedule (paragraph 10 of Schedule 7 to the 1991 Act).

Claims,[5] questions or differences to be determined.

Part I—

Claims made by the tenant.

Part II—

Claims made by the landlord.

Part III—

Questions or differences (including questions of rent in cases where the arbiter is not appointed by the Secretary of State or Scottish Land Court).

Part IV—

Variation of rent cases under section 13 of the 1991 Act in which the arbiter is appointed by the Secretary of State or Scottish Land Court.

In such cases a statement under the following headings must be provided as a Schedule to the Award and made available to the parties to the case and the Secretary of State—

(i)   a summary of the statement of case submitted by or on behalf of the landlord;

(ii) a summary of the statement of case submitted by or on behalf of the tenant;

(iii) details of any evidence of the condition of the holding, including the state of the landlord's and tenant's fixed equipment, which emerged at the inspection of the holding and were taken into account;

(iv) a summary of the relevant evidence considered at any hearing;

(v)   an appraisal of the evidence submitted under (i) to (iv);

(vi) details of any other evidence of open market rents for comparable subjects introduced by the arbiter on which the parties had the opportunity to comment and which the arbiter took into account;

(vii) the reasons for seeking evidence (in terms of the factors specifically listed in section 13(4) of the 1991 Act) other than evidence of open market rents for comparable subjects in the surrounding area;

(viii) details of the factors specified in section 13(4) of the 1991 Act which the arbiter considers it desirable to take into account;

(ix) an indication of the weight attached by the arbiter to the various criteria taken into account;

(x)   an explanation of any adjustment made by the arbiter to take account of differences in holdings used for comparative purpose;

(xi) any other explanation necessary to clarify the arbiter's decision.

1 Adapt to meet the circumstances.

2 Insert date from which revised rent is to run. (Where variation of rent under section 13 of the 1991 Act is concerned, the date will be the next ensuing day on which the tenancy could have been terminated by notice to quit given at the date of demanding the reference of the rent question to arbitration – usually a term of Whitsunday or Martinmas.)

3 Such parts of the following four paragraphs as may be appropriate should be incorporated in the award, adaptations to meet the particular circumstances being made as necessary.

4 The date of payment specified must not be later than one calendar month after the delivery of the Award.

5 Where claims are made under Schedules 3, 4, 5 or 6 to the 1991 Act, the amounts awarded must, if either party so requires, be shown separately against each numbered item as set out in those Schedules. Where claims are made by either party under agreement or custom and not under statute, the amounts awarded must be separately stated.

SCHEDULE 2

Form A

(Application for appointment by the Secretary of State of an arbiter to determine claims, questions or differences (except as to determination of rent) arising between the landlord and tenant of an agricultural holding.)

Agricultural Holdings (Scotland) Act 1991

To the Secretary of State,

In default of agreement between the landlord and the tenant of the holding specified in the Schedule to this application as to the person to act as arbiter and in the absence of any provision in any lease or agreement between them relating to the appointment of an arbiter, I/we hereby apply to the Secretary of State to appoint an arbiter for the purpose of settling the claims questions or differences set out in the Schedule to this application.

Signature(s) ....

[1] ....

Date ....

SCHEDULE

(Applicants seeking determination of a claim for compensation associated with questions and differences should answer questions 1 to 11 inclusive.)

Particulars required	Replies
SECTION A – *To be completed by all applicants*	
1. Name and address of holding	Holding: District: Region:
2. Name and address of landlord.	
3. Name and address of landlord's agent.[2]	
4. Name and address of tenant.	
5. Name and address of tenant's agent.[2]	
6. If the tenancy has terminated state date of termination.	
7. Approximate area in hectares of holding.	
8. Description of holding.[3]	
SECTION B – *To be completed ONLY by applicants seeking determination of a claim for compensation*	
9. If an extension of time has been granted under section 62(4) of the	

Agricultural Holdings (Scotland) Act
1991 for the settlement of claims,
state date on which extension
expires.

---

10. Nature of claim to be referred to
arbitration.
(a) State claim for compensation for
improvements by the tenant, and
give short particulars of any further
claims by the tenant.
(b) Give short particulars of any
claims by the landlord.

SECTION C – *To be completed ONLY by applicants seeking determination of
questions or differences*

11. State questions or differences to
be referred to arbitration.

---

1 State whether landlord or tenant. If an agent signs state on whose behalf he is signing. The
appointment will be expedited if the application is made by both parties.
2 If no agent, insert 'None'.
3 Describe holding briefly, eg, mixed, arable, dairying, market garden.

FORM B

*(Application for appointment by the Secretary of State of an arbiter to determine
the rent of an agricultural holding.)*

AGRICULTURAL HOLDINGS (SCOTLAND) ACT 1991

To the Secretary of State,
    In default of agreement between the landlord and the tenant of the holding
specified in the Schedule to this application as to the person to act as arbiter
and in the absence of any provision in any lease or agreement between them
relating to the appointment of an arbiter, I/we hereby apply to the Secretary
of State to appoint an arbiter to determine the rent to be paid for the said
holding as from   19   : (*enter appropriate date in accordance
with note 1 below*)

Signature(s) ....

2
    ....

Date ....

SCHEDULE

Particulars required	Replies
1. Name and address of holding.	Holding: District: Region:
2. Name and address of landlord.	
3. Name and address of landlord's agent.[3]	
4. Name and address of tenant.	
5. Name and address of tenant's agent.[3]	
6. Approximate area in hectares of holding.	
7. Description of holding.[4]	
8. Date of demand in writing for reference to arbitration.	
9. Date at which tenancy of holding could be terminated by notice to quit.	
10. (a) Date of commencement of tenancy. (b) Effective date of any previous increase of reduction of rent. (c) Effective date of any previous direction of an arbiter that the rent continue unchanged.	

1 Where variation of rent under section 13 of the 1991 Act is concerned, the date will be the next ensuing day on which the tenancy could have been terminated by notice to quit given at the date of demanding the reference of the rent question to arbitration – usually a term of Whitsunday or Martinmas.

2 State whether landlord or tenant. If an agent signs, state on whose behalf he is signing. The appointment will be expedited if the application is made by both parties.

3 If no agent, insert 'None' in second column.

4 Describe holding briefly, eg, mixed, arable, dairying, market garden.

FORM C

(Application to the Secretary of State by an arbiter for extension of time for making his award in an arbitration.)

AGRICULTURAL HOLDINGS (SCOTLAND) ACT 1991

To the Secretary of State,

As the time for making the Award in the arbitration detailed below will expire/expired on the   day of   19   , I hereby apply for an extension of the time for making the said Award to the   day of 19   .

(Signature of arbiter
or arbiter's clerk) ....

Date ....

Details to be supplied—
1. Name of holding and district and region in which situated.
2. Name and address of landlord (and agent, if any).
3. Name and address of tenant (and agent, if any).
4. Name and address of arbiter (and clerk, if any).
5. (a) Date on which arbiter appointed.
   (b) Whether appointed by agreement of parties or by the Secretary of State or Scottish Land Court.

EXPLANATORY NOTE

(This note is not part of the Order)

The forms specified in this Order take the place of the forms specified in the Agricultural Holdings (Specification of Forms) (Scotland) Order 1983 revised to take account of the provisions of the Agricultural Holdings (Scotland) Act 1991.

INDEX

Acts
  amendments and repeals of other, 222, 244–253
  commencement and dates of operation, 1–2
  construction of references in other, 222
  derivations and destinations, 254–261
  object of, 1
  savings and transitionals, 222, 251–252
Agreements
  compensation under, 195–196
  contracting out, 63–65
  forms of, 271, 309
  game damage, compensation for, 54
  landlord and incoming tenant, between, 276
  lease, where no written, 8
  notice to quit, agreed holding to be sold, 271
  settlement of claims on termination of tenancy, 204–205
  tenancy, demand for execution of, 272
  validity of, 214
Agricultural Holding, *see* Holding
Agricultural Land
  definition of, 3–4
Allotments, 4, 167
Appeal
  to Land Court, 16
Arable Areas Payment Scheme, 122–123
Arbiter
  acceptance of office, 12
    minute of, 304
  appointment of, 12, 85, 109, 115, 116, 232, 290
    by agreement, 85, 232, 290
    by Land Court, 78, 85, 233
    by Secretary of State, 12, 85, 95, 232, 336–340
    in writing, 85, 232
    joint intimation of completion, 291
    revocation of, 232, 291
    Secretary of State a party, where, 206
  award, *see* Award
  bias, showing, 99
  damages, power to assess, 111
  death of or unable to act as, 86, 111, 232
  devolution by, 111, 292
  discretion of, 13, 87
  disqualification and removal of, 86, 300
  documents, power to call for, 91, 293
  duties in valuations, 110
  expenses, power to award, 94, 233
  incidental orders by, 293–297

  interdict of, 77, 87
  interest in dispute, having, 86
  jurisdiction of, 7, 77, 84–85, 87
  law agent, entitled to call in, 90
  men of skill, assistance of, 90
  minute of submission, 87
  misconduct or improper conduct of, 87, 93, 98, 117, 234
  objection to competency of, 87
  oversman, *see* Oversman
  panel of arbiters, 205–206, 232
  personal knowledge of, 90
  powers conferred by statute, 28–29
  proposed findings, note of, 94, 296
  remuneration of, 95, 116, 205–206
  state a case, order to, 92, 299
  state a case, refusal to, 92
  valuations, duties in, 53
  variation of rents, duties in, 12, 72
Arbitration, 77–99
  arbiter, *see* Arbiter
  claims, *see* Claims
  clerk in, *see* Clerk in Arbitration
  death of party, 86
  evidence, 90–92, 232–233
  expenses of, 94–96, 233–234
  fixing of rent by, 1
  forms, 234, 290–305, 333
  hearing and inspection, 89–90
  irregularities in, 99
  Land Court, references to, *see* Land Court
  modification of demand to remedy, power of, 206–208
  procedure in, 87
  prorogation, minute of, 304, 305
  reference under s 2 of 1991 Act, 7
  reference under s 4 of 1991 Act, 146
  reference under s 5 of 1991 Act, 9, 146
  stated case, 16, 92–93, 106, 298
  statement of case and particulars of claim, 78, 83–84, 88, 116, 232, 234, 287
  submission, minute of, *see* Submission
  tenancy, matters arising out of, 83
  terms of lease, 82
  terms of lease, specifying unwritten, 8
Arbitrations and Valuations
  (outside Act), 106–111
Award, 96–98, 233, 334–336
  alteration or cancellation of, 97
  alternative, 97
  amounts awarded for claims stated separately, 97, 233
  common law submission, in, 303
  expenses to be included in, 94, 233–234

Award – *cont*
form of, 16, 96, 233
interim, 96, 233
mistakes in, 97, 233
reasons for, 15–16, 233
recording of, 97–98, 206
recovery of, 97–98, 206
reduction of, *see* Reduction of Award
setting aside, *see* Reduction of Award
time for making of, 96, 233
  extension by arbiter, 340
  extension by parties, 96, 292
  extension by Secretary of State, 96
time for payment of sums awarded, 97, 233

Bad Husbandry, *see* Certificate of Bad Husbandry
Bankruptcy of Tenant, 59, 152
Benefit
variation of rent, 72
Bequest of Lease, 1, 19–20, 139–141
contracting out of statutory power, 19, 63, 139
intimation of, 279
legatee, *see* Legatee
Bracken, etc, 45, 46–47, 277, 229, 230
Breach of Lease, *see* Lease
Bridges, Making of, 43, 227, 228, 230
Buildings and Fixtures
arbitrations, 59, 80
buildings as agricultural holding, 4
compensation for, 1, 58, 66
contracting out of the provisions, re, 63
definitions, *see* Words and Phrases
erection of, 227, 228, 230, 232
fixtures
  intention to remove, 58, 72, 81, 276
  landlord electing to purchase, 59, 82, 277
  purchased by landlord, payment for, 82
  tenant's right to remove, 58, 72, 81
  valuation of, 59
improvements which require consent, 43
maintenance and repair, 1
market garden improvements, 66
repairs
  compensation for, 45, 79, 228, 229
  notice of, 79
tenant's right to remove, 148–149

Canal, Making of, 167
Certificate of Bad Husbandry
application for, 27, 61, 121, 164–165
Chalking of Land, 45, 227, 229
Charge on Holding, 61–62, 325
Claims
arbiter, order by, for, 293
competency and relevancy of, 84–85
landlord, by, 83
notice, *see* Notice by Landlord and Notice by Tenant

particulars of, 83–84, 232
settlement of, on termination of tenancy, 106
  application to extend time for, 289
  by arbitration, 204–205
tenant, by, 41–56, 78–82, 306
Clay Burning, 227, 229, 230
Claying of Land, 227, 229, 230
Clerk in Arbitration
appointment of, 88, 304
  minute of acceptance, 304
fees, expenses, etc of, 88, 94, 95
forms, 295, 297
layman as, 90
Clover, 45, 228, 229, 231
Coal, Working of, 36, 167
Common Law
arbitration at, 78
Company as Tenant, 38, 64, 226
Compensation *See also under the particular subjects in respect of which claims are made*
agreements, under, 195–196, 233, 276
charging of estate with, *see* Charge on Holding
agreed scale, 53
compulsory acquisition, 74
fair and reasonable, 53
holding vested in more than one person, 192–193
milk quota, *see* Milk Quotas
not payable for anything done in compliance with the Act, 193–194
part of holding, in respect of, 49, 51, 192
recovery of, 206
substituted, *see* Substituted Compensation
tenant quits possession after notice to quit, 49
tenant's rights, 1
Compulsory Acquisition, 74–76, 197, 199, 201, 237–238
Consent of Land Court
improvement, to, 44
notice to quit, to, 25, 30, 32–36, 75, 155–165, 169, 197, 207
  conditions accompanying, 160–163, 165
  fair and reasonable landlord provision, 38–40, 161, 170
  grounds for consent, 37–38
Consent of Landlord
improvements
  compensation payable without consent or notice, 42
  consent required as condition of compensation, 42, 43
  notice required as condition of compensation, 42, 43–44
limited owners, power of, 212
market garden improvements, 66
Consents, Validity of, 214
Contracting Out, *see* Agreements
Corn, Consumption of, 45, 227, 229, 230

Cottages, Erection of, 167
Court of Session
  application to, 78, 84
  power to compel arbiter to proceed, 86, 111
    Crop, Away-going Valuations, 53, 107, 110, 111
Cropping
  custom of, 57, 136
  freedom of, 42, 47, 57–58, 134–135
    conditions attached to, 57
    contracting out of, 63
  let
    definite and limited period, for, 26
    seasonal becoming protected tenancy, 6, 26
  restrictions, 57
  system of, meaning of, 13
Crown Land
  application of Acts to, 214, 326
  Crown Estate Commissioners, 214

Dairying Plant, Fixed, 43, 230
Damages
  arbiter, assessment by, 58
  deterioration, for, 58, 134
  liquidated, 59, 191–192
Deer, see Game
Definitions, see Words and Phrases
Deterioration of Holding
  compensation for, 42, 55, 83, 189–190
    conditions for payment of, 55, 83
  damages for and interdict against, 58, 134
  notice of claim, see Notice by Landlord
Dilapidations, 15, 42
Disturbance
  compensation for, 1, 49–50, 66, 72, 80, 184–187
    amount of, 49
    conditions for payment of, 49–50
    contracting out of, 63
    valuation of stock and produce, etc, 50
  notice to quit, see Notice to Quit
  reorganisation payment, 50–51, 196
  sub-tenant, compensation to, 49
Documents
  arbiter's order, form of, 293
  production of, 232
Drainage
  improvements, 43, 227, 228, 230
Dung (see also Manure)
  benefit, 47
  compensation for, 46
  incoming tenant bound to take, 108
  succession, in question of, 46
  valuation of, 84, 107

Early Resumption, Compensation for, 51
Electrical Equipment, 43, 228, 230
Embankments, 43, 227, 228, 229, 230
Estate Management
  good, 139, 218, 223
    rules of, 331

sound, distinguished from good, 33, 161, 162, 198
Evesham Custom, 66
Evidence
  oath or affirmation, on, 91, 232
  perjury of, 92
  refusal to listen to, by arbiter, 90
  shorthand notes of, 90
  valuations, in, 13
  witnesses
    citation of, 91, 116
    skilled, 90
    subject to any legal objection, 91
Expenses
  agent and client basis, 95
  arbitration, 94–96, 233–234
  award by arbiter, 94, 111, 233
    considerations in, 95
  claim for compensation, 94
  clerk, of, 88, 94, 95
  discretion of arbiter, 94, 95
  disturbance claim, 94
  extrajudicial type, 95
  stated case, of, 94, 95
  taxation, subject to, 95, 233
  witnesses, of, 95

Fallow Ground
  incoming tenant bound to take bare, 108
  valuation of, 84, 107
Feeding Stuffs
  consumption on holding, 44, 45–47, 227, 229, 230
  unexhausted value, 107
Fences
  making of, 43, 227, 228, 23
  removal of, 227, 228, 230
  valuation of, 107, 110
Fiars Prices, 203, 204
Fire, Damage by, 223
Fixed Equipment
  compensation for failure to repair or maintain, 190
  definition of, 217
  provision and maintenance of, 8–10, 132
    arbitration, reference to, 9, 82, 133, 206, 273, 274
    statutory obligations, 9–10, 132
  record of, 80, 132
  repair of, 44, 132, 230
Fixtures, Machinery and Buildings, 58
Fixtures, see Buildings and Fixtures
Folds, 230
Fords, 230
Forms, 265–309
  list of, 262–264
Freedom of Cropping, see Cropping
Fruit Bushes, 66, 180, 227, 228, 229, 232
Fruit Trees
  planting of, 66, 232
  protection of, 227, 228, 230
  removal of, 66, 180

Game, Damage by
compensation for, 1, 54–55, 66, 81, 194–195
conditions of payment of, 55, 81
contracting out of, 54, 63
landlord's right to indemnity, 194, 195
notice of claim for, 55, 81, 194
forms, 277, 278
Gardens, 4, 167, 227, 228, 229
Grants, State, 17, 42, 53
Grass, 45, 108, 228, 229, 231
Grazing, 3, 130
seasonal grazing, 5, 6
Grouse, see Game, Damage by
Guardian
appointment of, to landlord or tenant, 214

Haulage, 229
Hay Sheds, 43, 230
High Farming, 52, 72, 137, 187–189, 284
Holding
charge on, 212–213
definition of, 3, 128, 217
test of predominant user, 3
deterioration of, see Deterioration of Holding
entry and inspection, 138, 215
extent of, determination of, 3
record of, see Record of Holding
references to definitions in earlier Acts, construction of, 222
sale of, see Sale of Holding
size of, 3
succession to, see Succession
transfer of part of, apportionment of milk quota on, see Milk Quotas
Husbandry
bad, see Certificate of Bad Husbandry
freedom of cropping, see Cropping
good, 32, 161, 198
rules of good, see Rules of Good Husbandry

Implements
payment for, 109, 150
sheds for, 230
Improvements
1923 Act improvement, 41, 44, 78, 170, 176
1931 Act improvement, 41, 44, 78, 170, 171, 176
buildings, to, see Buildings and Fixtures
compensation for, 1, 41–48, 66, 72, 170–179
'benefit' taken into consideration, 43, 175
conditions for payment of, 42
continuous adoption of special standard of farming, 43, 80, 187–189, 284 (see also High Farming)
customary, 172
feeding stuffs, 45

leases entered into before 1st January 1921, 171
notice of claim, 45
payment of, by incoming tenant, 173–174
payable without consent or notice, 42, 44
previous tenancy, where made in, 41, 171
reduction or exclusion, 42
time begun, may depend on, 41
compensation for new, 43, 45, 52–54, 79, 170, 171, 174, 176
amount of, 175
conditional on approval of Land Court, 178–179
conditional on prior consent of landlord, 42, 43, 79, 176
conditional on prior notice to landlord, 42, 43–44, 80, 177
compensation for old, 43, 45, 52–54, 79, 170, 171, 174, 227–229
amount of, 175
conditional on prior consent of landlord, 42, 43, 79, 176, 227, 228
conditional on prior notice to landlord, 42, 43–44, 79, 177, 227, 228
consent to, by Land Court, see Consent of Land Court
definitions of, 217
increase of rent due to, 16, 146
Land Court, certain questions referred to, 78
manurial improvements, 41, 45
market garden improvements, see Market Garden
notice by landlord, 17
notice of, agreement to dispense with, 44, 79, 177
old, 41
pasture, see Pasture
previous tenant's, 41
state grant for, 17, 42, 53
temporary, 44–45
value of, 52–54
variation of rent, on, 14
Inspection of Holding
by arbiter, 15
Insurance
liability for premiums, 9, 133
sums recovered under fire policies, 134
Interdict
arbiter, of, 77
landlord's remedy of, 58, 77, 134
Irrigation, 228, 229
Irritancy of Lease, 24, 59, 151, 154

Land Court
acquirer of lease, in case of objection to, 141
application to, 203, 263
apportionment of milk quota, joint application for, 115

Land Court – *cont*
certificate of bad husbandry, 61, 164–165
consent of, *see* Consent of Land Court
definition, 217
improvements, approval of, 178–179
legatee, application to be declared tenant, 19
legatee, in case of objection to, 139
market garden direction, 69, 82
powers of, 1
proceedings of, 216
record of holding, determination of questions or differences in, 60
references to, in lieu of arbitration, 7, 78
rent, variation of, by, 14
sheep stock valuations by, 210–211
Land Improvement Companies, 213–214
Landlord
agreement with incoming tenant, 107
claims by, 55, 83
charge on holding by, 212–213
Crown Lands in relation to, 214, 326
definition of, 2, 217
guardian to, appointment of, 214
objection to acquirer of lease by, 141
objection to legatee by, 139
power to enter holding, 139
Secretary of State, 215
Lands Tribunal for Scotland, 74, 217
Lease
abbreviated form of, 263
acquisition of, 280
'agreement' distinguished from, 64
bequest of, *see* Bequest of Lease
breach of conditions of, 27, 59, 155, 191
definition of, 2, 218
disputes
jurisdiction of court and arbiter, 7
intestacy of tenant, 20
irritancy of, 24, 59
ish, 23
lease entered into after 13th July 1991, 23
minimum term of, 4
exceptions to statutory provision, 5–7
mowing or grazing, for, 5–6
penalties in, 135
provisions required in, 223
resumption under, 68–73
series of lets, 5, 6
statutory provision, 5
set-aside schemes, 123
special destination, subject to, 18–19
succession to, 18
tacit relocation, held under, 5, 6, 7–8, 11, 23, 57, 82, 130
term days, statutory regulation of, 23–24
termination of, by landlord on tenant's death, 1
termination of, by landlord or executor on tenant's death, 327
termination on death of tenant, 18

terms, adjustment of, 57, 82, 131
conditions for, 82
terms as to permanent pasture, variation of, 57
terms of, 1
terms, variation of, 147
transfer to heir, method of, 1
written, provisions for, 8, 131–132
year, for less than, 5
year, for more than one, but less than two years, 5
year, for single, 5
year to year, less than from, 2, 4, 82, 129
Legatee
application to be declared tenant, 19
bequest of lease,
does not accept, 139, 327
must intimate, 139, 279
landlord objecting to, 19, 139, 279
notice to quit, 266
possession of holding pending proceedings, 19, 139
Liming of Land, 45, 227, 229, 230
Limited Owners, 212, 325
Liquidated Damages, 59, 191–192
Livestock Quotas
lease of, 121–122
notification of, deadline dates for, 122
ownership of quota, 121
sheep annual premium quotas (SAP), 121–122
suckler cow premium quota (SCP), 121–123
transfer of, with holding, 121–122
notification of, deadline dates for, 122
variation of rent, consideration in, 122

Machinery, 43, 80, 230
Manure
application of, as improvement, 44–46, 227, 229, 230
compensation, ascertaining, 53
conditions attending freedom of cropping, 57
dung, *see* Dung
full equivalent manurial value, 134
purchased, application of, 45, 227, 229, 230
termination of tenancy, removal on, 147
valuation of, 46, 108
valuation of, principles of, 110
Market Gardens, 1
compensation for improvements, 42, 43, 66–67, 82, 179–181
agreements as to, 183–184
conditions of, 82
definition of, 218
Evesham custom, 66
improvements, 66, 232
Land Court, direction by, 66, 82, 181–183
substituted compensation, 66
Marking of Land, 227, 229, 230

Martinmas, 23–24, 103, 108
Milk Quotas, 112–121
  appointment of arbiter, 115
  apportionments of, prospective
    apportionments of, 1, 114–117
    criteria applied in rent review, 117
    agreed, distinguished from
      apportionment by arbitration, 114–115
    excess quota, 118
    inadequate quota, 118
  arbiter's decision, 116
  areas used for milk production,
    determination of, 116
  categories of,
    additional milk products quota, 114
    allowed quota, 113
    special quota, 113–114
    transferred quota, 113
  compensation, 1, 114, 118–119, 203,
    314–316
    calculation of payment, 317
    contracting out of statutory provisions,
      314
    outgoing tenants, to, 310
    qualifying interest to claim, 119
    termination of tenancy in part of
      holding, in, 114
    written intimation of claim for, 118
  definition of, 112
  definitions, statutory, *see* Words and
    Phrases
  exempt transfer, 114
  joint application to Land Court, 115
  leasing of, 120–121
    approval of, 120
  limited owners, powers of, 325
  proceedings, conduct of, 116
  registered, 117
  regulations, 112–120
  rent review, in, 117–118, 310–312
  sub-tenants, 316
  standard quota, 317–320
    determination of, 323
  succession to lease of tenancy, on, 316
  sums payable, recovery of, 325
  tenant's claim, settlement on termination
    of lease of, 324–325
  tenant's fraction, 320–322
    determination of, 323
  termination of lease, settlement of tenant's
    claim, 324–325
  types of,
    direct sales quota, 113
    wholesale quota, 113
  valuation of, 120, 322–323
Minerals, Working of, 167
Mowing Lets, 5, 6, 130

Notice by Landlord
  acquirer of lease, objecting to, 141, 280
  breach of conditions of tenancy, to
    remedy, 155, 206–209, 269
  buildings and fixtures, electing to
    purchase, 148, 277
  change of landlord, 286
  claims, of, 55, 78, 83
  contract for sale of farm, of, 271
  deterioration, claim for compensation for,
    83, 190–191, 284
    conditions of, 83
  fixed equipment, claim for compensation
    for, 190–191
  improvements
    intending to execute, 283
    objection to, 283
  legatee, objecting to, 139, 266, 279
  notice to quit, *see* Notice to Quit
  removal of tenant from part of holding, for,
    270
  rent, for payment of, 269
  rent, increase of, due to improvements, 275
  rent, reference to arbitration, 142
  terminate tenancy, to, 66
  termination of tenancy claims, 83, 204
Notice by Legatee, 139
Notice by Tenant
  arbitration, requiring, 268
  buildings and fixtures, intention to remove,
    148, 276
  claims of, 45, 55, 78–82, 284, 285
  counter-notice, 25, 30, 63, 155, 159, 168,
    169, 184, 268
  game damage, claim for, 55, 81, 194, 277,
    278
  improvements,
    for approval of, 281
    consent required, 42, 43, 79
    consent or notice not required, 42, 44,
      79
    intention to make, 282
    notice required, 42, 43–44, 79, 80
  intention to claim compensation for
    disturbance, 80
  intention to claim compensation for high
    farming, 72, 80, 284
  intention to remove fixtures, 72
  notice to quit, counter-notice to, 25, 80,
    155, 168
  quit, of intention to, 23, 151
    period of notice required, 11, 23, 151
  rent
    arbitration as to, 81, 142
    variation of, 81
  sale of implements, stock, etc, 80
  sale of holding, notice to quit to remain in
    force following, 272
  termination of tenancy claims, 78–82, 83,
    204
Notice to Quit, 23–40, 151–170, 184, 196,
    216
  acquirer of lease by succession, to,
    163–164
  agreement to sell holding, effect of, on, 61
  apparent insolvency, 32

346

Notice to Quit – *cont*
arbitration, questions referred to, 26, 80, 159–160, 206–208
bad husbandry, certificate of, 27
breach of lease, 27–31
compulsory acquisition, 75–76
contracting out of, provisions for, 23
counter-notice by tenant, 25, 30, 63, 155, 159, 168, 169, 184
cropping lets, 26
form of, 23, 152
forms, statutory, 265–272
grounds for consent to operation of, 224–225
hardship, 34–35
Land Court, consent of, *see* Consent of Land Court
non-agricultural use, 26, 35–36
non-near relative successor, 32, 36
part of holding, 50, 160, 167
form, 270
right to treat as notice to quit whole, 168, 270
penalty for breach of conditions accompanying, 165–166
period of notice required, 11, 23, 151
removal of manure etc, 147
restrictions on operation of, 1, 24, 25, 82, 155–159, 169–170
sale of holding
effect on notice, 166
provisions in, 61
service of, 23
set-aside schemes, effect on, 123
statutory provisions, exclusion of, incompetent, 23
Notices
service of, 216, 325
statutory requirements, compliance with, 8

Obstacles to Cultivation, 227, 229, 230
Orchards, 227, 228, 229
Oversman
appointment of, 107, 109, 304
minute of acceptance, 304
arbiter, death of, 111
arbiter obstructive, where, 111
devolution by arbiter on, 110, 292
duties of, 110
valuation, in, 101, 107

Panel of Arbiters, *see* Arbiter
Partnership as Tenant, 38, 64, 119, 226
Partridges, *see* Game, Damage by
Pasture
arbitration, demand for reference to, 138
permanent
definition of, 47
improvement of, 43
improvement of, by cultivation and re-seeding, 230

laying down of, 227, 228, 229
notice to quit, 155
ploughing up, 193
variation of terms as to, 57
temporary, 45, 47–48
basis of value, 47
compensation in respect of, 45, 47, 171
definition of, 47
in England, 47
laying down, 47, 171, 228, 229, 231
laid down during previous lease, 48
Penal Rents, 59
contracting out of prohibition of, 63
Pens, 230
Permanent Pasture, *see* Pasture
Pheasants, *see* Game, Damage by
Pier, Making of, 167
Procedure in Valuations, *see* Valuation
Produce
definition of, 135, 218
disposal of, 57, 134–135
landlord agreeing to purchase, 82
payment for, on termination of tenancy, 82
sale of, 1, 42
Prorogation, Minute of, 304, 305

Quitting, *see* Removing

Railway, Making of, 167
Reclamation of Waste Land, 43, 227, 228, 230
Record of Holding, 59, 137
buildings and fixtures, 60
claim for compensation, in, 60
claim for dilapidations, in, 60
cost of making, 60, 137
fixed equipment, 59, 133, 137
fixtures and buildings, 137
form of, 60, 137
improvements in, 60, 137
Land Court to determine questions or differences, 60, 137
landlord or tenant may require, 60, 137, 278
Reduction of Award
ad factum praestandum, 98
ambiguity, 98
bias shown by arbiter, 99
bribery, 98
challenge, grounds of, 98
common law grounds, 98
corruption, 98
failure to issue within time-limit, 98
failure to show basis of sheep stock valuation, 98
falsehood, 98
fraud, 99
improper execution, 98
misconduct of arbiter, 98, 234
mistake admitted, 98
powers of arbiter exceeded (*ultra vires*), 98
reference not exhausted, 98

Reduction of Award – *cont*
  refusal to admit material evidence, 99
  refusal to state a case, 99
Removing
  expenses and loss attributed to, 184
  letter of removal, an agreement, 65
  non-payment of rent, for, 1, 59, 60–61,
    150–151
    contracting out of, 63
Rent
  arbitration, conduct of, 1
  arbitration, demand by landlord for, 11,
    83, 142, 274
  arbitration, demand by tenant for, 11, 81,
    142
  arbitration, provision for milk quota in,
    117–118
  basis of valuation, 12
  disturbance claims, in, 184–185, 196
  economic rent, 1
  fixing by arbitration, 1, 143
  increase of,
    improvements by landlord, 16–17, 81,
      146, 275
  non-payment, removal for, 1, 59, 60–61,
    150–151
  notice requiring payment of, 27, 155, 269
    contracting out of prohibition of, 63
  penal rent, 59, 191–192
  reduction of, where partly dispossessed,
    72, 168
  review of, 1
  revision of, 11–17, 81, 122, 142–145
    conditions for, 81
  variation of, by arbiter, 10, 81, 338–339
**Reorganisation of Tenant's Affairs, Sum
    for,** 50–51, 196
Repairs, *see* Buildings and Fixtures
Reservoirs, 167, 227
Resumption of Holding
  compensation for, 49, 80, 200–201
  notice of, 72
  part of holding, compensation for, 51, 72
  under lease, 68–73, 200
Roads, Making of, 43, 167, 227, 228, 230
Roots, 147
Rotation of Crops, 58, *see* also Cropping
Rules of Good Husbandry, 2, 49, 122,
    155, 165, 218, 223, 331–332

Sale of Holding
  notice by landlord to tenant, 166, 271
  notice to quit, agreement as to, 61, 271
  notice to quit, effect on, 166
Secretary of State
  applications to, 289
  approval of lease for term shorter than
    statutory minimum, 5
  arbiter, appointment of, 232, 333–340
  award, application for extension of time of
    making, 233, 340
  entry and inspection, powers of, 215

  expenses and receipts, 215
  power to vary Schedules 5 and 6, 211–212
Security of Tenure, 25–32
  contracting out of, 63–65
  exception from,
    seasonal grazing or mowing lets, 6
  restrictions on operation of notice to quit,
    25
  tenant's rights, 1
Set Aside, 122–123
Sewage, 43, 230
Sheaf Sheds, 43, 230
Sheep Dipping Accommodation, 43, 227,
    228
Sheep Pens, etc, 230
Sheep Stocks
  sheep annual premium quotas, *see*
    Livestock Quotas
  valuation of, 3, 57, 84, 100–105, 106, 107,
    208–211, 238–243
    questions as to value, 211
    questions of law, 210
Sheriff
  arbiter, removal of, application for, 300
  no appeal from sheriff to Sheriff Principal,
    93, 208
  order to state a case, application for, 92,
    99, 299
  review of taxation of expenses, 95
  stated case for opinion of, 92, 116, 234,
    29
Silage and Silos, 43, 108, 227, 228, 230
Sluices, 43, 227, 228, 229, 230
Smallholdings, Provision of, 167
Stated Case, 92–93
  appeal to Court of Session, 93
  application to sheriff for order on arbiter,
    299
  by arbiter to Land Court, 16
  expenses of, 94, 95
  for opinion of Court of Session, 117
  for opinion of Land Court, 92, 234
  for opinion of sheriff, 92, 116, 234
  refusal to state a case, 99
  remit for amendment, 93
  revisal by parties, 92
Strawberry Plants, 66, 232
Submission
  award in common law submission, 303
  form of, 300
  prorogation, minute of, 304, 305
Substituted Compensation
  under agreements, 53
Sub-Tenant
  disturbance, compensation for, 185
  notice of quit to, 64
  period of let to, 2
  right to claims competent to tenant, 2
Succession
  holdings, to, 18–22
    confirmation of executor, form of docket
      to, 330

Succession – *cont*
  where lease vests in executor, 20–21,
    327–329
  where successor a near relative, 20, 22,
    36, 225
  where successor not a near relative, 36
  provisions as to, 2
  termination of tenancies acquired by,
    163–164

Tacit Relocation, 5, 6, 7–8, 11, 23, 57, 64,
  130
  contracting out of, 63, 130
Taxation by Auditor
  arbitration expenses subject to, 95, 233
Temporary Pasture, *see* Pasture
Tenancy
  breach of conditions, notice to remedy,
    155
  joint tenancy, 64
  questions arising out of, 106, 202
  termination of, 22
    acquired by succession, 163–164
    claims arising out of, 22, 67, 84, 106,
      118, 204–205
    definition of, 218
    notice of, 1, 22
    settlement of claims on, 204–205
  terms of, *see* Lease
Tenant
  bankruptcy of, 59, 152
  charge on holding by, 212–213
  claims between outgoing and incoming,
    78, 107
  claims by, 41–56, 78–82, 306
  company as, 38, 64, 226
  definition of, 2, 218
  guardian to, appointment of, 214
  notice of intention to quit, 23, 151
  partnership as, 38, 64, 119, 226
  removal of, *see* Removing
  Secretary of State, 215
  sum for reorganisation of affairs, 50–51,
    196
Three-year Average Price, 102, 239–243
Threshing Mills, 43, 230
Time
  for adjusting claims, extension of, 289, 294
Tramway, Making of, 167
Tree Roots, 45, 227, 229, 230
Trees, Planting of, 66, 167

Valuation
  arbiter and oversman, appointment of, 109
  arbitrations etc outside Act, 106–111
  awaygoing, 106, 108
  common law, subjects of, 106, 107–109
  crops, of, *see* Crops
  dung, of, *see* Dung
  fallow of, *see* Fallow Ground
  fences of, *see* Fences
  improvements, of, 52–54

  incoming tenant's obligation to take over
    at, 107, 108
  milk quota, of, *see* Milk Quotas
  procedure and principles of, 110
  procedure in making, 111
  sheep stocks, of, *see* Sheep Stocks
  silage, of, *see* Silage and Silos
  straw, of, 107
  turnips, of, 110
  valuation and arbitration, distinction
    between, 106
Vegetable Crops, 66, 232

Warping of Land, 227, 228, 229
Water Courses, 43, 227, 228, 230
Water Meadows, 227, 228, 229
Water Power and Supply, 227, 228, 230
Weiring of Land, 227, 228, 229
Wharf, Making of, 167
Whitsunday, 23–24, 102, 108
Witnesses, *see* Evidence
Words and Phrases
  acclimatisation, 100
  acquiring authority, 201
  aggregate of agricultural land, 3
  agreement in writing, 172, 196
  agricultural holding, 3, 101, 128, 209, 211,
    217
  agricultural land, 4, 128, 217
  agricultural unit, 217, 226
  agriculture, 3, 4, 217
  all compensation, 183
  allocated quota, 313
  amalgamation, 225
  any benefit, 175
  arable lands, 135
  arbiter, 101, 211
  arbitration, 211
  basic ewe value, 102
  basic lamb value, 102
  benefit or relief, 169
  building, 217
  constitution of apparent insolvency, 183
  custom of the country, 172
  dairy cows, 318
  dairy improvement, 320
  default of agreement, in, 234
  delivery, 236
  dilapidation, deterioration, 189
  directly attributable, 186
  dominium utile, 212, 213
  during the tenancy, 188
  expenses reasonably incurred, 186
  fixed equipment, 217, 321
  full equivalent manurial value, 58, 134
  greater hardship, 162, 198
  hefting, 100
  holding, 112, 201, 312
  improvement, 217
  incapable of acting, 235
  Land Court, 217
  Lands Tribunal, 217

Words and Phrases – *cont*

landlord, 2, 217, 312
lease, 218
livestock, 218
market garden, 218
market value, 100
milk quota, 312
misconduct, 236
near relative, 225
near relative successor, 36
new improvement, 217
notice to quit, 185
old improvement, 217
open market value, 12
open valuation, 101
outgoing tenant, 204
possession, 200
prescribed, 218
produce, 218
producer, 112
protection of the landlord, for the, 183
reasonable amount, 318
reasonable opportunity, 195
registered, 312
relevant number of hectares, 318
relevant quota, 314
rent, 186–187

sheep – eild ewe, eild sheep, eild gimmer, ewe, ewe hogg, gimmer, lamb, regular cast ewes, shott, tup, 103–105, 241, 243
sheep stock valuation, 101, 211, 238–243
standard or system of farming, 188
standard quota, 317
standard yield per hectare, 318
statutory small tenant, 201
substantial and otherwise suitable person, 183
surface damages, 169
tacit relocation, 130
tenancy, 313
tenant, 2, 218, 313
tenant's fraction, 320
term of years, 5
terminate the lease, 330
termination, 313
termination of tenancy, 218
three-year average price, 102
trade or business, 3, 4, 129
transferred quota, 314
two-man unit, 225
unavoidably incurred, 186
used for agriculture, 4
value to an incoming tenant, 175